Varieties of Capitalism

*The Institutional Foundations
of Comparative Advantage*

edited by

PETER A. HALL
AND DAVID SOSKICE

OXFORD

UNIVERSITY PRESS

OXFORD
UNIVERSITY PRESS

Great Clarendon Street, Oxford OX2 6DP

Oxford University Press is a department of the University of Oxford.
It furthers the University's objective of excellence in research, scholarship,
and education by publishing worldwide in

Oxford New York

Athens Auckland Bangkok Bogotá Buenos Aires Cape Town
Chennai Dar es Salaam Delhi Florence Hong Kong Istanbul Karachi
Kolkata Kuala Lumpur Madrid Melbourne Mexico City Mumbai Nairobi
Paris São Paulo Shanghai Singapore Taipei Tokyo Toronto Warsaw

with associated companies in Berlin Ibadan

Oxford is a registered trade mark of Oxford University Press
in the UK and in certain other countries

Published in the United States
by Oxford University Press Inc., New York

British Library Cataloguing in Publication Data

Data available

Library of Congress Cataloging in Publication Data

Varieties of capitalism : the institutional foundations of comparative advantage
/ edited by Peter A. Hall and David Soskice.
p. cm
Includes bibliographical references and index.
1. Capitalism. 2. Institutional economics. 3. Comparative economics.
4. Competition, International. 5. Comparative advantage
(International trade) I. Hall, Peter A., 1950–
II. Soskice, David W., 1942–
HB501 V355 2001   330.12'2--dc21   2001033838

ISBN 0–19–924774–9
ISBN 0–19–924775–7 (pbk.)

1 3 5 7 9 10 8 6 4 2

Typeset by Florence Production Ltd, Stoodleigh, Devon
Printed in Great Britain
on acid-free paper by
T.J. International Ltd., Padstow, Cornwall

Jacket/cover illustration: *Work* by Ford Maddox Brown, 1852-1865.
Manchester City Art Gallery. © Manchester City Art Galleries

PREFACE

Are there fundamental differences in national political economies conditioning economic performance and social well-being? How should these differences be construed? Can we expect them to survive the pressures that integration into an international economy places upon nations? These have long been fundamental issues in the field of comparative political economy. They have acquired a new urgency in the contemporary era, as technological change and the developments associated with 'globalization' shift the climate for business around the world, calling into question many settled understandings.

This book outlines a new approach to the comparison of national economies that can be used to answer such questions. Building on the new economics of organization, it develops an approach to understanding the macroeconomy and the institutions within it that moves beyond earlier conceptions built on influential distinctions between 'strong' and 'weak' states or 'neo-corporatist' and 'pluralist' societies. It brings the firm back into a central position in our understanding of the political economy and, as such, should be of interest to scholars of business as well as political economists. It applies concepts drawn from game theory and the new institutionalism in economics to the problem of understanding national economies, effecting an integration between theories of the firm and conceptions of the macroeconomy relevant to economics as well as political science.

For many years, discussions of international trade have been dominated by theories of comparative economic advantage. However, recent patterns in the movement of goods across national borders have called into question classic theories of comparative advantage. At the same time, endogenous sources of growth based on economies of scope, learning by doing, and positive externalities have led some to argue that the institutional frameworks within which firms operate may condition what they can do. This raises the possibility that nations may derive comparative advantages from their institutional infrastructure, but few theories have been developed to explain precisely how institutions generate such advantages or in what they consist. The approach to comparative capitalism developed in this volume fills that gap, offering an account of how the institutions structuring the political economy confer comparative advantages on a nation, especially in the sphere of innovation.

This theory of comparative institutional advantage has wide implications. It generates predictions about what kinds of activities firms will move across national borders when international markets become more open and where they will move them. It provides a new analysis of the pressures governments experience as a result of globalization and one capable of explaining the diversity of policy responses that follow. It offers a novel perspective on the positions governments are likely to take in international economic negotiations. Perhaps most important, it calls into question the presumption that increasing international economic integration will force the institutions and regulatory regimes of diverse nations into convergence on a common model.

· The implications for policy-making of this approach to comparative political economy are equally radical. It casts the fundamental problems facing economic policy-makers in a new light, suggesting that their principal task is not to identify endeavors in which firms can excel and provide incentives for pursuing them, but rather the more difficult one of improving the capacities of firms to coordinate with other actors in the economy. It calls for a reexamination of social policy and a reinterpretation of the welfare state. Social policies are often seen as measures that impede the operation of markets, forced on an unwilling business community by labor or the political left. However, the essays in this volume suggest that many kinds of social policies actually improve the operation of markets and enhance the capacities of firms to pursue distinctive strategies, thereby inspiring active support in the business community.

Building on the distinction between 'liberal market economies' and 'coordinated market economies' that is central to the approach, the contributors to this volume explore many of the institutional complementarities found in such economies. They show how firms develop corporate strategies to take advantage of the institutional support available in any economy for particular modes of coordination, deriving from this a new perspective on issues in strategic management. They examine how national legal frameworks for contracting and standard-setting reinforce specific patterns of business coordination and the ways in which monetary regimes interact with industrial relations systems to generate distinctive patterns of economic performance. The result is a textured account of how some institutions in the political economy can reinforce the operation of others to generate nationally distinctive forms of capitalism.

Although grounded in large bodies of empirical research, the contributions to this volume are bold and bound to be controversial. Even at this length, the volume covers only some of the issues raised by this approach to comparative political economy and a few of the nations to which it can be applied. We construe the book, however, not as the end of a story but as its beginning. Above all else, it is an effort to open research agendas in multiple fields by suggesting new lines of inquiry and analysis. We hope that readers will find the contents as stimulating as we found the works on which we have built.

The artwork on the cover of this book, *Work* by Ford Madox Brown, is now in the Manchester City Art Gallery. Painted between 1852 and 1865 on Heath Street, Hampstead, it portrays two intellectuals, Thomas Carlyle and F. D. Maurice, observing work in its social context during an earlier era of intense economic change, much as the contributors to this book observe the processes of globalization today.

This volume has had a long gestation. It is the culmination of a project begun in 1992 as a collaborative effort between the Minda de Gunzburg Center for European Studies at Harvard University and the Wissenschaftszentrum in Berlin to bring together a group of young political economists to discuss the issues associated with varieties of capitalism that we led jointly with Suzanne Berger of MIT. The participants met twice a year over five years for intensive debate, and many spent extended periods of time at the WZB. These discussions provided some of the most exciting intellectual experiences of our lives, and we have learned more than we can ever acknowledge from those who took part in them.

We owe a particular debt to Suzanne Berger whose leadership was indispensable to the project and whose lively intelligence and empathetic criticism influenced many of the formulations in these pages. Tom Cusack, Geoffrey Garrett, and Jonas Pontusson were also mainstays of this project from the beginning whose intellectual contributions to it have profoundly influenced our thinking. Among those who participated in many of the sessions, we want to thank Carles Boix, Jonah Levy, Richard Locke, Paul Pierson, Peter Swenson, Anne Wren, and Nicholas Ziegler. Those who provided important contributions to specific sessions include: Richard Clayton, Elie Cohen, John Ferejohn, David Finegold, Andrew Glyn, John Griffin, Ellen Immergut, Wade Jacoby, Horst Kern, Desmond King, Peter Lange, Gerhard Lehmbruch, Ton Notermans, Claus Offe, Sofia Pérez, Fritz Scharpf, Wolfgang Streeck, Gunnar Trumbull, Steven Vogel, and John Zysman.

For the financial support that sustained this project, we are grateful to the Wissenschaftszentrum and the Program for the Study of Germany and Europe at Harvard. We thank Charles Maier, the Director of the Center for European Studies, Abby Collins, its Associate Director, and

Friedhelm Neidhardt, the President of the WZB, for active encouragement at crucial stages of the proceedings. Without the logistical support of Hannelore Minzlaff and Ilona Köhler at the WZB as well as Lisa Eschenbach at CES, our meetings would have not have been possible. As usual, we are deeply grateful to them. Support for the preparation of the Introduction was also provided through a grant from the research and writing initiative of the Program on Global Security and Sustainability of the John D. and Catherine T. MacArthur Foundation. Jessica Berger, Alison Fleig, Holger Frank, and Daniel Gingerich worked with efficiency and dispatch to prepare this volume for the press.

Over the years in which we have been working on this book, we have received encouragement and constructive criticism from so many friends and colleagues that it is impossible to list them all, but they should know we are grateful. Among those who deserve special thanks for the advice or close readings they provided are: Rainer Fehn, Peter Gourevitch, Michel Goyer, Rogers Hollingsworth, Peter Katzenstein, Stephan Leibfried, Margaret Levi, Philip Manow, Andrew Martin, and Jonathan Zeitlin as well as the anonymous readers for the press.

Finally, for intellectual stimulation and sustained support, we owe more than we can express to Nicola Lacey and Rosemary C. R. Taylor.

P.A.H.
D.S.

Cambridge and Berlin
January 2001

CONTENTS

Part III: Corporate Governance, Firm Strategy,
and the Law

LIST OF FIGURES

LIST OF TABLES

LIST OF CONTRIBUTORS

Steven Casper is a University Lecturer in the Judge Institute of Management at the University of Cambridge. He publishes in the areas of institutional theory, national systems of innovation, and the relationship between law and technical change. His current research investigates the diffusion of entrepreneurial business models in Europe.

Pepper D. Culpepper is Assistant Professor of Public Policy at the John F. Kennedy School of Government at Harvard University. He is the editor of *The German Skills Machine* and the author of a forthcoming book, *Rethinking Reform: The Politics of Decentralized Cooperation in the Advanced Industrial Countries*.

Margarita Estevez-Abe is Assistant Professor of Government at Harvard University. She is currently finishing a book on *Welfare and Capitalism in Postwar Japan* that examines institutional complementarities between the Japanese welfare system, employment, and financial systems.

Orfeo Fioretos is an Assistant Professor of Political Science at the University of Wisconsin, Madison. He has published several articles on international relations and is currently completing a book entitled *Creative Reconstruction: Globalization, European Multilateralism, and Varieties of Capitalism, 1973–99*.

Robert J. Franzese, Jr. is Assistant Professor of Political Science at the University of Michigan and the author of *Explaining Macroeconomic Policy: Interactions of Interests and Institutions in the Evolving Political Economies of Developed Democracies* as well as many articles about economic policy-making in democratic polities.

Peter A. Hall is Frank G. Thomson Professor of Government and the Director of the Minda de Gunzburg Center for European Studies at Harvard University. His publications include *Governing the Economy* and *The Political Power of Economic Ideas* as well as many articles on European politics and comparative political economy.

Bob Hancké is Lecturer in European political economy in the European Institute of the London School of Economics. His articles address restructuring in the French economy and comparative labour relations.

Torben Iversen is Professor of Government at Harvard University and the author of *Contested Economic Institutions: The Politics of Macroeconomics and Wage Bargaining in Advanced Democracies* as well as numerous articles on voting and political economy.

Mark Lehrer is Assistant Professor of Management at the University of Rhode Island. He has published many articles applying comparative institutional analysis to the governance of firms and sectors, especially in knowledge-intensive and high-technology areas.

Isabela Mares is Assistant Professor of Political Science at Stanford University. She is completing a book entitled *Negotiated Risks: Employers' Role in Social Policy Development*. Her articles examining the formation of cross-class alliances in the process of social-policy reform have been published in *Politics and Society*, the *Journal of Public Policy*, *Governance*, and a number of edited volumes.

David Soskice is Research Professor of Political Science at Duke University and Adjunct Research Professor in the Research School for the Social Sciences, Australian National University. He is on long-term leave of absence from the Wissenschaftszentrum in Berlin.

Jay Tate is a Research Associate at the Berkeley Roundtable on the International Economy (BRIE) and author of *Driving Production Innovation Home: Japan's Guardian State Capitalism and the Competitiveness of the Japanese Automobile Industry*. His research interests include knowledge capitalism, reinventing government, and the politics of work.

Gunther Teubner is Professor of Private Law and Legal Sociology at Frankfurt University and the London School of Economics. He has published widely on comparative law and social theory including *Global Law without a State*.

Kathleen Thelen is Associate Professor of Political Science at Northwestern University. She is the author of *Union of Parts* and co-editor of *Structuring Politics* as well as a number of articles on historical institutionalism and on labor politics in the developed democracies.

Sigurt Vitols is a senior research fellow at the Wissenschaftszentrum Berlin für Sozialforschung. His research interests include comparative corporate governance, financial regulation, and venture capital. Recent publications include contributions to *Small Business Economics*, *Industry and Innovation*, and a number of edited collections.

Stewart Wood is a fellow in politics at Magdalen College, Oxford University. He has written articles on contemporary political economy, public policy issues, and British politics and is currently writing a book comparing supply-side reforms in Britain and Germany during the post-war period.

1

An Introduction to Varieties of Capitalism

Peter A. Hall and David Soskice

1.1 Introduction

Political economists have always been interested in the differences in economic and political institutions that occur across countries. Some regard these differences as deviations from 'best practice' that will dissolve as nations catch up to a technological or organizational leader. Others see them as the distillation of more durable historical choices for a specific kind of society, since economic institutions condition levels of social protection, the distribution of income, and the availability of collective goods—features of the social solidarity of a nation. In each case, comparative political economy revolves around the conceptual frameworks used to understand institutional variation across nations.

On such frameworks depend the answers to a range of important questions. Some are policy-related. What kind of economic policies will improve the performance of the economy? What will governments do in the face of economic challenges? What defines a state's capacities to meet such challenges? Other questions are firm-related. Do companies located in different nations display systematic differences in their structure and strategies? If so, what inspires such differences? How can national differences in the pace or character of innovation be explained? Some are issues about economic performance. Do some sets of institutions provide lower rates of inflation and unemployment or higher rates of growth than others? What are the trade-offs in terms of economic performance to developing one type of political economy rather than another? Finally, second-order questions about institutional change and stability are of special significance today. Can we expect technological progress and the competitive pressures of globalization to inspire institutional convergence? What factors condition the adjustment paths a political economy takes in the face of such challenges?

The object of this book is to elaborate a new framework for understanding the institutional similarities and differences among the developed economies, one that offers a new and intriguing set of answers to such questions.[1] We outline the basic approach in this Introduction. Subsequent chapters extend and apply it to a wide range of issues. In many respects, this approach is still a work-in-progress. We see it as a set of contentions that open up new research agendas rather than settled wisdom to be accepted uncritically, but, as the contributions to this volume indicate, it provides new perspectives on an unusually broad set of topics, ranging from issues in innovation, vocational training, and corporate strategy to those associated with legal systems, the development of social policy, and the stance nations take in international negotiations.

As any work on this topic must be, ours is deeply indebted to prior scholarship in the field. The 'varieties of capitalism' approach developed here can be seen as an effort to go beyond three perspectives on institutional variation that have dominated the study of comparative capitalism in the preceding thirty years.[2] In important respects, like ours, each of these perspectives was a response to the economic problems of its time.

The first of these perspectives offers a *modernization approach* to comparative capitalism nicely elucidated in Shonfield's magisterial treatise of 1965. Devised in the post-war decades, this approach saw the principal challenge confronting the developed economies as one of modernizing industries still dominated by pre-war practices in order to secure high rates of national growth. Analysts tried to identify a set of actors with the strategic capacity to devise plans for industry and to impress them on specific sectors. Occasionally, this capacity was said to reside in the banks but more often in public officials. Accordingly, those taking this approach focused on the institutional structures that gave states leverage over the private sector, such as planning systems and public influence over the flows of funds in the financial system (Cohen 1977; Estrin and Holmes 1983; Zysman 1983; Cox 1986). Countries were often categorized, according to the structure of their state, into those with 'strong' and 'weak' states (Katzenstein 1978b; Sacks 1980; Nordlinger 1981; Skocpol and Amenta 1985). France and Japan emerged from this perspective as models of economic success, while Britain was generally seen as a laggard (Shonfield 1965; Johnson 1982).

---

[1] We concentrate here on economies at relatively high levels of development because we know them best and think the framework applies well to many problems there. However, the basic approach should also have relevance for understanding developing economies as well (cf. Bates 1997).

[2] Of necessity, this summary is brief and slightly stylized. As a result, it does not do full justice to the variety of analyses found within these literatures and neglects some discussions that fall outside them. Note that some of our own prior work can be said to fall within them. For more extensive reviews, see Hall (1999, 2001).

During the 1970s, when inflation became the preeminent problem facing the developed economies, a number of analysts developed a second approach to comparative capitalism based on the concept of *neo-corporatism* (Schmitter and Lehmbruch 1979; Berger 1981; Goldthorpe 1984; Alvarez et al. 1991). Although defined in various ways, neo-corporatism was generally associated with the capacity of a state to negotiate durable bargains with employers and the trade union movement regarding wages, working conditions, and social or economic policy.[3] Accordingly, a nation's capacity for neo-corporatism was generally said to depend on the centralization or concentration of the trade union movement, following an Olsonian logic of collective action which specifies that more encompassing unions can better internalize the economic effects of their wage settlements (Olson 1965; Cameron 1984; Calmfors and Driffill 1988; Golden 1993). Those who saw neo-corporatist bargains as a 'political exchange' emphasized the ability of states to offer inducements as well as the capacity of unions to discipline their members (Pizzorno 1978; Regini 1984; Scharpf 1987, 1991; cf. Przeworski and Wallerstein 1982). Those working from this perspective categorized countries largely by reference to the organization of their trade union movement; and the success stories of this literature were the small, open economies of northern Europe.

During the 1980s and 1990s, a new approach to comparative capitalism that we will term a *social systems of production* approach gained currency. Under this rubric, we group analyses of sectoral governance, national innovation systems, and flexible production regimes that are diverse in some respects but united by several key analytic features. Responding to the reorganization of production in response to technological change, these works devote more attention to the behavior of firms. Influenced by the French regulation school, they emphasize the movement of firms away from mass production toward new production regimes that depend on collective institutions at the regional, sectoral, or national level (Piore and Sabel 1984; Dore 1986; Streeck and Schmitter 1986; Dosi et al. 1988; Boyer 1990; Lazonick 1991; Campbell et al. 1991; Nelson 1993; Hollingsworth et al. 1994; Herrigel 1996; Hollingsworth and Boyer 1997; Edquist 1997; Whitley 1999). These works bring a wider range of institutions into the analysis and adopt a more sociological approach to their operation, stressing the ways in which institutions

---

[3] An alternative approach to neo-corporatism, closer to our own, which puts less emphasis on the trade union movement and more on the organization of business was also developed by Katzenstein (1985*a*, 1985*b*) among others (Offe 1981).

generate trust or enhance learning within economic communities. As a result, some of these works resist national categories in favor of an emphasis on regional success of the sort found in Baden-Württemberg and the Third Italy.

Each of these bodies of work explains important aspects of the economic world. However, we seek to go beyond them in several respects. Although those who wrote within it characterized national differences in the early post-war era well, for instance, some versions of the modernization approach tend to overstate what governments can accomplish, especially in contexts of economic openness where adjustment is firm-led. We will argue that features of states once seen as attributes of strength actually make the implementation of many economic policies more difficult; and we seek a basis for comparison more deeply rooted in the organization of the private sector.

Neo-corporatist analysis directs our attention to the organization of society, but its emphasis on the trade union movement underplays the role that firms and employer organizations play in the coordination of the economy (cf. Soskice 1990a; Swenson 1991). We want to bring firms back into the center of the analysis of comparative capitalism and, without neglecting trade unions, highlight the role that business associations and other types of relationships among firms play in the political economy.

The literature on social systems of production accords firms a central role and links the organization of production to the support provided by external institutions at many levels of the political economy. However, without denying that regional or sectoral institutions matter to firm behavior, we focus on variation among national political economies. Our premiss is that many of the most important institutional structures—notably systems of labor market regulation, of education and training, and of corporate governance—depend on the presence of regulatory regimes that are the preserve of the nation-state. Accordingly, we look for national-level differences and terms in which to characterize them that are more general or parsimonious than this literature has generated.[4]

Where we break most fundamentally from these approaches, however, is in our conception of how behavior is affected by the institutions of the political economy. Three frameworks for understanding this relationship

---

[4] One of the pioneering works that some will want to compare is Albert (1993), who develops a contrast between the models of the Rhine and America that parallels ours in some respects. Other valuable efforts to identify varieties of capitalism that have influenced us include Hollingsworth and Boyer (1997), Crouch and Streeck (1997b), and Whitley (1999).

dominate the analysis of comparative capitalism. One sees institutions as *socializing agencies* that instill a particular set of norms or attitudes in those who operate within them. French civil servants, for instance, are said to acquire a particular concern for the public interest by virtue of their training or the ethos of their agencies. A second suggests that the effects of an institution follow from the *power* it confers on particular actors through the formal sanctions that hierarchy supplies or the resources an institution provides for mobilization. Industrial policy-makers and trade union leaders are often said to have such forms of power. A third framework construes the institutions of the political economy as a *matrix of sanctions and incentives* to which the relevant actors respond such that behavior can be predicted more or less automatically from the presence of specific institutions, as, for instance, when individuals refuse to provide public goods in the absence of selective incentives. This kind of logic is often cited to explain the willingness of encompassing trade unions to moderate wages in order to reduce inflation.

Each of these formulations captures important ways in which the institutions of the political economy affect economic behavior and we make use of them. However, we think these approaches tend to miss or model too incompletely the *strategic interactions* central to the behavior of economic actors. The importance of strategic interaction is increasingly appreciated by economists but still neglected in studies of comparative capitalism.[5] If interaction of this sort is central to economic and political outcomes, the most important institutions distinguishing one political economy from another will be those conditioning such interaction, and it is these that we seek to capture in this analysis. For this purpose, we construe the key relationships in the political economy in game-theoretic terms and focus on the kinds of institutions that alter the outcomes of strategic interaction. This approach generates an analysis that focuses on some of the same institutions others have identified as important but construes the impact of those institutions differently as well as one that highlights other institutions not yet given enough attention in studies of comparative capitalism.

By locating the firm at the center of the analysis, we hope to build bridges between business studies and comparative political economy, two disciplines that are all too often disconnected. By integrating game-theoretical perspectives on the firm of the sort that are now central to microeconomics into an analysis of the macroeconomy, we attempt to connect the new microeconomics to important issues in macroeconomics.

[5] There are a few notable exceptions that influence our analysis, including the work of Scharpf (1987, 1997*a*) and Przeworski and Wallerstein (1982).

Ours is a framework that should be of interest to economists, scholars of business, and political scientists alike. We turn now to an elucidation of its basic elements.

1.2 The Basic Elements of the Approach

This *varieties of capitalism* approach to the political economy is actor-centered, which is to say we see the political economy as a terrain populated by multiple actors, each of whom seeks to advance his interests in a rational way in strategic interaction with others (Scharpf 1997a). The relevant actors may be individuals, firms, producer groups, or governments. However, this is a firm-centered political economy that regards companies as the crucial actors in a capitalist economy. They are the key agents of adjustment in the face of technological change or international competition whose activities aggregate into overall levels of economic performance.

1.2.1 A Relational View of the Firm

Our conception of the firm is relational. Following recent work in economics, we see firms as actors seeking to develop and exploit *core competencies* or *dynamic capabilities* understood as capacities for developing, producing, and distributing goods and services profitably (Teece and Pisano 1998). We take the view that critical to these is the quality of the relationships the firm is able to establish, both internally, with its own employees, and externally, with a range of other actors that include suppliers, clients, collaborators, stakeholders, trade unions, business associations, and governments. As the work on transactions costs and principal–agent relationships in the economics of organization has underlined, these are problematic relationships (Milgrom and Roberts 1992). Even where hierarchies can be used to secure the cooperation of actors, firms encounter problems of moral hazard, adverse selection, and shirking. In many cases, effective operation even within a hierarchical environment may entail the formation of implicit contracts among the actors; and many of a firm's relationships with outside actors involve incomplete contracting (cf. Williamson 1985). In short, because its capabilities are ultimately relational, a firm encounters many coordination problems. Its success depends substantially on its ability to coordinate effectively with a wide range of actors.

For the purposes of this inquiry, we focus on five spheres in which firms must develop relationships to resolve coordination problems central to their core competencies. The first is the sphere of *industrial relations* where the problem facing companies is how to coordinate bargaining over wages and working conditions with their labor force, the organizations that represent labor, and other employers. At stake here are wage and productivity levels that condition the success of the firm and rates of unemployment or inflation in the economy as a whole. In the sphere of *vocational training and education*, firms face the problem of securing a workforce with suitable skills, while workers face the problem of deciding how much to invest in what skills. On the outcomes of this coordination problem turn not only the fortunes of individual companies and workers but the skill levels and competitiveness of the overall economy.

Issues of coordination also arise in the sphere of *corporate governance*, to which firms turn for access to finance and in which investors seek assurances of returns on their investments. The solutions devised to these problems affect both the availability of finance for particular types of projects and the terms on which firms can secure funds. The fourth sphere in which coordination problems crucial to the core competencies of an enterprise appear is the broad one of *inter-firm relations*, a term we use to cover the relationships a company forms with other enterprises, and notably its suppliers or clients, with a view to securing a stable demand for its products, appropriate supplies of inputs, and access to technology. These are endeavors that may entail standard-setting, technology transfer, and collaborative research and development. Here, coordination problems stem from the sharing of proprietary information and the risk of exploitation in joint ventures. On the development of appropriate relationships in this sphere, however, depend the capacities of firms to remain competitive and technological progress in the economy as a whole.

Finally, firms face a set of coordination problems vis-à-vis their own *employees*. Their central problem is to ensure that employees have the requisite competencies and cooperate well with others to advance the objectives of the firm. In this context, familiar problems of adverse selection and moral hazard arise, and issues of information-sharing become important (see Milgrom and Roberts 1992). Workers develop reservoirs of specialized information about the firm's operations that can be of value to management, but they also have the capacity to withhold information or effort. The relationships firms develop to resolve these problems condition their own competencies and the character of an economy's production regimes.

1.2.2 Liberal Market Economies and Coordinated Market Economies

From this perspective, it follows that national political economies can be compared by reference to the way in which firms resolve the coordination problems they face in these five spheres. The core distinction we draw is between two types of political economies, liberal market economies and coordinated market economies, which constitute ideal types at the poles of a spectrum along which many nations can be arrayed.[6]

In *liberal market economies*, firms coordinate their activities primarily via hierarchies and competitive market arrangements. These forms of coordination are well described by a classic literature (Williamson 1985). Market relationships are characterized by the arm's-length exchange of goods or services in a context of competition and formal contracting. In response to the price signals generated by such markets, the actors adjust their willingness to supply and demand goods or services, often on the basis of the marginal calculations stressed by neoclassical economics.[7] In many respects, market institutions provide a highly effective means for coordinating the endeavors of economic actors.

In *coordinated market economies*, firms depend more heavily on non-market relationships to coordinate their endeavors with other actors and to construct their core competencies. These non-market modes of coordination generally entail more extensive relational or incomplete contracting, network monitoring based on the exchange of private information inside networks, and more reliance on collaborative, as opposed to competitive, relationships to build the competencies of the firm. In contrast to liberal market economies (LMEs), where the equilibrium outcomes of firm behavior are usually given by demand and supply conditions in competitive markets, the equilibria on which firms coordinate in coordinated market economies (CMEs) are more often the result of strategic interaction among firms and other actors.

Market relations and hierarchies are important to firms in all capitalist economies, of course, and, even in liberal market economies, firms enter

---

[6] In other works by the contributors to this volume, 'organized market economy' is sometimes used as a term synonymous with 'coordinated market economy'. Although all of the economies we discuss are 'coordinated' in the general sense of the term, by markets if not by other institutions, the term reflects the prominence of strategic interaction and hence of coordination in the game-theoretic sense in CMEs.

[7] Although we do not emphasize it here, this is not meant to deny the observation of Granovetter (1985) and others that market relations are usually underpinned by personal relationships of familiarity and trust.

into some relationships that are not fully mediated by market forces.[8] But this typology is based on the contention that the incidence of different types of firm relationships varies systematically across nations. In some nations, for instance, firms rely primarily on formal contracts and highly competitive markets to organize relationships with their employees and suppliers of finance, while, in others, firms coordinate these endeavors differently. In any national economy, firms will gravitate toward the mode of coordination for which there is institutional support.

1.2.3 The Role of Institutions and Organizations

Institutions, organizations, and culture enter this analysis because of the support they provide for the relationships firms develop to resolve coordination problems. Following North (1990: 3), we define institutions as a set of rules, formal or informal, that actors generally follow, whether for normative, cognitive, or material reasons, and organizations as durable entities with formally recognized members, whose rules also contribute to the institutions of the political economy.[9]

From this perspective, markets are institutions that support relationships of particular types, marked by arm's-length relations and high levels of competition. Their concomitant is a legal system that supports formal contracting and encourages relatively complete contracts, as the chapters by Teubner and Casper indicate. All capitalist economies also contain the hierarchies that firms construct to resolve the problems that cannot be addressed by markets (Williamson 1985). In liberal market economies, these are the principal institutions on which firms rely to coordinate their endeavors.

Although markets and hierarchies are also important elements of coordinated market economies, firms in this type of economy draw on a further set of organizations and institutions for support in coordinating their endeavors. What types of organizations and institutions support the distinctive strategies of economic actors in such economies? Because the latter rely more heavily on forms of coordination secured through

---

[8] This point applies with particular force to market relationships in which one or more of the participants has substantially more market power than the others, as in cases of oligopoly, oligopsony, and the relations found in some supplier chains. We are not arguing that all markets in LMEs are perfectly competitive.

[9] Note that, from time to time, we refer loosely to the 'institutions' or 'organization' of the political economy to refer to both the organizations and institutions found within it.

strategic interaction to resolve the problems they face, the relevant institutions will be those that allow them to coordinate on equilibrium strategies that offer higher returns to all concerned. In general, these will be institutions that reduce the uncertainty actors have about the behavior of others and allow them to make credible commitments to each other. A standard literature suggests that these are institutions providing capacities for (i) the *exchange of information* among the actors, (ii) the *monitoring* of behavior, and (iii) the *sanctioning* of defection from cooperative endeavor (see Ostrom 1990). Typically, these institutions include powerful business or employer associations, strong trade unions, extensive networks of cross-shareholding, and legal or regulatory systems designed to facilitate information-sharing and collaboration. Where these are present, firms can coordinate on strategies to which they would not have been led by market relations alone.

The problem of operating collaborative vocational training schemes provides a classic example. Here, the willingness of firms to participate depends on the security of their beliefs that workers will learn useful skills and that firms not investing in training will not poach extensively from those who do, while the participation of workers depends on assurances that training will lead to remunerative employment. As Culpepper's chapter in this volume indicates, it is easier for actors to secure these assurances where there are institutions providing reliable flows of information about appropriate skill levels, the incidence of training, and the employment prospects of apprentices (Finegold and Soskice 1988; Culpepper and Finegold 1999).

Similarly, the terms on which finance is provided to firms will depend on the monitoring capacities present in the economy. Where potential investors have little access to inside information about the progress of the firms they fund, access to capital is likely to depend on highly public criteria about the assets of a firm of the sort commonly found on balance sheets. Where investors are linked to the firms they fund through networks that allow for the development of reputations based on extensive access to information about the internal operations of the firm, however, investors will be more willing to supply capital to firms on terms that do not depend entirely on their balance sheets. The presence of institutions providing network reputational monitoring can have substantial effects on the terms on which firms can secure finance.

In short, this approach to comparative capitalism emphasizes the presence of institutions providing capacities for the exchange of information, monitoring, and the sanctioning of defections relevant to cooperative behavior among firms and other actors; and it is for the presence of such institutions that we look when comparing nations.

In addition, examination of coordinated market economies leads us to emphasize the importance of another kind of institution that is not normally on the list of those crucial to the formation of credible commitments, namely institutions that provide actors potentially able to cooperate with one another with a capacity for *deliberation*. By this, we simply mean institutions that encourage the relevant actors to engage in collective discussion and to reach agreements with each other.[10] Deliberative institutions are important for several reasons.

Deliberative proceedings in which the participants engage in extensive sharing of information about their interests and beliefs can improve the confidence of each in the strategies likely to be taken by the others. Many game-theoretic analyses assume a level of common knowledge that is relatively thin, barely stretching past a shared language and familiarity with the relevant payoffs. When multiple equilibria are available, however, coordination on one (especially one that exchanges higher payoffs for higher risks) can be greatly facilitated by the presence of a thicker common knowledge, one that extends beyond the basic situation to a knowledge of the other players sufficiently intimate to provide confidence that each will coordinate on a specific equilibrium (Eichengreen 1997). Deliberation can substantially thicken the common knowledge of the group.

As Scharpf (1987: ch. 4) has pointed out, although many think only of a 'prisoner's dilemma' game when they consider problems of cooperation, in the political economy many such problems take quite different forms, including 'battle of the sexes' games in which joint gains are available from more than one strategy but are distributed differently depending on the equilibrium chosen. Distributive dilemmas of this sort are endemic to political economies, and agreement on the distribution of the relevant gains is often the prerequisite to effective cooperation (Knight 1992). In some cases, such as those of collaborative research and development, the problem is not simply to distribute the gains but also the risks attendant on the enterprise. Deliberation provides the actors with an opportunity to establish the risks and gains attendant on cooperation and to resolve the distributive issues associated with them. In some cases, the actors may simply be negotiating from positions of

---

[10] One political economist who has consistently drawn attention to the importance of deliberation is Sabel (1992, 1994) and the issue is now the subject of a growing game-theoretic literature (see Elster 1998).

relative power, but extensive deliberation over time may build up specific conceptions of distributive justice that can be used to facilitate agreement in subsequent exchanges.

Finally, deliberative institutions can enhance the capacity of actors in the political economy for strategic action when faced with new or unfamiliar challenges. This is far from irrelevant since economies are frequently subject to exogenous shocks that force the actors within them to respond to situations to which they are unaccustomed. The history of wage negotiations in Europe is replete with examples. In such instances, developments may outrun common knowledge, and deliberation can be instrumental to devising an effective and coordinated response, allowing the actors to develop a common diagnosis of the situation and an agreed response.

In short, deliberative institutions can provide the actors in a political economy with strategic capacities they would not otherwise enjoy; and we think cross-national comparison should be attentive to the presence of facilities for deliberation as well as institutions that provide for the exchange of information in other forms, monitoring, and the enforcement of agreements.

1.2.4 The Role of Culture, Informal Rules, and History

Our approach departs from previous works on comparative capitalism in another respect.[11] Many analyses take the view that the relevant outcomes in economic performance or policy follow more or less directly from differences in the formal organization of the political economy. Particular types of wage settlements or rates of inflation and unemployment are often said to follow, for instance, from the organizational structure of the union movement. Because we believe such outcomes are the products of efforts to coordinate in contexts of strategic interaction, however, we reject the contention that they follow from the presence of a particular set of institutions alone, at least if the latter are defined entirely in terms of formal rules or organizations.

As we have noted, the presence of a set of formal institutions is often a necessary precondition for attaining the relevant equilibrium in contexts of coordination. But formal institutions are rarely sufficient to guarantee that equilibrium. In multi-player games with multiple iterations of the sort that characterize most of the cases in which we are

[11] Here we depart from some of our own previous formulations as well (cf. Hall 1986; Soskice 1990*b*).

interested, it is well known that there exist multiple equilibria, any one of which could be chosen by the actors even in the presence of institutions conducive to the formation of credible commitments (Fudenberg and Maskin 1986). Something else is needed to lead the actors to coordinate on a specific equilibrium and, notably, on equilibria offering high returns in a non-coooperative context.[12] In many instances, what leads the actors to a specific equilibrium is a set of shared understandings about what other actors are likely to do, often rooted in a sense of what it is appropriate to do in such circumstances (March and Olsen 1989).

Accordingly, taking a step beyond many accounts, we emphasize the importance of informal rules and understandings to securing the equilibria in the many strategic interactions of the political economy. These shared understandings are important elements of the 'common knowledge' that lead participants to coordinate on one outcome, rather than another, when both are feasible in the presence of a specific set of formal institutions. By considering them a component of the institutions making up the political economy, we expand the concept of institutions beyond the purely formal connotations given to it in some analyses.

This is an entry point in the analysis for history and culture. Many actors learn to follow a set of informal rules by virtue of experience with a familiar set of actors and the shared understandings that accumulate from this experience constitute something like a common culture. This concept of culture as a set of shared understandings or available 'strategies for action' developed from experience of operating in a particular environment is analogous to those developed in the 'cognitive turn' taken by sociology (Swidler 1986; DiMaggio and Powell 1991). Our view of the role that culture can play in the strategic interactions of the political economy is similar to the one Kreps (1990) accords it in organizations faced with problems of incomplete contracting.

The implication is that the institutions of a nation's political economy are inextricably bound up with its history in two respects. On the one hand, they are created by actions, statutory or otherwise, that establish formal institutions and their operating procedures. On the other, repeated historical experience builds up a set of common expectations that allows the actors to coordinate effectively with each other. Among other things, this implies that the institutions central to the operation of the political economy should not be seen as entities that are created at one point in time and can then be assumed to operate effectively afterwards.

---

[12] Culpepper documents this problem and explores some solutions to it in this volume and Culpepper (1998).

To remain viable, the shared understandings associated with them must be reaffirmed periodically by appropriate historical experience. As Thelen emphasizes in this volume, the operative force of many institutions cannot be taken for granted but must be reinforced by the active endeavors of the participants.

1.2.5 Institutional Infrastructure and Corporate Strategy

This varieties of capitalism approach draws its basic conceptions of how institutions operate from the new economics of organization. We apply a set of concepts commonly used to explain behavior at the micro level of the economy to problems of understanding the macroeconomy (Milgrom and Roberts 1992). One of the advantages is an analysis with robust and consistent postulates about what kind of institutions matter and how they affect behavior. Another is the capacity of the approach to integrate analysis of firm behavior with analysis of the political economy as a whole.

However, there are at least two respects in which our account deviates from mainstream views in the new economics of organization. First, although we make use of the influential dichotomy between 'markets' and 'hierarchies' that Williamson (1975) has impressed on the field, we do not think this exhausts the relevant variation. Markets and hierarchies are features of LMEs and CMEs but we stress the systematic variation found in the character of corporate structure (or hierarchies) across different types of economies and the presence of coordination problems even within hierarchical settings (Milgrom and Roberts 1992). Even more important, we do not see these two institutional forms as the only ones firms can employ to resolve the challenges they confront. In coordinated market economies in particular, many firms develop relationships with other firms, outside actors, and their employees that are not well described as either market-based or hierarchical relations but better seen as efforts to secure cooperative outcomes among the actors using a range of institutional devices that underpin credible commitments. Variation in the incidence and character of this 'third' type of relationship is central to the distinctions we draw between various types of political economies.[13]

Second, it is conventional in much of the new economics of organization to assume that the core institutional structures of the economy,

---

[13] Williamson (1985) himself acknowledges the presence of institutionalized relationships extending beyond markets or hierarchies, albeit without characterizing them precisely as we do here.

whether markets, hierarchies, or networks, are erected by firms seeking the most efficient institutions for performing certain tasks. The postulate is that (institutional) structure follows (firm) strategy (cf. Chandler 1974; Williamson 1975, 1985; Chandler and Daems 1980). In a restricted sense, this is certainly true: firms can choose whether to contract out an endeavor or perform it in-house, for instance, and they enjoy some control over their own corporate form.

However, we think it unrealistic to regard the overarching institutional structures of the political economy, and especially those coordinating the endeavors of many actors (such as markets, institutional networks, and the organizations supporting collaborative endeavor), as constructs created or controlled by a particular firm. Because they are collective institutions, a single firm cannot create them; and, because they have multifarious effects, it may be difficult for a group of firms to agree on them.[14] Instead, as Calvert (1995) observes, the construction of coordinating institutions should be seen as a second-order coordination problem of considerable magnitude. Even when firms can agree, the project may entail regulatory action by the government and the formation of coalitions among political parties and labor organizations motivated by considerations going well beyond efficiency (Swenson 1991, 1997).

As a result, the firms located within any political economy face a set of coordinating institutions whose character is not fully under their control. These institutions offer firms a particular set of opportunities; and companies can be expected to gravitate toward strategies that take advantage of these opportunities. In short, there are important respects in which strategy follows structure. For this reason, our approach predicts systematic differences in corporate strategy across nations, and differences that parallel the overarching institutional structures of the political economy. This is one of the most important implications of the analysis.

Let us stress that we refer here to broad differences. Of course, there will be additional variation in corporate strategies inside all economies in keeping with differences in the resource endowments and market settings of individual firms. The capabilities of management also matter, since firms are actors with considerable autonomy. Our point is that (institutional) structure conditions (corporate) strategy, not that it fully determines it. We also agree that differences in corporate strategy can be conditioned by the institutional support available to firms at the regional or sectoral levels (Campbell et al. 1991; Hollingsworth et al. 1994; Herrigel

---

[14] At the sectoral or regional level, of course, large firms may be able to exercise substantial influence over the development of these institutions, as Hancké shows in this volume (see also Hancké forthcoming).

1996). Many of the works making this point are congruent with our own in that they stress the importance of the institutional environment to firm strategy, even though there has been fruitful disagreement about which features of that environment matter most (cf. Streeck 1992*b*).[15]

However, we emphasize variations in corporate strategy evident at the national level. We think this justified by the fact that so many of the institutional factors conditioning the behavior of firms remain nation-specific. There are good reasons why that should be the case. Some of the relevant institutions were deeply conditioned by nationally specific processes of development, as are most trade unions and employers' associations. In others, the relevant institutions depend heavily on statutes or regulations promulgated by national states, as do many institutions in the financial arena and labor market, not to mention the sphere of contract law.

In sum, we contend that differences in the institutional framework of the political economy generate systematic differences in corporate strategy across LMEs and CMEs. There is already some evidence for this. For instance, the data that Knetter (1989) has gathered are especially interesting. He finds that the firms of Britain, a typical LME, and those of Germany, a CME, respond very differently to a similar shock, in this case an appreciation of the exchange rate that renders the nation's goods more expensive in foreign markets. British firms tend to pass the price increase along to customers in order to maintain their profitability, while German firms maintain their prices and accept lower returns in order to preserve market share.

Our approach predicts differences of precisely this sort. We would argue that British firms must sustain their profitability because the structure of financial markets in a liberal market economy links the firm's access to capital and ability to resist takeover to its current profitability; and they can sustain the loss of market share because fluid labor markets allow them to lay off workers readily. By contrast, German firms can sustain a decline in returns because the financial system of a coordinated market economy provides firms with access to capital independent of current profitability; and they attempt to retain market share because the labor institutions in such an economy militate in favor of long-term employment strategies and render layoffs difficult.

---

[15] It is possible to apply the general analytical framework of this volume to variations at the regional or sectoral level, as the chapter by Hancké does in some respects. From the perspective of this volume, institutional variation at the regional or sectoral level provides an additional layer of support for particular types of coordination and one that enhances a nation's capacity to support a range of corporate strategies and production regimes.

These are only some of the ways in which the institutional arrangements of a nation's political economy tend to push its firms toward particular kinds of corporate strategies. We explore more of these below with special emphasis on innovation.

To put the point in the most general terms, however, firms and other actors in coordinated market economies should be more willing to invest in *specific* and *co-specific assets* (i.e. assets that cannot readily be turned to another purpose and assets whose returns depend heavily on the active cooperation of others), while those in liberal market economies should invest more extensively in *switchable assets* (i.e. assets whose value can be realized if diverted to other purposes). This follows from the fact that CMEs provide more institutional support for the strategic interactions required to realize the value of co-specific assets, whether in the form of industry-specific training, collaborative research and development, or the like, while the more fluid markets of LMEs provide economic actors with greater opportunities to move their resources around in search of higher returns, encouraging them to acquire switchable assets, such as general skills or multi-purpose technologies.[16]

1.2.6 Institutional Complementarities

The presence of *institutional complementarities* reinforces the differences between liberal and coordinated market economies. The concept of 'complementary goods' is a familiar one: two goods, such as bread and butter, are described as complementary if an increase in the price of one depresses demand for the other. However, complementarities may also exist among the operations of a firm: marketing arrangements that offer customized products, for instance, may offer higher returns when coupled to the use of flexible machine tools on the shop floor (Jaikumar 1986; Milgrom and Roberts 1990, 1995).

Following Aoki (1994), we extend this line of reasoning to the institutions of the political economy. Here, two institutions can be said to be complementary if the presence (or efficiency) of one increases the returns from (or efficiency of) the other.[17] The returns from a stock market trading

---

[16] For examples in one sphere, see the essay by Estevez-Abe, Iversen, and Soskice in this volume.

[17] Conversely, two institutions can be said to be 'substitutable' if the absence or inefficiency of one increases the returns to using the other. Note that we refer to total returns, leaving aside the question of to whom they accrue, which is a matter of property rights, and we define efficiency as the net returns to the use of an institution given its costs.

in corporate securities, for instance, may be increased by regulations mandating a fuller exchange of information about companies.

Of particular interest are complementarities between institutions located in different spheres of the political economy. Aoki (1994) has argued that long-term employment is more feasible where the financial system provides capital on terms that are not sensitive to current profitability. Conversely, fluid labor markets may be more effective at sustaining employment in the presence of financial markets that transfer resources readily among endeavors thereby maintaining a demand for labor (cf. Caballero and Hamour 1998; Fehn 1998). Casper explores complementarities between national systems of contract law and modes of inter-firm collaboration, and we identify others in the sections that follow.

This point about institutional complementarities has special relevance for the study of comparative capitalism. It suggests that nations with a particular type of coordination in one sphere of the economy should tend to develop complementary practices in other spheres as well.[18] Several logics may be operative here. In some cases, the institutions sustaining coordination in one sphere can be used to support analogous forms of coordination in others. Where dense networks of business associations support collaborative systems of vocational training, for instance, those same networks may be used to operate collective standard-setting. Similarly, firms may pressure governments to foster the development of institutions complementary to those already present in the economy in order to secure the efficiency gains they provide.

If this is correct, institutional practices of various types should not be distributed randomly across nations. Instead, we should see some clustering along the dimensions that divide liberal from coordinated market economies, as nations converge on complementary practices across different spheres. Fig. 1.1 presents some support for these propositions. It locates OECD nations on two axes that provide indicators for the character of institutions in the spheres of corporate finance and labor markets respectively. A highly developed stock market indicates greater reliance on market modes of coordination in the financial

---

[18] Of course, there are limits to the institutional isomorphism that can be expected across spheres of the economy. Although efficiency considerations may press in this direction, the presence of functional equivalents for particular arrangements will limit the institutional homology even across similar types of political economies, and the importance to institutional development of historical processes driven by considerations other than efficiency will limit the number of complementarities found in any economy.

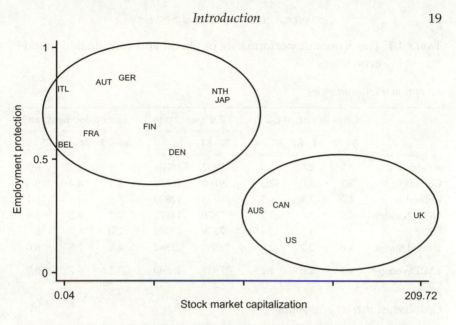

FIG. 1.1 Institutions across sub-spheres of the political economy

Note: Employment protection refers to the index of employment protection developed by Estevez-Abe, Iversen, and Soskice in this volume. Stock market capitalization is the market value of listed domestic companies as a percentage of GDP.

Source: International Federation of Stock Exchanges, *Annual Report*.

sphere, and high levels of employment protection tend to reflect higher levels of non-market coordination in the sphere of industrial relations.[19] Although there is some variation within each group, a pronounced clustering is evident. Nations with liberal market economies tend to rely on markets to coordinate endeavors in both the financial and industrial relations systems, while those with coordinated market economies have institutions in both spheres that reflect higher levels of non-market coordination.

Among the large OECD nations, six can be classified as liberal market economies (the USA, Britain, Australia, Canada, New Zealand, Ireland) and another ten as coordinated market economies (Germany, Japan, Switzerland, the Netherlands, Belgium, Sweden, Norway, Denmark,

---

[19] The employment protection index developed by Estevez-Abe, Iversen, and Soskice in their chapter for this volume is a composite measure of the relative stringency of legislation or collective agreements dealing with hiring and firing, the level of restraint embedded in collective dismissal rules, and the extent of firm-level employment protection. Stock market capitalization is the market value of listed domestic companies as a percentage of GDP.

TABLE 1.1 The economic performance of liberal and coordinated market
economies

Liberal market economies

	Growth rate of GDP			GDP per capita		Unemployment rate		
	61–73	74–84	85–98	74–84	85–97	60–73	74–84	85–98
Australia	5.2	2.8	3.3	7932	16701	1.9	6.2	8.5
Canada	5.3	3.0	2.3	9160	18835	5.1	8.4	9.5
Ireland	4.4	3.9	6.5	4751	12830	5.0	9.1	14.1
New Zealand	4.0	1.8	1.7	7378	14172	0.2	2.2	6.9
UK	3.1	1.3	2.4	7359	15942	2.0	6.7	8.7
United States	4.0	2.2	2.9	11055	22862	4.9	7.5	6.0
LME average	4.3	2.5	3.2	7939	16890	3.2	6.7	8.9

Coordinated market economies

	Growth rate of GDP			GDP per capita		Unemployment rate		
	61–73	74–84	85–98	74–84	85–97	60–73	74–84	85–98
Austria[a]	4.9	2.3	2.5	7852	17414	1.6	2.2	5.3
Belgium	4.9	2.0	2.2	8007	17576	2.2	8.2	11.3
Denmark	4.4	1.8	2.2	8354	18618	1.4	7.1	9.3
Finland	5.0	2.7	2.2	7219	15619	2.0	4.8	9.4
Iceland	5.7	4.1	2.7	8319	18285	0.6	0.6	2.5
Germany	4.3	1.8	2.2	7542	16933	0.8	4.6	8.5
Japan	9.7	3.3	2.6	7437	18475	1.3	2.1	2.8
Netherlands[b]	4.9	1.9	2.8	7872	16579	1.5	5.6	6.8
Norway	4.3	4.0	2.9	8181	19325	1.6	2.1	4.3
Sweden	4.2	1.8	1.5	8450	16710	1.9	2.3	4.8
Switzerland	4.4	.58	1.3	10680	21398	.01	0.4	2.5
CME average	5.1	2.4	2.3	8174	17902	1.3	3.6	6.1

Notes: Growth rate of GDP: average annual growth in GDP, averaged for the time-periods indicated. GDP per capita: per capita GDP at purchasing power parity, averaged for the time-periods indicated. Unemployment rate: annual unemployment rate.

[a] Unemployment series begins in 1964.
[b] Unemployment series begins in 1969.

Sources: Growth rate of GDP: World Bank, *World Development Indicators CD-ROM* (2000); except for Germany, for which data were taken from OECD, *Historical Statistics* (1997), for 1960–91, and *WDI* for years thereafter. GDP per capita: OECD, *OECD Statistical Compendium CD-ROM* (2000). Unemployment rate: OECD, *OECD Statistical Compendium CD-ROM* (2000).

Finland, and Austria) leaving six in more ambiguous positions (France, Italy, Spain, Portugal, Greece, and Turkey).[20] However, the latter show some signs of institutional clustering as well, indicating that they may constitute another type of capitalism, sometimes described as 'Mediterranean', marked by a large agrarian sector and recent histories of extensive state intervention that have left them with specific kinds of capacities for non-market coordination in the sphere of corporate finance but more liberal arrangements in the sphere of labor relations (see Rhodes 1997).

Although each type of capitalism has its partisans, we are not arguing here that one is superior to another. Despite some variation over specific periods, both liberal and coordinated market economies seem capable of providing satisfactory levels of long-run economic performance, as the major indicators of national well-being displayed in Table 1.1 indicate. Where there is systematic variation between these types of political economies, it is on other dimensions of performance. We argue below that the two types of economies have quite different capacities for innovation. In addition, they tend to distribute income and employment differently. As Fig. 1.2 indicates, in liberal market economies, the adult population tends to be engaged more extensively in paid employment and levels of income inequality are high.[21] In coordinated market economies, working hours tend to be shorter for more of the population and incomes more equal. With regard to the distribution of well-being, of course, these differences are important.

To make this analytical framework more concrete, we now look more closely at coordination in the principal spheres of firm endeavor in coordinated and liberal market economies, drawing on the cases of Germany and the United States for examples and emphasizing the institutional complementarities present in each political economy.

1.3 Coordinated Market Economies: The German Case

As we have noted, we regard capitalist economies as systems in which companies and individuals invest, not only in machines and material

---

[20] Luxembourg and Iceland have been omitted from this list because of their small size and Mexico because it is still a developing nation.

[21] The Gini Index used in Fig. 1.2 is a standard measure for income inequality, measured here as post-tax, post-transfer income, reported in the Luxembourg Income Study for the mid- to late 1980s. Full-time equivalent employment is reported as a percentage of potential employment and measured as the total number of hours worked per year divided by full-time equivalent hours per person (37.5 hours at 50 weeks) times the working-age population. It is reported for the latest available of 1993 or 1994.

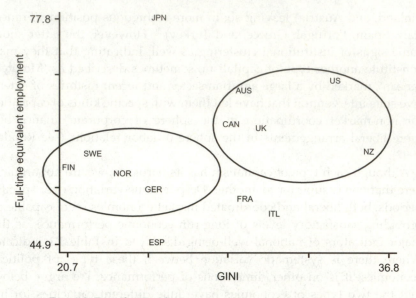

FIG. 1.2 Distributional outcomes across political economies

Note: Full-time equivalent employment is defined as the total number of hours worked per year divided by full-time equivalent hours per year per person times working age population. GINI refers to the gini ceffficient measuring post-tax, post-transfer income inequality.

Sources: For full-time equivalent unemployment: OECD (1996*a*). For GINI index: Spain, Japan, New Zealand are from Deiniger and Squire (1996); the remaining countries are from OECD (1996*a*).

technologies, but in competencies based on relations with others that entail coordination problems. In coordinated market economies, firms resolve many of these problems through strategic interaction. The resulting equilibria depend, in part, on the presence of supportive institutions. Here, we use the case of Germany to illustrate how non-market coordination is achieved in each of the principal spheres of firm endeavor. Of course, the institutions used to secure coordination in other CMEs may differ to some extent from those of Germany.

(i) The *financial system* or *market for corporate governance* in coordinated market economies typically provides companies with access to finance that is not entirely dependent on publicly available financial data or current returns. Access to this kind of 'patient capital' makes it possible for firms to retain a skilled workforce through economic downturns and to invest in projects generating returns only in the long run. The core problem here is that, if finance is not to be dependent on balance-sheet criteria, investors must have other ways of monitoring the performance of companies in order to ensure the value of their investments. In general, that means they must have access to what would normally be considered 'private' or 'inside' information about the operation of the company.

This problem is generally resolved in CMEs by the presence of dense networks linking the managers and technical personnel inside a company to their counterparts in other firms on terms that provide for the sharing of reliable information about the progress of the firm. Reliability is secured in a number of ways. Firms may share information with third parties in a position to monitor the firm and sanction it for misleading them, such as business associations whose officials have an intimate knowledge of the industry. Reputation is also a key factor: where membership in a network is of continuing value, the participants will be deterred from providing false information lest their reputation in the network and access to it suffer. CMEs usually have extensive systems for what might be termed 'network reputational monitoring' (Vitols et al. 1997).

In Germany, information about the reputation and operation of a company is available to investors by virtue of (*a*) the close relationships that companies cultivate with major suppliers and clients, (*b*) the knowledge secured from extensive networks of cross-shareholding, and (*c*) joint membership in active industry associations that gather information about companies in the course of coordinating standard-setting, technology transfer, and vocational training. Other companies are not only represented on the supervisory boards of firms but typically engaged closely with them in joint research, product development, and the like. In short, firms sit inside dense business networks from which potential funders can gain a considerable amount of inside information about the track record and projects of a firm.[22]

The overall structure of the market for corporate governance is equally important. Since firms often fund their activities from retained earnings, they are not always sensitive to the terms on which external finance is supplied. But they can be forced to focus on profitability and shareholder value if faced with the prospect of hostile takeover by others claiming to be able to extract more value from the company. Thus, the corporate strategies found in many CMEs also depend on tax provisions, securities regulations, and networks of cross-shareholding that

---

[22] In previous decades, the German banks were also important contributors to such networks by virtue of their control over large numbers of shares in industrial firms (Hall 1986: ch. 9). In recent years, the role of the large commercial banks has declined, as they divest themselves of many holdings (Griffin 2000).

discourage hostile mergers and acquisitions, which were very rare until recently, for instance, in Germany.

(ii) The *internal structure* of the firm reinforces these systems of network monitoring in many CMEs. Unlike their counterparts in LMEs, for instance, top managers in Germany rarely have a capacity for unilateral action. Instead, they must secure agreement for major decisions from supervisory boards, which include employee representatives as well as major shareholders, and from other managers with entrenched positions as well as major suppliers and customers. This structural bias toward consensus decision-making encourages the sharing of information and the development of reputations for providing reliable information, thereby facilitating network monitoring.

In the perspective we present, the incentives facing individuals, whether managers or workers, are as important as those facing firms. In CMEs, managerial incentives tend to reinforce the operation of business networks. Long-term employment contracts and the premium that firm-structure places on a manager's ability to secure consensus for his projects lead managers to focus heavily on the maintenance of their reputations, while the smaller weight given to stock-option schemes in managerial compensation in CMEs relative to LMEs inclines them to focus less on profitability than their counterparts in LMEs. The incentives for managers are broadly aligned with those of firms.

(iii) Many firms in coordinated market economies employ production strategies that rely on a highly skilled labor force given substantial work autonomy and encouraged to share the information it acquires in order to generate continuous improvements in product lines and production processes (Sorge and Warner 1986; Dore 1986). However, companies that adopt such strategies are vulnerable to 'hold up' by their employees and the 'poaching' of skilled workers by other firms, while employees who share the information they gain at work with management are open to exploitation.[23] Thus, CMEs need *industrial relations* institutions capable of resolving such problems.

The German industrial relations system addresses these problems by setting wages through industry-level bargains between trade unions and employer associations that generally follow a leading settlement, normally reached in engineering where the union is powerful enough to

---

[23] 'Hold up' is Williamson's (1985) term for the withdrawal of active cooperation to back up demands.

assure the labor movement that it has received a good deal. Although union density is only moderately high, encompassing employers' associations bind their members to these agreements. By equalizing wages at equivalent skill levels across an industry, this system makes it difficult for firms to poach workers and assures the latter that they are receiving the highest feasible rates of pay in return for the deep commitments they are making to firms. By coordinating bargaining across the economy, these arrangements also limit the inflationary effects of wage settlements (Streeck 1994; Hall and Franzese 1998).

The complement to these institutions at the company level is a system of works councils composed of elected employee representatives endowed with considerable authority over layoffs and working conditions. By providing employees with security against arbitrary layoffs or changes to their working conditions, these works councils encourage employees to invest in company-specific skills and extra effort. Their effectiveness is underpinned by the capacity of either side to appeal a disputed decision to the trade unions and employers' associations, who act as external guarantors that the councils function as intended (Thelen 1991).

(iv) Because coordinated market economies typically make extensive use of labor with high industry-specific or firm-specific skills, they depend on *education and training systems* capable of providing workers with such skills.[24] As Culpepper notes in his chapter, the coordination problems here are acute, as workers must be assured that an apprenticeship will result in lucrative employment, while firms investing in training need to know that their workers will acquire usable skills and will not be poached by companies that do not make equivalent investments in training. CMEs resolve these problems in a variety of ways.

Germany relies on industry-wide employer associations and trade unions to supervise a publicly subsidized training system. By pressuring major firms to take on apprentices and monitoring their participation in such schemes, these associations limit free-riding on the training efforts of others; and, by negotiating industry-wide skill categories and training protocols with the firms in each sector, they ensure both that the training fits the firms' needs and that there will be an external demand for any graduates not employed by the firms at which they apprenticed. Because German employer associations are encompassing organizations

[24] Compared to general skills that can be used in many settings, industry-specific skills normally have value only when used within a single industry and firm-specific skills only in employment within that firm.

that provide many benefits to their members and to which most firms in a sector belong, they are well placed to supply the monitoring and suasion that the operation of such a system demands as well as the deliberative forums in which skill categories, training quotas, and protocols can be negotiated. Workers emerge from their training with both company-specific skills and the skills to secure employment elsewhere.

(v) Since many firms in coordinated market economies make extensive use of long-term labor contracts, they cannot rely as heavily on the movement of scientific or engineering personnel across companies, to effect technology transfer, as liberal market economies do. Instead, they tend to cultivate *inter-company relations* of the sort that facilitate the diffusion of technology across the economy. In Germany, these relationships are supported by a number of institutions. Business associations promote the diffusion of new technologies by working with public officials to determine where firm competencies can be improved and orchestrating publicly subsidized programs to do so. The access to private information about the sector that these associations enjoy helps them ensure that the design of the programs is effective for these purposes. A considerable amount of research is also financed jointly by companies, often in collaboration with quasi-public research institutes. The common technical standards fostered by industry associations help to diffuse new technologies, and they contribute to a common knowledge-base that facilitates collaboration among personnel from multiple firms, as do the industry-specific skills fostered by German training schemes (Lütz 1993; Soskice 1997b; Ziegler 1997).

Casper's chapter in this volume shows that Germany has also developed a system of contract law complementary to the presence of strong industry associations that encourages relational contracting among companies and promotes this sort of technology transfer. Because of the many contingencies that can arise in close inter-firm relationships involving joint research or product development, tightly written, formal contracts are often inadequate to sustain such relationships. However, the German courts permit unusually open-ended clauses in inter-firm contracts on the explicit condition that these be grounded in the prevailing standards of the relevant industry association. Thus, the presence of strong industry associations capable of promulgating standards and resolving disputes among firms is the precondition for a system of contract law that encourages relational contracting (cf. Casper 1997; Teubner in this volume).

In these respects, German institutions support forms of relational contracting and technology transfer that are more difficult to achieve in liberal market economies. One of the effects is to encourage corporate strategies that focus on product differentiation and niche production, rather than direct product competition with other firms in the industry, since close inter-firm collaboration is harder to sustain in the presence of the intense product competition that tends to characterize LMEs. The chapter by Estevez-Abe, Iversen, and Soskice examines the linkages between these product market strategies, skill systems, and social-policy regimes.

The complementarities present in the German political economy should be apparent from this account. Many firms pursue production strategies that depend on workers with specific skills and high levels of corporate commitment that are secured by offering them long employment tenures, industry-based wages, and protective works councils. But these practices are feasible only because a corporate governance system replete with mechanisms for network monitoring provides firms with access to capital on terms that are relatively independent of fluctuations in profitability. Effective vocational training schemes, supported by an industrial-relations system that discourages poaching, provide high levels of industry-specific skills. In turn, this encourages collective standard-setting and inter-firm collaboration of the sort that promotes technology transfer. The arrows in Fig. 1.3 summarize some of these complementarities. Since many of these institutional practices enhance the effectiveness with which others operate, the economic returns to the system as a whole are greater than its component parts alone would generate.

1.4 Liberal Market Economies: The American Case

Liberal market economies can secure levels of overall economic performance as high as those of coordinated market economies, but they do so quite differently. In LMEs, firms rely more heavily on market relations to resolve the coordination problems that firms in CMEs address more often via forms of non-market coordination that entail collaboration and strategic interaction. In each of the major spheres of firm endeavor, competitive markets are more robust and there is less institutional support for non-market forms of coordination.

(i) Several features of the *financial systems* or *markets for corporate governance* of liberal market economies encourage firms to be attentive to current earnings and the price of their shares on equity markets. Regulatory regimes are tolerant of mergers and acquisitions, including the hostile

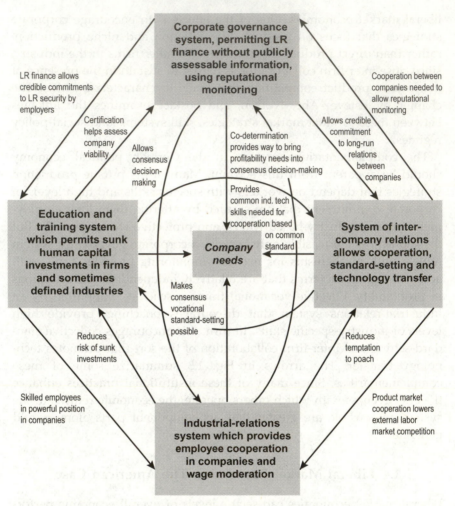

FIG. 1.3 Complementarities across subsystems in the German coordinated
market economy

takeovers that become a prospect when the market valuation of a firm
declines. The terms on which large firms can secure finance are heavily
dependent on their valuation in equity markets, where dispersed investors depend on publicly available information to value the company.
This applies to both bonds, share issues, and bank lending.[25] Compensation systems that reward top management for increases in net earnings

[25] Firms in LMEs tend to rely on bond and equity markets for external finance more
heavily than those in CMEs. However, bank lending in such economies also privileges
publicly accessible, balance-sheet criteria, since banks find it difficult to monitor the less-

or share price are common in such economies. Liberal market economies usually lack the close-knit corporate networks capable of providing investors with inside information about the progress of companies that allows them to supply finance less dependent on quarterly balance sheets and publicly available information. The relevant contrast is with CMEs, where firms need not be as attentive to share price or current profitability in order to ensure access to finance or deter hostile takeovers.

Of course, there are some qualifications to these generalizations. Companies with readily assessable assets associated with forward income streams, such as pharmaceutical firms with a 'pipeline' of drugs, consumer-goods companies with strong reputations for successful product development, and firms well positioned in high-growth markets, need not be as concerned about current profitability. New firms in high-technology fields can often secure funds from venture-capital companies that develop the resources and technical expertise to monitor their performance directly and trade ownership stakes in these firms for the high risks they take.[26] On the whole, however, the markets for corporate governance in LMEs encourage firms to focus on the publicly assessable dimensions of their performance that affect share price, such as current profitability.

(ii) In the *industrial relations arena*, firms in liberal market economies generally rely heavily on the market relationship between individual worker and employer to organize relations with their labor force. Top management normally has unilateral control over the firm, including substantial freedom to hire and fire.[27] Firms are under no obligation to establish representative bodies for employees such as works councils; and trade unions are generally less powerful than in CMEs, although they may have significant strength in some sectors. Because trade unions

obvious dimensions of corporate progress in an environment that lacks the close-knit corporate networks conveying such information in CMEs. Intense monitoring by a loan officer is feasible only when small sums are involved, since it exposes the bank to problems of moral hazard that are especially acute in countries where officers can take advantage of fluid labor markets to move elsewhere.

[26] Note that we avoid a distinction often drawn between countries in which firms can raise 'long-term' capital versus those in which only 'short-term' capital is available because this distinction is rarely meaningful. Many companies in LMEs with established market reputations can raise capital for projects promising revenues only in the medium to long term, and firms often finance the bulk of their activities from retained earnings. Of more relevance are the rules governing hostile takeovers, whose prospect can induce firms to pay more attention to corporate earnings and the price of their shares.

[27] Partly for this reason, the market valuation of firms in LMEs often depends more heavily on the reputation of its CEO than it does in CMEs.

and employer associations in LMEs are less cohesive and encompassing, economy-wide wage coordination is generally difficult to secure. Therefore, these economies depend more heavily on macroeconomic policy and market competition to control wages and inflation (see Franzese in this volume; Hall and Franzese 1998).

The presence of highly fluid labor markets influences the strategies pursued by both firms and individuals in liberal market economies. These markets make it relatively easy for firms to release or hire labor in order to take advantage of new opportunities but less attractive for them to pursue production strategies based on promises of long-term employment. They encourage individuals to invest in general skills, transferable across firms, rather than company-specific skills and in career trajectories that include a substantial amount of movement among firms.

(iii) The *education and training systems* of liberal market economies are generally complementary to these highly fluid labor markets. Vocational training is normally provided by institutions offering formal education that focuses on general skills because companies are loath to invest in apprenticeship schemes imparting industry-specific skills where they have no guarantees that other firms will not simply poach their apprentices without investing in training themselves. From the perspective of workers facing short job tenures and fluid labor markets, career success also depends on acquiring the general skills that can be used in many different firms; and most educational programs from secondary through university levels, even in business and engineering, stress 'certification' in general skills rather than the acquisition of more specialized competencies.

High levels of general education, however, lower the cost of additional training. Therefore, the companies in these economies do a substantial amount of in-house training, although rarely in the form of the intensive apprenticeships used to develop company-specific or industry-specific skills in CMEs. More often, they provide further training in the marketable skills that employees have incentives to learn. The result is a labor force well equipped with general skills, especially suited to job growth in the service sector where such skills assume importance, but one that leaves some firms short of employees with highly specialized or company-specific skills.

(iv) *Inter-company relations* in liberal market economies are based, for the most part, on standard market relationships and enforceable formal contracts. In the United States, these relations are also mediated by rigorous antitrust regulations designed to prevent companies from colluding to control prices or markets and doctrines of contract laws that rely heavily on the strict interpretation of written contracts, nicely summarized by MacNeil's dictum: 'sharp in by clear agreement, sharp out by clear performance' (Williamson 1985). Therefore, companies wishing to engage in relational contracts with other firms get little assistance from the American legal system, as Casper observes.

In some fields of endeavor, such as after-sales service, companies can engage successfully in incomplete contracting by building up reputations on which other parties rely. But extensive reputation-building is more difficult in economies lacking the dense business networks or associations that circulate reputations for reliability or sharp practice quickly and widely. Because the market for corporate governance renders firms sensitive to fluctuations in current profitability, it is also more difficult for them to make credible commitments to relational contracts that extend over substantial periods of time.

How then does technology transfer take place in liberal market economies? In large measure, it is secured through the movement of scientists and engineers from one company to another (or from research institutions to the private sector) that fluid labor markets facilitate. These scientific personnel bring their technical knowledge with them. LMEs also rely heavily on the licensing or sale of innovations to effect technology transfer, techniques that are most feasible in sectors of the economy where effective patenting is possible, such as biotechnology, microelectronics, and semiconductors. In the United States, the character of standard-setting reinforces the importance of licensing. Since few sectors have business associations capable of securing consensus on new standards, collective standard-setting is rarely feasible. Instead, standards are often set by market races, whose winners then profit by licensing their technology to many users (see also Tate in this volume). The prominence of this practice helps to explain the presence of venture-capital firms in liberal market economies: one success at standard-setting can pay for many failed investments (Borrus and Zysman 1997).

In LMEs, research consortia and inter-firm collaboration, therefore, play less important roles in the process of technology transfer than in CMEs where the institutional environment is more conducive to them. Until the National Cooperative Research Act of 1984, American firms engaging in close collaboration with other firms actually ran the risk of being sued for triple damages under antitrust law; and it is still estimated that barely 1 to 7 per cent of the funds spent on research and development in the American private sector are devoted to collaborative research.

It should be apparent that there are many institutional complementarities across the sub-spheres of a liberal market economy (see Fig. 1.4). Labor market arrangements that allow companies to cut costs in a downturn by shedding labor are complementary to financial markets that render a firm's access to funds dependent on current profitability. Educational arrangements that privilege general, rather than firm-specific, skills are complementary to highly fluid labor markets; and the latter render forms of technology transfer that rely on labor mobility more feasible. In

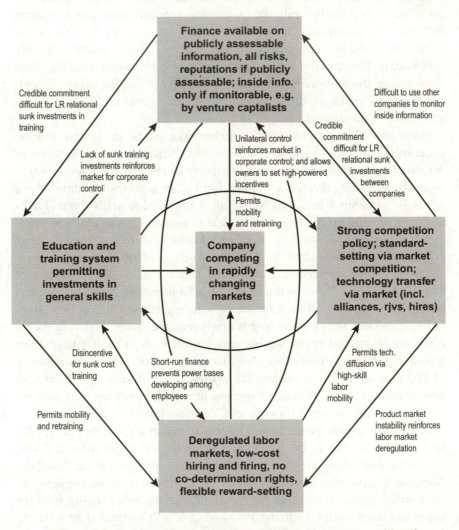

FIG. 1.4 Complementarities across subsystems in the American liberal market economy

the context of a legal system that militates against relational contracting, licensing agreements are also more effective than inter-firm collaboration on research and development for effecting technology transfer.

Special note should be taken of the complementarities between the internal structure of firms and their external institutional environment in liberal and coordinated market economies. In LMEs, corporate structures that concentrate authority in top management make it easier for firms to release labor when facing pressure from financial markets and to impose a new strategy on the firm to take advantage of the shifting market opportunities that often present themselves in economies characterized by highly mobile assets. By contrast, in CMEs, where access to finance and technology often depends on a firm's attractiveness as a collaborator and hence on its reputation, corporate structures that impose more consensual forms of decision-making allow firms to develop reputations that are not entirely dependent on those of its top management. By reducing the capacity of top management to act arbitrarily, these structures also enhance the firm's capacity to enter credibly into relational contracts with employees and others in economies where a firm's access to many kinds of assets, ranging from technology to skills, may depend on its capacity for relational contracting. Lehrer's chapter explores some of these linkages between corporate structure and the external environment in more detail.

1.5 Comparing Coordination

Although many of the developed nations can be classified as liberal or coordinated market economies, the point of this analysis is not simply to identify these two types but to outline an approach that can be used to compare many kinds of economies. In particular, we are suggesting that it can be fruitful to consider how firms coordinate their endeavors and to analyze the institutions of the political economy from a perspective that asks what kind of support they provide for different kinds of coordination, even when the political economies at hand do not correspond to the ideal types we have just outlined.

It is important to note that, even within these two types, significant variations can be found. Broadly speaking, liberal market economies are distinguishable from coordinated market economies by the extent to which firms rely on market mechanisms to coordinate their endeavors as opposed to forms of strategic interaction supported by non-market institutions. Because market institutions are better known, we will not explore the differences among liberal market economies here. But a few

words about variation in coordinated market economies may be appropriate, if only to show that variation in the institutional structures underpinning strategic coordination can have significant effects on corporate
strategy and economic outcomes.

One important axis of difference among CMEs runs between those that
rely primarily on *industry-based coordination*, as do many of the northern
European nations, and those with institutional structures that foster
group-based coordination of the sort found in Japan and South Korea. As
we have seen, in Germany, coordination depends on business associations and trade unions that are organized primarily along sectoral lines,
giving rise to vocational training schemes that cultivate industry-specific
skills, a system of wage coordination that negotiates wages by sector, and
corporate collaboration that is often industry-specific. By contrast, the
business networks of most importance in Japan are built on *keiretsu*, fam-
ilies of companies with dense interconnections cutting across sectors, the
most important of which is nowadays the *vertical keiretsu* with one major
company at its center.

These differences in the character of business networks have major
implications. In Germany, companies within the same sector often
cooperate in the sensitive areas of training and technology transfer. But
the structure of the Japanese economy encourages sharp competition
between companies in the same industry. Cooperation on sensitive
matters is more likely to take place within the *keiretsu*, i.e. among firms
operating in different sectors but within one 'family' of companies. The
sectoral cooperation that takes place usually concerns less sensitive
matters, including recession cartels, licensing requirements, and entry
barriers as well as the annual wage round (Soskice 1990*a*). Partly for this
reason, the attempts of MITI to develop cooperative research projects
within sectors have had very limited success; serious research and
development remains the preserve of the laboratories of the major
companies.

This pattern of *keiretsu*-led coordination also has significant implications for patterns of skill acquisition and technology transfer. Serious
training, technology transfer and a good deal of standard-setting take
place primarily within the vertical *keiretsu*. Workers are encouraged to
acquire firm- or group-specific skills, and notably strong relational skills
appropriate for use within the family of companies within which they
have been trained. In order to persuade workers to invest in skills of this
specificity, the large firms have customarily offered many of them lifetime employment. And, in order to sustain such commitments, many
Japanese firms have cultivated the capacity to move rapidly into new

products and product areas in response to changes in world markets and technologies. This kind of corporate strategy takes advantage of the high levels of workforce cooperation that lifetime employment encourages. To reinforce it, Japanese firms have also developed company unions providing the workforce with a voice in the affairs of the firm.

Japanese firms tend to lack the capacities for radical innovation that American firms enjoy by virtue of fluid market settings or for sector-centered technology transfer of the sort found in Germany. Instead, the group-based organization of the Japanese political economy has encouraged firms there to develop distinctive corporate strategies that take advantage of the capacities for cross-sector technology transfer and rapid organizational redeployment provided by the *keiretsu* system. These translate into comparative institutional advantages in the large-scale production of consumer goods, machinery, and electronics that exploit existing technologies and capacities for organizational change. Although Japan is clearly a coordinated market economy, the institutional structures that support group-based coordination there have been conducive to corporate strategies and comparative advantages somewhat different from those in economies with industry-based systems of co-ordination.

The varieties of capitalism approach can also be useful for understanding political economies that do not correspond to the ideal type of a liberal or coordinated market economy. From our perspective, each economy displays specific capacities for coordination that will condition what its firms and government do.

France is a case in point, and the chapters in this volume by Lehrer, Culpepper, and Hancké explore some of the implications of this approach for it. Collaboration across French companies is based on career patterns that led many of the managers of leading firms through a few elite schools and the public service before taking up their positions in the private sector. Lehrer observes that the top managers of many French firms, therefore, have close ties to the state and weak ties to the rest of the enterprise. As a result, he argues, they are less likely to pursue the corporate strategies found in Britain or Germany and more likely to look to the state for assistance than their counterparts in other nations. Using the case of vocational training, however, Culpepper shows that there are clear limits to what states can do in the absence of strong business associations capable of monitoring their members. Hancké examines how large French firms are adapting to these limits, suggesting that many are taking industrial reorganization upon themselves, sometimes devising new networks to coordinate their activities.

In sum, although the contrast between coordinated and liberal market economies is important, we are not suggesting that all economies conform to these two types. Our object is to advance comparative analysis of the political economy more generally by drawing attention to the ways in which firms coordinate their endeavors, elucidating the connections between firm strategies and the institutional support available for them, and linking these factors to patterns of policy and performance. These are matters relevant to any kind of political economy.

1.6 Comparative Institutional Advantage

We turn now to some of the issues to which this perspective can be applied, beginning with a question central to international economics, namely, how to construe comparative economic advantage. The theory of comparative economic advantage is important because it implies that freer trade will not impoverish nations by driving their production abroad but enrich them by allowing each to specialize in the goods it produces most efficiently and exchange them for even more goods from other nations. It can be used to explain both the expansion of world trade and the patterns of product specialization found across nations. The most influential version of the theory focuses on the relative endowment of basic factors (such as land, labor, and capital) found in a nation and suggests that trade will lead a nation to specialize in the production of goods that use its most abundant factors most intensively (Stolper and Samuelson 1941).

However, recent developments have dealt a serious blow to this account of comparative economic advantage. The most important of these include the expansion of intra-industry trade and increases in the international mobility of capital. If the theory is correct, nations should not import and export high volumes of goods from the same sector; and there is a real possibility that international movements of capital will even out national factor endowments. As a result, some economists have become skeptical about whether comparative advantages really exist, and many have begun to seek other explanations for the expansion of trade and the geographic distribution of production.

Some explain the growth of trade, and intra-industry trade in particular, as the result of efforts to concentrate production in order to secure returns to scale (Helpmann 1984). Others explain the concentration of particular kinds of production in some nations as the result of firms' efforts to secure the positive externalities generated by a group of firms engaged in related endeavors at the same site, whether in the form of appropriate labor pools, the availability of relevant intermediate products, or technological spillovers. This approach predicts that companies making similar products will cluster together, whether in Silicon Valley or Baden-Württemberg (Krugman 1991).

Both of these theories are valuable as far as they go, and nothing in our own is inconsistent with them, but we think they do not go far enough. Both explain why the production of some kinds of goods might be concentrated in a nation, but they say little about why production of *that* type should be concentrated in *that* particular nation, while other nations specialize in other kinds of production. Agglomeration theory explains why firms engaged in similar endeavors cluster in places like Silicon Valley or Baden-Württemberg, but it cannot explain why firms engaged in activities that entail high risks, intense competition, and high rates of labor turnover cluster in Silicon Valley, while firms engaged in very different activities that entail lower risks, close inter-firm collaboration, and low rates of labor turnover locate in Baden-Württemberg. We still need a theory that explains why particular nations tend to specialize in specific types of production or products.

We think that such a theory can be found in the concept of *comparative institutional advantage*. The basic idea is that the institutional structure of a particular political economy provides firms with advantages for engaging in specific types of activities there. Firms can perform some types of activities, which allow them to produce some kinds of goods, more efficiently than others because of the institutional support they receive for those activities in the political economy, and the institutions relevant to these activities are not distributed evenly across nations.

The contention that institutions matter to the efficiency with which goods can be produced receives considerable support from the growing body of work on endogenous growth. Many economists have observed that national rates of growth cannot be explained fully by incremental additions to the stock of capital and labor and fixed rates of technical change. Endogenous growth theorists have suggested that the institutional setting for production also seems to matter to national rates of growth; and various efforts have been made to specify what features of that setting might be important, generating suggestions that include: economies of scale available from oligopoly positions, economies of scope arising from experience in related endeavors, network externalities generated by firms engaged in similar activities, and the nature of property rights regimes (Romer 1986, 1994; Grossman and Helpmann

1992; Aghion and Howitt 1998).[28] There is now widespread recognition that the institutional context can condition rates of growth and technological progress.

To date, however, most efforts to specify these institutions have concentrated on market relationships and the legal framework for them, neglecting the non-market relations that may be equally important to such outcomes. The latter receive more emphasis in the literature on national innovation systems and some analyses of competitive advantage (Dosi et al. 1988; Porter 1990; Barro and Sala-i-Martin 1995; Edquist 1997). Most of this literature, however, looks for the ingredients of *absolute* advantage, i.e. it identifies factors more of which will improve the performance of any economy. We seek institutional features that might confer *comparative* advantage and, thus, be better suited to explaining cross-national patterns of product or process specialization (Zysman 1994).

The basic logic of our approach should be apparent. We have argued that, in some political economies, firms make more extensive use of non-market modes of coordination to organize their endeavors, while in others firms rely mainly on markets to coordinate those endeavors. Broadly speaking, these differences correspond to the level of institutional support available for market, as opposed to non-market, coordination in each political economy. Using a distinction between liberal and coordinated market economies, we have identified many of the institutional features of the political economy relevant to these differences and suggest that these correspond to cross-national differences in corporate strategy.

The important point to be added here is that the availability of these different modes of coordination conditions the efficiency with which firms can perform certain activities, thereby affecting the efficiency with which they can produce certain kinds of goods and services. In short, the national institutional frameworks examined in this volume provide nations with comparative advantages in particular activities and products. In the presence of trade, these advantages should give rise to cross-national patterns of specialization.

Although there may be types of comparative advantage that these institutional frameworks confer that we have not yet explored, we focus here on their impact on *innovation* since a firm's capacity to innovate is crucial to its long-run success. The key distinction we draw is between *radical* innovation, which entails substantial shifts in product lines, the development of entirely new goods, or major changes to the production

---

[28] Note that strategic trade theory focuses on a similar set of variables (cf. Krugman 1986; Busch 1999).

process, and *incremental* innovation, marked by continuous but small-scale improvements to existing product lines and production processes. Over the medium to long term, efficiency in the production of some kinds of goods requires a capacity for radical innovation, while, in other kinds of goods, it requires a capacity for incremental innovation.

Radical innovation is especially important in fast-moving technology sectors, which call for innovative design and rapid product development based on research, as in biotechnology, semiconductors, and software development. It is also important to success in the provision of complex system-based products, such as telecommunications or defense systems, and their service-sector analogs: airlines, advertising, corporate finance, and entertainment. In the latter, competitiveness demands a capacity for taking risks on new product strategies and for the rapid implementation of such strategies within large, tightly coupled organizations that employ a diverse personnel.

Incremental innovation tends to be more important for maintaining competitiveness in the production of capital goods, such as machine tools and factory equipment, consumer durables, engines, and specialized transport equipment. Here, the problem is to maintain the high quality of an established product line, to devise incremental improvements to it that attract consumer loyalty, and to secure continuous improvements in the production process in order to improve quality control and hold down costs.

Coordinated market economies should be better at supporting incremental innovation. This follows from the emphasis we have put on the relational requirements of company endeavors. It will be easier to secure incremental innovation where the workforce (extending all the way down to the shop floor) is skilled enough to come up with such innovations, secure enough to risk suggesting changes to products or process that might alter their job situation, and endowed with enough work autonomy to see these kinds of improvements as a dimension of their job. Thus, incremental innovation should be most feasible where corporate organization provides workers with secure employment, autonomy from close monitoring, and opportunities to influence the decisions of the firm, where the skill system provides workers with more than task-specific skills and, ideally, high levels of industry-specific technical skills, and where close inter-firm collaboration encourages clients and suppliers to suggest incremental improvements to products or production processes.

The institutions of coordinated market economies normally provide high levels of support for these relational requirements. Highly coordinated *industrial-relations systems* and *corporate structures* characterized by works councils and consensus decision-making provide employees with the guarantees that elicit their cooperation. The *training systems* of CMEs typically provide high skill levels and the requisite mix of company-specific and more general technical skills. Appropriate *contract laws* and *dense networks of inter-corporate linkages* allow firms to form relational contracts with other firms; and *systems of corporate governance* that insulate firms against hostile takeovers and reduce their sensitivity to current profits encourage long employment tenures and the development of the inter-firm and employee relations that foster incremental innovation. By encouraging corporate strategies based on product differentiation rather than intense product competition, these inter-corporate networks also tend to promote incremental, rather than radical, innovation. A reputation for risk-taking or cut-throat competition is rarely an asset in such networks.

By contrast, although some can occur there, the institutional features of liberal market economies tend to limit firms' capacities for incremental innovation. Financial market arrangements that emphasize current profitability and corporate structures that concentrate unilateral control at the top deprive the workforce of the security conducive to their full cooperation in innovation. Fluid labor markets and short job tenures make it rational for employees to concentrate more heavily on their personal career than the firm's success and on the development of general skills rather than the industry- or company-specific skills conducive to incremental innovation. The complexion of contract law and antitrust laws discourages inter-firm collaboration in incremental product development.

However, the institutional framework of liberal market economies is highly supportive of radical innovation. *Labor markets* with few restrictions on layoffs and high rates of labor mobility mean that companies interested in developing an entirely new product line can hire in personnel with the requisite expertise, knowing they can release them if the project proves unprofitable. Extensive *equity markets* with dispersed shareholders and few restrictions on mergers or acquisitions allow firms seeking access to new or radically different technologies to do so by acquiring other companies with relative ease, and the presence of venture capital allows scientists and engineers to bring their own ideas to market. As Lehrer's study of the airline industry shows, the concentration of power at the top typical of *corporate organization* in an LME makes it easier for senior management to implement entirely new business strategies throughout a multi-layered organization delivering complex system goods or services. Such firms can also acquire or divest subsidiaries quickly. *Inter-firm relations* based primarily on markets enhance the capacities of firms to buy other companies, to poach their personnel, and to license new products—all means of acquiring new technologies quickly.

By contrast, in CMEs, although dense inter-corporate networks facilitate the gradual diffusion of technology, they make it more difficult for firms to access radically new technologies by taking over other companies. Corporate structures characterized by strong worker representation and consensus decision-making make radical reorganization of a firm more difficult, as each of the affected actors contemplates the consequences for his relationship to the company. The long employment tenures that such institutions encourage make it less feasible for firms to secure access to new technologies by hiring in large numbers of new personnel.

In short, the institutional frameworks of liberal market economies provide companies with better capacities for radical innovation, while those of coordinated market economies provide superior capacities for incremental innovation. Therefore, to the extent allowed by transport costs and the efficiency of international markets, there should be national patterns of specialization in activities and products; and these should reflect rational responses to the institutional frameworks identified here rather than random geographic agglomeration.

Figs. 1.5 and 1.6 provide some evidence for these propositions. Using data from the European Patent Office, they report indices measuring the degree to which innovation in Germany and the United States is concentrated into any of thirty technology classes that vary according to whether technological progress in them is typically characterized by radical or incremental innovation.[29] Higher scores reflect greater specialization in that kind of technological innovation, and the charts include data from 1993–4 as well as 1983–4 to assess stability over time.

The striking finding is that Germany specializes in technological developments that are just the reverse of those in the USA. Fig. 1.6 is almost the mirror image of Fig. 1.5. Firms in Germany have been more active innovators in fields predominantly characterized by incremental innovation, including mechanical engineering, product handling, transport,

[29] The data are from the European Patent Office and calculated for thirty classes of technologies. For technology class *i* (e.g. machine tools) Germany's relative specialization is measured by the share of German machine-tool patents in total German patents *less* the share of global machine-tool patents in global patents. We are grateful to Tom Cusack for substantial assistance with the calculations for Figs. 1.5 and 1.6. See Cusack and Frosch 2000 and Grupp et al. 1995.

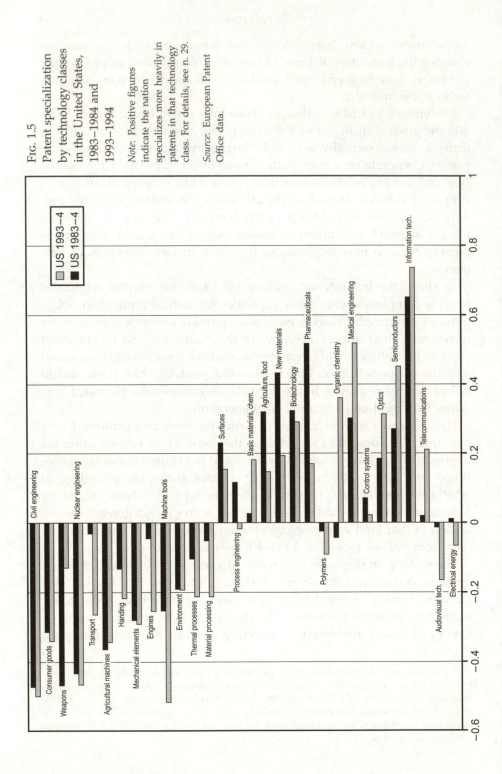

FIG. 1.5
Patent specialization
by technology classes
in the United States,
1983–1984 and
1993–1994

Note: Positive figures
indicate the nation
specializes more heavily in
patents in that technology
class. For details, see n. 29.

Source: European Patent
Office data.

US 1993–4
US 1983–4

Civil engineering
Consumer goods
Weapons
Nuclear engineering
Transport
Agricultural machines
Handling
Mechanical elements
Engines
Machine tools
Environment
Thermal processes
Material processing
Process engineering
Surfaces
Basic materials, chem.
Agriculture, food
New materials
Biotechnology
Pharmaceuticals
Polymers
Organic chemistry
Medical engineering
Control systems
Optics
Semiconductors
Information tech.
Telecommunications
Audiovisual tech.
Electrical energy

−0.6
−0.4
−0.2
0
0.2
0.4
0.6
0.8
1

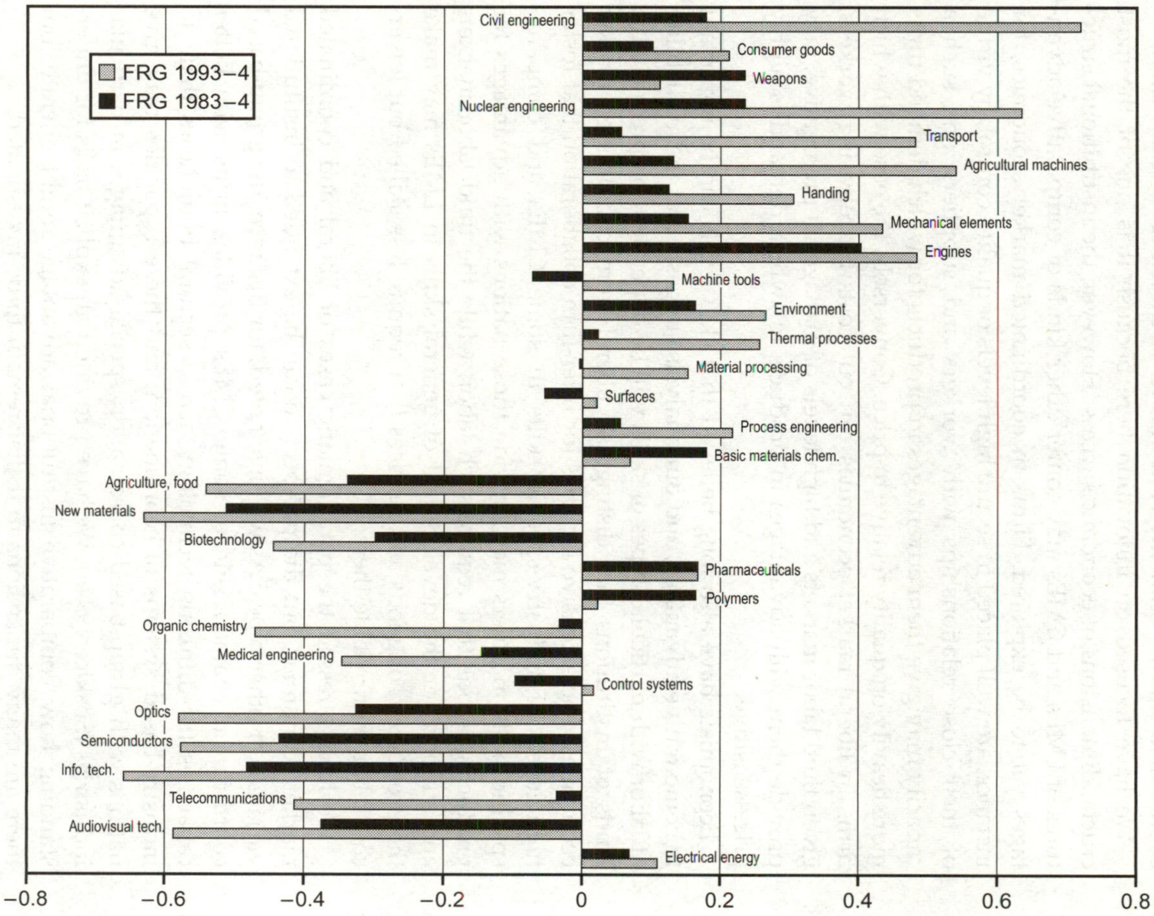

Fig. 1.6
Patent specialization
by technology classes
in the Federal Republic
of Germany, 1983–1984
and 1993–1994

Note: Positive figures
indicate the nation
specializes more heavily in
patents in that technology
class. For details, see n. 29.
Source: European Patent
Office data.

Legend:
- FRG 1993–4
- FRG 1983–4

Technology classes (above zero, specialized): Civil engineering, Consumer goods, Weapons, Nuclear engineering, Transport, Agricultural machines, Handling, Mechanical elements, Engines, Machine tools, Environment, Thermal processes, Material processing, Surfaces, Process engineering, Basic materials chem., Pharmaceuticals, Polymers, Control systems, Electrical energy

Technology classes (below zero): Agriculture, food, New materials, Biotechnology, Organic chemistry, Medical engineering, Optics, Semiconductors, Info. tech., Telecommunications, Audiovisual tech.

Axis scale: −0.8, −0.6, −0.4, −0.2, 0, 0.2, 0.4, 0.6, 0.8

consumer durables, and machine tools, while firms in the United States innovate disproportionately in fields where radical innovation is important, such as medical engineering, biotechnology, semiconductors, and telecommunications. These patterns are consistent over time and precisely the ones our analysis would expect. There does appear to be specialization in innovation across nations, with firms in the liberal market economy specializing in radical innovation, while those in the coordinated market economy concentrate on incremental innovation.

We have focused on innovation here because it is one of the most crucial dimensions of economic success. However, the institutional structures of LMEs and CMEs may confer other kinds of comparative advantages yet to be explored. Firms in coordinated market economies, for instance, are well placed to secure high levels of quality control, by virtue of their close relationships with workers and suppliers; and such a capacity may give them advantages in products for which demand turns more heavily on quality relative to price. Conversely, the ease with which firms in liberal market economies can cut costs by releasing workers, given fluid labor markets and high levels of managerial prerogative, may provide them with advantages in products for which demand is highly price-sensitive.

Economists have also long believed that skill levels can be important to comparative advantage, and our analysis suggests that the availability of labor with particular types of skills will be dependent on precisely the kinds of institutions that distinguish liberal from coordinated market economies. The extensive facilities for inter-firm collaboration that foster high levels of industry-specific skills in some CMEs and company-specific skills in others may provide those nations with advantages for producing goods that require such labor, while the fluid labor markets and support for the development of general skills in LMEs may make the production of goods and services that require less skilled but lower-cost labor more viable there.

We have stressed the paradigmatic cases of liberal and coordinated market economies, but the perspective can be extended to institutional variation of other types. As we have noted, for instance, the group-based coordination characteristic of some CMEs provides firms with better capacities for diffusing technology across sectoral boundaries than do industry-based systems of coordination; and these capacities may give nations with group-based coordination special advantages in particular industries (Soskice 1994*a*). We have provided an explicit basis for understanding how comparative institutional advantage might operate, but there are many dimensions to it that remain to be investigated.

1.7 New Perspectives on Comparative Public Policy-Making

Comparative political economists have been as interested in patterns of economic policy-making as in problems of economic performance. Accordingly, it is appropriate to note that the analytical framework developed in this volume also opens up substantial new perspectives on both economic and social policy-making with relevance for the domestic arena and international relations.

1.7.1 Economic Policy-Making

The approach we take to the political economy suggests some important revisions in the way we normally think about the problematic facing economic policy-makers, especially on the supply side of the economy. A substantial literature in comparative political economy, going back to Shonfield (1965), construes the problem facing policy-makers as one of settling on the actions that firms or other private-sector actors should take in order to improve economic performance and then devising a set of incentives, whether regulatory or financial, to induce them to take those actions. This was what the 'strong' states of France and Japan were once said to be so effective at doing (Johnson 1982; Zysman 1983). Broadly speaking, the problem was seen as one of inducing economic actors to cooperate with the government.

From our perspective, however, the principal problem facing policy-makers is quite different: it is one of inducing economic actors to co-operate more effectively with each other.[30] This follows from our view of the economy as an arena in which multiple actors develop competencies by devising better ways of coordinating their endeavors with one another. When firms coordinate more effectively, their performance will be better, and the result will be better overall economic performance. In some cases, more effective coordination among other actors, such as trade unions and employers, will also enhance performance.[31] Accordingly, one of the principal ways in which policy-makers can improve national economic performance is to secure better forms of coordination among private-sector actors.

[30] The formulations in these paragraphs are influenced by the work of Pepper Culpepper (1998, forthcoming) and owe a good deal to conversations with him.

[31] Here, as elsewhere in this chapter, when we refer to 'more effective' coordination, we mean coordination by the actors on actions providing equilibria that are Pareto-superior to those that preceded them in the sense that they make at least some of the actors better off without making others worse off.

In some cases, markets can be used to secure this coordination, and so the task facing policy-makers is to improve the functioning of markets. This is not always easy, but there are some well-known techniques for accomplishing this task. However, there are other cases in which firms can perform certain endeavors well (whether wage-bargaining, collaborating with other firms in research and development, or the like) only by coordinating with others in contexts of strategic interaction. Here, the problem is one of improving the equilibrium outcomes that arise from strategic interactions, and less is known about how to accomplish that. Culpepper describes this problem as one of securing 'decentralized co-operation'. It entails persuading private-sector actors to share information, improving their ability to make credible commitments, and altering their expectations about what others will do. As we have noted, the development of supportive institutions and the cultivation of a base of common knowledge may be crucial here (Ostrom 1990; Ramirez-Rangel 2000; Culpepper forthcoming).

This formulation highlights the difficulties facing economic policy-makers, especially when they are seeking to enhance non-market co-ordination. In such contexts, states cannot simply tell economic actors what to do, not only because the outcomes are too complex to be dictated by regulation but because states generally lack the information needed to specify appropriate strategies. States may establish agencies, but what agencies can do is limited. In many cases, effective strategic co-ordination depends on the presence of appropriately organized social organizations, such as trade unions and employer associations, that governments can encourage but not create. As Culpepper's analysis of vocational training shows, effective cooperation also requires common knowledge that may develop only out of experience over time. Where norms and institutions supporting effective cooperation already exist, policy-makers may be able to improve its operation with complementary regulations, but it is difficult to induce such cooperation *ex nihilo* (Culpepper 1998).

It follows that economic policies will be effective only if they are *incentive compatible*, namely complementary to the coordinating capacities embedded in the existing political economy (Wood 1997). In liberal market economies, where coordination is secured primarily through market mechanisms, better economic performance may demand policies that sharpen market competition, while coordinated market economies may benefit more from policies that reinforce the capacities of actors for non-market coordination. Because the institutional context of the British economy encourages the acquisition of general skills and militates against sectoral coordination, its government is likely to enhance skill levels more by expanding formal education than by trying to foster sectoral training schemes modeled on the German. Conversely, competition policies that serve Britain well might erode the capacities of German firms for non-market coordination.

Wood (1997 and this volume) goes beyond this to argue that the viability of policy depends not only on the organization of the political economy but on the organization of the political realm (see also Katzenstein 1978*b*, 1987).[32] Let us distinguish between 'market incentive' policies and 'coordination-oriented' policies. The former rely on market-based incentives to induce actors to perform more effectively. The latter attempt to improve the competencies of firms, such as their skill levels or technological capabilities, by addressing firm needs with relative precision. Thus, coordination-oriented policies must be based on high levels of information about the activities of the firm. But, as Wood points out, firms are reluctant to share such information with governments whose position as powerful actors under a range of unpredictable influences raises the risks that they will defect from any agreement and use the information they have acquired against the firm. The transaction costs to governments of coordinating the activities of many private-sector actors can also be prohibitively high. In short, this kind of policy-making is marked by information asymmetries, high transaction costs, and time-inconsistency problems.

The governments of coordinated market economies have taken advantage of the strong business associations, trade unions, and other para-public organizations in their political economies to resolve these problems. Because such associations are independent of the government and responsible to their member-firms, the latter are more inclined to trust them with enough private information to administer a coordination-oriented or 'framework' policy effectively. And because these associations are in a good position to monitor and even gently sanction their members, they can often secure the coordination that a policy demands with lower transaction costs. Thus, producer-group organizations enter into 'implicit contracts' with the government to administer the policy, drawing some benefits of their own in the form of enhanced resources and authority.

This is where the organization of the political realm matters. Business associations and their members will be willing to form such contracts,

---

[32] The analysis in the following paragraphs owes a great deal to Wood (1997) as well as his chapter in this volume.

which usually entail some information-sharing, only if the government's commitment to abide by them is credible. As Wood (1997) observes, however, that commitment will be more credible where the relevant producer groups have enough structural influence to punish the government for any deviations from its agreements. This structural influence may rest on a number of bases: the authority of producer organizations inside political parties, the entrenchment of neo-corporatist practices in enough spheres of policy-making that defection in one can be punished in another, or policy-making procedures decentralized enough to allow producer groups many points of access and some veto points. Of course, the influence of producer groups will also depend on the character of those groups themselves: they must be encompassing and powerful enough to mobilize a serious constituency if they need to sanction the government. In short, coordination-oriented policies should be more feasible in nations with both a coordinated market economy and a political system in which producer groups enjoy substantial structural influence.

Coordination-oriented policies will be more difficult to implement in liberal market economies because their business and labor associations usually lack the encompassing character required to administer such policies well. In addition, producer groups may be less willing to enter into such implicit contracts in nations where they do not possess enough structural influence to sanction the government for deviations from them. This should be an especially important problem in nations where the powers of the state are highly concentrated in the political executive or where the influence of producer groups inside political parties is very limited.

In contradistinction to some others, then, this analysis suggests that the attributes normally associated with the 'strength' of a state may prevent governments from implementing many kinds of policies effectively. Wood (1997) shows that the failures of successive British schemes for industrial rationalization were rooted, not in the 'weakness' of the British state, as many who underline the limited levers in the hands of the authorities have suggested, but in its very strength: the Westminster system concentrates so much power in the political executive that producer groups were reluctant to trust it (cf. Sacks 1980; Leruez 1975; Shonfield 1965). Despite its many powers, the French state has also had difficulty implementing schemes for regional or technological development that require coordination among private-sector actors, partly because it concentrates power in Paris and cannot find encompassing producer groups to operate them (Culpepper 1998; Levy 1999a).

In general, liberal market economies should find it more feasible to implement market-incentive policies that do not put extensive demands on firms to form relational contracts with others but rely on markets to coordinate their activities. These include regional development schemes based on tax incentives, vocational programs focused on formal instruction in marketable skills, and government subsidies for basic research. Because of the bluntness of the instruments available to states and the importance of markets to these economies, deregulation is often the most effective way to improve coordination in LMEs.

This analysis of institutional complementarities between political regimes and political economies raises some intriguing issues about the patterns observable in the developed world. Many liberal market economies have Westminster systems of government that concentrate power in the political executive, while coordinated market economies tend to be governed by consociational, coalitional, or quasi-corporatist regimes. Several factors could lie behind this congruence.[33] However, some amount of co-evolution cannot be ruled out. If regimes that provide structural influence to encompassing producer groups find it more feasible to implement coordination-oriented policies, while states in which power is highly concentrated have more success with market-incentive policies, the character of the political regime may contribute to the development of a particular type of economy. Levy (1999*a*) argues forcefully for a variant of this view in the case of France.

To put a similar point in more general terms, the character of the political regime may condition the levels of asset specificity found across nations (see Alt et al. 1996). We have already argued that the institutional structure of the economy encourages certain kinds of investments. The fluid market settings of liberal market economies encourage investment in switchable assets, while the dense institutional networks of coordinated market economies enhance the attractiveness of investment in specific or co-specific assets. Political regimes characterized by coalition governments, multiple veto points, and parties that entrench the power of producer groups may also be more conducive to investment in specific assets than ones that concentrate power in highly autonomous party leaders, because (i) regimes of this sort are well positioned to provide the framework policies that sustain the institutions supporting specific investments and (ii) because they provide producers with more direct influence over government and the capacity to punish it for deviating

---

[33] Since many LMEs were once British colonies, the diffusion of cultural norms in the economic and political spheres may be a factor here, and, of course, the USA provides a notable exception to this rule.

from its agreements, such regimes offer investors more assurance that policy will not shift in such a way as to damage the value of assets that cannot readily be switched to other uses.[34] Thus, we should expect to find more investment in specific assets in nations with such regimes. These are issues that merit further investigation.

1.7.2 Social Policy

The varieties of capitalism approach to political economy also opens up new perspectives on social policy. In particular, it highlights the importance of social policy to firms and the role that business groups play in the development of welfare states. Convention associates the development of social policy with organized labor and progressive political parties, on the assumption that business generally opposes such initiatives. However, Mares (1998a and this volume) shows that business groups have played key roles in the development of social policy for over a century and develops a parsimonious model to explain the policies in which various types of firms will have interests. Her work advances an important literature exploring the contribution that business groups have made to the construction of welfare states (Pierson 1995a; Martin 1999; Swenson 1997, 2001; Mares 1997b, 1998; Estevez-Abe 1999a).

The relational approach we take to company competencies naturally draws attention to the support that social policies can provide for the relationships firms develop to advance their objectives. Social policy is often thought to interfere with labor markets by raising labor costs or the reservation wage. But the contributors to this volume explore the ways in which social policies can improve the operation of labor markets, notably from the perspective of the firm. Unemployment benefits with high replacement rates, for instance, can improve the ability of firms to attract and retain pools of labor with high or specific skills. Disability benefits and early retirement benefits can allow firms that operate production regimes requiring employee loyalty to release labor without violating implicit contracts about long-term employment. There are many respects in which social policies can be crucial to the relational strategies of firms.

For this reason, there should be a correspondence between types of political economies and types of welfare states. And that appears to be the case. Virtually all liberal market economies are accompanied by

[34] Katzenstein (1987) shows how the structural features of the German political system hem in most governments, while Gamble and Walkland (1987) show how frequently British governments have changed regulatory regimes important to business.

'liberal' welfare states, whose emphasis on means-testing and low levels of benefits reinforce the fluid labor markets that firms use to manage their relations with labor (Esping-Andersen 1990). As Estevez-Abe, Iversen, and Soskice note, liberal social-policy regimes also encourage individuals to develop the general, rather than specific, skills that corporate strategies in LMEs tend to require.

Although the social-policy regimes that accompany coordinated market economies are more varied, there are many respects in which their distinctive features lend support to the corporate strategies found in such economies. Large companies in Japan find it easier to secure employee loyalty and company-specific skills because they provide many of the social benefits that might otherwise be the responsibility of the state (Estevez-Abe 1999*a*). Many of the firms in CMEs operate product market strategies and associated production regimes that require a workforce equipped with high levels of industry-specific skills. Workers must be persuaded to invest in such skills, however, especially given the risk that, if they are laid off and must take employment in another sector, they may never realize their investment. In such contexts, as Estevez-Abe, Iversen, and Soskice point out, the pension and unemployment-benefit schemes offering generous replacement rates closely tied to wages often found in coordinated market economies help to assure workers that they can weather an economic downturn without having to shift to a job in which their investment in specific skills does not pay off.

Governments introduce social legislation for many reasons, some of them conditioned by partisan competition and the demands of labor. But the contributors to this volume argue that business also has important interests in social policy and a role in its development. Mares (1998) traces the way in which social policy emerges from alliances between business groups, trade unions, and public officials in Germany and France, while Estevez-Abe (1999*a*) and Iversen and Soskice (2000) explore the politics that leads specific types of political economies toward distinctive welfare states. In the sphere of social policy, the varieties of capitalism approach is helping to open up several new research agendas.

1.7.3 National Interests in the International Arena

The international arena is also an important sphere for policy-making. What states cannot secure domestically, because of political resistance or transnational externalities, they often seek in negotiations about international regimes (Krasner 1983*b*; Keohane 1984; Putnam 1988). These regimes now have a substantial impact on national societies, especially in Europe where the regulations of the European Union have become almost as important as national policies. For this reason, it is important to understand how the rules or regulations of such regimes are determined, and a number of approaches can be taken to that problem. One of the most influential, however, argues that the character and regulations of regimes and of the EU are determined by their member states, operating from conceptions of national interest (Moravcsik 1991). In this context, it has become important to be able to specify what a government's conception of its national interest will be and whence such conceptions derive, especially in the economic sphere.

Analysts have taken several approaches to identifying the conceptions of national economic interest that motivate governments in international negotiations. Some formulations associate them with prevailing economic conditions, such as the levels of inflation or unemployment in the nation (Moravscik 1998). Others employ neoclassical economic doctrine to specify the welfare gains likely to accrue to the nation from a particular outcome, such as freer trade (Frieden and Rogowski 1996). The conceptions of national interest from which government officials operate in international negotiations are most often seen, however, as a response to pressure from domestic interests. The direction of that pressure can then be specified in a number of ways. Most who take this approach use an economic theory to identify the impact a decision will have on particular sectors and an institutional theory to predict which sectors will have more influence over the government (Milner 1988, 1997; Frieden 1991; Garrett and Lange 1996).

There is some value in all these approaches, especially for specific cases, but the conceptions of national interest they generate can be nebulous or of limited generality, especially when rooted in transitory economic conditions or shifting parallelograms of sectoral pressure. Without prejudice to the alternatives, the approach to comparative capitalism developed in this volume provides another way of specifying how states will define their national interests in international economic negotiations. It suggests that their stance toward new regulatory initiatives will be influenced by judgements about whether those initiatives are likely to sustain or undermine the comparative institutional advantages of their nation's economy. Governments should be inclined to support such initiatives only when they do not threaten the institutions most crucial to the competitive advantages their firms enjoy.[35]

[35] Note, of course, that governments can misperceive the impact of a proposed regulation and that other factors will often also enter into calculations of national interest. These formulations are deeply influenced by the work of Fioretos (1998).

In this volume and others (1998), Fioretos applies this perspective to the positions taken by Britain, Sweden, France, and Germany in negotiations leading up to the Maastricht Treaty. He argues that many of the conflicts between Britain and the other member-states of the EU, leading to its opt-out from the social charter, can be traced to British efforts to protect the institutions of its liberal market economy. The positions taken by member states in those negotiations toward the industrial policies of the EU also correspond to the concerns they were likely to have about preserving the distinctive institutional infrastructures of their nations and particular types of relations among firms.

This approach can be applied to a wide range of issues associated with the evolution of the European Union. Germany's reluctance to accept deep financial deregulation may derive, for instance, not simply from a desire to maintain the rents of its financial sector but from a concern to preserve the capacities for network monitoring that sustain the terms on which domestic capital is available to its firms (cf. Story and Walter 1997). Britain's efforts to secure regulations that enhance market competition in many sectors may reflect an interest in securing a competitive edge for its own firms, whose corporate strategies and structures are already appropriate for operating in such environments.

Even some of the positions that member-states have taken toward the development of the institutions of the European Union may be explicable in these terms. We have argued that the success of a national economy can depend on whether it is supervised by a state with institutions appropriate for supplying the kind of economic policies that sustain it. As the EU takes on additional economic responsibilities, its members may be concerned to ensure that the agencies and techniques used to administer them are congruent with the needs of their own economies. Thus, states and actors from coordinated market economies can be expected to seek institutions conducive to the formation of implicit contracts between public authorities and business associations, while those from liberal market economies should want to avoid agencies interventionist enough to interfere with the operation of market mechanisms. Such considerations cannot fully explain the design of European institutions, but they may figure in the process (cf. Schmidt 1997; Pollack 1997).

This perspective may help explain why it has been so difficult for the EU to secure full regulatory harmonization and why it has resorted, instead, to the 'mutual recognition' of national regulations (K. Nicolaides 1993). Transaction costs alone do not seem to provide enough of an explanation. If the structure of the European economies were broadly similar, it should be possible to agree on 'best practice', allowing a transition period for laggards to catch up. But there are profound institutional differences among the political economies of Europe, on which the firms of each nation have come to rely for competitive advantage. Although, as market economies, all can agree on some measures, to enforce high levels of regulatory homogeneity on the member-states would be to compromise the institutions and firm strategies on which national comparative advantages depend. It is not surprising that there has been no consensus on such matters. More than national tradition has been at stake. This suggests that, despite some significant effects, international negotiations are unlikely to be vehicles for the cross-national institutional convergence that some expect from them.[36]

1.8 The Dynamics of Economic Adjustment

Although we have emphasized differences among political economies that have been relatively durable, ours is not a static conception of the political economy. On the contrary, we expect the corporate strategies, policies, and institutions of each nation to evolve in response to the challenges they face, and our approach contains a number of conceptual tools for understanding both the nature of contemporary challenges and the shape this evolution is likely to take. In this section, we discuss some of the dynamic elements of the analysis that are covered in more detail in subsequent chapters.

1.8.1 The Challenge of Globalization

The developed economies are currently experiencing profound changes. A technological revolution is creating entirely new sectors, based on biotechnology, microprocessors, and telecommunications, whose products are transforming business practices across the economy. A wave of managerial innovations has seen companies around the world adopt new forms of supplier–client relations, just-in-time inventory systems, quality control, and team production. Economic activity is shifting from the industrial sector into the service sector. Capitalism seems to be in the midst of one of those 'cycles of creative destruction' that Schumpeter (1950) identified.

---

[36] As Streeck (1996b) and Scharpf (1995: ch. 2) have pointed out, precisely because they cannot legislate regulatory convergence, international regimes and the EU may resort to measures that enhance market competition, thereby intensifying the pressures for convergence that come from another direction, namely via processes of competitive deregulation. There is much to be said for this view. For further discussion, see the section on 'globalization' below.

If technology provided the spark for this revolution, the accelerant has been liberalization in the international economy. With declining transport and communication costs, more liberal trade and financial regimes have inspired vast new flows of goods and capital across national borders, including a large increase in foreign direct investment. All the developed economies are more open than they were twenty years ago, and intense international competition is enforcing innovation on many firms. The watchword for these developments has become *globalization* —a term summing up the hopes of some for global prosperity and the fears of many that their way of life will be lost to international forces beyond the control even of their government (Berger and Dore 1996; Keohane and Milner 1996; Friedman 1999).[37]

For political economy, the principal issue raised by globalization concerns the stability of regulatory regimes and national institutions in the face of heightened competitive pressure (Boyer and Drache 1996; Rodrik 1997). Will institutional differences among nations of the sort we have identified remain significant or will the processes of competitive deregulation unleashed by international integration drive all economies toward a common market model?

To these questions, the conventional view of globalization prominent in the press and much of the literature gives an ominous answer. It is built on three pillars. First, it sees firms as essentially similar across nations at least in terms of basic structure and strategy. Second, it associates the competitiveness of firms with their unit labor costs, from which it follows that many will move production abroad if they can find cheaper labor there. And, third, these propositions generate a particular model of the political dynamic inspired by globalization, of the following type.

In the face of threats from firms to exit the economy, governments are said to come under increasing pressure from business to alter their regulatory frameworks so as to lower domestic labor costs, reduce rates of taxation, and expand internal markets via deregulation. What resistance there is to such steps will come from trade unions, seeking to protect the wages of their members, and social democratic parties, seeking to preserve social programs. The precise effects that each nation suffers in the face of globalization will thus be determined by the amount of political resistance that labor and the left can mount to proposals for

---

[37] We use the term 'globalization' in this chapter to refer to the developments that have made it easier for companies to locate operations abroad, including the liberalization of trade, the deregulation and expansion of international financial markets, the new accessibility and expansion of markets in what was the communist world, and declining transportation or communication costs.

change. But, because international interdependence provides capital with more exit opportunities than it does for labor, the balance of power is said to have shifted dramatically toward capital. In short, this is a model that predicts substantial deregulation and a convergence in economic institutions across nations. Conventional views of globalization contain a 'convergence hypothesis' analogous in force, but considerably less sanguine in implications, to an earlier one based on theories of industrialism (Kerr et al. 1960; Graubard 1964).

To date, the principal challenges to this view have come in two forms. Some scholars argue that the internationalization of trade and finance has not been as extensive or unprecedented as is often believed. Others argue that national governments are not as defenseless in the face of these developments as they appear, because governments have simply used international institutions or the excuse of global pressure to pursue reforms they wanted in any case (Wade 1996; Boyer 1996; Cohen 1996). There is some validity to both arguments. However, the analysis developed in this volume provides another basis for reevaluating the effects of globalization.

1.8.2 Reconsidering Globalization

The varieties of capitalism approach calls into question each of the assumptions underpinning the conventional view of globalization. First, it suggests that firms are not essentially similar across nations. On the contrary, firms in LMEs and CMEs develop distinctive strategies and structures to capitalize on the institutions available for market or non-market coordination in the economy. There is substantial evidence that firms in different types of economies react differently to similar challenges (Knetter 1989). Thus, we should not expect identical responses from them to globalization.

Second, our perspective suggests that firms will not automatically move their activities off-shore when offered low-cost labor abroad. Cheaper labor that comes with commensurate skill and productivity levels is always attractive, but firms also derive competitive advantages from the institutions in their home country that support specific types of inter- and intra-firm relationships. Many firms will be reluctant to give these up simply to reduce wage costs. Comparative institutional advantages tend to render companies less mobile than theories that do not acknowledge them imply.

Of course, with international liberalization, there will be some movement of corporate activities across national borders, as firms seek access to new markets and new sources of supply, but our approach suggests dimensions to this movement that conventional views do not anticipate. It implies, for instance, that firms based in LMEs may be more inclined to move their activities abroad to secure cheaper labor than companies based in CMEs, because the former already coordinate their endeavors using the market structures that less developed nations usually provide, while the latter often pursue corporate strategies that rely on high skills and institutional infrastructure difficult to secure elsewhere.

Our concept of comparative institutional advantage also suggests that firms may exploit new opportunities for movement to engage in a form of *institutional arbitrage*. By this, we mean that companies may shift particular activities to other nations in order to secure the advantages that the institutional frameworks of their political economies offer for pursuing those activities. Thus, companies may move some of their activities to liberal market economies, not simply to lower labor costs, but to secure access to institutional support for radical innovation. This helps to explain why Nissan locates design facilities in California, Deutsche Bank acquires subsidiaries in Chicago and London, and German pharmaceutical firms open research labs in the United States. Conversely, companies may locate other activities in coordinated market economies in order to secure access to the quality control, skill levels, and capacities for incremental innovation that their institutional frameworks offer. General Motors locates its engine plant in Düsseldorf rather than in Spain. Over time, corporate movements of this sort should reinforce differences in national institutional frameworks, as firms that have shifted their operations to benefit from particular institutions seek to retain them.

Finally, our perspective calls into question the monolithic political dynamic conventionally associated with globalization. It predicts one dynamic in liberal market economies and a different one in coordinated market economies. In the face of more intense international competition, business interests in LMEs are likely to pressure governments for deregulation, since firms that coordinate their endeavors primarily through the market can improve their competencies by sharpening its edges. The government is likely to be sympathetic because the comparative advantage of the economy as a whole rests on the effectiveness of market mechanisms. Organized labor will put up some resistance, resulting in mild forms of class conflict. But, because international liberalization enhances the exit options of firms in LMEs, as noted above, the balance of power is likely to tilt toward business. The result should be some weakening of organized labor and a substantial amount of deregulation, much as conventional views predict.

In coordinated market economies, however, the political dynamic inspired by globalization should be quite different. Here, governments should be less sympathetic to deregulation because it threatens the nation's comparative institutional advantages.[38] Although there will be some calls for deregulation even in such settings, the business community is likely to provide less support for it, because many firms draw competitive advantages from systems of relational contracting that depend on the presence of supportive regulatory regimes. In these economies, firms and workers have common interests to defend because they have invested in many co-specific assets, such as industry-specific skills. Thus, the political dynamic inspired by globalization in these countries is likely to entail less class conflict and to center around the formation of cross-class coalitions, as firms and workers with intense interests in particular regulatory regimes align against those with interests in others (cf. Swenson 1991, 1997).[39]

This analysis explains several outcomes in the spheres of policy and politics that are otherwise puzzling. Globalization was expected to weaken trade unions across the industrialized world. But comparative data show that trade union membership and the locus of collective bargaining has dropped far more substantially in some nations than in others (Lange et al. 1995; Ebbinghaus and Visser 2000). Our analysis predicts most of the patterns observed (see Table 1.2). Trade unions have been weakened by business initiatives and deregulation in LMEs but remain strong in CMEs where cross-class coalitions help to preserve them and some degree of wage coordination (see also Thelen in this volume).

Instead of the monolithic movement toward deregulation that many expect from globalization, our analysis predicts a bifurcated response marked by widespread deregulation in liberal market economies and limited movement in coordinated market economies.[40] This is precisely

---

[38] Note that we are not claiming all types of non-market institutions contribute to the efficiency of the economy. We have identified some specific types of inter- and intra-firm relations and supporting institutions that we associate with effective firm performance. There are other 'non-market' institutions in many economies that simply generate economic rents or detract from economic efficiency. The point is to distinguish among them and not to label all 'non-market' institutions efficient or inefficient.

[39] Note that this observation corresponds to the predictions of Frieden and Rogowski (1996) that class conflict is more likely in economies where switchable assets predominate and sectoral conflict characterized by cross-class coalitions more likely in economies where asset specificity is high. However, because firms and workers share some interests in all economies, we do not exclude the possibility that some cross-class coalitions will also be formed in liberal market economies, as Swenson (1997) suggests.

[40] We use 'deregulation' as a convenient shorthand to refer to policies that remove regulations limiting competition, expand the role of markets in the allocation of resources, or

TABLE 1.2 Changes in trade union density and the level of collective bargaining, 1950 – 1992

Liberal market economies

	Trade union density			Bargaining level[a]		
	1950 – 73	1974 – 84	1985 – 92	1950 – 73	1974 – 84	1985 – 92
Australia[b]	54	52	49	3.0	3.1	3.0
Canada	30	33	32	1.0	1.8	1.0
UK	45	51	41	1.7	2.1	1.0
United States	29	23	15	1.3	1.0	1.0
LME average	39	40	34	1.7	2.0	1.5

Coordinated market economies

	Trade union density			Bargaining level[a]		
	1950 – 73	1974 – 84	1985 – 92	1950 – 73	1974 – 84	1985 – 92
Austria	63	58	55	2.2	2.0	2.0
Belgium	48	68	69	2.0	2.9	2.5
Denmark	59	77	81	4.0	3.3	2.8
Finland	41	78	88	3.2	2.8	2.8
Germany	38	40	37	2.0	2.0	2.0
Japan	34	31	25	1.4	2.0	2.0
The Netherlands	40	36	28	3.7	3.4	2.1
Norway	58	61	63	3.8	3.6	3.6
Sweden	71	86	95	3.7	3.7	2.9
Switzerland	37	35	29	2.0	2.0	2.0
CME average	49	57	57	2.8	2.8	2.5

[a] 1 = plant-level wage-setting; 2 = industry-level wage-setting; 3 = central wage-setting without sanctions; 4 = central wage-setting with sanctions. Value recorded is the average for the period indicated.
[b] Trade union series ends in 1989.

Sources: Visser (1996). Compiled in Golden et al. (1997).

the pattern of policy across the OECD in recent decades. Deregulation has been far-reaching in the liberal market economies of Britain, the United States, New Zealand, Canada, and Australia but much less extensive in the coordinated market economies of northern Europe and east

sharpen market incentives in the economy. Of course, we recognize that all deregulation is implicitly a form of reregulation (Vogel 1996).

Asia (Vogel 1996; Ellis 1998; Story and Walter 1997; Wood 1997; King and Wood 1999).[41] Moreover, Wood and Thelen report finding just the sort of politics this approach would lead one to expect in both liberal and coordinated market economies in recent years (this volume; Wood 1997; Thelen 2000).

Ultimately, it is not surprising that increasing flows of trade have not erased the institutional differences across nations. After all, world trade has been increasing for fifty years without enforcing convergence. Because of comparative institutional advantage, nations often prosper, not by becoming more similar, but by building on their institutional differences.[42]

1.8.3 Developments in the Market for Corporate Governance

There is another side to globalization, however, with effects that some argue are more ambiguous. It lies in the pressures stemming from the internationalization of finance, where developments have recently been dramatic, if not unprecedented.[43] International flows of capital have grown exponentially in the past two decades, raising levels of both direct and portfolio investment (cf. Simmons 1999). This puts pressure on the institutions of coordinated market economies in several ways. International financial markets have become increasingly important sources of capital for large firms. But, lacking the facilities to monitor the progress of a company closely, distant investors usually prefer to supply capital on arm's-length terms that emphasize transparent, balance-sheet criteria. Therefore, firms seeking access to these funds face pressure to revise their accounting standards, appoint independent directors, and deliver the high rates of return associated with 'shareholder value'.

Even more important is the wave of international merger and acquisition activity that has taken place over the past decade, as firms of all sorts reposition themselves to take advantage of the liberalization of world markets. It has had several effects. Firms based in coordinated

---

[41] We predict some, if more limited, deregulation in CMEs because, alongside non-market institutions, they also use market mechanisms whose operation can be improved by a measured amount of deregulation.

[42] The effects of trade integration seem to have fallen, less substantially on the differences between CMEs and LMEs, and more heavily on practices of state intervention of the sort once prominent in France and the developing world, as governments found that *dirigiste* policies cannot ensure competitiveness on international markets (cf. Hall 1990; Ziegler 1997; McArthur and Scott 1969).

[43] As Zevin (1992) points out, international capital markets were probably more integrated in the decades before World War I than they have ever been since.

market economies, such as Germany, that have usually not been as concerned about their rate of return on capital or share price as American firms have acquired a new interest in such matters because many hope to use their own shares to make foreign acquisitions to consolidate their competitive position in global markets that are opening and reconfiguring rapidly.[44] Shares that are highly valued can be a significant asset in merger and acquisition contests.

Similarly, some of the large banks and insurance companies in CMEs that once cultivated close relations with manufacturing firms have been disengaging from them in order to free up resources for global expansion. The German government has recently facilitated such moves by lowering capital-gains taxes on the sale of corporate shareholdings. Where steps such as these reduce cross-shareholding enough to undercut the protection it provides firms against hostile takeovers or government regulations on such acquisitions are relaxed, the heightened dangers of takeover could also provoke changes in corporate strategy in CMEs. Many firms would have to become more attentive to the value of their shares and earnings in order to deter takeovers.

These developments threaten traditional practices in CMEs in several ways. On the one hand, they could disrupt the intricate systems of cross-shareholding and inter-corporate linkage that provide capacities for network monitoring, thereby reducing the access of firms to capital that is not tied to current profitability. On the other, they could force firms whose strategies and structure have reflected responsiveness to a wide range of stakeholders, including employees, to become more attentive to shareholders and rates of return; and this might reduce their capacity to make credible commitments to long-term collaborative relationships with other firms and employees. That could engender shifts in strategy extending all the way down to production regimes.

However, while important, the impact of international financial developments can easily be misinterpreted. There is no doubt that large companies in CMEs will have to make the long-run, risk-adjusted real rates of return demanded by world financial markets. But that is not inconsistent with internal management practices that maximize comparative institutional advantage. These pressures have led many companies to develop closer relationships with works councils rather than the reverse, simply because employee cooperation becomes more, not less, important in such contexts. Moreover, it is not a rational strategy for

---

[44] We are grateful to Michel Goyer for drawing our attention to this point (see Goyer 2001).

shareholders to insist on Anglo-Saxon management practices if that has the effect of lowering rates of return.

Germany provides a case in point. Although the large German banks are seeking a global role, they are still engaged with German industry and regional banks maintain important *Hausbank* relationships (cf. Ziegler 2000; Griffin 2000; Vitols 2000).[45] Many German firms have embraced international accounting standards, but there are still few independent directors on their boards and 'shareholder value' has been used mainly as a slogan to justify reorganizations that would have been dictated in any case. Although hostile takeovers have become more common in France, they remain rare in Germany, where regulatory regimes and cross-share-holding militate against them.[46] The market for corporate governance is changing but at a pace that may allow firms to retain many aspects of their long-standing strategies.

1.8.4 Analyzing Change in National Systems

Much of the work on comparative capitalism lacks developed concep-tions of how national systems change. As a result, the literature on glob-alization tends to cluster around two poles. On one side are works that focus on institutions and the ways in which they reproduce stable patterns of behavior. Their relatively static view implies that national systems are unlikely to change very much in the face of globalization. On the other are works that attribute great force to the pressures associ-ated with globalization. They tend to see national practices as inertial factors that will be transformed by these pressures.

Our approach offers a more dynamic conception of national political economies in the sense that it anticipates change in them and contains specific propositions about the processes through which it will occur. Some of these should already be apparent from the account we have given of globalization. However, it may be useful to summarize some of the key implications about dynamics in this approach.

We see national political economies as systems that often experience external shocks emanating from a world economy in which technologies, products, and tastes change continuously. These shocks will often un-settle the equilibria on which economic actors have been coordinating

---

[45] The important role played by the German banks in the rescue of the construction group Philip Holzmann provides one example.

[46] As of 1999, the combined equity stake of hard-core shareholders and the shares voted by German banks in the firms on the German DAX-30 still averaged 39% of those firms' shares (figures supplied by Michel Goyer).

and challenge the existing practices of firms. We expect firms to respond with efforts to modify their practices so as to sustain their competitive advantages, including comparative institutional advantages. Thus, much of the adjustment process will be oriented to the institutional recreation of comparative advantage. In its course, firms and individuals will modify their relational investments, seeking new competencies that entail new relations with other firms or employees.

To do so, they will call on the existing institutional structures supporting coordination in the economy, including those that allow for deliberation and the making of credible commitments. In many cases, firms will need the cooperation of government, but we expect governments to be responsive to efforts to restore coordination, because they will come under pressure from producer groups and voters with substantial interests in existing institutions to do so (Iversen and Soskice 2000; Wood this volume). If coordination entails strategic interaction, however, more than institutional support is required to establish it. As we have noted, this sort of coordination also depends on the presence of a common knowledge set of beliefs that reflect relatively complete understandings of the roles and interests of the participants in the arrangement, as well as some confidence in the trustworthiness of the relevant institutions. Economic shocks and interim attempts to cope with them can unsettle such understandings. Therefore, their restoration will be a crucial, and difficult, component of the adjustment process.

Several points follow from this perspective. First, although we expect firms to attempt to sustain or restore the forms of coordination on which their competitive advantages have been built, after an economic shock, these efforts may entail changes to existing institutions or practices in the economy. Second, the importance of common knowledge to successful strategic interaction implies some asymmetry in the development potential of these systems. Because they have little experience of such coordination to underpin the requisite common knowledge, LMEs will find it difficult to develop non-market coordination of the sort common in CMEs, even when the relevant institutions can be put into place. Because market relations do not demand the same levels of common knowledge, however, there is no such constraint on CMEs deregulating to become more like LMEs. However, we have noted that the business communities of CMEs will not automatically support deregulation, since many firms may want to retain competitive advantages that depend on high levels of regulation.

Institutional complementarities should play an important, if ambiguous, role in these processes of adjustment. On the one hand, they raise the prospect that institutional reform in one sphere of the economy could snowball into changes in other spheres as well. If the financial markets of a CME are deregulated, for instance, it may become more difficult for firms to offer long-term employment. That could make it harder for them to recruit skilled labor or sustain worker loyalty, ultimately inspiring major changes in production regimes (cf. Aoki 1994). Financial deregulation could be the string that unravels coordinated market economies. On the other hand, institutional complementarities generate disincentives to radical change. Firms and other actors may attempt to preserve arrangements in one sphere of the economy in order to protect complementary institutions or synergies with institutions elsewhere that are of value to them. Many German firms have devoted energy to revising rather than abolishing their vocational training schemes because they operate production regimes that demand particular types of skills.

The types of adjustment problems encountered in a coordinated market economy are well illustrated by some of the recent difficulties afflicting the German system of wage coordination.[47] For many years, the capacity of this system to generate wage increases moderate enough to sustain the competitiveness of German industry has depended on the ability of employers' associations to mount resistance to exorbitant wage demands, if necessary orchestrating lockouts of the workforce. In many cases, the major firms in a sector would resist high industry settlements, even if they could afford them, in order to maintain solidarity with smaller firms that could not afford them, increasing their own workers' wages only after an industry agreement had been reached.

In some sectors, the large firms have now rationalized their operations to take advantage of the opportunities presented by higher levels of international integration, moving some operations off-shore and reconfiguring supply chains. As a result, they have become increasingly sensitive to interruptions in production and inclined to veto lockouts. But this shift in stance has disrupted the existing equilibrium. Without the cooperation of large firms, employers' associations can no longer mount effective resistance to wage demands. As a consequence, some smaller or less efficient firms are dropping out of them; and trade union leaders who would normally be inclined to accept moderate wage increases in order to preserve employment are now finding themselves unable to do so because of pressure from their militants, who are no longer deterred by

---

[47] We owe this example to Kathleen Thelen (see Thelen and Kume 1999*a*; Thelen and Wijnbergen 2000).

the threat of lockouts.[48] The result has been a deterioration in the effectiveness of wage coordination and of employers' associations in some German sectors (Thelen and Kume 1999*a*; Thelen and Wijnbergen 2000; see also Manow and Seils 2000).

This is the type of adjustment problem that often arises in coordinated settings. However, there are good reasons for thinking that effective coordination can be restored in most such cases. As Thelen points out, such problems are not unprecedented in coordinated market economies. The equilibrium outcomes on which actors coordinate have been unsettled by economic shocks many times in the past. In each case, new equilibria have been found through processes of negotiation and compromise. The process of adjustment may well entail a period of conflict and suboptimal outcomes, as each side tests the power and resolve of the other. But the presence of institutions that entrench the power of the actors, whether employers or trade unions, give them strong incentives to cooperate with each other, and the availability of deliberative institutions facilitates coordination.

In 'negotiated economies' such as these, adjustment is often slower than it is in economies coordinated primarily by markets; but markets do not necessarily generate superior outcomes. Where encompassing producer groups have extensive 'strategic capacity' and strong incentives to reach agreement, the results can be equally satisfactory.[49] Coordinated market economies have a track record of meeting these kind of challenges (Hall 1997; Global Economic Forum 2000). In Sweden, for instance, peak-level bargaining broke down during the 1980s because it was no longer meeting the needs of firms facing new technologies and greater international competition; but the trade unions and employers developed new forms of wage-bargaining recoordinated at the sectoral level rather than revert to purely liberal arrangements (Pontusson and Swenson 1996).

In sum, this is an approach to political economy designed not only to identify important patterns of similarity and difference across nations but also to elucidate the processes whereby national political economies

---

[48] Of course, with the advent of economic and monetary union, the Bundesbank no longer has the capacity to discipline union members by threatening tighter monetary policies, and the capacity of the European central bank to do so is much lower now because it stands at one remove from the German economy (see Hall and Franzese 1998).

[49] By 'strategic capacity', we mean the capacity to formulate a collective strategy for the group and to mobilize support for it among the group. Typically, this entails highly articulated organization.

change. It anticipates institutional change in all the developed democracies, as they adjust to contemporary challenges, but provides a framework within which the import of those changes can be assessed.

The chapters that follow elaborate many of the themes raised in this introduction. Each uses the basic approach outlined here to explore a more specific set of issues, but we have not imposed a rigid template on the contributors and there are differences of emphasis among them. These essays encompass a wide range of cases, issue areas, and methodologies. They illuminate both the potential in the approach and the scope of the research agenda it opens up. Since we have referred to many chapters in the course of this Introduction, we will simply outline the organization of the volume here.

Part I of the volume displays the wide range of topics for which the varieties of capitalism approach has implications. The first two chapters explore issues in industrial relations with an emphasis on the institutional complementarities relevant to this sphere. Thelen examines recent developments in the industrial-relations arena, showing how institutions at the macro and micro levels of the economy interact to generate a politics that produces different outcomes in liberal and coordinated market economies. Franzese shows how the institutions for wage coordination and monetary policy-making interact with each other and with the sectoral composition of the organized workforce to influence national patterns of economic performance. These essays show why different types of economies can be expected to react quite differently to economic challenges.

The next two chapters investigate some of the implications of this approach for our understanding of social policy. Estevez-Abe, Iversen, and Soskice examine the relationship between particular varieties of capitalism and social-policy regimes, emphasizing the way in which different types of social policies encourage workers to develop specific or general skills, thereby reinforcing the product market strategies characteristic of firms in various types of economies. Mares makes a more general case for the contention that employers have strong interests in social policy and will want to influence its development. She devises a parsimonious model to elucidate the interests of different types of firms in social policy and presents case-study evidence to show that the interests they have articulated conform to her model. This work suggests that it is time to reevaluate the welfare state: social policies that were once seen as impediments to the operation of markets, imposed by labor or the left on business in the name of social protection, may actually be important adjuncts to markets with real value for firms who have been actively involved in their design.

Fioretos concludes this part of the book by indicating how a varieties of capitalism approach can be used to address important issues in international relations, particularly the problem of how national interests are constructed for the purposes of international negotiations. He argues that the conceptions of national interest applied in such contexts are often rooted in the organization of their political economy and shows that the differences between German and British capitalism can explain many of the positions taken by these nations in the negotiations leading up to the Maastricht Treaty of the European Union.

Part II of the volume displays some of the new perspectives on public policy-making that this varieties of capitalism perspective opens up. Wood compares the development of labor market policy in Britain and Germany with a view to showing how the organization of the political realm interacts with the organization of the political economy to generate distinctive patterns of policy across liberal and coordinated market economies. Culpepper takes on issues of reform, exploring efforts to transplant vocational training schemes of the sort practiced in West Germany to East Germany and France. His analysis shows how difficult it is for governments to secure such coordination and how dependent the results are on the presence of supportive employer organizations. Hancké focuses on the case of France, arguing, contrary to conventional images of its *dirigiste* regime, that recent industrial adjustment there has been led, not by the state, but by large firms using the business networks available to them.

Part III of the book explores issues of corporate governance, firm strategy, and the law. Vitols provides a detailed comparison of the systems for corporate governance found in Britain and Germany and argues that, despite recent challenges, they remain distinctive. Lehrer takes the analysis down to the level of corporate strategy, developing a varieties of capitalism approach to strategic management that links the structure of the political economy closely to corporate strategy. Using the case of the airline industry, he shows how the approach can be used to explain national differences in corporate strategy. The chapters by Casper and Teubner show how a varieties of capitalism approach can be used to integrate work in comparative political economy with legal studies. Casper explores the way in which contract law and corporate strategies interlock in Germany and the United States. He shows that specific types of legal systems support distinctive forms of business coordination and that the latter influence the development of the law. Teubner also explores the co-evolution of law and corporate behavior. Taking up 'good faith' doctrine in the British case, he argues that the character of a nation's production regimes will influence its receptivity to specific legal concepts and the application of those concepts. Finally, Tate examines the differences in systems of standard-setting characteristic of different varieties of capitalism, stressing the impact that collective arrangements for standard-setting can have on corporate behavior.

Together these essays suggest that a varieties of capitalism approach can be the basis for fruitful interchange among scholars interested in many kinds of issues in economics, industrial relations, social policy-making, political science, business, and the law.

PART I

GENERAL THEMES AND DIVERSE APPLICATIONS

2

Varieties of Labor Politics in the Developed Democracies

Kathleen Thelen

2.1 Introduction

Industrial-relations systems in the advanced industrial countries are experiencing serious new strains as a result of intensified market competition and adjustment pressures. More volatile international markets since the 1980s have intensified conflict with employers who are seeking greater flexibility through a retreat from uniform, national standards in favor of local bargaining on issues such as wages, working times, and work reorganization. Although expressed in different ways in different countries, two important and pervasive changes have occurred in the past two decades. The first involves widespread structural pressures by employers for more flexibility to respond to changing market conditions, sometimes though not always linked with a push for more decentralized wage-bargaining. These structural pressures are in turn associated with a second, substantive shift in the content of bargaining, away from macroeconomic steering and full employment policies of previous decades and toward greater emphasis on production issues. Both trends are related to broader developments (often subsumed under the rubric of 'globalization') and their combined effect has been to reorient labor politics in the advanced capitalist countries away from labor's traditional national distributional agendas toward employers' firm-level concerns with productivity and efficiency.

This chapter explores the implications of these changes for labor and for labor scholarship through an examination of recent trends in industrial relations across several countries. I take issue with 'globalization' theories that view contemporary changes as part of a universal move on the part of employers to deregulate labor relations, and which attribute

I wish to thank Nils Elvander, Peter Hall, Chris Howell, Harry Katz, Richard Locke, Marino Regini, Peter Swenson, Lowell Turner, Michael Wallerstein, and the participants in the 'Varieties of Capitalism' project for helpful comments on this chapter. Christa van Wijnbergen provided invaluable research assistance.

cross-national differences in outcomes primarily to the differing capacities of unions to resist these changes. Instead, I argue that recent trends in industrial relations are better captured through what the editors of this volume are calling a 'varieties of capitalism' approach that distinguishes different *types* of political-economic systems and explores the different institutional arrangements and behavioral 'logics' that sustain them. Contemporary changes are best understood not as movement along a continuum (deregulation culminating in convergence) but rather in terms of continuing and if anything increasing divergence between the 'coordinated' and 'liberal' market economies (Thelen 1996; Kitschelt et al. 1999b; Iversen and Pontusson 2000).

Furthermore, I argue that the divergence in outcomes between the two types of economies at the macro level (in the structure of bargaining, in the overall position of labor) goes back to fundamental differences in the *micro-level* strategies pursued by employers as they respond to the new terms of competition. In the liberal market economies, employers' 'search for flexibility' (Boyer 1988) at the plant level has brought them sharply into conflict with overarching union structures. Here, collective bargaining institutions rested more on union strength than on employer organization and were always less encompassing than in the coordinated market economies. In the absence of complementary institutions (long-term financing and collective provision of skills, for example) employers falling within the purview of union-enforced mechanisms for labor regulation experienced these as constraining. As the deregulation literature suggests, they have taken advantage of the prevailing political and market climate since the 1980s to restore 'managerial freedom.' Even those employers who have sought to meet the demands of high-quality production with intensified cooperation with labor have done so in ways that clash with traditional union structures, pursuing strategies that sever the link between plant-based industrial relations and overarching institutions for the collective representation of labor. Thus, where organized labor has not been left behind altogether, employers have frequently demanded and won changes in union structures and rights that bring these in line with internal labor markets.

Things look rather different in the coordinated market economies. In these countries, employers have also sought (and largely achieved) changes in traditional bargaining institutions that give them greater flexibility in personnel and wage policy at the plant level. In these cases, however, overarching (sectoral) bargaining institutions have proved more resilient. The reason for this lies again in the connection between national collective bargaining structures and plant-level strategies. Here the joint regulation of labor markets is embedded in other institutional arrangements that have taken employers further in orienting their competitive strategies around high-quality, high value-added production that depends on a high degree of stability and cooperation with labor (Streeck 1991; Hall and Soskice, this volume). In such countries, national-level bargaining institutions have been shored up not just by strong unions, but by employers who realize the extent to which the plant-level cooperation that they seek with labor is *underwritten and sustained* by the collective management of labor markets above the plant level.

While illustrating the analytic leverage afforded by the 'varieties of capitalism' approach elaborated in this volume, I also advocate further development of this approach, focusing especially on two issues that have not received sufficient attention in this literature. The first is the *alternative logic* of employer strategies in the liberal market economies. The dynamics of LMEs have been explicitly outlined for some areas (e.g. especially technology policy, see Soskice 1996*a*), but in the industrial relations literature, LMEs are more a residual category. Such systems are mostly characterized in negative terms, that is, in terms of what they lack (above all, employer coordination), rather than analyzed in terms of the alternative logic that animates them (see also Crouch and Streeck 1997*a*: 8–9). This tendency is reminiscent of the corporatism literature of the 1970s, which heaped attention on a relatively small number of northern European countries, while other economies were defined more in terms of what these systems *were not* (namely corporatist) than what they were.

The second issue that merits more attention is the *political dynamics* behind non-market coordination in the coordinated market economies. Much of the literature in this area treats such coordination as a 'thing' that some countries have and others lack, when in reality coordination is a political process, and an outcome that has to be actively sustained and nurtured. The varieties of capitalism literature has given us powerful tools for understanding differences in the logic of employer strategies in different countries. But the language of equilibrium sometimes obscures the significant changes taking place even in the coordinated market economies, all of which are in fact in the midst of a fundamental renegotiation of the terms of coordination and in some cases of the political settlement on which it is based.

This chapter proceeds as follows. First, I address the continuing legacy of the corporatism literature and discuss the way that this has framed conventional understandings of the effects of globalization on labor unions in the advanced industrial countries. The traditional framework was essentially built around a continuum, in which cross-national differences were conceived as differences in degree ('more' versus 'less' corporatist countries) and in which, in consequence, change within countries over time was viewed in terms of movement along this continuum. Just as the traditional corporatism literature saw any decentralization of bargaining as a move away from corporatism and toward pluralist fragmentation, so too do many contemporary globalization theories equate decentralization with deregulation.

Second, against the traditional view, I set an alternative perspective that distinguishes the different logics of employer strategies within the liberal market economies and the coordinated market economies. I begin with an overview of developments across a wide range of advanced industrial societies, showing how employers in different contexts pursue similar goals through very different strategies, with radically different consequences for labor and for the collective regulation of labor markets generally. This is followed by a more detailed treatment of five countries —Germany, Sweden, and Italy as examples of coordinated market economies, and Britain and the United States as examples of liberal market economies. The goal here is to trace in more detail the distinctive trajectories of change in the two types of systems.

The concluding section returns to the two issues flagged above, the alternative logic of employer strategies in the liberal market economies and the political dynamics that sustain non-market coordination in the coordinated market economies. While building on the varieties of capitalism framework developed in the introduction to this volume, I attempt to advance the debate a step further. For the liberal market economies, I argue that employers seeking to pursue high-quality production (and lacking the strong non-market coordination mechanisms that support this in the CMEs) often turn to strategies that involve internalizing skill formation and instituting various plant-based mechanisms for securing labor cooperation and peace. However, the lack of complementary institutions renders such strategies in industrial relations unstable, and employers more often than not fall back on the lower-cost route of pure deregulation. For the coordinated market economies, I elaborate the political dimension of the institutional equilibrium described by the editors. By exploring the power relations on which different equilibria are founded, we can see that non-market coordination, far from being a self-sustaining feature of particular systems, in fact involves a political settlement and indeed one that has to be renegotiated periodically.

2.2 Against Convergence

Traditional conceptions of what industrial relations consist of—and especially of what distinguishes different industrial relations systems from each other—continue to exert a strong pull. Much of the contemporary literature implicitly embraces the underlying logic of the corporatism literature of the 1970s.[1] In particular, observed trends toward decentralization and flexibility are often viewed in very zero-sum terms, that is, decentralization is explicitly or implicitly equated with a general weakening of labor because it impinges on the ability of unions to establish and enforce uniform national standards. The globalization literature sees change in terms of a seemingly inexorable, inevitable slide toward deregulation, as high unemployment and increased capital mobility allow employers to dispense with strategies based on accommodating labor and instead to shop for the best (i.e. least restrictive, least expensive) labor regime. The result is a convergence theory that sees changes in the 'strong labor' countries as moving them in the direction of the weak labor countries in ways that are very reminiscent of the 'continuum' thinking of the corporatism literature.

These formulations, however, fail to make sense of observed trends, both at the cross-national level and at the level of individual countries. First, this literature's predictions of convergence and homogenization through competitive deregulation have simply not been borne out (Ferner and Hyman 1992*a*; Hyman 1994; Berger and Dore 1996; Boyer 1996; Zysman 1996*b*; Iversen 1996, 1999*a*; Wallerstein et al. 1997; Regini 2000). The deregulation literature appears to apply rather well to some economies, like the United States and Britain, where the decline of unions and of collective bargaining has continued unabated. But developments elsewhere are more complicated. Sweden and Denmark, for example, have abandoned peak-level negotiations but retained systems of highly coordinated multi-industrial bargaining. In Italy and Spain, the trend has been toward *centralization* not decentralization and the renewal of tripartite bargaining (Regini 1997*b*; Regini and Regalia 1997; Pérez 2000).

Second, the causal connections at the heart of conventional theories are not borne out by the evidence. Against the idea that unemployment is what gives the employer offensive its momentum, we find that unions are more embattled in countries (such as the United States and Britain) where unemployment is among the lowest in the advanced industrial world. By most conventional measures (union membership, for example),

---

[1] I have explored the implications of this at length elsewhere; see Thelen (1994).

unions in much of continental Europe have weathered the crisis rather better than their Anglo Saxon colleagues, despite much higher levels of unemployment. Finally, against the common characterization of the crisis of industrial relations as a neo-liberal employer offensive against embattled unions, we find that in countries like Germany, the tensions in traditional bargaining institutions go back not so much to union weakness but above all to a lack of *employer* solidarity (Thelen and Kume 1999*a*; Thelen 2000; Thelen and van Wijnbergen 2000).

These empirical anomalies underscore the need for a somewhat more decisive break with traditional concepts and categories. The alternative perspective developed in this chapter is built on several observations that depart from the assumptions and the logic of the conventional model. First, and following Soskice and others, I take issue with conceptualizations that see industrial relations as an entirely zero-sum game between employers and unions. In fact in many settings employers need unions and find them useful in regulating competition among themselves, and —nowadays, especially—in ensuring peace and predictability on the shop floor. Second, I maintain that a dichotomous understanding of centralization and decentralization obscures important changes in the *relationship between* bargaining at the two levels. As I show below, in some economies, employers' goals in decentralized bargaining are not incompatible with—indeed, in many ways they rest on—continued coordination and negotiation at higher levels (Thelen 1991, 2000).

To set the context for the analysis that follows, I submit that a very important source of pressure toward 'disorganization' in industrial-relations systems today goes back to the new terms of market competition rather than simply efforts on the part of employers to 'get out from under' union regulation. The received wisdom is that globalization— understood mostly as capital mobility or the threat of exit—has shifted the balance of power decisively toward capital. I do not wish to dispute this general claim; indeed there is much evidence to support this view, particularly in the liberal market economies. However, I want to suggest that there is another face to globalization, and one that in fact has rather different implications for labor relations. Increasingly integrated global markets have heightened the competitive pressures that many firms face. Where firms compete on the basis of quality and reliability in the context of just-in-time production, the capacity to adjust depends rather heavily on stable and cooperative relations with labor at the plant level. Recognizing this aspect of contemporary market relations is necessary to explain why in countries such as Germany and Sweden, employers are in fact extremely reluctant to undertake full decentralization, why they are 'deathly afraid' (as one German employer put it) of industrial conflict, and why some of their traditionally most potent weapons (above all the lockout) are looking increasingly obsolete.

To understand how this alternative face of globalization plays out cross-nationally, we need to focus on the link between employer strategies at the plant level and macro structural changes. For both the CMEs and the LMEs, changes in national-level institutions and processes have been driven in part by the changing interests of labor and employers at the *firm* level. To understand the nature of this link it is useful to begin with a distinction between 'collectivist' and 'segmentalist' strategies.[2] Very briefly, and in ideal-typical terms, collectivist strategies involve the collective regulation of labor markets, and are generally sustained in large part through negotiations by highly organized employer associations and unified and encompassing labor movements. Collectivist governance of labor markets serves employers' interests in labor market stability through measures that dampen competition among firms for labor (especially skilled labor), coordinate wage formation, share the costs of skill formation, and monitor and punish poaching. 'Segmentalism' is another strategy designed to stabilize labor markets, but it is based on very different principles. Here individual employers attempt to shield themselves from competition over labor by erecting barriers to the outside labor market. This translates into measures such as internal career ladders, seniority wages, and company-based training.[3]

For firms whose competitive strategies depend on a high degree of social peace and cooperation with labor at the plant level, context is everything. In the CMEs, where labor markets are regulated in a collectivist fashion, plant-level cooperation relies in important ways on continued coordination between unions and employers at higher levels. Collective bargaining above the level of the firm supports plant-level cooperation by 'bracketing' divisive distributional issues and 'depersonalizing' industrial conflict (see esp. Streeck 1996a: 36). The mediating effects of bargaining outside the firm are particularly important where plant-level labor representatives enjoy extensive participatory rights. Studies have shown that in such contexts, local bargaining over wages

---

[2] This distinction was very much inspired by and draws on the one made by Peter Swenson between 'solidaristic' versus 'segmentalist' strategies (Swenson 2001). I substitute the term collectivism for solidarism only because Swenson's definition of the latter is more specific and invokes some elements (e.g. the creation of labor market scarcity through institutions that set wages below the level at which the market will clear) that are not part of the argument I develop here.

[3] In addition to Swenson's characterization, see also the literature on dual labor markets and labor market segmentation, e.g. Doeringer and Piore (1971) and Edwards et al. (1975).

undermines the constructive, efficiency-enhancing effects of plant-based co-determination (Freeman and Lazear 1995; Sadowski et al. 1995).

The situation is very different in LMEs such as Britain and the United States. Here we find widespread attempts to impose unilateral managerial control, and where there are attempts at fostering cooperation with labor, these are more often undertaken in conflict with (and directed against) unions. Here again, the context is decisive. In the LMEs, employers lack the coordinating capacities that characterize the CMEs (supporting standardized wages and the collective provision of skills, for example). They are thus more likely to try to stabilize their core workforce and to enhance peace on the shop floor through strategies built on strong internal controls—in-house training and company-based participation schemes for labor, for example. Whereas collectivist strategies rely on encompassing unions and national bargaining structures, segmentalist strategies clash with both. This is why we find that where employers in LMEs are pursuing such strategies, it is frequently without unions (as in Japanese transplants, but also large companies such as IBM). Where deals have been struck *with* unions, they have frequently involved cutting the local union off from national-level bargaining structures and negotiating trade-offs—typically, job security for a core workforce in exchange for internal labor market flexibility—that conform to the dictates of segmentalism.

2.3 Contemporary Industrial-Relations Systems: an Overview

Space does not permit a full survey of developments across the whole range of advanced industrial democracies (but see Thelen and Turner 1997). However, a cursory review reveals that if anything, the gap between the 'liberal market economies' and the 'coordinated market economies' is growing (see also Kitschelt et al. 1999b; Iversen and Pontusson 2000). In the former, it is entirely appropriate to talk about a trend toward deregulation, including attempts to escape union regulation at all levels. The coordinated market economies, by contrast, appear to be seeking flexibility through controlled decentralization (not deregulation but reregulation of various issues at lower bargaining levels), but along with a continued commitment to coordination (especially of wage-bargaining) at the multi-industrial level (though less and less at the confederal level).

Moreover, one trend that appears to be common, cutting across both types of economies (CMEs and LMEs alike), is the growing importance of shop-floor bargaining, often combined with attempts on the part of employers to secure labor's cooperation in enhancing firm productivity and efficiency. In both the CMEs and the LMEs, this has been expressed in a strong preference on the part of employers for a reliable, responsible, and unitary bargaining partner at the plant level. However, in the LMEs this frequently translates into strategies that are specifically designed to undercut union influence or hold unions at bay.

The following sections consider broad, cross-national trends in two areas: the link between centralized and plant-level bargaining and shop-floor institutions.

2.3.1 The Link between Centralized and Plant-level Bargaining

As noted above, analyses that posit a general trend toward deregulation through bargaining decentralization fail to capture important aspects of the *interaction* between centralized and decentralized bargaining. Where —as in the CMEs—employers possess institutions that facilitate coordination among themselves and where they (employers) confront strong unions, the attempt so far has not been to deregulate industrial relations, though we can certainly speak of a widespread trend toward a renegotiation of the relationship between centralized collective bargaining and local bargaining (Thelen 1996). Such a characterization would capture the gist of important changes in Sweden (where the shift from confederal to industry-level bargaining has been accompanied by changes allowing more room for plant-level flexibility, especially with respect to plant wage structures). But it would also capture the intent of reforms in Italy in the 1990s which went in the opposite direction—*recentralizing* bargaining but at the same time clarifying the link between central and plant-level bargaining and establishing the primacy of central contracts which lay down the parameters for local negotiations (Locke and Baccaro 1999). Rather than deregulation through decentralization, employers in these countries appear to be groping toward changes that will continue to capture the benefits of national coordination (which include dampening competition for skilled labor but also facilitating cooperation with labor on production issues at the plant level by explicitly bracketing distributional issues). But these efforts are combined with reforms that allow firms to adjust more flexibly to changes in market conditions through decentralized negotiations.

All of this, however, contrasts sharply with the recent experiences of the liberal market economies. In these cases, wage-bargaining (less centralized and encompassing to begin with) has been further decentralized—to the level of the plant if not the individual worker—a process accompanied by a further weakening of unions, along often with the collapse of important employers' associations (e.g. the Engineering Employers' Federation in Britain). King and Wood (1999) have suggested why labor market deregulation recommends itself especially in the LMEs. Because employers' ability to coordinate among themselves is low and non-market regulation of labor is primarily a matter of union organization, employers do better by deregulating their relations with labor as well. Thus, we find in these countries not just a decline of union capacities, but also (further) erosion of employers' own institutions and capacity for collective action. This divergence is significant in light of the large literature that emphasizes the economic benefits (e.g. in the area of skill formation) that can flow from employer coordination, usually in the context of strong unions (Soskice 1990*b*, 1991; Streeck 1992*b*).

2.3.2 Shop-floor Institutions

A second theme that runs through recent developments in industrial relations across the advanced industrial countries is strong evidence of employers' increased interest in a predictable and constructive relationship with labor on the shop floor, linked to a distinct preference for a *unitary* bargaining partner at that level (Thelen 1996). This commonality cuts across very different political economies. For example, the strategy of some British employers to replace multi-unionism with single-union agreements shares many similarities with Danish employers' goal of 'one company, one agreement' and with initiatives toward 'co-worker' agreements in some large Swedish firms, despite the very different institutional arrangements governing labor–management relations in these three countries. In both Denmark and Sweden, the national-level restructuring mentioned above has in fact been explicitly connected to plant-level initiatives designed to neutralize divisions on the shop floor that are rooted in national-level cleavages—between white- and blue-collar representation (in Sweden) and between skilled and unskilled unions (in Denmark). Likewise in Italy, in the context of a series of major industrial relations reforms in 1993, employers insisted on rules for shop-floor representation that were designed to prevent further fragmentation of labor by strengthening the 'most representative' unions against growing challenges by new and often more militant local organizations (Locke and Baccaro 1999: 253–4).

Indeed, even in some cases in which firms have been on the attack against unions, employers have at the same time pursued policies designed to give them the stable and responsible interlocutor at the plant level that they think they need to adapt to changing market conditions. In Britain, for example, companies that have 'derecognized' unions nonetheless have sometimes allowed the old representatives to retain 'some form of representative and/or consultative rights.'[4] The same type of apparently contradictory policies toward local unions are on display as well in the United States. Those American employers who are not trying actively to avoid unions (and many that are) are often attempting at the same time to enlist labor's cooperation and participation in new forms of collective bargaining and 'cooperative' plant structures, although almost invariably in exchange for concessions in traditional union job controls (Turner 1991; Cutcher-Gershenfeld et al. 1996). Finally, several observers have noted that France leads the rest of Europe in the introduction of quality circles, a fact that is probably not unrelated to the collapse of unionism and the crisis of shop-floor representation there. Hyman (1994: 7) has even suggested that the extensive introduction of quality circles in France may be best understood as an effort 'not to bypass . . . [but] to compensate for the lack of "normal" mechanisms of effective interest representation.'

This strong interest in promoting or preserving reliable, responsible, and wherever possible unitary bargaining partners at the local level is perhaps best understood in the context of the new strategic problems that employers face. These involve the need to manage ongoing adjustment to market conditions that are more volatile than ever before (Streeck 1987: 285). It appears that employers across a range of countries see cooperative relations at the plant level as a precondition for such adjustment, though differences in institutional starting points have led them to pursue this goal in different ways cross-nationally.

Summing up, the cross-national evidence does not point toward convergence across industrial-relations systems, but rather, if anything, to a growing gap between LMEs and CMEs. Despite many differences among the CMEs, employers in general have (1) settled for or actively supported continued coordination (especially in wage-bargaining) while at the same time in most cases they have (2) sought changes in the link between plant-level negotiations and industry-level bargaining that allow greater flexibility—in plant wage structures and in work organization, for example—to adapt to rapidly changing markets. The experience in these counties has thus been quite different from that in the LMEs, where employers have been more likely (1) to eliminate higher-level bargaining

---

[4] *European Industrial Relations Review*, June 1994: 24, based on a survey of companies that had 'derecognized' unions.

structures altogether (in the process, dismantling their own coordinating capacities while attacking those of the unions), and (2) to drive unions off the shop floor entirely, or to force a radical renegotiation of organized labor's rights and role at that level.

2.4 Trajectories of Change in CMEs and LMEs

As we have seen, the broad distinction between 'coordinated' versus 'liberal' market economies represents a crucial (even if not perfectly 'clean') distinction that sheds considerable light on the very different patterns of industrial relations across the developed democracies. By identifying distinct types of systems that operate according to different logics, this approach gives us greater analytic leverage in explaining the lack of convergence in industrial relations, despite the putatively common trend toward globalization. In order to understand the different trajectories of change in the two types of economies, we need to delve deeper into recent developments in individual countries. Thus, this section reviews evidence from five cases—Germany, Sweden, and Italy as examples of coordinated market economies, and the United States and Britain as examples of liberal market economies. The idea is not so much to provide a full account of recent developments in each country, but to demonstrate in each case how micro-level strategies have affected the macro-level dynamics of change in the CMEs and the LMEs.

2.4.1 Germany

Cross-national studies have coded Germany as a paragon of stability (e.g. Wallerstein et al. 1997) but such characterizations mask substantial tensions and also important changes within still stable formal institutions. The German system consists of multi-industrial 'pattern' bargaining, typically led by the metalworkers' union (IG Metall). This system of coordinated wage-bargaining has survived pressures by employers for more flexibility, though there has been an important shift toward the increasing importance of plant-level negotiations on other (non-wage) issues.

Struggles over flexibility in Germany date back to the 1980s, when a major conflict between employers and unions over working-time reduction was resolved through a trade-off between lower overall working hours and more plant-level variation in working times. This compromise brought an end to a costly dispute in 1984, and it helped to avoid further strife in subsequent negotiations over working-time reduction. However, the terms of the deal activated previously dormant cleavages within key employer associations like Gesamtmetall (the association for metal-working employers). The working-time contracts turned out to be particularly expensive for small and medium-sized firms (i.e. Germany's large and important *Mittelstand*), which had to absorb the costs of overall reductions in working hours, but were not generally capable of taking advantage of the compensating 'flexibility' clauses (Silvia 1997: 194–8). The result has been growing disgruntlement in the 1990s on the part of the *Mittelstand*, chafing against the domination of the large firms within Gesamtmetall.

These conflicts have intersected with new tensions within the employers' associations in the wake of unification. Given the substantial gaps in productivity between firms in the East and West, many eastern companies have stayed out of the employers' associations in order to avoid being bound to the wage and working-time contracts they negotiate with the unions (Schroeder and Ruppert 1996; Silvia 1997). Defections are of two sorts and they are no longer limited to eastern firms. In some cases, firms opt out of the employers' association, sometimes to join new organizations that offer many of the benefits of association membership (e.g. legal assistance) but that are not parties to collective agreements with the unions. In other cases, member companies simply ignore the terms of the central bargain, certainly with the knowledge of the works council and often with its blessing. The combined effect has been seriously to weaken the coordinating capacities of associations like Gesamtmetall.

These developments have opened up a major debate within Germany on the appropriate balance between centrally bargained parameters and plant-level flexibility. The direction of change so far has been to shore up industry-level coordination by 'flexibilizing' central contracts, in the process delegating more bargaining competencies to plant-level works councils. This is in some ways a continuation of previous patterns (Thelen 1991), but flexibility clauses increasingly are used to address the concerns of firms that might otherwise exit national bargaining arrangements altogether. In extreme cases, flexibility has been extended to cover wages, where works councils (legally) have no independent jurisdiction. Thus, for example, in 1996 the chemical workers' union agreed to an opening clause in the central contract that allows works councils in struggling firms to negotiate wage reductions of up to 10 per cent in exchange for employment guarantees. More often, however, central contracts delegate new bargaining responsibilities to works councils over other issues, leaving wages set at the industry level. For instance, a 1997 agreement in metalworking allows works councils and managers to negotiate deals that ease elderly workers out of the workforce on rather generous terms, in exchange for new hires.

In short, recent collective bargaining rounds—in metalworking but more generally—have moved in the direction of dealing with contemporary strains, both between unions and employers but especially within the employers' associations themselves, through the flexibilization of central contracts and the delegation of new bargaining competencies to works councils. This has resulted in a partial renegotiation of the terms of coordination, but not the abandonment of industry-wide bargaining. Against conventional accounts, however, this outcome is not solely the result of unions' successfully resisting employers' push for decentralization. Instead, employers' *own interests*, as much as German unions' continued strength, accounts for the resilience of traditional bargaining institutions in Germany (Thelen and Kume 1999*a*; Thelen 2000).

In fact, a number of collective bargaining rounds in the mid- to late 1990s dramatically revealed the extent to which the competitive strategies that German employers are pursuing in the market have rendered them deeply ambivalent about abandoning sectoral bargaining arrangements. When (in 1995) IG Metall initiated a strike in Bavaria—a bastion of hardliners and disgruntled *Mittelständler*—it appeared that the union was in for an existential fight. However, while the union held together, the employers' militant strategy quickly collapsed as individual employers worried openly about the effects of a conflict on the cooperative relations they had painstakingly built with their works councils over the past years.[5] In the face of mounting resistance from within their own ranks, the employers' association (Gesamtmetall) abandoned its hard-line position, and dropped its plans for a lockout. Even the unions were taken aback at how quickly employers settled (at a very high level of wages); the agreement was widely viewed as a 'catastrophic' defeat for Gesamtmetall. Employers publicly bemoaned the fact that they could no longer hold out against the union and argued that something needed to be done to redress the 'lack of parity' (favoring *labor*) in collective bargaining.[6]

---

[5] For a full account of the strike, see Thelen (2000).

[6] *Handelsblatt*, 19 Dec. 1996; *Tageszeitung*, 19 Dec. 1996; *Wirtschaftswoche*, 13 Dec. 1996; and *Süddeutsche Zeitung*, 10 Dec. 1996.

Subsequent skirmishes—in 1996 over sick pay, in the East German steel industry in 1998, and in the 1999 wage round—followed a similar script. Gesamtmetall now avoids conflict like the plague and speaks of trying to achieve its goals through a 'new partnership' with labor (Gesamtmetall 1999).

The rhetoric among German employers has been quite militant at times. However, at the end of the day, most of them would much prefer to reform the current system rather than dismantle it.[7] What employers clearly like about industry-level bargaining is the predictability and peace it sustains at the plant level. These are features that have if anything become more dear to them in the context of tightly coupled production and the need to deliver high-quality products on a just-in-time basis (Thelen and Kume 1999*a*). Industry-level bargaining removes divisive distributional issues from the shop floor and it provides a uniform and concentrated timetable for negotiations—thus protecting firms from disruptive rolling wage disputes (Streeck 1996*a*).

For these reasons, German employers have been approaching the issue of bargaining decentralization very gingerly. Previous calls for a revision in the Works Constitution Act that would allow plant-level works councils to negotiate wages (under the current law, a right restricted to the industrial unions unless opening clauses in central contracts specifically allow local bargaining) have been all but abandoned. A recent report on workplace co-determination, adopted unanimously by a committee composed of representatives of labor and employers, argues instead that while works councils can be vehicles for 'controlled flexibilization' no changes in the law should be contemplated. The report explicitly acknowledges the 'relief' functions afforded by the (industry-level) collective bargaining contract, and argues that without it, 'cooperative relations between works councils and employers would be difficult to achieve.'[8] The tension within key employers' associations such as Gesamtmetall remains a serious threat to the system (Thelen and van Wijnbergen 2000). At this writing, however, the most striking feature of recent developments in Germany—in contrast to Britain and the United States—is the lengths to which most employers have been willing to go to manage new pressures for flexibility within traditional institutions.

---

[7] 'Arbeitgeber lehnen eine Änderung des Tarifrechts ab,' *Frankfurter Allgemeine Zeitung*, 27 Jan. 1998: 11.

[8] Arbeitsausschuß 'Mitbestimmung und Tarifwesen' 1997: 2.

2.4.2 Sweden

A great deal of attention has been devoted to the breakdown of the Swedish model, and situating this case within the varieties of capitalism framework can help resolve ongoing debates about whether Sweden is exceptional or exemplary.[9] The central feature of what was known as the 'Swedish model' was the highly centralized (confederal-level) system of wage-bargaining and the labor movement's policy of solidaristic wages, which had resulted in a substantial narrowing of wage differentials across the national workforce. As the comparative literature of the 1970s emphasized, these structures and policies helped to dampen inflation in the 1950s and 1960s and to promote the movement of Swedish firms out of low-productivity sectors and technologies and into more efficient and productive technologies and industries.

Developments in the late 1960s and early 1970s, however, put new strains on the system and contributed to the eventual breakdown of the Swedish model (see esp. Pontusson and Swenson 1996). First, the less-productive public sector, which had been excluded from solidaristic wage policy as it was originally conceived, demanded and won agreements that brought its workers' wages in line with those of the higher-productivity private sector. Second, early solidaristic wage policy focused only on intersectoral wage disparities and did not touch differences between skilled and unskilled workers. However, in the late 1960s, unskilled workers were able to use their political power within the central union confederation (LO) to win new clauses in central contracts that would compensate them for skilled workers' previous year's wage drift. These clauses resulted in an overall, institutionalized ratcheting up of wages, as wage drift in manufacturing rose in the 1980s to 50 per cent for both white- and blue-collar workers (Elvander 1997: 13). Apart from their inflationary effects, these developments complicated national-level wage-bargaining because negotiators had to adjust their positions and adapt the bargain to take account of anticipated plant-level drift.

These changes in the meaning and scope of solidaristic wage-bargaining contributed to a revolt on the part of employers in key industries against peak-level bargaining. In 1983, the employers' association for the metalworking industry (Verkstadsföreningen, now Verkstadsindustrier, VI) withdrew from confederal negotiations and struck a separate deal at the industry level (with the metalworkers' union, Metall)

---

[9] Pontusson and Swenson (1996) treat it as exemplary of broader trends (e.g. post-Fordism), while Wallerstein and Golden (2000) see it as exceptional.

that traded more generous wage increases for an elimination of the clauses that linked skilled and unskilled workers' wages. Some of the organization's most influential members—firms like Ericsson, Volvo, and ABB—saw this as a first step toward full decentralization of bargaining to the company level.

However, events in the 1990s stabilized industry-level bargaining and have even promoted a degree of recentralization on new terms.[10] First of all, it became clear that VI was quite isolated within the employers' confederation, SAF. Whereas VI sought to push negotiations down to the company level, most of the other sectoral associations were content to stop at industry-level bargaining. Second, it turns out that full decentralization was controversial even within VI, as the organization's smaller firms expressed a strong preference to preserve collective negotiations at the industry level. Third, the radicals within VI encountered stiff resistance to their drive for full decentralization, even from unions that on the surface might have appeared easiest to co-opt.[11]

Most consequentially, however, events of the mid-1990s revealed the pitfalls of full decentralization in a context in which employers have become increasingly vulnerable to industrial strife (and in which, as in Germany, unions' capacity to organize strikes remains high). In 1995, negotiations in the Swedish engineering industry were disrupted by an abrupt and very high settlement by employers and unions in the (then booming) paper and pulp industry. Confronted with demands by the engineering workers' union (Metall) for a similar wage increase—backed up with overtime bans and strike threats—VI could not resist the pressure to settle. As Elvander (1997: 49–50) notes, lean production and just-in-time scheduling had rendered engineering firms extremely sensitive to disruptions in production, and so they were 'unable to use their strongest weapon, the big lockout, without hurting themselves' (see also Kjellberg 1998: 91, 95 ff.).

The events of 1995 underscored the disadvantages of uncoordinated bargaining, and thus set the scene for a broader accommodation between unions and employers across the entire industrial sector. In 1996, eight major employers' associations responded to an invitation by their

[10] This account is based on interviews in 1998 and 1999 with representatives of Metall, VI, Almega, and LO.

[11] For instance, Ericsson attempted to strike a decentralized deal with the local chapter of the Union of Graduate Engineers (CF), but the national union prohibited its local branch from even engaging in negotiations, citing the commitment it had made to other unions to support industry-wide coordination.

counterpart unions to engage in joint negotiations over wage formation and mediation procedures.[12] The result, less than a year later, was a new 'Agreement on Industrial Development and Wage Formation' designed to support 'constructive negotiations' and to avoid 'the need to resort to industrial action' (18 Mar. 1997, appendix A, paragraph 1). The Agreement provides for an impartial chairman to accompany industry-level wage negotiations and to facilitate peaceful compromise. The new framework also supports coordination in bargaining across the export sector as a whole (also between blue- and white-collar unions), though importantly, not a return to confederal bargaining (something that both employers and unions in manufacturing oppose).[13] For the unions, but especially for Metall, the Agreement marks the abandonment by VI of its earlier efforts to push for full decentralization, thus ending years of struggle in this key industry over the structure of negotiations. Employers, for their part, praise the new conflict mediation procedures that lie at the center of the Agreement and that they see as crucial to managing their heightened vulnerability to strikes.

The Swedish case thus provides another good illustration of how the strategies of employers at the plant level can affect relations with labor and bargaining structures at higher levels and vice versa. The dramatic events of the early 1980s did not turn out to be the first step in a full-fledged decentralization of industrial relations. Indeed, employers' new-found interest in mediation and recent agreements with labor make it quite clear that Swedish employers do not think they can get what they need through deregulation. The overall result in Sweden is not a breakdown of coordination though there has been a fundamental renegotiation of the terms of coordination—from national-confederal bargaining to a more flexible system of coordinated multi-industrial bargaining—along with increased reliance on mediation to achieve compromise without industrial strife.

2.4.3 Italy

Italy is often seen as an ambiguous case in the varieties of capitalism literature. However, when it comes to industrial relations, the trajectory of change parallels developments in the CMEs much more closely

[12] See *Dagens Nyheter*, 1 June 1996: A4, where the unions extended the invitation for employers to negotiate.

[13] The LO is quietly opposed to the agreement for the very reason that it precludes a recentralization on the old terms, i.e. coordination among blue-collar unions across all sectors.

than those in the LMEs. As in Germany and Sweden, we find in Italy evidence of a renegotiation of the relationship between national-sectoral and plant-level bargaining, although in this case these developments have involved important elements of *recentralization*, especially in wage-bargaining.

The fragmentation of Italian unions along ideological lines is well known, and this certainly distinguishes Italy from the other CMEs considered here. However, while relations among the three competing union confederations deteriorated at the national level in the 1980s, labor organizations continued to work with one another and with employers at the local level (Regalia and Regini 1995: 131). As Ferner and Hyman (1992*a*: 591) put it: 'the importance of company-level accommodations was increased following the splits between the main unions in 1984, which disrupted not only interconfederal relations but also national sectoral bargaining.' Local cooperation and accommodation might not have persisted where, as in Britain, the cleavages that separate unions are directly 'activated' by production reorganization (which precipitates jurisdictional disputes among craft unions). The fact that Italian unions divide along ideological rather than skill or job lines may thus help to account for why 'workplace trade union unity has often proved resilient even in the case of national disagreements' among the main union confederations (Ferner and Hyman 1992*a*: 543–4).

The persistence of local cooperation during the 1980s is cited as an important factor in preventing a major assault on unions in Italy (Regalia and Regini 1995: 159). Regalia (1995: 224–5) has noted that since the mid-1980s Italian managers assigned works councils more and more consultative functions. She suggests that 'many councils were to a large extent sustained by a growing managerial need to find effective and not too expensive ways to obtain greater and more active worker consent.' Among the positive functions with which managers credit Italian councils are that 'they facilitate internal communication at lower cost than separate managerial channels and programs, they help settle individual and collective grievances, and they operate as a feedback mechanism on the operation of middle management' (Regalia 1995: 236). Moreover, as Regalia (1995: 236) notes, 'Case studies of industrial readjustment in the 1980s have shown that the existence of active and well-rooted councils made innovation and reorganization of production easier for firms while making the management of redundancies and changes in work practices less traumatic for employees.' It is important to note that this is not merely a case of employer co-optation. In fact, 'personnel managers of multi-plant companies pointed out their preference for strong and even militant councils that are the undisputed leaders of the workers, as compared to representative bodies that are weak and poorly supported. In the former case, joint decision-making, through consultation or collective bargaining, would lead to much more reliable and therefore in the end more efficient outcomes, while in the latter case, apparently more convenient results might easily turn into a bothersome waste of time' (Regalia 1995: 236).

Continued cooperation at the plant level in Italy also appears to have provided a foundation for renewed national tripartism in the 1990s (Regalia and Regini 1995: 154; Locke and Baccaro 1999). In 1993 the government, unions, and employers reached a historic agreement that abolished the national cost of living index (*scala mobile*), instituted a loose incomes policy, and overhauled collective bargaining institutions.[14] Far from fighting recentralization, Italian employers strongly favored this move, among other reasons to secure wage restraint (Pérez 2000; Regini 2000: esp. 272–3). But as Locke and Baccaro (1999) point out, the reconfiguration of wage-bargaining institutions at the national level was closely linked to the parallel renegotiation of the institutions for labor representation at the plant level, and the fates of the two sets of reforms are closely intertwined.

Italy's previous factory committees (*Rappresentanze Sindacali Aziendali*, or RSAs) had been dominated by the three main union confederations, but by the late 1980s these were increasingly facing challenges from autonomous unions and militant rank and file committees (COBAS) which among other things opposed the unions' egalitarian wage policies. The 1993 reforms replaced the RSAs with new unitary union structures (*Rappresentanze Sindacali Unitarie*, or RSUs) subject to new election rules. Two-thirds of the members are elected by a vote of all workers, but one third of the members are to be appointed by the unions that are parties to the national industrial contract with employers. The one-third provision shores up the position of the three main union confederations. Importantly, this provision was included at the insistence of *employers* who wanted to make sure that there was a strong institutional link between bargaining agreements at the national and plant levels (Locke and Baccaro 1999: 253).

The precise nature of that link was also defined in the 1993 Accords. Previously, the relationship among the various bargaining levels in Italy had been unclear and contested (Regalia and Regini 1995: 135). In the

---

[14] The Accords are summarized in detail in *European Industrial Relations Review*, Sept. 1993: 15–19 and Locke and Baccaro (1999: esp. 247–8).

reforms, Italian employers sought to limit local negotiations (an interesting reversal of the dominant trend in Europe, where employers have more often been pushing for less centralized negotiations and more local bargaining). At unions' insistence, the Accord specifically allows for continued local negotiations; however, it imposes restrictions on bargaining at that level and subordinates it to industry-level bargaining (Locke and Baccaro 1999: 247–8). In particular, pay increases are to be set at the industry level and in line with national tripartite discussions (taking account of the projected inflation rate) and company or local increases must be linked to productivity and other factors related to a firm's economic performance. In addition, the Accord established the primacy of sectoral bargaining by specifying that company bargaining should deal with matters 'different from, and not overlapping with' those issues that are regulated in sectoral agreements (*European Industrial Relations Review*, Sept. 1993: 15–19).

2.4.4 The Cases Compared: Signs of Convergence?

The conventional literature tends to emphasize differences between Sweden and Germany (with Sweden being coded as a case of institutional breakdown and Germany one of institutional stability; e.g. Wallerstein and Golden 1997), and to draw an even sharper distinction between these two countries and Italy. But a closer look at the dynamics of change reveals that all three cases involve a renegotiation of traditional institutional arrangements, the results of which have if anything brought them closer together. Most obviously, the move in Sweden away from confederal dominance and toward coordinated industry-level bargaining represents a shift in the direction of the German model (Thelen 1993; Pontusson 1997). Italy appears to be moving in that direction as well, albeit from a rather different starting point. Motivated by a desire to control inflation and reduce labor conflict, Italian employers pushed for changes that established the primacy of industry-level bargaining over local bargaining on wages and strengthened the links between plant-based labor representation and national institutions by shoring up the main unions against their rivals at the local level.

There are also signs of at least partial convergence in plant-level relations as well. For example, in the past it was common to stress the differences between Germany's legalistic versus Sweden's more negotiated versions of co-determination (Thelen 1991). However, in Germany, there are signs that the specific legal rights that works councils enjoy under the law are receding in importance relative to the new *delegated* bargaining competencies they have acquired through industry-level bargains (a consequence of the trends cited above as well as the emergence of new problems that are not covered in the law). To the extent that German works councils are thus put in the position of negotiating over a wider range of issues (but not subject to conciliation because not covered in the law), this arguably brings their functions closer to that of Swedish shop stewards (and where the inability of Swedish local unions to strike is the functional equivalent of German works councils' 'peace obligation'). Italian unions, for their part, are still possessed of much weaker plant-level rights. However, the new RSU structure, as we have seen, was designed specifically to counteract union fragmentation and as such represents an attempt to move a step closer to unitary shop-floor representation of the sort found in Germany.

2.4.5 United States

The trend in US industrial relations over the last several decades has been toward declining union influence at both the industry and plant levels. Here, the language of 'deregulation' and a neo-liberal offensive against organized labor is appropriate. Union membership has fallen more or less steadily for forty years, and unions now represent less than 10 per cent of the private-sector labor force (e.g. Troy 1999).

At the same time, however, US industrial relations has also been the site of innovations aimed at enlisting worker participation in various 'employee involvement' schemes, suggesting a somewhat more complex development than just a 'return to the market.' There has actually been a dual trend. Some companies are pursuing new 'human relations/industrial relations' (HR/IR) strategies that involve an intensification of cooperation with labor at the plant and company levels (either with or without unions), while others have simply sought to reimpose managerial unilateralism, often through intense conflicts with unions (Weinstein and Kochan 1995; Katz and Darbishire 1999). Examples of the latter include the highly publicized cases of Eastern Airlines, Caterpillar, Greyhound Bus Lines, and Pittston Coal (Wever 1995: 7).

To make sense of the overall trend, it is useful to distinguish two aspects of employer strategies—first with respect to coordinated bargaining (which was already more tenuous and incomplete than in the CMEs), and second with respect to labor at the plant level. In terms of coordination, the trend in the United States has been toward severing company- and plant-level bargaining from previous forms of coordination. Wage-bargaining in the United States was never as centralized or encompassing as in many European countries, but it became even more decentralized from the 1980s with the breakdown of pattern bargaining in industries such as coal, steel, rubber, and transportation. Even in the automobile industry, coordination has declined significantly, as more and more firms are outside the pattern. Supplier firms have opted out in large numbers, Japanese transplants have resisted unionization, and even where union influence remains relatively strong, some of the more innovative contracts in the past two decades (e.g. Saturn) involve separate deals with the United Auto Workers, UAW. In other industries (e.g. trucking and coal mining), multi-employer bargaining has similarly declined, as companies have withdrawn from master agreements negotiated with the relevant union (Katz and Darbishire 1999: 28).

The changes at the shop-floor level have been equally dramatic. Since the 1970s, under growing pressure from international competition, American managers have worked aggressively to reduce job classifications, renegotiate traditional work rules and seniority provisions, and reorganize production along more flexible lines. Such changes clashed directly with traditional union rights and structures, which is one reason why production reorganization was originally pioneered in the non-union sector (Kochan et al. 1986). However, there are also a number of cases in which work reorganization was negotiated with unions. The most publicized examples were in the automobile industry, e.g. the GM–Toyota joint venture (NUMMI) in California and the Saturn project in Tennessee, where the UAW agreed to trade in traditional rights and controls for increased participation through other channels designed to encourage more consensual decision-making (Katz and Darbishire 1999: 41–2). Similarly successful examples of labor–management partnership at unionized workplaces were forged in the aerospace, communications, steel, electronics, and other industries as well. Companies that instituted such practices include Boeing, Bethlehem Steel, AT&T, NYNEX, BellSouth Telecommunications, Xerox, Corning, United Airlines, John Deere, and Levi-Strauss (see e.g. Wever 1995: 5, 67, and 89 ff.).

In many other companies, however, the renegotiation of work rules provoked major industrial strife, fomented internal union conflict, and encouraged employers to pursue elaborate union avoidance strategies.[15] Many employer-created and dominated programs for worker participa-

---

[15] And in the United States, 'cooperative' deals are often extorted from unions, as management pits different workforces against each other by promising to retain production sites where unions agree to the new arrangements. See, for example, Katz and Darbishire (1999: 28).

tion have been specifically designed to sideline and replace unions by establishing alternative channels of communication between the workforce and management. This is the logic behind 'human resource management strategies' in non-union companies such as Hewlett-Packard, Proctor and Gamble, Eastman Kodak, and Motorola (Katz and Darbishire 1999).

Clearly, the neo-liberal trend in US industrial relations rests on a set of political and political-economic conditions—shareholder value, short-term financing, restrictive labor law—that are biased against union organization and collective labor representation. A large number of the most innovative new programs to enlist workforce participation in improving quality and enhancing firm efficiency were either specifically designed to replace organized labor, or, if negotiated with unions, involved a complete renegotiation of traditional union structures and rights. In line with a more segmentalist approach, the trend has been toward the destruction of coordinating capacities across firms (demise of pattern bargaining) along with innovations in HR/IR that tie workers to internal labor markets and co-opt them into company communities. Where unions have been party to these sorts of innovations, the deal has often been one in which they agree to co-administer more flexible internal labor markets in exchange for no-layoff guarantees—in other words, agreements that are very much in sync with segmentalist strategies (e.g. Weinstein and Kochan 1995: 16).

It should be noted that the US labor movement has shown new signs of life in the past few years. Under the inspired leadership of John Sweeney, the AFL-CIO has made organization drives a focus of attention and effort. After years of setbacks, organized workers have scored some significant strike victories (UPS, Boeing, and Verizon), and launched important new initiatives (e.g. Justice for Janitors). These are trends worth watching, but at this writing it is doubtful that they will be sufficient to restore the US labor movement to anything close to its previous stature and membership levels. Among other things, lasting success would almost certainly require significant reforms to existing labor law, the prospects for which are currently anything but bright.

2.4.6 Britain

As in the United States, the trend in British industrial relations in the last twenty years has been in the direction of deregulation in the sense of sharply declining union influence at all levels. And here again, we can distinguish two trends—the collapse of coordinated bargaining and the changing relationship between unions and employers at the plant level. The changes in Britain have in many ways been more dramatic, since British unions at their peak were better organized than in the United States and collective bargaining coverage much higher.[16]

In Britain, the collapse of traditional bargaining institutions was vigorously promoted by the Thatcher government which, beginning in 1979, undertook a series of reforms that encouraged individualized bargaining between an employer and his or her employees while actively discouraging collective bargaining and labor representation through unions (Howell 1995, 1996: 516). Legislation under the Conservative governments of the 1980s and 1990s included measures that made it more difficult for unions to initiate industrial action and secure collective bargaining rights, and that eliminated completely previous mechanisms for extending the terms of agreements in unionized plants to other firms in the same sector (Dickens and Hall 1995; Undy et al. 1996).

Combined with changes in employer strategies due to the market forces cited at the outset, the legislative assault on organized labor helped bring about a broad and thoroughgoing shift toward deregulation. This is reflected in three related trends: the collapse of multi-employer bargaining, the rise of enterprise-level bargaining, and an overall shrinking of the number of workers covered by collective agreements of any sort. First, there has been a dramatic decline in Britain of multi-employer bargaining as employers have step by step dismantled what apparatus existed for the collective, joint regulation of the labor market. Fourteen major industry agreements were dismantled between 1985 and 1995 (Howell 1995: 161–2). More generally, whereas, in 1980, 43 per cent of workplaces were involved in multi-employer bargaining, by 1998 this was down to 14 per cent (Cully et al. 1999: 228–9).[17]

The collapse of two-tier (usually industry or regional plus plant-level) bargaining has in some cases given way to single-enterprise agreements. Brown, Marginson, and Walsh (1995: 137) report that 'by 1990 of the somewhat under five out of ten employees then covered by a collective agreement, for four in ten they were . . . single employer, but for only 1 in 10 were they multi-employer agreements.' They note that one of the advantages for employers of enterprise bargaining is that 'it allows employers to cultivate internal labour markets. When much skill acqui-

---

[16] In 1979, British unions organized 53% of the total working population, as against US unions which peaked at 35% in the 1940s (Edwards et al. 1992: 31–2).

[17] These figures refer to workplaces with twenty-five or more employees. The picture is even more bleak if one singles out the private sector, where only 4% of such workplaces engaged in multi-employer bargaining in 1998 (Cully et al. 1999: 229).

sition is on the job and technological change is constant and incremental, there are advantages in having fluid job titles, predictable trajectories, and more stable internal salary structures' (1995: 138).

However, an even more pronounced trend is a decline in the number of workers who are covered by any kind of collective bargain. As employers' willingness and capacity to coordinate have disintegrated, so too have the coordinating capacities of unions suffered. In Britain there was an automaticity to union recognition embedded in industry-level bargaining, and so the demise of the latter has had disastrous effects on union coverage. The proportion of employees whose wages are set by collective bargaining with unions has fallen steadily, from 70 per cent in 1984 to 41 per cent by 1998 (Cully et al. 1999: 241–2).

The effects of these trends on union membership have been disastrous. The closed shop, once quite pervasive, is virtually gone, and a growing number of new companies have opted not to recognize unions in the first place (Howell 1995: 153, 162). Union membership plunged over the years of conservative rule, falling by 40 per cent, from over 13 million to 7.9 million workers (Howell 1999: 29).[18] In strong contrast to Sweden and Germany where employers are, as we have seen, deeply worried about industrial strife, British employers face a much more docile union movement. In Britain in the 1990s there were fewer stoppages and days lost than at any time since records began being kept at the end of the last century (Howell 1996: 517; see also Edwards 1995).

There have also been important changes in shop-floor institutions and practices, in both the (declining) union sector and beyond. Similar to the United States, work reorganization emerged in the 1970s and 1980s as a key point of conflict between unions and employers. In Britain, the structure of the unions has been a long-standing source of rigidity, and one reason employers prefer single-union agreements is to eliminate craft-based multi-unionism. In such agreements, 'a union agrees to complete flexibility in the use of labor, various forms of arbitration to prevent strikes, and the equivalent of a works council, in return for exclusive union recognition' (Howell 1995: 153). First introduced by Japanese firms in Britain, these arrangements have been copied by British firms, especially new ones. In fact, it appears that single unionism is virtually the only form of union recognition occurring in the past decade (Howell 1999: 38).[19]

[18] Trade union membership appears to have stabilized, albeit at these low levels, since Labour took office.

[19] Unions have in some cases met this trend by coordinating their demands more closely and engaging in what is called 'single table bargaining' (Howell 1999: 54; see also Geary 1995: 375).

As Howell (1995: 153) summarizes: 'As an indicator of the trajectory of British industrial relations, it is now the case that newly created firms will almost never adopt traditional forms of collective bargaining, preferring either to forgo union recognition altogether or to opt for a single union agreement.' Compared to the United States, outright derecognition remains relatively rare in Britain, but partial derecognitions (i.e. derecognizing particular unions or categories of employee) are on the rise, and appear to be part of employer strategies to 'rationalize' plant-based labor representation. Sisson and Marginson (1995: 112), for example, report that 'almost one in five companies with over 1,000 employees reported that recognition for negotiating purposes had been partially or wholly withdrawn on their established sites.'

The kinds of employer-dominated worker involvement 'HR/IR' schemes that have flourished in the United States have not been as popular among British employers (Howell 1999: 39; also Sisson and Marginson 1995). However, against the backdrop of employers' need for stability and predictability at the plant level, it seems significant that shop steward presence has fallen off somewhat less than overall union membership (Millward et al. 1992: 117).[20] Even in cases of outright derecognition, employers have sometimes allowed stewards to retain some representation or consultation rights (*European Industrial Relations Review*, June 1994: 24). Geary (1995: 375) reports that case studies show that management often continues to rely on shop stewards to smooth the implementation of shop-floor changes (for example, work reorganization), and he cites examples in which 'management had not sought, nor wished, to dismantle representative structures completely.' As Terry (1995: 224) argues, one factor shoring up steward organization is that 'for many employers, despite the adoption of "union free" approaches, no thoroughgoing alternative to steward based collective bargaining has been pursued. The basic infrastructure for wage and conditions bargaining remains intact in many areas.' Apparently, even in the context of the massive attack on unions, British employers continue to believe that there are advantages to having labor representatives to consult and work with at the plant level (Sisson and Marginson 1995: 112). However, as Howell (1999: 39) notes, firms want a particular kind of bargaining partner: 'The CBI [Confederation of British Industry] sees a continued role for shop stewards, but . . . a very limited role for trade unions

---

[20] Although of course the decline in union recognition reduces shop steward representation overall. Terry reports that while in 1984, a steward was present in 54% of all firms in the WIRS survey, by 1990, the figure was 38% (Terry 1995: 213).

external to the firm. This implies a preference, where unions do exist, for something akin to enterprise unions, though employers do not use the term.'

In sum, and very similar to the trajectory of change in the United States, the two most dominant trends in Britain have been (1) escape from all forms of union regulation, or where this is impossible or impractical (2) a strong preference for dealing with labor representatives that are cut off from national-level bargaining structures and with local unions that have been reorganized along unitary lines.

Responding to years of decline, British unions in the 1990s reversed their historic commitment to voluntarism and began clamoring for legislative changes to help them stanch the tide (Howell 1996: 535; also Dickens and Hall 1995: 295 ff.). Since coming to power, the new Labour government has delivered on several of its promised reforms, including a national minimum wage, British inclusion in the EU Social Charter, and a new Employment Relations Act that includes, among other things, a statutory right to union recognition. While certainly a far cry from the policies served up by the Conservatives, it is not yet clear whether these measures will turn things around for the British labor movement. As Chris Howell (2000: 27–8, 34) points out, New Labour has not shown much interest in restoring organized labor to its previous position in the political economy, and indeed many of the recent reforms reflect this, since they involve legal regulation through the state rather than collective regulation by unions.

2.4.7 The Cases Compared: Convergence Again?

In the LMEs, employers confronted the more turbulent markets of the 1980s and 1990s with a different set of opportunities and constraints. The opportunities to escape union regulation are many and they also appear to be quite irresistible to employers. King and Wood's (1999) argument —that because employers in the LMEs lack strong coordinating capacities of their own, they prefer to deregulate relations with labor as well —appears to be confirmed, for in the countries considered here we find strong tendencies to escape union regulation at all levels. Firms that compete on the basis of quality and reliability may seek to foster cooperative relations with their workforces. However, they are likely to do so in a radically different way from the CMEs—through strategies that either attempt to sideline unions completely, or, failing that, to renegotiate union structures and rights in such as way as to bring them in line with segmentalism (breakdown of pattern or industry-level bargaining; enterprise or single-union agreements in Britain; 'human resource management' strategies in the USA).

2.5 Conclusion: Beyond Equilibrium

This concluding section returns to the two issues flagged at the beginning of this chapter—namely the alternative logic of employer strategies in the LMEs and the political dynamics that sustain non-market coordination in the CMEs.

First, in the LMEs there is ample evidence to support the claims of the deregulation literature, manifest in a widespread move to eliminate collective representation and restore 'managerial freedom.' At the same time, in the United States and Britain, we also find examples of employer initiatives that are designed to enlist worker involvement and to encourage shop-floor peace, sometimes through practices or concessions that do not fit the strict dictates of neo-liberalism—e.g. long-term employment guarantees and personnel policies that favor internal over external (i.e. hire and fire) flexibility. Such strategies recommend themselves in LMEs for the reasons that King and Wood (1999) point to, namely, that they do not require strong overarching institutions for non-market coordination. Indeed, such strategies constitute one way in which at least the largest firms can compensate for the labor market instabilities and collective action problems that a lack of coordination—for example, in training—can generate.

Firms in the USA and UK that have established innovative arrangements designed to promote cooperative relations at the plant or company level exhibit some similarities to core firms in the Japanese economy, and indeed many of them have been more or less explicitly modeled on the Japanese example. The bias toward segmentalist strategies for labor market regulation that all these countries share helps to explain why Japan clusters with the LMEs on many dimensions—highly segmented labor markets, low redistribution, limited labor strength at the national political level (Rueda and Pontusson 2000). At the same time, we know that these arrangements are both less pervasive in the large firm sector in the USA and UK than they are in Japan, and that they are also much less stable.[21] To explain this we need to consider the broader institutional context in which these arrangements are embedded. One important difference is that, in Japan, segmentalist strategies do not require a fundamental renegotiation of labor's traditional organization and strategies, for the obvious reason that the structure of Japanese unions already fits

---

[21] See Wever (1995) on the failure of these practices to diffuse widely, and Weinstein and Kochan (1995) on the high failure rate of many of the more innovative programs for employee involvement in the United States.

with (and historically, actually promoted) such strategies on the part of firms (Thelen and Kume 1999*b*).

While it seems clear that segmentalist strategies are not compatible with strong overarching unions, merely the absence of such unions does not suffice to produce stable segmentalism. Here our attention is drawn to other features of the Japanese political economy, features that explain why Japan is frequently classified as a CME in 'varieties of capitalism' research. First, the large firm sector in Japan has demonstrated a greater capacity for coordination, especially in wage-bargaining, than that in the UK and the USA. This is important, because as Swenson (2001) has pointed out, segmentalist strategies will not necessarily succeed without some coordination, at least among the segmentalists. Among other things, seniority-based wages only keep workers in place as long as other firms agree to hire workers only at entry-level wages. Second, long-term financing arrangements in Japan have shored up stable internal labor markets to the extent that they have allowed Japanese employers to go to extreme lengths to avoid reneging on lifetime employment guarantees (Kume 1998; Thelen and Kume 1999*a*). Operating on a shorter financial leash, employers in Britain and the United States have proven much more likely to respond to market downturns by laying off workers.[22] The general point is that plant-based cooperation between labor and employers itself often depends for its stability on collateral institutions (a degree of employer coordination, long-term financing). Lacking these, American and British firms frequently revert to the default—managerial unilateralism.

Second, my analysis of the CMEs shows that, compared to the LMEs, national-level collective bargaining institutions and joint (with labor) regulation of labor markets remains relatively strong. However, most contemporary analyses tend to attribute this stability either to institutional inertia, or to the functional benefits of continued coordination. The present analysis, by contrast, sees non-market coordination as a political process, a dynamic equilibrium that is premised on a particular set of power relations—both within employer associations and between unions and employers. Historical analysis has shown that the process of centralization in Sweden was accomplished only when export sectors were able to prevail over and dominate sheltered industries within the employers' associations (Swenson 1989). And so it comes as no surprise

[22] For example, Xerox and Kodak, two companies with especially strong reputations for employment stability and long-term commitments to their workforces, ultimately resorted to massive layoffs in the context of restructuring (Osterman et al. forthcoming: ch. 2, pp. 8–9).

that shifts in the balance of power—brought about by the decline of LO–SAF hegemony and the rise of the public sector, above all—resulted in a destabilization of traditional industrial-relations institutions there (Iversen, this volume).

A similar story could be told for Germany, where historically industry-level bargaining had to prevail against a coalition that favored confederal bargaining led by the DGB (Pirker 1979), and where the leadership role played by IG Metall has survived ongoing tensions through compromise with other industrial unions (above all, the chemical workers' union). On the employer side, associations like Gesamtmetall have always had to reconcile differences of interest among its extremely diverse membership base, something that as we have seen has become more difficult in recent years as a result of the often diverging opportunities that globalization affords to large versus small firms. The outcome of this internal struggle has enormous implications for the stability of traditional bargaining institutions. This is certainly clear to the actors involved, not least union leaders who understand very well that the strength and position of organized labor within the political economy requires continued coordination and unity on the employer side as well (*Frankfurter Allgemeine Zeitung*, 6 Apr. 1995, *Augsburger Allgemeine Zeitung*, 1 Apr. 1996).

From the foregoing analysis it also seems clear that labor's continued strength in the CMEs has been an especially important factor in sustaining non-market coordination in industrial relations. In Sweden and Germany, as we have seen, employers' heightened sensitivity to industrial conflict is what has brought them rushing back to the bargaining table with central unions, in an effort to maintain peace at the plant level. Employers' current vulnerability is in part the result of the way in which their competitive strategies in the market accommodated labor's (past) strength. This is what, over time, pushed them along the trajectory of the kind of high-quality, high-skill, high value-added production strategies that have now rendered them so dependent on labor's active cooperation on the shop floor (Streeck 1992b: ch. 1). The 'labor power' dimension to their strategies is only dimly visible if we limit ourselves to a 'snapshot' of the situation in the 1990s (Pierson 1996b). To take one aspect, the functional contribution of strong co-determination to economic success in these countries should not obscure the fact that, historically speaking, employers in both Germany and Sweden opposed the strengthening of labor's rights at the plant level. Now that they have organized their competitive strategies around these institutions, they find that they can scarcely do without them. We can see this as an equilibrium situation—employers' dependence on labor cooperation shores up the power of unions which in turn keeps employers focused on strategies that depend on labor cooperation. But if so, it is also clear that this is an equilibrium that is founded on a particular balance of power.

Summary

The trends in labor relations in the advanced industrial democracies sketched out above cannot be captured in the dichotomies that have served as benchmarks for much traditional theorizing—stability versus breakdown, centralization versus decentralization. I have argued that the 'varieties of capitalism' approach elaborated in this volume provides a more reliable foundation for theorizing because it takes us beyond the formal structures to identify the quite different behavioral logics that characterize various political economies. The distinction between co-ordinated and liberal market economies, in particular, sheds light on the sources of resiliency in labor institutions in the CMEs as well as the fragility of traditional institutions in the LMEs. Despite important changes in some CMEs (in particular, Sweden and Denmark), wage-bargaining has re-equilibrated at a rather centralized level (multi-indus-trial rather than national-confederal). While significant, these changes do not amount to a wholesale deregulation, or to the return of widespread employer unilateralism, as in the LMEs.

In this chapter I have specifically focused on the interaction between national level institutional arrangements and plant-level bargaining, for in all cases this interaction is key to understanding sources of stability and trajectories of change. In the CMEs, where labor representatives at the plant level enjoy rather extensive participatory rights and are linked closely to strong overarching unions, employers' dependence on stability and cooperation at the firm level has helped to shore up coordination at higher levels. In the LMEs, by contrast, employer strategies at the firm level have brought them into conflict with traditional union structures and strategies at both the industry and plant levels. Here, employers have seized on the current permissive political and economic environ-ment to eliminate union influence altogether, or to force a reconfigura-tion of industrial relations along lines that move them even further away from the coordinated market economies.

I have also argued that the varieties of capitalism literature needs to go beyond existing, somewhat functional, accounts to incorporate the political dynamics that sustain the contrasting trajectories of the two types of economies. In the case of the CMEs, recent developments have involved a renegotiation of the terms of coordination, more dramatic perhaps in Sweden than in Germany, but in both cases, placing new limits on the capacity of central unions to directly determine plant outcomes. In these cases, we can talk of a shifting balance within structures that still afford labor an important role at both the industry and plant levels. Not so in the LMEs, where recent developments signal a more fundamental renegotiation of labor's position at both levels and, indeed, in the political economy as a whole. In both Britain and the United States, the overall trend has been toward sharply reduced union influence and the question is not just how well organized labor will survive but also what kinds of unions will emerge from this process.

3

Institutional and Sectoral Interactions in Monetary Policy and Wage/Price-Bargaining

Robert J. Franzese, Jr.

3.1 Introduction

Institutional political economists interested in politico-economic management of inflation and unemployment have confronted two disparate and partially contradictory literatures. One approach derives from the modern neoclassical economics of monetary policy and stresses the monetary authority's anti-inflationary conservatism and credible autonomy from the current government. The central claim is that credibly autonomous and conservative central banks achieve nominal (e.g. inflation) benefits at no real (e.g. employment) costs on average. The other derives from the study of interest intermediation in democracies and stresses institutions in labor and, more recently, goods markets. Its central claim is that coordinated wage/price-bargaining fosters restrained settlements by internalizing certain externalities inherent to the bargains, thereby providing real and perhaps also nominal benefits. Each argument emphasizes a single institution in the macro political economy: the degree of central-bank independence from political authority or of wage/price-bargaining coordination across the economy. This exclusivity of focus clearly facilitated theoretical development; the two literatures are now among the most influential in political economy, academically and practically. However, monetary policy and wage/price-bargaining

I gratefully acknowledge funding during the development of these ideas from summer 1993 to present from the National Science Foundation (1991–4), the Harvard-MIT Research Training Group in Positive Political Economy (1994–5); the Harvard Center for European Studies, the Wissenschaftszentrum Berlin (1993); the Mellon Foundation (1995–6); and the University of Michigan (1996–present). Gratitude for comments, criticisms, and suggestions are due especially to Peter Hall and David Soskice, and to James Alt, Alberto Alesina, Thomas Cusack, Geoff Garrett, and Torben Iversen. Remaining shortcomings, inexcusable given this wealth of valuable input, are my own. Complete estimation results and all data available from http://www-personal.umich.edu/~franzese.

are intimately related exercises, so the sorts of institutional interactions emphasized in this volume are especially likely to operate in this setting.

Building on these well-developed arguments and several recent contributions[1] beginning to combine their insights, I argue that the institutions of monetary policy-making and wage/price-bargaining interact, with each other and with the sectoral composition of the bargainers, in macroeconomic regulation. Specifically, *central-bank independence, coordinated wage/price-bargaining, dominant traded sectors, and dominated public sectors are generally substitutes in producing low inflation and complements in producing low unemployment.* More broadly, the incentives facing politico-economic actors are determined by *multiple interactions* among the *set* of institutions and structures of their environments. Macroeconomic regulation of unemployment and inflation, for example, rests not on any single institution, central-bank independence or wage/price-bargaining coordination, but rather on the broader configuration of the set of relevant institutions and structures characterizing the political economy.

I structure the chapter to substantiate these arguments as follows. Sections 3.2 and 3.3 review each literature, offering a simple heuristic model designed to highlight its principal theoretical contentions and reproduce its core empirical predictions. Reconsideration of each argument and associated evidence reveals their contradictory theoretical foundations and claims and some lingering empirical issues. Section 3.4 addresses these contradictions and issues by merging the literatures' insights and stressing a sectoral-structure extension of that synthesis, again offering a heuristic model to guide the argumentation. This synthesis and extension restores theoretical coherence and demonstrates the operation at the macro-political-economic level of certain institutional complementarities of the sort emphasized in this volume. Section 3.5 employs the post-Bretton Woods macroeconomic experiences of developed democracies to evaluate the emergent hypotheses empirically. Section 3.6 concludes.

---

[1] Scharpf (1984, 1987, 1991) presages. Franzese (2000) reviews later advances (Cubitt 1989, 1992, 1995); Yashiv 1989; Agell and Ysander 1993; Franzese 1994, 1996, 1999a, 1999b, forthcoming; Garrett and Way 1995a, 1995b, 1999, 2000); Gylfason and Lindbeck 1994; Hall 1994; Rama 1994; Jonsson 1995; Bleaney 1996; Iversen 1996, 1998a, 1998b, 1998c, 2000; Jensen 1997; Ozkan et al. 1997; Skott 1997; Calmfors 1998; Forteza 1998; Hall and Franzese 1998; Soskice and Iversen 1998, 2000; Cukierman and Lippi 1999; Velasco and Guzzo 1999; Grüner and Hefeker 1999; Iversen et al. 2000; Sibert 1999; Zervoyianni 1997; Franzese and Hall 2000; Sibert and Sutherland 2000).

3.2 Central-bank Independence

3.2.1 Central-bank Independence: Reviewing the Neoclassical Argument

Institutional political economists in the 1980s and 1990s argued convincingly that central-bank independence lowers inflation.[2] Due to credibility advantages such central banks enjoy over elected governments, the inflation benefit is argued to come without real economic costs (e.g. unemployment) on average. Simplifying and summarizing, the argument proceeds thus.

First, given nominal and real rigidities in the economy, such as those created by wage/price-bargaining, the monetary authority has incentives to create 'surprise' inflation, thereby lowering real wages (prices) and thus spurring employment (real demand). Second, the private sector is, however, aware of these incentives and incorporates their inflationary consequences into its wage/price-setting. Thus, in rational-expectations equilibrium, monetary authorities cannot systematically surprise bargainers, so real wages (prices) and thus employment (output) are unaffected on average while inflation is higher. Third, if, contrarily, monetary authorities could *credibly* promise to refrain from inflationary policy, bargainers could set lower wages (prices) without fear so that, again, real wages (prices) and so employment (output) would be unaffected on average, while inflation could be lower than without such credible commitment. Lastly, institutionalizing a conservative central bank with relative autonomy from political officials is held to provide such credibility; therefore, central-bank independence provides nominal benefits without adverse real effects on average.

Looking more closely, the neoclassical model begins by specifying the utility function, $V^m(\cdot)$, of the monetary policy-maker (see Cukierman 1992: 27–45):

$$V^m = -\left[\tfrac{1}{2}A(N^* - N)^2 + \tfrac{1}{2}\pi^2 \right] \tag{1}$$

i.e., policy-makers dislike deviations of employment and inflation from their targets ($N-N^*$ and $\pi-\pi^*$, with $\pi^* = 0$ for simplicity).[3] A here reflects

---

[2] *Independence*, in this literature, means *autonomy and conservatism*. Core works include Barro and Gordon (1983a, 1983b); Rogoff (1985); Lohmann (1992). Cukierman (1992) provides textbook compilation, and Eijffinger and De Haan (1996) offer a briefer review of theory and evidence.

[3] Any real quantity (e.g. output) can substitute for employment here. Notice (1) actually implies policy-makers derive *disutility* from *too high* employment. To avoid this odd

policy-makers' weight on employment relative to inflation; *conservative* can therefore be defined as having lower A, N^*, and/or π^*.

Next, with nominal contracts and market power, unexpected money growth spurs employment beyond its natural rate (N_n), giving the economy as an expectations-augmented Phillips Curve:

$$N = N_n + \alpha(\pi - \pi^e) \tag{2}$$

where π^e is expected inflation and α the slope of the Phillips Curve (i.e. the real effectiveness of surprise money). Finally, given rational expectations and no uncertainty, abstracting from real growth or velocity shocks, and assuming for simplicity that monetary authorities directly control inflation, equilibrium inflation absent any commitment devices is found by substituting (2) into (1), maximizing with respect to π, and then applying rational expectations by setting $\pi = \pi^e$:

$$\pi_d^* = A\alpha(N^* - N_n) \tag{3}$$

Since this *discretionary equilibrium inflation* (π_d^*) involves only parameters known with certainty by the private sector (A, α, N^*, N_n), expected inflation (π^e) is actual inflation (π_d^*), so employment (N) does not deviate from its natural rate (N_n) in rational-expectations equilibrium.[4] If, however, the bank could credibly commit to lower inflation (say its target rate, zero), expected and actual inflation would again be equal (at zero), so equilibrium employment would still be the natural rate (N_n). Call this *commitment inflation*: $\pi_c^* = 0$. The argument then equates central-bank independence with credible commitment to conservative inflation policy and thus concludes that independence lowers inflation without real costs on average.[5]

That central-bank independence lowers inflation without real costs on average has been extensively empirically tested. Typically, post-war averages of inflation and of some real outcome are regressed on indices of independence in cross-sections of fifteen to twenty-one OECD countries; rarely are the data temporally disaggregated or any controls included.[6]

---

implication, Cukierman (1992: 28) stipulates $N^* > N$; alternatively, assume a full-employment target.

[4] Actually, as Gylfason and Lindbeck (1994) note, the standard model assumes this result *ab initio*, given rational expectations and (2), in which natural rates are exogenous.

[5] Adding information asymmetry, uncertainty, and/or incomplete information to this model, independence produces more-variant real outcomes (a real cost), but credible commitment still lowers inflation without affecting real variables on average (see Cukierman 1992).

[6] Alesina and Summers (1993) could serve as graphical summary of the standard approach. Eijffinger and De Haan (1996) review the empirical literature, revealing few exceptions.

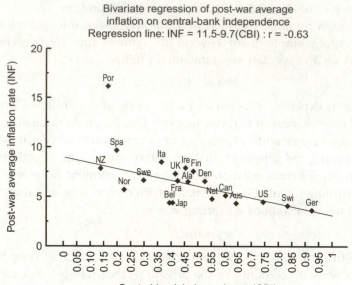

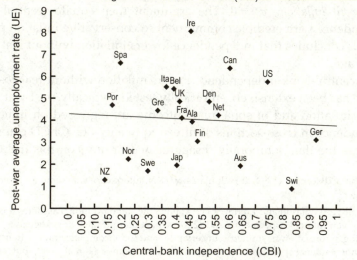

FIG. 3.1 Bivariate relations of central-bank independence with
inflation and unemployment

Such cross-sections reveal impressively strong negative correlation between central-bank independence and inflation and no significant bivariate correlation in those small samples between independence and virtually any real outcome. Fig. 3.1 graphically summarizes the statistical case for the neoclassical model.

Prominent *real-world* examples also bolstered the case. Germany, Switzerland, and the USA have famously independent central banks and share experiences of relatively low inflation while their unemployment experiences differ considerably. Such eloquently logical argument, simple but striking quantitative evidence, and prominent empirical anecdotes have apparently convinced wide academic and policy-making audiences. Raising central-bank independence has become a policy priority around the world recently; and many have moved in this direction: Italy and New Zealand most notably among developed democracies. The requirements for European Monetary Union and the European Central Bank were also clearly designed with these arguments, with this evidence, and with the template of the Bundesbank in mind.

3.2.2 CBI: Lingering Theoretical Issues and Empirical Anomalies

First, even in its own terms, the model indicates more than has generally been explored theoretically or empirically.[7] Beyond central-bank independence lowering inflation, (3) implies also that anything that increases the (i) government's weight on employment relative to inflation, A, (ii) real effectiveness of surprise money, α, (iii) government's employment or inflation targets, N^* or π^*, or that decreases the (iv) natural rate of employment, N_n, raises discretionary inflation. Central-bank independence then lowers actual inflation from this discretionary level toward the bank's target level (here zero). Accordingly, it lowers inflation more (less) the higher (lower) discretionary inflation would have been. Points (i) and (iii), for example, suggest that independence reduces inflation more under left than right government because the left places greater weight on unemployment relative to inflation or has higher employment or inflation targets (higher A, N^*, or π^*). More importantly here, points (ii) and (iv) begin to suggest one possible avenue for synthesizing central-bank-independence and coordinated-wage/price-bargaining theories since the

---

[7] Jonsson (1995), Bleaney (1996), Simmons (1996), Clark et al. (1998), Hall and Franzese (1998), Iversen (1999*b*) are partial exceptions. Franzese (1999*a*, 1999*b*) gives the general treatment.

institutional features of the wage/price bargain directly impact the real effectiveness of monetary expansion (α) and the natural rate of employment (N_n).

Previous estimations of the anti-inflationary impact of central-bank independence were, therefore, mis-specified.[8] Defining CBI as the *degree of central-bank independence*, 0 $\equiv$ none and 1 $\equiv$ complete, the theory more precisely predicts:

$$\pi = CBI \cdot \pi_c^* + (1 - CBI) \cdot \pi_d^* \tag{4}$$

where π_d^* is the discretionary inflation from (3), and π_c^* is commitment inflation. Thus, the argument suggests that the anti-inflationary impact of central-bank independence depends on everything that determines discretionary inflation differently from commitment inflation, i.e. everything to which the inflation policies of central banks and governments would respond differently. Thus, even the neoclassical theory of central-bank independence and inflation, correctly conceived, implies that *the inflation effects of central-bank independence depend on many other domestic and international structural and institutional features of the political economy in which the central bank interacts.* On that, neoclassical central-bank-independence theory, coordinated-wage/price-bargaining theory, and the synthesis and extension offered here agree. I explore this partial agreement further below.

The theoretical and empirical problems in the standard model extend further though; central banks' behavior and public announcements are also anomalous from that view. For example, the US Federal Reserve frequently announces and acts upon its intention to raise interest rates 'to defuse incipient inflationary pressures' or lower them 'to prevent recession'. However, *incipient inflationary pressures* do not exist in this model since the bank controls inflation directly; nor does relaxing that assumption, which was merely simplifying and known false anyway, correct matters. Theoretically, inflation is a weighted average of discretionary and commitment inflation (π_d^* and π_c^*) as in (4). π_d^*, in turn, is a function of A, α, N^* and N_n as in (3), but none of these vary cyclically in a manner consistent with Fed behavior. By *incipient inflationary pressures* the Fed means a strong real economy. If the government's relative weight on or target for employment (A, N^*), monetary real efficacy (α), and the natural rate (N_n) vary at all cyclically it would be to lower

---

[8] At best, they might be reasonable estimates of the *average* inflation impact of independence across the various configurations of other relevant factors occurring in their particular sample.

A, α, and $N^* - N_n$ in booms. That is, when the economy is pushing capacity, governments tend to fret more over inflation than employment (A lower), the real efficacy of monetary policy (α) diminishes by the law of diminishing returns, and the gap from target to actual employment ($N^* - N$) shrinks. Thus, by this theory as seen in (3), *incipient inflationary pressures* should concern central banks *less* in booms than busts. Also, by this theory, by announcing its intention to lower interest rates, the bank weakens that very policy's effect in stemming any coming slowdown. The Fed's behavior is therefore anomalous.[9]

The Bundesbank behaves somewhat differently, but equally anomalously. It often directs its pronouncements specifically to wage/price-bargainers or the government, more or less overtly threatening to respond to upcoming wage/price settlements or public budgets that it views as inflationary by raising interest rates.[10] Thus, the Bundesbank identifies the sources of the *incipient inflationary pressures* it perceives: budgets and wage/price bargains. Again, though, neoclassical theory cannot explain Bundesbank behavior. First, public budgets do not affect inflation in this model, leaving little reason to address the government except as a price-setter for public goods and as the public-sector employer. Second, more revealingly, wage/price-bargainers here simply add expected money growth to desired real wage growth. No need to threaten a *response* then; a credible bank announcement of *fixed* intended money growth will suffice.

Thus, the behavior and pronouncements of both Bundesbank and Fed seem to contradict the theory. Moreover, that the Bundesbank speaks differently and to different actors than the Fed is also inexplicable from the neoclassical view. Finally, the theory has been inappropriately tested, even in its own terms, especially on the nominal side because (4) demands interactive empirical models, but also on nominal and real sides because necessary controls have usually been omitted. The proposed synthesis and extension, which will resolve these anomalies and begin to fill the empirical gaps, requires that we next consider wage/price-bargaining institutions.

[9] Furthermore, the 'financial-stability motive' for the observed counter-cyclical policy (see Cukierman 1992: 117–35) cannot explain the justification the Fed offers for its behavior.

[10] The Fed, contrarily, rarely mentions wage/price-bargainers. Examples of the Bundesbank's quite different announcements are easily found: see e.g. Kennedy (1991: 27–53) or *Financial Times* (24 June 1993: 14).

3.3 Coordinated Bargaining

3.3.1 Coordinated Wage/Price-Bargaining: Reviewing the Basic Argument

A largely unconnected literature developed contemporaneously showing that encompassing (Olson 1965) wage/price-bargaining can achieve real, and perhaps nominal, wage and price restraint and thereby has beneficial employment, and perhaps inflation, effects.[11] The argument, simplified and summarized, proceeds thus. One person's wage earnings (output price) are another's wage cost (input price). Therefore, if wage/price bargains occur in highly fragmented units, this and any other aggregate externality are ignored, so fragmented wage/price settlements will be higher than optimal. They will include increments to offset expected increases elsewhere in the economy.[12] If, contrarily, bargaining occurs in encompassing or coordinated units, this externality is internalized and such increments are unnecessary. Thus, coordinated wage/price-bargaining induces wage/price restraint and therefore lowers unemployment and inflation.

A heuristic model derived from these first principles will prove useful later. Following the early literature, I begin with wage-bargaining from labor's perspective. First, identify the value functions of the j worker-bargaining units (*unions*). The core of the argument is that these j unions derive utility from the real consumption value of their wages, ω_j^c, and from their employment prospects, ε_j, which latter are increasing in, *inter alia*, aggregate output growth, y:[13]

$$V_j^u = V^u(\omega_j^c, \varepsilon_j(y, \cdot)) \quad with \quad V_1^u \equiv \frac{\partial V^u}{\partial \omega^c} > 0, \tag{5}$$

$$V_2^u \equiv \frac{\partial V^u}{\partial \varepsilon} > 0, \ \varepsilon' \equiv \frac{\partial \varepsilon}{\partial y} > 0$$

[11] Headey (1970) foreshadows. Core works include Berger (1981); Lehmbruch and Schmitter (1982); Cameron (1984); Lange (1984); Lange and Garrett (1985); Bruno and Sachs (1987); Calmfors and Driffill (1988); Soskice (1990a). Carlin and Soskice (1990) and Layard et al. (1991) provide textbook treatments; Calmfors (1993) is an excellent briefer review.

[12] The multiple bargains are often viewed as prisoner's dilemma in which i's preferences order thus: all units except i, all, none, and lastly only i exercise restraint. NB this ordering assumes market power since being the only unit raising wages (prices) is most preferred, which is only likely if employment (demand) is relatively wage (price) inelastic, which defines market power.

[13] This sensitivity of the unions' members' employment prospects to aggregate economic performance drives the incentive for wage restraint in the standard model. It, in turn, responds to an individual union's wage settlement in proportion to the encompassingness of its bargain. The assumed monotonicity of these relationships has been much criticized recently (see below).

Defining terms in log changes (growth rates) for comparability with the previous model, the growth of real consumption wages for the jth union (ω_j^c) is the difference between its nominal wage growth (w_j) and the growth in consumer prices (inflation, π):

$$\omega_j^c = w_j - \pi \tag{6}$$

The perceived marginal value to any union $_j$ of gaining higher nominal wage growth for itself (w_j) is found by substituting (6) into (5) and differentiating with respect to w_j:

$$\frac{\partial V_j^u}{\partial w_j} = V_1^u \left(1 - \frac{\partial \pi}{\partial w_j}\right) + V_2^u \left(\frac{\partial \varepsilon_j}{\partial y} \cdot \frac{\partial y}{\partial w_j}\right) \tag{7}$$

(7) reveals the central conclusion. Unions perceive more value from nominal wage-gains, and so exercise less *wage restraint*, the larger this expression; the lower this derivative, the more wage restraint unions are likely to exercise.[14] The first term on the right indicates that the real wage gains union j expects from any given nominal wage increase are lower the more j expects aggregate-price inflation, π, to parallel its wage inflation (w_j). At one extreme, j's bargain is all-encompassing, so j expects inflation to move one for one with its settlement: $d\pi/dw_j = 1$. Union j expects no real wage gains because it knows the rest of the economy will exactly follow its own nominal gains. At the other extreme, when individual bargains are vanishingly small relative to national aggregates, no union perceives aggregate inflation to respond to its little settlement: $d\pi/dw_j \approx 0$. In short, nominal wage gains are perceived to produce real wage gains in proportion to wage/price-bargaining fragmentation. The second term in (7) reflects the adverse aggregate-output effects of aggregate (or average) wage gains: $dy/dw < 0$;[15] unions perceive employment prospects to decline with aggregate wage gains. Once again, though, the response of *aggregate* output to an *individual* bargain's settlement (dy/dw_j) is more negative, and union j's employment prospects respond more to aggregate output ($d\varepsilon_j/dy$), the more encompassing j's bargain. On both real-wage-gain and employment-prospect-cost side, then, unions are more disposed to deliver wage restraint the more encompassing their bargaining unit or, equivalently, the greater the coordination across bargaining units.

As with central-bank independence, an impressive amount of evidence amassed to support the coordinated-wage/price-bargaining argument

---

[14] More precisely, more (less) wage restraint is exercised the lower (higher) w_j (wage inflation) at which $\partial V/\partial w = 0$.

[15] This relationship was usually under-specified. Bruno and Sachs (1987), Carlin and Soskice (1990), and Layard et al. (1991) later specified it more exactly; the negative relationship remains.

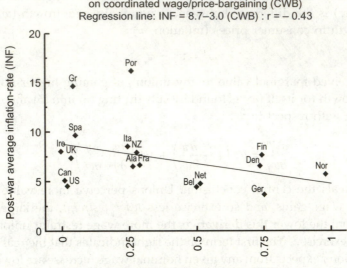

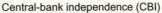

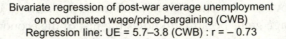

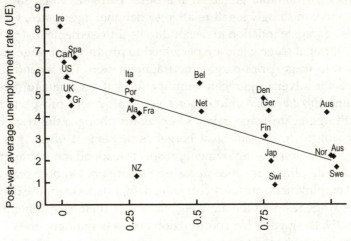

FIG. 3.2 Bivariate relations of coordinated wage/price-bargaining with inflation and unemployment

(see e.g. Cameron 1984; Bruno and Sachs 1987). Again, the quantitative evidence has typically[16] involved regressing post-war averages of unemployment and inflation (or some other real and nominal variables) on an index of coordination. Fig. 3.2 illustrates (the CWB index employed is described later), and, again, prominent real-world examples added to the argument convincingly. The Scandinavian countries and Austria were well known to exhibit considerable bargaining coordination, admirable unemployment, and moderate inflation. As with central-bank independence later, the intuitive argument, striking evidence, and real-world examples put wage/price-bargaining coordination on many economic policy agendas. Some countries (e.g. the UK and Italy) scrambled for a time, though mostly unsuccessfully, to institute such bargaining in their economies (Regini 1984).

3.3.2 Coordinated Wage/Price-Bargaining: Recent Theoretical and Empirical Extensions

Recent work extends this literature in two directions. Swenson (1989, 1991), Soskice (1990a), and Layard et al. (1991) draw attention to the, previously virtually ignored, employer side of the wage/price bargain (the *employer-side amendment*). Calmfors and Driffill (1988), Layard et al. (1991), and Calmfors (1993) draw attention to market-power assumptions implicit in the union preferences assumed by the early literature (the *market-competition amendment*).

To consider these amendments, I reformulate the simple model slightly. First, unions do not unilaterally set wages; rather, *wage/price* settlements emerge from *bargains* between unions and their counterpart employer groups (*firms*). Thus, whereas previous focus lay on the marginal utility unions perceive from nominal wage gains, these must now be considered relative to the marginal disutility firms suffer from ceding such gains and their respective bargaining strengths. Start as before with j unions that value the real consumption value of their wages and their members' employment prospects, which are now more sensibly modeled as increasing in the output of group j firms. Those j firms care about profits, which are a function of, *inter alia*, product real wages (i.e. input costs: ω_j^p) and demand for their firms' products (y_j):[17]

---

[16] Exceptions were less rare in this case (e.g. Alvarez et al. 1991; Layard et al. 1991).

[17] I assume exogenous productivity growth for simplicity; given that, assuming it is zero and dropping it from these formulations is no further loss of generality.

$$V_j^u = V^u(\omega_j^c, \varepsilon_j(y_j, \cdot)) \ \text{with} \ V_1^u > 0, \ V_2^u > 0, \ \varepsilon' > 0 \tag{8}$$

$$V_j^e = V^e(\omega_j^p, y_j, \cdot) \ \text{with} \ V_1^e < 0, \ V_2^e > 0 \tag{9}$$

(8) and (9) clarify that employers and workers bargain over wages understanding that prices will be a mark-up over wages, so they are actually bargaining over how to trade (a) wages against employment, (8), and (b) prices against demand, (9), and (a) against (b). Thus, the first conclusion of the employer-side amendment is that the institutional and structural organizations of labor *and* goods markets are *jointly* relevant to wage/*price*-bargaining regulation.

Next, assuming union–firm dyads Nash-bargain over nominal wage growth, some tedious algebra yields the common-sense conclusion that wage/price-bargaining settlements will reflect unions' propensity to offer restraint and firms' arduousness in demanding it proportionately to the relative strengths of their current bargaining positions.[18] Thus, for our purposes, derivatives of (8) and (9) will suffice, as those of (5) did above, to characterize the wage/price-restraint implications of coordination, larger derivatives again implying less restraint. First, define new terms in (8) and (9). Growth of *product* real wages (ω_j^p) is nominal wage growth minus growth of j's *product* prices (π_j), not *consumption*-price inflation (π_j) as for *consumption* real wages:

$$\omega_j^p = w_j - \pi_j \tag{10}$$

Demand for and thus output of j's products is increasing in aggregate income and, importantly, decreasing in j's price growth relative to its competitors' price growth ($\pi_{i(j)}$):

---

[18] Nash bargaining is both convenient and especially appropriate because, though a cooperative-game solution concept, it produces equilibria identical to a non-cooperative game of offers and counter-offers such as wage/price-bargaining (Rubinstein 1982). Nash-bargaining solutions are found by maximizing bargaining-power-weighted products of the bargainers' utilities with respect to variable(s) being bargained, here nominal-wage growth (w_j):

$$\underset{w_j}{\text{Max}} \, [V^u(\omega_j^c, \varepsilon(y_j))]^a \, [V^e(\omega_j^p, y_j)]^b$$

The solution sets a weighted sum of the marginal utilities to unions (firms) of getting (ceding) a nominal wage gain to zero. The weights reflect the exogenous bargaining powers and the initial utility levels of the unions and the firms.

$$\frac{a}{V_j^u} \cdot \frac{\partial V_j^u}{\partial w_j} + \frac{b}{V_j^e} \cdot \frac{\partial V_j^e}{\partial w_j} = 0$$

Franzese (1994, 1996) details derivation of this solution.

$$y_j = y_j(y, \pi_j - \pi_{i\{j\}}) \text{ with } y_1 > 0 \text{ , } y_2 < 0; \text{ define } \rho \equiv \pi_j - \pi_{i\{j\}} \qquad (11)$$

Now, substituting (6), (10), and (11) into (8) and (9), and differentiating with respect to w_j, gives the marginal (dis)utility unions (firms) perceive from attaining (ceding) a nominal wage gain:

$$\frac{\partial V_j^u}{\partial w_j} = V_1^u \left(1 - \frac{\partial \pi}{\partial w_j}\right) + V_2^u \cdot \frac{\partial \varepsilon_j}{\partial y_j} \cdot \frac{\partial y_j}{\partial y} \cdot \frac{\partial y}{\partial w_j}$$

$$+ V_2^u \cdot \frac{\partial \varepsilon_j}{\partial y_j} \cdot \frac{\partial y_j}{\partial \rho_j} \cdot \left(\frac{\partial \pi_j}{\partial w_j} - \frac{\partial \pi_{i\{j\}}}{\partial \pi_j} \cdot \frac{\partial \pi_j}{\partial w_j}\right) \qquad (12)$$

$$\frac{\partial V_j^e}{\partial w_j} = V_1^e \left(1 - \frac{\partial \pi_j}{\partial w_j}\right) + V_2^e \cdot \frac{\partial y_j}{\partial y} \cdot \frac{\partial y}{\partial w_j}$$

$$+ V_2^u \cdot \frac{\partial y_j}{\partial \rho_j} \cdot \left(\frac{\partial \pi_j}{\partial w_j} - \frac{\partial \pi_{i\{j\}}}{\partial \pi_j} \cdot \frac{\partial \pi_j}{\partial w_j}\right) \qquad (13)$$

The employer-side amendment, embodied in these two equations, highlights three obvious but previously underemphasized points. (*a*) Consumption real wages matter to unions while product real wages matter to firms, and unions derive utility from their real wage growth while firms derive disutility from theirs, so firms are more disposed than workers to demand (offer) restraint. (*b*) Though workers' employment concerns virtually mirror employers' output concerns, the term $\partial \varepsilon_j / \partial y_j$ reflects employment responses to output growth and underscores a key difference over how much labor will be input for the amount of output demanded at any given price. (*c*) Most importantly here, the term $\partial \pi_j / \partial w_j$ indicates the response of group j's price growth to its wage growth; i.e. it reflects mark-up adjustments (e.g. fixed mark-ups $\Rightarrow$ $\partial \pi_j / \partial w_j = 1$). Part of any wage/price bargain, then, is a battle over the share of the product-price increases the market will bear that will accrue to wage-earners, i.e. over how to distribute productivity growth and extra-normal profits between workers and employers. The degree to which this battle will be zero-sum depends critically on the competitive situation of group j firms. Specifically, as price competition faced by j's firms increases (decreases), their arduousness in resisting wage restraint increases (decreases). The critical role that price competition among firms plays in regulating wage/price-bargaining is central to the synthesis and extension offered below. However obvious, points (*a*)–(*c*) underscore that the institutions and structures of goods and labor markets interact to structure the incentives facing bargainers. *Wage bargains* are more correctly conceived as *wage/price bargains*; the labor market position of unions, their institutions and structure, are no more central to wage/price restraint than the goods market position of firms, their institutions and structure.

Regarding the *market-competition amendment*, compare (7) with (12) and (13). The first two terms of (12) and (7) are identical. Thus, all the (dis)incentives for unions to exercise wage restraint discussed in 3.1 are still present, and firms share or exceed them, but the third terms of (12) and (13) add another consideration. Namely, union j's employment prospects and firm j's profits increase in group j's output, which in turn decreases in the relative price of j's products ($\partial y_j / \partial \rho_j < 0$). Thus, the more nominal-wage increases for j cause price increases for j's products that its competitors less than match (i.e. the greater $\partial \rho_j / \partial w_j$), the more union (firm) j will have incentive to exercise (demand) restraint. Therefore, group j's propensity to deliver restraint also depends on their expectations of the responsiveness of competitors' prices to its own.

Therefore, as Calmfors and Driffill (1988) argued, very competitive and very coordinated market structures both induce wage/price restraint. Under perfect competition in labor and goods markets, workers cannot garner wages exceeding the marginal value of their product, and, since competitors' prices do not respond to j's, firms cannot pass the cost increase of wage gains to consumers. Any nominal gains in excess of productivity growth (i.e. any lack of restraint) will drastically harm employment prospects and profits; indeed, atomized bargainers facing perfectly competitive labor (goods) markets who exercise insufficient restraint simply lose all their jobs (demand) with certainty. The force of this incentive makes the externality consideration that the early coordinated-bargaining literature stressed irrelevant under perfect competition. Conversely, under perfect bargaining coordination across the entire economy, all concerns about prices relative to *domestic* competitors vanish since all *domestic* wages will rise with one's own. Under these conditions, incentives to exercise restraint stem only from considerations of national competitiveness, exactly as argued in the earliest literature. Between the extremes, some mix of incentives applies. More specifically, Calmfors and Driffill (1988) argue that industry-level bargaining allows workers and firms some shelter from competitive-pricing considerations—their competitors, being within the industry, will have the same wage/price settlement—but, no industry being terribly large relative to the whole, national-level concerns will still mostly be ignored. They conclude, therefore, that intermediate levels of coordination in bargaining are inferior to both zero and full coordination, yielding the now-famous hump-shaped hypothesis.

Summarizing, modern coordinated-wage/price-bargaining theory stresses economy-wide coordination; institutions and structures of labor and goods markets are equally key. Modern theory also hypothesizes a hump-shaped relation between coordination and wage/price restraint. Zero and full coordination achieve restraint, but intermediate levels do less well. However, as with central-bank-independence theory, theoretical and empirical issues linger.

3.3.3 Coordinated Wage/Price-Bargaining: Theoretical and Empirical Problems

Three empirical controversies continue to plague theoretical development. First, much disagreement remains over the degree of coordination characterizing certain country-times. Calmfors and Driffill (1988) and Soskice (1990*a*), for example, dispute Japan and Switzerland. Second, a wider debate lingers over whether and how well union-membership structure might proxy for effective coordination.[19] A third, more theoretically central, debate involves whether the 'hump' exists, what shape it takes, and where empirically nations lie on the hump. That is, coordination and restraint may relate curvilinearly, but whether the hump rises very quickly from zero coordination and then gradually declines, vice versa, or anything in between is theoretically ambiguous. Also unknown with any precision is where countries lie on that hump whatever its true shape since, however one resolves the measurement issue, how the resulting *empirical* index places relative to *theoretical* zero and full coordination would remain unknown.[20]

Current theory insists that empirical measures consider bargaining coordination across the economy, among employers as well as unions; they cannot derive solely from the structure of union membership.[21] Moreover, estimated coordination-restraint relationships must reflect both the competition and coordination effects of labor and goods market

---

[19] On this point, compare e.g. Franzese (1994, 1996, forthcoming), Hall (1994), Garrett and Way (1995*a*, 1995*b*, 1999, 2000), Iversen (1996, 1998*a*, 1998*b*, 1998*c*, 2000), Hall and Franzese (1998), Cukierman and Lippi (1999), Franzese and Hall (2000).

[20] Zero and full coordination can be excluded though. Bargaining *ipso facto* implies some market power since perfect competition in labor and goods markets allows only market-clearing wages and prices. Conversely, any international mobility in goods or labor excludes full coordination among all relevant bargainers.

[21] Golden (1993), Golden and Wallerstein (1995), and Lange et al. (1995) add more considerations.

institutions and structures. The curvature of the relationship between effective, economy-wide coordination and wage/price restraint must be estimated directly as in Iversen (1998a), or the competition-impacting and coordination-impacting features of wage/price-bargaining institutions must be separated. I follow Layard et al. (1991) in attempting the latter, relying on union density to capture competition-reducing and a subjective index of economy-wide coordination to represent coordination-increasing aspects of bargaining organization.

Two important theoretical omissions also remain. First, as noted above, the central-bank-independence literature hinders consideration of interactions between wage/price-bargaining and monetary institutions by assuming monetary authorities control inflation directly. Coordinated-wage/price-bargaining theory is equally ill positioned to consider such interactions because it has generally assumed passive or accommodating monetary policy, yet autonomous and conservative central banks would certainly react to inflationary wage/price settlements. As stressed in central-bank-independence theory, bargainers must consider this reaction in their bargaining; wage/price-bargaining and monetary policy interact, so theory must consider them jointly. Second, work in the bargaining tradition has also generally assumed homogeneous unions and firms, yet traded-sector bargainers have different interests, both in general and vis-à-vis monetary policy, than do sheltered- (i.e. private-non-traded-) and especially public-sector bargainers. I turn now to a synthesis addressing these theoretical holes and the implied institutional-structural interactions.

3.4 Theoretical Synthesis and Extension

Summarizing, the central-bank literature predicts centrally that independence produces low inflation without real costs on average. This prediction has been extensively considered empirically with apparently favorable results. However, the theory actually predicts considerably more, implicitly describing how much independence reduces inflation under various political, economic, institutional, and structural conditions. These predictions have gone virtually unexplored theoretically and empirically. Moreover, the actions and pronouncements of monetary authorities contradict these more precise predictions. Meanwhile, wage/price-bargaining theory predicts centrally that coordination induces nominal and real wage restraint, and thereby helps reduce both unemployment and inflation. This too has been subjected to extensive empirical analysis. Two recent theoretical amendments may have expanded

our understanding but have yet to overcome several empirical controversies. However, this literature has evolved largely without considering
either possible monetary policy reactions to wage/price settlements or
the sectorally determined interests of different types of bargainers.

Both lines of research provided indubitably valuable insights, mini-
mally underscoring the institutional characteristics of monetary policy-
makers and wage/price-bargainers as key variables in the politico-
economic management of the macroeconomy, yet the incompatibility of
their underlying assumptions hinders combination of their insights. On
one hand, central-bank theory has typically assumed banks directly
control inflation and that bargainers set wage growth to equal expected
money growth plus their target real wage, which is assumed independent of labor and goods market structures. However, if wages and prices
are bargained, inflation is determined by the settlement of these bargains;
monetary policy matters because it affects these settlements. That distinction is important. Moreover, wage/price-bargaining implies market
power, leaving the possibility that workers (employers) may desire and
obtain different wages (prices) depending on expected monetary reactions and their institutional and sectoral structure. On the other hand,
coordinated-bargaining theory typically (implicitly) assumed that monetary policy does not respond to wage/price bargains,[22] yet monetary
policy, whoever controls it, aims to manage inflation, and so must respond to wage/price settlements. Any proposed synthesis, then, must
begin by redressing these contradictions.

3.4.1 A Proposed Neoclassical Synthesis

One possible redress, call it a *neoclassical synthesis*, I began to describe
above. Cukierman (1992) notes that, in the neoclassical model, the incentive to create surprise inflation only exists and thus there is an inflationary bias to discretionary monetary policy only if real wages are
excessive, possibly due to the monopoly power of unions.[23] The advance
is to model the natural rate of employment (N_n) as decreasing in real
wage excessiveness (ω) and that excessiveness increasing in *union power*

---

[22] Scharpf's (1984, 1987, 1991) work is exceptional (both senses), foreshadowing the
synthesis emerging from the references in n. 1 from which this current offering builds.
[23] Specifically: 'employment [must be] a decreasing function of the real wage rate . . .
[i.e.] . . . own effects [must] dominate cross-effects in labor demands or . . . the supply of
labor in the competitive segment of the labor market [must be] relatively irresponsive to
the real wage rate, or . . . both conditions [must] hold' (p. 41). If any unemployment is
involuntary, then labor supply is effectively in excess and therefore wage inelastic, so
Cukierman's conditions will hold.

(*UP*). That is, unions with some monopoly power target real wages exceeding market clearing, thus creating incentives for 'surprise' inflation. Thus, under discretion, inflation increases in union power because, by (3), $\pi_d{}^*$ is increasing in (N^*-N_n), and now N_n is decreasing in ω, which finally is increasing in *UP*.

We could simply add to this the argument that coordination in bargaining, as opposed to *union power*, produces wage/price restraint rather than excessive real wages. Thus, the natural rate (N_n) increases in coordination and decreases in union power (without coordination):

$$N_n = N_n(\omega(UP, CWB), \cdot) \ \ with \ \ \frac{\partial N_n}{\partial \omega} < 0, \ \frac{\partial \omega}{\partial UP} > 0, \ \frac{\partial \omega}{\partial CWB} < 0 \qquad (14)$$

This neoclassical additive combination of the two arguments would conclude that:

(*a*) Unemployment is decreasing in coordination,
(*b*) Inflation is decreasing in independence, but less so the higher is coordination,
(*c*) Inflation is decreasing in coordination, but less so the higher is independence, and
(*d*) Unemployment is unaffected on average by independence.

The weighted average in (4) implies the interactive hypotheses (*b*) and (*c*) as follows. *Discretionary* inflation rises as the natural rate of employment (N_n) falls, implying independence lowers inflation less the higher is N_n. The natural rate in turn increases with coordination. Thus independence lowers inflation less the greater is coordination. Conversely, coordination raises the natural rate, which lowers discretionary inflation, implying that coordination lowers inflation but less so the less discretionary is inflation (i.e. the higher is independence).

3.4.2 A Fuller Synthesis

The neoclassical synthesis retains the real/nominal divide by assuming that monetary policy directly controls inflation and that unions set wages in real levels, with expected inflation simply added thereafter, in a manner that does not depend on the monetary stance regardless of the bargainers' institutional or sectoral structure. However, wage/price-bargaining with market power in labor and goods markets cannot be so compartmentalized. These bargains set nominal wages *and prices*, leaving the monetary authority discretion over how monetary policy will react to these settlements rather than direct control over inflation.[24] Moreover, unions and firms may respond to expected monetary reactions differently depending on their institutional and structural configuration. The neoclassical synthesis is therefore insufficient.

To see how, return to the heuristic model of wage/price-bargaining, but now allow the monetary authority to respond to wage/price settlements.[25] As before, analyzing the marginal values to unions (firms) of getting (ceding) nominal wage hikes ($\partial V_j^u / \partial w_j$, $\partial V_j^e / \partial w_j$) will suffice:

$$\frac{\partial V_j^u}{\partial w_j} = V_1^u \left(1 - \frac{\partial \pi}{\partial w_j} - \frac{\partial \pi}{\partial m} \cdot \frac{\partial m}{\partial w_j} \right)$$

$$+ V_2^u \left(\frac{\partial \varepsilon_j}{\partial y_j} \cdot \frac{\partial y_j}{\partial y} \right) \cdot \left(\frac{\partial y}{\partial w_j} + \frac{\partial y}{\partial m} \cdot \frac{\partial m}{\partial w_j} \right)$$

$$+ V_2^u \left(\frac{\partial \varepsilon_j}{\partial y_j} \cdot \frac{\partial y_j}{\partial \rho_j} \right) \cdot \left(1 - \frac{\partial \pi_{i(j)}}{\partial w_j} - \frac{\partial \pi_{i(j)}}{\partial m} \cdot \frac{\partial m}{\partial w_j} \right) \tag{15}$$

$$\frac{\partial V_j^e}{\partial w_j} = V_2^e \cdot \frac{\partial y_j}{\partial y} \cdot \left(\frac{\partial y}{\partial w_j} + \frac{\partial y}{\partial m} \cdot \frac{\partial m}{\partial w_j} \right)$$

$$+ V_2^e \cdot \frac{\partial y_j}{\partial \rho_j} \cdot \left(1 - \frac{\partial \pi_{i(j)}}{\partial w_j} - \frac{\partial \pi_{i(j)}}{\partial m} \cdot \frac{\partial m}{\partial w_j} \right) \tag{16}$$

The new considerations here are the terms involving $\partial m / \partial w_j$, which are how the jth bargaining unit expects the money supply to respond to *its* settlement. Call this the *monetary threat*. That is, the central bank announces that it will not accommodate excessive *aggregate* settlements. If the bank can make that threat sufficiently large and credible for bargaining unit j's expected cost of getting (ceding) a nominal wage gain to outweigh benefits, j will refrain from inflationary settlements and the threat need not be enacted. The neoclassical synthesis ends there: a credible enough bank, wielding a big enough threat, achieves low inflation at no average cost.

Note, though, that central banks cannot threaten to respond to each individual settlement differently. With only one money, monetary policy

---

[24] Cukierman et al. (1992) implicitly recognize this, positing (not deriving from explicit bargaining) price inflation as determined jointly by money and nominal-wage growth.

[25] For expositional simplicity, I now assume prices are fixed mark-ups on wages, thus reducing the variables being bargained to the nominal wage growth rate, w_j.

can respond only to aggregates, implying that the perceived monetary threat, $\partial m / \partial w_j$, involves three substantive parts: the magnitude of the central bank's threatened response to aggregate wage growth, $\partial m / \partial w$, that threat's credibility, c, and the degree to which bargaining unit j expects its settlement to affect the aggregate, $\partial w / \partial w_j$:

$$\frac{\partial m}{\partial w_j} \equiv \frac{\partial m}{\partial w} \cdot c \cdot \frac{\partial w}{\partial w_j} \tag{17}$$

Obviously, central-bank independence increases threat credibility, c, but it also increases the maximum acceptable employment/inflation trade-off since *independent* means *conservative* and autonomous. Higher central-bank independence thus shifts the expectations-augmented Phillips Curve inward (credibility) but also increases the slope at which the monetary authority's indifference curve is tangent to the Phillips Curve (conservatism). In other words, independent banks, by virtue of their greater credibility, can trade inflation for employment at better rates than could discretionary (i.e. political) authorities; but such banks will also accept higher unemployment for any given inflation rate than a government would if trades must be made.

The questions, therefore, are whether trades must be made, i.e., whether banks must enact monetary threats, and, if so, what the likely (real) effects are. The answers hinge critically on the institutional and sectoral structure of wage/price-bargaining. Recall that $\partial w / \partial w_j$ increases in bargaining coordination. When coordination is nearly full, all wages and prices are effectively set in the central or lead bargain ($\partial w / \partial w_j \approx 1$), so all of the bank's threat is directly perceived by that one bargaining unit. Contrarily, when coordination is nearly nil, unions and firms do not perceive other wages to rise with their own ($\partial w / \partial w_j \approx 0$), so atomistic bargaining units directly perceive little. Therefore, when coordination is very low, the threat, $\partial m / \partial w$, times its credibility, c, must be extremely high to restrain bargainers without being enacted. In fact, the threat would have to be *incredibly* large if coordination was not moderately high.

For example, suppose some professors have some market power and are bargaining with their university, which also has some market power. By their market power, the professors can demand excessive wages (beyond their productivity growth), and, by its own, the university can cede them if it must. The settlement is likely to be inflationary. An independent central bank could threaten to respond to *aggregate* inflationary signs with monetary contraction, but this academic unit is so small relative to the aggregate that from their perspective, however credible the threat, either the bank will contract the money supply or it will not and nothing they do will alter that. Any aggregate threat would have to be catastrophically large for such atomistic bargainers to feel it sufficiently to restrain their settlement appreciably, but catastrophic threats are (*trembling-hand*) *incredible*. No democratic government would idly watch its bank inflict catastrophe.

More generally, settlements become increasingly inflationary as market power rises (absent bargaining coordination). To restrain inflation, the monetary authority must create real contraction by enacting its threat, thereby raising unemployment (lowering output), thus making the next bargain less inflationary by reducing bargainers' market power and shifting power within bargains toward employers. Equilibrium obtains when bargainers wish nominal increases the bank will tolerate. This explains central bankers' concerns over *incipient inflationary pressures*. A bargaining perspective predicts more-excessive settlements as market power rises, and market power in labor and goods markets increases in booms and decreases in recessions. Booms (recessions) also raise (lower) unions' bargaining power relative to firms. Thus, incipient inflationary pressures are located in wage/price-bargaining, and banks defuse them by preventing the real economy from becoming 'too strong'. The final step in the argument is that how strong the real economy may become before triggering incipient inflationary pressures depends on the institutional and structural configuration of the political economy as I demonstrate below.

With perfect credibility ($c = 1$) and no uncertainty, monetary threats need never be enacted (so the neoclassical conclusions will hold), but, absent full credibility or certainty, threats must periodically be enacted to work. Thus, the neoclassical conclusion that greater *credibility* is beneficial remains intact because credibility helps reduce size or frequency of threat enactment. However, in practice, central-bank independence brings both credibility and conservatism. In (17), the former corresponds to higher c, which is unambiguously beneficial, the latter to greater willingness to increase the magnitude of the threat ($\partial m/\partial w$) at any given credibility level. With periodic threat enactment, the latter is ambiguous, implying the usual Keynes/Phillips trade-off between inflation and unemployment.[26]

The next logical question regards the conditions under which this unavoidable trade-off is more or less costly. Simply and abstractly put:

---

[26] One neglected line of research, then, is the degree to which the concepts *monetary conservatism* and *monetary credibility* are theoretically and practically separable.

anything that lowers (raises) the enacted threat required to restrain bargainers improves (worsens) the trade-off. As just noted, credibility improves the trade-off, as the central bank literature would suggest, but (17) also reveals that greater bargaining coordination does also by increasing $\partial w / \partial w_j$. Coordinated bargainers perceive monetary threats more directly than do fragmented bargainers, so threats can be smaller/ less frequently enacted when coordination is high than they must be when it is low. This explains the difference between the Bundesbank's and the Fed's behavior. The Bundesbank addresses its monetary pronouncements to wage/price bargainers because Germany's labor and product market actors have the institutionally and structurally determined incentives and *strategic capacity* (Iversen's apt phrase) to respond. The Fed has no such actors to threaten.

Further implications follow from the differential impact of monetary constriction, which raises interest rates and causes exchange appreciation, across various economic sectors. Refer to (15) and (16). Higher interest rates reduce investment and so hurt employers and workers in sectors dependent on domestic demand, i.e. all *private* sectors ($\partial y / \partial m < 0$, $\partial y_j / \partial y > 0$ ∀ private sector j). Public-sector workers, contrarily, are unharmed or even benefit by this because public employment is counter- or a-cyclical ($\partial y_j / \partial y \leq 0$ ∀ public sector j). The investment-reducing effect of enacted threats therefore hurts private- more than public-sector actors, so private-sector bargainers will be more responsive to monetary threats. Thus, the aggregate economy must suffer disproportionately less (more) when the bank must restrain private- (public-)sector actors.

The exchange-rate appreciation caused by enacted threats has three impacts. First, appreciation reduces total demand for domestically produced goods and so, again, harms all sectors dependent on private-sector demand while the public sector remains relatively unharmed or benefits. Second, appreciation raises the price of tradables relative to nontradables and so is especially painful to bargaining units competing in tradables ($\partial p_{i(j)} / \partial m < 0$ ∀ traded sector j). Finally, exchange appreciation lowers import prices thus reducing the consumption-price index. By raising consumption real wages, this actually works against enforcing restraint from unions,[27] but I suspect this last effect is dominated by the others. Note, though, that it implies again that employer-led coordination is more conducive than labor-led coordination to wage/price restraint.

Adding all of these considerations, monetary-threat enactment would be most costly to bargainers in the private and especially the private-

---

[27] Employers *qua* employers are unaffected, but, of course, they benefit as consumers.

traded sector and least costly to bargainers in the (non-competing) public sector. Accordingly, traded-sector bargainers will be most responsive to monetary threats and public-sector actors least responsive, so the aggregate economy must suffer less to restrain trade-sector-led than public-sector-led wage/price-bargaining. Moreover, coordinated wage/price-bargainers are more responsive to monetary threats, and, finally, all bargainers are more responsive the greater the credibility of the monetary authority. Thus, important institutional complementarities operate at the macroeconomic level: *central-bank independence reduces inflation most efficiently (i.e. at least real cost) in political economies characterized by traded-sector-led coordinated wage/price-bargaining and least efficiently in those characterized by uncoordinated bargaining or public-sector-led coordinated bargaining.*

A related set of interactions operates between bargaining coordination and sectoral structure. Public-sector bargainers have little incentive to exercise restraint or to respond to monetary threats appropriately; contrarily, traded-sector bargainers are especially disposed to exercise restraint and to respond to monetary threats appropriately. Thus, coordinated bargaining operates differently depending on the sectoral composition of the economy and the way it is institutionalized in wage-price bargaining. Coordination is most effective, both *per se* and in its interaction with monetary authorities, when traded-sector actors dominate bargaining and public-sector actors follow. Provided the traded sector continues to dominate, coordination will be more beneficial the larger the public sector 'brought into line'. Conversely, if public sectors dominate, coordination is less efficient *per se* and in interaction with monetary authorities; public-sector-led coordination may even be costly since a *lack* of restraint may be coordinated across bargains. Provided the public sector leads, coordination will be less beneficial (more costly) the larger the traded sector because the traded sector will most bear the costs of monetary authorities' attempts to restrain public-sector bargainers. In both cases, sheltered sectors are intermediate.

In sum, then, the proposed synthesis and extension implies:

(*a*1) *Central-bank independence has interactive real effects:* it is less costly (or more beneficial) when bargaining is coordinated and traded-sector-led and more costly when bargaining is uncoordinated or coordinated but public-sector-led.

(*a*2) *Central-bank independence has interactive nominal effects:* it reduces inflation less when bargaining is coordinated and traded-sector-led and more when bargaining is uncoordinated or coordinated and public-sector-led.

(b1) *Coordinated wage/price-bargaining has interactive real effects:* when traded-sector-led, it is more beneficial the higher central-bank independence; when public-sector-led, it is less beneficial (or more costly) the higher central-bank independence.

(b2) *Coordinated wage/price-bargaining has interactive nominal effects:* it reduces inflation more when traded-sector-led and less (possibly increasing it) when public-sector-led. Greater central-bank independence dampens these effects.

(c) *Sectoral structure has interactive real and nominal effects:* Traded-sector dominance enhances the efficacy of coordinated bargaining in delivering wage/price restraint and so has more beneficial real effects the higher coordination and central-bank independence and larger (smaller) beneficial inflation effects the higher coordination (central-bank independence). Provided the traded sector continues to dominate, these effects are magnified by larger public sectors. Public-sector (sheltered-sector) dominance works oppositely (intermediately).

Broadly, this theoretical synthesis and extension uncovered a highly interactive political economy; the effect of any single institutional or structural feature on both real and nominal macroeconomic outcomes depends on the wider configuration of other institutions and structures present. More specifically, central-bank independence and coordinated wage/price-bargaining with traded-dominating public sectors are generally complements in producing beneficial real outcomes—they tend to augment each other's efficacy in, e.g., reducing unemployment—and substitutes in producing beneficial nominal outcomes—either can suffice to reduce inflation.[28]

---

[28] The difference with the neoclassical synthesis offered above is primarily (a1) that central-bank independence has real effects (on average). These arguments extend and modify Franzese (1994, 1996) by partitioning the monetary threat in (17), addressing the difference between sectoral size and sectoral dominance, and more directly considering the nominal implications and the interaction of wage/price-bargaining institutions with sectoral structure. They extend and modify Hall and Franzese (1998) and Franzese and Hall (2000) in these ways and by considering sectoral structure. Cukierman and Lippi (1999) and Velasco and Guzzo (1999) differ in that wage-bargainers may also dislike inflation *per se*. They reach some different substantive conclusions, but share core real-side implications. Iversen (1996, 1998a, 1998b, 1998c, 2000) argues differently that independence has real benefits when *centralization* (not coordination) is intermediate, costs when centralization is high, and little effect when bargaining is decentralized. The differences arise because his wage-bargainers also have a preference for wage equality and because he incorporates the hump-shaped hypothesis into the theoretical analysis differently. A resolution of these differences is offered below. Franzese (2000, forthcoming) elaborates on this resolution; the former also offers a fuller review of this burgeoning literature (see n. 1).

3.5 Empirical Evidence

I offer first a brief review of evidence amassing in favor of existent syntheses and extensions and then some new evidence that, in addressing the present theory, extends and modifies previous offerings and may resolve one emerging controversy.

3.5.1 A Brief Review of Previous Evidence

The empirical trail begins with Hall (1994) who, charting post-war average inflation and unemployment by wage/price-bargaining coordination and central-bank independence, noted an interactive pattern. Hall and Franzese (1998) summarize that pattern tabularly, showing post-war average (a) inflation declines in independence and in coordination, (b) unemployment declines in coordination, but that (c) the unemployment costs of independence (benefits of coordination) decrease as coordination (increase as independence) increases—real-outcome *complementarity*—and (d) the inflation benefits of independence and coordination each decrease as the other increases—nominal-outcome *substitutability*. Their regression analyses employing post-war average, decade frequency, and annual data in eighteen OECD countries support these conclusions.

Using decade frequency data in twenty-one OECD countries, Franzese (1994, 1996) tests several hypotheses regarding interactive real effects of independence, coordination, and sectoral structure. Beyond interactions of independence and coordination, which yielded substantively congruent and statistically stronger results than Hall and Franzese (1998), these models include traded- and public-sector employment shares and their interactions with independence. Results strongly supported that public-sector employment share and independence interact detrimentally in unemployment regulation. When independence is high, increasing public-sector employment share increases unemployment whereas, when it is low, increasing public-sector employment share lowers unemployment. That traded-sector employment share improves unemployment outcomes and more so the greater independence was also supported, though less strongly.

Garrett and Way (1995a) criticize Hall (1994) and Franzese (1994) for their subjective coordination indices. Replacing those indices with 'union strength' (union concentration plus wage-bargaining coverage)—a procedure argued against here, following Swenson (1989, 1991) and Soskice (1990a)—they nonetheless find similar institutional interactions. Using post-war quinquennial data in thirteen OECD countries, they conclude central-bank independence and union strength interact beneficially in regulating inflation, unemployment, and real growth. Garrett and Way (1995*b*, 1999, 2000) provide more-direct evidence of the adverse effect of public-sector employment share on coordinated bargainers' ability to deliver wage/price restraint. They estimate, in the same sample, a curvilinear relation between union strength and unemployment, allowing 'public-sector strength' (public-sector share of total union membership) to alter that relation. They found a hump-shaped relation between union strength and unemployment when public-sector strength is low (low and high union strength producing low unemployment) that becomes increasingly linear-positive as public-sector union-membership share rises (low (high) public-sector-led union strength producing low (high) unemployment).

Iversen (1996, 1998*a*, 1998*b*, 1998*c*, 2000) provides further evidence of real effects of monetary conservatism that depend on wage/price-bargaining institutions and vice versa, but his findings differ importantly. He argues that monetary conservatism reduces unemployment when wage-bargaining *concentration*—not coordination—is intermediate and increases (has little effect on) unemployment when it is high (low). His findings from quinquennial data in fifteen OECD countries 1973–93 support these predictions. The sample and the measure of bargaining *concentration* differ from the rest, the latter notably regarding placement of Japan and Switzerland, which reflects the empirical controversy between Calmfors and Driffill (1988) and Soskice (1990*a*). The measure of monetary conservatism and credibility also differs, using actual exchange-rate movements additionally to an independence index. These differences are still disturbing, though, because Iversen finds monetary conservatism to have unemployment *benefits* over most of the sample range and unemployment *costs* in the most concentrated-bargaining countries: almost opposite previous results. I suggest below that the present synthesis and extension resolves the apparent controversy, but, first, I emphasize the agreement across all these studies.[29]

First, all agree that wage/price-bargaining and monetary policy-making institutions interact in determining *both* real and nominal outcomes. The classical divide between the real and nominal economy was misleading, so institutional analysis must consider, as far as possible, the functioning of *networks* of institutions since the effects of any particular institution depend on the others operating in that environment. Second, all agree that central-bank independence operates more efficiently at

---

[29] Cukierman and Lippi (1999) also share these agreements. See Franzese (2000) for elaboration and a more complete review.

intermediate than at low coordination. They disagree more regarding high coordination. Third, the nominal effects of central-bank independence and bargaining coordination, and of their interaction to the degree it has been explored, are broadly agreed.[30]

3.5.2 Empirical Evidence on this Theoretical Synthesis and Extension

Empirical evaluation of theory involves determining the relevant sample, measuring the variables identified (plus controls), specifying the model suggested by theory, estimating that model, and inferring from the results to the theory. First, regarding sample selection, all these arguments presuppose wage/price-bargaining in relatively liberal market economies and that central banks can attain legal autonomy from current governments, if only partially, and conduct appreciably distinct national monetary policy. These considerations suggest restricting the sample to larger, established capitalist democracies. I count twenty-one such countries: USA, Japan, Germany, France, Italy, UK, Canada, Austria, Belgium, Denmark, Finland, Greece, Ireland, the Netherlands, Norway, Portugal, Spain,[31] Sweden, Switzerland, Australia, and New Zealand. Further, I exclude the Bretton Woods fixed-exchange-rate era as it limited national monetary autonomy and to increase comparability with Iversen (1996, 1998a, 1998b, 1998c, 2000). Wage/price-bargaining occurs at most annually, so annual data in these twenty-one countries 1974–90 comprise the sample.

Second, regarding variable measurement, the theory emphasizes three independent variables—central-bank independence, wage/price-bargaining coordination, and sectoral structure—and two dependent variables—inflation and unemployment. I measure inflation (π) by consumer-price inflation (IMF and OECD sources).[32] Unemployment (U) are internationally comparable figures (OECD sources). Central-bank independence (I) is indexed 0–1, averaging five commonly used indices.[33] Wage/price-bargaining coordination (C) is indexed subjectively

---

[30] As shown above, even the neoclassical synthesis agrees on the last point. See also Franzese (2000).

[31] Dummy variables for Greece, Portugal, and Spain, and one for authoritarian periods therein included in both equations, acknowledging those country-years' ambiguous sample membership.

[32] *IMF sources* = IMF IFS CD-ROM 6/96. *OECD sources* = *OECD Economic Outlook* 61 and Historical Supplement diskettes, and *OECD Main Accounts II*, Detailed Tables diskettes.

[33] Cukierman's (1992) LVAU and QVAU; Grilli et al.'s (1991) EC and POL; Bade and Parkin's (1982) CBI. Averaging expands coverage and, under plausible assumptions, reduces measurement-error variance.

as in Hall and Franzese (1998) and valued (0, 0.25, 0.5, 0.75, 1). C builds from Soskice's (1990) EWC, Layard et al.'s (1991) BO and LO, and secondary sources, and is extended here, using Layard et al. (1991), to Greece (0), Portugal (0.25), and Spain (0). C is intended to reflect economy-wide coordination, whether employer- or labor-led, as theory has suggested. Regarding sectoral structure, the theory distinguishes public, sheltered, and traded sectors. The *desired* data are the proportions of employment covered by wage/price-bargaining in sectors whose products respectively do not compete in the market, do not compete with foreign products, and compete with foreign products. The *available* data are government employment and employment by single-digit ISIC sectors[34] as shares of total employment (OECD sources). Since the theory predicts oppositely for traded and public sectors with sheltered sector intermediate, government employment (G) divided by manufacturing employment (M) may serve as a proxy for public-relative-to-traded sectoral-structure (S).[35] Appendix 1 details the controls employed; note that union density is included (union members' share of total employment) as section 3.3 suggested. I indicate these controls below by $\alpha' X_1 + \gamma' X_2$ where the first term represents the constant, time-serial controls, dummies for non-democratic country-times, and their coefficients, and the second represents the other, more substantive, controls and their coefficients.

Third, regarding model specification, (4) showed inflation to be a weighted average of what it would be if the political authority fully controlled monetary policy, π_a^*, and if a fully autonomous and conservative central bank controlled inflation, π_c^*, with the weight on the latter given by the degree of central-bank independence. The present theory emphasizes wage/price-bargaining coordination, sectoral structure, and their interaction among potential determinants of discretionary inflation, π_d^*, and of unemployment, U, though a weighted average form is not expected on the real side. Finally, in both cases, the impact of sectoral structure (G/M) should differ according to whether the public (numerator) or the traded (denominator) sector dominates. That is, the impact

---

[34] Agriculture, extraction, construction, manufacturing, utilities, exchange, transport-shipping-communications, finance, other services, other.

[35] 'Government employees' may contain workers who do not bargain wages, and some public-sector workers as defined theoretically will not be counted in 'government employment' as measured. Most manufacturing is traded and conducts wage/price-bargaining, but manufacturing certainly omits many other traded sectors. Plus, manufacturing is likely more unionized than most sectors, and government employees are variably unionized and able to bargain across countries, typically more unionized and able to bargain in countries with large public sectors than small. All these considerations may confound G/M as a

of G/M should be non-linear in a manner most easily enabled by entering G/M and $(G/M)^2$ in the regressions. The specifications matching the theory are therefore:

$$\pi = \alpha'_{\pi} X_1 + (1 + \beta_{i,2} I) \cdot \gamma'_{\pi} X_2 + \beta_{i,1} I + (1 + \beta_{i,2} I) \cdot$$

$$[\beta_c C + \beta_{s,1} S + \beta_{s,2} S^2 + \beta_{cs,1} C \cdot S + \beta_{cs,2} C \cdot S^2] + \varepsilon_{\pi} \qquad (18)$$

$$U = \alpha'_u X_1 + \gamma'_u X_2 + \theta_i I + \theta_c C + \theta_{s,1} S + \theta_{s,2} S^2 + \theta_{ic} I \cdot C + \theta_{is,1} I \cdot S$$

$$+ \theta_{is,2} I \cdot S^2 + \theta_{cs,1} C \cdot S + \theta_{cs,2} C \cdot S^2 + \theta_{ics,1} I \cdot C \cdot S + \theta_{ics,2} I \cdot C \cdot S^2 + \varepsilon_u \qquad (19)$$

The expression inside square brackets in (18) reflects the interaction of bargaining coordination with sectoral structure in determining discretionary inflation. The term $(1 + \beta_{i2} I)$, which multiplies that and the controls, reflects the prediction that central-bank independence lowers inflation from discretionary levels toward the bank's target level as independence increases. If this is true, we should estimate $\beta_{i2} < 0$ (see Franzese 1999*a*, 1999*b*).

The modeled effects of central-bank independence, wage/price-bargaining coordination, and sectoral structure on inflation are all interactive. For example, the impact of independence on inflation ($\partial \pi / \partial I$) is:

$$\frac{\partial \pi}{\partial I} = \beta_{i,1} + \beta_{i,2} \cdot \gamma'_{\pi} X_2 +$$

$$\beta_{i,2} \cdot [\beta_c C + \beta_{s,1} S + \beta_{s,2} S^2 + \beta_{cs,1} C \cdot S + \beta_{cs,2} C \cdot S^2] \qquad (20)$$

We expect this to be generally negative, but its magnitude will depend on the degree of bargaining coordination and the sectoral structure.[36] The modeled effect of wage/price-bargaining coordination on inflation ($\partial \pi / \partial C$) is:

$$\frac{\partial \pi}{\partial C} = \beta_{i,2} \cdot I \cdot [\beta_c + \beta_{cs,1} S + \beta_{cs,2} S^2] \qquad (21)$$

We expect this to be generally negative also, but the magnitude will depend on the degree of central-bank independence and the sectoral

---

measure of public-relative-to-traded-sector structure as theoretically defined, but the proxy seems the best possible at this time.

[36] The effect also depends on all X_2 given the weighted-average form in (4); see Franzese (1999*a*, 1999*b*). Franzese et al. (1999) offer guidance for interpreting interactive terms in regression.

structure. Coordination may even increase inflation if public-sector employment sufficiently dominates traded (i.e. if S is high enough). Finally, the modeled effect of sectoral structure on inflation, specifically of an increase in government-relative-to-manufacturing employment ($S \equiv G/M$), is:

$$\frac{\partial \pi}{\partial S} = \beta_{i,2} \cdot I \cdot [\beta_{s,1} + 2\beta_{s,2}S + \beta_{cs,1}C + 2\beta_{cs,2}C \cdot S] \tag{22}$$

which analogously depends on C and I and also on the level of S itself since sectoral structure has non-linear effects. We expect increases in S generally to increase inflation, especially when G is large relative to M, though this will depend on degrees of independence and coordination.

Likewise, (19) reflects our contention that the unemployment effects of bargaining coordination, central-bank independence, and sectoral structure are interactive. The modeled effect of independence on unemployment ($\partial U / \partial I$) is:

$$\frac{\partial U}{\partial I} = \theta_i + \theta_{ic}C + \theta_{is,1}S + \theta_{is,2}S^2 + \theta_{ics,1}C \cdot S + \theta_{ics,2}C \cdot S^2 \tag{23}$$

which depends on bargaining coordination and sectoral structure. The effect may be positive or negative since independence has both conservatism and credibility effects, but it should generally be decreasing as coordination rises when the traded sector dominates (low S) and generally be increasing as coordination rises when the public sector dominates (high S). Symmetrically, the modeled effect of bargaining coordination on unemployment ($\partial U / \partial C$) is:

$$\frac{\partial U}{\partial C} = \theta_c + \theta_{ic}I + \theta_{cs,1}S + \theta_{cs,2}S^2 + \theta_{ics,1}I \cdot S + \theta_{ics,2}I \cdot S^2 \tag{24}$$

which should generally be negative but depends on I and S, and may even become positive for large enough public-relative-to-traded sectors and high enough central-bank independence. Finally, the modeled effect of sectoral structure on unemployment ($\partial U / \partial S$) depends on the degrees of independence and coordination and upon its own level as follows:

$$\frac{\partial U}{\partial S} = \theta_{s,1} + 2\theta_{s,2}S + \theta_{is,1}I + 2\theta_{is,2}I \cdot S + \theta_{cs,1}C + 2\theta_{cs,2}C \cdot S$$

$$+ \theta_{ics,1}I \cdot C + 2\theta_{ics,2}I \cdot C \cdot S \tag{25}$$

We expect a positive effect when independence, coordination, and public-relative-to-traded sector (S) are large because under these conditions public sectors are large in the economy and dominate any coordinated bargains, and central banks react with costly real consequences. Conversely, when the public sector is not so large as to dominate, increases in G/M actually increase the value of coordination and independence, and so (25) could be negative at lower S.

Finally, regarding model estimation and inference, (18) and (19) were both estimated by least squares with robust standard errors.[37] Table 3.1 summarizes the inflation-equation estimation. The central result is clear: central-bank independence, bargaining coordination, and sectoral structure interact in determining inflation. That central-bank independence interacts with bargaining coordination and sectoral structure (and the controls, X_2) to determine inflation is reflected in the coefficient b_{i2} being negative and highly statistically significant.[38] Similarly the interaction of bargaining coordination and sectoral structure is strongly supported by the estimated coefficients b_{cs} and b_{cs2} (joint significance, $p \approx .0001$).[39] One cannot read the substantive meaning of these statistically significant results from the coefficient estimates directly or simply because the impact of each factor depends on many other institutional and structural variables as shown in (20)–(22). I defer substantive discussion until after reporting the unemployment results to consider the real and nominal effects together.

Central-bank independence, bargaining coordination, and sectoral structure equally clearly interact in determining unemployment. The joint significance of coefficients (e)–(k) firmly establishes the relevant interactions: $p \approx .02$. That central-bank independence has real effects, implying that the neoclassical synthesis is insufficient, is established by the joint significance of coefficients (b), (e)–(g), and (j)–(k) (i.e. those on variables involving I): $p \approx .003$. The analogous tests for bargaining coordination and sectoral structure also strongly support the broad claim of

---

[37] Specifically, I employ weighted (W) two-stage (2S) least squares (LS). WLS is necessary because high unemployment and inflation both exhibited greater (stochastic) variance than low. The weights are $1/(1 + Y)^5$, with Y the dependent variable. I use 2SLS to mitigate endogeneity concerns regarding contemporaneously measured independent variables; instruments are simply the one-year lag of all variables. White's robust standard errors are reported since scale is unlikely to be the only source of heteroskedasticity. The inflation equation is estimated by non-linear (N) W2SLS since its weighted-average (convex-combinatorial) form is not linear. The reported results are robust across applications of any subset combination of these techniques.

[38] Indeed, b_{i2} is not unreasonably far from the -1 one would expect if the functional form of (18), its variables, and their measurement were all exact.

[39] Wald F-tests, more appropriate with robust standard errors, reported here.

TABLE 3.1 Estimation results for the inflation equation (18)

Coefficient (associated variable)	Estimated coefficient	Standard error	t-statistic	Two-sided p-level
$b_c(C)$	−28.150	5.818	−4.838	0.000
$b_s(S)$	−34.834	9.968	−3.495	0.001
$b_{s2}(S^2)$	+16.000	5.301	3.018	0.003
$b_{cs}(C \cdot S)$	+43.699	11.734	3.724	0.000
$b_{cs2}(C \cdot S^2)$	−19.267	5.955	−3.235	0.001
$b_{i1}(I)$	−8.954	11.748	−0.762	0.447
$b_{i2}(I(\cdot [\bullet]))$	−0.691	0.157	−4.413	0.000

Summary statistics: number of observations 347; degrees of freedom 323; R-squared 0.523; standard error of regression 1.960; adjusted R-squared 0.489; Durbin−Watson stat. 1.976.

Notes: Non-germane results suppressed to conserve space. Complete results available at http://www-personal.umich.edu/~franzese. Estimation by weighted, two-stage, non-linear least squares with White's robust standard errors (see n. 36).

institutional and structural interaction. Again the substantive meaning of these statistically significant coefficients is not clear from the coefficients in Table 3.2 alone because the effects of independence, coordination, and sectoral structure on unemployment are interactive (as shown in equations (23)−(25)).

The substantive import of these results is revealed by the estimated impact of each variable over a relevant sample range of the other variables. I covers 0.15−0.95 in the sample; C covers 0−1; and most $S \equiv G/M$ observations lie between 0.25 and 1.25). Consider, for example, the estimated inflation-impact of a 0.1 increase in the central-bank-independence index (about the spacing in the ascending sequence Sweden−Italy−Ireland−the Netherlands−Austria−USA−Switzerland−Germany). That effect depends on the degree of bargaining coordination and on the sectoral structure within which such bargaining occurs. Setting all other variables to their means, our estimates indicate that the effect is as shown in Table 3.3.

All theory suggests central-bank independence will generally lower inflation. Every entry but the extreme top right—and the sample has no observations with those characteristics—is indeed negative. The syntheses implied further that independence should lower inflation less when the institutional and sectoral structure of wage/price-bargaining is anti-inflationary anyway and more when the institutional and sectoral structure is less anti-inflationary itself. That is, the issue is how much the central bank must do by itself (i.e. monetarily) to constrain inflation since

TABLE 3.2 Estimation results for the unemployment equation (19)

Coefficient (*associated variable*)	Estimated coefficient	Standard error	t-statistic	Two-sided p-level
(a) C	+11.826	3.847	3.074	0.002
(b) I	+20.314	6.885	2.951	0.003
(c) S	+14.921	7.132	2.092	0.037
(d) S^2	−4.924	4.372	−1.126	0.261
(e) I·C	−29.423	9.204	−3.197	0.002
(f) I·S	−35.596	15.317	−2.324	0.021
(g) I·S^2	+14.163	8.753	1.618	0.107
(h) C·S	−22.523	8.465	−2.661	0.008
(i) C·S^2	+8.385	4.740	1.769	0.078
(j) I·C·S	+54.697	20.051	2.728	0.007
(k) I·C·S^2	−22.201	10.651	−2.084	0.038

Summary statistics: number of observations 347; degrees of freedom 320; R-squared 0.907; standard error of regression 0.637; adjusted R-squared 0.899; Durbin–Watson stat. 2.082.

Notes: Non-germane results suppressed to conserve space. Complete results available at http://www-personal.umich.edu/~franzese. Estimation by weighted, two-stage, linear least squares with White's robust standard errors (see n. 36).

central-bank independence, bargaining coordination, and traded-dominating public-sectoral structure are *substitutes* in producing low inflation. Thus, the estimated anti-inflationary impact of independence should be less as bargaining coordination increases, which the table affirms.

Further, as public-relative-traded-sector size increases beyond some point it begins to reflect public-sector dominance, and public-sector dominance is inflationary, so independent central banks should have to do more monetarily to reduce inflation as S increases beyond that point.

TABLE 3.3 Estimated inflation impact of increasing central-bank independence

	CWB = 0.00	CWB = 0.25	CWB = 0.50	CWB = 0.75	CWB = 1.00
G/M = 0.25	−1.20	−0.88	−0.57	−0.25	+0.07
G/M = 0.50	−0.81	−0.62	−0.42	−0.23	−0.04
G/M = 0.75	−0.55	−0.44	−0.34	−0.23	−0.12
G/M = 1.00	−0.43	−0.37	−0.30	−0.24	−0.18
G/M = 1.25	−0.45	−0.39	−0.33	−0.27	−0.20

Notes: Cell entries give the estimated first-year impact of a 0.1 increase in CBI in a political economy with the CWB and G/M listed in that column and row. The equation is dynamic, so these impacts will accumulate over time if the hypothetical CBI increase is permanent.

TABLE 3.4 Estimated inflation impact of increasing coordination of wage/price-bargaining

	CBI = 0.15	CBI = 0.35	CBI = 0.55	CBI = 0.75	CBI = 0.95
G/M = 0.25	−4.13	−3.49	−2.86	−2.22	−1.58
G/M = 0.50	−2.49	−2.11	−1.72	−1.34	−0.95
G/M = 0.75	−1.39	−1.18	−0.96	−0.75	−0.53
G/M = 1.00	−0.83	−0.70	−0.58	−0.45	−0.32
G/M = 1.25	−0.81	−0.69	−0.56	−0.44	−0.31

Notes: Cell entries give the estimated first-year impact of a 0.25 increase in CWB in a political economy with the CBI and G/M listed in that column and row. The equation is dynamic, so these impacts will accumulate over time if the hypothetical CWB increase is permanent.

Conversely, prior to that point, the traded sector dominates and so provides greater anti-inflationary benefits the larger the public sector it dominates, leaving less for independent central banks to do with brute monetary force. Thus, the anti-inflationary impact of independence should initially decline and then begin to rise again beyond some point as *G/M* increases. Table 3.3 exhibits just such a pattern. In fact, how large the public sector must be before it begins to dominate appears to decline as coordination increases, suggesting that public sectors dominate coordinated bargaining more easily than uncoordinated bargaining.[40]

Consider next the inflation impact of a 0.25 increase in bargaining coordination. First, theory suggests such coordination should generally reduce inflation, and indeed every entry in Table 3.4 is negative. Second, coordination should reduce inflation less the greater central-bank independence since, with a more independent central bank, coordinated bargainers need reduce inflation less on their own: a substitute property. Reading the table left to right confirms this. Finally, as public sectors grow relative to traded sectors, coordination should become less able to deliver anti-inflationary wage/price restraint. Reading top to bottom, the estimates support this also since the estimated impact of coordination on inflation is less negative as *G/M* increases.

The remaining derivatives, representing the inflation effects of increases in public-relative-to-traded-sector employment, *G/M*, are more difficult to present because they depend on three factors—central-bank independence, bargaining coordination, and the level of *G/M* itself—and so require three dimensions. Summarizing those results (see Franzese forthcoming), public-sector dominance increases inflation most when

---

[40] This supports an argument of Garrett and Way (1995*b*, 1999, 2000).

TABLE 3.5 Estimated unemployment impact of increasing central-bank independence

	CWB = 0.00	CWB = 0.25	CWB = 0.50	CWB = 0.75	CWB = 1.00
G/M = 0.25	+1.23	+0.80	+0.37	−0.06	−0.48
G/M = 0.50	+0.61	+0.42	+0.22	+0.03	−0.16
G/M = 0.75	+0.16	+0.14	+0.11	+0.09	+0.07
G/M = 1.00	−0.11	−0.04	+0.04	+0.12	+0.20
G/M = 1.25	−0.21	−0.10	+0.01	+0.11	+0.22

Notes: Cell entries give the estimated first-year impact of a 0.1 increase in CBI in a political economy with the CWB and G/M listed in that column and row. The equation is dynamic, so these impacts will accumulate over time if the hypothetical CBI increase is permanent.

coordination is high and independence is low. That is, as argued, increased public-sector dominance when coordination is high increases the degree to which coordinated bargains are inflationary, producing largest net inflationary effects absent a central bank sufficiently autonomous and conservative to resist that effect monetarily.

We argued that the unemployment impact of central-bank independence may be positive or negative but should decrease (increase) in coordination if the latter is traded-sector (public-sector) dominated. Reading Table 3.5 from left to right shows that indeed the unemployment effect of central-bank independence becomes less positive (more negative) as bargaining coordination increases when government-relative-to-manufacturing employment is low (below about one) and reverses direction once government comes to dominate manufacturing employment.[41] Thus, *central-bank independence and traded-sector-dominant/public-sector-dominated coordinated wage/price-bargaining are complements in the production of low unemployment. Reverse the sectoral structure, and independence and coordination become complements in the production of high unemployment.*

Finally, consider the estimated unemployment impact of a 0.25 increase in wage/price-bargaining coordination. Theory suggests coordination generally reduces unemployment, and indeed our estimates broadly

---

[41] However, when coordination is low, central-bank independence actually has less detrimental (more beneficial) unemployment effects as G/M increases. Perhaps the different bargaining rights and strengths of public relative to traded-sector actors in high- and low-coordination countries is behind this result. Especially in low-coordination countries, public-sector workers may be relatively powerless in wage/price-bargaining or even be legally denied bargaining rights. If so, their increase relative to traded workers will not force central bank enactment of monetary threats because it decreases the proportion of the economy that bargains. This requires further exploration but should not distract from the strong central conclusion summarized in the text.

TABLE 3.6 Estimated unemployment impact of increasing coordination of wage/price-bargaining

	CBI = 0.15	CBI = 0.35	CBI = 0.55	CBI = 0.75	CBI = 0.95
G/M = 0.25	+1.04	+0.18	−0.68	−1.53	−2.39
G/M = 0.50	+0.38	0.00	−0.38	−0.76	−1.15
G/M = 0.75	−0.12	−0.17	−0.21	−0.25	−0.30
G/M = 1.00	−0.46	−0.31	−0.16	0.00	+0.15
G/M = 1.25	−0.65	−0.43	−0.22	−0.01	+0.21

Notes: Cell entries give the estimated first-year impact of a 0.25 increase in CWB in a political economy with the CBI and G/M listed in that column and row. The equation is dynamic, so these impacts will accumulate over time if the hypothetical CWB increase is permanent.

support that claim: most Table 3.6 cells are negative. Furthermore, provided the traded sector dominates, coordination should reduce unemployment more the more independent the central bank because its monetary threats help enforce restraint by coordinated traded-sector bargainers and, vice versa, coordinated traded-sector bargainers respond best to such monetary threats. However, if the public sector comes to dominate coordination, the relationship can reverse. Independent central banks will fight against coordination on public-sector-led bargaining because it tends to be inflationary; thus, the impact of coordination when both independence and *G/M* becomes less salutary. With a sufficiently adverse sectoral structure, coordination will be detrimental to unemployment performance *if* the central bank is sufficiently autonomous and conservative to resist the inflationary results of such coordination monetarily.

The estimated unemployment effects of sectoral structure require three dimensions to present (see Franzese forthcoming), but may be summarized succinctly: increasing government-relative-to-manufacturing employment when the public sector already dominates, coordination is high, and the central bank is independent, increases unemployment, as expected.

3.6 Conclusion

The arguments and evidence presented here synthesize and extend two literatures central to institutional political economy: central-bank independence and coordinated bargaining.

First, contrary to much neoclassical theory, central-bank independence does have real, rational-expectations-equilibrium and on-average effects; their manifestation depends on the institutional structure of wage/price-bargaining and the sectoral composition of bargainers. The real effects of a central bank's anti-inflationary stance depend not only on the credibility of that stance, as previously emphasized, but also upon the incentives and capacity of wage/price-bargainers to respond. Central-bank independence is most costly in real terms when coordination is low or when it is high but characterized by public-sector dominance of the traded sector and least costly or even beneficial when coordination is high and traded-sector-led. These are complementary relationships: the real economic efficiency of central-bank independence and traded-sector-led coordinated bargaining are each enhanced by a high degree of the other. Second, central-bank independence lowers inflation less (more) the more (less) anti-inflationary is the rest of the political economy. These are substitute relationships: an independent central bank needs to do less monetarily to control inflation if wage/price-bargaining (and other factors) are already conducive to low inflation. Third, these new arguments and evidence resolve two empirical anomalies for previous theory regarding the actions and announcements of central banks. The Bundesbank speaks differently and to different entities than does the US Federal Reserve because their audiences are differently structured institutionally; and both the Fed and the Bundesbank react to real strength in the economy as *incipient inflationary pressure* because real strength weakens the incentives of bargainers to exercise wage/price restraint.

Conversely, the coordinated-wage/price-bargaining literature has virtually ignored the likely response of monetary policy to wage/price settlements and the impact of sectoral structure on the incentives of wage/price-bargainers to exercise restraint autonomously and to respond to expected monetary reactions. I have argued and the evidence supports that the impact of coordination, on both nominal and real outcomes, depends upon the sectoral composition of those being coordinated and upon the institutional characteristics of the monetary authority. Coordinated bargaining most reduces unemployment when traded-sector actors dominate public-sector actors, especially when monetary policy is controlled by a conservative and credibly independent central bank. Coordination least reduces (or even increases) unemployment when public sectors dominate traded sectors, especially when monetary policy is credibly conservative. These are complementary relationships. Conversely, traded-sector-led coordinated bargaining reduces inflation but less so when the central bank is independent because then inflation would have been low anyway. These are substitute relationships.

Finally, previous studies of interactions between central-bank independence and coordinated wage/price-bargaining have highlighted individual interactions between some two of independence, coordination, and sectoral structure. I have argued and shown empirically that the impact of *each* of these politico-economic features depends on both of the others.

This consideration may also resolve one key point of contention in those previous studies. Iversen (1996, 1998a, 1998b, 1998c, 2000) found *monetary conservatism* to have beneficial unemployment effects under intermediate bargaining *centralization* and detrimental effects under high *centralization*. Others found *central-bank independence* uniformly more beneficial as *coordination* increased. The italicized differences notwithstanding, these findings seemed disturbingly different. The theory and evidence here, showing a beneficial interaction of coordination with independence when traded sectors dominate public sectors but the reverse relationship when public sectors dominate, suggest a resolution. Adverse sectoral structure combined with coordination could explain the detrimental unemployment effects of independence Iversen observed at high centralization. In Iversen's model, bargainers seek wage equality and achieve it more the greater is centralization. Since economies become increasingly service oriented as they advance, and since productivity growth in services lags behind that in industry, wage equalization makes private-sector service provision increasingly costly in growing economies where wage/price-bargaining achieves wage equality. With the private sector 'priced out' of service provision, public-sector service provision must rise or growth and employment will suffer. Thus, centralization or coordination *with wage equalization* virtually forces governments in growing economies to increase public-sector employment, but that sectoral trend will eventually weaken the ability of coordination to produce beneficial nominal and real outcomes as shown here. In this situation, governments increasingly must choose between a high-inflation/low-unemployment equilibrium without monetary conservatism, or a low-inflation/high-unemployment one with it. In this light, much less dispute exists between Iversen's arguments and findings and these and others' arguments than first appears. In fact, together, they suggest that coordination accompanied by wage-equalization might be inherently unstable in the long run because jointly they tend to produce public-sector growth, which is incompatible with coordination on wage/price restraint.

Concluding most broadly, this analysis demonstrated that and explained how several institutional interactions, exhibiting both substitute and complement relations, operate at the macroeconomic level. That is, the politico-economic regulation of inflation and unemployment depends on the broad network of institutions and the structural setting within which wage/price-bargainers and monetary policy-makers inter-. act. More specifically, I have shown how central-bank autonomy and conservatism and the coordination and sectoral structure—traded, sheltered, and public—of wage/price-bargaining interact in regulating inflation and unemployment.

APPENDIX 3.1
CONTROLS IN THE REGRESSION EQUATIONS

Equations (18) and (19) included time-serial controls,[42] dummies for Greece, Portugal, Spain, and for the authoritarian periods therein,[43] trade-openness (O: exports-plus-imports share of GDP), terms of trade (T: export–import price-index ratio), their product, the natural log of real GDP *per capita* (Y), the partisan left–right center of the current government (CoG), a pre-election year indicator (ELE), and union density (UD). (18) also controlled for financial-sector employment share (F) and average inflation in the other twenty countries in that year (π_a: inflation abroad). Similarly, (19) controls for average unemployment abroad (U_a). In the text, X_1 refers to the time-serial controls plus dummies and X_2 to the other factors. Table 3.7 gives sample descriptive statistics.

TABLE 3.7 Descriptive statistics for the data

	π	U	π_a	U_a	O	T	Y	CoG	ELE	F	UD	CWB	CBI	G/M
Mean	8.7	6.1	9.0	6.2	0.5	1.0	9.3	5.5	0.3	6.8	0.4	0.4	0.5	0.8
Median	7.7	5.7	8.8	6.7	0.5	1.0	9.3	5.6	0.2	6.8	0.4	0.3	0.4	0.7
Maximum	29.0	21.0	15.0	8.6	1.4	1.5	9.8	10.0	1.4	11.6	0.8	1.0	0.9	1.8
Minimum	−0.7	0.0	4.0	2.4	0.1	0.7	8.5	2.8	0.0	2.1	0.1	0.0	0.2	0.3
Std. dev.	5.6	4.0	3.2	1.7	0.3	0.1	0.3	1.6	0.3	2.3	0.2	0.4	0.2	0.3

[42] Three lags of the dependent variable proved sufficient in each equation. The resulting residuals exhibited no significant serial correlation, and coefficients on the lags added to well below one, erasing any unit-root or correlated-residual concerns.

[43] Spain's dummy was significantly negative in (18) and positive in (19); Greece's and Portugal's were small and insignificant in both. The authoritarian dummy was small and insignificant in (19) and negative and nearly significant in (18).

4

Social Protection and the Formation of Skills: A Reinterpretation of the Welfare State

Margarita Estevez-Abe, Torben Iversen,
and David Soskice

4.1 Introduction

Social protection does not always mean 'politics against markets.' In this chapter we argue, as did Polanyi (1944), that social protection rescues the market from itself by preventing market failures. More specifically, we contend that social protection aids the market by helping economic actors overcome market failures in skill formation. We show, in this chapter, that different types of social protection are complementary to different skill equilibria.[1]

The market failure problem in the provision of skills is generally attributed to employers' reluctance to invest in transferable skills. Here we pay more attention to workers' reluctance to invest in specific skills. Young people are less likely to invest in specific skills if the risk of loss of employment opportunities that require those specific skills is high. Employers who rely on specific skills to compete effectively in international markets therefore need to institutionalize some sort of guarantee to insure workers against potential risks. Without implicit agreements for long-term employment and real wage stability, their specific skills will be under-supplied. Employers' promises are not, however, sufficiently credible by themselves. This is why social protection as governmental policy becomes critical.

Original version prepared for presentation at the 95th American Political Association Meeting at the Atlanta Hilton and the Marriott Marquis, 2–5 Sept. 1999. We wish to thank Robert Fannion for his excellent research assistance. Thanks also to Paul Pierson and the participants at the European Political Economy Workshop at the Center for European Studies, 5–6 Nov. 1999 for many helpful comments. Torben Iversen gratefully acknowledges financial support from the Hoover Institution while working on this paper.

[1] For a discussion of complementarity, see the Introduction to this volume.

The upshot of this chapter is that the shape of social protection has bearings on national competitive advantage in international markets and choice of product market strategies. Relative abundance in certain skills in a given country constitutes a comparative advantage for firms in that country. But relative abundance in, for instance, a highly flexible multi-skilled workforce does not simply come by as an accumulative result of individual firms' decisions. Firms' product market choices are constrained by the availability of necessary skills. Availability of specific skills, in turn, requires appropriate forms and levels of social protection.[2] Institutional differences that safeguard returns on specific skills explain why workers and employers invest more in specific skills. The absence of such institutions, in countries such as the USA and UK, gives workers a strong incentive to invest in transferable skills. In such an environment, it then also makes more economic sense for firms to pursue product market strategies that use these transferable skills intensely.

We refer to the set of product market strategies, employee skill trajectories, and social, economic, and political institutions that support them, as *welfare production regimes*. A primary objective of this chapter is therefore to identify the main varieties of welfare production regimes and their consequences for distribution and economic outcomes. In the rapidly growing 'varieties of capitalism' literature, production regimes are conceptualized as institutional complementarities that reinforce one another and particular ways of producing and competing in international markets (cf. Hollingsworth and Boyer 1997; Kitschelt et al. 1999*b*; Hall and Soskice, this volume). We contend that the welfare state can also be understood as a complement in national production systems. Our chapter thus is part of the new efforts to understand the link between models of capitalism and welfare states (Swenson 1997, forthcoming; Mares 1998; Scharpf and Schmidt 2000; Estevez-Abe 1999*a*; Huber and Stephens 2001).

The model of micro-level links between skills and social protection we develop in this chapter has important policy implications. First, our model predicts what types of political alliance are likely to emerge in support of a particular type of social protection. For example, in economies

---

[2] We are not arguing that social protection is the sole institution that makes a particular skill formation possible. Other institutions are also necessary: for instance, in the case of industry skills, strong employer associations are needed to develop agreed vocational training standards; and in order for the social protection institutions to function effectively strong employee representative organizations are required. Furthermore, different product market strategies require access to different kinds of finance: the longer term the commitments companies have to make, the longer term the finance has to be. Thus a range of complementary institutions need to be in place.

where companies engage in product market strategies that require a combination of firm- and industry-specific skills, and where a large number of workers invest in such skills, a strong alliance between skilled workers and their employers in favor of social protection advantageous to them is likely to emerge—even if this means reducing job opportunities for low-skilled workers. By contrast, where business has no common interest in the promotion of specific skills, it will have no interest in defending any of the three components of social protection (cf. Mares, this volume). Second, we show that different systems of social protection have deeper ramifications for inequality than commonly assumed. Some skill equilibria—sustained by different systems of social protection—produce more inequalities based on the academic background of workers, while others produce more inequalities based on gender.

That said, it should be emphasized here that our model *is not* intended to explain the origin of specific social policies. Although our model helps understand intra-class differences in policy preferences, we do not claim to make a historical argument about origins.[3] The path-breaking work by Mares (1998) and Swenson (1997, forthcoming) shows the potential insights that can be gained from studying questions about origins from a political economy perspective of the sort we advocate here. But this is not a study of origins.

The chapter is divided into four sections. Section 4.2 outlines the basic argument. Section 4.3 ties the welfare–skill links to broader issues of income inequality across different groups of citizens. Section 4.4 provides empirical support for our argument. The final section concludes.

4.2 Product Market Strategies, Skill Types, and the Welfare State

We explore the logical links between product market strategies and their welfare implications in two steps. First, we identify three types of skills and argue that different product market strategies are facilitated by a workforce with particular skill profiles. Second, we then spell out how different types of social protection influence the propensity of individuals to invest in particular skills, which, in turn, determines the skill profile of an economy.

---

[3] There is a significant amount of work that evaluates the role of business in shaping welfare policies, although authors disagree in terms of the actual influence of economic interests (cf. Skocpol and Ikenberry 1983; Skocpol and Amenta 1985; Quadagno 1984; Martin 1995; Pierson 1995*b*, 1996*a*; Hacker and Pierson 2000; Mares 1998; Estevez-Abe 1999*b*).

4.2.1. Skills and Product Market Strategies

This chapter distinguishes three types of skills associated with different product market strategies: (i) firm-specific skills; (ii) industry-specific skills; and (iii) general skills.[4] These skills differ significantly in terms of their asset specificity (i.e. portability). Firm-specific skills are acquired through on-the-job training, and are least portable. They are valuable to the employer who carried out the training but not to other employers. Industry-specific skills are acquired through apprenticeship and vocational schools. These skills, especially when authoritatively certified, are recognized by any employer within a specific trade. General skills, recognized by all employers, carry a value that is independent of the type of firm or industry. Of course, any actual production system will involve all three types of skills to some degree. Nonetheless, we can characterize distinctive product market strategies based upon the 'skill profile' they require.

A Fordist mass production of standardized goods does not require a highly trained workforce. Production work is broken into a narrow range of standardized tasks that only require semi-skilled workers. Traditional US manufacturing industries such as automobile and other consumer durables fall into this category. There is, however, a variant of mass production called diversified mass production (DMP). The DMP strategy, in contrast, aims at producing a varied range of products in large volumes. Japanese auto-makers and domestic electronic appliances industry are good examples. This production strategy depends on workers capable of performing a wide range of tasks to enable frequent product changes in the line (Koike 1981). Workers are also expected to solve problems that emerge in the production line themselves to minimize downtime (Shibata 1999). The tasks these workers perform involve high levels of knowledge about their company products and machineries in use, and hence are highly firm-specific.

There are product market strategies that do not mass produce. One strategy is a high-quality product niche market strategy. It requires a highly trained workforce with industry-specific craft skills. The prototype of this production strategy does not involve any scale merit, and

---

[4] Our framework builds upon Gary Becker's distinction between general and specific skills (1964: ch. 3). In Becker's definition, firm-specific training increases productivity only in the firm where training takes place. General training, in contrast, raises productivity equally in all firms. In an analogous manner, industry-specific training can be defined as training that raises productivity in all firms in the industry, but not in other industries. Firm-, industry-, and general skills are skills acquired through firm-specific, industry-specific, and general training.

the process tends to involve highly craft-intensive workshops. Custom-made clothing, jewelry, and fine porcelain may be examples of such production. Another strategy is a hybrid. It pursues high-quality product lines, but takes the production out of small-scale craft shops in order to increase the volume of production. Streeck (1992*b*) calls this diversified quality production. This production strategy requires firm-specific skills in addition to high levels of craft skills. Germany is a prototype of this type of production.

All the above strategies require firm-specific and industry-specific skills to varying degrees. It is important, however, to note that relative abundance of high levels of general skills (i.e. university and postgraduate qualifications) brings comparative advantages in radical product innovation. Let us take the example of the USA to illustrate this point. For example, start-up software companies in the USA take advantage of a highly flexible labor market with university-educated people combining excellent general skills with valuable knowledge about the industry acquired from switching from one job to another. Another example would be American financial institutions, which have taken advantage of an abundant supply of math Ph.D.s to develop new products such as derivatives. Complex systems development (for e-commerce, for example), biotechnology, segments of the telecommunications industry, and advanced consulting services are other examples that fall into this class of industries.

4.2.2 The Welfare–Skill Formation Nexus

We make the three following assumptions about workers' economic behavior:

(*i*) *People calculate overall return to their educational/training investment before deciding to commit themselves. (The investment cost of further training and education can be conceptualized in terms of wages forgone during the period of training and education, in addition to any tuition or training fees incurred.)*

(*ii*) *People choose to invest in those skills that generate higher expected returns, provided that the riskiness of the investments is identical.*

(*iii*) Ceteris paribus, *people refrain from investing in skills that have more uncertain future returns (i.e. people are risk averse).*

From these assumptions, it follows that a rational worker must consider three factors in making skill investment decisions: (i) the initial cost of acquiring the skills as, for instance, when a worker receives a reduced wage during the period of training; (ii) the future wage premium of specific skills; and (iii) the risks of losing the current job and the associated wage premium.

The core skills required by an industry are critical for this analysis because they vary in the degree to which they expose workers to the risk of future income losses. Highly portable skills are less risky than highly specific skills because in the former case the market value of the skill is not tied to a particular firm or industry. Faced with future job insecurity, a rational worker will not invest his or her time and money in skills that have no remunerative value outside the firm or industry. In other words, in the absence of institutional interventions into workers' payoff structure, general rather than asset-specific skill acquisition represents the utility-maximizing strategy.

Let us now examine what types of institutions are necessary in order to protect investments in asset-specific skills. We can distinguish three different types of protection, which might be called *employment protection, unemployment protection*, and *wage protection*. *Employment protection* refers to institutionalized employment security. The higher the employment protection, the less likely that a worker will be laid off even during economic downturns. *Unemployment protection* means protection from income reduction due to unemployment, and can thus reduce the uncertainty over the wage level throughout one's career. *Wage protection*, finally, is an institutional mechanism that protects wage levels from market fluctuations. In this section, we first contrast the significance of *employment protection* and *unemployment protection* for firm-specific and industry-specific skills. We will discuss wage protection in a separate section, because it is generally not considered to be part of the welfare system.

Firm-specific skills are, *ex hypothesi*, worthless outside that specific firm, and they therefore require a high level of *employment protection* in order to convince workers to invest in such skills (Aoki 1988). Since workers will only be paid the value of their non-firm-specific skills in the external market, the greater their investment in specific skills the greater the discrepancy between current wages and the wages they could fetch in the external market. In order to invest heavily in firm-specific skills, workers therefore need assurances that they can remain in the company for a long enough period to reap the returns on such investments (see Lazear and Freeman 1996; Osterman 1987; Schettkat 1993). If not, the expenditures of training must be commensurably lower, and/or the premium on future wages higher. In either case, the cost of training for the firm goes up, and it will offer less training.

Because rational workers weigh higher expected income later in their career against the risks of losing their current job, the only way to encourage workers to carry a substantial part of the costs of firm-specific training is to increase job security and/or reduce the insecurity of job loss. Hence we can interpret institutionalized lifetime employment, or subsidies to keep redundant workers within the firm, as safeguarding mechanisms for firm-specific skill investment.

It should be noted here that this argument appears to conflict with Becker's (1964) famous proposition that companies will pay fully for company-specific skills, since they need to pay only marginally above the market wage for the employee's marketable skills in order to retain the employee, and can thus appropriate the full return on the investment.

Becker's argument, however, makes two critical assumptions that are not generally satisfied. The first is that the acquisition of company-specific skills does not reduce the maximum present value of the employee's marketable skills, either marketable skills which the employee currently possesses or marketable skills in which the employee will invest in at some future point. This assumption is reasonable where relatively minor specific skills are concerned—for example, the understanding of specific office routines. It is implausible where the company-specific skills constitute a major part of the employee's skill portfolio. There are three broad reasons for this.

First, the greater the proportion of company-specific skills, the less likely is the employee to use preexisting marketable skills; since most skills are maintained by use, refreshment, and updating, the employee's marketable skills will deteriorate. Second, after full-time education, a large proportion of marketable skills are acquired by most employees at low cost during their employment by doing different jobs (often within the same company) and being taught, for example, the different software packages which each job requires. If a company, however, invests heavily in an employee's company-specific skills, the company is likely to want the employee to focus on using those skills, hence not to move around. Third, the greater the importance of company-specific skills across a sector in general, the less valuable will marketable skills be to employees in that sector. Workers will therefore only work for firm-specific skill companies if they know the chances of job loss are very low, and this in turn presupposes high employment protection.

A second critical assumption which Becker makes is that company-specific skills confer no 'hold-up' power on employees. If they do, as is often the case, then the ability of companies to appropriate the full return no longer holds, and then companies will seek credible guarantees from their workforce. This typically involves cooperative arrangements with unions, such as works councils, which in turn is made possible because employees have made investments in company-specific assets. In order to encourage employees to make these investments, employees require some measure of credible protection.

For industry-specific skills, employment protection *per se* matters less. If skills are truly specific only to the industry, not the firm, workers can in principle move between firms without loss of income. Instead, what becomes important for workers' incentives to invest in industry-specific skills is the protection of 'skilled wages,' regardless of employment status. Unemployment protection achieves this in part by securing earning-related benefits and also by helping to keep the skilled wages high even when the supply of skills exceeds the demand for those skills. In part, generous unemployment protection is also important in so far as it allows workers to turn down job offers outside their previous industry or occupation. If compelled to accept a job offer outside the worker's core competencies, either because of low benefits or a strict requirement to accept almost any job offer, this undermines the worker's incentives to invest in industry-specific skills.

A high replacement ratio, especially when the unemployment benefits are earnings-related, rewards the worker for his or her specific skill investment even when the worker is out of work. A high replacement ratio also eliminates the downward pressure on specific skilled wages, as unemployed skilled workers do not have to take job offers at discounted wages. Benefit duration and the administration of require-ments to accept a 'suitable job' further reinforce this mechanism. A longer benefit duration permits the unemployed industry-specific skill-holders enough time to find another job that matches their skills, especially if they are permitted to turn down jobs that are outside their core compe-tencies. This ensures that their reemployment will generate the same skilled wages as before, simultaneously reducing downward pressures on the skilled wages. In short, these two components of *unemployment protection*—a high replacement ratio and 'secure' benefits—guarantee return on skill investment sufficient to compensate for economic fluctu-ations.

For firms pursuing product market strategies which depend heavily on firm- and industry-specific skills, promise of employment and unem-ployment security can thus provide a cost-effective path to improving the firms' competitive position in international markets (cf. Ohashi and Tachibanaki 1998; Koike 1994). Contrary to conventional neoclassical theory, which sees efforts to increase protection against job loss as an interference with the efficient operation of labor markets, measures to reduce future uncertainty over employment status—hence uncertainty over future wage premiums—can significantly improve firms' cost effectiveness (Schettkat 1993). And the more successful these firms are, the greater their demand for specific skills. We are in a specific skills equilibrium.

If there is little protection built into either the employment or the unemployment system, the best insurance against labor market risks for the worker is to invest in general, or portable, skills that are highly valued in the external labor market. If general skills are what firms need for pursuing their product market strategies successfully, low employment protection can thus give these firms a competitive edge. Indeed, if most firms are pursuing general skills strategies, then higher protection will undermine workers' incentives to invest in these skills, *without* significantly increasing their appropriation of specific skills (because there is little demand for such skills). In this general skills equilibrium the neoclassical efficiency argument for little protection is more valid.[5]

The predictions of the argument are summarized in Fig. 4.1, which identifies the four main welfare production regimes and gives an empirical example of each (discussed below). The empirical details will be discussed in section 4.4.

4.2.3 Wage-Bargaining Institutions and Wage Protection

The previous section argued that the greater the uncertainty attached to employment in the use of particular skills the greater the incentive to invest in general skills which permit mobility. The proper calculation relates to the uncertainty of income, namely employment multiplied by earnings. If there is uncertainty in the earnings from particular skills, this is as much of a disincentive to sink investments in those skills as uncertainty in employment.

We suggest that some wage determination systems provide what we call *wage protection*. *Wage protection* reinforces the effects of *employment* and *unemployment protection* by reducing the risk that the wage levels for specific skills might drop radically in the future. In other words, *wage*

---

[5] Since the general skills are portable, there is no risk associated with separation from current employer. See Gary Becker (1964). This does not mean that high turnover in countries with more general skills does not produce negative welfare consequences from the economy-wide efficiency perspective. For an interesting elaboration on this issue, see Chang and Wang (1995).

154 Estevez-Abe, Iversen, and Soskice

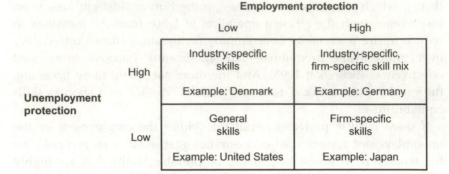

FIG. 4.1 Social protection and predicted skill profiles

protection makes it possible for workers to calculate viable lifelong earnings if they were to invest in specific skills. This possibility is arguably as important as employment and unemployment protection in making sunk investments in human capital. In the absence of a credible lifetime earnings, any major investment in specific skills is unlikely to result. Thus the wage determination system should be seen by political economists not just in macroeconomic terms but as a critical linking institution between the welfare state and the production regime. Just as the nature of employment and unemployment protection is contingent on the type of skill investments, so too is wage protection.

At a rough first cut, then, it is necessary to provide wage protection in order to induce front-end investments in company- or industry-specific skills. The natural interpretation of a wage protection system is where wage determination provides a broadly stable proportionate distribution of earnings across different occupations. This is the result when there is a high degree of coordination in a system of wage determination. Thus institutionally we would expect to find coordinated wage-bargaining systems in economies in which specific skills are important, and non-coordinated systems where they are not. And in terms of outcomes we would expect to find stable distributions of earnings across occupations in the first, but not necessarily the second case.

There is one complication to the above which is worth noting. A distinction can be made between wage protection for the employed and for the unemployed: for the employed wage protection means simply that wages do not fall out of line with wages in other occupations. For the unemployed, a natural definition of wage protection is that there is some guarantee that the wage at which the unemployed person is rehired is the same as the wage at which he or she was previously employed.

(The unemployment benefit, it will be remembered, is part of unemployment protection.)

As far as the three cases of industry-specific, industry- and company-specific, and general skills are concerned, employed wage protection and unemployed wage protection are the same. In the first two cases, they are both high; in the third case they are both low. But in the case of company-specific skills employed wage protection is high but unemployed wage protection is low. This mirrors the (very) high employment and low unemployment protection in the Japanese case. And it can be explained in the same way: if an employee has a 'lifetime' employment and employed wage protection guarantee, at least so long as he works effectively, this constitutes an effective incentive for the potentially responsible employee to invest appropriately in company-specific skills. Low unemployment and unemployed wage protection serve as a disincentive to leave the company or to work in such a way as might lead to dismissal.

The association between skills and wage-bargaining has implications for the distribution of earnings. Wage-bargaining systems have consequences for the wage structure for three associated reasons. First, as implied by our argument, intra-occupational compression of wages serves as a complement to employment and unemployment protection because it helps insure against a big drop in income if a worker loses her job. Secondly, to the extent that collective bargaining systems are designed to prevent poaching, they limit the ability of individual firms to pay wages that are significantly above the negotiated rate. The third reason has to do with the effect of collective bargaining arrangements on the relative bargaining power of different income groups. Collective bargaining at the industry or higher levels brings diverse income groups into a collective decision-making process, and this affords low-income groups opportunities to influence the distribution of wages that they lack in more fragmented systems.

4.3 Self-reinforcing Inequalities and Political Preferences

So far the discussion has focused on the efficiency aspects of social protection. In this section we extend the core argument to unravel two sets of previously neglected logics by which welfare production regimes perpetuate inequalities. First, we point out that general skill systems are more likely to create a 'poverty trap.' Second, we cast light upon the gender inequality consequences of different product market strategies. Finally, we discuss how these distributive implications of different welfare state regimes are reproduced and perpetuated through distinct patterns of political support for social protection.

4.3.1 Distribution, Poverty Traps, and Product Market Strategies

Our argument has far-reaching implications for equality and labor market stratification, some of which are poorly understood in the existing welfare state literature. Product market strategies that rely on high levels of industry-specific and firm-specific skills are likely to create more egalitarian societies than product market strategies based on general skills. They therefore help us understand large and persistent cross-national differences in the distribution of wages and incomes. The existing literature can only account for these differences in so far as they are caused by redistributive state policies. This is far too narrow an approach. We contend that most inequalities result from particular welfare production regimes (i.e. combinations of product market strategies, skill profiles, and the political-institutional framework that supports them).

The basic logic of our argument is straightforward. We argue that different skill systems and accompanying training systems have important economic implications for those who are academically weak and strong respectively. For the bottom one third, or so, of the academic ability distribution, a highly developed vocational training system offers the best opportunities for students to acquire skills that are valued by employers. When entry into vocational training is competitive, these students have an incentive to be as good as they can academically in order to get into the best training programs with the most promising career prospects (Soskice 1994b). Therefore, countries with well-developed (and competitive) vocational training systems provide a stable economic future even to those students who are not academically strong. General education systems, in contrast, offer these students relatively few opportunities for improving their labor market value outside of the school system. As a result, there are fewer incentives for them to work hard inside the school system.

In firm-specific skill-training systems, employers develop strong stakes in overseeing the quality of potential employees (i.e. trainees) and developing clear job entry patterns.[6] Since employers are committed to make

---

[6] It is worth noting that monitoring the quality of the general education system becomes important where a lot of human capital investment takes place beyond the general education system, because poor general education increases the cost of training workers in industry-specific and firm-specific skills.

significant initial human capital investment in new job entrants, they will be interested in monitoring the quality of the pool of the new school leavers. As a result, they are likely to establish a working relationship with various schools for systematic hiring of new school leavers. Since employers in a firm-specific skill system carry out initial job training, new school graduates have a chance of building careers as skilled workers. This gives young schoolgoers a strong incentive to work hard in school. The 'from-school-to-work' transition is likely to be more institutionalized (Dore and Sako 1989).

Similarly, in the case of industry-specific skills where employers are involved, employers take an interest in ensuring the quality of vocational training and the certification of skills (Finegold and Soskice 1988). In these systems, education–work transition is also relatively institutionalized (Ni Cheallaigh 1995; Blossfeld and Mayer 1988).

In general skill regimes, in contrast, the 'from-school-to-work' transition is less institutionalized (see Allmendinger 1989). Hiring is more flexible. Employers hire new job entrants with different educational backgrounds. Promotion and opportunities for further skill training are themselves contingent upon the job performance of the worker. There is not so much initial human capital investment by employers as there is in firm-specific skill systems. Because of the absence of a clear vocational track, systems based on general skills therefore tend to disadvantage those who are not academically inclined. Regardless of the presence or absence of vocational schools and apprenticeship programs, for employers who emphasize general skills a certificate from a vocational school does not add much value to the worker. Potential workers therefore have to demonstrate their competence in terms of general scholarly achievement, and getting a tertiary degree becomes an essential component. Because there is a hierarchy of post-secondary schools, if the student thinks there is a possibility of making it into the tertiary educational system, he or she has a strong incentive to work hard. For those who are not academically inclined, by contrast, the system produces the unintended consequence of undermining the incentive to work hard in school. In the absence of a specialized vocational track, unless a student believes that he or she can make the cut into college, there is not much gained by being a good student.

In short, in general skill systems, since the completion of elementary and secondary school does not qualify them for a vocational certificate that leads to secure jobs, academically weak students face lower returns from their educational investment. Since the opportunity for vocational training—both on the job and off the job—for these students will remain low, it creates an impoverished labor pool. In contrast, at the top end of the ability distribution, a general education system offers the largest returns to those with advanced graduate and postgraduate degrees. These returns tend to be more modest in specific skills systems because a large number of companies depend more on industry-specific and firm-specific skills than professional degrees or broad academic qualifications. General skill systems, therefore, reward those students who are academically talented in terms of labor market entry. Distribution of academic aptitude thus translates into distribution of skills, and consequently into a very skewed distribution of earnings. As a consequence, academically weak students in general skill regimes are worse off than their counterparts elsewhere: they are more likely to be trapped in low-paid unskilled jobs.

4.3.2 Gender Equality and Skill Types

Compared to men, women face an additional set of issues when making skill investment choices (see Estevez-Abe 1999*b*). In addition to the probability of layoff, women have to take into consideration the likelihood of career interruption due to their role as mothers (see Daly 1994; Rubery et al. 1996). For a woman to invest in specific skills, she has to be assured that potential career interruptions will not (i) lead to dismissal; or (ii) reduce her wage level in the long run. A high probability of dismissal reduces the incentives to acquire firm-specific skills. A high probability of reduction in wages after becoming a mother—because of time off due to childbirth and -rearing—reduces the incentives to invest in either firm-specific or industry-specific skills.

For women, therefore, employment protection necessarily involves two factors in addition to the employment and unemployment protection discussed earlier. These two factors are (i) protection against dismissal, such as maternity, parental, and family leave policies; and (ii) income maintenance during leaves and guarantees of reinstatement to the same job at the same wage level upon return to work.

As for industry-specific skill investments, leave programs and generous income maintenance during the leave function in the same way as unemployment protection for male skilled workers. A higher wage replacement ratio thus encourages specific skill investment. Firm-specific and industry-specific skills again require slightly different institutional guarantees. While income maintenance during leave is sufficient for industry-specific skills, firm-specific skill investment by women faces another issue. In firm-specific skill regimes, reinstatement to the original job after the leave means that women fall behind their male cohort in skill formation and promotion. This means that despite generous income replacement during the leave, time off due to childbirth and -rearing reduces women's overall earnings. The very fact that the child-rearing years for women coincide with the critical early years of employment compounds the problem. Therefore, for women to invest in firm-specific skills, affordable childcare is more important than a family leave policy.

In short, compared to men, it takes more institutional support to encourage women to make specific skill investments. This means that employers' incentives differ significantly from the earlier descriptions of employment and unemployment protection. From the employers' perspective, it costs more to provide incentives for women to invest in specific skills than it does for men (Spence 1973). Not only do additional income maintenance and childcare create a greater financial burden, but they come with the organizational cost of hiring replacement workers during regular workers' maternal and childcare leaves. And not only is it expensive to hire highly skilled workers as replacement workers, but it is also very difficult to seek those skills in the external labor market— especially in the case of firm-specific skills.

Given these additional financial and organizational costs, employers are unlikely to support family leave or childcare programs except under two circumstances: (i) when someone other than the employer covers the program expenses; or (ii) when there is an acute shortage of men willing to invest in the skills they need.

From a woman's perspective, this means that it does not pay to invest in skills for which there is an abundant supply of males. Even if a woman invests to acquire a specific skill, as far as there is an abundant supply of male skilled workers, her skill investment will not be protected to the same degree as men's. Given this situation, women are more likely than men to invest in general skills. Furthermore, even women who are willing to invest in skill training will rationally choose trades and profes- sions where there are few men. Hence a vicious cycle of occupational segregation of women arises. In countries where there is an established vocational training system, women's enrollment choices will reflect women's tendency to avoid 'male jobs.'

In short, product market strategies that rely on firm-specific and industry-specific skills are more gender segregating than product market strategies based on general skills. As we argued, general skills provide more flexibility without penalizing career interruptions, precisely because they do not require any external guarantee and reinforcement. We can thus predict that economies with a large presence of companies with specific skill strategies demonstrate high occupational gender segregation, while general skill systems are more gender neutral.

4.3.3 Employers, Core Workers, and Median Voters

The argument presented so far explains the complementarity between different combinations of welfare programs and product market strategies, and their distributional implications. From this, it follows that rational employers who pursue distinctive product market strategies can benefit from welfare programs and policies that favor their production strategy. Complementary welfare programs and policies reduce employers' cost of providing adequate rewards to persuade workers to invest in the skill required for specific product market strategies. We can assume, as in the case of workers, that employers are rational and that they are aware of the incentive structure affecting workers' skill investment decisions. In other words, a rational employer who is interested in specific skills will support policies that ensure an adequate return for workers who make investments in those skills. Given such benefits, employers are likely to develop preferences for the 'right' sets of programs and policies (Mares 1998, this volume; Swenson 1997; Estevez-Abe 1999*a*). Similarly, rational workers who have made investments in specific skills will prefer welfare programs and policies that reward and protect these investments in the future (Iversen and Soskice 2000).

One of the most salient divisions in employers' preferences over types of social protection is *firm size* (Mares 1998). Small firms are more severely affected by restrictions on their ability to hire and fire because they do not have the same organizational capacity to adapt to the business cycle as do large firms. Moreover, small firms with limited R&D capacity typically depend more on industry technologies and skills than do large firms, which are often in a position to develop proprietary technologies based on their own R&D effort. Depending on their particular product market strategy, and hence skill needs, large firms are therefore more likely to favor high employment protection than small firms, who tend to view such protection as an unnecessary financial burden and excessive restriction on their manpower flexibility. For small firms a much more important resource in developing a healthy supply of workers with the appropriate industry-specific skills is generous and publicly financed unemployment benefits. This allows small firms to 'park' some of their skilled workers in the unemployment-benefit system during downturns, without undermining the incentives of workers to invest in relevant skills.

Particular welfare programs and policies also have advocates among workers. Workers who have invested in asset-specific skills have vested interests in retaining institutions that protect the value of these assets. Such support will tend to be much lower among workers with heavy investments in general skills since these workers share equally in the costs of social provision, yet are less likely to benefit from social protection. The presumed negative relationship between income and support for social protection, as implied by a standard Meltzer–Richards median voter model (Meltzer and Richards 1981), is thus mediated by the asset specificity of workers' skill investments (Iversen and Soskice 2000). Consequently, the greater the significance of a specific skill system in the overall national employment structure, the greater the number of workers who possess the 'key skills,' and the more likely it is that the median voter would be someone with an interest in supporting generous social protection. Because the interests of these workers would be well aligned with most employers, there would be a formidable political coalition in favor of retaining and strengthening existing institutions.[7]

We can find empirical examples of such cases in northern Europe and Japan. For instance, employers and unions in Germany and the Nordic countries collaborate in setting industry-specific skilled wages, and unions intervene to maintain earnings of skilled workers by means of combining welfare benefits and wages. In so far as industry-specific skills are core skills in a particular economy, not only are the key private unions likely to protect favorable institutions in place but the proportion of the skilled workers in the overall voting population is likely to be significant. Those not possessing the core skills would be shot out of the most attractive jobs, and in many specific skills countries this has meant a secondary position for women in the labor market.

In Japan, where a large number of employers rely on firm-specific skills, employers advocate wage subsidies during economic downturns in order to avoid layoffs. Japanese unions, composed by protected core workers from large corporations, support these policies. In Germany, where large manufacturers rely on a combination of firm-specific and industry-specific skills, we also observe that large German employers and unions are interested in minimizing layoffs. Like Japan, Germany provides wage subsidies from the unemployment insurance in order to reduce layoffs. The *Mittelstand* sector of small firms complain about the

---

[7] For detailed empirical support for this hypothesis see Iversen and Soskice (2000), who use comparative public opinion data to show the effects of skill type on social policy preferences among mass publics.

costs of these protections, and advocate deregulation of hiring and firing rules, but they have not been able to impose their preferences on the German political economy (Thelen and Kume 1999*a*).

In contrast to firm-specific and industry-specific skills, general skills do not require any institutional guarantee. Indeed, employment and unemployment protection undermines the incentives of workers to invest in general skills. Employers pursuing product market strategies based on general skills thus have no incentive to support either the employment or unemployment protection we discussed above. Because the median voter tends to have a good general education and understands that expanding benefits and job security can have adverse effects on competitiveness, such opposition is likely also to carry the day in electoral politics. We might therefore expect that countries where the dominant product market strategy is based on general skills will have meager employment protection and unemployment benefits. The USA and UK provide good examples here.

4.4 Comparative Patterns

Our argument implies a tight coupling between employment protection, unemployment protection, and skill formation. The dominant mode of firm structure, as well as circumstances in the historical development of different welfare production regimes, have led some countries to emphasize *employment protection* over *unemployment protection*, or vice versa. As we noted in the theoretical discussion, political opposition to strong *employment protection* legislation will be greater in countries with a high proportion of small firms.

The predictions of our model are summarized in Fig. 4.1 above. When *neither* employment *nor* unemployment protection is high, workers have a strong incentive to protect themselves against labor market insecurities by investing heavily in highly portable skills. Since workers are reluctant to take on specific skills in this scenario—or at least unlikely to share much of the cost of training such skills—firms have an incentive to use technologies that rely least on specific skills. This, in turn, increases demand for general skills, and availability of general skill jobs makes general education more attractive for workers, thus creating a self-reinforcing dynamic. In this case we expect skill profiles to be heavily tilted toward general and broad occupational skills, with a weak or absent vocational training system.

When employment and unemployment protection are both high, on the other hand, workers will find it more attractive to invest in firm- and industry-specific skills. In turn, this makes it more cost-efficient for firms to engage in production that require large inputs of labor with specific skills. As firms specialize in this type of production, the job market for general skills shrinks. Note here that a standard trade argument supports the idea of self-reinforcing dynamics in both types of systems: institutional comparative advantage makes an intensive use of relatively more abundant skills an efficient production strategy.

Yet, not all countries necessarily conform to these two ideal types. Where companies can offer very high levels of job protection and a large and attractive internal labor market, firm-specific skill formation can flourish in the absence of strong unemployment protection (represented by the south-east corner of Fig. 4.1). If career opportunities are extensive within the firm, and if the firm makes credible commitments to job security, the external labor market will be small and workers will have an incentive to take advantage of internal career opportunities by investing in company-specific skills. This, essentially, is the Japanese situation (see Aoki 1988; Koike 1981). In most other cases, firms neither have the size nor the resources and institutional capacity to commit credibly to lifetime employment. It is for this reason that we would *ordinarily* expect the development of firm-specific skills to be coupled with generous protection against unemployment.

On the flip side of the Japanese system, we find welfare production regimes with extensive unemployment protection, but low or only modest employment protection. Especially in economies dominated by small firms, with small internal labor markets and little organizational capacity to adapt to business cycles, employment protection is a costly and unattractive option for employers. Denmark is an archetypal example of an economy with a small-firm industrial structure. Yet, generous unemployment protection for skilled workers is still a requisite for workers to invest in industry-specific skills in these cases, much the same way as employment protection is a requisite for investment in firm-specific skills. In effect, unemployment protection increases employment security *within the industry*, as opposed to security within a particular firm. At a high level of abstraction, therefore, the *industry* in a country with high unemployment and low employment protection becomes functionally equivalent to the *firm* in a country with low unemployment and high employment protection.

4.4.1 Measuring Protection

There are no direct measures of job security, such as the risk of non-voluntary dismissals, that can be used consistently across national cases.[8]

---

[8] See OECD (1997c: 147) for a discussion of these measurement problems.

However, a series of indirect measures pertaining to legal and quasi-legal rules governing individual hiring and firing have been developed by the OECD to gauge the strictness of employment protection legislation (EPL). The composite EPL index is based on provisions in the legal code as well as in collective bargaining agreements, hereunder what constitutes just cause for dismissals, required length of advance notice, mandated severance pay, compensation for unfair dismissals, the rights of employee representatives to be informed about dismissals and other employment matters, and the rights of workers to challenge dismissals in the courts. The OECD constructed this index to reflect as accurately as possible the costs to employers of dismissing workers, and this is directly relevant to our argument since such costs can be seen as a measure of employer commitment to retain the workers they hire.

The composite EPL index is constructed for both regular and temporary employment, but our argument is only relevant for the former since neither employers nor employees have much of an incentive to invest in firm-specific skills when employment is time-limited. The regular employment EPL index is calculated for two periods, the late 1980s and the late 1990s, but since it is nearly perfectly correlated between the two periods (r = 0.99) we have simply used an average (shown in the first column of Table 4.1). The index is based on the regulation of individual contracts and does not incorporate measures for protection against collective dismissals. In OECD's latest update of the index (*OECD Employment Outlook* 1999) a separate index was created to reflect the regulation of collective dismissals, which is shown in the second column of Table 4.1.

Neither of the OECD measures fully takes into account the employment protection that is built into the firm governance structure or into the workings of the industrial relations system. As the OECD acknowledges, 'non-legislated employment protection tends to be more difficult to measure and may therefore be under-weighted' (*OECD Employment Outlook* 1999: 51). Japan illustrates the problem because companies in Japan offer greater protection against dismissals for their skilled workers than the EPL index would suggest (see *OECD Employment Outlook* 1994: 79–80). Indeed, dismissals and layoffs are extremely rare in Japan compared to other countries (OECD 1997c: table 5.12).[9] Instead, large Japanese firms engage in special workforce loan practices with their suppliers, called 'Shukko', which enable them to retain workers during

---

[9] These data are not fully comparable across countries, but the figure for Japan is of an order of magnitude smaller than in any other country for which data are available.

TABLE 4.1 Employment protection in eighteen OECD countries

	(1) Employment protection legislation (EPL)[a]	(2) Collective dismissals protection[b]	(3) Company-based protection[c]	(4) Index of employment protection[d]
Sweden	2.8	4.5	3	0.94
Germany	2.8	3.1	3	0.86
Austria	2.6	3.3	3	0.84
Italy	2.8	4.1	2	0.81
The Netherlands	3.1	2.8	2	0.80
Japan	2.7	1.5	3	0.76
Norway	2.4	2.8	2	0.66
Finland	2.4	2.4	2	0.64
France	2.3	2.1	2	0.61
Belgium	1.5	4.1	2	0.56
Denmark	1.6	3.1	2	0.53
Switzerland	1.2	3.9	2	0.49
Ireland	1.6	2.1	1	0.36
Canada	0.9	3.4	1	0.30
New Zealand	1.7	0.4	1	0.29
Australia	1.0	2.6	1	0.27
United Kingdom	0.8	2.9	1	0.25
United States	0.2	2.9	1	0.14

[a] Index of the 'restrictiveness' of individual hiring and firing rules contained in legislation and collective agreements (high numbers mean more restrictive regimes). Weight: 5/9.

[b] Index of the 'restrictiveness' of collective dismissal rules contained in legislation and collective agreements (high numbers mean more restrictive regimes). Weight: 2/9.

[c] Measure of company-level employment protection based on three criteria: (i) the presence of employee-elected bodies with a significant role in company manpower decisions; (ii) the existence of strong external unions with some monitoring and sanctioning capacity (especially through arbitration); and (iii) the systematic use of employee-sharing practices between parent companies and subsidiaries or across companies. Where at least two of these conditions are met to a considerable degree, we assigned a score of 3; where all three are largely absent, we assigned a score of 1. Intermediary cases were assigned a score of 2. The French case has been assigned a score of 2 even though company-level protection is weak. The reason is that the Inspectorat du Travail can and does intervene to prevent redundancies, and this is not captured by OECD's legal measure of employment protection. Weight: 2/9.

[d] Weighted average of columns (1)−(2) after each indicator has been standardized to vary between 0 and 1.

Sources: *OECD Employment Outlook* (1998: 142−52, 1999); Income Data Services (1996); Soskice (1999).

recessions. In other countries, and to some extent also in Japan, firms have to consult with works councils or other employee representative bodies before making decisions about layoffs, and often industry unions are in a strong position to oppose collective layoffs. This is only partly reflected in the EPL index since it considers only the need for firms to *notify* works councils or unions about impending dismissals—not the power of unions or works councils to prevent or modify the implementation of decisions to dismiss.

We have captured these 'private' employment protection arrangements in column 3 of Table 4.1 by a simple index that measures the strength of institutions and practices at the firm level that increase the job security of especially skilled workers in a company. The measure is based on three criteria: (i) the presence of employee-elected bodies with a significant role in company manpower decisions; (ii) the existence of strong external unions with some monitoring and sanctioning capacity (especially through arbitration); and (iii) the systematic use of employee-sharing practices between parent companies and subsidiaries or across companies. Where at least two of these conditions are met to a considerable degree, we assigned a score of 3; where all three are largely absent, we assigned a score of 1. Intermediary cases were assigned a score of 2. With the exception of Japan the index of company-based protection is consistent with the rank-ordering implied by the composite index.

The final column combines the OECD and company-based measures in a composite index that captures both the legal and more informal aspects of employment protection. The index is a weighted average with the following weights: 5/9, 2/9, and 2/9. The first two weights are adopted unchanged from OECD's own weighing scheme (*OECD Employment Outlook* 1999: 118), and reflect the fact that collective dismissal rules tend to build on individual dismissal rules, which are already part of the EPL index. Since the influence of employee representative bodies over firm-level manpower decisions is also partly captured by the EPL index, we assigned the same (low) weight to the company protection indicator. We feel that the resulting index of employment protection is about as accurate as possible, and although some would quibble with the assignment of weights the relative numbers are not very sensitive to changes in these weights.

Looking at the ranking of countries, it is not surprising to find the Anglo-Saxon countries at the low end, and Japan and many of the continental European countries at the high end of protection. Belgium, Denmark, and Switzerland are in the lower half of the table, most likely because these countries have relatively large small-firm sectors, but in terms of actual numbers the break in the employment protection index is between this group of countries and the Anglo-Saxon countries.

The measurement of unemployment protection is more straightforward, although there are some non-trivial issues concerning the *administration* of unemployment-benefit systems. The most obvious indicator, and the most commonly used, is unemployment replacement rates; i.e. the portion of a worker's previous wage that is replaced by unemployment benefits (see column 1 of Table 4.2). We are here considering a 'typical' worker, defined as a 40-year-old industrial production worker, 'averaged' across several different family types (single, married to working spouse, and married to non-working spouse), and we are looking at *net* replacement rates where cross-national differences in tax systems and non-income subsidies for unemployed have been adjusted for (such as rent support). Given that taxation of unemployment benefits varies considerably across countries, gross replacement rates (for which much more detailed data exist) can be quite misleading.

As in the case of employment protection, the Anglo-Saxon countries again score at the bottom. But note that the three continental European countries falling in the lower half of the employment protection index —Belgium, Denmark, and Switzerland—now figure at or near the top of the table. On the other hand, two countries—Italy and Japan—have very low replacement rates compared to their position on the employment protection indicators. The pattern is broadly similar, though not identical, when we look instead at the actual amount of money the government spends on unemployment benefits (as a share of GDP), compared to the number of unemployed people (as a share of the population). As before, the three countries in northern Europe with relatively low employment protection are among the five countries with the most generous unemployment-benefit systems.

Table 4.2 also includes a more qualitative measure of the administration of unemployment benefits: the restrictiveness of the definition of a 'suitable job.' All national unemployment systems stipulate that in order to receive benefits a person cannot refuse a 'suitable' job, but what constitutes a 'suitable job' varies significantly from one system to another. In principle, such variation is important for our purposes. For example, if a skilled worker is required to take any available job, regardless of whether it is commensurate with the worker's skills, high unemployment benefits are of limited value from the perspective of reducing the riskiness of specific skills investments. In practice it is difficult to get any precise comparable figures for this variable. We therefore pieced together only a very simple three-tiered classification based on a variety of

TABLE 4.2 Unemployment protection in eighteen OECD countries

	(1) Net unemployment replacement rates[a]	(2) Generosity of benefits[b]	(3) Definition of 'suitable' job[c]	(4) Index of unemployment protection[d]
Denmark	60	76	3	0.91
The Netherlands	58	74	3	0.89
Switzerland	(40)	94	2	0.86
Belgium	57	99	2	0.82
Austria	43	78	3	0.81
Germany	43	66	3	0.77
Norway	40	40	3	0.64
Sweden	30	52	3	0.63
France	48	44	2	0.54
Finland	45	20	2	0.43
Ireland	(38)	59	1	0.37
Japan	10	48	2	0.33
Canada	32	49	2	0.30
New Zealand	31	44	1	0.27
Australia	32	30	1	0.22
Italy	5	18	2	0.18
United Kingdom	23	15	1	0.11
United States	14	26	1	0.10

[a] Net unemployment replacement rates for a 40-year-old representative worker. Net figures for Ireland and Switzerland are missing from the source and have instead been estimated by taking gross replacement rates for these countries as proportions of average gross replacement rates and then multiplying these proportions by average net replacement rates.

[b] The share of GDP paid in unemployment benefits as a percentage of the share of unemployed in the total population. Average for the period 1973–89.

[c] Index that measures the restrictiveness of the definition of a 'suitable job' in the administration of benefits to unemployed. (1) Any job qualifies as a suitable job; (2) Skilled unemployed are given some discretion in rejecting jobs they deem unsuitable to their skills, but choice is restricted in time and/or to certain job categories; (3) Skilled unemployed exercise wide discretion in accepting or rejecting jobs on the grounds of the suitability of the job to their skills.

[d] Average of columns (1) – (3) after each indicator has been standardized to vary between 0 and 1.

Sources: Col. 1: Restricted OECD data reported in Esping-Andersen (1999: table 2.2, p. 22); OECD, *Database on Unemployment Benefit Entitlements and Replacement Rates* (undated). Col. 2: Huber et al. (1997); *OECD Economic Outlook* (various years); OECD, *Labour Force Statistics* (various years). Col. 3: OECD (1991: 199 – 231); European Commission, *Unemployment in Europe* (various years); and national sources.

national and international sources. Though basically reinforcing the pattern revealed by the other two indicators, it does affect the rank-order position of some countries slightly.

As in the case of employment protection, we combined the various indicators into an index of unemployment protection (see column 4). With the possible exception of Italy, this index gives a good sense of cross-national differences in the extent of unemployment protection. The number for Italy probably underestimates the extent of protection because of quasi-public insurance schemes that do not show up in the official statistics. Thus, about a third of (mainly large companies) covered by Casa Integrazione have replacement rates between 70 and 80 per cent, and there are normally good unemployment-benefit schemes for artisans (i.e. craftsmen) administered at the regional level by associations representing small firms, in cooperation with regional governments.[10]

4.4.2 Measuring Skill Profiles

Workers' skills are difficult to measure because they are not directly observable. However, we can rely on a number of indirect measures. The first is median enterprise tenure rates—the median number of years workers have been with their current employer (based on national labor force surveys). These numbers contain relevant information about the firm specificity of skills because firms and individuals investing heavily in such skills become increasingly dependent upon one another for their future welfare. The greater the investment, the higher the opportunity costs of severing the relationship, and the lower the incentive for either party to do so. Indeed, short tenure rates may not only be an indicator of the *absence* of firm-specific skills, but a positive measure of *presence* of general skills. The reason is that general skills are developed in part by accumulating job experience from many different firms.

The drawback of using tenure rates to measure firm-specific skills is that they may also in part reflect the costs of dismissing workers as a result of employment protection. However, if higher tenure rates were unrelated to the extent of firm-specific skills, then the association between employment protection and tenure rates would be weak at best since most job switching is known to be voluntary. But, in fact, the cross-national association between the two variables is rather high (r = 0.75), and where data are available tenure rates are strongly negatively related to quit rates. From this it seems clear that at least part of the effect of

---

[10] We thank Michele Salvati for providing this information.

TABLE 4.3 Skill profiles in eighteen OECD countries

	(1) Median length of tenure[a]	(2) Vocational training share[b]	(3) Vocational training system[c]	(4) Upper-secondary/ university education[d]	(5) Skill profile[e]
Austria	6.9	22	Dual apprenticeship	71 6	Firm/industry/ occupational
Germany	10.7	34	Dual apprenticeship	81 13	Firm/industry/ occupational
Sweden	7.8	36	Vocational colleges	74 13	Firm/industry/ occupational
Norway	(6.5)	37	Vocational colleges	82 16	Industry/ occupational
Belgium	8.4	53	Mixed	53 11	Industry/ occupational
Japan	8.3	16	Company-based	n.a. n.a.	Firm/ occupational
Finland	7.8	32	Vocational colleges	67 12	Industry/ occupational
Italy	8.9	35	Company-based	38 8	Firm/ occupational
France	7.7	28	Company-based	60 10	Firm/ occupational
Ireland	5.3	6	Weak	50 11	Occupational/ general
The Netherlands	5.5	43	Mixed	62 22	Industry/ occupational
Switzerland	6.0	23	Dual apprenticeship	80 10	Industry/ occupational
Denmark	4.4	31	Mixed	66 15	Industry/ occupational
Canada	5.9	5	Weak	76 17	Occupational/ general
Australia	3.4	9	Weak	57 15	Occupational/ general
New Zealand	n.a.	7	Weak	60 11	Occupational/ general
United Kingdom	5.0	11	Weak	76 13	Occupational/ general
United States	4.2	3	Weak	86 26	Occupational/ general

employment protection on tenure rates must go through the effect of the former on the stock of firm-specific skills. This interpretation is supported by considerable evidence showing tenure rates across industries *within* countries to be closely associated with the skill intensity of these industries (*OECD Employment Outlook* 1993: 141–5).

Used as a measure of firm-specific skills (column 1 in Table 4.3), tenure rates suggest that the stock of such skills is low in the Anglo-Saxon countries compared to Japan and most of the continental European countries where workers stay with their firms for significantly longer periods of time. The exceptions are Denmark, the Netherlands, and Switzerland, where firm tenure rates also tend to be quite short.

The pattern of training suggested by tenure rates is reflected in the character of vocational training systems (columns 2 and 3). Whereas such systems are weak or absent in the Anglo-Saxon countries and Ireland, in all the others vocational training is widespread and highly institutionalized. The share of an age cohort that goes through a vocational training in the former varies between 3 and 11 per cent (counting short-term post-secondary degrees, such as the American junior college system), and there is little involvement of companies in the training system. In the remaining countries, the percentage of an age cohort going through a vocational training is generally between a quarter and one half of an age cohort. The figure for Japan is only 16 per cent, but much training in this country goes on in large companies and is not recorded in the data.

The main difference among the countries with strong vocational training systems is in the emphasis on company- as opposed to industry-level training. Whereas in Japan, and to a lesser extent in France and Italy, the emphasis is on company training, the remainder have some

---

Notes for Table 4.3

[a] The median length of enterprise tenure in years, 1995 (Norwegian figure refers to 1991).

[b] The share of an age cohort in either secondary or post-secondary (ISCED5) vocational training.

[c] The character of the vocational training system according to whether most of the training occurs at the company level (as in Japan), through a dual apprenticeship system (as in Germany), through vocational colleges (as in Sweden), or through some mixture of the latter two (as in the Netherlands). Where vocational training is weak, we have not distinguished between the type of system.

[d] First entry is the percentage of 25–34-year-olds with an upper-secondary education; the second entry is the percentage of 25–34-year-olds with a university degree (1996 figures). Data are not available for Japan.

[e] Average of columns (1)–(4) after each indicator has been standardized to vary between 0 and 1.

Sources: Col. 1: *OECD Employment Outlook* (1997: table 5.5). For Norway: *OECD Employment Outlook* (1993: table 4.1). Col. 2: UNESCO (1999). Col. 3: Streeck (1992*b*); Finegold and Soskice (1988); Soskice (1999). Col. 4: OECD (1999).

combination of on-the-job training and school-based training, with heavy involvement of employer organizations and unions. Formally, the systems can be divided into apprenticeship systems of the German type, vocational school systems of the Swedish type, or mixtures between the two, but all combine theoretical, industry-specific, and direct workplace training (column 3). The weight between the three is difficult to gauge, but Belgium, the Netherlands, and the Scandinavian countries (less so Sweden) tend to place more emphasis on school-based training (i.e. provision of non-firm-specific skills) than do Austria or Germany.

An additional indicator of skill profiles is the share of young people with post-compulsory education (column 4). Unlike tenure rates, there is no indication on this measure that Anglo-Saxon countries are less skill intensive than continental European countries (no comparable data are available for Japan). As in any advanced economy, a high average standard of living in the Anglo-Saxon countries depends on heavy investment in human capital. Indeed, there is some indication that countries with only a modest stock of firm-specific skills compensate by investing more heavily in higher education. For example, there is a negative relationship between tenure rates and university degrees. The USA can here be highlighted as an archetypal case of a country with a weak company and vocational training system, but a very advanced higher education system. Indeed, a college education in this country is widely considered the only effective insurance against an otherwise highly volatile and uncertain labor market.

The figures for upper-secondary education hide more subtle differences in the *content* of this education. In the Anglo-Saxon countries university education tends to be very general, and even engineering and business schools provide very broad training that is not linked to particular industries or trades. By contrast, in Japan and most continental European countries, many university degrees are more specialized and there tend to be close linkages between engineering and trade schools to private industry. Combined with the other two indicators, this paints a fairly clear picture of the skill profile in different countries, summarized in column (5) of Table 4.3. Needless to say, all training systems produce a whole range of skills, but each system can be roughly characterized according to its emphasis on firm, industry, occupational, or general skills.

4.4.3 Putting the Pieces Together

Fig. 4.2 plots the eighteen OECD countries on the employment and unemployment protection indexes. Countries are distributed along a primary

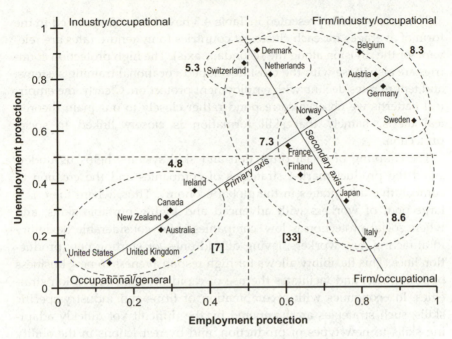

Fig. 4.2 Social protection and skill profiles

Notes: Bolded numbers are mean tenure rates for the cluster of countries circled; bracketed numbers are the percentage of an age cohort going through a vocational training.

Source: See Tables 4.1, 4.2, and 4.3.

axis, corresponding to the south-west–north-east diagonal in Fig. 4.2, with some countries further divided along a secondary axis, corresponding to the north-west–south-east diagonal in Fig. 4.2. The main axis separates countries into two distinct welfare production regimes: one combining weak employment and unemployment protection with a general skills profile, represented by the Anglo-Saxon countries and Ireland; and one combining high protection on at least one of the two social protection dimensions with firm- and/or industry-specific skills, represented by the continental European countries and Japan. The secondary axis divides the latter group into one with greater emphasis on employment protection and the creation of firm-specific skills, exemplified primarily by Japan and Italy,[11] and one with greater emphasis on unemployment protection and the production of industry-specific skills, exemplified by Denmark, the Netherlands, and Switzerland.

[11] Although the position of Italy is probably exaggerated by the failure to account for semi-public unemployment insurance arrangements, as noted above.

The data on skills presented in Table 4.3 have been summarized in the form of averages for each cluster of countries (only tenure rates are relevant for the division along the secondary axis). The high protection countries are also those with the most developed vocational training systems, and tenure rates decline with employment protection. Clearly, the empirical patterns we observe correspond rather closely to our main theoretical thesis, namely that skill formation is closely linked to social protection.

The coupling of social protection and skill systems helps us understand the product market strategies of companies and the creation of comparative advantages in the global economy. Thus, where there is a large pool of workers with advanced and highly portable skills, and where social protection is low, companies enjoy considerable flexibility in attracting new workers, laying off old ones, or starting new production lines. This flexibility allows for high responsiveness to new business opportunities, and facilitates the use of rapid product innovation strategies. In economies with a combination of firm- and industry-specific skills, such strategies are hampered by the difficulty of quickly adapting skills to new types of production, and by restrictions in the ability of firms to hire and fire workers. On the other hand, these welfare-production regimes advantage companies that seek to develop deep competencies within established technologies, and to continuously upgrade and diversify existing product lines ('diversified quality production' in the terminology of Streeck 1991).

There is considerable case-oriented research to support these propositions (see especially Porter 1990; Soskice 1999; and Hollingsworth and Boyer 1997), and they can be bolstered by quantitative evidence constructed by Thomas Cusack from US Patent Office data. Broken into thirty technology classes, Cusack counted the number of references to scientific articles for patents in each technology class and country, and then divided this number by the world number of scientific citations per technology class.[12] The idea is that the number of scientific citations, as opposed to citations to previous patents and non-scientific sources, is a good proxy for the extent to which national firms are engaged in radical innovation strategies. The results are shown in the first column of

[12] The data are coded into references to previous patents and others, where many of the latter are references to scientific articles. To get a good estimate for the number of scientific articles in the 'other' category, the proportion of scientific references to other references was calculated for a random sample (6,000) for each country and technology class. These factors were then used to correct the overall dataset so as to get a better measure of scientific citations.

TABLE 4.4 Scientific citation rates and low-wage service employment in eighteen OECD countries

	(1) Scientific citation ratio[a]	(2) Private service employment[b]
Ireland	1.514	—
United States	1.310	23
New Zealand	1.267	—
Canada	1.032	20
United Kingdom	0.837	16
Australia	0.804	26
Sweden	0.757	14
The Netherlands	0.754	14
Norway	0.690	17
Switzerland	0.639	—
France	0.601	11
Belgium	0.598	13
Germany	0.592	14
Japan	0.586	—
Austria	0.575	—
Finland	0.552	11
Denmark	0.536	11
Italy	0.491	9

[a] The average number of scientific citations per patent by national firms in each of 30 technology classes as a proportion of the average number of citations in each class for the entire world.

[b] The number of people employed in wholesale, retail trade, restaurants and hotels, and in community, social and personal services, 1982−91 as a percentage of the working-age population.

Source: Col. 1: United States Patent Office Data. Col. 2: OECD (1996*b*).

Table 4.4, with countries ranked by the average ratio of scientific citations for patents secured by national firms. As it turns out, the Anglo-Saxon countries and Ireland all have ratios that are significantly higher than in the specific skills countries of continental Europe and Japan. Precisely as we would expect.

At the low-tech end of product markets, we have to rely on a different type of data to detect cross-national differences. In column (2) of Table 4.4 we used the proportion of the working-age population employed in private social and personal services as a proxy. As argued by Esping-Andersen (1990: ch. 8) and Iversen and Wren (1998), firms that rely heavily on low-skilled and low-paid labor for profitability tend to be concentrated in these industries. Although we only have data for a subset of countries, the numbers display a rather clear cross-national pattern. Producers of standardized and low-productivity services thrive in general skills countries such as Australia and the United States because they can hire from a large pool of unskilled workers who are afforded much job protection and whose wages are held down by low unemployment protection. By contrast, firms trying to compete in this space in specific skills countries such as Germany and Sweden are inhibited by higher labor costs and lower flexibility in hiring and firing. These differences have magnified during the 1980s and 1990s, and Britain is now closer to the mean for the general skills countries.

In an open international trading system, differences in product market strategies will tend to be perpetuated, which in turn feed back into organized support for existing social protection regimes. Contrary to the popular notion of a 'race to the bottom' in social policies, differences across countries persist and are even attenuated through open trade. Correspondingly, from the 1970s to the 1980s and 1990s, unemployment benefits remained stable or rose in most continental European countries, but they were cut in Ireland and all the Anglo-Saxon countries with the exception of Australia.[13] Moreover, whereas labor markets have become even more deregulated in the latter countries, employment protection has remained high in the former. Although some countries have seen a notable relaxation in the protection of temporary employment, there is no reduction in the level of protection for regular employment (*OECD Employment Outlook* 1999). This evidence, and the theoretical explanation we provide for it, seriously challenge the notion, popular in much of the economic literature, that social protection is simply inefficient forms of labor market 'rigidities.' Social protection can provide important competitive advantages. By the same token we question the prevalent approach in the sociological and political science literature, which understands social protection solely in terms of its redistributive effects.

4.4.4 Implications for Labor Market Stratification

That said, we are not implying that welfare production regimes are irrelevant for distributive outcomes. To the contrary, our argument has important implications for equality and labor market stratification, and it helps account for the political divisions over the welfare state. Partly these effects are direct consequences of particular product market strategies and their associated skill profiles; partly they reflect the effects of

---

[13] Based on gross unemployment replacement rates published in OECD's *Database on Unemployment Benefit Entitlements and Replacement Rates* (undated).

the collective wage-bargaining system that is itself an important component of the wage protection system.

With respect to wage protection, the most important issue is what we have previously referred to as wage protection for the unemployed. Such protection implies that workers with similar skills are paid the same amount across firms and industries, and in practice this is accomplished through collective wage-bargaining at the industry level or at higher levels. It is striking, though not surprising, that all countries with a strong emphasis on industry-specific skills have developed effective wage co-ordination at the industry level. Conversely, general skills countries, and countries with a strong emphasis on firm-specific skills (Japan in particular), lack such coordination.

Very extensive evidence has now been accumulated that demonstrates the importance of the structure of the wage-bargaining system for the wage structure (see especially Rowthorn 1992; Wallerstein 1999; and Rueda and Pontusson 2000), but we believe the skill system is equally important. Fig. 4.3, which uses the incidence of vocational training as the indicator for skill system, clearly shows the empirical association between skills and earnings equality, and there is a good reason. Because specific skills systems generate high demand for workers with good vocational training, young people who are not academically inclined have career opportunities that are largely missing in general skills systems. Whereas a large proportion of early school leavers in the former acquire valuable skills through the vocational training system, in the latter most early school leavers end up as low-paid unskilled workers for most or all of their working lives.

In combination, the wage-bargaining system—i.e. whether it is industry coordinated or not—and the skill system—i.e. whether it is specific skills or general skills biased—provides a powerful explanation of earnings inequality as we have illustrated in Fig. 4.4. The figure shows earnings and income inequality for each combination of bargaining and skill system. The big drop in earnings equality occurs as we move from specific skills systems with industry-coordinated bargaining to general skills systems where industry-coordinated wage-bargaining is lacking. By themselves this pair of dichotomous variables account for nearly 70 per cent of the cross-national variance in income inequality.[14] Yet, despite their importance for explaining inequality, neither variable is

---

[14] The estimated regression equation is :

Income equality $= 0.23 + 0.048 \times$ Specific skills $+ 0.055 \times$ Industry coordination, where $R^2 = 0.69$

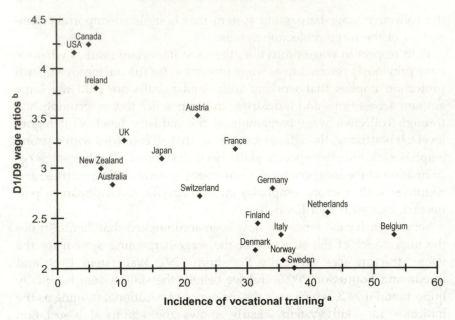

FIG. 4.3 Vocational training and wage inequality

[a] The share of an age cohort in either secondary or post-secondary (ISCED5) vocational training.
[b] The earnings of a worker in the top decile of the earnings distribution relative to a worker in the bottom decile of the earnings distribution.

Sources: D1/D9 wage ratios: UNESCO (1999). Incidence of vocational training: OECD, *Electronic Data Base on Wage Dispersion* (undated).

accorded much attention in the established welfare state literature, notwithstanding the focus on distribution in this literature. In our theoretical framework, on the other hand, they are integral parts of the story, even though we have focused on micro mechanisms that emphasize the importance of efficiency.

The hypothesized relationship between product market strategies, skill composition, and equality points to another, and quite different, source of evidence: academic test scores. Because specific skills systems create strong incentives among young schoolgoers to do as well as they can in school in order to get the best vocational training spots, whereas those at the bottom of the academic ability distribution in general skills systems have few such incentives, we should expect the number of early school leavers who fail internationally standardized tests to be higher in general skills countries than in specific skills countries.

Although the data are limited in coverage, this is in fact what we observe (see Fig. 4.5). Whereas the percentage failing the test varies

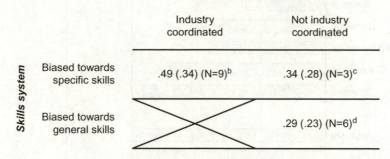

FIG. 4.4 Skills, the bargaining system, and equality[a]

[a] Numbers are D9/D1 earnings ratios based on gross earnings (including all employer contributions for pensions, social security, etc.) of a worker in the bottom decile of the earnings distribution relative to a worker in the top decile. Figures are averages for the period 1977–1993. Numbers in parentheses are D9/D1 income ratios based on disposable income of a person in the bottom decile of the earnings distribution relative to a person in the top decile. Most figures are from the early 1990s, with a few from the 1980s.

[b] Austria, Belgium, Denmark, Finland, Germany, the Netherlands, Norway, Sweden, Switzerland.

[c] France, Italy, Japan.

[d] Australia, Canada, Ireland, New Zealand, UK, USA.

Sources: Skills: see Table 4.4. Bargaining system: see Iversen (1999*a*: ch. 3). Inequality measures: see *OECD Employment Outlook* (1991, 1996); Gottschalk and Smeeding (2000: fig. 2).

between 15 and 22 per cent in the Anglo-Saxon countries, it is only between 8 and 14 in the countries emphasizing more specific skills for which we have data. Although these differences could be due to the overall quality of the educational system, it is not the case that the Anglo-Saxon countries spend less money on primary education, and there is no systematic difference in average scores. This points to the importance of incentives outside the school system, which vary systematically according to the dominant product market strategies of firms and their associated demand for particular skills.

But general skills systems are not necessarily bad for all types of inequality. They perform better in terms of gender equality at work (Estevez-Abe 1999*b*). When we compare degrees of occupational segregation, specific skills systems fare worse than general skills systems. Specific skills systems segregate women into 'female occupations' such as low-rank clerical and service jobs. Table 4.5 shows the occupational breakdown of women employed expressed in terms of a percentage of women over total workforce within the same category. While the data are not conclusive, it nonetheless shows that countries (see Germany and Sweden

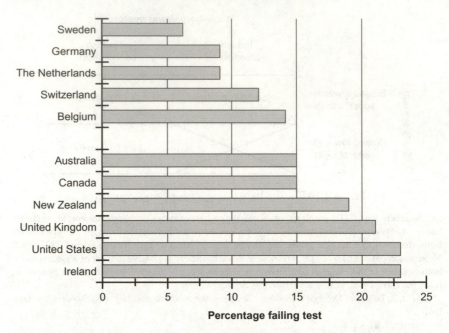

Fig. 4.5 The failure of early school leavers to pass standardized tests in
eleven OECD countries

Notes: The numbers are the percentage of all early school leavers taking the test who get a failing
score. Average across four test categories. The Belgian figure refers to Flanders only.

Source: OECD (2000).

in Table 4.5) that adopt high-quality product market strategies—thus
dependent on high industry-specific skills—employ women for production jobs to a lesser degree. The USA, the archetypal general skills system,
shows significantly higher ratios of women in technical and managerial
positions when compared to specific skills systems. Our findings support
Esping-Andersen's argument about the US employment system being
more gender equal than that found in Germany and Sweden (Esping-
Andersen 1999). Our explanation, however, differs from his.

4.5 Conclusion

Protection of employment and income is widely seen in the welfare state
literature as reducing workers' dependence on the market and employers
('decommodification' in Esping-Andersen's terminology). In turn, this is
argued to reflect a particular balance of power between labor and capital.
We reject both theses. Although strong unions and left governments

TABLE 4.5 Share of women by occupation (%)[a]

	(1) Professional, technical, and related workers	(2) Adminis- trative and managerial workers	(3) Clerical and related workers	(4) Sales workers	(5) Service workers	(6) Production and related workers
USA (1989)	22	26	70	33	30	30
Japan (1988)	10	7	58	11	40	39[b]
Germany (1986)	15	11	59	52	67	21
The Netherlands (1993)	14	0	55	32	45	12
Sweden (1989)	15		57	25	72	24
Australia (1987)	8	18	20	43	76	31

[a] Percentages represent the ratio of women over the total of men and women employed within each occupational category.

[b] The female ratio for occupational category (6) in Japan is exceptionally high due to a demographically shrinking pool of young male workers (Estevez-Abe 1999*b*).

Source: ILO (1989–90).

undoubtedly affect distributive outcomes, we have argued that employment and income protection can be seen as efforts to *increase* workers' dependence on particular employers, as well as their exposure to labor market risks. Moreover, social protection often stems from the strength rather than the weakness of employers.

The key to our argument is the link between social protection and the level and composition of skills. In a modern economy, skills are essential for firms to compete in international markets, and depending on the particular product market strategy of firms, they rely on a workforce with a certain combination of firm-specific, industry-specific, and general skills. To be cost-effective firms need workers who are willing to make personal investments in these skills. And if firms want to be competitive in product markets that require an abundance of specific skills, workers must be willing to acquire these skills at the cost of increasing their dependence on a particular employer or group of employers. Because investment in specific skills increases workers' exposure to risks, only by insuring against such risks can firms satisfy their need for specific skills.

The particular combination of employment protection and unemployment protection determines the profile of skills that is likely to emerge in an economy. Thus employment protection increases the propensity of workers to invest in firm-specific skills, whereas unemployment protection facilitates investment in industry-specific skills. The absence of both gives people strong incentives to invest in general skills. These predictions are borne out by the comparative data, which show that most countries combine either low protection with general skills, or high protection with specific skills.

Two factors contribute to the distinctiveness and resilience of particular welfare production regimes. The first is that such regimes tend to be reinforced by institutions—collective wage-bargaining systems, business organizations, employee representation, and financial systems—that facilitate the credible commitment of actors to particular strategies, such as wage restraint and long-term employment, that are necessary to sustain cooperation in the provision of specific skills. The second is that those workers and employers who are being most advantaged by these institutional complementaries also tend to be in strong political positions, in terms of both economic clout and sheer numbers. For example, the more a welfare production system emphasizes the creation of specific skills, the more likely it is that the median voter will be someone with considerable investments in specific skills, and the more likely it is that employers' interest organizations will be dominated by firms pursuing specific skills strategies. Both will contribute to perpetuating institutions and policies that advantage firms and workers with heavy investments in specific skills.

Our argument has broader implications for our understanding of the welfare state that reach well beyond the immediate effects of employment and income protection. In particular, earnings dispersion, by far the most important determinant of the overall distribution of income, is closely related to particular skill systems as well as the wage-bargaining institutions that tend to go with these systems. Similarly, the combination of particular product market strategies and skills has distinct effects on the career opportunities of particular groups, especially women. Thus, our theory implies that gender-based segmentation of the labor market varies systematically across welfare production systems.

Clearly, what we have done in this chapter is to outline a broad research agenda for the study of the welfare state rather than testing a specific set of hypotheses that follows from it. Much work needs to be done, for example, in testing whether public opinion, voting behavior, and the preferences of employers conform to the predictions of the theory. Another big task is to rewrite social history to take into account the preferences of employers, and the attempt by firms to engage in particular product market strategies. This new emphasis on firms differs from the earlier focus on the role of welfare capitalists—particularly in case studies of the American social policy—in its explicit effort to highlight links between skills, product markets, and different welfare systems. Some work has already been undertaken (cf. Estevez-Abe 1999*a*; Mares 1998; Swenson 1997, forthcoming), but there are ample opportunities to expand on their pioneering research. Finally, much work remains to be done to explore the implications of our argument for labor market stratification. We have indicated the empirical relationship between skill profiles, wage-bargaining systems, and labor market stratification (including women's position in the labor market); most of the empirical work is still to be done.

5

Firms and the Welfare State: When, Why, and How Does Social Policy Matter to Employers?

Isabela Mares

5.1 Introduction

A widely shared understanding of the functions of social policy that informs the literature developed by welfare state scholars characterizes social insurance as a compensation of workers for their disadvantaged position in the labor market. By providing benefits to workers during employment-related risks, social policies lower their dependence on the labor market—or, using the terminology developed by these studies, they 'decommodify' labor (Esping-Andersen 1990). Political and economic associations representing employees, such as trade union organizations or social democratic parties, share a strong, unambiguous interest in the provision of social insurance and in the expansion of the generosity and coverage of social policies and regard the welfare state as an important institutional arrangement that can offset the structural asymmetry of the employment relationship.

It is indisputable that these labor-centered analyses capture a central and significant component of the politics of welfare state development. Yet the relentless search for the centrality of labor's role in the dynamics of social policy expansion that has been characteristic of several 'generations' of research on the welfare state (Shalev 1983) has overshadowed a broad range of questions and issues related to the significance of social insurance to *employers*. Fundamentally simple questions pertaining to firms' relationship to the welfare state remain, so far, poorly specified theoretically. What does social policy represent to *firms*? Is the welfare state only a constraint on firms, which comes in the form of higher costs

I would like to thank Carles Boix, Peter Hall, Peter Katzenstein, Philip Manow, and David Soskice for comments on previous versions of this chapter. For financial support in writing this chapter, I am grateful to the Center for German and European Studies, Georgetown University.

or unnecessary labor market rigidities, or does it also provide some tangible and immediate benefits to employers? When do the benefits offered by the welfare state to firms outweigh the costs imposed by social policies on business? We currently lack a theory of the significance of social policies to employers that specifies the sources of business interest in social policy and the conditions under which particular firms will actively support different social policy arrangements.

This chapter will fill this analytical gap, by providing a theory of business preferences towards different social policy arrangements which, as announced in the title, will explore 'when', 'why', and 'how' social policy matters to employers. The first goal of the chapter is to identify those institutional features of different social policies that have a high salience for employers and specify the relevant policy *trade-offs* faced by firms during the process of social policy development. The second goal of the chapter is to formulate a number of hypotheses about the causes of inter-sectoral disagreement among employers during the process of social policy reform. I will develop a number of propositions about the effects of both firm and industry characteristics (reliance on a skilled workforce, incidence of different labor market risks etc.) in determining the *sensitivity* of the firm towards institutional features of different social policies—the degree of risk redistribution characterizing a social policy, the participation retained by employers in the administration of social insurance, the indexation of social policy benefits to wages, and so on. This analysis will generate strong comparative statics results identifying the ideal social policies preferred by different firms.

The model developed in this chapter seeks to contribute to the new direction of research in comparative political economy that places firms at the center of the analysis and explores cross-national differences in the nature of business involvement in the formulation and implementation of public policies (Soskice 1996b, 1999; Hall and Soskice, this volume; Wood 1997, this volume; Culpepper 1998). While sharing this analytical aspiration with most of the contributions to the volume, the chapter simultaneously attempts to establish a link to another important body of literature—comparative research on the welfare state (Mares 1996, 1998; Estevez-Abe 1999a; Manow and Ebbinghaus forthcoming). The analysis of business interests in social policy presented in this chapter is only a first step towards a synthesis between the 'varieties of capitalism' and the 'varieties of welfare regimes' literature and needs to be supplemented by a fuller model specifying the different pathways of business influence during social policy development and the conditions facilitating the emergence of different coalitions among unions and employers (Swenson

1991, 1997; Pierson 1995*a*; Mares 1997*a*, 2000). Yet it provides important *microfoundations* for the understanding of the institutional complementarities between different systems of skill provision and other institutions facilitating the coordination of employers, on the one hand, and institutions of social protection on the other hand (Manow and Seils 1999).

Social policies create indirect, but strong institutional advantages to employers. By providing support to workers during various employment-related risks—such as unemployment, disability, or sickness—social policies raise the reservation wage of workers, allowing them to reject jobs that do not correspond to their skill qualifications. Thus, indirectly, social policies support the investments in skills made by *employers*. Several characteristics of institutional design of social policies—such as the indexation of social policy benefits to wages, restrictions on the type of jobs that recipients of benefits can accept—'reproduce' the wage and skill hierarchies of a particular firm during moments in which the employment relationship is temporarily interrupted. (For a lengthier elaboration of this argument see Mares 1998.) Social policies are of particular importance to employers in coordinated market economies, where a dense network of background institutions facilitates intensive firm-level investment in the skill formation of the workforce but also to individual firms in liberal market economies that have made investments in the training of their workforce (Mares 1998; Hall and Soskice, this volume; Manow 2000).

The analytical framework developed in this volume provides important insights for the understanding of the sources of business interest in social policy. The skill profile of a firm—and the relative mix of firm-specific and more 'portable' skills—remains a significant predictor for the interest of a firm towards different social policy arrangements and the willingness of a firm to discount the costs and financial burden imposed by a social policy in exchange for the institutional advantages provided by the welfare state (Mares 1996; Estevez-Abe et al. this volume). However, this chapter will argue that to characterize the preferences of employers during the process of social policy reform, we need to consider the importance of additional variables, most significantly firm size and the incidence of a risk facing the employees of a firm. The empirical analysis of the role played by employers in the development of the German welfare state reveals that we encounter strong intersectoral conflict among employers when confronted with policy dilemmas surrounding the design of new institutions of social insurance. These intersectoral disagreements among employers cannot be predicted by differences in the skill profiles of firms alone. Firm size, the incidence of a risk, and the skill composition of a firm *interact* in determining the *sensitivities* of firms towards various questions pertaining to the design of a new social policy and in explaining the variation in the social policy preferences of different firms.

To lay out and test this argument, this chapter will proceed as follows. In the following section, I will identify the most important policy trade-offs encountered by employers during the process of social policy development. Next, I will present a formal model of firms' utilities towards different social policy arrangements that specifies more rigorously the conditions under which the utility of different types of firms attains its maximum in different points in the social policy space. Using the insights generated by the model, I will explore the position of employers during three episodes in the political history of the German welfare state: the introduction of disability insurance and unemployment insurance and the development of early retirement policies during recent decades. I conclude by exploring the implications of the analysis for our understanding of the linkage between 'varieties of capitalism' and 'varieties of welfare regimes.'

5.2 The Universe of Social Policies: The Trade-off between Risk Redistribution and Control

Social insurance—the provision of income compensating for employment-related risks—comes in a variety of institutional forms. The level and generosity of social policy benefits, the relative mix between tax- and contribution-based financing, the criteria used in the determination of eligibility for insurance or assistance—vary dramatically across policies. To get a theoretical grip on this institutional diversity, the model developed in this chapter will assume that the empirical variety among existing social policies can be summarized in two aggregate variables.

These two dimensions, which will be called *risk redistribution* and *control*, form the axes of the social policy space represented in Fig. 5.1. The horizontal axis—*risk redistribution*—ranks different social policies based on their ability to 'reapportion the costs of risks and mischance' (Baldwin 1990: 1). The degree of risk redistribution of a social policy is the aggregate effect of two features of institutional design. The first concerns the boundary of the risk pool, in other words, how many occupations are part of the common pool of risk created by social insurance. Is the social policy restricted to the participants of a single firm (as in some private social policies) or does the insurance cover several occupations that are affected in dissimilar ways by a risk? Secondly, the

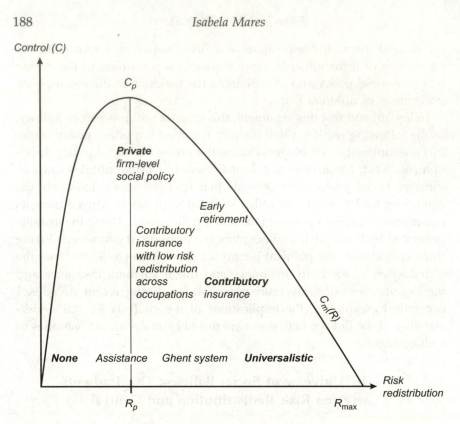

FIG. 5.1 The social policy space

degree of risk redistribution of a social policy is affected by a number of policy decisions that establish a relationship between the incidence of a risk and the level of social insurance contributions. Risk redistribution is lower if social insurance contributions mirror and reflect the actuarial incidence of a risk; it is higher in those social policies that loosen this relationship.

The vertical axis of the social policy space—labeled *control*—denotes the residual responsibilities in the administration of social insurance retained by employers. In other words, control seeks to capture the participation and involvement of employers in a variety of administrative decisions—ranging from the calculation of the level of social insurance contributions (and their modification in response to sudden changes in the incidence of a risk) to the determination of the level and duration of social policy benefits and so on.

Fig. 5.1 situates a variety of social policies within the social policy space bounded by the two axes—*risk redistribution* and *control*. At one extreme of the social policy space, we find universalistic social policies that take high values of *risk redistribution* and low values of *control*. A comprehensive risk pool that includes all occupations and flat-rate social policy benefits that are divorced from the incidence of a risk guarantee that for these policies 'the community of risks coincides with the entire human community' (Baldwin 1990: 3). Since business plays no role in the administration of social insurance, these policies take very low values along the control axis. At the other extreme of the social policy space, we find private-level social policies. In these policies, risk redistribution is very low, since the risk pool is restricted to the members of a single firm. Control, on the other hand, is very high—since private social policies can be administered exclusively by employers, who retain a high level of discretion in initiating and withholding insurance benefits, in targeting these benefits to particular groups of employees, etc. Contributory insurance solutions take intermediate values along both axes. In these social policies, employers participate with bureaucratic representatives and trade unions in the administration of social insurance. The degree of risk redistribution is lower if compared with universalistic social policies. The risk pool is not comprehensive, as a number of occupations are generally excluded from insurance. In some forms of contributory insurance, the insurance contributions required by employers and employees mirror the incidence of a risk, as high-risk industries and occupations pay higher insurance contributions—a policy characteristic that further lowers the degree of risk redistribution of the policy.

Early retirement policies occupy a special position in the social policy space. These policies are characterized by a very high involvement of firms in the initiation of the policy, the determination of the benefits of early retirees, etc. Thus, early retirement policies can be ranked along the axis control in immediate vicinity to private-level social policy. However, early retirement policies are simultaneously characterized by a very high redistribution of risks across several subsystems of the welfare state—unemployment, old-age, and disability insurance. It follows that the values along the horizontal axis (*risk redistribution*) are higher than the values for a contributory insurance policy. Early retirement is, in fact, characterized by a unique combination of *control* and *risk redistribution* which positions it in the upper right corner of the social policy space.

A few additional considerations about Fig. 5.1 are, perhaps, necessary at this point. It is important to point out that social policies characterized simultaneously by high values along both axes, risk redistribution and control, do not exist. A hypothetical example for a policy situated in the upper right-hand corner of the social policy space would be a social policy entirely administered by the firm (or an association of employers), with no participation of labor representatives or the state, but which remains universalistic in its character—tax financed, including all occupations, and involving no differentiation in contributions across industries. Such policies remain historically unknown. I will model this as a constraint on the set of possible social policies—which is represented in Fig. 5.1 by the upper boundary of the social policy space.

The second observation about the distribution of the different social policies in the social policy space concerns the presence of a *policy trade-off between risk redistribution and control.* The diagonal axis in Fig. 5.1 linking private-level social policies to contributory insurance to universalistic social policies represents the policy trade-off between risk redistribution and control faced by employers during the process of social policy development. Employers are never able to achieve a maximal degree of risk redistribution and a maximal control at the same time: policies characterized by a maximal control of employers (private social policies) remain ultimately incompatible with a very high degree of risk redistribution; conversely, in policies characterized by a high degree of risk redistribution (universalistic social policies), control is very low. The existence of this trade-off raises, however, the interesting questions: What firms are more interested in the advantages of risk redistribution and what firms are more interested in the advantages of control? One of the goals of the model developed in this chapter is to formulate a number of hypotheses about the reasons why different firms prefer social policies situated at different points along the diagonal axis of the social policy space.

To lay the groundwork for the formal model of firms' preferences towards different social policies, it is important at this point to provide a more rigorous description of the social policy space and to spell out the assumptions about the combinations of risk redistribution and control that remain possible. The above discussion has suggested that we can model the social policy space by a convex region in a plane bounded by the *risk redistribution* axis and a curved 'boundary'.

To be more specific, we can regard the upper boundary of the social policy space as the graph of a function $C_m = C_m(R)$ which models the maximum level of *Control* (C) available to employers for social policies with a level of *Risk Redistribution* (R). I will make the following hypotheses about the function C_m.

Hypothesis P 1: $C_m(0) = 0$.

At the origin of the social policy space, the point where both control and risk redistribution take values of 0, only one outcome is possible—this outcome will be labeled *None*. This hypothesis models the constraint that if $R = 0$, C can take only the value 0, i.e. at a point of no risk redistribution, we cannot find several different social policies that differ in their degree of control.

Hypothesis P 2: $C_m(R_{max}) = 0$.

Universalistic social policies are policies characterized by very high levels of risk redistribution (in this model $R = R_{max}$). As the discussion in the previous section has pointed out, in universalistic social policies employers play virtually no role in the administration of social insurance, which remains entirely in the hands of the state. According to the previous discussion, this means no control. Therefore, this constraint will be modeled by setting $Cm = 0$ at the point R_{max}.

Hypothesis P 3: There exists a level of risk redistribution R_p, such that C_m is increasing on $[0, R_p]$ and decreasing on $[R_p, R_{max}]$.

I will describe the significance of R_p through an example. Let us imagine a social policy in which employers' control is maximal, $SP_p(C_p, R_p)$. Let us think, for example, of a firm-level pension policy in which the benefits are not based on contributions of the employee, but are entirely financed by the employer to reward the loyalty of the workers and a lifelong career in the same firm. No benefits are paid to those employees that leave the firm prior to retirement or who change employers during their careers. Such social policy arrangements—encountered most often during the early industrialization—approximate a point of maximal control of employers ($C_p = C_m(R_p)$).

Social policies situated on the left-hand side of SP_p (where both the control of employers and the level of risk redistribution are lower) can be interpreted as 'scaled-down' versions of the same policy. For example, we can imagine possible versions of the same policy situated on the left-hand side of SP_p—characterized by lower levels of risk redistribution (the policy is directed to fewer employees) and lower levels of control (for example employers do not exercise unilateral discretionary power in the administration of these benefits, some consultation with the employees is in place). The shape of the boundary of the social policy space in the interval $[0, R_p]$ models the constraint on employers' control posed by the low levels of risk redistribution that can be achieved in this private social policy.

The second part of hypothesis 3 (C_m decreases in the interval $[R_p, R_{max}]$) models the trade-off between risk redistribution and control identified in the previous section. Let us assume a firm offering a social policy (that can be approximated by the policy R_p) which desires to move to a social policy characterized by a higher level of risk redistribution. We can imagine a social policy with $R > R_p$ as a social policy organized and administered by a group of employers of the same industry, involving thus a risk redistribution among the participants of this risk pool, but no cross-occupational risk redistribution. The higher level of risk redistribution would, however, come at the price of a decrease in control—as social policy benefits would now become transferable across different firms (to accommodate the increase in risk redistribution). Individual firms would have to relinquish part of discretionary authority over the distribution of social policy benefits in exchange for the advantages of risk redistribution. If follows that $C_m(R) < C_m(R_p)$

Hypothesis P 4: $C_m(R)$ is concave as a function of R.

This is equivalent to asking that the social policy space be convex. This hypothesis becomes very natural once we model the social policy space as a continuum and not as a discrete collection of different social policies. By definition, convexity of policy space requires that if two different social policies SP_1 and SP_2 exist, then all policies situated on the line segment linking SP_1 to SP_2 are also situated in the social policy space. This requirement is satisfied, since all social policies on the line segment between SP_1 and SP_2 can be thought of as weighted combinations of SP_1 and SP_2.

5.3 Firms' Utilities for Different Social Policies

We are now ready to turn to the main question of the analysis: the question of firms' preferences towards different social policies. I will approach this question as follows. I will first analyze the variation in the utility of firms along the *risk redistribution* dimension of the social policy space and I will then discuss the variation along the second axis, *control*. For each of the two dimensions of the social policy space, I will identify both the benefits and costs to the firm brought about by an increase in *risk redistribution* and *control* and will develop a number of hypotheses about the relative magnitude of the two effects for different firms. Next, I will specify the conditions under which the utility of the firm will attain its maximum at different points in the social policy space.

5.3.1 Firms' Utilities for Risk Redistribution

How does the utility of different firms vary along the risk redistribution dimension of the social policy space? How do employers choose among different social policies characterized by *similar* levels of control, but *different* levels of risk redistribution? What firm and industry character-istics are more likely to influence the importance of risk redistribution for the individual firm?

As discussed above, a movement along the horizontal dimension of the social policy space from private to universalistic social policies involves both a gradual expansion of the risk pool (through the inclu-sion of additional occupations in social insurance) and a weakening of the insurance principle in the determination of the level of contributions required by the employer and employee. To characterize the utility of employers along the horizontal axis, we need to model the relative magnitude of two separate effects: the set-up costs of a social policy versus the benefits brought about by the participation in a common pool of risks. In other words, the utility towards risk redistribution of the firm (at a constant level of control C_0) is

$$U(R, C_0) = B^R - K^R$$

where B^R denotes the benefits of risk redistribution, while K^R denotes the costs of the expansion of the risk pool.

Let the parameter ι_R denote the incidence of a labor market risk for a particular firm. The factors that affect the magnitude of ι_R are risk-specific and vary thus across different labor market risks. The level of mech-anization and other variables characterizing the level of technological development of the particular industry affect the incidence of the risk of workplace accidents. Iron- and steel-producers or producers of mechan-ical equipment employing new and complex technologies are 'high-risk' industries; artisans and other producers involving a lower level of mech-anization are 'low-risk' industries. The volatility in the demand for a firm's product or the reliance of the firms on external markets affect the incidence of the risk of unemployment. The demographic composition of the workforce of a firm affects the incidence of yet another labor market risk—the risk of old age.

The incidence of a risk has immediate effects on the relative magnitude of B^R—the benefits of risk redistribution for the individual firm—and K^R—the costs of participating in a common pool of risk. In fact, a central hypothesis of the model will be that *an increase in the incidence of a risk will increase the net benefits of risk redistribution for the individual firm*. For these firms, private forms of insurance are often costly and extremely ineffective, since sharing 'good' and 'bad' risks is very rarely possible in these narrow risk pools. However, as the size of the risk pool increases, the advantages of high inter-occupational risk redistribution can offset the costs of social insurance to the firm. It follows that firms characterized by a high incidence of a risk are expected to support social policies taking high values along the risk redistribution axis.

The related hypothesis suggests that a *decrease in the incidence of a risk will lower the benefits of high risk redistribution*. For firms in low-risk industries, highly redistributive social policies may be unattractive ($B_R < K_R$), since the inclusion in a social policy characterized by high inter-occupational risk redistribution turns these firms into subsidizers of high-risk industries. It follows that the utility of firms in low-risk industries will decrease along the risk redistribution dimension of the social policy space. We can formalize the above hypotheses as follows:

Hypothesis R: For a constant level of control, C_0, the utility function of firms, $U(R, C_0) = B^R - K^R$ is monotonic in R. There are two cases. If the costs associated with an increase in risk redistribution outweigh the benefits, then $U(R, C_0)$ decreases strictly as control increases. Conversely, if the benefits of risk redistribution outweigh the costs, then $U(R, C_0)$ increases strictly, as risk redistribution increases.

Hypothesis R 1: For firms affected by a high incidence of a risk, $B_R > K_R$. Denoting by λ_R the partial derivative of $U(R, C_0)$, we can hypothesize that for high-risk industries $\lambda_R > 0$.

Hypothesis R 2: For firms characterized by a low incidence of a risk, $B_R < K_R$, thus $\lambda_R < 0$.

To recapitulate, the above analysis has hypothesized that the sensitivity for risk redistribution of a firm ($\lambda_R = \partial U / \partial R$) is affected by the incidence of a risk. The sensitivity for risk redistribution is expected to be positive for industries characterized by a high incidence of a labor market risk and negative for industries facing a low incidence of a risk. High-risk industries are expected to favor highly redistributive social policies—such as universalistic social policies or contributory insurance solutions characterized by high inter-occupational risk redistribution— while low-risk industries are expected to oppose an expansion of the size of the risk pool and the introduction of additional policy instruments that increase the degree of risk redistribution of a social policy.

5.3.2 Firms' Utilities for Control

Let us now turn to the second dimension of the social policy space and analyze the variation in the preferences of employers for *control*. As defined above, control refers to the residual responsibilities in the administration of social insurance retained by employers. We can think of control as a bundle of institutional features that captures the authority retained by employers in the determination of both social insurance contributions and social policy benefits, involving policy decisions such as changes in the mode of financing of social policy in response to the expansion or contraction of the contributory basis of social insurance, the modification of administrative criteria defining the conditions of entitlement of social policy benefits, and so on.

Similar to the above analysis of the utility of firms for risk redistribution, I am interested in comparing the relative magnitude of the benefits (B^C) and costs (K^C) of an increase in control, at constant levels of risk redistribution. In other words, the utility of a firm along the control axis of the social policy space, at constant levels of risk redistribution, can be written as:

$$U(C, R_0) = B^C - K^C$$

An increase in the level of control from universalistic social policy (where control is assumed to be zero) to private social policies involves an increase in the firms' share of the costs of social insurance. While universalistic social policies are generally financed by income taxes and thus do not affect employers directly, both contributory insurance and private social policies are financed preponderantly by payroll taxes. Yet an increase in the level of control can bring about significant benefits to the individual firm as well. We can consider two type of benefits of social policies characterized by a high level of control. One type of advantage of contributory insurance or private social policies is the *tight coupling* between insurance benefits and the wage hierarchy established within the firm. Earnings-related contributions and benefits provide guarantees to employers that the distinctions based on skill qualifications will not be undermined during periods in which the employment relationship is temporarily interrupted (such as unemployment), acting, *de facto*, as a mechanism for skill retention (see also Mares 1997*b*; Manow 1997). (These policy resources are unavailable to employers in universalistic, tax-financed social policies in which flat-rate social policy benefits attempt to 'counteract' the wage and status distinctions established during the employment relationship (see Esping-Andersen 1990).) Secondly, in policies taking high values along the control dimension of the social policy space the discretionary ability of firms to deploy social policy as a resource stabilizing the demand for labor during economic downturns is very high. The most significant example of an expansion in firms' use of the welfare state as an instrument of adjustment is early retirement policies, which have experienced a rapid increase in all OECD countries during recent years. It follows that the utility of firms along the control dimension of the social policy space (assuming a constant level of risk redistribution R_0) can have both a positive and negative sign, depending on the relative magnitude of B^C and K^C. If $B^C > K^C$, the utility of firms will be increasing along the vertical axis of the social policy space; if the sign of the inequality is reversed, the utility will decrease along this dimension.

Two variables are likely to affect the sensitivity to control of a firm—the skill intensity of a firm and its size. The skill intensity is likely to exert a strong effect on the relative magnitude of the benefits and costs of control for the firm. In the presence of skilled workers, the firm will derive considerable advantages from social policies that protect its investment in the training of its employees, either by 'tying' the worker to the firm (through private social policies) or by ensuring that social policy benefits 'reproduce' and 'mirror' the wage differentials established within the firm, and thus create additional incentives for workers to invest in these skills. These considerations enable us to hypothesize that, in the presence of skilled workers, the benefits of social policies characterized by higher levels of control can outweigh their costs.

Similarly, size will affect the sensitivity for control of a firm. The costs of social policies characterized by high levels of control—such as private or contributory social policies—form a lower proportion of the total labor costs of large firms, as opposed to small firms. Facing tougher financial constraints, small firms have a lower (or often no) ability to develop private-level social policies, even if the firm might potentially derive advantages from these policies. We can thus hypothesize that for large firms, the benefits of control outweigh the costs, while for small firms, the costs of an increase in control are higher than the benefits. Summarizing this discussion:

Hypothesis C: For a constant level of risk redistribution, R_0, the utility functions of firms $U(R_0, C) = B_C - K_C$ is monotonic in R. There are two cases. If the costs associated with an increase in risk redistribution outweigh the benefits, then $U(R_0, C)$ decreases strictly as control increases. Conversely, if the benefits of risk redistribution outweigh the costs, then $U(R_0, C)$ increases strictly as risk redistribution increases.

Hypothesis C 1: For large firms or firms employing skilled workers, $B_C > K_C$. Denoting by λ_C the partial derivative of $U(R_0, C)$, I hypothesize that for these firms $\lambda_C > 0$.

Hypothesis C 2: Small firm or firms that do not employ high-skilled workers derive little advantages from an increase in the level of control. For these firms $B_C < K_C$, thus $\lambda_C < 0$.

The above analysis has suggested that the utility of firms towards the two dimensions of the social policy space will be influenced primarily by the incidence of a risk, the size and dependence of the firm on a skilled workforce. Both a high incidence of labor market risks and an increase in the number of skilled workers within the firm are expected to contribute to a relative increase in the benefits of risk redistribution and control to firms. In the presence of all these factors, the utility of firms is expected to increase along both axes of the social policy space. Summarizing the above hypotheses, Table 5.1 presents a first classification of firms, according to the type of their sensitivities.

Using the above hypotheses, we are now ready to analyze the preferences of firms in the entire social policy space. Due to the existence of a policy trade-off between risk redistribution and control, we can explore the conditions under which firms will prefer more 'private-type' policies (characterized by a high level of control and low level of risk

TABLE 5.1 Predicted effects of incidence of risk, size, and skill intensity on firms' sensitivities for risk redistribution and control

	Size and skill intensity	
	High	Low
Incidence of risk		
High	$\lambda_R > 0, \lambda_C > 0$	$\lambda_R > 0, \lambda_C < 0$
Low	$\lambda_R < 0, \lambda_C > 0$	$\lambda_R < 0, \lambda_C < 0$

redistribution) and contrast them to cases in which firms will favor more universalistic social policies. Summarizing the above discussion, we can write the objective function modeling the utility of a firm over the entire social policy space as

$$U(R, C) = \lambda_R R + \lambda_C C$$

in other words, as linear function of R, C.[1] This specification of the utility function makes the important assumption that λ_R and λ_C have a constant sign in the policy space.

An analysis of the indifference curves of firms allows us to locate the maximum of the utility function of firms in the policy space. Let $C = C(R)$ be an indifference curve, such that $U(R, C(R)) = constant$.[2] By implicit differentiation, we obtain

$$\frac{\partial C}{\partial R} = -\frac{\partial U/\partial R}{\partial U/\partial C} = -\frac{\lambda_R}{\lambda_C}.$$

This implies that the slopes of the indifference curves ($\partial C/\partial R$) have a constant sign throughout the policy space. The indifference curves of firms can be upward sloping throughout the policy space, if λ_R and λ_C have the same sign. If λ_R and λ_C have opposite signs, the indifference curves of firms will be downward sloping in the social policy space. The two cases are represented in Fig. 5.2.

The signs of λ_R and λ_C help us also determine the direction in which the utility of firms increases throughout the social policy space. Let us analyze each case separately. Consider first the case in which λ_R and λ_C have the same sign. As represented in Fig. 5.2 (*a*), if both λ_R and λ_C are positive, the utility of firms increases upward, towards social policies characterized by high levels of control. If both λ_R and λ_C are negative, the utility of firms decreases, as control increases. The analysis is analogous for the case in which firms' sensitivities to risk redistribution and control have opposite signs. We can distinguish two additional cases. If $\lambda_R < 0$ and $\lambda_C > 0$, the utility of firms increases towards the upper boundary of the social policy space. If $\lambda_R > 0$ and $\lambda_C < 0$, the utility of firms increases in the direction of the horizontal axis of the social policy space.

This discussion allows us to determine the location of the maximum of the utilities of firms. We can distinguish four cases. If $\lambda_C > 0$ and λ_R

---

[1] A more elaborate analysis of the utility of firms, which involves a more complicated functional form of λ_R can be found in chapter 2 of my dissertation 'Negotiated Risks: Employers' Role in Social Policy Development'.

[2] This analysis of the shape of indifference curves of firms follows from the assumption of constant sign of $\partial U/\partial C$ and $\partial U/\partial R$.

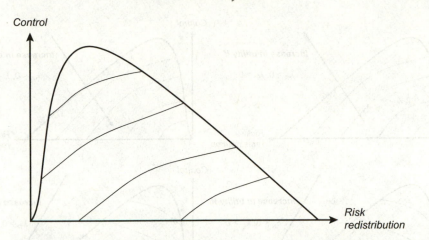

(*a*) Indifference curves if λ_R and λ_C have opposite signs ($\partial U/\partial C > 0$)

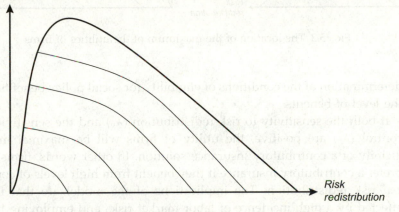

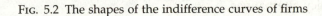

(*b*) Indifference curves if λ_R and λ_C have similar signs ($\partial U/\partial C < 0$)

FIG. 5.2 The shapes of the indifference curves of firms

< 0, firms' utilities will peak on the upper boundary of the social policy space, in the vicinity of a 'private-type' social policy. The sign of λ_R—the utility of the firm along the risk redistribution dimension of the social policy space—indicates that the firm does not benefit from social policies characterized by a significant pooling of risks, such as contributory insurance solutions or universalistic social policies. On the other hand, for these firms the benefits of control outweigh the costs ($\lambda_C > 0$), implying that they will favor social policies in which employers retain discretionary authority in the administration of social insurance and the

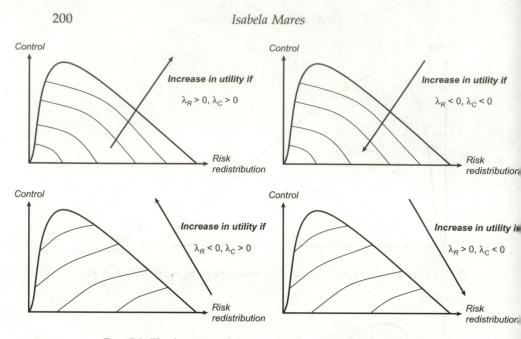

FIG. 5.3 The location of the maximum of the utilities of firms

determination of the conditions of eligibility for social policy benefits and the level of benefits.

If both the sensitivity to risk redistribution (λ_R) and the sensitivity to control (λ_C) are positive, the utility of firms will be maximal in the vicinity of a contributory insurance solution. In other words, firms will prefer a contributory insurance if they benefit from high levels of control *and* risk redistribution. The implications of the model are that firms affected by a high incidence of labor market risks and employing high-skilled workers will prefer contributory insurance solutions to all other social policy alternatives.

Thirdly, the firms will prefer a universalistic social policy if the sensitivity to risk redistribution (λ_R) is positive, but the sensitivity to control (λ_C) is negative. The analysis implies that firms who face a high incidence of a labor market risk (and thus benefit from risk-sharing) but which do not rely on skilled workers (and remain uninterested in relying on social policies as a mechanism of protection of their investment in skills) will rank universalistic social policies higher than all other social policy alternatives.

Finally, firms will reject all social policies, if both the sensitivity to risk redistribution (λ_R) and the sensitivity to control (λ_C) take negative values. The model above has suggested that the costs of all social policies

TABLE 5.2 Preferred social policy

	Size and skill intensity	
	High $\lambda_C > 0$	Low $\lambda_C < 0$
Incidence of risk		
High $\lambda_R > 0$	Contributory	Universalistic
Low $\lambda_R < 0$	Private	'None'

outweigh their benefits if the firm does not rely on skilled workers and if the incidence of the labor market risk is low. These four conclusions of this analysis are summarized in Table 5.2.

The model generates simultaneously a number of comparative statics results specifying the changes in the location of the ideal policy preferred by the firm as a result of changes in the relative magnitude of the two sensitivities, λ_R, the sensitivity of the firm to risk redistribution, and λ_C, the sensitivity of the firm to control. To illustrate these results, let us start from a situation in which both sensitivities are positive. As shown above, in this case the social policy favored by the firm is a contributory insurance. Assume now that the sensitivity of the firm towards risk redistribution (λ_R) increases relative to the sensitivity of the firm for control (λ_C). These increases in the benefits of risk redistribution for the individual firm can be the result of an increase in the incidence of a risk facing the firm or of a decrease in the costs of risk-sharing due to a simultaneous decrease in the incidence of a risk for other high-risk industries. The consequence of this increase in the sensitivity of the firm towards risk redistribution is a change in the slope of the indifference curves of firms ($\partial C / \partial R = - \lambda_R/\lambda_C$)—so that the slope becomes more negative. This change is illustrated geometrically in Fig. 5.4 below. The optimal social policy preferred by the firm shifts now towards a universalistic social policy. Conversely, if the sensitivity for control (λ_C) increases, while the sensitivity for risk redistribution remains unchanged, the maximum of the utility moves towards a private social policy. More generally, we can observe that the maximum of the utility of a firm is displaced towards a universalistic social policy if λ_C becomes very small or λ_R becomes very large. The maximum shifts towards a private social policy if λ_C becomes very large or λ_R becomes very small.

The model of business preferences developed in this chapter has suggested that the incidence of a risk and the intensity in the level of skill of the workforce are variables which predict the cleavages formed

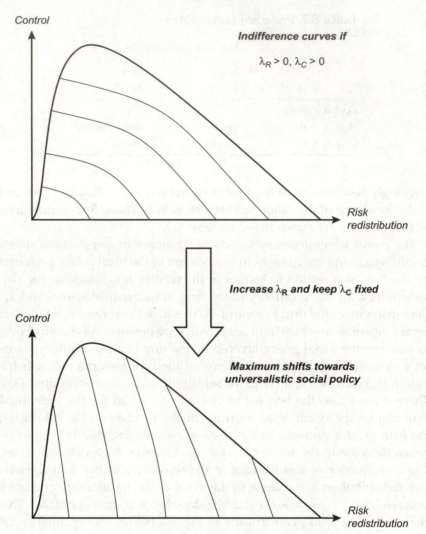

FIG. 5.4 Illustration of comparative statics results

among employers during the introduction of a new social policy. To put it succinctly, firms employing high-skilled workers are expected to favor the participation of employers in the administration of social insurance, as an institutional guarantee for the maintenance and further reproduction of the skill differentiation established within their own enterprise. In contrast to these employers, firms that do not rely on skilled workers are expected to be uninterested in these institutional characteristics of social policy. The second source of disunity and conflict among employers is the conflict over the degree of risk redistribution of a social policy. Firms in industries strongly affected by a risk are expected to favor the expansion of the risk pool, the inclusion of additional industries into social insurance, and the separation of the link between insurance contributions and the incidence of a risk. Firms characterized by a lower incidence of a risk are expected to oppose highly redistributive social policies, fearing to become subsidizers of high-risk industries.

To test the main propositions of the above model, I will examine the policy demands voiced by German employers during key political junctures in the history of the German welfare state. (For a systematic analysis that involves cross-national comparison see Mares 1998.) Chronologically, these episodes cover the introduction of disability insurance during Imperial Germany, the creation of compulsory unemployment insurance during the Weimar period, and the rapid growth of early retirement policies during the last two decades. These cases allow me to test the implications of the model for the most important risks covered by social insurance—disability, unemployment, and old age—and to determine the ways in which incidence of a risk, size, and skill intensity interact in determining the shape of the utility of a firm's utility.

5.4 Employers and the Introduction of Disability Insurance

During the last few decades of the previous century, questions about the legal and material remedies available to victims of workplace accidents triggered an intense process of legal and political experimentation in all countries undergoing rapid industrialization (Ewald 1986, 1991, 1996; Rabinbach 1996). What started as an attempt of legal experts and politicians to develop new legal justifications on the basis of which these victims could seek compensation from their employers culminated with the creation of disability insurance and the political 'invention' of a number of institutions and practices central to the modern welfare state. Germany was in the forefront of this process of political reform, setting through the introduction of compulsory accident insurance in 1884 a policy example that was emulated by reformers in other European countries during the following decades.

As documented by a number of historians of the German welfare state, employers in large firms have been a crucial actor in the process of policy reform that replaced a private law solution to the risk of workplace accidents (the Employers' Liability Act (*Reichshaftpflichtgesetz*) of 1871) with a compulsory disability insurance (Ullmann 1979; Breger 1982, 1994;

Tennstedt and Winter 1993). As early as 1881, German employers submitted to the Reichstag a proposal favoring the elimination of questions
of liability of either employer and employee as a precondition for the
distribution of disability benefits to the victims of workplace accidents
(*Bericht der Industrie- und Handelskammer Bochum* 1881, reprinted in
Tennstedt and Winter 1993: 343–9). This reform proposal of large firms—
named, after its initiator, the Baare bill of disability insurance—recommended the creation of an accident insurance fund (*Arbeiterunfalls-
versicherungskasse*) distributing benefits to the victims of workplace
accidents and financed by contributions of employers (half of amount),
employees (one quarter), and the local community (one quarter) (see
Tennstedt and Winter 1993: 346). The employers' draft bill—which contained the basic principles of modern social insurance—exceeded in
radicalism all policy alternatives debated at the period, which recommended only incremental and minor tinkering with the existing liability
laws.

There existed significant disunity among employers over the relative
advantages of a compulsory insurance over private insurance of firms
against the risk of workplace accidents. Powerful industries among
German employers, such as iron-and-steel producers, were supporters of
a social insurance establishing a unitary pool of risks (Verein Deutscher
Eisen- und Stahlindustrieller 1884*a*: 177, 1884*b*: 107). The number of
workplace accidents for these producers—a measure of their incidence
of risk—was two and a half times as high as the number of workplace
accidents in industries such as textiles (Zumpe 1961). To lower the insurance contributions of their firms and to achieve a high level of inter-occupational redistribution of risks, high-risk industries militated for the
inclusion of agriculture and other non-industrial occupations as part of
social insurance, a measure which would have justified higher levels
of public interventions (Bueck 1901: 83; Protocol of conference of German
employers of Bochum 1880: 52; Breger 1994: 32).

Proposals favoring a compulsory insurance aroused the fierce opposition of associations representing employers characterized by a lower level
of mechanization and by a lower incidence of the risk of accidents—who
denounced the plans submitted by iron- and steel-producers as a 'con-
spiracy of large firms' (Ullmann 1979: 588; Breger 1982: 81). A survey commissioned by the Prussian Statistical Office in 1881 among sixty-one
chambers of commerce found about 65 per cent of employers opposed to
the plans for a compulsory accident insurance favored by the
Centralverband der Deutschen Industrie (Francke 1881: 397–416). These
employers opposed the high level of risk redistribution of this policy and

demanded that the contributions paid by each industry to social insurance reflect differences in the incidence of the risk of workplace accidents. (For these views see Chambers of Commerce Giessen and Mannheim in Francke 1881: 413–15.) Other employers viewed the unification of insurance as extremely problematic and preferred the reliance on 'competitive private insurance' (Chambers of Commerce of Bremen, Pforzheim, and Altenberg, see Francke 1881).

During this early episode in the political history of the German welfare state, the question of control—the distribution of responsibilities in the administration of social insurance among the state and private actors— proved to be equally divisive for employers. On numerous occasions, employers signaled their readiness to accept a compulsory insurance, if they could participate in 'the administration of insurance, in the classification of individual firms, the determination of the level of contributions and the measurement of the social insurance benefits' (Chamber of Commerce Osnabrück in Francke 1881: 401; for similar demands, see Chambers of Commerce Mühlheim and Duisburg in Francke 1881: 407). The peak association representing German employers, the Centralverband der Deutschen Industriellen, opposed Bismarck's plans to create a unified social insurance (administered by a centralized bureaucracy) and advocated decentralization in the organization of social insurance and the creation of occupational risk pools (*Berufsgenossenschaften*) (see Centralverband Deutscher Industrieller 1881: 26). According to employers, these occupational risk pools allowed for the necessary self-administration of insurance and were an instrument that could counterbalance the administrative power retained by the state. These demands of the Centralverband were accommodated in the final disability insurance bill, which delegated the administration of insurance to associations of employers.

Many associations representing small firms remained uninterested in retaining administrative control in the newly established social insurance and were unopposed to Bismarck's plans to centralize these responsibilities in the hands of the state. The most important political concerns of these firms remained the minimization of the share of insurance contributions financed by employers (*Zeitschrift für Handel und Gewerbe* 1888: 374). To lower this burden, these firms demanded a greater financial involvement of the state in the new insurance solution and the lowering of the benefits paid to the victims of workplace accidents. Small firms remained largely disappointed with the final disability insurance law, which eliminated both contributions of employees and the financial participation of the state in social insurance (*Zeitschrift fur Handel und Gewerbe* 1890: 320–1).

5.5 Business and the Development of
Unemployment Insurance

Similar conflicts among employers over the institutional design of social insurance arose during the policy deliberations surrounding the introduction of a set of policies compensating against the effects of unemployment during the Weimar period (see also Führer 1990; Lewek 1992; Mares 1997*b*). While high-risk industries favored an expansion of the scope of unemployment insurance and the inclusion of occupations characterized by a low incidence of the risk of unemployment (such as agriculture), low-risk industries opposed insurance schemes altogether or demanded the strict adherence to actuarial criteria in the design of the new social policy. Firms relying on high-skilled workers showed a strong support for a contributory insurance solution to the risk of unemployment and demanded the introduction of social insurance benefits that mirrored and reflected preexisting wage hierarchies.

During the development of unemployment insurance, the question about the relative advantages of 'control' led to a strong disagreement among employers over the relative merits of the insurance versus assistance solution. As early as 1920, employers in large firms rejected the existing policy of unemployment assistance (*Erwerbslosenfürsorge*) introduced in the aftermath of World War I and demanded the establishment of a compulsory unemployment insurance (Reichsverband der Deutschen Industrie 1920). Large manufacturing producers developed two distinct theoretical justifications in support of a contributory insurance. The first of these arguments suggested that it was important to institutionalize the participation of employers in the determination of the level of unemployment compensation and of the definition of the criteria of eligibility for unemployment benefits (Vereinigung der Deutschen Arbeitgeberverbände 1925). In the policy of unemployment assistance, these important decisions remained in the hands of the communes, causing serious labor market disturbances and the coexistence of labor shortages and high levels of structural unemployment. According to employers, the failure of the policy of unemployment assistance was the consequence of the inability of those decision-makers responsible for the distribution of unemployment benefits to monitor effectively the 'willingness to work' and the true need of the unemployed (Vereinigung der Deutschen Arbeitgeberverbände 1925).

The second argument in support of a contributory unemployment insurance developed by the peak association representing German firms is of greater relevance for the analysis developed in this chapter because it highlights the importance of unemployment insurance as a mechanism for skill protection. Under the existing policy of unemployment assistance, unemployment benefits were flat-rate and not tied to the pre-existing wages of the unemployed. For employers relying on high-skilled workers, flat-rate unemployment benefits had two undesirable consequences. On the one hand, they raised the relative income of low-skilled workers, lowering their incentive to search for jobs during periods of unemployment. For high-skilled workers, flat-rate unemployment benefits had the opposite effect. Because these benefits lowered the relative income of high-skilled workers, they pressured these workers to accept jobs that did not correspond to their skill qualifications, undermining employers' investment in the skills of their employees (Vereinigung der Arbeitgeberverbände 1927: 164). To counteract these undesirable consequences of a means-tested policy of unemployment assistance, large German firms favored a policy with earnings-related benefits that tied unemployment benefits to the existing wage and skill hierarchies established within their firm—a *Lohnklassensystem*. For these firms, a contributory unemployment insurance became an important institutional framework protecting the investment in their skills.

Firms that did not rely on skilled workers did not share this enthusiasm for the insurance solution, objecting to the high costs of a policy financed through the contributions of employers (Reichsverband des Deutschen Handwerks 1923). In numerous writings addressed to the Imperial Employment Office, chambers of commerce and associations representing small firms opposed an institutional solution to the risk of unemployment bearing close resemblance to the other subsystems of the German welfare state (Verband Mitteldeutscher Industriellen 1920; Reichsverband des Deutschen Handwerks 1925). For some employers, the preferred outcome remained no policy at all (Handelskammer Hanover 1922). Other small firms proposed to reform the existing means-tested policy of unemployment assistance (Handelskammer Bremen 1920) or supported a tax-financed solution, where the costs of unemployment were not carried by employers and employees, but by the entire community of workers (Handwerkskammer Kassel 1921).

A second source of disagreement among employers was the question of inter-occupational redistribution of risk within unemployment insurance. Employers in export industries (such as chemical electrical or machine tools) favored a social policy characterized by high levels of inter-occupational redistribution of risk. Faced with persistent high levels of unemployment (that resulted from high fluctuations in the demand for their products), these employers argued that 'high-risk' industries were unable to pay higher unemployment insurance contributions than other industries; they favored a policy characterized by high levels of inter-occupational risk redistribution (Vereinigung der Deutschen Arbeitgeberverbände 1920: 470–6; Handelskammer Leipzig 1920: 117). The concrete policy proposals developed by these employers suggested the expansion of the risk pool of unemployment insurance and the inclusion of 'low-risk' occupations (such as agriculture or forestry) and the separation of the unemployment insurance contributions from the incidence of the risk of unemployment (Vereinigung der Deutschen Arbeitgeberverbände 1920: 470–6; Handwerkskammer Kassel 1925).

In contrast to these high-risk industries, employers facing a low incidence of the risk of unemployment opposed the equalization of risk within social insurance. The Central Federation of German *Handwerk* raised strong objections against a unitary risk pool and supported a proposal that 'divided firms into risk categories (*Gefahrenklassen*), because this measure would require higher contributions from larger firms with their risks than from the *Handwerk*' (Reichsverband des Deutschen Handwerks 1926, 1927). Voicing similar demands, other chambers of commerce protested 'against an insurance that placed the same burden on industries in which unemployment is rare as on occupations with high seasonal unemployment' and demanded the differentiation of unemployment contributions required from employers based on the incidence of the risk of unemployment of their industry (Handelskammer Lübeck 1920).

5.6 The Role of Employers in the Development of Early Retirement

One of the most significant social policy development of the last decades has been the massive withdrawal of elderly workers from the labor market and their transformation into a new clientele of the welfare state (Kohli et al. 1991; Naschold and de Vroom 1994; OECD 1994*b*). In Germany, labor force participation rates of male elderly workers (aged 55 to 65) declined from 80.1 per cent in 1970 to 52.7 per cent in 1995, a decline steeper than in most OECD countries (OECD 1997*a*). Early retirement policies began as a process of dispersed practices of labor shedding of large firms—facilitated by a permissive legislation designed to protect the labor market chances of elderly workers at the end of their careers—but evolved towards complex policy arrangements, as other political actors (such as unions, political parties, and bureaucratic representatives) attempted to exercise influence over the initiation of these measures. In the development of these policies, both questions of 'control' (the distribution of administrative responsibilities in the initiation of these measures) and questions of the redistribution of the financial burden of this new risk across different subsystems of the welfare state were highly contested political issues among these actors.

Large manufacturing firms have played a key role in the initiation of early retirement policies in Germany (Mares 1997*a*; Manow and Seils 1999). A number of decisions of the Federal Social Court, changes in the German pension system, as well as labor market policies introduced during the early 1970s created a policy environment that opened up the legal possibility for retirement prior to the official retirement age (Bundessozialgericht 1970; Jacobs and Schmähl 1988). Making use of these legal provisions, firms responded to the economic slowdown by developing complex compensation packages for their elderly employees that induced these to accept an 'early' termination of their employment, sometimes even ten years prior to the official retirement age. The use of these social policy instruments by large firms generally mirrored the ups and downs of the business cycle. Early retirement was both a cushion during economic downturns, a mechanism of stabilization of firms' demand for training, as well as a convenient way for firms to avoid the costly dismissal route (Jacobs and Schmähl 1988; Mares 1996). According to the estimates of the Federal Social Ministry, during the decade between 1970 and 1980, every second large firm made use of early retirement as a labor market policy instrument (Kühlewind 1986: 209–32).

The demographic structure of the workforce—a measure of the incidence of a risk—remained a variable strongly predicting the use of early retirement by large firms. Firms in industries with unfavorable demographic structure used early retirement more extensively, as compared to firms with a younger age structure. As indicated by studies of the German Federal Employment Office, the use of early retirement was highest in the construction, chemical, and electro-technical industries— industries that had a higher percentage of elderly workers as compared to the economy-wide average (IAB Kurzbericht 1988*a*, 1988*b*).

In contrast to large firms, employers of the *Mittelstand* made almost no use of the early retirement option (Zentralverband des Deutschen Handwerks 1982). The Central Federation of German *Handwerk* denounced on repeated occasions the reliance on early retirement by large firms as a misuse of the generosity of the German social insurance system (Deutsches Handwerksblatt 1982: 649), and demanded decisive legislative action ending these practices (Zentralverband des Deutschen Handwerks 1983: 417, 591–3, 754, 1984: 214). According to a publication of small firms, policies encouraging the reduction of the working life posed a fundamental threat to the existence of the *Mittelstand*, by encouraging illegal employment and by increasing the non-wage labor costs faced by all German firms (Zentralverband des Deutschen Handwerks 1982: 11).

This process of firm-based early retirement had important financial implications for the German welfare state. Early retirement practices of large firms created a new 'category' of social policy recipients, whose benefits were financed, in different degrees, by old-age, unemployment, and disability insurance. As a result of early retirement, boundaries between different subsystems of the German welfare state that had been once clearly institutionalized were now blurred. (On this 'blurring of risks', see also Guillemard 1997; Mares 1998.) The contraction in the contributory base of the welfare state was financed through an increase in social insurance contributions and not through a different source of fiscal revenue. Employers of large firms succeeded in shifting the costs of the risk of unemployment of elderly workers to the broader community of contributors to the German welfare state.

The offensive of the German Labor Ministry to stop this 'fiscal hemorrhage' of the German welfare system was largely unsuccessful. For a brief interlude between 1984 and 1988, the Early Retirement Act (*Vorruhestandsgesetz*) moved control over the initiation of early retirement to peak associations of employers and employees (Mares 1997*a*; Jacobs et al. 1991). The law was rescinded in 1988, due to its costly consequences to the German welfare state and to failure of firms to rehire new workers to fill the vacancies created as a result of early retirement. After 1988, the German government introduced a number of measures that attempted to increase firms' share of the costs of early retirement and which required employers to compensate social insurance systems for early retirement (Schmähl 1993). These measures failed to undermine the externalization strategy of German firms and to increase labor force participation rates among elderly workers.

While these policy changes failed to end early retirement, they exacerbated the polarization and disunity among German employers (Mares 1997*a*). Despite their rhetoric complaining against the costly character of the German welfare state, large German firms continued to favor the status quo and to benefit from a policy which financed the costs of enterprise reorganization through social insurance. In a number of recent publications and statements, the Bundesvereinigung der Deutschen Arbeitgeberverbände (the peak association representing the social policy interests of large firms) developed an extensive range of proposals for change in the other subsystems of the German welfare state (sickness insurance, long-term care insurance), but no proposal for the elimination or reduction of early retirement (Bundesvereinigung der Arbeitgeber-verbände 1997, 1998: 16–31; Bundesarbeitgeberverband Chemie 1997). To use the conceptual framework developed in the first part of the chapter, for large firms the status quo represented an ideal combination of risk redistribution and control. The losers of this system remained firms of the *Mittelstand*, squeezed by the costs of ever-rising contributions and unable to offer the same generous 'private' compensation packages to induce elderly workers to stop working prior to the retirement age. Yet they remained unable to find the political allies necessary to facilitate a dramatic reversal of policy.

5.7 Conclusions

The recent resurgence of interest in the study of employers and the elaboration of firm-centered analyses of the political economy is a development that has important analytical implications. These new perspectives—pioneered by Wolfgang Streeck and Philippe Schmitter, and refined in some of the recent varieties of capitalism approaches—introduce microfoundations into the corporatist studies developed by political economists during the 1970s and offer important insights into the dynamics of policy change in advanced industrial societies during recent decades (Streeck and Schmitter 1986; Kitschelt et al. 1999*b*; Hall and Soskice, this volume).

This chapter has been motivated by an attempt to develop similar microfoundations for the study of social policy—and to establish a theoretical link between the 'varieties of capitalism' and the 'varieties of welfare regimes' approaches. (For recent studies sharing a similar intention see Stephens et al. 1999; Manow 1997; Manow and Ebbinghaus forthcoming.) Until recent years, comparative politics scholars have focused predominantly on the macro-level linkages between various welfare states and systems of collective bargaining (Wilensky 1975; Esping-Andersen 1990), leaving out issues about the micro-level interaction between the firms of a political economy and different welfare states, or, in other words, questions about the ways in which different social policy arrangements support and sustain the organization of the employment relationship within firms.

The model developed in this chapter has argued that social policies can offer distinct institutional advantages to employers and has attempted to identify the conditions under which the benefits provided by social policy outweigh the costs of social policy to firms. I have argued that a number of features of social policies—such as the wage index-ation of social policy benefits, the conditionality of social policy benefits on a broad set of factors related to employment performance—reinforce employers' investment in the provision of skills and reproduce the skill and wage differentiation established at the firm level during moments in which the employment relationship is temporarily interrupted. A second important consideration of employers is the degree of risk redis-tribution of a social policy. The analysis of this chapter has suggested that the incidence of a risk will generate significant cleavages among employers, between firms who gain from highly redistributive social policies and firms who lose from the participation in a broad pool of risks.

To specify the causal role played by employers in the development of the modern welfare state, the theory of business preferences towards different social policy arrangements developed in this chapter needs to be supplemented by additional analyses exploring the pathways of busi-ness influence and the broad political conditions facilitating the forma-tion of different coalitions among unions and employers. While political economists and business historians such as Peter Swenson, Cathie Jo Martin, Colin Gordon, or Sanford Jacoby have begun to explore these issues during recent years, the difficulty posed by the collection of data on firms' preferences and business influence has, until now, strongly constrained more systematic cross-national analyses and theory-building (Swenson 1997; Gordon 1991; 1994, Jacoby 1997; Martin 1995, 1999). Specifying not only business preferences for different social policies, but also when and how employers matter in the formulation and imple-mentation of different social policies, remains an important question of future research for political economists and scholars of the welfare state.

6

The Domestic Sources of Multilateral Preferences: Varieties of Capitalism in the European Community

Orfeo Fioretos

6.1 Introduction

The Treaty on European Union (TEU) of December 1991 is considered by many as causing the most extensive abdication of national sovereignty in modern times. Popularly known as the Maastricht Treaty, it created the European Union (EU) by adding two new 'pillars' to the existing architecture in the form of a common foreign and security policy and greater cooperation in justice and home affairs. However, the decision to include these areas formally as part of a European Union did less in terms of adding competencies than 'formaliz[ing] the *status quo ante*, since . . . the two new pillars built on established circles of intergovernmental cooperation' (Wallace 1996: 56). Instead, it was agreements affecting the organization's economic architecture—formally labeled the European Community and known as 'Pillar 1' after Maastricht—that placed limits upon the economic autonomy of member-states and that signaled a new era of economic cooperation. This gave some observers the impetus to declare that the Treaty had 'the potential to change the EC beyond recognition by the end of the century,' and to call the new organization a 'superstate.'[1] These characterizations of unity, however, mask crucial and consequential differences in member-states' interests in the Treaty,

I thank the participants in the Varieties of Capitalism workshop at the Wissenschaftszentrum Berlin (June 1997) and Nick Ziegler for helpful suggestions, and in particular Steve Casper, Priya Joshi, David Soskice, and the matchless Peter Hall for additional and extensive feedback.

[1] This chapter focuses on events leading up to the Maastricht agreement and emphasizes the first pillar of the European Union and thus primarily uses the designation 'European Community.' It employs the label EU when discussing the organization in general and for events after November 1993 when the EU formally began to operate. The quotations are from the *Journal of Commerce*, 12 Dec. 1991: 1A, and the *Houston Chronicle*, 11 Dec. 1991: 21.

differences that were articulated in the extensive and acrimonious negotiations preceding the agreement.

Explaining why—rather than how—individual member-states agreed
to the TEU, particularly their preferences over the shape of the first pillar
concerning economic cooperation, takes us away from the traditional
emphasis on intergovernmental bargaining in studies of European integration and leads us to consider more seriously the domestic bases for
a member's decisions. The EU is an organization where bargaining
among members tends to be positive-sum, frequent, and regularized, and
where time-horizons often are long, information extensive, sanctions
possible, and decision-rules set. In such an organization, the nature of
states' 'national preferences' thus becomes a key determinant in defining
the shape of common multilateral institutions (Moravcsik 1998). This
chapter argues that with the help of the varieties of capitalism framework developed in this volume, two matters of importance to current
scholarship in International Relations (IR) can be explicated: first, why
two countries may have different preferences over the structure of the
same policy area in a multilateral organization; and second, why individual member-states may adopt divergent preferences across issue areas
in that organization.

In studying national preferences we must avoid two common problems in the literatures of IR and European integration. We must resist
taking national preferences as given, because, as Robert Jervis reminds
us, 'by taking preferences as given we beg what may be the most important question of how they were formed . . . [and draw] attention away
from areas that may contain much of the explanatory "action" in which
we are interested' (1988: 324–5). Moreover, we must avoid being overly
general in our definition of preferences. In studies of the EU, assessments
of states' positions are often confined to broad dichotomies, such as for
or against deeper integration. For example, while Germany is often identified as a vigorous champion of greater cooperation (Bulmer and
Patterson 1987), Britain is typically characterized as a reluctant supporter
of European integration (George 1990). However, such general statements not only conceal the fact that the positions of the two countries
are reversed in some cases, but also mask the reality that countries individually prefer different degrees of integration across issue areas. A
theory of national preference formation should not only explain how
preferences are formed, but also be able to account for cross-national
variations, as well as why varying preferences across issue areas are
internally consistent in the case of individual countries. Section 6.2 briefly
examines alternative IR explanations of state preferences.

The central proposition advanced in this chapter may be stated simply: the shape of multilateralism that an EC member espouses depends primarily upon the potential or actual implications of the form of multilateralism on the ability of that country to sustain the comparative institutional advantages provided by its specific variety of capitalism. If this proposition holds, then we should observe patterns of national preferences that differ across market economies. Additionally, we should observe that the variation in states' preferences across issue areas is consistent with the internal logic of individual market economies. This chapter tests that proposition by examining the variation in British and German multilateral preferences during the Maastricht negotiations in core economic areas. The two countries represent, respectively, a liberal and a coordinated market economy and are described in section 6.3.

Sections 6.4 and 6.5 review the Treaty on European Union and discuss the potential implications that multilateral institutions have for national regulatory frameworks. Particular attention is given to how the structures of the British and German market economies shape their national preferences over the structure of the TEU's provisions for common European monetary, social, and industrial policies. The chapter concludes with a discussion of a set of contemporary research topics at the intersection of comparative and international political economy.

6.2 Explanations of National Preferences

'[E]xplicit attention to preferences helps illuminate enduring issues in international relations, both at the theoretical level and in empirical applications,' writes Jeffrey A. Frieden (1999: 41). Andrew Moravcsik adds that 'The first stage in explaining the outcome of an international negotiation is to account for national preferences' (1998: 24). However, despite the pivotal importance of accounting for the shape of states' preferences, there is little consensus among scholars on what determines national preferences over multilateral institutions. As a preamble to how the varieties of capitalism framework can be used to explain the structure of states' multilateral preferences, a brief review follows of two alternative approaches that privilege either the international or the domestic environment as the key determinant.

6.2.1 Realism and Institutionalism

Realism and institutionalism—two dominant IR theories—both treat states as unitary actors and explain national preferences as a function of

the anarchic nature of the international environment. While realism privileges the balance of power among states in explaining why one point
on the Pareto frontier—i.e. the universe of possible outcomes—triumphs
(Krasner 1991), institutionalism emphasizes the conditions under which
states reach the frontier itself.

Realism explains states' support for European integration as a function of their efforts to improve security and to enhance their *relative* position vis-à-vis competitors in other economic regions such as East Asia
and North America. More specifically, it accounts for the timing of the
Maastricht Treaty in terms of western Europe's efforts to boost its security as the Cold War was coming to an unexpected end, and it explains
the shape of the Treaty with reference to the balance of power within the
EC (Grieco 1995). According to this perspective, the content of the Treaty
reflected a compromise between the three most powerful member-states
—Germany, France, and Britain—with some side-payments made to
smaller states for their support of the Treaty. However, this account of
the TEU is not fully persuasive, since both the fact and content of the
Treaty had been planned before the Cold War's sudden demise. More
importantly, realism cannot explain why the preferences of the core
member-states—whose relative power within the EC is very similar—
varied significantly. The emphasis on states as unitary actors also makes
it difficult for realism to spell out why individual states' preferences
diverge across issue areas and why they favor different points on the
Pareto frontier.

While institutionalism—often termed functional regime theory—
shares realism's ontological core, it maintains that international institutions can mitigate the effects of international anarchy and allow states to
focus on the absolute gains from multilateralism (see Baldwin 1993).
Institutionalism has paid particular attention to the importance of shared
and converging preferences among states in fostering cooperation.[2] The
process of preference convergence is intensified by higher levels of
economic interdependence and by membership in international regimes
like the EC which constitute a set of 'principles, norms, rules, and decision-making procedures around which actor expectations converge in a
give issue-area' (Krasner 1983a: 1). For institutionalism, then, the timing
and shape of the Maastricht Treaty was not so much a function of the
end of the Cold War, but a consequence of converging state preferences
caused by long-term membership in the same multilateral organization

---

[2] The renaissance of European integration in the 1980s has been debated in such terms
(Keohane and Hoffmann 1991; Moravcsik 1991).

and by higher levels of international economic exchange. However, like realism, institutionalism's emphasis on the unitary nature of states and the exogenous environment as the source of their preferences makes it difficult to explain why states that are structurally similar and are faced with cognate constraints adopt diverse preferences. For example, institutionalism cannot explain why, as the Maastricht negotiations demonstrated, the empirical record of the EC suggests a continuation— and in some cases an intensification—in the *divergence* of member-states' preferences over the structure, scope, and degree of European integration. Thus, while institutionalism may account for *how* the Pareto frontier was constructed (i.e. which alternatives were possible), it can neither explain the *shape* of that frontier (Moravcsik 1997: 543) nor *why* member-states prefer some points along it more than others.

Institutionalism, then, like realism, cannot explain why a member-state prefers a particular institutional make-up at the European level. The emphasis on the fact rather than the form of multilateralism in these theories is problematic considering that negotiations within the EC take place exactly because member-states vary in their preferences over the structure of common institutions. Thus, without a better understanding of the process that determines national preferences, we are unlikely to provide the 'explanatory action' that Jervis advises us to search for.

6.2.2 Domestic Explanations of National Preferences

In order to address the shortcomings of the systemic realist and institutionalist accounts of international cooperation and to give greater clarity to why states adopt particular economic policies and support international cooperation, scholars in recent years have created a renaissance in the study of the domestic sources of international relations (e.g. Milner 1997; Moravcsik 1998). These theories have ascribed causal significance to national political and economic variables in the analysis of inter-state relations, and these theories have been deemed particularly important in establishing the source of states' policy preferences and choices (e.g. Keohane and Milner 1996; Gourevitch 1996). The focus on the process that leads states to adopt specific preferences is both appropriate and important since it 'is analytically prior to both realism and institutionalism because it defines the conditions under which their assumptions hold' (Moravcsik 1997: 516, emphasis omitted). It is exactly because the prospects of successful multilateralism rest on the credibility of national commitments to those institutions (Ruggie 1993; Cowhey 1993) that the sources of national preferences deserve analytical emphasis.

Among the more sophisticated versions of the domestic approach to IR is the so-called societal school that has developed strong microfoundations for explaining why interest groups (usually firms) have distinct policy preferences and how governments aggregate these preferences to arrive at a specific policy choice. The societal school operates with a broadly pluralist model and suggests that 'the national interest will be the sum of the preferences of different interest groups as weighted by their access to policy-making institutions' (Milner 1992: 494). Consequently, it has focused much of its research agenda on determining what variables shape the preferences of interest groups. Particular emphasis has been given to relative factor endowments (Rogowski 1989; Shafer 1994), and other material elements such as asset specificity (Frieden 1991) and export orientation (Milner 1988) in deriving actors' preferences. Changes in actors' preferences are typically explained with reference to alterations in exogenous economic conditions.

Because of its methodological rigor, theoretical parsimony, and ability to bridge international and comparative political economy, the societal school has become one of the dominant approaches in studies of economic policy-making. However, it has difficulties accounting for some crucial variations across countries. Although recent contributions in this tradition have given greater weight to how domestic political institutions shape the interaction between governments and interest groups (Milner 1997), the approach has not devoted much attention to how national economic institutions shape the *institutional* preferences of actors. Thus, why actors of the same category (say firms with the same type of relative factor endowments) in different countries have divergent policy or institutional preferences is not easily accounted for by this approach. Rather, the societal approach assumes that economic agents like firms that are, *ceteris paribus*, embedded in different national contexts will adopt the *same* preferences. Hence, like the study of the firm in neoclassical economics, this approach assumes that firms do not have 'discretionary powers' or 'autonomous qualities,' and therefore, this approach 'militates against paying attention to firm differences as an important variable affecting economic performance' (Nelson 1991: 197–9). The claim that actors' preferences are exogenously determined also presents a problem for the societal approach's claim of how interests are aggregated. As Geoffrey Garrett and Peter Lange note, 'it is assumed that the effects of internationally generated changes in the constellation of domestic economic preferences will be quickly and faithfully reflected in changes in policies and institutional arrangements within countries' (1996: 49). Consequently, the societal approach cannot fully explain why two countries with similar material profiles and interest groups that share their general policy preferences—such as, for or against monetary cooperation—advocate very different institutional structures in, and across, policy domains.

This chapter suggests that we can fruitfully supplement the societal school with insights from the varieties of capitalism research agenda outlined in this volume as a way of understanding how differences in national economic institutions shape actors' preferences and political outcomes in distinct, divergent, and predictable ways across countries. It further suggests that by building on the strengths of the societal school and by supplementing it with a more dynamic theory of what defines economic actors' preferences from the varieties of capitalism literature, we are in a stronger position than are the two approaches individually when coming to terms with how domestic and international politics are interlinked, as well as why governments promote specific institutional configurations in multilateral settings.

6.3 Varieties of European Capitalism

The varieties of capitalism approach that informs this volume starts from the premiss that countries exhibit distinct, historically determined, national institutional equilibria that tie together a number of building blocks (such as the industrial relations, financial, corporate governance, and vocational training systems) in a coherent fashion that defines particular and differentiated market economies (see also Zysman 1994; Crouch and Streeck 1997*b*; Hollingsworth and Boyer 1997). It suggests that institutional complementarities prevail between the constituent units of a market economy—that is, the efficiency and returns on some building blocks depend upon, and frequently increase with, the presence of others (Richardson 1990; Milgrom and Roberts 1992: 108–13). The sum of the building blocks is thus greater than its parts, and shapes the behavior of economic agents in ways that transcend the limits and possibilities of an economy's constituent units. Since the manner in which the institutional building blocks are integrated differs across countries, agents have access to divergent comparative institutional advantages and, therefore, their core capacities and product market strategies often vary (Hall and Soskice, this volume; cf. Porter 1990).

Based on this holistic and relational understanding of advanced capitalism, the varieties approach makes important claims. For example, it suggests that existing institutions significantly shape policy and institutional preferences of economic actors, and that similar types of firms embedded in different market economies are likely to support divergent policies and institutions. As such, and in contrast to the theoretical traditions reviewed earlier, the varieties approach endogenizes agents' preferences.

This has important consequences for how we study processes of institutional change and continuity. For example, the varieties approach suggests that because the transformation of one market economy to another is a very costly, long, and uncertain process (due to the difficulties of achieving a new and stable institutional equilibrium) economic agents have strong stakes in protecting existing structures. Some studies have demonstrated that even in times of rapidly changing external economic circumstances, economic agents do not seek to transform the existing institutional equilibrium, but prefer to engage in marginal institutional reform for the purposes of *adapting* the existing market economy to new circumstances (e.g. Hancké and Soskice 1996; Muller 1997; Fioretos 1998; Thelen 2000). The varieties approach expects economic agents' institutional preferences to be relatively inelastic, and institutional change to be incremental and in accordance with the logic of the existing institutional make-up (cf. Hall 1986; North 1990; Steinmo et al. 1992). A comparison of the structure and development of Britain's and Germany's economic institutions bears these points out.

6.3.1 Britain and Germany

The manner in which economic coordination is structured differs significantly in Britain and Germany, a fact that has important implications for how economic agents in the two countries respond to changes in their economic and institutional environments. Britain's liberal market economy (LME) is characterized by low levels of business coordination and state intervention, and deregulated markets serve as the primary coordinating mechanism for economic activity. As a consequence, firms are often unable to resolve collective action problems and are rarely in a position jointly to provide basic supply-side goods that sustain vocational training, R&D, and long-term finance. In contrast, Germany's coordinated market economy (CME) is distinguished by extensive coordination among firms that is facilitated by encompassing and overlapping business associations. Whereas membership in business associations in Britain is below 50 per cent in most sectors (Edwards et al. 1992: 21), 95 per cent of German firms belong to the Federation of German Industry (von Alemann 1989: 76). These associations have allowed German firms to overcome collective action problems and to secure long-term vocational training, R&D, finance, and technology diffusion.

This fundamental difference, sustained by disparities in the legal architectures of the two countries, that mandates and provides incentives for non-market coordination in Germany, has produced different institutional equilibria with far-ranging consequences. For example, Britain has struggled with a low-skill, low-wage equilibrium because a deregulated labor market has produced an industrial-relations system that discourages producers from making long-term investments in their employees (Finegold and Soskice 1988). In contrast, Germany has relatively inflexible labor markets that have produced a high-skill, high-wage equilibrium, where there are institutional incentives for employers to invest in their employees' skills acquisition (Soskice 1994*b*). Extensive deregulation throughout the economy allows and sometimes forces firms in LMEs to adjust rapidly and cut their operational costs. The relatively extensive social and economic regulations in CMEs, on the other hand, encourage firms to adjust in incremental ways and to overcome short-term costs by emphasizing the long-term benefits of gradual product development. As a consequence, producers in LMEs tend to be more sensitive to relative costs than firms in CMEs who stress the importance of increasing the quality of their products.

Because of the structural disparities in the two countries, producers are provided with different institutional advantages that bias them toward adopting distinct product market strategies. The conventional picture of Germany as a country with strengths in advanced medium-tech manufacturing, and Britain as one with a concentration in basic manufacturing, is accurate (Matraves 1997). Unlike in Germany, where the industrial-relations and financial systems emphasize long-term product development and productivity growth (Streeck 1991), British producers have predominantly emphasized short-term profits because of a financial system that promotes rapid turnover and an industrial relations system that encourages employers to adopt cost-cutting practices (Rubery 1994).

While the institutional infrastructure of the German economy presents competitive advantages in areas that benefit advanced manufacturing (so-called specialized supplier and scale-intensive industries in Fig. 6.1) and are characterized by incremental innovation patterns, differences in the financial and innovation systems have allowed Britain to outpace Germany in high-tech areas characterized by radical innovation patterns (Soskice 1997). Not only did the British science-based sector show a

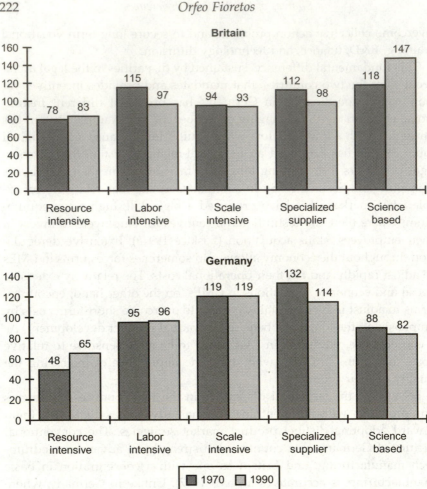

FIG. 6.1 The revealed comparative advantage of British and German
manufacturing industry

Note: Revealed comparative advantage 'for a particular industry (or industry grouping) is
defined as the ratio of the share of the country's exports in that industry in its total manufacturing exports to the share of total exports by that industry (or industry grouping) in OECD
manufacturing exports.'

The industry classification is based on core factors that determine competitiveness, and is
divided into: resource-intensive (food, beverages, tobacco, leather, wood, paper products, petro-
leum-refining, cement, and clay); labor-intensive (textiles, apparel, footwear, furniture, non-
ferrous and fabricated metals, other manufacturing); scale-intensive (printing, industrial
chemicals, rubber and plastics, pottery and glass, iron and steel, shipbuilding, railroad equipment, cars, and other transport); specialized supplier (non-electrical machinery excluding
computers, electrical machinery excluding telecommunications and semiconductors); and
science-based (pharmaceuticals, computers, telecommunications and semiconductors, aircraft,
scientific instruments, and other chemicals industries).

Source: OECD (1992: 158–9).

strong and growing competitive advantage in the 1970–90 period (Fig. 6.1), but it was twice the size of its German equivalent and grew much faster.[3] While there has been great continuity in the British and German industrial profile, changes in the external institutional environment of the two countries due to deeper European integration challenge firms' abilities to exploit the comparative institutional advantages of the respective national models.

6.4 National Institutions and European Integration

How can the varieties approach, which is primarily designed to address issues of economic performance and institutional change at the national level, be used to give greater clarity to a state's preferences over the structure of multilateral institutions? The following pages suggest that attention to how common European regulatory frameworks affect the institutional equilibrium of national market economies allows us to uncover why interest groups and governments prefer particular forms of European multilateralism.

Common regulatory frameworks on the European level present a challenge to member-states because EC regulations can both consolidate and undermine national institutions through intergovernmental agreements (Moravcsik 1998) or through spontaneous processes of up- and downward regulation (Vogel 1995; Scharpf 1997*b*). Thus, for example, while European agreements on low social standards may protect British interests in this area, it is often feared that it would undercut Germany's ability to maintain higher standards. Because the potential benefits or costs of institutional change at the national level as a result of EC agreements may be high, domestic interest groups and governments pay strong attention and invest great resources in influencing and anticipating the direction of common European regulations (Andersen and Eliassen 1993). However, interest groups or governments are not necessarily relegated to passive 'takers' in this environment, but have extensive opportunities to voice their preferences.

From the vantage point of member-states, EC institutions can generate three general effects on national regulatory structures. First, multilateral institutions can lock in national regulatory regimes at the multilateral level. The Single European Market (SEM) and Single European Act

---

[3] In 1990, the science-based sector in Britain made up 9.12% of industrial production, while the figure in Germany was 4.67%. In Britain the sector grew by 78.3% between 1976 and 1990, and in Germany by 39.4%. Calculations based on figures reported in OECD (1997*b*).

(SEA), for instance, have served to strengthen the liberal free-trade policies of EC member-states. Similarly, common minimum regulations in the social and environmental areas prevent processes of competitive deregulation from undermining core features of national frameworks. Second, multilateral institutions may facilitate new institutional growth trajectories at the domestic level that a country might have difficulties achieving on its own. Many governments and business groups, for example, support European-wide research programs in areas where existing national institutions are unable to facilitate rapid advances in the high-tech sector. I call this *positive institution-building* because the basic purpose of supporting the multilateral institution is to supplement national institutions with a common European-level institutional structure for the purposes of achieving goals that member-states are unable to achieve on their own. Third, multilateral institutions may undermine specific domestic institutional constructs that governments or producers are dissatisfied with. Efforts by producers in some countries (e.g. large firms in Germany) to undermine national antitrust and merger laws that are more restrictive than those of the EU are an example of this scenario. I call this *negative institution-building* since the objective is to undo and reduce certain national institutional frameworks that are deemed detrimental to achieving the desired policy outcome.

In brief, the EC should not only be seen as an institutional constraint on member-states, but also as an organization that presents opportunities for institutional reform that may be difficult to achieve on a purely national scale. In that sense, joining national with European institutions presents member-states with an opportunity to explore and achieve novel institutional complementarities.

While many of the chapters in this volume demonstrate that significant complementarities exist between the building blocks of national market economies, this chapter focuses on national political processes that lead member-states to adopt specific preferences over the structure of the EC in order to achieve complementarities between their national institutions and those at the European level. The rationale for this focus is simple: since the form of European multilateralism may have long-term implications for the structure of national economic institutions, member-states should hold specific preferences over those EC structures that may affect the institutional landscape at home. 'Selecting institutions', as George Tsebelis notes, 'is the sophisticated equivalent of selecting policies or selecting outcomes' (1990: 118).

As noted in the earlier discussion of alternative approaches to studying preferences, the formation of a national preference—that is, the position that a country's government will promote at the EC level—is a process that requires us to address a set of issues. Key political actors and their preferences in applicable policy areas must be determined.[4] How their often diverse preferences are aggregated into a 'national preference' is the next step, and for that purpose I use the structure of state–society relations to ascertain the domestic balance of power (Katzenstein 1978*b*). Since the likelihood of realizing the national preference in the EC depends on the distribution of preferences among other member-states and the environment in which EC institutions are negotiated—in particular the nature of voting rules in the relevant issue area—attention must also be given to the strategic environment that faces member-states (Moravcsik 1998; Pollack 1996). Following a brief overview of the Maastricht Treaty, I examine how these three factors shaped the British and German institutional preferences in crucial policy areas of the Treaty.

6.4.1 The Maastricht Treaty

The Maastricht Treaty consisted of seven titles divided into nineteen articles that partly amended previous treaties and partly added new competencies to the organization. Additionally, seventeen 'Protocols' were appended that added and expanded aspects of the Treaty, including among other things, special 'opt-outs' for some member-states (most notably for Britain and Denmark), protocols on social policy (No. 14), economic and social cohesion (No. 15), the structure of the European Central Bank (No. 3), and a timetable (No. 10) and criteria (No. 6) for an economic and monetary union (EMU).[5] Here, the focus falls on three core policy areas that were subject to negotiations at Maastricht, namely, the structure of EC monetary, social, and industrial policies.

Monetary Policy

Perhaps the most remarkable aspect of the Maastricht Treaty was the decision to set a timetable, define the criteria, and establish the structure for an EMU to begin in January 1999. If EMU was the most remarkable achievement in Maastricht, it has also proven to be its most controversial aspect. The Treaty provided for the introduction of a single currency and the transfer of monetary authority from national branches to the

---

[4] In the following, I make an assumption that interest groups and governments largely share a commitment to maximizing the comparative institutional advantages of their respective market economy. Elsewhere I explore the conditions under which such a situation does not hold (Fioretos 2000).

[5] For detailed accounts of the Maastricht Treaty, see Church and Phinnemore (1994).

European Central Bank (ECB). As such, it provided a blueprint for the relinquishment of national policy autonomy in this area and the introduction of a new supranational policy domain. The Treaty stipulated that member-states consider their economic policies a matter of common concern and that they meet strict economic requirements to qualify for EMU.

EMU had remained an elusive goal to the member-states since the 1970s, and the text adopted in Maastricht was preceded by many alternative designs and proposals (Ungerer 1997). Despite the agreement in Maastricht to form EMU, many of the twelve member-states were reluctant to support it. While Germany and France were strong advocates, others like Britain and Denmark were given opt-out (or better, opt-in) clauses which allowed them to defer the decision on whether to join EMU.

Social Policy

In the 1957 Treaty of Rome there was a small section devoted to employment and working conditions. However, it was not until after the SEA was adopted in 1987 that a more extensive discussion about the competence of the EC in this area took place and that the Community was given explicit authority to work for the advancement of a dialogue between management and labor and for the improvement of health and safety in the workplace. With the enactment of the SEM the discussion continued and was generally couched in terms that some member-states might undermine the internal market by engaging in 'social dumping' by maintaining low social standards. As a consequence, attempts were made to introduce a 'social dimension' to the economic dimension that was quickly emerging. The Social Charter of 1989 entailed provisions concerning social security benefits, freedom of association, fair compensation, and the dialogue between the labor market parties. The Charter was accepted in December 1989 by all member-states except Britain. Eventually, most of the Social Charter was appended to the Maastricht agreement and was called the Social Protocol (rather than Chapter) because of Britain's opt-out. Although this protocol does not entail any far-reaching provisions that will seriously undermine national authority in this domain—in fact, the Protocol states that 'the Community and the Member States shall implement measures which take account of the diverse forms of national practices' (Art. I)—it was subject to divisive negotiations and was only signed by eleven of the twelve member-states at the time.

Industrial Policy

If EMU and the Social Protocol have proven to be the most debated, cele-
brated, and to some extent most controversial issues in the aftermath of
the Maastricht meeting, then the provision for a common industrial
policy is an area that has received much less attention since the agreement. Before the Maastricht Treaty, the EC's industrial policy had
primarily been designed for market liberalization and the abolishment
of discriminatory subsidies (P. Nicolaides 1993), and nowhere could one
find a statement suggesting that the Community have an activist and
interventionist industrial policy. However, the debate surrounding
Article 130 of the Treaty, which was interpreted as potentially giving
the EC the authority to pursue an industrial policy, was very heated.
The Article establishes that '[t]he Community and the Member States
shall ensure that the conditions necessary for the competitiveness of the
Community's industry exist'; that '[t]he Commission may take any useful
initiative to promote . . . coordination [between Member States and the
Commission]'; and that the Council may design 'specific measures in
support of action taken in the Member States.' The Article was largely
the result of the demands by some member-states (France and Italy)
and industry groups for a more proactive European Commission with
the authority to initiate and sustain programs that would enhance the
competitiveness of European industry. This was primarily to be done
through programs that facilitated inter-company collaboration and large-
scale industrial projects on a precompetitive basis so that European
producers would be better positioned to meet the competition from non-
European manufacturers.

Although vague statements were made to the coordinating function of
the Commission, Article 130 is in fact very much of the same essence as
previous EC policies and has not been used to justify interventionist
practices in the spirit of national industrial policies that were common
during the 1970s or 1980s. Instead, the Article's general message—that
the pursuit of competitiveness should take place 'in accordance with a
system of open and competitive markets'—and its emphasis on creating
a favorable environment for business cooperation and development
remains the guiding principle of the EC's industrial policy. Nevertheless,
the heated debate prior to and during the Maastricht meeting clearly
revealed the great diversity in member-states' attitudes in this area.
While France espoused an interventionist form of industrial policy reminiscent of its *dirigiste* tradition, Britain advocated a minimalist version
and at times objected to the idea of the Article, and Germany adopted a

middle-of-the road position that corresponded relatively closely with the final outcome. How do we explain the variation in these policy positions, and the fact that Britain and Germany not only advocated different forms of industrial policy, but also different designs for EC's social and monetary components?

6.5 Unmasking Britain and Germany at Maastricht

The central hypothesis in this chapter states that the underlying determinant of a country's preferences over the structure of multilateralism is the composition of its market economy. If this is correct, then we should observe that individual countries' preferences constitute a coherent and internally consistent strategy across areas, and that there are distinct differences between countries' multilateral choices if their market economies differ. This section examines this proposition in the British and German cases in the context of the Maastricht agreement.

6.5.1 Britain

The common perception that Britain, under the Conservative governments of Margaret Thatcher and John Major, was persistently opposed to increased European integration is a great exaggeration. A closer examination of British policy positions in various issue areas reveals that the logic of its engagement in the EU does not reflect a general antipathy to the EU, but rather a calculated policy informed by the economic and institutional rationale of its national market economy. During the 1980s Britain supported many institutional programs that could only be characterized as entailing more integration and less national autonomy, including a strong commitment to the full implementation of the SEM and a highly centralized competition policy. While less interested in deeper integration during the Maastricht negotiations, it is clear that Britain's institutional preferences during those negotiations also reflected its attempts to promote and protect key features of its liberal market economy.

The structure of state–society relations in Britain gives the government a relatively high degree of autonomy from societal pressures in formulating its policy due to the considerable centralization in policy-making and the low organizational capacity of interest groups (Katzenstein 1978b). During the Maastricht negotiations, Prime Minister Major's domestic battles were therefore less with economic interest groups and more directed at appeasing the disparate interests of domestic federalists, Euroskeptics (especially in his own party), and an electorate which was bound to treat him harshly in the 1992 election if he was perceived to have given up key national interests. While the demands of these political constituencies constrained the availability of policy options to the Conservative government, they did not compromise—but rather reinforced—the government's objective of ensuring that the institutions of the EC would serve a complementary function to its economic policy program at home.

Originating in the Thatcher government's commitment to market deregulation and neo-liberalism, the Major government formulated a policy which aimed at making Britain the 'Enterprise Centre of Europe' by offering a business environment with highly deregulated labor and financial markets (see HMSO 1996*a*). This setting, it was argued, would provide the appropriate institutional infrastructure for British companies to flourish in global markets and to attract foreign companies to Britain. The SEM played a key role in achieving this objective. However, the Maastricht Treaty was seen as a potential threat to the competitive advantages offered by Britain's market economy because the structure and development in key areas were to be determined by qualified majority voting (QMV) and thus could potentially force Britain to implement EC regulations that would undermine the institutional logic of its LME (HMSO 1996*b*: 25). The Major government's strategy at Maastricht was therefore primarily concerned with ensuring an EC that would not undermine mechanisms that sustained and reinforced market coordination in Britain.

Monetary Policy

While Britain has cooperated on and off with the other member-states in monetary affairs, it was adamant not to sign on to the criteria and timetable for EMU during the Maastricht negotiations. After lengthy negotiations, Britain managed to secure an opt-out from EMU, which effectively gave it full autonomy in deciding if and when it wishes to join the single currency area. While the Tory government's reluctance to sign on to EMU to some extent was a function of its fear of antagonizing Euroskeptics within its own ranks, the decision also reflects a larger institutional rationale associated with the LME.

The British market economy provides an institutional framework that gives a competitive advantage to firms emphasizing relatively low-cost production, and has therefore made British producers particularly concerned with the potential effects of a fixed exchange-rate system. Currency devaluation becomes a particularly important mechanism to restoring competitiveness in Britain since its LME lacks a coordinated wage-determination system that can control labor costs (cf. Soskice 1996c), and provides a quick solution to restoring cost-competitiveness should prices rise too quickly at home. Accordingly, the British were more reluctant to give up national autonomy over the exchange rate than countries that had alternative means for controlling wages or that depended less on low labor costs for their competitive advantage. The reluctance to commit to 'irrevocably' fixing its exchange rate within a monetary union was expressed in its insistence on receiving an opt-out from the three-stage plan to construct EMU. For similar reasons, if Britain were to enter, it was concerned with entering with an exchange rate that was competitive vis-à-vis its partners. This reasoning urged a delayed decision as to when to enter the currency area.

Social Policy

The dependence of British manufacturers on a low-cost and deregulated business environment gave the British government a strong incentive to ensure that EC-level agreements did not impose high social regulations that would undermine the rationale of its 'Enterprise Centre of Europe' strategy. Economic coordination in Britain's LME is secured primarily via the market mechanism and it is generally by maintaining that mechanism—and the discipline it enforces on individual actors in a deregulated setting—that superior levels of coordination are achieved. Accordingly, the British were adamant in their opposition to EC regulations that would erode the market incentives on which the competitive advantage of the economy to a large extent is constructed. This logic extended itself most pointedly to social policy. Extensive social regulations were perceived to undercut the market incentives facing the workforce since higher levels of social benefits tend to raise the reservation wage, thereby raising labor costs for firms that, in many cases, depended on relatively low labor costs for their competitive edge. During the Maastricht negotiations, the Major government thus demanded a singular opt-out from the Treaty's Social Protocol. Upon securing the opt-out, Prime Minister Major summarized the rationale for its strong opposition to European-level legislation in this area: 'Europe can have the social chapter. We shall have employment . . . Jacques Delors accuses us of creating a paradise for foreign investors; I am happy to plead guilty' (quoted in Leibfried and Pierson 1995: 49). The opt-out allowed the government to retain a cost-competitive business environment at home, as well as full access to EC's other programs without committing, as John Major put it, 'a betrayal of our national interests' (quoted in *Daily*

Telegraph, 19 Dec. 1991). While the importance Britain has paid to its opt-out from the Social Chapter is only one example of its relationship to the EC, it signifies the importance the country attaches to structuring that relationship in a way that is consistent with its market economy. The Social Protocol, explained one government official, 'is absolutely anathema to freeing up labor markets . . . [and] it makes absolutely no sense to import European-level labor market regulations to Britain.'[6]

'Today, the UK has the best of two worlds: free access to 370 million consumers and low social costs,' were the words used by another official when summarizing the rationale for the British position.[7] Without membership in the EC, the government reasoned, its ability to attract foreign investment or even maintain domestic investments would have been seriously jeopardized. However, membership in the EC had to be on terms that did not erode the comparative institutional advantages of Britain's market economy. The strategy thus became one of encouraging foreign direct investment by maintaining a cost-competitive business environment and being a member of the internal market. Opting out of the Social Chapter was part of that strategy on both a rhetorical and practical level. This arrangement, as the government officials suggested, has allowed Britain to deregulate its economy, attract the largest share of incoming foreign direct investments in Europe, and exploit the consistency of this policy in an effort to secure the comparative institutional advantages of the LME.

Industrial Policy

Industrial policy arose as an issue during the Maastricht negotiations primarily with regard to whether the European Commission should have the authority to orchestrate an interventionist industrial policy. While the French championed such a solution, Britain was strongly opposed to this initiative. The varieties of capitalism framework suggests why it would. Since the British economy secured superior performance largely by enhancing the market mechanism, Commission-directed interventions that provided firms with alternative market incentives were seen as a source of likely distortions to economic coordination in the British economy. Instead, in the general area of industrial policy, Britain wanted to implement a more rigorous competition policy which in part would contribute to undermining the multiple forms of cooperation found else-

[6] Author's interview with Peter Bunn, director of EU Internal, Trade Policy, and Europe Directorates, Department of Trade and Industry, London, United Kingdom (19 June 1996).
[7] Author's interview with Stephen Lillie, head of section, European Union Internal, Foreign and Commonwealth Office, London, United Kingdom (25 June 1996).

where in Europe (in particular in CMEs) often described as cartels. Thus, the primary concern for the British was to extend the economic area regulated by the EC in a fashion that would enhance the market mechanism and provide British firms with an environment they were accustomed to and that would ensure their competitive edge.[8]

At the center of the discussion concerning a European industrial policy was how the EC could contribute to industrial competitiveness by supporting large-scale European R&D programs. Although Britain would be a net monetary beneficiary of some of these programs (George 1990: 199), the government paradoxically opposed most of these programs and insisted that this area of Community activity be governed by unanimity voting to ensure that Britain could influence the size and structure of future R&D programs. Again, the varieties framework suggests an answer to the government's and business community's reluctance to give the Commission greater resources and authority in this area. The institutional infrastructure for technology diffusion that exists in CMEs does not exist in Britain, and as a consequence the results of these programs were questioned (Buxton et al. 1994). Moreover, since British companies were already doing comparatively well in the high-tech sector (Fig. 6.1) that a common European industrial policy was to target, they might potentially have been relative losers from these programs within the EU.

There was a strong logical coherence to Britain's preferences over the structure of the Maastricht Treaty premissed on how common European regulations would impact its LME. It was reluctant to support common European monetary, social, and industrial policies for fear that they would undermine the institutional foundation of the British market economy and the basis of its strategy to attract investments and promote economic recovery. Its position at Maastricht was primarily an attempt to prevent the introduction of negative institutional growth trajectories at home, which could have eroded the basis of the LME's comparative institutional advantages.[9] 'Mr. Major can . . . claim that the "Thatcher

---

[8] The British government also objected to a common EU industrial policy because it maintained that member-states would have greater recourse to engage in competitive bidding for advanced and high-tech manufacturing (so-called 'subsidy auctions') by enticing investors with direct monetary contributions. Since the government was committed to minimizing public expenditures (most EU programs must be matched by national funds), and since it did not have the administrative apparatus to implement such programs in the early 1990s, the government feared that a common industrial policy within the EU would jeopardize Britain's attraction for foreign investors who had chosen Britain over other countries because of its competitive business environment (HMSO 1994: 84–6).

[9] It should be noted that the support for multilateral institutions during the Maastricht negotiations that would prevent negative institution-building at home has not been a

Revolution" is safe from the encroachment of Brussels,' were the words used by one observer when describing the British 'success' (Jenkins 1991: 1). The intensity of its preferences were not in doubt. Faced with the potential reality that it would be outvoted under the Community's rules of QMV, it insisted, in an unprecedented move and at considerable political costs, on receiving opt-outs from participation in the Social Chapter and EMU to ensure that the LME remained intact. For similar reasons, Britain refused to accept QMV in the industrial policy area and insisted on, and won approval for, unanimity voting in matters relating to common R&D programs. This outcome gave John Major cause to claim 'Game, set, match for Britain' (*Independent*, 15 Dec. 1991: 14) and ensured a strong endorsement in the House of Commons. The support of the business community for his achievements was also unequivocal: 'The prime minister and his colleagues have achieved exactly what business needs—an agreement on economic and monetary union which has left the way open for UK participation in a single European currency, steps to secure more even enforcement of Community legislation, and no extension of Community powers that could threaten international competitiveness,' concluded the director general of the Confederation of British Industry (*Financial Times*, 12 Dec. 1991: 4).

6.5.2 Germany

In strong contrast to the common perception of Britain as a diffident member of the EU, Germany is often described as its *Musterknabe* and a firm supporter of extensive economic integration (Bulmer and Patterson 1987). However, if the view of Britain as always reluctant to increased European integration is an exaggeration, then the claim that Germany is always a champion of integration is no less an overstatement. While EU's structure—including the emphasis on federalism and subsidiarity—is more similar to the German system than to the British, this does not necessarily mean that Germany is always supportive of deeper integration. Like Britain, Germany's institutional preferences within the EU are closely linked to the implications of deeper integration for the structure of its national market economy (cf. Anderson 1997).

The manner in which a German government ensures national support

persistent pattern in British policy. During the 1980s, Britain strongly espoused multilateral institutions that would lock in a liberal trade and extensive competition policy through the construction of new institutions. In both instances Britain's EU policy reflects the liberal bias that has existed for decades in its economic policy and its precise multilateral institutional preferences have depended on how common European regulatory programs affect the workings of its LME at home.

for its policies differs in crucial respects from that of its British counterpart. Because of high levels of party discipline in the Bundestag, German governments have generally little reason to worry about ratifying an international agreement in parliament. Instead, because of the decentralized nature of the German state and the high organizational capacity of economic interest groups, German governments must more actively consider the input of key societal interests and ensure their support for the implementation of policies (Katzenstein 1978*b*). As a consequence, Chancellor Helmut Kohl worried less about partisan political differences than his British counterpart during the Maastricht negotiations. Instead, his attention was directed towards guaranteeing the endorsement of the Bundesbank, and raising support from the national business and labor communities (Moravcsik 1998: ch. 6). However, these domestic constituencies posed relatively few constraints on the Kohl government during the Maastricht negotiations since their general interests were also broadly directed at ensuring that the Treaty did not erode key institutional domains of the German economy.[10]

The Kohl government, with strong support from the national business community, used the SEM and SEA as vehicles to secure the country's dependence on the European market and to dampen the effects of price competition from East Asia. These were important concerns because the strength of national labor unions made it difficult to reformulate Germany's industrial strategy to one that would focus on lowering costs. The internal market also cut transaction costs in Europe and was met with optimism because German firms' superior productivity was seen as a sure way to enhance market shares in Europe. However, as the SEM was being implemented, concerns grew regarding the potential effects the internal market could have in Germany if a stronger European social dimension and greater monetary cooperation were not achieved. The potentially negative effects on the German political and economic landscapes of an EU without stronger protection of the country's social regulations and its monetary regime—both core components of Germany's social market economy—became defining features of the Kohl government's approach to the Maastricht negotiations. A closer examination of Germany's policy and institutional preferences during the negotiations illustrates nicely not only the differences between Britain and Germany, but also the logical coherence to the Germany policy and

---

[10] If anything, the political opposition and the Bundesbank wanted the Kohl government to insist on more detailed regulations on social and monetary policy. The general direction and content of Kohl's policy, though, were not disputed (Beuter 1994).

the crucial role institutional considerations played in the formulation of its institutional preferences.

Monetary Policy

Germany's CME is centered around structures that maintain a great deal of non-market coordination, and it has contributed to the development of competitive advantages based on the capacity to sustain high quality control, customization of products, and incremental innovation in products and production processes. Fig. 6.1 showed the extent to which this structure has made Germany particularly strong in specialized supplier and scale-intensive goods which characterize advanced manufacturing. However, sustaining this kind of production system also comes at a price; in particular, German products tend to be relatively costly to manufacture. While cooperative arrangements at home make it unlikely that producers are undercut in terms of the price of goods, they are vulnerable to foreign competitors who may produce goods of similar quality at lower cost. German producers, unions, and politicians were particularly wary of the ability of other advanced European economies to devalue their currencies and price German products out of competition in the SEM. The risks that other members of the EC would use devaluations to strengthen their competitiveness was, therefore, of particular concern to Germany since it does not have recourse to the same option because of constitutional and political constraints (protected in large part by a fiercely independent Bundesbank). For this reason, EMU was particularly attractive to Germany—especially to manufacturers who dominate the economy—because it would impose limits on the ability of other European countries to undercut German competitiveness. Moreover, by fixing exchange rates within EMU, German producers calculated that they would be able to rely on their relatively superior productivity and the flexibility of their industrial-relations system to increase the quality and competitiveness of their products and thus enlarge their market shares.[11] The government also reasoned that with institutional provisions guaranteeing price and currency stability through EMU, Germany would be able to maintain a domestic environment that encouraged private investments and limited public spending (Waigel 1993).

While geopolitical concerns also played a role in the minds of Europe's political leaders during the Maastricht negotiations, the varieties approach aids in explaining both why Germany preferred a particular

---

[11] Author's interview with Hans-Joachim Haß, head of section, General Trade and Industry, Federation of German Industry (BDI), Bonn, Germany (25 April 1996).

shape to EMU and why it could pursue this policy confident of strong
domestic support. Germany's interest in EMU should not simply be seen
as a consequence of its historical commitment to a tight monetary policy.
Rather, it must be seen within a context that pays attention to the implications of European multilateralism for the institutional structure that
underpins its market economy. Key domestic political and economic
forces feared that this structure would be undermined in the absence
of a multilateral monetary arrangement like that agreed upon at
Maastricht.[12]

Social Policy

Germany is one of the strongest supporters of a 'social dimension' to
European economic integration. It is frequently thought that because
Germany has relatively high social standards and extensive labor market
regulations, it promotes upward harmonization of the Community's
social policy and that its support for the social dimension is premised
on this logic. However, this is a misrepresentation of the German government's objectives, as well as of the preferences of the business and labor
communities. There was a political logic behind the government's efforts
to broaden EC's social dimension during the Maastricht negotiations
because of the potential political costs that organized labor and the
electorate could impose on the government if it gave up the coveted
social program at home. The content of Germany's policy was premised
on how an integrated Europe would affect Germany's CME. More
specifically, Germany supported the establishment of common minimum
social regulations (as opposed to harmonization). This preference was a
function of a set of interrelated considerations.

The major German concern was to prevent the introduction of
processes of competitive deregulation in Europe because of their poten-

---

[12] Events following the Maastricht meeting also show the extent to which Germany's
position on EMU is shaped by the implications of non-EMU on its national market economy
and product markets. Despite enormous social costs of meeting the Maastricht convergence
criteria, Germany insisted throughout the 1990s that even a mini-EMU be implemented
with the countries that qualify. This at first sight is puzzling since we would expect
Germany to want as many countries as possible to be part of the arrangement. However,
since the countries that qualified (or nearly qualified) were countries that produce in similar
product markets to those of German companies, Germany was particularly keen that EMU
be implemented (author's interview with Eberhard Meller, head of Brussels Bureau,
Federation of German Industry, Brussels, Belgium (27 June 1996)). The fact that many
member-states who did not seem to qualify for EMU produce in markets where German
companies are weak was not a major concern for Germany since they do not pose a significant threat to German producers if their currencies depreciate.

tial threat to the regulatory coherence of the German economy. Because of the political difficulties of lowering social regulations at home, it was feared that 'social dumping' might place German producers at a distinct cost disadvantage. Under such circumstances it was argued that Germany would have to abandon key regulatory structures that underpin its economy and thus undermine the foundation of the CME, which receives a large part of its comparative institutional advantage from the 'productive constraints' imposed by relatively strict social regulations (Streeck 1991; Vitols 1997). In contrast, common minimum regulations would ensure that there was a floor under which no country would allow its social regulation to fall, while at the same time giving Germany the flexibility to exceed common standards as it saw politically and economically fit. Agreeing on minimum standards also had the benefit of increasing Germany's chances of finding support for its policy under QMV rules governing this area; in contrast, insisting on applying German standards across the Union would have ensured the opposition of many member-states and thus presented the possibility of minimal European social regulations.

An associated reason Germany did not support upward harmonization was because such an arrangement would lock in common regulatory arrangement and would limit the future flexibility of producers and instead establish high social costs across the EU. If that were the case, German producers argued, industry in most of the Union would be unable to produce competitive products and demand increased economic support from the wealthy countries, which would translate into higher taxes for German producers.[13] By the same token, high common social regulations would make changes to existing structures in times of external economic changes subject to the political will of a qualified majority of the EC, which would impose a slow, burdensome, and uncertain process of regulatory change.

Industrial Policy

On the issue of a European industrial policy, the outcome at Maastricht and the language in Article 130 corresponded closely to the German national preference—roughly between the British minimalist and the French maximalist positions. Unlike Britain, Germany was favorably disposed to including an article that would commit the Community to a horizontal industrial policy that encouraged large-scale cooperative

---

[13] This point is stressed both by the business community (author's interview with Haß 1996) and in government publications (Deregulierungskommission 1991: 187).

research projects within the EU and that would entail provisions to employ the kind of framework regulations that characterize Germany's regulatory architecture. Unlike the French, however, Germany was opposed to giving the Commission increased powers which could be used to direct the disbursements of collective funds towards specific industrial projects in particular sectors or firms. The rationale behind the German position rests on regulatory principles that are consonant with the principles of the CME, and the calculation that a limited EC industrial policy may have beneficial effects for German producers in areas (especially high-tech) where the German market economy has been relatively weak (cf. Grewlich 1984).

In a CME like Germany, the effectiveness of industrial policy and the provision of supply-side goods depends on the ability of the government to make credible commitments to the national business community that it will support firms' objectives without direct intervention. These commitments are a combination of explicit and often implicit contracts between the government and business, where the former provides important resources—frequently based on regulatory mandates—that are administered by business associations and para-public institutions (Katzenstein 1987; Streeck 1983). Such agreements are used to enhance the non-market coordination of the economy and improve the capacity of business to coordinate the provision of, among other things, vocational training, R&D, and technology diffusion. Aware of the benefits of this system to both the government and firms, the German government and the business community supported a similar type of arrangement at the EC level. A highly interventionist national or European industrial policy would be detrimental to this kind of arrangement since it assumes that public officials have the requisite private information that business possesses and would instead increase the power of the Commission to act in an arbitrary fashion.

Germany's position on an EC industrial policy was in practical terms also associated with attempts to provide German producers in the high-tech sector with the opportunity to cooperate with firms in other member-states. The German high-tech sector was relatively weak and showed little growth in the 1980s (Gerstenberger 1992). A common European industrial policy that encouraged cross-European inter-firm relations was very attractive to the German government and industry since it would supplement an area in which its national market economy was comparatively weak. Moreover, since the German form of industrial policy emphasizes the diffusion of technology (Ziegler 1997), a European industrial policy that follows that tradition as well as providing new opportunities in the high-tech area would allow German producers to make use of the comparative institutional advantages of the CME in technology transfer and diffusion while improving its innovation potential in high-tech industry. Thus, in this context, the EC actually served the purpose of facilitating a positive institutional growth trajectory which Germany, only with great difficulty and costs, would be able to achieve alone. In other words, Germany's preference in this area was shaped also by efforts to acquire expertise that its CME had difficulties providing and not, like Britain, by efforts to limit the involvement of the EU.

Like the British Prime Minister, the German Chancellor also claimed success at Maastricht stating that the outcomes 'fully reflect German conditions and interests' (quoted in *UPI*, 11 Dec. 1991). However, while Britain sought to preserve essential components of its domestic market economy by opting out from common arrangements, Germany approached Maastricht as an opportunity to lock in features of its CME by participating in EC-wide regulations. Although the Kohl government was not greeted with the same ringing endorsement at home as Major was, there was general consensus that its ability to push through the Social Protocol and EMU despite British and Danish opt-outs was a major achievement (Beuter 1994). In particular the principles embodied in EMU that were broadly consonant with those of the Bundesbank, and the emphasis on framework regulations akin to the principles of Germany's *Ordnungspolitik*, were hailed as crucial milestones in ensuring a European Community congruent with Germany's economic system.

6.6 Conclusion

A global economy and EC membership has heightened the tension between national and European institutions in recent decades, and it has become more important for countries to ensure that national and international institutions function in a complementary fashion. This chapter has suggested one way of understanding the underlying political and economic motivations that shape a country's preferences over how national and European institutions should be integrated. More specifically, I have suggested that a country's preferences over the structure of multilateralism are primarily a function of how international cooperation will affect the workings of its national market economy, and how the preferences of actors with a stake in that process are aggregated into a national position. The case studies of the British and German positions on the structure of the Maastricht Treaty support this claim. The cases also showed that common generalizations in the academic literature on

European integration and in the media that use stark dichotomies to portray member-states' interests in the EU mask crucial differences within and between states. Thus they often distort the source of states' support for specific forms of international cooperation. This chapter has sought to provide a framework for a more nuanced understanding of why states espouse particular institutional preferences and why these vary across countries and issue areas.

In grounding the analysis of the process of institutional preference formation within the varieties of capitalism literature, this chapter reaches different conclusions than prevailing IR theories. It disputes many of the traditional arguments in IR that rely on the relative distribution of power among states as the primary determinant of a state's international bargaining position, as well as those that expect long-term international cooperation to produce similar policy preferences across countries. Instead, this chapter has employed the varieties literature as a way of supplementing existing societal theories of IR in order to address how domestic actors are affected by the institutional architecture of differentiated market economies and how existing institutions shape their multilateral preferences. As such, the chapter provides additional theoretical depth and empirical breadth to societal theories of international relations by explaining why countries with similar compositions of interest groups support different institutional programs in the EU.

One of the strengths of the varieties of capitalism approach is that, unlike many theories in IR, it endogenizes actors' preferences and does not assume that actors have static preferences over time or issue areas. Rather, this framework emphasizes how institutional preferences vary across areas depending on how changes in one domain of the market economy will affect the institutional infrastructure of the economy as a whole and the complementarities it furnishes. As such, it provides a more empirically nuanced account of events, as well as a theoretically more precise approach to understanding the domestic sources of multilateralism. At the same time, by illustrating the importance that economic actors attach to achieving an institutional match between domestic and European institutions, this chapter provides a theoretical and empirical extension of the varieties of capitalism research program, which has limited itself primarily to events at the national level.

A competing explanation that has not been addressed thus far concerns the explanatory value of partisan differences. In short, could a model premissed on the notion that the ideology of the political party in office determines national preferences explain the variation in British and German approaches at Maastricht? This chapter suggests that such an explanation has serious limitations on both empirical and theoretical grounds. During the negotiations, right-of-center parties were in power in both countries, and yet their institutional preferences during the negotiations differed greatly. A partisan explanation would suggest greater similarities. More importantly, there has been a great deal of continuity in the two countries' policies vis-à-vis European integration despite recent changes in governments. Though beyond the limited scope of this chapter, events following the Maastricht negotiations are illustrations of this effect. In Britain, the Labour Party's electoral victory in 1997 did not fundamentally change that country's multilateral preferences within the EC. Despite Prime Minister Tony Blair's emphatic promise to improve his country's somewhat tarnished reputation within the EU, his government 'broadly followed the path taken by the Conservatives' (Driver and Martell 1998: 145; cf. Holmes 1991). While signing on to the Social Protocol, the Blair government claimed that the Protocol 'will not impose the so-called German or European model of social and employment costs,' and promised to oppose such movements 'if necessary by veto' (*Financial Times*, 11 Mar. 1997). Instead, Blair pledged that there would be no fundamental change in Britain's market economy or its attraction to foreign investors by promising that there would be a minimum of new social regulations (*Financial Times*, 11 Mar. 1997: 8). In fact, Blair's slogan of 'a nation of entrepreneurs' sounded surprisingly similar to Major's 'Enterprise Centre of Europe' strategy.[14]

The 1998 victory of Gerhard Schröder in Germany illustrated a similar path of continuity. His party's electoral manifesto echoed the policy of the Kohl government and stressed the importance of 'renewing the social market-economy,' using the European Union for the purposes of maintaining key framework regulations and common social minimum regulations, as well as utilizing the EU to improve the German high-tech sector, and employing EMU in order to prevent 'currency-dumping' from undercutting Germany's competitiveness (SPD 1998: 6, 9, 54–6). Finally, the manner in which Blair and, in particular, Schröder backtracked from their joint July 1999 statement of a 'third way' for Europe was indicative of the practical limitations of fashioning an economic architecture in the European Union that would meet the goals of both national constituencies.[15]

---

[14] Another instance of remarkable continuity in British policy is its lasting reluctance to commit to EMU. This is in part due to concerns with the potentially negative consequences that a fixed exchange rate and the limited recourse to currency depreciation would pose for producers in Britain (cf. *Financial Times*, 21 Nov. 1997: p. vii).

[15] The text of the joint statement, as well as other details on the Schröder government's *Neue Mitte*, are found in Hombach (2000).

The varieties framework suggests why there is such strong continuity in the institutional preferences of the two countries. It considers the political and economic calculations that policy-makers and interest groups make when evaluating the consequences of institutional change. The framework suggests that institutional continuity and adaptation are often a shared interest among these actors because a transformation of the existing institutional environment is seen as costly, uncertain, and time-consuming. Under such circumstances, European integration is approached, usually without regard to political partisanship, as a process that must be managed with the general economic and institutional interests of the national market economy as a whole in mind. Deeper European integration under appropriate terms helps both governments and interest groups to achieve their joint goals in strengthening the structural competitiveness of the economy in which they are embedded. This framework, then, suggests that there are parameters within which the preferences of policy-makers will be shaped and that these are defined by the extent to which national and European institutions will function in a complementary fashion, and not significantly by changes in the ideological make-up of governments.

No doubt the subject of how national and international institutions interact deserves more scholarly attention in the future as their interactions intensify. This chapter has suggested one way of approaching this issue, and in doing so it offers a set of implications for related topics of interest. For example, on both empirical and theoretical grounds it disputes the claim that economic globalization and long-term membership in international organizations like the EC necessarily lead to policy convergence or institutional isomorphism among states. Instead, the chapter shows that economic actors process external economic signals in a manner consistent with existing institutions and that because of the costs associated with moving from one institutional equilibrium to another—that is, with replacing one market economy with another—states seek to promote existing comparative institutional advantages. Therefore, we expect a continuation in varieties of market economies and, as a consequence, also continued differences in states' multilateral preferences.

Some scholars of the EC assert, however, that institutional convergence is a prerequisite for the successful achievement of important economic gains (Heylen and van Poeck 1995). While it is beyond the scope of this chapter to address the solutions that the EU has devised to resolve institutional differences and conflicting demands among member-states, this chapter questions the general claim that states' preferences will converge over time if they are members of the same organization. Thus, if diverse forms of advanced capitalism continue to coexist within the EU, the analytical emphasis in the future should not be on how convergence can be promoted, but rather on how divergence can be accommodated. Under these circumstances, it becomes increasingly important to uncover the source of members-states' institutional preferences in order to understand the basis of their negotiating positions, as well as under what circumstances members are willing to compromise. This chapter suggests that the varieties of capitalism literature can serve as a domestic theory of international relations in order to address these issues.

A second implication of this chapter concerns the terms on which states engage in international cooperation. It has been asserted that states' primary goal in international organizations is to transfer the structure of their national regulatory regimes to the international level in order to minimize the costs associated with institutional change or to maximize their advantages over competitors (e.g. Kahler 1995: 2). This chapter provides a more nuanced picture of states' terms of engagement at the multilateral level. It shows that states do not necessarily seek to replicate their national regulatory systems at the multilateral level, but that they also use multilateral cooperation to reach objectives which they are unable or have great difficulties achieving on their own. Thus, for example, the German case demonstrated attempts at positive institution-building when Germany sought to acquire greater strength in the high-tech sector through common EC programs. Conversely, knowing that it would not be able to replicate its LME within the EU, Britain sought to lock in significant parts of its comparative institutional advantages by opting out of some areas of European cooperation like parts of its social and monetary spheres.

This volume as a whole discusses significant issues relating to institutional change among advanced capitalist countries, and this chapter has addressed more specifically the interaction of national and European institutions. It shows that in an integrated Europe, institutional change at the national level happens neither spontaneously or independently of the institutional environment that the European Community embodies, nor is the direction of institutional change independent of existing constructs at home. Rather, existing national institutions shape the institutional preferences of economic agents in distinct ways, and European institutions provide opportunities to solidify desired outcomes. Using the intellectual framework of the societal approach to international relations and adding an institutional lens with the help of the varieties of capitalism literature, this chapter has argued that the nature of a country's market economy fundamentally shapes its multilateral preferences. As such, it demonstrates the importance of examining institutional change and national preference formation in Europe with a nuanced perspective that pays attention to the interaction between domestic and European-level institutions. In this context, it employs the varieties of capitalism literature as a domestic theory of international relations and potentially opens up a new avenue of research for scholars interested in narrowing the gap between comparative and international political economy as a means to acquire a fuller understanding of the contemporary political economy of Europe.

PART II

CASE-STUDIES IN PUBLIC POLICY, CONTINUITY, AND CHANGE

7

Business, Government, and Patterns of Labor Market Policy in Britain and the Federal Republic of Germany

Stewart Wood

The central focus of the 'varieties of capitalism' literature is the persistence of differences in the organization of national political economies. Variations between CMEs and LMEs in the structure, activities, and strategies of companies, and in the structure of inter-firm relationships, are well documented in the contributions to this volume. Similarly, many of the chapters demonstrate how resilient these institutional characteristics have been in the face of new political and economic challenges since the 1980s. At the same time, however, the 'varieties of capitalism' approach tends to underplay the importance of the *political* dimensions of political economies. Economic activity is not only situated within distinctive constitutional and political contexts, but depends upon the legislative and regulatory activities of governments for its viability. In striving for a firm-centered account of contemporary political economy, it is important not to marginalize the importance of public policy to the bundle of institutional complementarities that characterize CMEs and LMEs.

Just as the organization of economic activity in CMEs and LMEs has remained distinct in an era of supposed institutional convergence, so have the varieties of public policy pursued within each variety of capitalism. Generous welfare policies, for example, were supposed to be economically unsustainable in the face of highly mobile capital, and politically unsustainable as European electorates crept to the center-right. Yet the core features of different worlds of welfare capitalism remain firmly in place (Stephens et al. 1999). Convergence has been equally unforthcoming in the case of policies towards organized labor. Contrary to expectations that the rights and functions of trade unions in advanced industrial nations would be eroded by a combination of stronger employers, ideologically hostile governments, and high unemployment, differences in the role of organized labor across OECD countries remain (Wallerstein et al. 1997; Wood 2001). In short, the kinds of welfare and labor market policies that are pursued in CMEs and LMEs remain different, and different in systematic ways.

How can we explain these continuing differences in national policy patterns? And in what way are the institutional characteristics of varieties of capitalism linked to the policies governments pursue in them? This chapter explores this key relationship between public policy and the organization of economic activity in LMEs and CMEs, focusing on the case of labor market policy in Britain (an LME) and the Federal Republic of Germany (a CME).[1] It derives the policy regimes that characterize these two cases from the very different patterns of *business–government relationship* in each variety of capitalism. This understanding of policy-making adopts Hall and Soskice's firm-centered approach to political economy elaborated in the Introduction, and understands public policy in terms of the role it plays in supporting distinctive production regimes in CMEs and LMEs. A government's policy options are, I argue, fundamentally constrained, or biased, by the different organizational capacities of employers in CMEs and LMEs.

However, it is still governments rather than companies that make public policy. Governments may face strong pressures to deliver policies that are congruent with production regimes and company strategies, but they are also prone to a variety of other pressures—ideological, political, and electoral—that compete for attention, and that may result in (often sudden) changes in the direction of policy. Consequently, while the *content* of labor market policy in Britain and the FRG is derived from the preferences of employers, the *stability* of policy regimes over time is largely determined by the power of governments to initiate reform or reversals. In each case, the degree of constraint on central government is fundamental to employers' ability to pursue those production strategies that distinguish each variety of capitalism. First, because employers require the state to deliver certain kinds of complementary policies. Second, because the coordination of economic activities requires a guarantee of the stability of these policies across time. In the German case, the presence of institutional guarantees that limit the degree and

[1] References to 'Germany' can be misleading if the historical period covered straddles reunification. This chapter addresses themes in West Germany prior to reunification, as well as in Germany after 1990. The term 'the Federal Republic of Germany', or FRG, is used to refer to both throughout the article. Similarly the adjective 'German' is here always used to describe aspects of the Federal Republic, either before or after 1990. In section 7.2, where the discussion turns to policy developments in the 1980s, I also refer to the FRG as 'West Germany'.

type of government intervention is central to the logic of supply-side coordination. In Britain, the absence of such guarantees makes institutions of non-market coordination difficult to sustain.

The chapter is divided into two sections. In the first section, a theoretical framework for understanding business–government relations in the FRG and the UK, and the public policies they produce, is developed. For each country, the argument proceeds in three steps. First, employers' preferences about public policy are derived from the properties of CMEs and LMEs identified by Hall and Soskice. Second, an examination of the constitutional and political sources of government power in Britain and the FRG suggests significant variation in the expected stability of policy regimes. Finally, the two variables—the preferences of employers and the structural capacity of governments—are combined to produce two different paradigms of business–government relations, each with distinctive institutional and incentive properties. The second section offers an empirical illustration of the framework with the case of labor market policy in Britain and West Germany during the 1980s. In Great Britain this was a decade of unprecedented neo-liberal reform, propelled by the combination of employers agitating for the restoration of a liberal market economy and a powerful central government under Margaret Thatcher. In West Germany, however, the 1980s was a decade in which reform impulses were frustrated. German employers successfully protected the institutions and policies of supply-side coordination in the labor market. At the same time, a variety of veto players within the governing coalition prevented the Kohl administration from effecting any substantial liberalization at all.

7.1 Business–Government Relations in Britain and West Germany

7.1.1 Employers' policy preferences in CMEs and LMEs

In the Introduction to this volume, Hall and Soskice chart the main differences in the production regimes of CMEs and LMEs. One of the central implications of their framework is that the structure of supply-side relations shapes the company strategies that are available to firms in each variety of capitalism.

In CMEs, capital coordination facilitates product market strategies which employ the collective goods it makes possible. In particular, coordination between firms enables them to produce high value-added products targeted at niche export (as well as domestic) markets, involving highly and flexibly skilled workers. Capital coordination also allows a strategy of incremental innovation in production to maintain the qualitative advantage of products as technology, skills, and markets change. It is important to note that these strategies are not merely the product of capital coordination over one production input—such as skilled labor, or the provision of stable long-term finance—but over a *range* of them. There are, in other words, a number of interlocking 'subsystems of production' (Carlin and Soskice 1997) that together direct firms towards a quality-based competitive strategy employing incremental innovation. Consequently, coordination, and the company strategies it facilitates, exhibits strong self-reinforcing tendencies.

In LMEs, where capital coordination is absent, strategies employing supply-side collective goods and incremental innovation are unavailable to firms. The supply-side collective goods that are provided by and for business in CMEs cannot be provided in LMEs. Firms are therefore constrained in the sorts of product market strategies they can adopt. Where marketable skills, long-term finance, encompassing employer and labor organizations, and investment in technological development are absent, firms are forced to concentrate on products that can be produced at low cost using standardized production methods. These products must compete not on the basis of quality advantages, but primarily in terms of *cost* advantages. And work organization, rather than emphasizing flexible tasks or teamwork among highly skilled workers, will be based upon a more rigid and conventional division of tasks.

As Hall and Soskice explain, LMEs have their own distinctive variety of institutional complementarities. Just as company strategies in CMEs rely upon the institutions of capital coordination, so in LMEs company strategies rely upon *markets* to organize production inputs. The 'lock-in' effects of these complementarities are as strong as in CMEs. Where markets rather than non-market coordination determine the type of skills, technology, finance, and industrial relations available to companies, cost-based competitive strategies involving more standardized organization of work will be highly resilient. Efforts to stimulate supply-side coordination are thus likely to be unsuccessful for two 'path-dependent' reasons—first, because of employers' interests in maintaining their existing form of competitive advantage; and second, because employers in LMEs are faced with enormous collective action problems in the absence of institutions and practices of coordination.

How do these differences in company strategies in CMEs and LMEs influence employers' *policy* preferences? The connection is straightforward—employers will look to public policy to maintain and reinforce the variety of institutional competitive advantage upon which they rely. Public policy, in other words, is an important pillar of support for the governance structures of both CMEs and LMEs. In particular, public policy is central to the maintenance of the *incentive-compatibility* of the organization of various production inputs (skills, finance, technology, etc.), without which the viability of company strategies may be threatened. Employers will therefore look to government policy to perform two related functions.

First, *framework legislation* is required to underpin the institutional architecture supporting production in both CMEs and LMEs. The sorts of framework legislation required will vary sharply between the two. In CMEs, business sees the state's function as one of ensuring that the rich networks of business coordination are protected. Fundamental to these governance structures is the provision, and periodic renewal, of the legislative frameworks that invest private bodies with the (often exclusive) authority to regulate economic activities on the supply side. Vocational training in the FRG, for example, is governed by framework laws that establish chambers of commerce (*Kammern*) as the sole 'competent authorities' (*zuständige Behörde*) for oversight of training activities within companies (Streeck et al. 1987). Framework legislation such as this is crucial not only in providing legal authority for the coordinating activities of companies and their associations, but also in establishing areas protected from intrusion by the state itself. The special importance of such protection in CMEs stems from the circulation of information required for the coordination and monitoring of company activities. As Soskice observes, 'governments impinge across the whole range of a company's operations; there is no guarantee that information will not be used against the company in some other context, since ultimately governments are sovereign and cannot commit themselves or their successors' (Soskice 1991).

While in CMEs business looks to the state to protect the institutions of coordination, business in LMEs sees the state as an agent of *market preservation*. In the absence of business coordination, companies' competitive strategies depend upon maintaining deregulated product and labor markets, and maximizing flexibility in contractual relationships with employees. Employers will therefore look to the state for framework legislation to remove obstacles to market-clearing, and to locate decision-making power unambiguously in companies. For example, public policy should ensure that wage-bargaining or vocational training remain activities controlled by companies, rather than regulated through collective bargaining by sectoral representatives.

A second function of public policy is to provide *supporting incentives* for companies that reinforce their reliance upon distinct institutional comparative advantages. Policy can, in this sense, act like an institution and provide an additional, reinforcing complementarity (Pierson 2000). An important example in the area of social policy is provided by Estevez-Abe, Iversen, and Soskice (this volume). In their view, employment and unemployment protection policies can be understood as systems of skill protection. In CMEs, these policies provide income guarantees for those contemplating the decision to invest in the acquisition of specific skills. Generous replacement rates are therefore central to a coordinated market economy's ability to ensure an adequate and continuing supply of skilled labor. The opposite is true for LMEs, where company strategies do not depend upon collective provision of transferable skills. In LMEs companies view high replacement rates as simply distorting the functioning of labor markets and increasing their costs. Consequently, their policy preferences will be for minimal replacement rates to maximize the incentive for the unemployed to reenter employment as quickly as possible.

The case of labor market policy illustrates these differences in employers' preferences, and the way they reinforce company strategies. In CMEs, product market, innovation and work-organization strategies depend upon collaboration with organized labor (Hall and Soskice, this volume). One key role of public policy is therefore to maintain framework legislation that protects workers' organizations, and protects their role as partners in negotiated outcomes (Swenson 2001). A second role of public policy is to offer additional incentives for employers to adopt the characteristic strategies of CMEs. Legislation can be used to impose 'benign constraints' on companies, such as statutory limits on employers' ability to hire and fire at will. These constraints reinforce their dependence on long-term employee contracts and good industrial relations, and force them to invest in the productivity of their workers (Streeck 1992*b*). This in turn gives employers an incentive to participate in the provision of the relevant supply-side collective goods, and the governance structures that make this possible.

In LMEs, however, employers' preference is to weaken organized labor as much as possible. Where firms do not rely upon production strategies that render organized labor a virtue—in collective bargaining, or managing process innovation, for example—they will see strong trade unions and strong employment protection as fetters on their ability to compete on the basis of lowering production costs. In contrast to CMEs, the desirable role of framework legislation will be to provide statutory limitations on the power of organized labor, at both the sectoral and the company level. Supporting legislation will also be demanded which minimizes employment protection, and which maximizes flexibility in contractual relationships with employees.

Employer preferences over public policy therefore differ systematically between CMEs and LMEs. The extent to which public policy outcomes actually reflect these preferences, however, is a function of the relationship between business and government in specific national contexts. Clearly there are many factors that will influence what governments are able and willing to do. Ideological, electoral, and political influences are all important to a full understanding of any government's policy agenda. The framework of business–government relations developed here, however, concentrates on the factors that determine the ability (or inability) of governments to deliver those public policies demanded by business. The next section, therefore, explores the type and amount of power enjoyed by central government in the two national cases explored in section 7.2—the FRG and Great Britain.

7.1.2 The Power of Government in Britain and the FRG

The policy-making power of national governments is determined by two sets of factors. First, governments find themselves in different *constitutional* contexts that concentrate or disperse power in different ways (Huber et al. 1993; Bonoli 1999). Some constitutions dictate that public power be divided or shared between multiple institutions—both 'horizontally', between the executive, the legislature, and a constitutional court, and 'vertically', between national and subnational government. In these cases governments' policy autonomy is low, as they are forced to placate multiple veto players in their attempts to initiate policy change. In other constitutions, where power is highly concentrated, governments need only sustain a majority in the legislature to ensure their dominance over policy-making. Second, governments face *political* constraints on their ability to pursue distinct policy agendas. The most severe political constraint is that imposed by the necessity of coalition with other parties under different electoral systems (Huber et al. 1993). Parties in power may also be hamstrung by their electoral or financial dependence on key constituencies of support that constrain their leaders' room for policy maneuver (Kitschelt 1994).

The degree of constitutional and political constraint on governments in the FRG and the UK could not be more different. The German federal government's constitutional position is highly constrained. First, constitutionally protected federalism bars the government from intervention in certain designated policy areas, and mandates cooperation in the administration of most of those areas over which it has legislative jurisdiction (Jeffery 1996). Second, German bicameralism is of a particularly strong variety. The second chamber, the Bundesrat, exercises coequal powers with the lower house, the Bundestag, over most important policy issues. Furthermore, the two houses are often governed by different partisan majorities. Even when this is not the case, the federal basis of representation in the Bundesrat can generate strong inter-chamber tensions (Paterson and Southern 1994). Third, responsibility for many key policy areas in the FRG lies outside the boundaries of the state altogether. 'Para-public institutions' such as the Bundesbank and chambers of commerce are private bodies invested with public power, and are protected against central government by administrative and constitutional law (Katzenstein 1987). Fourth, the German government is subject to the rulings of a powerful Federal Constitutional Court (*Bundesverfassungsvericht*), with powers of review that are comparable to those of the US Supreme Court (Stone 1994). Together these external constraints on German governments suggest a state that is truly 'semi-sovereign' (Katzenstein 1987).

Political constraints on governments are equally strong. The German electoral system (AMS) has made coalition government necessary throughout the history of the Federal Republic (with a brief exception after 1957). Since the formation of the Grand Coalition in 1966, disputes between coalition partners over key policy proposals have plagued the legislative agendas of all German governments. A further political constraint stems from the way in which the main *Volksparteien* are organized. The CDU in particular has the character of a broad coalition of component groups, ranging from the free-market *Mittelstandsvereinigung* and *Wirtschaftsflügel* (business wing) on the economic 'right' to the union-affiliated Social Committees on the 'left' (Braunthal 1996). The party's links with trade unions have been crucial in counterbalancing the more economically liberal agenda of these groups and of the FDP (Wood 1997). Strong federalism compounds this internal institutional diversity, producing powerful subnational groups within the party that are not easily controlled by the federal party elites. Most conspicuous in this respect is the Christian Social Union (CSU)—the CDU-affiliated party in Bavaria —which has proven to be both socially conservative on religious and educational issues and reluctant to concede the retreat of the state from interventionist industrial policy.

The British case could hardly provide a stronger contrast. Although (or perhaps because) Britain does not have a written constitution, the degree of power enjoyed by central government is exceptional. A combination of the doctrine of parliamentary sovereignty, a first-past-the-post electoral system, and strong, internally hierarchical political parties gives Britain enormously powerful single-party governments. Once in power, single-party majorities in the Commons are little if at all hindered by the formal powers of other institutions. Since 1911 the second chamber, the House of Lords, has been reduced to exercising delaying rather than veto power. British courts are limited to the review of the implementation of statutes passed by Parliament, but as Parliament is sovereign, their review does not extend to the content of statute law. Local government in Britain has been reconstituted a number of times this century and enjoys no constitutional protection. Neither do the new devolved assemblies in Scotland and Wales, which were created, and thus may be dismantled, by simple Acts of Parliament. The implication of these constitutional features is that, once elected, Westminster governments can do almost anything they want. It is a degree of formal power unmatched anywhere in advanced industrial democracies (Hennessy 1994).

Similarly, British governments enjoy few political constraints on the exercise of their vast constitutional power. Britain's first-past-the-post electoral system almost always delivers single-party governments with stable majorities. Parties in opposition are powerless, reduced to 'heckling the steamroller' of the government legislative machine. Inside the House of Commons, party discipline is ruthlessly enforced by powerful party whips; voting defections are extremely rare, and on important policy matters are punishable by expulsion from the parliamentary party. Cabinets of both Conservative and Labour parties have consistently acted autonomously of their own party organizations once in power, often to the intense anger of the extra-parliamentary party (Kavanagh 1998). This autonomy is particularly pronounced for Conservative governments. Unlike the German CDU, the British Conservative Party's parliamentary leadership is completely autonomous of extra-parliamentary organizations in matters concerning party policy and electoral strategy (Norton 1996).

The severity of constraints on the power and autonomy of national governments thus differs markedly between the two cases. While German coalition governments are strongly constrained, both constitutionally and politically, British single-party governments benefit from an extreme concentration of power and a high degree of policy autonomy on the part of cabinets. One implication of this difference is that policy is likely to be more stable across electoral cycles in the FRG than in the UK. Similarly, radical policy initiatives are more likely to succeed in the UK than in the FRG. However, these differences in the feasibility of policy change affect the content of policy in deeper and more subtle ways. To understand this requires combining the preceding analyses to develop an account of the structural relationship between business and government in each national case.

7.1.3 The Structure of Business–Government Relations in the UK and the FRG

In one sense, the nature of business–government relations in any country is likely to vary across time in much the same way as relations between government and other interest groups do. But as Lindblom observed, the relationship between business and government is a special one, as business occupies a 'privileged position' among the ranks of other interest groups (Lindblom 1977). For Lindblom, the unique importance of the business–government relationship stems from a condition of mutual dependence in capitalist democracy. While the state is reliant upon business for the investment and growth that will produce economic success, and hence political success, business is reliant upon government to deliver a congenial regulatory environment. Lindblom referred to the power exercised by business in virtue of its privileged position as *structural* power, largely to distinguish it from the conception of interest-group power advanced by pluralists.

The argument developed here shares much of Lindblom's basic insight, and certainly shares his justification for the primacy of the nexus between business and government. However, of central interest in this chapter is the way in which the organization of business and the limits on state power combine in different national contexts to produce different policy regimes. These factors affect policy in three general ways. First, they determine what business and government want and are able to do; second, they bias the policy options available to governments; and third, they determine the credibility of commitments to the continuation of existing policy.

The FRG: Coordinated Business, Constrained Government

As shown above, business in the Federal Republic is highly coordinated, but faces a central government with severely constrained power and limited autonomy. This combination is crucial to the long-run maintenance of the institutions of coordination.

First, the capacity of any German government to erode the institutional complementarities that support coordination is small. This is not simply because of the political obstacles to radical policy change that exist; employers also enjoy a collective political strength that is in part an 'organizational externality' of supply-side coordination. With high levels of coordination, and strong collective control over the provision of supply-side public goods, German business is well placed to defend the governance structures that serve its interests, while governments with designs on undermining these structures (either through political centralization or deregulation) are unlikely to succeed. Taken together, these features serve to assure companies that the institutions of coordination are protected from injurious state intervention in the long run. This is crucial to business coordination because the investments required of companies in CMEs are specific or co-specific investments (such as industry-specific skills, or specialized technologies). These investments are costly and risky, with returns that may only be reaped over a long period. Although the institutions and networks of coordination in CMEs make these investments profitable, the limits to government power in the FRG provide an additional assurance that the returns to these investments are safe.

The fact that the institutions of coordination are difficult to undermine increases not only the likelihood of these institutions remaining in place, but, more specifically, the likelihood that employers will continue to *control* these institutions (Mares 1998). Again, the importance of employer control lies in the assurance it provides to nervous employers. The main purpose of business coordination is to enable the long-run provision of supply-side investments for high value-added production. One key problem associated with these investments is that they are plagued by classic collective action problems—each firm has an incentive to free-ride on the investments of others, and to poach the workers that others train or the process innovations that others have developed. Coordinated business solves this problem in part through ensuring the circulation of information between companies, between business and banks, and particularly between companies and 'monitors' such as employers' associations and chambers of commerce. In order to cooperate willingly in providing this information, companies must be assured that the monitors who have access to it are credibly distanced from government. The assurance of long-term control of the institutions of business coordination by business is therefore central to the functioning of coordination.

As both of these examples show, the fact that government power is highly constrained in the FRG is central to the long-run integrity of institutions and networks of coordination. In turn, the fact that companies enjoy a strong expectation that these institutions will remain in place, and will remain under the control of business, increases their willingness to share information and to undertake risky specific investments. What looks at one level like the weakness of the German state is therefore at another level its great strength. For its very weakness is an important assurance to companies whose cooperation is required to make coordination work.

A second effect of the combination of coordinated business and a constrained central government is its influence on the policy options available to governments in the FRG. Whatever their ideological preferences, German governments know that policies that challenge the governance structures of business coordination are not likely to succeed. The flipside of this constraint is that policies that are incentive-compatible with existing institutional complementarities are more likely to be successful. Thus, the fact that business is highly coordinated combined with the limits on government power *biases* governments towards policies that exploit those institutional advantages associated with CMEs. The point can be made in a different way. Governments may see advantages in policies that delegate control over supply-side investments to business. In order for such policies to be effective, however, business must be organized in a highly coordinated way—in the case of training policy, so that it is capable of standard-setting and firm-monitoring, for example. Where business is highly coordinated, therefore, government will be significantly more disposed to pursue incentive-compatible policies.

The structure of the business–government relationship in the FRG therefore produces an *equilibrium policy outcome*. Business requires framework and supporting legislation of a certain kind in order to maintain the governance structures on which successful economic performance depends. However, these structures also require a credible restraint on the power of government to undermine these governance structures. The constitutional and political fetters on the power of German governments overcome this problem by credibly committing governments, of whatever partisan stripe, to the institutions and policies supporting coordination. Furthermore, the presence of strong business coordination biases the policy options of governments towards policies that are incentive-compatible with existing institutional complementarities.

The UK: Uncoordinated Business, Unconstrained Government

In stark contrast to the FRG, business in the UK is uncoordinated, while British governments face no significant constitutional or political checks on their legislative power. What are the implications of this combination of organizational features for the structure of business–government relations, and the public policies that result?

First, the legislative strength of British governments brings uncertainty to the political economy, and thereby further confirms the unavailability of supply-side coordination. Because governments have the capacity to introduce radical changes of policy at will, companies are unwilling to make the risky long-term investments that would be necessary for constructing networks of coordination. Governments are also unable to credibly distance themselves from the sorts of business-led governance structures that characterize CMEs. As a result companies face over-whelming incentives to withhold rather than share information, and to resist other behavioural requirements of coordination. The sizeable power and autonomy of British governments therefore makes the sort of institutional guarantees observed in the German case impossible.

Second, the absence of coordination in British business offers strong incentives to governments to deliver the market-enhancing policies demanded by employers. Policies predicated on supply-side coordina-tion among employers will simply not work (their failure is heavily over-determined!); policies to stimulate such coordination face the incentive and credibility problems outlined earlier. Policy options are therefore constrained by the absence of organizational capacities on the part of British business, by business' preferences, and by existing 'liberal' insti-tutional complementarities.

These considerations suggest that the structure of business–govern-ment relations in the UK should produce its own brand of equilibrium policy outcome, one in which the institutional complementarities of an LME are maintained over time. However, the structure of business–government relations in Britain is less stable than the corresponding relationship in the FRG.

The problem arises from the weakness of constraints on the power of government in Britain, and the policy inconsistencies to which this can give rise. While it is true that government has an incentive to produce policies that reinforce the comparative institutional advantage of an LME, its structural power means that it is not constrained to respond to these incentives. There are few institutional obstacles to British govern-ments pursuing whatever policy experiments they choose. Indeed, between 1961 and 1979 both Labour and Conservative governments launched a series of supply-side policies that aimed, in different ways, to bring about greater degrees of coordination in the areas of industrial training, investment, research and development, and wage-bargaining. These policies were inspired by a mixture of intellectual fads and interest-group pressure, together with a pervasive sense of the need for new policies to arrest declining growth rates (Wood 1997). Nevertheless, while it is true that British governments are *able* to initiate policies that are not incentive-compatible with the institutional complementarities of LMEs, these policies are unlikely to succeed. The 1961–79 period offers ample evidence for this; it is a period littered with failures to entice business into replacing liberal with coordinated governance structures. These policy failures were an important factor in the emergence and electoral success of Margaret Thatcher, and of her programme for the restoration of Britain's liberal market economy.

What does this imply for the stability of Britain's LME? Clearly strong incentives exist on the part of business and government to pursue corporate and policy strategies characteristic of LMEs. The power of governments in the Westminster model, however, means that radical departures from this 'equilibrium' outcome are possible; governments always have the *capacity* to disturb the market-based governance structures favoured by business. Where this occurs, the incentive-incompatibility of such policies with company strategies is likely to defeat the policy, and impose political costs on the governments that introduced them. Over time, it is therefore likely that governments will abandon these policies, and choose those policy options that sustain existing institutional advantages.

7.2 Labor Market Policy in Britain and West Germany in the 1980s

The preceding section outlined a framework for understanding the structure of business–government relations in Britain (an LME) and the FRG (a CME), and the broad patterns of public policy associated with them. The discussion that follows does not attempt to illustrate all the arguments suggested in section 7.1; nor does it present evidence over a range of public policies. Instead, it focuses on a 'snapshot' of business–government relations in one policy area—labor market policy—during the 1980s. Labor market policy is central to production regimes in LMEs and CMEs, while employer preferences about it differ strongly between the two. It is also a policy area that became highly politically charged during the 1980s in both the UK and the FRG (in both cases as a result of industrial action). Most contentious of all was the question of the role of organized labor, and it is this aspect of labor market policy on which this section focuses.[2]

---

[2] This section draws heavily on research presented in greater detail in Wood (1997).

7.2.1 Britain in the 1980s: The Attack on Organized Labor

A legislative assault on trade unions was the dominant theme of the Conservative Party's successful electoral campaign in 1979. Trade union power had accumulated as a result of a variety of factors during the post-war period, not the least of which were the policies of preceding governments. Successive governments had sought to govern in collaboration with trade unions—through incomes policies and peak-level consultation over growth targets, for example. Associated with this were attempts to give unions statutory power in a variety of policy areas, such as industrial training and collective bargaining. These policies failed in large part because they assumed a degree of internal cohesion on the part of the trade union movement that did not exist. Individual trade unions remained largely autonomous of the central leadership of the Trade Union Congress (TUC); and within unions, increasingly powerful shop stewards at the plant level fragmented authority and control even further. The culmination of these developments was the collapse of the Labour government's attempt at a voluntary incomes policy in 1978, and the resulting wave of public- and private-sector strikes that crippled the country during the 1978–9 'Winter of Discontent' (Middlemas 1991).

Margaret Thatcher ended government consultation with trade unions —'beer and sandwiches at Number 10'—immediately. More subtly, Thatcher transformed the main peak-level corporatist institution, the Manpower Services Commission (MSC), from being an instrument of national manpower and training policy to a mechanism for legitimizing unemployment. The MSC's tripartite composition enabled the government to enlist employers and unions in the management of its unemployment commitments. 'Training' policy gradually evolved into a series of stop-gap measures designed to reduce the visibility of the swelling ranks of the unemployed (King 1993). Employers supported the new MSC regime *not* because of its tripartite constitution, but because the training programs that it administered provided short-term, cheap labor to companies.

The MSC survived until 1988, when government and employers developed a new regime for the management of skills and local employment that marginalized organized labor more explicitly. In 1988 the TUC withdrew support for the government's Employment Training Scheme because they interpreted it (correctly) as a device to cut wage costs (King 1995). In its place, and after collaboration with the main employers' confederation (the Confederation of British Industries, CBI), the government established regional Training and Enterprise Councils to administer government training programs. These Councils were to consist of leading local employers but made no provision for the representation of unions or employees whatsoever. Training and (un)employment policy was thus by 1988 removed from the sphere of worker influence altogether (Wood 1999).

A second element of the government's policy aimed to empower employers — individually rather than collectively — to resist trade union demands. Measures of this variety largely took the form of restricting trade union powers and immunities in common law, and were among those for which British employers pushed most vociferously. The legislation that effected this transformation in industrial relations was pursued in stages, and began somewhat falteringly. In 1980 the Conservatives passed their first Employment Act, which set out to eliminate perceived 'excesses' of union activity in the second half of the 1970s. The Act is notable for three measures that set the trend for the future. First, it prohibited coercive recruitment by unions of new members for the purposes of expanding an industrial dispute; second, it placed severe restrictions on picketing activity; and third, it empowered employers to resist industrial action by making a range of common-law sanctions available to them. Statutory recognition of unions was also limited, as was the right of recourse to wage arbitration proceedings. In the same year the Social Security Act limited the payment of supplementary benefit to dependants of strikers if the latter were receiving strike payments from union funds (Davies and Freedland 1993).

A comprehensive package, perhaps, but behind the Act lay a struggle for power within the Conservative Party between the reformers and the revolutionaries. The split was clearly an ideological one, between those committed to a consensual process of gradualist reform, and those who saw trade unions as a political and economic menace in need of restraint. A different sort of split could be observed among British employers. While all employer organizations approved of the thrust of the legislation, some, such as the Engineering Employers' Federation (EEF), thought the 1980 Act did not go far enough. On the more radical wing, the Institute of Directors and small employers in particular advocated a complete ban on all secondary picketing activity, coupled with the introduction of *criminal* proceedings for strikes deploying certain prohibited forms of industrial action. On the more moderate side, the CBI supported the 1980 program, and initially seemed content to reject the need for further statutory measures (Auerbach 1990).

The turning point came in 1981, when the moderates within industry and the Conservative government swung decisively towards a more radical legislative agenda. Key to this acceleration of radicalism were two developments. The first came in mid-1981 when Chancellor Geoffrey Howe delivered a sharply contractionary budget in the middle of a downturn in the economic cycle. It was crucial in signalling to employers that the government was strongly committed to driving down inflation (and driving up unemployment), and hence that there would be no repeat of the economic policy U-turn of the previous Conservative government in 1970–2 when it too had tried, unsuccessfully, to contain union power. Unlike Heath, Thatcher's onslaught on trade unions combined a statutory attack on their legal standing with a macroeconomic policy that reduced their membership and undermined their economic power. The second key development was the split in the Labour Party caused by the formation of the Social Democratic Party in autumn 1981. In the context of a first-past-the-post electoral system this split gave the Thatcher government a degree of electoral immunity from the effects of its more radical economic policies. Furthermore, business also came to believe that the government's *electoral* prospects would not be harmed by the resolute pursuit of its economic and industrial-relations goals (Taylor 1993). This impression was reinforced by the rise in real wages for the 'Tory majority' in the south, coupled with the evident unpopularity of trade unions in the country at large.

The CBI remained more cautious than some other employer organizations, but after the 1981 Budget its position was consistently more hard-line than before. Auerbach notes that '[t]he CBI moved from an attitude of considerable skepticism, if not hostility, towards the Government's policies, towards robust and concerted support for its legislative proposals at the end of the year' (Auerbach 1990: 73). By 1981 the CBI was advocating the complete removal of the immunity in tort of trade unions, aligning itself with the radical suggestions of the Institute of Directors (CBI 1981).

The following three years saw the most concerted attacks by employers and the government on trade unions. Norman Tebbit's 1982 Employment Act promulgated further restrictions on closed-shop and 'union-only' practices, again by stripping trade unions of long-standing common-law immunities from prosecution. Perhaps more significant was the empowerment of employers through the curtailment of two other types of common-law immunity — trade disputes immunity, and the removal of tort immunity for damages caused to a company during a dispute. Both immunities had been in place since legislation overturning the famous Taff Vale decision of 1906, and both were the direct product of pressure from employers' organizations to allow legal action to be taken against unions.

For the CBI in particular the removal of trade union immunities was the central task of industrial-relations policy. Trade unions were also made liable for the actions of their leaders, and given strong incentives to rein in militant groups in order to avoid further liability. Unions thus found themselves constrained both by legal restriction of their activities, and increased liability for damages incurred by their actions (Taylor 1993).

Two years later the government turned to a new tactic for limiting union power—recasting the relationship between unions and their members. The 1983 Green Paper entitled *Democracy in Trade Unions* had spelled out possible legislation on reforming internal structures of trade unions. This document revealed the government's obsession with strikes as the root of the ailing British economy's problems. Rather than extend direct regulation of strike activity, the government chose to inhibit major strike action by requiring more stringent use of pre-strike ballots. The government's proposal was modeled on a specific analysis of trade union militancy conducted by irresponsible shop stewards and union leaders, who were vulnerable to more moderate rank-and-file members if the latter could be armed with statutory powers in the name of 'extending democracy' (Auerbach 1990).

Interestingly, employers' responses to the proposals were initially luke-warm. Both the EEF and CBI warned of the dangers of imposing strike ballots on union members before industrial action. For one thing, the strategy could backfire by providing a statutory tool for union leaders to legitimize increased militancy in the workplace. Employers instead expressed a preference for a continuation of the path trodden by the 1982 Employment Act; increasing union liability for strike action, and expanding the scope for employers to engage the courts in restraining industrial action.

Despite this divergence between employers and government, however, employers' associations were quick to pick up on the implications of the regime that emerged from the 1984 Trade Union Act. In its final form the Act did not give union members the power to require the holding of a ballot, but rather gave employers the option of a remedy through the courts *subsequent* to a failure to hold a ballot. The kernel of the legislation was thus an incentive for unions to hold a ballot, coupled with an increase in employers' recourse to damages, *without* any more significant form of state intervention. Soon after passage of the Act both the EEF and CBI issued documents instructing member firms of the strategic possibilities it opened up, even offering advice on alternative tactics that employers could use against unions. The tone of these documents resembles that of a military strategist on the eve of battle, and 'provide[s] a striking illustration of the extent and potential of the strategic weapon of legal action which the legislation placed into the hand of employers' (Auerbach 1990: 145–6).

Many considered the 1984 Trade Union Act the final word in legislative reform of industrial relations. Employers were, however, restless for further restrictions, and issued further pamphlets pressing for action on strikes in essential services, as well as for measures requiring greater observance of procedures as a prerequisite for statutory immunity (e.g. IoD 1985). Ironically, the next development in the government's legislative agenda was suggested by internal legal struggles within the National Union of Miners (NUM) that had taken place during the year-long miners' strike of 1984–5. After the refusal of Arthur Scargill, NUM president, to hold a ballot on strike action, a series of civil actions were brought against the national and area unions by individual NUM members. This internecine struggle suggested to employers' associations and to government the possibilities for further control of union activity through empowering individual union members with legal control rights. Although skeptical about the value of 'extending democracy' within trade unions in 1983–4, employers now embraced the idea with zeal.

In May 1986 the IoD published a document that would provide the template for the 1988 Employment Act. Its proposals included controls over the use of union funds, new members' rights to inspect union accounts, restrictions on union rules permitting indemnification of members, controls on union trustees, and, most significantly of all, the extension of the 1984 Act to allow individual workers to *appeal* against a union decision to take industrial action that had not yet received approval via a ballot (Grunfeld and Bloch 1986). That the Act which was passed by Parliament in 1988 mirrors the IoD recommendations so closely suggests how strong the influence of employers over the Thatcher administration's industrial-relations policy was. It is important to recognize that the 1988 Act explicitly combines the goal of desolidarizing trade unions with that of achieving a more flexible *labor market*. Section 3 gave individual trade union members the right to refuse to participate in industrial action, even when a majority had agreed to it in a ballot. In a similar vein, employers' dismissal powers were increased if closed-shop practices were suspected, or strikes were conducted in illegal ways. The rationale for these measures made explicit reference to the political goal of upholding democratic practices within trade unions, but also to the *economic* goal of eliminating obstacles to the 'proper' functioning of the labor market. In this sense, as with previous Acts, political and economic motivations reinforced one another.

The strength of the employer–Tory alliance of the 1980s in industrial-relations reform was based on their agreement on the aim of restoring employer power in a deregulated labor market. Employers' central aim (after a period of anxious moderation in 1979–80) was the pursuit of more flexible labor markets through a weakening of the powers of unions, a strengthening of employers' recourse to litigation, and a severing of the link between the interests of the union and those of the individual worker. For the government, attacking the trade unions was part of an integrated economic and industrial relations policy, as well as an attack on political opponents. From the moment Norman Tebbit arrived at the Ministry of Employment the government explicitly recognized and supported the economic argument advanced by employers for weakening organized labor in order to free up labor markets. Ironically, therefore, employers relied upon a powerful and radical Conservative government to deliver their longed-for restoration of a 'liberal' industrial-relations regime.

7.2.2 West Germany in the 1980s: The Deflected Attack on Organized Labor

The emergence of Helmut Kohl's CDU-led coalition after the 1983 general election suggested that West Germany might adopt its own version of 'Thatcherism'. Trumpeting the slogan 'less state, more freedom', Kohl's electoral campaign had been deliberately pitched towards neo-liberal themes. As Soltwedel observed,

Many voters had high hopes and firm expectations that the new government would in fact start with a comprehensive, systematic, and fundamental turn-around to lift the heavy hand of government, to cut taxes and subsidies, and to open markets through privatisation and deregulation. Seldom before had a market-oriented approach been announced so frankly in an election campaign and gained so much credit even in depressed regions with high long-term unemployment such as the Ruhr. (Soltwedel 1989: 73–4)

Within a year a range of measures of fiscal 'consolidation' had been introduced in an attempt to control public expenditure and state intervention. In the field of labor market policy, commentators such as Sengenberger suggested that Kohl's administration was on the verge of a radical overhaul of the industrial-relations model, supported, no doubt, by employers keen for a reduction in wage costs (Sengenberger 1984).

But the rights and standing of unions and workers were never seriously threatened in the 1980s, despite the neo-liberal tenor of the early years of the CDU-led government. By the time of unification in 1989, the role of trade unions at sectoral and company level was as secure as it had been ten years earlier. Nevertheless, this reform impetus gave rise to two major legislative proposals during the 1980s which aimed at weakening organized labor in different ways, and which provoked enormous controversy. Each was aimed at a specific institution or policy that was pivotal to the coordination of industrial relations. The first concerned the ability of trade unions to pursue strike activity; the second centered on the organization of worker representation within companies.

The 1984 metalworkers' strike over the issue of reduced working time raised a technical but fundamental issue regarding state neutrality during strikes. In 1984, workers directly involved in strike action were not eligible for state benefit from the Bundesanstalt für Arbeit (Federal Labour Office, FLO). However, strikes in one firm lead to disruptions in other firms linked via supply chains, and employers are empowered under German labor law to cease production temporarily if affected indirectly in this way. A central problem in these cases is: what means of support should be available to workers who lose wages as a result of a strike outside their own bargaining region (so-called 'indirectly affected workers')? Paragraph 116 of the 1969 Work Promotion Act (AFG) laid down a principle of payment of unemployment benefit to such workers, subject to two restrictions: the strike could not aim at changing the terms and conditions of the firm where the 'indirectly affected' workers were employed; and payment of the benefits should not influence the outcome of the strike. The decision about the applicability of these criteria in individual cases was left to the FLO.

Payment of benefits to these workers is a crucial issue for the unions. If indirectly affected workers forfeit income as part of a strike conducted elsewhere, the union's solidarity of interests across bargaining units is severely undermined. And if the union wishes to continue the strike action, it would be forced to finance these payments out of its own funds. In this sense, an apparently obscure ruling about strike benefit is at the heart of the collective power of trade unions in West Germany—if removed, the payment of benefits would have seriously undermined the unions' ability to bargain with employers from a comparable position of strength (Silvia 1988).

Employers, however, contested the provision from its creation, arguing for a more precise definition of the conditions under which payments can be said to 'influence' the outcome of a strike. An FLO ruling in 1973 had stated that benefit must be forfeited when the claims in the non-striking region were 'equivalent in scope and content' to those in a striking region. But employers had been angered by the courts' insistence on a reading of this 'equivalence' criterion that was sympathetic to trade unions. The last straw came in the 1984 strike—regional labor courts overruled an FLO decision that the commonality of the working-time issue across regions prohibited indirectly affected workers from receiving strike benefit.

Prompted by many employers' concerns, the CDU-FDP coalition announced before the end of the dispute that it would legislate on the issue. Yet the history of the reform was to testify to the divergence in motivations between German employers and those elements of the coalition who wanted to weaken trade unions. To the Free Democratic Party (FDP) and some members of the business wing of the CDU, the organization of the German labor market imposed excessive burdens on the private economy. In March 1985 a group of 150 FDP and CDU Bundestag representatives proposed an amendment to paragraph 116, according to which payment would be denied to *all* workers indirectly affected by a strike, irrespective of their regional location. Their motivation was clearly to attack the solidarity of organized labor in *general*.

Employers' organizations, however, did not share this zeal. Certainly they wanted a change in the rules governing strike behavior. But more important to employers was retention of the principle of *Tarifautonomie* —collective bargaining free from state interference. In June 1985, Otto Esser, president of the German Confederation of Employers (BDA), argued for a voluntarist rather than a statutory solution. Legislation, he argued, would only create more latitude and need for intervention by the courts and the FLO. By the end of 1985 it was clear that trade unions were opposed to a voluntary accord, and the BDA reluctantly agreed to legislation. But in its view, the purpose of legislation should remain limited to a moderate redressing of the balance of power during strike activity. What employers feared was intervention in the name of enforcing neutrality. Once 'in,' the BDA feared, it would be difficult for the state to retreat. State intervention would also politicize industrial relations to an unacceptable degree. The limited ambition of state intervention was therefore repeatedly emphasized by leading employers during this period. What was needed was clarity to prevent the need for further intervention, not a first step towards a class battle between organized labor and business.

Meanwhile, within the coalition the CDU's Social Committees saw the suggested amendment as an unambiguous assault on the position of German unions, with whom they enjoyed such strong links. This placed the CDU leadership in a difficult position; support for the FDP was important for the coalition, but the cost of such support seemed to be alienation of a crucial constituency within the party, whose links to worker organizations were extremely important in maintaining the CDU's claim to be a *Volkspartei*. The 'left' of the party, moreover, found themselves supported in their opposition to the more radical demands of the FDP by *both* the union movement and employers' organizations.

After two years of protracted negotiations, the amendment to paragraph 16 of the 1969 Act was passed in March 1986. It reflected a classic compromise between the two positions. The principle of state support for indirectly affected workers remained in place, *contra* the wishes of the FDP. Payments would be withheld, however, if demands of workers in the indirectly affected region were 'in scope and content equivalent to the main demands of the strike, without necessarily corresponding exactly' (Silvia 1988). On the surface, this gave great power to coordinated employers. If the similarity of demands was a ground for prohibiting essential payments to striking workers by the state, employers were in a strong position to press for the regional differentiation of claims by unions, while unions would be unable to coordinate nationwide strikes in pursuit of national goals. In practice, however, the new wording of paragraph 116 does not limit *wage* demands, partly because it is common practice to vary regional wage demands, and partly because the new wording actually encourages unions to differentiate their wage claims *even further*. On qualitative issues, therefore, the new legislation does indeed empower employers to undermine unions' solidarity in strike action.

But what has been noticeable since 1986 has been the *reluctance* of employers to use the new ruling to their advantage. During the 1987 bargaining round metalworking unions succeeded in concluding a highly favorable deal (reducing the working week to 35 hours) without employer recourse to the revised paragraph 116. In 1995, on the other hand, when industrial action *was* employed by IG Metall, it was conspicuous that only final assemblers in one region (Bavaria) were targeted, rather than supplier firms in the traditional region of North Baden-Württemberg (Thelen 2000). As a result the level of disruption to production was minimized, suggesting that the reform had indeed produced its desired behavioral effect of *ordering* rather than *undermining* strike action. To understand this self-restraint on the part of German employers it is important to appreciate that, in their view, the aim of the reform was different from the aims of British employers in supporting the Conservatives' labor market reforms. Changing the terms of receipt of strike payments was a way of raising the costs of strike action to the union movement, thus ensuring that neither party to a collective bargain had a disproportionate incentive to reject discussion in favor of industrial action. Employers thus advocated reforming the law as a way of re-aligning the incentives facing unions, thus promoting more orderly collective bargaining *without* relying upon statutory intervention.

No less controversial was the simultaneous attempt by the coalition to reform works council election procedures. The CDU-led administration, neo-liberal voices within the coalition, renewed the battle over works councils that had followed the passage of the 1976 Co-determination Act. But the battle of the 1980s was not about the formal standing of works councils before the law, as it had been in the 1950s and 1970s. Nor did it tackle head-on the sets of issues over which works councils had co-determining powers. Rather, the debate in the 1980s centred around two separate initiatives pertaining to the *de facto* monopoly of power exercised by the DGB—the main trade union confederation—within the works council system. The first of these was concerned with the protection of minority unions (and non-unionized workers) on works councils, and particularly in elections to these bodies; the second concerned the establishment of representative bodies for 'middle management' distinct from those covering the conventional workforce. Taken together, these legislative moves amounted to an indirect but highly significant assault on the unity of the German trade union movement, and its control of works councils. In this chapter I concentrate on the first of these proposals.

Control of works councils by the dominant DGB-affiliated union in each sector was secured, *inter alia*, by the election laws to works councils adumbrated in the 1972 Works Constitution Act. Candidates (or slates of candidates proposed by a union) had to receive the signatures of one tenth of the eligible workforce in order to be nominated. Given that no other federated union covered anywhere near 10 per cent of the total workforce, this had the effect of guaranteeing that non-DGB-affiliated unions would obtain limited representation on works councils in certain sectors only, and thus exaggerated the degree of dominance enjoyed by the DGB in the workforce. In the coal-mining industry, for example, between 1960 and 1975 about 93 per cent of elected works councillors were members of the DGB-affiliated German miners' union (IGBE; Streeck 1981: 488). The 1984 strike, however, severely dented the reputation of the DGB, not least because of a number of scandals about manipulation of works council elections by DGB officials. The same year saw over a quarter of works council seats going to non-unionized representatives for the first time (Wood 1997). In November the 10 per cent threshold requirement for signatures was ruled unconstitutional by the Constitutional Court, as it generated a *de facto* monopoly of the DGB.

Once again the FDP was at the forefront of support for reform of the law, seeing an opportunity to limit the strength of the DGB on works councils, and thus to hamper the collective voice of organized labour at the plant level. In this endeavour it was strongly supported by the Christian Social Union (CSU), keen to bolster the position of the Christian trade union confederation (CGB) in German works councils. The coalition announced its intention in 1985 to introduce a new, lower signature threshold of 3 per cent (the so-called *Lex-CGB*). However, the CDU's Social Committees once more showed a marked reluctance to support any measure that could have implied a weakening of the position of trade unions. Their strategy was to offer conditional support for the proposal in return for obtaining concessions on two other 'linked' issues —the extension of co-determination to questions of introducing new technology (which they supported); and the compulsory establishment of 'middle management committees' (which they vehemently opposed). Kohl found himself yet again embroiled in a tussle between groups inside his party and his coalition.

German employers maintained strong opposition to these proposals, even though the intention of the reform was to fragment union power at the plant level. The logic of this position is only comprehensible if we understand the logic of coordination in industrial relations. Given the fact that bargaining with the plant workforce is required by law over certain issues, it is rational for employers to ensure that the internal discipline of the works council delegation is as strong as possible—i.e. to ensure that the works council 'speaks with one voice.' Employers have an interest in preventing divisions between unions within the workplace, both because it complicates the process of bargaining and consultation, and because fragmentation of worker representation brings with it the possibility of the politicization of works councils. Thus, the nature of employers' support for works councils is contingent on the form of worker representation within the councils themselves.

Public declarations of employers from early on in the dispute confirm this interpretation. The lack of employer support for the reforms was attributed to the fact that '[b]usinessmen are worried about industrial peace. What they would like most of all is not to disturb the Works Constitution Act, as each amendment threatens to bring unrest.' Employers clearly rejected the idea that they saw the reform aspirations of the government as an opportunity to further a 'divide and rule' strategy in the workplace. Instead, 'most employers . . . would prefer companies and works councils with as unified a representation of interests as possible' (*Die Zeit* 1984). The initiative aiming to strengthen minority unions raised the likelihood of radical groups finding their way into works councils. As the employers' association in the chemicals industry argued, the proposals raised the spectre of a permanent electoral war within works councils.

A similar argument was used to reject the suggestion of introducing a proportional representation principle into the allocation of works council committee chairs and sabbatical posts—the move 'could only, as the unions also argued, strengthen the competition for interest representation in the works council, generate power struggles, expand the opportunities for radical groups, and significantly impede the work of the works council' (*Frankfurter Allgemeine* 1985). One of the ways in which the proposal suggested that minority unions could be strengthened was to vest them with a right to propose a slate of their own candidates. As the employer associations pointed out, however, this merely strengthened the individual unions' ability to compete with each other in works councils.

Within the coalition, opponents of the electoral reform engineered a complex web of concessions encompassing four different co-determination issues. As a result, and as with the 'strike payments' case, a new law was eventually passed, but its main provisions were diluted. The coalition of employers, Social Committees, and moderates in the leadership succeeded in getting the signature threshold reduced to 5 per cent rather than to 3 per cent as the CSU had wanted. Most significantly of all, although proportional representation was introduced to decide the crucial positions on works council committees, it was only applied to groups that received over 25 per cent of the total vote. These concessions to employers and the CDA effectively preserved the DGB's monopoly control of works councils and their committees. In the next round of works council elections in 1987, the DGB unions scored their *highest* total vote across all sectors since passage of the 1972 Act (Wood 1997). What remained of the initial proposal to democratize works council politics was little more than legislative compliance with the Constitutional Court's requirement that the 10 per cent threshold be lowered.

7.3 Conclusion

The cases of policy towards organized labor in West Germany and Britain demonstrate the differences in employer preferences spelt out in section 7.1. In Britain, despite an initial reluctance to countenance an aggressive attack on the legal supports for organized labor, employers supported most of the substance of the Conservatives' industrial-relations reforms.

Indeed in some areas they thought the government had not gone far enough. The West German case exhibits quite different employer preferences. There, despite the militancy of IG Metall during the 1984 strike and a history of opposition to the extension of *Mitbestimmung*, employers expressed a strong collective preference against legislation that would have weakened the organizational strength of both trade unions and works councils. These differences in employer preferences clearly derive from differences in the production regimes and company strategies of each variety of capitalism.

In both examples, employer influence was central to the outcome of the respective policy initiatives. In West Germany, employers were influential during the formulation of policy in diluting the radical ingredients of the government's proposals. They were assisted in this by the constraints imposed on the CDU by its coalition partners, and by the need to appease powerful groups within the CDU, particularly the Social Committees. Even when watered-down versions of both proposals were passed, their force was further limited by employers' collective refusal to use the legislation in the manner intended by its proponents. In Britain, employers were as weakly coordinated as they had been during the 1960s and 1970s, when the tide of legislation went against their policy preferences. However, in the 1980s their representative associations worked closely with the Thatcher government to produce a sequence of policies that annihilated the formal and informal powers of British trade unions. What made the Thatcher government's restoration of market-based governance in labor markets possible was the massive concentration of power given to it by the Westminster model and a first-past-the-post electoral system.

I conclude with two reflections on the framework used in this chapter. The first returns to the question of equilibria. In the case of CMEs, the German example indicates that a highly constrained government tends to produce a stable institutional and policy equilibrium. The combination of a CME with a weakly constrained central government may lead to problems in sustaining supply-side coordination in the long run. An illustration of this problem is Swedish employers' aggressive response to what they saw as excessive legislative radicalism under Social Democratic governments in the 1960s and 1970s, culminating in the dismantling of centralized wage bargaining after 1983 (Pestoff 1991). In the case of LMEs, the British example is less suggestive of an equilibrium. Powerful central governments have oscillated wildly between liberal and 'collectivist' policies in the post-war period. A stable institutional and policy equilibrium in LMEs *also* seems to require constraints on the interventionist capacity of governments, once market-based governance structures have been firmly established. The instructive example here is that of the USA, where a Madisonian constitution that disperses power, limits the reach of the state, and inhibits legislative radicalism, reinforces liberal market governance structures (King and Wood 1999). In *both* CMEs and LMEs, therefore, equilibrium tendencies are more conspicuous where the power of the state is constitutionally limited.

Secondly, the argument advanced in this chapter informs our conception of what constitutes effective policy-making in different varieties of capitalism. It rejects the *dirigiste* conception of policy-making, according to which coordination is secured by designing a set of sanctions and incentives and imposing these patterns of behavior on firms. Instead, it suggests that governments should produce policies that complement the institutional comparative advantage of their respective market economies. In an LME, where relations between firms are mediated by markets, the state will be more effective if it restores and 'sharpens' market mechanisms. In a CME, effective policy consists in supporting the institutions and networks of coordination that connect companies. What it is wise for governments to do depends upon the type of market economy in which they find themselves. Acknowledging the force of this conclusion may dent the transformative ambitions of governments, but they will be less likely to founder in the pursuit of bold but ultimately fruitless policy experiments.

8

Employers, Public Policy, and the Politics of Decentralized Cooperation in Germany and France

Pepper D. Culpepper

8.1 Introduction

The analytical framework of varieties of capitalism can be grim reading for public policy-makers. If their countries lack the institutional framework necessary for sustaining non-market coordination, then the counsel of many of the chapters in this volume is simple: stick with the policies that are compatible with the existing institutional framework of your country, even if that means abandoning goals that could improve both the competitiveness of firms and the wages of workers. In this chapter I argue that the *diagnosis* generated by the varieties of capitalism framework is indeed compelling; many modern problems of economic and social policy-making are in fact problems of coordination among companies, such that the goals of state policy-makers will frequently involve convincing actors to act in concert to achieve desirable social ends. Yet the *prognosis* of this chapter is rather more hopeful than others in this volume for political initiatives that aspire to create coordination in policy areas where it has previously not existed. Such initiatives *can* succeed, even when countries lacking the framework of a coordinated market economy attempt to create non-market coordination *de novo*.

The empirical case through which I demonstrate this proposition is the showpiece of the coordinated market economies: their system of vocational education and training. The German dual system of apprenticeship

This chapter has been improved thanks to the comments of Peter Hall, Bob Hancké, Peter Katzenstein, two anonymous reviewers, and participants in panel discussions at the Twelfth International Conference of Europeanists and the 1997 Annual Meeting of the American Political Science Association. I bear full responsibility for any remaining shortcomings. The author gratefully acknowledges financial support from the National Science Foundation, the Center for European Studies at Harvard University, the Wissenschaftszentrum Berlin, the Social Science Research Council, and the Bourse Chateaubriand.

training has confounded predictions that companies will not invest in the transferable skills of their employees, since other companies should then free-ride on these investments by poaching the newly minted skilled workers (Becker 1964; Harhoff and Kane 1997; Acemoglu and Pischke 1998). If enough companies can be persuaded to invest in transferable skills, the German case demonstrates that it is possible to sustain a 'high-skill equilibrium' through institutions of employer coordination: associations can negotiate the content of skill qualifications with unions, while circulating information about training behavior that is necessary to ensure that firms continue to invest heavily in apprenticeship training (Soskice 1994b). Once established, the system is also stabilized by a number of self-reinforcing incentives and constraints. Individual young people, knowing that the path to lucrative firm-internal labor markets runs through apprenticeship, will have an incentive to work hard in school to get the best available apprenticeships (Finegold and Soskice 1988). Companies, which know that they can count on a supply of young people with a broad base of transferable skills willing to work for lower wages than a skilled worker, can invest in an organization of production that maximizes the comparative advantage of their skilled workforce (Culpepper and Finegold 1999). Unions and employers can divide the lucrative product of the performance of these companies in export markets, so that the high-skill equilibrium is also a high-wage equilibrium (Streeck 1997b).[1] Moreover, the German model of apprenticeship training has captured increasing international attention as a way to provide intermediate skills relevant to the working world while simultaneously creating a smooth transition to work, which keeps German youth unemployment relatively low (OECD 1994a; BMBW 2000).

Yet for those countries not already in possession of a high-skill equilibrium, it is extremely difficult to get there from here. If any individual company attempts to invest heavily in the provision of transferable skills, it leaves itself open to predation by those companies that do not make such investments. So governments that want to emulate the high-skill equilibrium established in western Germany have to devise some method

---

[1] As argued in the chapter by Estevez-Abe et al. in this volume, the character of the welfare state can also provide additional incentives for workers to invest in different sorts of skill sets. Yet these policies are only capable of *stabilizing* an existing high-skill equilibrium, rather than convincing companies to *establish* a high-skill equilibrium. The structure of the welfare state does not in itself enable employers to overcome the problem of coordination at the heart of apprenticeship training, which is the analytical problem addressed in this chapter.

of persuading employers to move *en masse* to initiate such training practices. Public policy, in other words, must find a way to convince firms to coordinate their actions. Yet governments that have tried to convince employers to make such a move, in the absence of the institutions of the coordinated market economy, have typically failed (Layard et al. 1994; Boyer 1995).

Both Germany and France confront this stylized problem of transition to a high-skill equilibrium: the German government in transferring the dual apprenticeship system to the new federal states of eastern Germany, and the French government in its attempts to overhaul the in-firm youth training system in France since 1984.[2] Prior to embarking on their reforms, neither economy had any of the institutions of a coordinated market economy. The reforms in eastern Germany were of course more daunting, because they involved the transformation of a command economy to an advanced capitalist economy; but the eastern Germans also enjoyed the compensating advantage of organizational assistance from western German employers' associations and unions. The French economy, while already an advanced capitalist system, lacks the strong associations of employers and labor that are necessary to sustain a high-skill equilibrium. In both political economies, national governments attempted to develop a self-sustaining system of vocational training loosely based on the model of the western German dual system, in which companies pay the bulk of the costs of in-firm training while public funds support the provision of complementary education in schools.

In this chapter I propose a theoretical framework to explain the causes of success and failure in an attempted transition to a high-skill equilibrium. The argument developed here grows out of a larger research project in which I have argued that we can better understand such attempted transitions as a politics of decentralized cooperation, in which governments try to convince private actors to cooperate with each other (Culpepper forthcoming). In this chapter I focus particularly on the roles that employers' associations and governments can play in facilitating the emergence of decentralized cooperation among companies in different regions. The key to securing decentralized cooperation is the acknowledgment of the central role of uncertainty in blocking change. In such a situation of transition, the uncertainty of how other actors will behave undermines the effectiveness of the tool of sanctioning, either by the state

[2] Throughout this chapter, I use the terms East Germany and West Germany only to denote those independent states before German unification in 1990; I refer to eastern and western Germany when discussing these distinct, geographically defined political economies of the politically unified Germany after 1990.

or by private associations. Instead, what is important is to develop policies that target the most likely cooperators in the population, a group I
designate as 'waverers.' Designing policies that can disproportionately
attract waverers requires inside information about the cooperative
proclivities of firms, and this is information that governments will not
be able to acquire on their own. States are good at standardizing
measures, not at assessing contextual information (Scott 1998). Such policies can only be crafted if state policy-makers incorporate the private
information accessible to employers' associations in the design of public
policies.

In the second section of the chapter I critique existing approaches that
explain the outcome of reforms by focusing primarily on the capacity
of employers' associations *or* of the state. In the third section, I suggest
a theoretical synthesis and extension of the two approaches, arguing
that the two must be articulated in particular ways to maximize the
chances for success of an attempted transition to the high-skill equilibrium. From this framework I derive a set of testable hypotheses, and
in the fourth section I confront the hypotheses with data from firms in
France and Germany. On the basis of this evidence, we can see the
two different routes to decentralized cooperation attempted in eastern
Germany and France. Employers' associations from the west have
succeeded in facilitating the establishment of strong organizational
capacity among eastern German associations, but state governments
have not all taken advantage of the information to which these associations have access. In France, the general weakness of employers' organizations has hobbled regional policies, but success has been achieved
where a strong organization has formulated a program targeting national
subsidies at waverers. The final section considers the implications of
these findings for broader problems of reform.

8.2 The Explanatory Framework

How can companies be persuaded to cooperate with one another to
improve the skill level of the workforce?[3] Existing theories in political

---

[3] Throughout this chapter, I refer in general to problems of coordination as well as to
the specific cooperative structure of the decision facing individual firms in training investment. Coordination problems require that actors come to similar expectations about an
iterated interaction, given multiple potential equilibria. For the companies discussed here,
the problem of 'decentralized cooperation' requires a cooperative move in a given interaction, i.e. forgoing the possible immediate gains to defection, in view of the long-term
benefits to mutual cooperation. Achieving this cooperation over repeated interactions is
itself a coordination problem (Calvert 1995).

economy suggest at least two alternative means of encouraging companies to invest in high-skill training practices: private interest governance or the state. Employer-led private interest governance is the most widely accepted model for understanding the functioning of the high-skill equilibrium in western Germany (Finegold and Soskice 1988; Soskice 1994*b*). The alternative solution to overcoming the coordination problems created by a reform of the skill provision system is for the state to underwrite and regulate the achievement of decentralized cooperation (cf. Reich 1991). Indeed, who better than the state, whose legitimization is much more bound up with the public weal than is that of private employers' associations, to ensure the provision of the 'public goods' that would be provided by large employer investments in vocational training? However, as I will argue in this section, neither a capable employers' association nor active state intervention will suffice for such reforms to succeed in securing decentralized cooperation. Both mechanisms are handicapped by the uncertainty created by a situation of reform, and the key to solving problems of uncertainty is information. What sorts of information are important, and how this information can be incorporated into public policy, are the criteria for developing a theoretical framework capable of explaining when reforms are likely to succeed and when they are doomed to fail.

8.2.1 Employers' Associations, the State, and Problems of Coordination

The premiss underlying a model of private interest governance is that employers and unions know best the requirements of a firm-based skill system, so they should be left to regulate it themselves, with minimal state intervention (Ayres and Braithwaite 1992; Cohen and Rogers 1992). Using the schematic division of coordinating functions identified by Hall and Soskice in the Introduction to this volume, we can identify four potential roles played by the institutions of employer coordination in vocational training reform: information circulation, deliberation, monitoring, and sanctioning. Capable private interest groups are likely to be better equipped than the state to fulfill the roles of information circulation and deliberation, because they have greater access to information about their members. The information to which these groups need access relates to the functioning of training practices, as well as to the predispositions of different groups of member firms. How are existing requirements being taught through in-firm practice? What requirements in the system of training regulations need to be updated to take account of new skill demands in production? Which firms are most likely to find an investment in apprenticeship training beneficial? An association needs to be able to draw this information up, from a wide base of member firms, in order to formulate positions for negotiation on changing the manner in which the system functions, or to create or modify new qualifications. Likewise, the association must be able to diffuse information back down to member companies, so that they are aware of new training regulations and practices, as well as of subsidies or other advantages from which they can benefit.

The *deliberative* function involves capacities for the negotiation and resolution of internal disagreements, and it presupposes an ability for organizations to pursue and modify these collective positions in negotiations with representatives of labor and the state. The deliberative capacity entails, first, a forum for negotiation, where members with different interests can bargain over outcomes that will favor some actors more than others. However, collective position-taking capacity must also include a means for reflection among members as to the strategy to be pursued in a given situation. Deliberation requires that organizations balance the sometimes competing interests of different members in a context in which the outcome of any given strategy to be chosen is uncertain. Thus, deliberation is more than just a forum for bargaining, though it is that, too.

When it comes to the more demanding capacities of monitoring and sanctioning, however, private interest governance often falls short of what the state can provide. Monitoring only has meaning when the association has regularized access to information about company compliance with some regulations or policies for which it is responsible; that is to say, information that it will use to try to exact compliance from companies, which may not be information that the company would voluntarily share with the association. A firm will only allow its association this access when it is confident that other firms are also allowing equivalent access, and that the advantages of mutual verification outweigh the potential benefits of secrecy. Monitoring usually occurs in a context in which sanctions are exacted for non-compliance. Sanctioning obviously requires that the association can credibly threaten to deprive firms of something that they value. For a voluntary organization, this is not easily done, because these organizations are subject to the demands of being able to attract members voluntarily. As Elinor Ostrom's (1990) work has brilliantly shown, graduated sanctions can be very effective in limiting free-riding in common pool resource dilemmas. Yet, sanctioning by private interest organizations is only likely to work well when operating in 'the shadow of the state,' since only the state is likely to be a credible sanctioner of last resort (Scharpf 1997*a*).

The state is strong where private associations are weak, but it is also weak where they are strong. The greatest empirical successes of the state in promoting information circulation and deliberation are those cited in the literature on neo-corporatism, in which states grant employers' organizations and labor unions power over the implementation of policy in return for organizational participation in achieving the goals pursued by the state (Schmitter and Lehmbruch 1979; Goldthorpe 1984; Keeler 1987). Yet the drawbacks of state intervention are readily apparent if we reconsider the functions played by employers' associations in the stylized model of the western German dual system. Information circulation and deliberation only function effectively in this model because employers have confidence that their organizations—that is, organizations ultimately responsive and accountable to them—are the conduits for the flow of information and the arenas for deliberation among firms. An individual company cannot ensure that its own views will prevail within the employers' organization, but the employers' association must have the confidence of companies that it does in fact respond to their demands to enjoy the coordinating capacity exercised by associations in the western German model. In fact, however, an association that ties itself too closely to the state runs the risk of alienating members who perceive it as having been co-opted by the state. This problem is exacerbated when it comes to monitoring company behavior. As Soskice (1994*b*) has argued, the ability to monitor requires that companies reveal sensitive inside information to their organizations. When employers believe their organization is as much a creature of the state as of business firms, they will balk at giving that organization access to this information.

While these weaknesses of state intervention are all valid, the state also has some compensating virtues that employers' organizations lack. As noted previously, the state has a greater capacity to sanction companies than do individual associations. Its potential sanctions include imposing (or threatening to impose) more intrusive state regulations on companies, or instituting levies that force non-training companies to pay penalties for not engaging in apprenticeship training. No association has the same sort of capacity to impose costs on companies. Yet, as I will argue below, the capacity for sanctioning to promote cooperative behavior becomes problematic in cases of sweeping policy reform. Thus, in these reform situations, the most important capacity of the state is budgetary: the state has much deeper pockets than any association, which enables it to offer subsidies for cooperative action. The fiscal capacity of governments in the industrialized countries is not limitless, and the goal of the vocational training reforms studied here is eventually to induce companies to make substantial investments in human capital development through in-firm training contracts. Compared to associations, though, the ability of governments to offer transitional subsidies is an important tool that can help encourage companies to begin adopting high-skill training behavior. Finally, although states cannot replace the information circulation function of associations, they can provide a corps of experts at the disposal of companies, associations, and unions, which can make reliable information available to all actors involved about the likely consequences of certain courses of action.

Both the state and private associations find their coordinating capacity reduced under the pressures of sweeping reforms aimed at securing decentralized cooperation. An attempted transition from one skills equilibrium to another creates conditions that make these functions more difficult to fulfill than is the case in an already existing equilibrium. Moving to a high-skill equilibrium requires that firms be convinced to invest in the provision of transferable skills. This problem is overcome by the western German dual system. The fact that the dual system already functions lowers the barriers to cooperation by individual companies: each benefits from the history of cooperation embodied in an already functioning system, in which previous companies have made the investments and derived the rewards of cooperation.

The cooperative dilemmas inherent in changing a training system are concomitantly more difficult, because actors lack the track record of a preexisting system: there is no history of cooperation on which to build. Even companies that have a pressing need for workers with a higher level of general skills will not want to invest in training apprentices if no other firm is going to make that investment. If they were to do so, other firms could quickly lure away their workers with slightly higher wages, and the first firm would never get the return to its investment in the skills accumulation process. *If* a certain number of firms can be convinced that other firms will respond to the policy reform by investing heavily in apprenticeship training, then (given a sufficiently low discount rate) that equilibrium is also supportable; this is the implication of the folk theorem. Because reform changes the incentives facing companies, individual companies cannot rely so heavily on past experience to suggest how their counterparts will respond. So any attempted policy-led move to the high-skill equilibrium must overcome the uncertainty of companies about how others will behave.

The mechanisms described previously would seem to have a solution to this problem: the coordinating capacities of employers' associations and/or the state would help stabilize the expectations among firms about how other firms will respond. But the fact that these reforms encourage new sorts of training behavior usually means that they require the state and private associations to play roles that they have not ever played before. New institutions, or institutions being called on to play new functions, do not have an established track record of providing these specific collective goods. Thus, even if they are technically capable of providing the goods in question, such as the information circulation that is required for the fine-tuning of a new training program, the institutions have not established a pattern of having done it before, so actors may attach a lower probability to their capability than they would in a situation in which they have seen the institution(s) function normally. If employers' associations and the state are not perceived by potential cooperators as being able to circulate information well, it follows logically that they will not have the access to information that would allow them to be effective monitors.

In the area of sanctioning, both theories suffer from the fact that a new sort of behavior is being called for, and thus a new set of responses is being designated as 'sanctionable.' There is going to be some uncertainty about what exactly constitutes 'defection' and what constitutes 'cooperation'—on the part of both the potential sanctioner and the sanctionee—in this new realm of cooperation. Consider the case of sanctions as stigma, alluded to by Finegold and Soskice (1988). It is simply not credible in a situation of reform that behavior that has not previously been considered 'out of bounds' instantaneously becomes a subject of social stigma. This is particularly true for employers' associations, which have to maintain the confidence of dues-paying members; if a majority of members deviates from a newly adopted standard, an association cannot risk alienating more than half of its members by trying to sanction them. Thus in times of reform, not only do the institutions lack credibility to monitor deviations from cooperation, but the nature of sanctionable behavior is itself uncertain. In short, the very uncertainty created by governments trying to change the political economic equilibrium drastically reduces the credibility of the institutions that will be called on to facilitate that reform.

Finally, the attempted transition to high skill creates uncertainty about whether the causal mechanisms that supposedly generate the high payoff to cooperation actually do deliver that outcome. In other words, does cooperation—in the case of vocational training, high-level investment in apprentices—actually produce a higher long-term payoff than defection?

Iida (1993) has called this latter concept 'analytic uncertainty' to distinguish it from the more familiar problem of strategic uncertainty, which pertains to uncertainty about the attributes of other actors. Analytic uncertainty refers to the misapprehension of one's own payoff matrix, as well as the opponent's payoff, because the causal mechanisms of the new system are not clear or well understood. A reform of the political economy often asks players to move to a mutually beneficial pattern of cooperation when the actors are skeptical that the causal model of policy-makers accurately predicts the payoff they (the actors) will receive. If the causal mechanisms underlying one's own payoff matrix are uncertain, then there is a problem of 'pure learning' about the real causal mechanisms at work in the world (Iida 1993).

8.2.2 Policy Design and Private Information

The prerequisite to understanding the sources of success and failure in securing decentralized cooperation is the recognition of the central role of information and the reduced role of sanctioning. The synthetic theoretical framework I propose here satisfies these criteria by recognizing the respective strengths of private groups and public policy-makers in securing decentralized cooperation. My argument builds in particular on two capacities discussed earlier: the ability of associations to get access to and be able to circulate private information, and the ability of the state to provide transitional aid (subsidies) to hesitant new cooperators. The inside information to which private groups alone are likely to have access is a necessary ingredient to develop policies that can target the most likely potential cooperators in the population. State aid and private information must be articulated so as to create clusters of supported cooperation, in which wavering companies are able to gain confidence not only in the ability of institutions to perform their prescribed roles in supporting high-skill training, but of the training investment itself to provide a positive benefit.

The fundamental importance of employers' associations lies in their access to information about the cooperative propensities of member firms. Depending on the variables of size, product market, and managerial strategy, the propensity of companies to engage in decentralized cooperation is heterogeneously distributed across the economy. Companies are aware of this heterogeneity, and so is their association. Yet companies have an incentive to hide their individual propensities to cooperate from the state, because it is well known that the state is willing to subsidize potential cooperators. States thus face a problem of asymmetric information in designing their policies, and it is one they cannot over-come on their own. This inside, relational information about company propensities to cooperate is analogous to local information, which states also have a difficult time acquiring and categorizing (Scott 1998).

This general handicap of the state—an inability to get access to reliable inside information from companies—is exacerbated in transitional situations characteristic of sweeping reform. In situations in which the incentive framework facing companies is stable, the state can at least try to predict the future behavior of these companies based on their past responses. When policy-makers change this incentive framework, though, they lack any reliable method of predicting how companies will respond to the policy changes. In normal times, companies distrust the state and are leery of sharing information with it; in times of transition, their distrust is only magnified by their uncertainty about the motives of the state in trying to convince them to train.

The employers' association is the only intermediary to which employers will be willing to grant access to their internal information. States do of course have access to formidable technical expertise, through the bureaucracy or special research institutions set up to study a particular policy area. Yet the information the state can acquire by using its own research potential is conditioned by the difficulty a corps of state experts will have in getting access to firm-internal information. Like the drunk in the dark who looks for his keys under the lamppost—because that is where he can see them—the sort of information available to bureaucrats and experts is constrained by what their tools enable them to observe. And what they are very good at observing is aggregate outcomes: How many total apprenticeship contracts were signed in a given area? What occupations are particularly sharply characterized by a shortage of apprenticeship places? What demographic groups have the most difficulty finding apprenticeships? While the advantage of the state in transitional situations is its ability to provide subsidies to promote the sorts of behavior it wants to encourage, the form of subsidies it can craft remains dependent on the information to which it can get access about the obstacles that confront firms that want to begin training. Without access to inside information of companies, the state can only target subsidies at the aggregates it can measure, and none of those provides a clear window into which firms are actually investing (or willing to invest in the future) in training.

The foregoing discussion yields two testable hypotheses relevant to state policies:

H_1: *State policies devised without inside information will target only those aggregate problems that state bureaucracies can measure.*

H_2: *State policies devised with inside information will be designed disproportionately so as to attract the most likely cooperators in the population.*

In addition to their access to inside information, employers' associations will play two further roles that greatly improve the odds of success of encouraging decentralized cooperation: deliberation and mobilization. Rather than a mere compiling of the grievances of companies in the wake of reforms, employers require a collective deliberative capacity that can enable them to make decisions about which grievances to prioritize to suit the broadest constituency of companies. The second, expressly political capacity of employers' organizations is not generally underlined in the varieties of capitalism framework: *to mobilize* companies in favor of positions agreed on collectively, such that those companies begin investing themselves in apprenticeship-style training. In part, the mobilization function represents an extension of the information circulation and deliberation functions. As information flows up, from individual companies to regional affiliates to national organizations, so must information on framework considerations about training and national policy innovations be diffused to the firms for which it is intended. Companies will presumably demand a much greater amount of information when the very framework of the training system is in the process of mutation, especially with respect to special dispensations or programs aimed at firms with particular needs. At the same time that it delivers this information, the association is uniquely well qualified to remind companies of the collective interests of employers in the goal of skill provision. Indeed, the association may have sought the development of a subsidy policy that corresponds to the obstacles encountered by a given firm, which gives the association legitimacy in encouraging the company to begin training, using the available subsidies.

In light of its role in acquiring private information, deliberation, and mobilizing capacity, we have the following general hypothesis:

H_3: *The presence of employers' organizations with capacities of information circulation, deliberation, and mobilization is a necessary condition for reforms premised on securing decentralized cooperation to succeed.*

Moreover, it is equally important to underline the presence of the dog that does *not* bark in the night, according to my theoretical framework: sanctioning. This leads to another testable implication:

H$_4$: *In times of transition, associations possess no credible sanctioning mechanism to deter free-riding.*

What is the hypothesized role of the state in this process? The nature of the reform undertaken is such that the state wants to convince private companies that it is in their individual interest to use apprenticeship training, because it is in the collective interest if enough of them do so. Therefore, what the state most wants to do with its principal tool for encouraging coordination—that is, its ability to subsidize—is to use it to encourage *those* companies to begin training that show promise of being *future* investors in the training system. It does not want to subsidize training permanently; that would vitiate the whole point of adopting the western German model. However, the state wants to encourage firms that acknowledge the promise of apprenticeship-style training, but that remain reluctant to invest in it when they are unsure if other (like-minded) firms will invest in it. It is these firms, the waverers, that the state most wants to convince to engage in high-skill training practices, because they are the ones most likely to be easily convinced of the inherent merits of such training. This suggests a final testable implication of my framework:

H$_5$: *Programs specifically targeted at waverers are likely to succeed, whereas those subsidy policies that distribute aid indiscriminately will fail, in securing decentralized cooperation.*

8.3 Two Routes to Decentralized Cooperation

The cases I use to test these hypotheses are the reforms of vocational education and training systems undertaken in France since 1984 and in eastern Germany since 1990. The two cases constitute that most serendipitous of events for a social scientist: roughly contemporaneous reforms motivated by similar rationales and end-points—the West German high-skill equilibrium. We take our experiments as we find them, and there are certainly many dissimilarities between France, which is one of the advanced capitalist political economies, and the reforming state-socialist political economy of eastern Germany. In the area of vocational education and training, though, the reforms they attempted are conceptually quite similar, such that comparisons within and between the two cases yield significant new understanding of the dynamics that underlie attempted transitions to a new societal equilibrium.

The securing of decentralized cooperation followed different patterns in eastern Germany and France, and these different patterns reflected the different capacities of employers' associations in the two economies. German employers' associations have succeeded in establishing capable organizations across the new states of eastern Germany; these organizations have access to the private information necessary to target waverers. The divergence in results in eastern Germany grows out of the different extent to which governments have incorporated employers' associations into the policy-making process. The successful German employment zones in my sample are both located in the state of Saxony, and it is the policy of that state that is responsible for those successes. As I demonstrate in the second part of this section, Saxon policy-makers drew on the informational resources of employers and unions in designing state subsidies, which allowed them to develop policies that could successfully attract wavering companies on the threshold of cooperation. Saxony-Anhalt, whose policy-makers gave little input to representatives of private interest groups, developed policies that did not target aid to the most likely cooperators. The resultant policy mix in the state has failed to secure widespread decentralized cooperation, as indicated by the failures observed in my sample from that state. This policy mix has in fact only encouraged the growth of apprenticeship training in sectors characterized by low investment in skills (Lutz and Grünert 1999).

The major story of the French reforms is one of weak organizations of employers proving unable to serve as interlocutors for regional governments trying to design policies to encourage decentralized cooperation among firms. Although some regions have *attempted* to incorporate private information into the policy-making process, the weakness of these organizations in acquiring this information has undercut that effort (Comité de Coordination 1996). Thus, in the only successful case in my French sample—the Valley of the Arve—a private association has developed its own program for targeting waverers, using the national subsidy programs available to all firms. Unable to influence the shape of policy itself, this organization has influenced the course of its implementation through mobilizing only those companies perceived as most likely to be persuaded of the long-term benefits of investment in youth training. This success case is in many ways idiosyncratic, and it may be difficult to replicate elsewhere in France. But its existence demonstrates that successful reform is indeed possible, even in an economy lacking a history of coordinated action.

8.3.1 An Overview of the Reforms in
Eastern Germany and France

The attempted transformation of the training system took place in the context of German reunification after 1990, where training was but one of a multiplicity of institutions transferred to the new federal states of eastern Germany. In focusing on the training practices of companies within certain regions, this chapter does not directly address the sometimes dramatic problems of transferring to eastern Germany the associational infrastructure associated with the operation of the dual system in the west: employers' associations, unions, and chambers. The organizational challenges facing these groups are important, and they have been analyzed elsewhere (Wiesenthal 1995; Fichter 1997). Because the central theoretical issue in this chapter is how employers coordinate their action, I focus on how *companies* perceive the role played by these collective actors, and how this role has influenced firm-level decision-making about apprenticeship training.

The GDR enjoyed an established practice of industrial apprenticeship and shared with the Federal Republic the historical roots of apprenticeship training in Germany. What was radically new in post-unification training, as in many other aspects of life in eastern Germany, was the primacy of the market in the making of company decisions. In highly stylized form, then, the conceptual challenge of apprenticeship training in eastern Germany has been to convince (newly) private firms to invest in the costs of training apprentices, as in any other long-term investment. And it had to persuade them to make this long-term investment despite a context of dramatic economic restructuring that resulted in the bankruptcy of many companies and the unemployment of large portions of the workforce (Wagner 1999).

In the decade since unification, eastern German firms overall have not invested in apprenticeship training at levels that constitute anything like a high-skill equilibrium. Whereas the hallmark of the western German system is that firms pay for the in-firm costs of apprenticeship training, *70 per cent of the new contracts signed in eastern Germany in 1998 were subsidized by the federal or state governments*. This raises the question of how to evaluate different types of subsidies that states are offering, and how effectively they are being used as transitional measures to convince firms of the long-term benefits of high levels of investment in apprenticeship training. We return to a reconsideration of these questions below.

In France, too, the challenge of in-firm training is to convince a large number of firms to invest in the development of the skills of their workforces through in-firm youth training contracts. Historically, in-firm training has occupied a much less significant place in the French than in the German political economy: the number of students enrolled in purely school-based professional training routinely exceeds the number of young people trained in company-based training contracts. The challenge in France is not, therefore, to convince companies to invest in a market context, which is nothing new to French companies. It is, rather, to convince them to increase their investment in in-firm training contracts for young people, rather than leaving the provision of general skills exclusively to the educational system (cf. Maurice et al. 1986; Géhin and Méhaut 1993). The governments that introduced three reforms of the training system (in 1984, 1987, and 1993) adopted these laws so as to move away from a system in which apprentices occupy a lowly social and economic position, and do not develop broad, transferable skills, to a high-skill equilibrium *à la française*.

We know that in the period since the passage of the 1993 reform, the number and educational levels of those young people hired by French firms in training contracts have increased (Comité de Coordination 1996). Yet much of this increase is due to the increased state subsidies available for youth training contracts, and it is not clear from aggregate indicators the extent of the *net* investment by companies in the transferable skills of their young employees. Recall that the problem of securing decentralized cooperation is to convince companies to move in a coordinated fashion to high levels of net investment, even though they cannot be protected from poaching by other firms. Thus, to ascertain whether or not France has made the jump to a high-skill equilibrium, we need to know whether or not employers are investing substantially in these contracts as a future means of procuring their skilled labor force. The data I collected from employers in nine employment zones in the two transitional political economies provide considerable insight into these questions.[4]

Table 8.1 depicts a summary of the findings across the nine employment zones I studied. Some might argue that the success or failure of high-skill training will be solely a function of the preexisting demand for skilled labor, and that this in turn is a function of the existing level of unemployment. The figures in the second column, showing unemployment figures around the time the data were gathered, certainly rule out the existence of any mechanistic relationship between unemployment and the presence of high-skill training. The third column shows the

---

[4] See the appendix to this chapter for a discussion of the criteria used in assembling and evaluating these data.

TABLE 8.1 Overall results by employment zone

	Unemployment[a] (%)	Group capacity[b]	Subsidies	Outcome[c]	N
Arve	9.0	High	Yes	*Success*	5
Plauen	16.5	High	Yes	*Success*	5
Leipzig	18.0	High	Yes	*Success*	7
Strasbourg	8.5	Low	Yes	Failure	9
Lyon	12.0	Medium	Yes	Failure	4
Vimeu	14.5	Medium	Yes	Failure	7
Amiens	14.5	Low	Yes	Failure	4
Halle	16.5	High	Yes	Failure	5
Sangerhausen	22.0	High	Yes	Failure	6

[a] Unemployment rates are rounded to the nearest half per cent; rates for French employment zones refer to the departmental unemployment level. Rates refer to the period during which interviews were conducted in firms in the respective areas.

[b] Group capacity is measured by the ability of employers' associations to circulate information, deliberate, and mobilize members; my estimations are based on information collected from firms and associations, and are explained more fully in Culpepper (forthcoming). Associational capacity among eastern German organizations I studied was uniformly high, but the greater variation in French associational capacity required that I designate three categories. Groups in the 'medium' category do not fulfill the requirements of employer coordination described above; however, they demonstrate a limited capacity for information-circulation, which distinguishes them from the exclusive service-provision orientation of the associations categorized as 'low.'

[c] Success is measured according to whether or not the proportion of companies training according to the standards of the high-skill training model in western Germany exceeds 34%, which is the benchmark of the western German model (Wagner 1999). See the appendix to this chapter for a further discussion of these methodological issues.

Source: Interviews conducted in 1995 and 1996 in France and Germany.

degree of employer organizational capacity, which is invariably high in the four German zones but varies quite a bit across the French zones. Finally, we see that subsidies are a constant in these transitional political economies: firms in every employment zone had access to some sort of governmental subsidy aimed at promoting conformity with the training objectives of the government. As we shall see below, however, the design of subsidies varied substantially among zones.

Two results are worth noting immediately. First, success only occurs in one third of the cases studied. In other words, decentralized cooperation is not easy to secure, and indeed the majority of zones in my sample failed in trying to secure it. Second, the data in Table 8.1 immediately confirm hypothesis H$_3$: success is unlikely in the absence of an employers' association with the capacities of information circulation, deliberation, and mobilization. Only those zones credited with high group capacity enjoy the capabilities of information circulation, deliberation, and mobilization of members that I have argued are the prerequisites for success. Yet group capacity is a necessary, but not a sufficient condition: the results in the employment zones of Halle and Sangerhausen testify to the fact that a high degree of employer organizational capacity does not ensure success in promoting high-skill training practices.[5] As I show in the next section, what distinguished the three success cases from the more numerous failures was the particular blend of private information with public policy.

8.3.2 Eastern Germany

The signal fact of training in eastern Germany is that small and medium-sized firms encounter the most difficulty in trying to begin investing in training. Most of the current apprenticeship places in eastern Germany are subsidized, and almost all the subsidies to firms go to companies in the *Mittelstand*. Most of the large, private firms in eastern Germany are owned by western German companies; these companies have, by virtue of their ownership ties with western German companies, married into the stabilizing influences and rigidities of the classic coordinated market economy model characteristic of western Germany (Culpepper 1999). Their access to the financial and informational resources of their western German ownership has allowed them to move quickly to adopt high-skill training practices. Yet large firms in the western German model comprise a very small proportion of the overall training places in the economy. As the government is well aware, in order for the transfer of the dual system of apprenticeship training to eastern Germany to succeed, it must convince small and medium-sized companies to invest heavily in youth training through apprenticeship. The question is how.

It is clear from the evidence in my study that private-sector sanctioning will not be sufficient to compel companies to engage in decentralized cooperation. As representatives of firms in my eastern German sample readily volunteered, the employers' association possesses no sanctioning capacity other than expulsion of members, and this was not a plausible avenue to prevent poaching. Even very large firms in my sample admitted to the lack of recourse available through the employers' association

---

[5] If the theory of transition that I am putting forward is correct, this finding creates particular problems for France, where only one of the five employers' associations studied manifested a high level of organizational capacity; I return to the particular case of the Valley of the Arve below.

to punish firms that poached their most highly skilled workers, thus confirming hypothesis H_4. One very large eastern German firm in my sample was compelled to raise its wages to parity with the western rate in 1991, because it had no other means of holding on to its skilled workers, who were being poached by firms in the west. The association lacked a viable sanctioning mechanism to prevent this problem. Even in the case of collectively bargained wage rates, which is the original *raison d'être* of the employers' association, companies in eastern Germany defy their association with impunity (Ettl and Heikenroth 1995). These associations, concerned with the stagnation of membership numbers in eastern Germany, admit that they have no credible sanctioning mechanism against free-riding companies, and the companies know it.

Faced with the inability of private interest actors to solve the crisis of the eastern German apprenticeship market on their own, state governments have subsidized firms heavily to induce them to hire apprentices. As predicted by hypothesis H_1, these general state policies have targeted those problems which states can easily observe. In particular, there are four sorts of subsidies that dominate state-level aid for in-firm training, which all the new federal states in the east have offered. First, there are subsidies for newly founded firms, or firms that are training apprentices for the first time. From the perspective of the individual states, this seems like an intuitively obvious way to help firms begin training that have not done so before. Second, there are subsidies for firms that hire 'supplementary' apprentices; that is, apprentices they would not normally hire to meet their own needs, but whom they hire to help ease problems on the labor market. Third, and similarly structured, are the subsidies for firms that hire apprentices from other firms that have gone bankrupt. Again, the state is paying for a reduction of the problems on the labor market, and allowing the apprentices to finish their training and receive their certification. Finally there is in almost every state of eastern Germany subsidy money available for firms that hire young women in 'atypical' female professions, which in practice usually means technical, industrial professions.

Rather than trying to determine *which* sorts of firms are likely to be convinced of the merits of investing heavily in training, these subsidies manifest the *inability* of the states to discriminate between firms that are likely to continue training and those that are not. What the state can determine, though, is whether or not a firm is new, and so it imposes that as a criterion for subsidizing firms. The other three common sets of subsidies are targeted at observable social problems that their constituents care about: in the second group, the overall supply of places is recognized as insufficient; in the third, the problem of apprentices in bankrupt firms is acknowledged;[6] and in the fourth, a demographic group particularly affected by the shortage of apprenticeship places is aided. These goals are certainly defensible on social grounds, yet only the first addresses directly the overriding concern of the German government to transfer a system based on firm responsibility for apprenticeship training to the eastern states. And it does so in a way that fails to identify the firms that are most likely to continue investing in training, without subsidies, in the future. Rather, as noted in a report on subsidies commissioned by the government of Saxony-Anhalt, these subsidies are leading to training in qualifications for which there is little future demand and for professions in which subsidies reduce the level of firm investment to almost zero (Lutz and Grünert 1999).

What employers' associations and unions *could* observe, from the vantage point at the firm level, is that these indiscriminate subsidies were not encouraging companies to invest heavily in apprenticeship training. In 1995, employers and unions lobbied eastern German state governments to adopt the one policy that appeared most likely to target the firms most interested in investing heavily in apprenticeship training: the *Verbund* (training cooperative) policy. The *Verbund* policy had two elements that made it especially likely to attract waverers among the firm population. First, it phased the aid over the duration of the apprenticeship contract, with most aid concentrated in the first year of training, which is the year of general training that small and medium-sized firms in Germany find most onerous. Apprentices require an especially heavy net investment in their first year, as they are relatively unproductive for the firm, because they principally receive broad general training. The high cost of this first year of training posed the largest obstacle for the firms that wanted to invest in trainees. While eastern German states had previously experimented with subsidizing partnerships among firms, the *Verbund* laid out for the first time the explicit condition of subsidizing over the course of an apprenticeship, with most aid coming the first year. Those companies seeking the most lucrative subsidy might not choose the *Verbund*, but those closest to being persuaded of the value of high-skill training would. Moreover, once they had chosen the *Verbund*, they were engaged with other companies in training the apprentices, which gave them the opportunity to observe the experiences of other firms

---

[6] Lest this seem like an isolated phenomenon, recall that between 1989 and 1991 two-thirds of the jobs in the eastern German manufacturing sector had ceased to exist.

investing in apprenticeship training over the three-and-a-half-year course during which their apprentices were training.

Employers' associations teamed with unions across eastern Germany to urge adoption of this policy by state governments in 1995. Why, then, did Saxony adopt such a phased *Verbund* program in 1995 when Saxony-Anhalt did not? Both the Saxon and Saxon-Anhalt employers' associations had reliable inside information about the needs of training companies, which informed their advocacy to their respective state governments. The CDU government of Saxony included employers' organizations in working groups tasked with designing a solution to the apprenticeship crisis, and this working group proposed the *Verbund* policy that was eventually adopted. By contrast, the red-green coalition government of Saxony-Anhalt turned a deaf ear to the demands of employers in designing apprenticeship subsidies in 1995, despite the fact that *Verbund* aid was also favored by union representatives.[7] Whereas the Saxon Economics Minister relied heavily on the informational resources provided by employers' organizations, the employers' representative in Saxon-Anhalt lamented the routine unwillingness of the state government to incorporate its advice (Schramedei 1995).

In my firm sample, several companies received training subsidies of the type discussed previously, some more generous than Saxon *Verbund* aid, but only the *Verbund* aid was cited as leading eastern German firms to train, which would not have done so otherwise, at levels associated with the high-skill equilibrium in western Germany. One firm in my sample from Saxony-Anhalt, which was not training any apprentices at the time of interview, summarized the uncertainty about the value of training that prevented wavering firms from investing: 'if we were going to train, we would want to be certain that apprentices were learning their craft, and not just being cheap labor. To do that, you need the right equipment and the right personnel.' In focusing aid on exactly the concerns that prevented wavering firms from training, the Saxon *Verbund* succeeded in creating pockets of cooperation. By refusing to adopt such a policy early on, and relying instead on the more traditional, indiscriminate state measures, the government of Saxony-Anhalt has limited the ability of its subsidies to facilitate the emergence of decentralized cooperation. Hypothesis H_5 is confirmed. When the Saxon-Anhalt govern-

---

[7] The Saxon-Anhalt government opted to continue its 'cooperation' subsidy in 1995, but it did not concentrate aid in the first year and was one of the least generous apprenticeship subsidy programs in the state, offering a maximum of only one tenth the aid available in Saxony (DM 1,200 vs. DM 12,150).

ment commissioned an impartial review of its subsidy policies in 1998, this is the same conclusion to which the authors came: 'since apprenticeship *Verbünde* could be extremely important in securing higher quality training in an overwhelmingly small-firm economy, it is recommended that the state look into the low utilization of this policy—especially in comparison to neighboring states—and seek a remedy for it' (Lutz and Grünert 1999: 88).[8]

Are there alternative explanations that can account for the divergence in policies and outcomes between Saxony and Saxony-Anhalt? Certainly the difference in outcomes observed between the two states has nothing to do with level of the state subsidies for apprenticeship training. Saxony-Anhalt spends more per capita on the subsidization of apprenticeship, and subsidizes more places per capita, than does the Saxon government. It is possible to argue that the CDU majority government in Saxony was more likely to adopt an employer-friendly policy than the SPD-Green coalition government in Saxony-Anhalt. However, a Grand Coalition government in Berlin and an SPD government in Brandenburg both incorporated employer demands on a *Verbund* policy into their subsidy packages in 1995. Those governments, like the one in Saxony, delegated significant influence to the social partners in designing state policies (Culpepper forthcoming). Finally, some readers might believe that Saxony is in fact far more endowed with social capital than is Saxony-Anhalt. Using the associational density measure of Robert Putnam (1993), though, the differences between the two states are negligible. Moreover, in each state I selected the employment zone with the highest (Plauen, Sangerhausen) and lowest (Leipzig, Halle) density of secondary associations. This difference in social capital had no effect on the propensity of actors to cooperate with each other.

The different policies adopted in Saxony and Saxony-Anhalt were based on the different types of information available to governments in

---

[8] Once other states began to show the good results from having a *Verbund* policy, the government in Saxony-Anhalt eventually (in 1997) overhauled its existing 'cooperation' subsidy to concentrate aid in the first year, while increasing the available amount to DM 6,500 over the course of the apprenticeship for firms that wanted to train in cooperation with other firms or training centers. However, the program remains small in comparison with Saxony's: while Saxony has just over twice the population of Saxony-Anhalt, in 1999 it subsidized more than *nine* times as many apprenticeship places through its *Verbund* program as did Saxony-Anhalt through its cooperation program. The Saxon program, developed with the private information available through employers' associations, has apparently been better able to attract the firms most interested in investing in high-skill training than the policies on which Saxony-Anhalt has relied.

the two states, as predicted by my theoretical framework. In addition, it is clear from the evidence presented above that the *Verbund* policy has been far more effective than other policies in encouraging companies to cooperate with each other through an investment in high-skill training. This success is a function of the policy design, made possible by access to private information, which directly targeted the problems of greatest concern to those small and medium-sized companies most likely to be persuaded of the value of long-term cooperation.

8.3.3 France

The French reforms have largely failed in securing decentralized cooperation. There are two major causes of this failure: the interests of large companies and the organizational incapacity on the part of employers generally. Thanks to the weakness of French unions, French large firms have considerable autonomy in choosing their product market and skill provision strategies. Unlike their large counterparts in eastern Germany, large French firms do not face a regulatory situation that compels them to pursue a strategy of incremental innovation (Regini 1997*a*; Culpepper 1999). Adopting this sort of strategy would require that workers possess the broad, transferable skills taught through the German dual system, which would lead large companies in France to favor the widespread practice of investing heavily in youth training contracts. However, given the inability of the unions to push companies toward a strategy of incremental innovation, large French firms are able to get away with a flexibly Fordist production model, in which they use the education system to provide general skills and then train only in firm-specific skills at the firm level (Boyer 1995). Thus, French large firms have no interest in investing in high-skill firm contracts, and they have accordingly done nothing to promote the achievement of this goal in the wake of the French training reforms.[9] This assessment is borne out by the empirical data in my firm sample, in which not a single company with more than 500 employees invests in training at levels consistent with western German practice.

---

[9] This view of large-firm activity in France is somewhat at odds with that developed by Hancké in his chapter in this volume. While it is true, as Hancké argues, that large firms are central figures in relations with their suppliers, there is no evidence that they provide any collective benefits for their suppliers in the area of vocational training. In fact, some of the firms in my sample that had moved furthest in the direction of high-level training investment were making training investments so as to enable them to acquire new, better product market niches, as a way of *diminishing* their dependence on large automotive companies.

Thus, as in eastern Germany, the potential cooperators among French companies are to be found among the small and medium-sized firms.[10] But these companies hesitate to invest in firm-based training when they are uncertain how other companies will react. And it is here that the organizational weakness of French employers has severely undermined the reform project of the French government. Unlike in Germany, French regional governments have no set of organizational interlocutors with the capacities of information circulation and deliberation that would be necessary to design policies based on private information about the obstacles facing waverers (cf. Bunel 1995). Even in the region in which policy-makers have gone to the most exaggerated lengths to incorporate the input of employers—Rhône-Alpes—the regional association has not been up to the task of providing such detailed information about its member firms, and the reforms appear to have had no direct impact on firm training behavior. The regional governments in France have adopted a wide array of policies in the area of training, but none is designed to identify and appeal specifically to the concerns of the most likely cooperators in the population (Comité de Coordination 1996). National aid policy is similarly indiscriminate, being available to any firm that hires trainees. This experience emphatically confirms the predictions of hypothesis H_1: state policies made without inside information about the identity of waverers will target only those aggregate problems they can measure.

The sole case of success that I observed in France lies in the Valley of the Arve. The Arve is the heart of the French bar-turning industry: 60 per cent of French bar-turning production comes from the valley, with production dominated by small and medium-sized firms. This density of firms with similar needs for basic and advanced technical skills has led even small firms to develop a close relationship with the national trade association for bar-turning (SNDEC), whose offices are located there (Poleyn 1996). In the mid-1980s the industry had faced a problem of acute labor shortage that led the SNDEC to delegate responsibility for industrial training to its technical center, the CTDEC. The CTDEC, relying on its close contacts with firms and in consultation with the SNDEC, was able to canvass firm needs exhaustively and then provide a site of

---

[10] Lacking the market power of their large compatriots, French small firms do not have the capacity to force the social partners or the Education Ministry to tailor degrees narrowly to their firm-specific requirements. They can be convinced to provide transferable skills through training if it helps them attract candidates and also train them in skills specific to the company.

reflection about how multiple firm needs could be met most efficiently with new qualifications. The SNDEC lobbied for these new qualifications at the national level and succeeded in having them adopted. On the basis of the new qualifications, the bar-turning association announced its program to train '1,000 technicians' by the end of the century, and the CTDEC has become an aggressive lobbyist for more training from individual companies to meet this goal. The threshold of 1,000 new technicians was surpassed in 1999, one year ahead of schedule.[11]

As we would expect, given hypothesis H_4, the SNDEC had to meet this goal despite the fact that it lacked a credible sanctioning capacity. Given the labor shortage in the industry, the association would have to convince individual companies to invest despite the ever-present risks of poaching. Multiple firms in my sample had themselves poached employees in the past, or lost them to poaching. Yet the CTDEC had no recourse to prevent this poaching. In fact, shortly after beginning the initiative to promote in-firm training, the association sent a delegation to Paris to try to introduce a *contrat de fidélité* that would require workers to stay at a company for a certain period of time after their training there. The bar-turning association, in other words, sought legal recourse for its firms to close off the poaching problem, as it lacked an effective means itself to prevent poaching. The proposed amendment was incompatible with French labor law, and so was rejected by the Parliament. The '1,000 technicians' program would therefore be forced to succeed without the benefit of any sanctioning capacity, from either the state or private associations.

Only the access to inside information about companies by the SNDEC and the CTDEC enabled the association to use an indiscriminate set of national subsidies to target waverers in the population. As summarized in an interview with the director of the CTDEC, the strategy was explicit and deliberate: 'other places in France, the big firms hire 20 young people and only want to hire one. Our firms hire one person and they want to keep them.' The association targeted the analytic uncertainty of the waverers by investing in the improvement of the training center of the CTDEC, which could then serve a function equivalent to that of German large firms in the Saxon *Verbund*: ensuring SMEs that their investment in training would result in higher-level skills of workers. By convincing

---

[11] The department of Haute-Savoie benefited from this program by showing a substantial increase in the total number of highly skilled workers in the 1990s, whereas this proportion remained unchanged in France as a whole (Poleyn 1996: 2).

these companies to work together through the training center, it allowed them to exchange information with one another, and thereby to be persuaded of the intrinsic value of in-firm training. In other words, the sectoral association was able to take existing national government subsidy programs and propose a clear risk reduction to companies: 'you get some money to cover training, and you know our center has the capacity to produce highly skilled workers.'

As a result, on every available metric of high-skill training, the evidence from my sample of companies shows that the firms in the Arve invest more than other companies of the same size in France. They maintained an average training ratio that was more than twice that of companies of this size in my sample that were not from the Arve. They retained almost 90 per cent of those they trained, whereas firms throughout France, in all sectors and size groups, retain only a miserable 29 per cent of their trainees after the conclusion of the qualification contract (Charpail and Zilberman 1998). The educational level of the trainees in small firms in the Arve and elsewhere is equally, dramatically different: 70 per cent of the trainees in Arve Valley firms had at least a *bac*, and over half of those had two additional years after the *bac*; in the small firms in the rest of France, 75 per cent of trainees had qualifications below the *bac* level.[12] The sorts of figures that we observe from firms in the Arve are characteristic of western German firms making a substantial investment in youth training. Moreover, company attitudes towards subsidies further support this finding. Four of the SMEs located outside the Valley of the Arve— including one firm in the bar-turning industry, but from a different region of France—would train fewer or no young people in the absence of state subsidies; none of the training firms in the valley of the Arve would take on fewer young trainees in the absence of public subsidies to training. These subsidies have helped companies in the Arve to make the decision to begin training, and their experience in cooperative training has already led them to revise upward their estimates of the returns to that investment in human capital development. As predicted by hypothesis H_5, the clever combination of subsidies with private information in the Valley of the Arve has led to a situation of uncommon success in securing decentralized cooperation.

The case of the Arve is, in the French context, somewhat unusual: a territory featuring a high density of small and medium-sized firms

---

[12] The *baccalauréat* (or *bac*) is the general education certificate for the completion of secondary school in France.

producing for similar product markets. Yet this is also the case of another French industrial district included in my study, the Vimeu. And, as shown in Table 8.1, the Vimeu has failed in eliciting high-skill training behavior from its companies. The reason for the difference is that the association located in the Vimeu adopted an indiscriminate strategy of targeting national aid to attract wavering companies.[13] The counterexample of the Vimeu similarly undercuts the explanatory power of social capital, given that the associational density of the two districts is virtually identical. While the general findings support the argument of Levy (1999a) about the weaknesses of French regional institutions that require effective secondary associations in order to function, the clear success of the Arve demonstrates that French civic associations are not doomed to fail. It is possible for the coordinating capacity of employers' associations in France to be mobilized effectively to support experiments in decentralized cooperation, in cases where associations develop that capacity. But to be successful, they must find a way to transform indiscriminate policies into targeted policies that will disproportionately attract waverers and persuade them of the benefits of engaging in decentralized cooperation.

8.4 Conclusion

An employers' association, or some instrument controlled by employers that can mimic the functions of an association, is a necessary condition to facilitate the emergence of decentralized cooperation in the area of apprenticeship training. Yet it is not a sufficient condition. There is a role for public policy here, and it is not a role that can easily be played by private actors. Associations are uniquely well suited to acquire private information that is not readily obtained by the state, information about the real barriers that keep firms from engaging in a new system of vocational education and training. The association has insight about which firms are most likely to be candidates for long-term investment in high-skill training, and this information can help policy-makers craft policies that target these firms specifically. State policy divorced from this private information can only target the aggregate problems that are easily observed, and such subsidies do not appear to facilitate the transition to durable practices of high-skill training; this is the lesson of French policy in most of the regions I studied. Yet the results from Saxony-Anhalt show

---

[13] For an extended comparison of the two areas, see Culpepper (2000).

that coordination is not enough: the problems of transition are severe, and even capable employers' associations alone are usually incapable of engineering the transition to a high-skill equilibrium.[14]

These findings provide a way to rethink, in some fundamental respects, the contemporary problems of state intervention in the economy of the advanced capitalist countries. Vocational training reform is one of a subset of policies aimed at promoting economic adjustment on the supply side of the economy, policies that frequently demand that social actors (especially companies) cooperate not with the state, but with each other (cf. Katzenstein 1985*b*; Garrett and Lange 1991; Boix 1998). Governments that want to adopt such policies must realize that they frequently lack the information necessary to design policies that can solve these problems of coordination. Private associations have access to information the state cannot itself acquire, and this information appears to be a crucial ingredient in formulating the policies that can help convince private actors to begin cooperating with each other. Especially in the political economies that lack the organizational infrastructure characteristic of the coordinated market economies, the role of the state may paradoxically be to encourage the development of associations that it cannot control. Without the assistance of these associations, the state can only rely on its own informational resources, whose limits I have repeatedly underscored.

Two points of general significance for political scientists studying policy reforms should be emphasized here. First, the importance of reliable, credible information is hard to overstate. This is a finding that converges with those of rational choice theorists who have argued that even though talk is cheap, when communication cannot be backed up by sanctions, communication and credible carriers of information are the requisites of any attempt to establish cooperation from scratch (Calvert 1995; Ostrom 1998). It is for this reason that I have laid such a heavy emphasis on the importance of employers' associations in circulating information among companies, as well as on their capability to facilitate deliberation among member companies about the best strategies to

---

[14] Although I have not emphasized it in this chapter, there is of course a fundamental prerequisite to convincing firms to invest in high-skill training: they must have a demand for these skills in their production processes. If companies do not need the skills taught through an apprenticeship system, no amount of employer coordination and deftly designed public policy will convince them to invest in the training of apprentices. The difficulty of moving to a high-skill equilibrium when a political economy is not currently in one will therefore be influenced by the preexisting demand of firms for skills, as well as the alternative means (besides apprenticeship) of procuring skilled workers (Culpepper 1999).

pursue to assure that company skill needs are met. The capability of associations to facilitate collective deliberation enables them to serve both as
a forum for bargaining among different companies about skill needs and
as a collective mechanism for devising strategy under conditions in
which the boundedness of individual rationality is exacerbated by the
uncertainties introduced by the reforms of the training system.

The second point of general interest is that sanctioning is overrated as
the ultimate means of resolving problems of decentralized cooperation
(cf. Ostrom 1998). Sanctions are only useful when they are credible. This
is typically the case in an environment where the rules are clear, expectations are well established, and violations are easily observable. Reforms
that require the securing of decentralized cooperation violate, *ex hypothesi*,
the first two conditions; and the third is often difficult to measure in
practice. As the cases of vocational training reform in eastern Germany
and France demonstrate with clarity, the uncertainty created by reforms
premissed on decentralized cooperation is substantial. An important component of this uncertainty is the estimation by actors of the returns to
requited cooperation. Lacking a history of cooperation on which to build,
they are unsure not only of the trustworthiness of other players in the
game, but also of how they will fare if their cooperative overture is not
exploited. It is well known that many experiments in cooperation fail
because people prefer a certain status quo to an uncertain future benefit
(Ostrom 1990). The lesson of this study is that policy-makers will often be
well advised to subsidize potential cooperators—thus offsetting the risk
that, according to the status quo bias, keeps these waverers from cooperating. Such an approach provides an opportunity for people to assess the
real-world costs of cooperation, which helps to overcome the problem of
analytic uncertainty. Adopting such policies will be more effective
than devising implausible sanctioning schemes, provided the state is able
to procure credible information about how to identify the most likely
cooperators in a population.

The analytic tool kit of the varieties of capitalism approach is extremely
useful in understanding the challenges posed by the politics of decentralized cooperation. Countries that lack existing mechanisms for
achieving non-market coordination face long odds when they undertake
reforms premissed on convincing private actors to cooperate with one
another. To succeed, they will need to invest in building up the power
of private associations, associations that they will not be able to control.
But, although the odds are long, they are not hopeless. When there are
serious gains to be made from cooperation, policy-makers have resources
they can mobilize to defray risky experiments, and associational actors

can be very creative in devising strategies to get the most likely cooperators to take small steps on the road to reform. If private information is
prudently used to inform public policy, private actors can be convinced
to reap the gains of cooperation from any societal terrain, regardless of
its institutional history.

APPENDIX 8.1
METHODOLOGICAL NOTES ON MEASURING
HIGH-SKILL TRAINING

The high-skill equilibrium is a theoretical construct, not an easily measurable empirical phenomenon: there are no readily available data on the extent of 'high-skill' training behavior by companies, even in western Germany. In order to study the progress toward high-skill training in France and eastern Germany, I assembled my own sample of companies in specific areas in the two political economies studied, such that I could ascertain the level of their investment in youth training and investigate its links with national and state policies. The sample cited in this chapter comes from fifty-two companies from the metal and electronics industries, all belonging to the chambers of industry and commerce in France and in eastern Germany.[15] As the most significant industrial sector in both political economies, the metal sector is also the sector whose outcomes are most likely to influence the overall success or failure of the reform effort. The central goal of the vocational training reforms attempted in the two political economies was to increase firm participation in apprenticeship training and its equivalents (i.e. the French qualification contract) as paths for the creation of high-skill workers. As western German training is the baseline for assessing these reforms, I used two measures—the ratio of apprentices to total workforce, and the rate of post-apprenticeship retention in a job—to compare training practices in the two countries with those patterns characterizing the western German high-skill equilibrium.

These measures highlight the feature of German training that is most elusive for other political economies, and most difficult to explain: why do western German industrial companies make significant net investments in the costs of conferring both general and firm-specific skills on their workers? The first of these two measures, which I call the training ratio, measures the stock of apprentices currently in training. While the figures vary, depending on a firm's exact market positioning, sector, and phase of growth, a typical training ratio for western German industrial metalworking companies lies somewhere between 4 and 8 per cent. Think of this as the replacement rate of young workers coming in the

---

[15] Since the metalworking and electronics sectors share a collective bargaining arrangement, it is customary to refer to companies in these sectors as members of the metal industry.

pipeline to take over new jobs in the wake of departures from the work-force.[16] This ratio assumes a very high rate of retention of apprentices in their training company, which is the second measure I use.[17] *Ceteris paribus*, we would expect that the higher the net investment of com-panies in the training of their apprentices, the more of their apprentices they will hire into regular employment after the apprenticeship. High retention of apprentices is a signal of the sort of significant firm invest-ment in apprenticeship training that governments have tried to encourage in France and eastern Germany in order to facilitate the move to the high-skill equilibrium. Similarly, having trainees with higher educational backgrounds suggests that companies are likely to invest heavily in their apprentices, since those with higher existing levels of human capital are less likely to be willing to accept an apprenticeship that does not further improve their future earning power.

To test the propositions about the role of employers' associations and public policy in securing decentralized cooperation, I designated the employment zone as the appropriate unit of analysis.[18] There are four eastern German employment zones included in the sample: Plauen and Leipzig are located in the state of Saxony, Halle and Sangerhausen in the state of Saxony-Anhalt. The five French employment zones are located in three regions: Lyon and the Valley of the Arve are situated in Rhône-Alpes, Amiens and the Vimeu are in Picardy, and Strasbourg is in Alsace. For each employment zone I developed a 'high-skill training index,' summarizing the proportion of firms in the sample that trained at levels approximating the western German standard. Only those zones where at least 34 per cent of companies were training at this level were classi-fied as successes. This figure is also based the western German standard (Wagner 1999). These criteria are explicated at much greater length in Culpepper (forthcoming).

---

[16] If companies are training at a much higher level, they are either in a period of rapid growth, or they do not retain the large majority of those they train. The latter is typical practice in German craft firms. If companies train at a much lower level, they are either shrinking or using other means of recruitment than apprenticeship training to satisfy their labor force needs.

[17] Because retention refers to the hiring of apprentices after their apprenticeship, a large number of eastern German companies (which had only very recently started training again when I conducted my interviews in 1995–6) had no data on retention. Assessment of eastern German training in my sample was made on the basis of the training ratio alone.

[18] In eastern Germany, these subnational units are delimited by the jurisdictional bound-aries of the employment offices (*Arbeitsämter*), while in France they correspond to employ-ment zones as designated by the French statistical service, INSEE.

Revisiting the French Model: Coordination and Restructuring in French Industry

Bob Hancké

9.1 Introduction

Recent newspaper reports of takeover battles between large French firms which were once considered close allies and between banks at the heart of the French financial system, OECD data on French economic performance, corporate reorganizations and business profitability in France, and the wave of international alliances where French firms take the lead must come as a surprise even to those only remotely familiar with the French model of economic organization. Instead of a blocked society unable to reform the institutions that were at the basis of its rapid post-war economic growth but which failed to deliver under global competitive pressures, the French political economy has instead displayed a remarkable capacity for adjustment, and is increasingly held up by many liberal observers as an example for other west European economies to follow.

Both liberal and left observers seem to agree on the causes of these changes—even though they disagree widely on their implications for French society: the increasing importance of the market, and the simultaneous reduction of the state's role in the economy. This chapter argues that both these versions of the argument contain some truth, but misunderstand the dynamics underlying the adjustment of the French economy. The old French model has disappeared and a new model has emerged, which still relies on many elements of the old French system, in which the state and the large firms are critical actors, but it does so against a corporate governance background which is integrated in the international (Anglo-Saxon) capital market.

The author would like to thank Bruno Amable, Suzanne Berger, Richard Bronk, Benjamin Coriat, Michal Federowicz, Michel Goyer, Peter Hall, Horst Kern, Richard Locke, Andrew Martin, David Soskice, and Eric Verdier for discussions on the topic of this chapter and comments on earlier versions. The usual disclaimers apply.

This chapter argues that understanding this transition requires an analysis of the shifts in the French production regime during the period 1980–95. During those fifteen years, the French political economy went through a crisis of dramatic proportions and resolving this crisis irreversibly shifted the balance of power from the state to the management of the large firms. After having gained autonomy from both the state and the capital markets through a complex system of cross-shareholdings, these economic elites set out on an adjustment path which allowed them to pursue a series of profound internal corporate reorganizations. The outcome of this adjustment process was that by the mid-1990s, French firms were sufficiently profitable to competitively tender for foreign capital on the rapidly grown Paris stock market.

Given the importance of the adjustment in the period between 1985 and 1996 for an understanding of the French political economy today, this chapter will concentrate on corporate restructuring in France during that period. After a short review of the positions in the debate on French economic adjustment, the balance of section 9.2 will discuss the basic mechanism at the heart of the adjustment: the particular French mode of coordination, which encompassed elites in the state, business, and finance. Section 9.3 will present the story in full: how the crisis of the French production regime challenged the basic parameters of the French model, how the state and the elite reacted, and how these reactions led to a new organization of the French production regime. Section 9.4 concludes by summarizing the main points and by raising the question how the mode of elite coordination is reacting to the shifts in corporate governance structures since the mid-1990s and speculating on what this might imply for the French model.

9.2 Explaining Adjustment in France

In 1982, after one year of rule by the first left-wing government under the Fifth Republic, France appeared more than ever as an exception among western political economies. More than one third of manufacturing GDP was under the state's direct control, the main channels for industrial credit were state-directed, resulting in a highly autarchic investment regime, the government attempted an expansive Keynesian policy which resulted in high inflation rates, and the state was pursuing highly activist industrial policies. In the workplaces low-skilled workers performed extremely narrow tasks: as late as 1982, almost 60 per cent of all workers in France were semi- and unskilled (d'Iribarne 1989). In comparative perspective, France not only had a much higher supervisors to workers ratio (Maurice et al. 1986, 1988), but also employed, controlling for other relevant variables, simply more people (Lane 1989). Labor questions were resolved through social conflicts, and attempts at organizational change invariably faced fierce opposition from the labor unions. Suppliers to industry consisted primarily of small firms, more interested in their own survival than in the conquest of new markets and therefore perennially under-financed and technologically backward. The corporate governance system, finally, was a mixture of direct state control via ownership and indirect state control through the state-centered credit system, and the planning apparatus, all run by a small elite (Shonfield 1965; Zysman 1983).

In 1998, with another left government in power, many of the large firms and banks in France have been partially or entirely sold off to the private sector, FDI in France is higher than elsewhere in continental Europe, and French inflation is lower than in Germany. Workplaces still have a strong Taylorist flavour, but instead of isolated jobs performed by unskilled workers, the shop floor in many companies is made up of teams of polyvalent workers today (Benders et al. 1999; Duval 1996, 1998). Labor unions have by all accounts become irrelevant in the contemporary French political economy. Only some 9 per cent of the workforce is organized today, and in the private sector alone, the organization rate has dropped to 5 per cent. Despite their monopoly in works councils elections, labor unions have lost these to non-union slates (Daley 1999). In comparative perspective, France has become a low-strike country: between 1980 and 1990, strike rates were converging on the low German one, and diverging from the much higher rates in Italy and the UK (Boltho 1996). Strikes and other social conflicts increasingly take place outside (and often against) the labor unions, and are organized by independent contractors, small sectional associations of public-sector personnel and hospital workers, or concentrate on narrow firm-centered demands (Daley 1999).

Small firms and their links with large firms have changed as well. More than half of the small firms make a substantial share of their turnover as suppliers to large firms: between 1980 and 1990, the proportion of subcontracting small and medium-sized enterprises (SMEs) rose from below 40 per cent to roughly 55 per cent (Duchéneaut 1995: 199). In order to keep their customers, the SMEs had to become much stronger technologically and organizationally: almost without exception suppliers are certified according to the prevailing international ISO 9000 quality management standard and, as a result, they now are an active, technologically able partner to the large firms (Casper and Hancké 1999).

Finally, between 1986 and 1993, many formerly state-owned companies were privatized, the system for industrial credit was transformed around the stock market, and, as a result of its increased autonomy, management is considerably more immune to state intrusion.

How should we understand these changes? Both the literature on economic change in advanced capitalism and the debate on the French political economy in particular have produced two broad perspectives to understand the transition reflected in these data. According to the first interpretation, which has been developed in many studies of the post-war French growth miracle, change as such is nothing new. Through the industrial policy apparatus, the planning mechanism, and its ownership of strategic sectors of the economy, between 1946 and 1980 the French state succeeded in creating the conditions for a profound transformation of the French economy from a largely agricultural society to a modern industrial power (Berger 1972; Estrin and Holmes 1983; Hall 1986). This policy-making apparatus, slightly modified to meet the challenges of the new situation, was also at the basis of recent developments. The state conceived policies that the main economic actors had to follow, and then used industrial policy, economic planning, and the broader legislative process to induce the latter to do so.

This interpretation explains how, as a result of direct state intervention, the French car industry rebounded after a profound crisis that led the two national car producers into virtual bankruptcy (Hart 1992). It understands the reorganization of the French steel industry after its own succession of crises since the late 1970s as a result of state policies that helped companies restructure and corporate and labor union interests converge on a new industrial plan for the industry (Daley 1996). This argument is also at the basis of an account of the process of privatization in France after 1986 and how it contributed to a profound restructuring in many industries, and led to a substantial evolution of management styles (Schmidt 1996).

However, these accounts do not tell the whole story. The equally dramatic failures of some of the state policies in other industries, for example in the computer and machine-tool industries (Ziegler 1997; Zysman 1977) should raise questions about the *omniscient* and *omnipotent* French state. Precisely at the moment, for instance, that the machine-tool industry required higher skills and more flexible forms of work organization in order to position itself in more quality-oriented and less cost-sensitive markets, the French state attempted to modernize the industry by imposing policies copied from the large firms competing in mass markets (Ziegler 1997).

The state-centered argument also ignores an even more important policy development of the 1980s. What probably characterized French economic and industrial policy most during that decade were the attempts by the state to retreat from direct economic and industrial policy-making. After a nationalization wave in 1981, governments (of all political colour) have put considerable energy into privatizing the state-owned companies. Labor relations were reorganized in such a way that the state played a smaller role, and unions and employers were presented with the possibility of negotiating change on their own. And in a far-reaching attempt to reorganize the state apparatus, a series of decentralization laws was passed that aimed at creating new regional and local partnerships for economic development. All these policies were informed by what has become known as 'Toquevillian liberalism,' which implied a simultaneous reduction of central state involvement in policy-making, and a devolution of power to local and regional societal actors—the opposite, in short, of a state-centered, *dirigiste* policy.[1]

An alternative interpretation builds precisely on the reduced state role in contemporary France. What explains the transition, in this view, is that firms were subjected to new forms of competition, a process in which the state actively participated. By deregulating the environment of companies—in capital markets with the financial deregulation of 1984, and in labor markets since the mid-1980s—competition in these areas was intensified, and economic actors—banks, companies, and workers —were forced to cope with this new situation. This interpretation has strong adherence in France itself, mainly among progressive Gaullist and left-wing observers, who deplore the grip of international capital markets on the French economy and how globalization jeopardizes the traditional, mainly state-organized bonds of solidarity (Commissariat Général du Plan 1996; Hoang-Ngoc 1998; Lipietz 1998; Todd 1998).

Without denying that economic adjustment in France over the last two decades has had disruptive social consequences, it is hard to see how this could have been a direct effect of deregulation and increased competition. By all accounts, industrial concentration has increased in France during this period: in response to the crisis that the large exporting

---

[1] These government initiatives ultimately failed: neither the labor unions nor employers were strong enough to carry through the reforms, and the regionalization hit very poor soil in the regions, where no local actors could be found (or created) to provide an underpinning for the policies. Whether they failed or not, however, is not important for the purposes of this argument. What matters is that they were attempts by the state to disengage itself from these different fields of economic policy-making. See Levy (1999a) for full details of these policies and their failures.

industrial companies faced in the first half of the 1980s, the restructuring of industrial sectors frequently entailed a further reduction of the
number of large firms in these sectors. In the automobile industry, for
example, two firms, Renault and Peugeot, roughly equal in size (in terms
of turnover and employment), make up the sector. The steel industry,
which was made up of a few large and many small producers before,
was consolidated into one gigantic steel conglomerate in the mid-1980s.
And the government used its ownership of the chemical industry to
restructure the industry into a small number of complementary rather
than competing firms. Overall, in most industries, one or very few large
companies accounted for over 50 per cent of turnover in 1994 (INSEE
1996). A systematic and detailed econometric analysis of industrial
restructuring in the 1980s (Amar and Crépon 1990) in fact reveals that
the increase in industrial concentration during this period has been a
major factor in improving the competitiveness of French exporting
industry.

More importantly, the abrupt and extensive deregulation of the financial sector in 1984—perhaps the main instance where a policy was introduced which explicitly aimed at increasing competition—did not result
in a competitive capital market characterized by a high merger and
takeover activity, but in a highly orchestrated system of cross-shareholdings, which were formed precisely in an attempt to prevent rampant
competition (Bauer 1988; Maclean 1995; Morin 1995). In short, none of
the outcomes conventionally associated with a market-led adjustment
process can be found in France.

Understanding adjustment in France over the last two decades requires
going beyond the state–market opposition that is central in political
economy, and bringing in firms—in the case of France the large exporting companies in particular—as the key actors. The modernization
of the French economy over the last two decades was not a state- or
market-led process, but a firm-led one, whereby large firms used public
resources and institutions on their own terms and for their own adjustment, and then induced other actors, through power, competition, and
cooperation, to act in a manner which supported their trajectory.

Anybody familiar with the post-war French economy will hardly be
surprised by the central role of large firms in the adjustment process.
The entire Gaullist modernization program was constructed around them
as the engines of economic development, and after the arrival of the left
in office in 1981, the nationalizations of the same year announced themselves as the logical continuation of the Gaullist strategy. In this situation,
however, the large firms were—with only a slight sense of exaggeration

—instruments for broader social, economic, technological, and regional development goals pursued by the state. In exchange, the state provided them with an institutional infrastructure in labor relations, regional development agencies, and technology transfer systems that offered them stable growth. Today, however, large firms have more autonomy in designing their goals while relying considerably less upon state initiatives in their implementation. Instead of being the objects of state policies, the large firms had become the agents of a profound modernization process.

The organizational basis for this shift toward a large firm-led adjustment model was the mode of coordination in France, which is based on a particular configuration, different from both the German associational model and the Anglo-Saxon market model of economic coordination discussed in other chapters in this volume. It entails a system whereby the state, banks, and large firms are intertwined through a complex elite network. In the course of their education, the *best and the brightest* of a given age cohort are selected through a series of difficult exams, which allows them to go on to study at the *grandes écoles*, from where they are recruited into the top of the state administration. After a career in the state apparatus, these people then move into other areas as top managers in large companies or banks, and almost invariably start circulating between these three spheres (Birnbaum 1994; Bourdieu 1989; Suleiman 1979; Suleiman and Mendras 1995). In the 1980s as much as in the 1960s and 1970s, most CEOs in France have, in fact, followed this typical career path over the *grandes écoles* into the state apparatus and the government and then into finance or business—and back, when duty called (Bauer and Bertin-Mourot 1995).

This mode of coordination relies upon several mechanisms. The first is the meritocratic selection mechanism, which imbues all participants with an elitist ethos, giving the business elite a relative autonomy on the basis of educational credentials (Bourdieu 1989). Different studies in different eras demonstrated that the social distance between top management and the rest of the company (who have not followed this elite education trajectory) is vast in France (Crozier 1964; Hofstede 1980). The meritocracy also socializes the members of the elite into one basic world view. Empirical studies of the financial elite in France, one of the pillars of the system, show, for example, that the educational background in the *grandes écoles*, more than political convictions and similar experience, provides the social cement for interaction among this group (Kadushin 1995). Finally, after this initial period of socialization, the monitoring and sanctioning mechanisms within the elite secure compliance with high standards. As a result of the relatively small size of the group, the track record of individual members who pursue a career is in principle knowledge shared by all in the elite, and forms the basis for further career advances. The individual reputation in this elite network, with its roots in the state, therefore is the currency used among the financial, economic, and bureaucratic elites in France.

In the early 1980s, a profound crisis hit the French production regime, and this elite coordination structure became the organizational framework for the subsequent adjustment. It filtered the effects of both the financial deregulation of 1984 and the privatizations of 1986 and thus allowed a reorganization of the corporate governance system. Deregulation and privatization could—and were designed to—impose a regime of intense competition upon CEOs, which included detailed scrutiny by investors. In effect, however, the elite coordination mechanism led to the opposite situation: it allowed for a large sphere of autonomy for top management, by shielding the CEOs of large firms from outside influences—both the state and capital markets—during the process of internal corporate reorganization. Because of this relative insulation, CEOs were now able to pursue their conception of competitiveness and profitability with considerably more vigor than under the state's aegis.

However, as the literature on the inertia of the French model predicted, firms could not simply move out of the old situation by CEO *fiat*. In order to pursue their internal adjustment, the companies relied heavily on public resources. The firms used the panoply of regional government agencies, technology institutes, and training centres, as well as the different laws dealing with the labor market, as instruments to fill the holes in their own adjustment capacities. By doing so, they also ended up inducing the other relevant actors—small firms, labor unions, and workers, but also the state—to act in a manner congruent with the path they took.

The remainder of this chapter will develop this argument, first by showing how exactly top management increased its autonomy, and then by detailing how companies reorganized their ties with workers and suppliers.

9.3 The French Political Economy in the 1980s

Between 1980 and 1985, the French production regime experienced two separate but mutually reinforcing crises. The first was an internal crisis of the large firms, the second a crisis of the supporting macroeconomic policy regime. Despite the mass production strategies based on economies of scale—which themselves were relatively successful, since many large firms had become European market leaders in the early 1980s—the companies posted dramatically low profits in this period: aggregate profitability in France was among the lowest in the G7 (Glyn 1997). Moreover, because of the implicit soft budget constraints for many among them which resulted from the state's willingness to finance their growth, their expansion had led to a situation where they found themselves with an extremely high debt burden, the highest in the OECD (Hall 1986). Third, labor productivity was low by European standards. Detailed comparative assessments of car production, for example, demonstrated that the French automobile industry, at that moment a market leader in Europe, was less productive even than FIAT: Peugeot calculated that it produced 8.3 cars per worker per year in 1983 (down from 9 in 1979), FIAT almost 12 (up from 10) cars, and Ford-Europe 13.2 (up from 10.4) (Loubet 1998). Finally, massive social conflicts in those sectors that spearheaded the French economy exacerbated the internal problems: semi-skilled workers refused the organization of work and the concurrent lack of career perspectives that came with it. Combined, these four elements led to a collapse of French industry: between 1981 and 1985, the large firms, many of which were owned by the state, lost over FF 100 billion (Schmidt 1996: 108).

A profound crisis of *external* conditions accompanied this internal turmoil. The expansionary policies pursued by the left-wing government after May 1981, rapidly led to profound macroeconomic disequilibria. International capital markets began to speculate against the franc, and the government was increasingly running into budgetary problems as a result of the macroeconomic expansion and the nationalizations (which had cost over FF 130 billion). In March 1983, the government therefore decided, after serious debate (Cameron 1996; Halimi 1992), to leave the *socialism in one country* policy and adopt a more restrictive macroeconomic stance (Hall 1986). The political decision to stay within the Exchange Rate Mechanism, and thus reorient French economic policy in order to strengthen the franc by fighting inflation, provided the broad macroeconomic background for the crisis of the French production regime.

The macroeconomic policy adopted after 1983, with the euphemistic name of *competitive disinflation*, had two goals. The first and most important one was to create the domestic economic conditions for a stabilization of the franc after the devaluations of 1982–3. The instrument was straightforward wage restraint by imposing inflation targets on wage negotiations. As a result, France became, after Portugal and Greece, the country with the lowest real wage growth in the EU after 1985 (Taddéi and Coriat 1993). The second goal followed from the first and was an attempt to emulate the hard currency environment that had been so beneficial to German industry: unable to rely on competitive devaluations for export success, the argument went (Albert 1991), German industry was forced to search for competitiveness in quality rather than price.

These macroeconomic policies radically changed the broader environment of companies. In the short run, the *franc fort* policy raised French interest rates to the highest level in the OECD, while, more structurally, adherence to the Exchange Rate Mechanism also implied an acceptance of the broader framework of competition rules regarding subsidies for ailing companies within the EU. The high interest rates hit the companies at the worst possible moment. Not only did they sharply raise the price of much-needed productive investments, the highly indebted companies were severely punished by this situation: for some of them debt servicing accounted for more than 15 per cent of annual turnover! Finally, budgetary constraints and the adoption of EU competition rules led to a structurally new situation: the well-known option of having the state finance the losses until the business cycle picked up again was increasingly becoming impossible as a viable option.

9.3.1 State-Led Corporate Survival

Despite the formal restrictions on state involvement, the state played a crucial role in the first phase of the adjustment process. Having assumed ownership of many large firms after its advent to power in 1981, the government could now shelter the large companies from bankruptcy and foreign takeovers, by allowing them to become recipients of massive state aid.[2] Combined, the state-owned large firms received over FF 64 billion in subsidies, three-quarters of which went to the steel companies Usinor and Sacilor (subsequently merged and restructured) and Renault alone (Schmidt 1996: 108). Without these massive capital injections survival would have been impossible, and new productive investment would not have taken place. It is estimated that between 1981 and 1986, the government invested twenty times more in the state-owned companies than the

---

[2] While nationalizing the industry and the credit sector in the first year of the Mitterrand presidency were actions primarily couched in anti-capitalist terms, broader strategic objectives, evoking the Gaullist program of maintaining a strong national industrial basis as a precondition for political *grandeur*, were never far away. Mitterrand expressed this idea powerfully when he presented the nationalizations to the public in September 1991, and explained that if nationalizations did not take place, 'these companies would rapidly be internationalized' (quoted in Cohen 1996: 227).

private sector had done in these companies between 1967 and 1981 (Schmidt 1996: 124).

Importantly, however, in all cases, the subsidies were accompanied by the negotiation of a detailed business plan. The goal of these plans in the different industries was invariably a rapid restructuring in order to redress the dramatic financial situation. The first effort in this regard was the negotiation of a series of social plans to rapidly reduce the workforce in the companies. Between 1984 and 1987, Renault thus reduced its total workforce by almost 30,000, or 20 per cent (Freyssenet 1998). The Peugeot group did the same: between 1980 and 1987, 57,000 workers were laid off (23 per cent of the workforce) (Loubet 1998). The steel industry, where the crisis had set in a few years earlier, reduced employment in the sector by 45 per cent between 1980 and 1987 (Daley 1996). Overall, the large companies shed 20 per cent of their jobs in the 1980s (INSEE 1993; SESSI 1997; Berger 1995).

Since hard layoffs were (and still are) very difficult in France—in contrast to the Anglo-Saxon economies—the large firms were forced to search for other ways to reduce employment. These were found in the wide array of state programs made available to workers in early retirement and the measures associated with more restrictive immigration policies (Guillemard 1991). More than half of the workforce reductions in the car industry were financed by these measures (and for the remaining ones, the companies relied upon other state programs for industrial conversion), the massive workforce reductions in the steel industry were almost entirely state-financed through the early retirement system (Daley 1996), and even the SNCF managed its workforce restructuring through reliance upon the state (Cauchon 1997).

The second big cost-cutting move by the large firms was a rapid extension of subcontracting by means of outsourcing production and services. Between 1979 and 1985, for example, the vertical integration rate of Renault and PSA fell from 26 per cent to 19 per cent for the first and from 35 per cent to 26 per cent for the second. Électricité de France, the large state-owned utility company, did the same: instead of hiring new workers, the company hired subcontractors for the maintenance of its nuclear plants and network, and for local customer service. EDF workers that were hired, furthermore, were hired with regular labour contracts, not any longer on the civil servant statute typical of EDF workers (Duclos and Mauchamp 1994).

These subcontracting operations had the advantage of rapidly clearing the balance sheets, since many of the supporting activities associated with the subcontracted tasks were eliminated as well: product development, process engineering, training, and quality control. In assembly industries subcontracting also implied just-in-time delivery of parts upon demand, which had the additional financial advantage of reducing capital tied up in the inventory of parts to a minimum. Between 1984 and 1987, for example, Renault used these plans to reduce its stock of cars that were made but not yet sold by 55 per cent, and, despite the increase in outsourcing, reduced its purchasing/turnover ratio by 8 percentage points between 1984 and 1988, due to the renegotiation of prices with suppliers (Freyssenet 1998).

Through a reorganization of the production and service chain, and as a result of dramatic cuts in their workforce, the large firms in France thus managed a serious reduction of their immediate production costs. The most remarkable example of such a turnaround is probably Renault: whereas the company lost over FF 11 billion per year in 1984 and 1985, from 1987 onwards, Renault posted high profits—and continued to do so for the following ten years. The same happened in other large companies. After the crisis of the early 1980s, for example, the French steel industry, now concentrated in Usinor-Sacilor, became one of the most profitable on the Continent (Smith 1998), and EDF managed to turn structural operating deficits into an operating surplus despite the government's claims on its revenue. In short, by 1987, and as a result of the cost-cutting measures, the large firms had secured their financial survival.

9.3.2 Elite Coordination and Corporate Adjustment

While these restructuring plans solved the short-term cost problems and thus helped stabilize the French political economy in the short run, they created a series of entirely new challenges for the large firms. Sustained profitability, which had become the main goal by the mid-1980s, was only possible through a series of organizational innovations that increased productivity. Two areas were, given the existing weaknesses of French organizations, of crucial importance: workforce skills and the organization of work, on the one hand, and subcontractors and suppliers, on the other. The post-mass production era required broadly trained teams of workers instead of unskilled workers as well as sophisticated suppliers to address the volatility of demand (Piore and Sabel 1984).

Yet these were precisely the type of reorganizations that had traditionally proven to be difficult in France. Despite the *presidentialism* of French management and the relative weakness of labor unions, corporate reorganizations were difficult, for different reasons: the state kept a close watch on the social policies of large firms, French workers were insufficiently trained for them to be deployed flexibly, structures for workers' participation on the shop floor did not exist, and unions managed to mobilize possible sources of discontent in shop-floor reorganization and thus thwart shop-floor adjustment strategies. Moreover, increased outsourcing was certain to raise union resistance, because it implied huge job losses. In short, a reorganization of work could succeed only if management proved able to neutralize both the state and the labor unions.

Suppliers, on the other hand, had traditionally been treated as simple executors of large firm orders, were technologically unsophisticated without proper innovation capacities as a result, and were therefore incapable of dealing with any new demands from large firms. Since any reorganization of the supplier networks of large firms would entail a dramatic restructuring of the small-firm sector, which included dropping some altogether and reorganizing the others through technology programs and mergers, governments would be hard put to accept the social consequences of such a reorganization. Again, a strategy based on technologically well-equipped small firms could only succeed if management had a free hand in restructuring its supplier base.

Top management autonomy thus became a necessary condition for internal reorganizations. Autonomy from the state (and from the labor unions, who relied on the state) was necessary to be able to drop a broad social and political dimension from management decisions and concentrate solely or at least primarily on profitability; fortunately, that was also the Fabius government's message to CEOs in the midst of the crisis of corporate France in the early 1980s. Yet being shielded from the immediate impact of the stock market was equally important, since corporate reorganizations announced themselves as a relatively long-term process, which required patient capital: without protection from the short-termness of the stock market, many companies would have been unable to survive the financial pressures they were exposed to under an open capital market.

The elite-based coordination mechanism, which had tied the large firms to the state, provided the conditions for management autonomy from both the state and the stock market. As discussed before, the set-up was one in which top management was sealed off from the rest of the company, but tightly linked to the administrative apparatus. The privatizations of the 1980s and 1990s grafted themselves upon this system, but led to a profound change in the way it operated: they created a protective circle of core shareholders recruited from the elite, which gave the CEO more autonomy from the state while protecting the company against takeovers.

Understanding how this happened requires going back to the end of the 1970s and early 1980s, before the financial reforms was implemented. The core of the relationship between industry and the banks in France was the vital importance of long-term debt for the financing needs of large firms. As late as 1980, French firms were the most highly indebted companies in the OECD, which put the banks in a position of serious influence over the affairs of industry; and because most of the debt was medium to long term, these banks generally took an active interest in the production and marketing strategies of the firms they supported in order to safeguard their investment (Cohen et al. 1985: 47; Hall 1986).

Most of these credit institutions were specialized banks which, combined, collected and disposed of two-thirds of all deposits in the French banking system. Beside these, there was a set of public invest-ment funds, administering several billions of francs, that were used for joint projects with private banks and as a discount fund for their loans (Zysman 1983; Hall 1986).

The main problem in the system was that, by discounting the loans, the government in fact ended up assuming the risk and thus banks were, despite the close relationship between finance and industry, especially poor at long-term monitoring (Goyer 1998). In order to deal with this issue, the government's aim was to reorganize the financial system in two ways: dismantling the sectoral credit monopolies by allowing most banks to become universal banks, thus installing competition for loans and deposits between them, and liberalizing the system of industrial credit through a series of fiscal regulations that made investing in stocks more appealing to households. These reforms thus led to a situation in which households had a variety of ways to save, and companies a variety of ways to obtain (a variety of) money: they could rely on long-term bank financing, issue shares to investors, and rely on retained earnings for investment.

The financial reform of 1984 was followed by the privatizations (under the right-wing government after 1986) of many of the companies brought under the state's control only a few years before. The formal goals of this reform were simple: selling off the nationalized large firms with the tools that had become available after the financial reform and thus creating a popular capitalism of the Anglo-Saxon kind (Schmidt 1996; Goyer 1998).

However, the privatizations took place in a profoundly different way. Instead of being sold to a wide collection of potential owners, the com-panies were sold to five categories of investors only: the first was a hard core of stable shareholders, the so-called *noyau dur*, the second the work-force, the third, quantitatively most important part, the public at large (i.e. using the financial instruments that were born out of the financial reform), and the fourth and fifth French and foreign institutional investors (Cohen 1996: 237–8). The privatizations were designed so that employees were given a preferred shareholder status by reserving them up to 10 per cent of shares and offering discounts on the purchase (Schmidt 1996: 156–7). Furthermore, in many cases the government limited the maximum number of shares that individuals could buy, thereby assuring that ownership was not concentrated. And in order to avoid speculative bursts and unwanted swaps, shares that were not sold for a longer period (up to eighteen months) were rewarded with an extra share or tax advantages. Thus an ownership structure of loyal investor cores emerged, which consisted of groups of banks, insurance companies, and industrial companies that acted as long-term institutional investors and were supposed to help govern the company and protect it from takeovers (Schmidt 1996: 157–63).

As a result of this gigantic financial engineering operation, two stable groups of cross-shareholdings emerged, each one constructed around a giant utility company, a holding, a major bank, and a large insurance company. The first one had the Lyonnaise des Eaux, the holding Suez, the Banque Nationale de Paris and the Union des Assurances de Paris at its core, the other the Générale des Eaux, PARIBAS, the Crédit Lyonnais, the Société Générale and the insurance company Assurances Générales de France (Morin 1995). Together, these financial cores had direct and indirect controlling stakes in each other and almost all publicly quoted large companies. For example, the UAP-BNP core held 8.8 per cent in Air France, over 15 per cent in Saint-Gobain, 9.2 per cent in Elf, and 7.5 per cent in Péchiney. The AGF-Paribas group held 20 per cent in Aérospatiale, 20 per cent in Usinor-Sacilor, 14 per cent in Rhône-Poulenc, and 7.2 per cent in the oil company Total.

Because of the particular corporate governance structure in France, where small shareholders are neither directly nor indirectly represented (something the proxy voting system in Germany allows), this particular mode of privatization should have amounted to an extraordinary control by these hard cores of investors over industry (Morin 1995). Yet the opposite was the case. Shareholders did get a better look at the inside of the companies—a result of the publication and accounting requirements following the opening up of the capital market—but that did not imply more control over management. Instead of reducing management autonomy, the reorganization of the corporate governance system opened the way for the management of large firms to construct a broad sphere of independence from outside influences.

The privatization package included a set of rules on the selection of members of the board of directors, which gave the CEO the right to appoint most of the board members and of the hard core of investors more generally him- or herself. Since the companies that these people represented were frequently entangled in complex cross-ownership arrangements with each other and with the company on whose board they sat, control was, if it took place at all, far from tough. Secondly, more management autonomy also implied more financial freedom. As a last effective safeguard against unwelcome surprises, many CEOs thus created or took control of subsidiaries that allowed them to buy back their floated shares. Even if the representatives of those companies on the board took their job seriously, they were, needless to say, more than careful not to press too hard for control. Their career depended, after all, on the CEO that they formally controlled (see Schmidt 1996: 374–7 for full ownership details). François Morin, one of the most prominent observers of the restructuring of French capital, aptly calls this set-up *self-management by management* (Morin 1989).

Large firms used their own privatization to construct a situation in which they were able to pursue internal reorganizations without being burdened by the traditional social policy, regional development, and other non-financial considerations. Thus, this situation sheltered firms from hostile takeovers during the crisis years, while it assured the companies of the capital needed for the necessary restructuring. Secondly, this holding structure also created a situation of autonomy in relation to the state and the labor unions: it allowed firms to be reorganized through massive layoffs if this proved necessary, since the state was no longer the only, often socially conscious, owner. This enabled the large companies to pursue more relentless workforce reduction policies and increase subcontracting and outsourcing as a way of cutting direct production costs. It also allowed, where necessary, international corporate alliances, as in the case of GEC-Alsthom or the planned merger between Renault and Volvo. In sum, the internal reforms—which frequently entailed a brutal externalization of costs onto workers and small firms—could be pursued without state intrusion and against the will of the labor unions.

The following two sections discuss two central areas of internal corporate reform: the labor-relations system writ large, and the supplier system. Both areas were at the heart of the initial restructuring to stop the crisis in the early years: massive layoffs and rapid externalization of immediate production costs. A thorough redefinition of the French production regime, however, required more than a simple reorganization to cut costs. Without the organizational prerequisites for a move into more flexible mass markets (combining high volume with high quality and product differentiation), the crisis of the French model was bound to repeat itself, probably no later than during the next downturn in the business cycle.

9.3.3 Restructuring Work and Labor Relations

A redefinition of the French production regime critically hinged on shop-floor restructuring, and that, in turn, required a reorganization of the broader labor relations system. Such a reorganization implied solving two different but related problems. The first dealt with the basic configuration of work organization and skills. French firms were traditionally highly Taylorist; as a result organizational structures were inefficient, and they incorporated a wide array of obstacles to change. Repositioning in new market segments implied a profound overhaul of the work organization system. The second issue had to do with union politics. French unions are radical and, mirroring the workplace relationships based on distrust, they are unwilling, and most likely unable, to take reform proposals, even by progressive management, seriously. However, because of their *de facto* capacity to block changes, a reorganization of the workplaces depended either upon the labor unions' goodwill (which was not forthcoming), or upon a strategy that sidelined them.

The reorganization of the internal labor market followed very rapidly after the first measures that secured the survival of the companies. Since the early 1980s, the goal of official government policy has been to assure that by the mid-1990s, four out of five young people had a certificate of finished secondary studies—until the age of 18 or 19, the so-called *baccalauréat* or *bac*. In effect, by 1995, around 75 per cent of the 1977 age cohort passed the *bac* exam, up from some 40 per cent in 1984 (Courtois 1995). As a direct result, higher education also increased tremendously: almost half the students of the 1975 cohort (aged 18 in 1993) went on to some form of higher education: 22 per cent to university, 8.5 per cent to the *écoles supérieures*, and 16 per cent to short-term higher education (the so-called *bac* +2, a technical-commercial degree) (Courtois 1995).

Alongside this quantitative increase in education, the contents of the vocational and technical training programs were reorganized as well, with France attempting to emulate the German dual training system. As was to be expected, this attempt fell considerably short of its stated ambitions, since—as the French discovered along the way (Möbus and

Verdier 1997)—many of the institutional preconditions that made the German training system work, such as strong unions and employers' associations, were simply not present in the French context. However, in their implementation, curriculum reforms echoed the actual needs of large firms. Some of the firms even managed to have new technical diplomas created and sanctioned by the Ministry of Education only for them (Verdier 1997).

While it was an important step, the revision of the vocational and technical training programs did not solve the workplace reorganization problem. The educational system may have been producing skills that were considerably more attuned to the needs of the large firms, but many of the older workers who were relatively ill equipped for the new forms of work organization remained in the factories. In response, most large firms accelerated their existing workforce reduction programs—this time, importantly, not to cut costs, but to qualitatively adjust their workforce to the new product market strategies they were adopting. Thus, as elsewhere in Europe as well (Kohli et al. 1991), the French government financed the restructuring by including many of the older workers in early retirement programs, the so-called *Fonds National de l'Emploi* (FNE) and the *Fonds Industriels de Modernisation* (FIM). They kept their income but disappeared from the factories without showing up in the unemployment statistics (Guillemard 1991). Most importantly, it allowed the large firms to replace relatively old, relatively under-skilled workers with younger, better-trained workers (Béret 1992; Midler and Charue 1993).

Thus, the basic parameters in the human resources policies of the large firms were fundamentally changed. The evolution of the educational system raised and customized the skill basis of the young workers, creating a large skills reservoir. These skills were not—and cannot be, given the initial situation—of the 'deep' technological kind that the German system produces (Soskice 1997), but involved general skills such as mathematics, languages and their application in industrial and commercial activities, software and computer knowledge, and a large set of 'social' skills, enabling the exchange of information between workers, production units inside the company, and the company and suppliers. In other words, they included a wide variety of skills peripheral to most production processes—administrative skills for low-level personnel and inventory management, as well as the skills required for quality control and interaction between different units inside the company—but that were essential to the large firms, since they allowed a restructuring of tasks and a reorganization of work. The early retirement packages, then, made sure that these younger workers could replace the older ones.

Deploying all these very different policy instruments enabled the large firms to integrate a series of tasks that had been outside the purview of production workers into their jobs, which allowed them to pursue entirely novel, more sophisticated product market strategies, away from classical mass production (Salais 1988, 1992).

It is important not to misunderstand this outcome. French workplaces are still highly Taylorist (Linhart 1991). In fact, a survey of workplace practices (Duval 1996) emphasizes that between 1984 and 1990, the central period in workplace restructuring, the number of workers in the French engineering sector who said they performed repetitive work, where the working rhythms were imposed by machines (typical characteristics of Taylorist mass production), increased by almost a third. Yet that was exactly the point of the new education programs and the way they articulated with the new workplaces: they left the core contents of the job largely untouched, but provided employers with skills for the administrative tasks *surrounding* the actual work. Since historically these had been exactly the types of jobs—administration, supervision, and maintenance—of which French companies had disproportionately many more than similar companies in other countries, *reorganizing* those tasks offered serious potential productivity increases, while the possibility to engage broader skills bases allowed for an increase in product and process complexity.

Copying practices that already existed abroad, large firms thus reorganized the production process in such a way that small groups of workers reappropriated many of the peripheral tasks: such teams of workers now perform primary maintenance tasks, low-level personnel administration (such as job rotation and holidays), quality control, inventory management, and sometimes on-line contacts with suppliers. It may still be Taylorism, but it certainly takes on a different form.

Workplace reorganization was intimately tied up with the labor-relations system, because of the capacity by the labor unions to block far-reaching changes. Thus, restructuring workplaces also required installing forms of workplace communications that circumvented the unions. To create those, firms redeployed a series of institutional innovations in the labor relations system proposed by the left-wing governments of the early 1980s to their own advantage.

In 1981 and 1982, the Assemblée passed a series of laws, the Auroux laws, which introduced new methods of direct workers' participation on the shop floor that were no longer monopolized by the labor unions. While usually the unions regarded government initiatives with a mixture of defiance and suspicion, for these reforms, both the communist CGT and the left-socialist CFDT, the two main unions at that moment, dropped their radical rhetoric and attempted to make the reforms work. The local union people, however, who were meant to implement the reforms, were incapable of playing this novel role. Since unions had been highly centralized prior to the reforms, the local union sections had in fact little or no experience with the type of *social democratic* workplace union activities that the Auroux laws had carved out for them (Eyraud and Tchobanian 1985). The fundamental discrepancy between local union capacities and the new requirements of the situation made the unions almost collapse under the weight of the new situation.

Employers' positions developed in the opposite direction. The Auroux reforms initially appeared as a fifth column to them, and it came therefore as no surprise that the employers' association CNPF and most managers resisted their introduction (Weber 1990). Gradually, however, employers began to see the advantages of the new institutions for shop-floor workers' participation that the laws created (Morville 1985). This was related to the structure of the Auroux reform project itself, which consisted of two very different reform projects, one hidden underneath the other: the first project was a blend of *German-style* social democracy and self-management ideas carried over from the 1960s, while the second was *Japanese-style* workers' integration (Howell 1992). Since the unions —the necessary ingredient for the first project to succeed—stood helplessly to the side, the second scenario of the flexible workplace revealed itself. As soon as the boom of expression groups was tapering off, French industry witnessed an explosion of management-led quality programs and shop-floor teams: from roughly 500 in 1981, the year of the Auroux reform, to over 10,000 in the summer of 1984 (Weber 1990: 446). For their internal reorganization, large firms thus simply picked from the labor-relations policies those elements that allowed them to neutralize the labor unions. In other words, what was initially a worker-oriented reform package became a management tool that helped defuse the conflict-ridden formal industrial-relations institutions and allowed for a partici-pative management model integrating workers' skills into the production system without integrating unions in the corporate decision-making structure. Put differently still, in their search for competitiveness, the large firms had simply deployed the existing policies that dealt with the training and education system, the labor market, and labor rela-tions in such a way that the measures ended up serving *their* needs, regardless of the initial intentions.

A similar argument helps to explain the reorganization of supplier relationships. Here as well, management of large firms exploited the effects of government policies for their own purposes, and used them to raise their suppliers' general technological and organizational capabilities.

9.3.4 Reorganizing Supplier Networks

The changes in the supplier relationships of the large firms have to be understood in light of the dramatic financial problems they faced in the early 1980s. Gigantic losses, high debt, and high interest rates put serious cost pressures on the large firms and, in order to clear their balance sheets, large firms attempted to externalize as many of the costs as possible. The most convenient way to resolve the financial problem was to drastically reduce in-house inventory, because it eliminated the capital costs required to carry the inventory while imposing a new mode of production which assured that these costs never reappeared. The answer was therefore the forced introduction of just-in-time delivery systems in French industry.[3]

Very soon, however, large firms realized that their suppliers were unable to meet the organizational and technological demands that these new, considerably more fragile systems imposed. The causes of these adjustment problems are historical: the upshot of the Gaullist-inspired large-firm-led development model in France (Kuisel 1981) was that small industrial firms were neglected in the modernization plans, if not downright eliminated (Ganne 1992). Despite lip service paid to the small firms, industrial policies were, in fact, almost exclusively oriented toward the large firms.[4] As a consequence, by 1980, when adjustment relied on closer relations between large and small firms in a subcontracting relationship, the industrial landscape in France in effect offered the opposite of what was needed for the reorganization: the engineers of the large firms detailed the specifications, delivery times, and work processes, and the SMEs diligently carried out the orders (Rochard 1987; Veltz 1996: 24–9). When, as a result of their own internal reorganization, the large firms imposed new complex organizational arrangements nonetheless, the suppliers suddenly faced high costs for the externalization of inventory associated with just-in-time parts delivery—so high, in fact, that the

---

[3] The first mention of *KanBan* delivery systems in the car industry is 1982–3 (Labbé 1992); other industries followed suit rapidly and by the end of the 1980s, just-in-time delivery systems were generalized in France (Gorgeu and Mathieu 1993).

[4] The French state was careful, of course, to further small artisanal firms because of their role as a political reservoir for the right, and the numerical flexibility they provided for the mass-producing large firms (Berger and Piore 1980), but not with targeted industrial policies.

adjustment process of the large firms itself was endangered by the inability of the small firms to follow adjustment.

Again, the large firms appealed to existing policies to fill the gaps in their own capabilities. The economic decentralization policies passed by the first left-wing government aimed at creating a vibrant tissue of small and medium-sized firms in the regions. While these reforms failed miserably in that goal (Levy 1999*a*), they had the inadvertent effect of providing the large firms with a wide array of regional institutional resources that they could tap into in order to *modernize* their suppliers' networks.

These reforms were geared at regions which had, as a result of the regional development program of the 1960s, in fact become industrial monocultures: even today, in almost all of the twenty-one regions outside *Île-de-France*, one large firm dominates the region in terms of output and (direct and indirect) employment (see the data per region in Quélennec 1997, and the analysis in Hancké forthcoming). As a result of their weight in those regions, the large companies were easily able to use the institutions created by the decentralization programs of the 1980s to their own advantage: they were the organizational interface between the regional institutions created or mobilized by the government, and the small firms that the policies were meant to address.

In the late 1980s, for example, Peugeot PSA used the local engineering school in the Franche-Comté region, in the east of the country, to help its steel suppliers upgrade their technologies and products to meet the new corrosion standards that the car manufacturer was adopting in its next generation of cars (Levy 1999*a*: 180 ff.). A similar rearrangement of regional resources took place in the Marseilles area, where the steel company Sollac, again the largest local company, drew on the regional training funds to adapt the skills of its workforce to the technological turn that the company was taking (Hildebrandt 1996). In cooperation with the central Ministry of Education and a local training institution, the company first created two new industry-specific technical diplomas and then used its own training center to organize the courses—financed by the public authorities. The same centre was also used to retrain the suppliers' workforce, again mainly funded by the regional authorities. Aérospatiale in Toulouse (Morin 1994), Citroën in Brittany (Gorgeu and Mathieu 1996), and chemical companies around Lyon have adopted a similar strategy of appropriating public resources for their own adjustment: local schools and training programs, regional technical universities, and the battery of local employment agencies, regional offices of the Ministries of Industry and Regional Development, as well as the Foreign

Trade Office were used to help the small firms upgrade organizationally and technologically and then support them in finding new markets.

Importantly, however, all this attention to suppliers has not led to an increase of their power in the relationship with the large firms. Despite their technological capabilities, they are rarely closely involved in product development. Product design remains heavily centralized in the large firms' product development departments, which design new products as a collection of discrete, standardized, and in principle independent modules (Ulrich 1995). The gains of this product development method for the large firms are obvious: they offer the benefits of advanced design and flexibility without losing control over the process as a whole. Despite the increased sophistication of the suppliers, the situation remains structurally biased in favour of the customers (Hancké 1998).

The new supplier policies of the large firms, and the increased reliance of the large firms upon their suppliers for system development and JIT logistics for production, thus eventually ended up reorganizing French industry into a series of regional production networks, constructed around one large firm, dominating the region in every aspect: employment, output, regional investment. Increasingly, France began to resemble a collection of quasi-autarchic regional economies, in which the SMEs subordinated themselves to the exigencies of the large firms' local plants, precisely because they were technologically and organizationally closely integrated. The regional network that thus emerged was, in turn, subordinate to the strategies conceived and developed in corporate headquarters, usually located in the Paris area. In embryonic form, this multiple-layered hierarchical structure had always existed, but after the crisis of the early 1980s, it became a building block for the large firms in their reorganization.

9.4 Corporate Reorganization in the Late 1990s

The decade between 1985 and 1996 is, as this material indicates, best seen as a hinge period between the old state-led French model, and a new set-up in which large firms are exposed to a flexible capital market. The transition from a state-led, growth-oriented model in the early 1980s to a privately owned, profit-oriented corporate sector depended critically on the capacity of management to gain autonomy which allowed them to restructure the companies.

Recent developments in the French corporate sector suggest, however, that the elite coordination mechanism which was at the core of this adjustment process has come under tremendous pressure, as a result of what looks like a second wave of corporate restructuring. Even though these events are too new to be analysed in full, a few remarks—some based on data, other of a more speculative nature—may help put these new developments in perspective by tying them to the analysis that preceded.

In late 1996, one of the cross-shareholding structures collapsed, and the years 1998–2000 have seen takeover attempts, mergers, and acquisitions among firms at the core of the French elite coordination model. At the same time, the closed French corporate governance model was rapidly replaced by a structure which relied more on outside directors (Goyer 2001), and new international institutional investors appeared on the Paris Bourse: currently 35 per cent of the shares of top forty (*CAC 40*) firms are held by foreign investors (against 11 per cent in Japan, 10 per cent in Germany, and 9 per cent in the UK—Jeffers and Plihon 2000). All this took place against a background of French companies looking abroad for acquisitions and joint ventures: since 1998, Renault has acquired a controlling stake in Nissan, EDF bought up electricity companies in Germany and the UK, Rhône-Poulenc merged with Hoechst in the new life sciences company Aventis, France Télécom acquired a large share in the German Mobilcom, and Cap Gemini has taken over the business consulting firm Ernst & Young. Compared with the tight and closed structure which existed only a few years before, by the late 1990s, the elite coordination mechanism, which had proven so useful in restructuring French firms, undoubtedly had lost a lot of its power.

On first glance, these recent changes are a direct consequence of the restructuring of the French production regime analysed before. The typical product market strategy of French exporting firms is based on rapid model cycles to stay ahead of the market, and where strategic decisions regarding product development remain centralized with the OEM. However, because it is top-heavy and evolves rapidly, such a product market strategy requires heavy investment in product development, machinery, and marketing—much more, in all likelihood, than the counterparts of French firms in other countries, who rely on more long-term product market strategies, would have to expend.

As a result of the cross-shareholdings, a lot of the capital to cover such investments was simply not available. In some cases, as much as 40 per cent of the market capitalization of the top forty firms listed on the Paris Bourse was tied up in these cross-shareholdings in the late 1990s, and combined, they immobilized FF 100 billion (*Nouvel Économiste*, 28 June 1996). These funds were badly needed at a time when competition heated up again after the recession of the early 1990s, and the fastest way to have access to it, and assure a steady flow in the future, was by opening up the capital structure of the companies. It allowed the large firms to productively invest their retained earnings and, since the volume of shares floated after the privatizations of the early 1990s was simply too large to be absorbed by French capital alone, to have access to international capital markets. Expressed in more general terms, the unravelling of the *noyaux durs* had become a necessary condition for French exporting companies to pursue an innovation path that exploited their comparative advantages, and to assure foreign investors of the transparency necessary for them to be able to evaluate corporate performance.[5]

The effects of this shift in the governance structures of the French economy are, however, far from clear. Despite the massive shift toward capital markets which are no longer organized around either banks or the state, many of the investors seem to offer a functional equivalent of long-term capital in this new set-up. The majority of the large French firms are family-owned, and the state holds large minority blocks in many of the privatized companies (*Alternatives Économiques*, June 2000). Those institutional investors which have appeared on the French scene since 1997 are themselves relatively long-term investors such as pension funds (see the data in Morin 2000), which leave the actual running of the company to management. Rather than a prima facie short-term capital structure, French companies thus appear subjected to a mitigated long-term financial regime, but one which requires and imposes much more openness on management.

Against this background, the particular French model of company organization is bound to remain relatively long term as well. Workplaces are organized on the basis of high general skills, non-union workers' participation schemes, and clearly defined training and career opportunities. Relations between large exporting firms and their suppliers, which have become relatively large firms since they passed their own wave of restructuring, may be hierarchical and highly centralized, but

---

[5] Note that this strategy is not without problems. The French innovation trajectory in the 1990s (and before) in fact consisted of two models. The first one was the flexible mass production path discussed in detail in this chapter. The other was (and is) a much more challenging form of innovation based on networking capacities that are in part provided through the state and in part through cross-shareholdings. This latter model is exemplified in telecommunications, high-speed trains, electricity provision through nuclear power, and complex armament systems—all sectors where France is among the world leaders (see a forthcoming issue of *Industry and Innovation* in the fall of 2001 on these sectors). The question is therefore if the beneficial effects of the unraveling of the system for one sector will be offset by its negative effects in the other, which still appears to rely crucially on co-ordination across different companies.

also very long term—in part because the innovation strategies of companies rely on long-term collaboration between top engineers, whose careers are determined by the internal labor markets of the large firms.

In short, the actual elite coordination mechanism is losing importance, because it may simply not be as central anymore to the operation of the French model as before. Over the last ten to fifteen years, the large exporting firms have developed the internal capabilities—often because they were sheltered by the elite system—for sustained profitability, which has both pushed and allowed them to open up their corporate governance structures. At the same time, however, the internal operations of companies seem well attuned to these new ownership structures, by offering high profits—while keeping long-term orientations in the organization of the labor market and the suppliers' structures.

In this new set-up the state organizes the background conditions for corporate profitability. As Levy (1999b) argues, social policy has now taken the place of activist industrial policy by providing companies with the tools that they need to rapidly restructure their workforce; the discussion earlier about the shifts in the educational system also indicates that the state sees its role as one of providing a high level of general skills to industry. Moreover, recent state initiatives in the labor market—most importantly, the introduction of a law generalizing a 35-hour working week in the French economy—are informed as much by a sense of social justice (lowering working hours will reduce the unemployment rate) as by an attempt to offer companies—especially the large firms—more flexible working-time arrangements: 35 hours is the annual average hours worked, thus allowing companies to flexibly adjust their work volume to immediate customer and production needs (Trumbull 2001).

9.5 Conclusion: Reinterpreting the Political Economy of France

After a crisis in the early 1980s, French industry went through a dramatic adjustment phase. During the first years of the 1980s, large firms in France were forced to search for rapid measures to rebalance the books and then set out to reorganize their internal structures to secure competitiveness. This internal reorganization was conditional upon increased management autonomy, especially from the state. The internal reorganization that followed allowed French firms to pursue new human resources policies, introduce new methods of supplier integration, and generally position themselves in new markets. At the end of this process, French firms had become among the most profitable in the OECD (Glyn

1997), able to survive even the tough 1992 recession and capable of attracting foreign investment.

While the central role of the large firms in the adjustment process heralds a profound continuity with the post-war large firm-centered French political economy, the wider strategic context for management is different. Under the old regime, large firms were policy instruments for the state; precisely that configuration is fundamentally different today. Instead of a state-led path, the French adjustment trajectory was a firm-led one. Despite some *dirigiste* attempts in the 1980s, the French state today plays a considerably smaller role in the economy than before, and has lost much of its capacity to direct industrial and economic adjustment. However, and equally important, the gap that emerged was not filled by the market, but by a mode of coordination which included elites in the state apparatus, large firms, and *haute finance*, which assured that large firms were able to construct a novel institutional environment for their own adjustment and then induce other relevant actors—the state, labor unions, the workforce, other companies, and the financial world—to act according to their preferences.

This novel perspective on France—firm-led instead of state- or market-led adjustment—not only helps make sense of the developments since the early 1980s, it also sheds new light on an old theme in the study of France—the *société bloquée*. According to this perspective, reforms are difficult to implement in France, because they are conceived with strong societal actors in mind (in recent years because they were *technocratically* copied from the successful German experience), but the actors are too weak to become the social bearers of the policies. The result is policy failure—and a more general fundamental inability of the country to reform its political economy. The financial deregulation, for example, led to elite-controlled cross-shareholdings instead of popular capitalism (Bauer 1988; Maclean 1995), because the banks were incapable of playing the new monitoring role designed for them (Goyer 1998). The Auroux workplace reform resulted in weaker instead of—as intended—stronger labor unions, because the unions were incapable of turning the institutional innovation into advantages for themselves (Howell 1992). And the decentralization of policy-making led to an increased dependence on Paris instead of the construction of new policy-making systems in the regions to support industrial development, because the regional associations were unable to provide the type of interface between the firms targeted and the regional institutes that were supposed to serve them (Levy 1999*a*). Reforms turned into failures because the social actors that were critical for their implementation were too weak.

Changing the perspective to the large firms as the central agents in the French political economy puts these apparent failures into a fundamentally different light. In their adjustment the large firms deployed the resources provided by these policies on their own terms. The financial deregulation allowed large-firm CEOs to construct a broad sphere of autonomy; the Auroux laws provided large firms with institutions to defuse the perennial workplace conflict; and the administrative decentralization policies offered the large firms instruments to upgrade their regional supplier base. In short, by shifting the perspective to strategic adjustment by the large firms, policy initiatives that are documented as dramatic failures take the shape of institutional resources for the large firms—a very different idea indeed than what is offered by the *société bloquée* and one which suggests that this notion is up for reevaluation (Suleiman 1995).

Recent developments in the French political economy leave little doubt that the country is passing through a second wave of corporate restructuring: many of the elite networks that proved crucial to adjustment in the last two decades have disintegrated, and the corporate governance system of the large companies that has driven economic adjustment in France since the mid-1980s has been entirely restructured as well with the massive advent of foreign investors.

The jury is still out on what this implies for the French production regime. While many argue that this heralds a fundamental shift to the Anglo-Saxon regime, a careful look at some of the data indicates that the French political economy retains, even after capital markets have become more flexible, specifically French characteristics. Corporate profitability is and remains high, companies have found a functional equivalent of long-term capital on the Paris Bourse, the internal organization of companies retains a long-term orientation, and the state plays a strong role in supply-side adjustment.

The main difference between the old and the new French political economy is that today the state no longer directly intervenes in the economy (as the low-key role of the Ministry of Finance in the bank takeover attempt in the summer of 1999 and in the Elf–Total merger in that year suggest), but concentrates on offering a social policy framework which furthers economic restructuring and competitiveness. While it may still be an activist state in comparative perspective (compare with Boix 1998), French governments today, of all political colour, seem to be working on the assumption that corporate needs for flexibility and profitability, instead of economic growth and broader technological and social policies, should be at the heart of policy-making.

PART III

CORPORATE GOVERNANCE, FIRM STRATEGY, AND THE LAW

10

Varieties of Corporate Governance: Comparing Germany and the UK

Sigurt Vitols

A key concern of the varieties of capitalism (VoC) approach is the topic of corporate governance, one aspect of which is the relationship between firms and external providers of finance (see the Introduction to this book). The literature on corporate governance, which originated in the USA and UK, initially was concerned with a fairly narrow set of issues: how can shareholders monitor and motivate management to act in their interests, i.e. to improve 'shareholder value' through increasing share price (Keasy and Wright 1997; Prowse 1994; Williamson 1988)? In recent years, however, comparative work in this area has increasingly taken a broader view of the relationships involved in running companies, and it is now commonplace to distinguish between two different models of corporate governance: the 'shareholder' model, in which the maximization of shareholder value is the primary goal of the firm and only shareholders enjoy strong formalized links with top management; and the 'stakeholder' model, in which a variety of firm constituencies—including employees, suppliers and customers, and the communities companies are located in—enjoy 'voice' in the firm and whose interests are to be balanced against each other in management decision-making (Kelly et al. 1997). Most comparativists in this area have claimed that one or the other model is economically superior and that, over time, we should see convergence towards this model of 'best practice'. Although the shareholder model was heavily criticized in the early 1990s for the tendencies to under-invest and focus on short-term results (Porter 1990), at present the majority view is that the shareholder model will prevail due to the increasing dominance of institutional investors on international capital markets (Lazonick and O'Sullivan 2000).

This debate is of great interest to the VoC approach for a number of reasons. First of all, VoC offers a framework within which the linkages

This chapter draws on the results of a joint WZB–LSE project funded by the Anglo-German Foundation and conducted 1995–7 as well as on subsequent research by the author.

between external investors and other actors relevant to the firm can be
systematically explored. The concepts of coordinated market economies
(CMEs) and liberal market economies (LMEs) provide a broader institutional context within which stakeholder and shareholder models of
governance, respectively, can be analyzed. Secondly, since VoC stresses
the embeddedness of national institutions as well as the possibility of
'complementarities' between different combinations of these institutions,
VoC hypothesizes that responses to internationalizing capital markets
other than convergence are possible. Companies may respond very
differently to similar sorts of pressures and distinct sets of 'best practice'
contingent on the national context may emerge.

This chapter attempts to apply such a broader approach to corporate
governance by examining the interaction between large firms and
national institutions in Germany and the UK in the context of internationalizing capital markets. The first section relates the discussion on
shareholder versus stakeholder models of corporate governance to VoC
through an analysis of the major sets of institutions influencing post-war
company decision-making—institutions concerning ownership, industrial relations and employee representation, and the structure of management. Germany, a CME, has 'non-market' institutions, which not only
allow for inter-firm coordination, but also regulate the interaction
between owners and managers, between employees and firms, and
among top managers. In the corporate governance literature Germany is
one of the foremost examples of the stakeholder model, since the different firm constituencies enjoy a strong formal 'voice' in decision-making
through representation on company boards. In contrast, in the UK, an
LME, markets play a much more significant role not only in influencing
inter-firm relationships but also in regulating the interactions between
the actors mentioned above. The UK is one of the primary examples
of the shareholder model of governance due to the weak formalized role
of constituencies other than shareholders in firm decision-making.

The second section of this chapter examines changes in institutions
affecting corporate governance in the two countries in recent years,
in particular reforms in financial regulation, labor law, and company
law. A widespread view is that, since international capital markets are
increasingly dominated by diversified portfolio investors (such as
mutual funds and pension funds) seeking higher returns, companies
must adopt the shareholder model or be starved of the external capital
needed to invest and survive. Thus, in order to promote the competitiveness of 'their' firms, governments in countries where the stakeholder
model is predominant are forced to abandon the institutions promoting

stakeholding. The analysis in this section shows that, with the partial exception of financial regulation in Germany, these developments can be clearly characterized as incremental—rather than fundamental—changes in existing ownership, employee representation, and top management institutions.

The third section of this chapter relates the above discussion on institutions to the different comparative advantages enjoyed by large companies and the financial and innovation strategies pursued by these companies in the two countries (see Table 10.1). Non-market institutions in Germany, which give 'voice' to the different constituencies of the firm, encourage firm-specific investments but also discourage radical innovation and organizational changes due to high 'sunk costs.' Market relationships in the UK in contrast represent weaker and less costly barriers to radical innovation but also pressure companies to exit markets quickly when profitability decreases. Drawing on examples mainly from financial services and diversified chemical/pharmaceutical firms, this section highlights two key differences between companies in the two countries in responding to the demands of international investors. One difference is that, although greater attention is being paid to institutional investors in both countries, 'shareholder value' principles in the UK are typically implemented in a top-down manner by the chief

TABLE 10.1 Corporate governance institutions and firm strategies in the UK and Germany

	UK	Germany
Dominant ownership structure	Small shareholdings by portfolio investors	Large shareholdings by strategic investors
Employee representation institutions	Voluntarist	Corporatist (board-level co-determination)
Top management institutions	Single board dominated by CEO	Dual board Multiple power centers
Primary corporate goal	Profitability	Multiple goals: profitability, market share, and employment security
Competitive strategy	Radical innovation in new sectors Price competition in established sectors	Non-price competition through incremental innovation

executive officer (CEO). In Germany, in contrast, consensus on changes is generally reached before implementation through negotiation among top managers with different functional responsibilities and between top managers and employee representatives ('negotiated shareholder value'). This difference has significant consequences for the types of employment bargains and the kinds of performance incentives that are evolving in companies in the two countries. A second difference is that, although investors are increasingly pressuring diversified companies in the two countries to sell off or close down peripheral operations in order to focus on 'core competencies,' large German companies are generally either relocating their 'radically innovative' activities in the UK or USA or exiting these types of activities entirely. As a result, country specialization in different types of innovative activities appears to be increasing rather than decreasing.

10.1 Corporate Governance Institutions in the UK and Germany

Traditional approaches to corporate governance, which developed in the USA and UK, have been concerned mainly with the fundamental conflict of interest between shareholders and top management. Whereas shareholders primarily have a financial interest in increasing the value of their shares in the firm, management may be more interested in private consumption (such as luxurious corporate headquarters or a fleet of corporate jets) or the status enjoyed with creating a large, highly visible company through mergers ('empire-building').

Although this problem was flagged in the academic literature as early as the 1930s (Berle and Means 1932), its appearance as a significant policy issue is intimately linked with the rise of the 'institutional investor'. These investors are primarily pension funds or mutual funds that manage huge pools of financial assets using modern portfolio techniques, i.e. by investing relatively small amounts of capital in a large number of diversified companies. Companies are monitored mainly through a limited number of quantifiable financial variables and decisions on entering or exiting investments are made on the basis of fairly simple decision rules. Institutional investing is increasingly characterized by intense competition to outperform standardized 'benchmarks' such as the weighted share performance of Standard and Poors's largest 500 companies in the USA or the *Financial Times* (FTSE) top 100 companies in the UK. Outperformance of these indexes is important for mutual funds to attract retail customers. Pension funds are also increasingly contracting out much of the monitoring and investment work to professional 'money managers' whose performance is evaluated on an annual basis.

The literature of corporate governance in the USA and UK initially was largely concerned with the point of view of institutional investors and with the relationship between these investors and management as 'the' key problem in running companies: what kinds of institutions are available to monitor and motivate management? In this model of corporate governance other problems, such as the nature of company strategy and human resources policy, were subordinated to this primary issue. As a broader range of countries were examined, however, it became apparent that this conception of corporate governance was dominant in only some countries. In many countries shareholders are considered to be only one of a number of key constituencies of the firm, and increasing share price through boosting profitability may be only one of the top priorities (or even a secondary priority) of the firm. Interestingly enough the characterization of this alternative as a 'stakeholding' model of corporate governance was coined in the UK by critics of the shareholder model (Hutton 1995; Kelly et al. 1997). According to them one of the strongest contrasts to the UK is provided by Germany, which has not only very different *ownership patterns* and *financial institutions*, but also has a very different structure of *industrial relations* and *employee representation* and also *organization of the firm*. Significantly, markets (as opposed to non-market institutions) regulate all of these kinds of relationships to a much greater extent in the UK than in Germany. These institutional differences are reflected in different corporate practices, including longer investment time-horizons and a greater concern with the impact of decisions on different constituencies of the firm. It is worthwhile to go into these differences in some detail and to paint a stylized picture of the models as they currently exist, before turning to the issue of recent regulatory changes and the possibility of fundamental change in corporate governance in the future.

10.1.1 The Institutions of Ownership

The relationship between owners and large companies in the UK is regulated by one of the most highly developed national equity markets. The major investors in the UK—investment funds, pension funds, and (to a certain extent) insurance companies—take a 'portfolio' approach to risk management by taking small stakes in a large number of companies. Furthermore, these portfolio investors are generally solely interested in a high return on their shares (and thus primarily on the profitability of

TABLE 10.2 Percentage of total shares in circulation held by different sectors in Germany and the UK, end of 1995

	Germany	United Kingdom
Households	14.6	29.6
Enterprises	42.1	4.1
Public sector	4.3	0.2
Banks	10.3	2.3
Insurance enterprises and pension funds	12.4	39.7
Investment funds and other financial institutions	7.6	10.4
Rest of world	8.7	13.7
Total	100.0	100.0

Source: Deutsche Bundesbank (1997: 29).

the company invested in). These portfolio investors together hold 50 per cent of shares in the UK (see Table 10.2). Households, which for the most part also have small shareholdings, account for another 30 per cent of ownership. Thus the types of investors generally taking smaller shareholdings account for 80 per cent of shareholdings in Britain. The types of investors more likely to take large strategic shareholdings—enterprises, the public sector, and banks—account for less than 7 per cent of shareholdings.

Owner–company relationships in Germany in contrast are much more likely to be characterized by one or more large shareholders with a strategic (rather than purely share value maximization) motivation for ownership. Ninety per cent of listed companies in Germany have a shareholder with at least a 10 per cent stake in the company (Seibert 1997). The types of investors likely to have strategic interests—enterprises, banks, and the public sector—hold 57 per cent of shares (or 42.1 per cent, 10.3 per cent, and 4.3 per cent respectively). Enterprises generally pursue strategic business interests. Large German banks have tended to view their shareholdings as a mechanism for protecting their loans and strengthening their business relationships with companies rather than as a direct source of income. They often are able to multiply their effective voting power through the extensive use of proxy voting rights, particularly for households. The state generally pursues some public goal. In contrast, the ownership types having smaller shareholdings—

investment funds, pension funds/insurance companies, and households —account for only 35 per cent of total shareholdings (or 7.6 per cent, 12.4 per cent and 14.6 per cent respectively).

Thus the UK is characterized by dispersed ownership by share-price-oriented financial institutions while Germany is characterized by concentrated ownership by actors pursuing a mix of financial and strategic goals.

10.1.2 The Institutions of Employee Representation

A second important institutional difference between the two countries relates to the area of employee representation. Employees in large German companies enjoy strong 'voice' through corporatist bargaining and co-determination. Every plant with at least five regular employees is entitled under the Works Constitution Act of 1972 (*Betriebsverfassungsgesetz*) to elect a works council. This works council has the right to negotiate key issues with management, including the hiring of new employees, introduction of new technology, use of overtime and short-working time, and, in the case of mass redundancies, the negotiation of social plans (*Sozialpläne*) covering redeployment, severance payments, and early retirement.

Employee representatives are also included on German supervisory boards under the 1976 Co-Determination Act (*Mitbestimmungsgesetz*), which applies to almost all companies with 2,000 or more employees.[1] This law has the following key provisions:

- Employee representatives are to comprise half of supervisory board representatives and shareholder representatives the other half. Shareholders, however, elect the chairperson, who may cast a tie-breaking vote in case of a 'deadlock' between shareholder and employee blocks.
- The number of supervisory board seats are to total 12 in the case of companies with between 2,000 and 10,000 employees, 16 in the case of companies with between 10,000 and 20,000 employees, and 20 in the case of companies with above 20,000 employees.
- In the case of companies with between 2,000 and 20,000 employees, two employee representatives can be union functionaries (i.e. non-employees); in the case of companies with more than 20,000 employees, three may be union functionaries.

[1] A second, stronger form of co-determination applies only to companies mainly involved in steel and coal mining (*Montanmitbestimmung*). A third, weaker form of co-determination under the Works Constitution Act of 1952, as amended in 1972, applies to most companies with between 500 and 2,000 employees.

In practice there is typically a close overlap between co-determination at the board level and plant level; the head employee representative on the supervisory board is typically a leading works council member.

In Britain, in contrast, there are no legal provisions for employee representation on company boards. In only a few exceptional cases is there an informal practice of including a union representative on the board. The establishment of European Works Councils (EWCs) in larger British firms has up to now had little influence on company practice due to the limitation of most EWC meetings to information exchange, differences in industrial-relations traditions, and the inexperience of many employee representatives.

10.1.3 The Institutions Structuring Top Management

The different strengths and interests of owners and employees in the two countries are expressed in the different board systems and corporate constitutions in the two countries. German large companies are characterized by a pluralist system whereas British companies are characterized by a CEO-dominated system.

The clearest manifestation of pluralism in large German companies is the dual company board system. Strategic decisions such as major investments, mergers and acquisitions, dividend policy, changes in capital structure, and appointment of top managers are made by the supervisory board (*Aufsichtsrat*). The day-to-day running of the company in contrast is the responsibility of the management board (*Vorstand*), which generally meets once a week and includes between five and ten top managers in the company. The management board is clearly separated from the supervisory board. No individual is allowed to be simultaneously a member of both the supervisory and management board. While the management board has a chair or 'speaker', his or her role is generally the case of 'first among equals.' Top managers have a great deal of autonomy in their individual areas of responsibility (generally defined by function such as finance, production, personnel and social policy, etc.). Major decisions or proposals to the supervisory board are reached through consensus. The separate appointment of managers by the supervisory board reduces the dependency of individual members on the chair/speaker.

Large British companies in contrast are generally run by a CEO-dominated single board. This CEO is often also the chair of the board and either hand-picks or plays a major role in choosing the other members of the board. The typical leadership style is for the CEO, after a period of consultation with other managers, to make major decisions alone and to take sole responsibility for these decisions.

10.1.4 Summing Up

Relationships between the typical large German company and its various constituencies are largely governed by non-market institutions. Owner-ship in Germany is highly concentrated in the hands of long-term, strategic actors with multiple links with the company; a corporatist system of employee representation gives employees formal participation rights on both the plant and company level; and German company law creates a framework for consensus bargaining between different func-tional areas of the firm by dispersing authority among the top level of management. Relationships in the UK, in contrast, are regulated to a much greater extent by markets. Equity markets in the UK are charac-terized by dispersed ownership by financial institutions mainly inter-ested in increasing share price; the voluntarist labor-relations system in the UK provides employees with no formal 'voice' in corporate decision-making; and the authority of managers is much less structured than in Germany and more dependent upon the current market situation.

10.2 Changes in the Institutions Involved in Corporate Governance

Although it is clear that there are significant differences between the UK and Germany in the institutions involved in corporate governance, a key question is how enduring these differences are within the context of 'globalization.' In the early 1990s a vocal minority within the UK and USA claimed that the stakeholder model would have to be adopted in these countries if they wanted their industries to remain competitive in world markets. As the stakeholder models in Germany and Japan ran into their own sets of competitive problems, however, the debate has shifted to focus much more on the power of institutional investors to force convergence to a shareholder model. Institutional investors are increasingly willing to invest outside of their 'home country' and now 'scan the world' in search of investment opportunities offering the poten-tial of higher returns. In order to attract the capital needed to modernize industry from these investors, it is claimed, countries in which the stake-holder model is dominant will have to abandon the institutions supporting stakeholding (Jürgens et al. 2000).

The VoC approach, however, recognizes that the barriers to fundamental institutional change are very high and is therefore skeptical about wholesale convergence arguments. Institutions derive from deeply rooted historical traditions and typically are defended at the least by vested interests if not by powerful actors within national systems who will recognize the comparative advantages of their institutions. The typical nature of institutional change should therefore be incremental, reflecting the politics of bargaining between 'traditionalists' and 'modernizers.'

To what extent has change in the institutions involved in corporate governance in the UK and Germany actually followed this 'incrementalist' path? Advocates of radical change can in fact be found in both the UK and Germany. In the UK parts of the left wing of the Labour Party and segments of the trade union movement have advocated the importation of the German model of 'stakeholder capitalism' to combat an alleged short-termism in industry (Kelly et al. 1997). In Germany vocal advocates of a radical 'free-market' approach to corporate governance and financial regulation can be found (Rosen 1997). Nevertheless, it is striking that these advocates are clearly in the minority and have little actual influence on the process of change in the two countries. An analysis of change in the areas of financial regulation, labor law, and company law shows that, with the partial exception of financial regulation in Germany, changes can be clearly characterized as incremental.

10.2.1 Institutional Change in Germany

The most important legal changes in Germany in the past few years in the area of corporate governance have been in the areas of *company law* and *financial regulation*. In terms of company law change can clearly be characterized as incremental; the case of financial regulation is more complex, but the elements of continuity are perhaps more striking than the fundamental changes that have been made.

The first significant reform of company law in over twenty years was effected through the Law for Control and Transparency in Large Companies (*Kontrag*) (taking effect in 1998), which modifies the Joint Stock Company Law of 1965 (*Aktiengesetz*). The first significant point is that the reform effort was motivated much more by corporate scandals rather than the desire to adopt Anglo-American corporate principles. The law was an initiative of the Kohl government as a political response to a number of major failures of supervisory board oversight (Metallgesellschaft, Bremer Vulkan, Balsam). Thus the most significant provisions of the law strengthen the supervisory board vis-à-vis management, for example in allowing the supervisory board to choose and independently meet with the firm hired to audit company accounts. The law also modifies the personal liability of corporate directors to try to make lawsuits a more credible mechanism for ensuring accountability of board members for their decisions. While the law also authorizes the use of stock options for managers and share buy-back programs to allow German companies to adopt 'typical' Anglo-American practices, this was clearly a secondary goal of the reform, and support from German industry was lukewarm.

Altogether then what is most significant about the *Kontrag* reform is how many fundamental aspects of German company law were not changed. Neither the dual board system nor the principle of employee board representation were ever seriously questioned. The basic principle of the Joint Stock Company Law of 1965, that is, that neither shareholders, top managers, nor employees should exert unilateral control in the company (Hefermehl 1991), remains intact. Even a relatively minor proposal contained in the draft legislation, which did not question the concept of stakeholder representation on the board but in fact would have reduced the size of supervisory boards, was not included in the ultimate version of the law due to opposition of trade unions.[2]

A somewhat more complex case is posed by a set of laws reforming financial regulation (Second and Third Laws for the Promotion of Financial Markets) in Germany. After more than a decade of opposing pressure from the USA to substitute corporatist regulatory mechanisms with American-style financial reform through establishing an independent oversight agency modeled on the Securities Exchange Commission, Germany has taken important steps in the 1990s (through the Second and Third Laws for the Promotion of Financial Markets) to introduce some Anglo-American-style institutions into its financial markets. These changes have been supported mainly by the large private German banks (particularly the Deutsche Bank and the Dresdner Bank), who have become pessimistic about the chances of achieving high profits through traditional corporate lending, and now wish to compete with US and UK investment banks for more capital-market-based income such as underwriting, asset management, derivatives, and trading on own account (Lütz 1996). This small but powerful group of private banks clearly do

---

[2] Although the principle of parity employee representation would have been preserved, a reduction in the total number of board seats would have meant a reduction in the total number of employee representatives sitting on boards. The remuneration associated with holding a board seat is an important means for rewarding works council and trade union activists.

see the USA as 'the model' for financial regulation and have pushed for financial reform to try to increase the significance of capital markets (and thus market-related business) in their 'home territory.' Thus the Second Law (from 1991) established oversight of securities markets through an SEC-style Bundesaufsichtsamt für Wertpapierhandel and imposed insider-trading prohibitions. The Third Law (passed in 1997) liberalizes restrictions on mutual funds and venture capital companies and allows more liberal listing requirements to try to encourage more German and foreign companies to list on the German stock exchange.

Although these reforms have led to a more liquid and transparent stock exchange for the largest German companies (particularly the largest thirty companies contained in the Deutscher Aktienindex or DAX), what is perhaps more significant about these laws is the elements of continuity that remain. The vast majority of German companies are in fact not listed on the stock exchange, remain embedded in 'relational networks' including their local banks, and continue to receive their external finance mainly in the form of bank loans. The most important banking group—especially for the vast *Mittelstand* (i.e. small and medium-sized companies)—remains the publicly owned municipal savings bank sector (*Sparkassen*), which continues to account for more than half of all banking system assets in Germany. Furthermore, although a slight trend in investment in favor of stocks can be noted, in fact no steps have been taken to radically change the distribution of ownership of financial assets or the distribution of these assets between different categories. The biggest step that could be taken in this direction is to promote US- and UK-style pension funds and mutual funds by creating tax incentives for employers and employees to defer compensation. Such a proposal was in fact made by the nascent mutual fund industry in Germany (and in fact included in the draft of the Third Law), but due to opposition from the insurance industry this was dropped. Thus although financial markets have been somewhat liberalized, the increase in the relative importance of the types of institutional investors dominant in the UK, i.e. pension funds and mutual funds, will be limited.

10.2.2 Institutional Change in the UK

The debate on the need for significant changes in British corporate governance dates back at least to the issue of short-termism in British industry in the 1960s and 1970s. The Labour Party had endorsed the nationalization of the top 100 companies and industrial-relations commissions recommended a statutory requirement for works councils-style institutions. While this debate died down during the Thatcher government in the 1980s, the deep recession of the early 1990s revitalized it. An extensive argument for a German-style stakeholder model of governance (Hutton 1995) achieved best-seller status and the concept was tentatively endorsed by the then candidate Tony Blair in his famous Singapore speech.

However, change under the Conservative governments in the 1990s took the form of the voluntary acceptance of codes rather than statutory change. The most significant developments here were the recommendations of the Greenbury, Cadbury, and Hampel committees:

- The Cadbury Committee, which was established in 1991 in response to a number of large corporate failures (Polly Peck, BCCI, the Maxwell companies), was given a mandate to investigate problems in financial aspects of the UK corporate governance system. The Committee issued recommendations for a voluntary 'code' of best practice. The Cadbury Committee recommendations have led to a focus on *accountability* and the role of boards and non-executives: how are the activities of chief executives to be controlled?
- The Greenbury Committee, which was set up in 1995 in response to the public perception that the top management of privatized utilities were receiving excessive pay increases, focused on the issue of determination of executive remuneration.
- The Hampel Committee, the successor to the Cadbury Committee, has recently issued a draft report and is planning to propose a 'supercode' combining and updating the Cadbury and Greenbury codes. While the Cadbury and Greenbury committees were concerned more with the *accountability* of top management, the Hampel Committee is striving to address also the forward-looking issue of business prosperity or entrepreneurship.

What is significant about these reports is that they all recommended the voluntary acceptance of codes of best practice. None of these codes suggested implementing corporatist labor practices such as the inclusion of employee representatives on the boards, nor the encouragement of large shareholders. Although the Cadbury Code did recommend that the posts of CEO and chairperson be held by two separate people to reduce unilateral control, this recommendation has not been followed by many prominent companies (e.g. Glaxo/Wellcome, the largest pharmaceutical company in the UK).

Although Tony Blair appeared to endorse the concept of stakeholding before the elections of 1998, since the Labour victory he has stressed the need to carefully study the issue of corporate governance and to reach consensus with the business community before making any significant changes. A large commission has in fact been appointed to study corporate governance and to make concrete recommendations and does include a number of strong advocates of the stakeholder model. However, the long-time period granted to the commission (three years), the minority position of stakeholder advocates and their pragmatic decision to push for changes which are limited yet 'feasible', and the context of a Labour government unwilling to take measures opposed by business clearly mean that this commission is unlikely to be a vehicle for introducing serious 'stakeholding' elements into the British political economy.

10.3 Impact of Corporate Governance on Product Market and Innovation Strategies

This section explores the relationship between these institutions and company strategy regarding product markets and innovation. It will be claimed that, although both British and German companies are responding to the internationalization of capital markets by paying more attention to institutional investors and (particularly in the case of highly diversified companies) by focusing more on their areas of 'core competencies,' in fact there are two significant differences in the typical adjustment pattern of the two groups of companies. First, whereas shareholder value principles tend to be introduced unilaterally by the CEO in British companies, these principles have to be negotiated on a consensus basis among top management and between management and the works council before implementation. This 'negotiated shareholder value' has consequences for the types of performance incentives and employment relations that are evolving in the two groups of companies.[3] The second difference is that British companies tend to define their core competencies more clearly in new, often 'radically innovative', markets than German firms, which focus more on traditional, 'incrementally innovative' markets. Thus a tendency to divest non-core operations actually leads to a stronger pattern of industrial specialization rather than the convergence of industrial profiles between the UK and Germany.

---

[3] See Wever (1995) on the related concept of 'negotiated competitiveness' in Germany.

10.3.1 Institutions and Firm Strategies

Most sectors are characterized by some degree of heterogeneity in products and innovation strategy with regard to the introduction of new or improved products. Thus firms are faced with the strategic questions of how to position themselves within given product markets as well as whether they wish to be market leaders or market followers with respect to the introduction of new products (Porter 1990). A firm-based approach to political economy seeks to establish the link between variation in national corporate governance institutions and typical product market and innovation strategies of companies based in different countries.

As reviewed in the last section, in the UK the dominant owners are portfolio investors who are primarily interested in share price and diversify shareholdings across many companies. Due to this diversification of risk, they are willing to accept higher risk of individual investments as long as the overall expected return on the portfolio is higher. Although these dispersed, portfolio-based shareholders exercise little 'voice' in company decision-making, they support high-profitability strategies through buying shares and withdraw support by 'exiting' through the sale of shares. The CEO has a direct interest in the profitability of the company and share price (through tying a higher proportion of remuneration to performance and providing this in the form of stock and stock options). As a result, the incentives of the CEO and dominant investors are strongly aligned toward strategies involving moving quickly into new product markets and developing new products. At the same time, companies have a strong incentive to move out of stagnating or declining industries, i.e. industries in which competitive pressures are increasing and thus profitability is declining.

This shareholder interest is supported by flexible external labor markets and internal promotion and remuneration practices. Due to the weak attachment of employees to firms, British companies can quickly hire and reward (through strong performance incentives) 'top talent' in new areas. This top talent is needed to pursue radical innovation strategies involved in developing products in new fields (Soskice 1997). At the same time, these companies can have mass layoffs fairly easily, both because unions are weak and because qualified employees have a good chance of finding a new job.

In Germany, pressures to undertake higher-profitability, higher-risk strategies are weaker and countervailing pressures for conservative strategies are stronger. Profitability and share price play a weaker role in the interests of the dominant shareholders. Other companies invest for strategic reasons; they generally have invested because of strategic interests and thus are equally or more concerned with market share or technological developments. Banks may have a strong interest in conservative policies to preserve the value of their loans (and also to protect the value of investments of their retail customers). The state is concerned with promoting public goals. Thus there is not as much pressure to enter new markets or exit stagnating or declining industries. This is reinforced by employee representatives and co-determination. Representatives have an interest in a strong commitment to existing sectors, thus the preservation of jobs and the build-up of firm-specific human capital.

There is considerable evidence supporting this stylized picture of the differences between German and British companies. At the macro level, a much higher proportion of chief executives in British companies said that they would protect dividends at the expense of employment (89 per cent versus 41 per cent for Germany) (Itami 1999). Overall manufacturing, and particularly medium-tech manufacturing (specialized products in traditional areas such as chemicals, machinery, and autos), plays a much more prominent role in Germany than in the UK. However, high-tech manufacturing (such as pharmaceuticals and information technology) is relatively more important in the UK than in Germany (BMBF 1996; Matraves 1997). The extent of corporate restructuring—e.g. selling off of divisions, mergers with other companies, and acquisition of new operations—is much more extensive in the UK than in Germany (Richter 1997).

A close look at the sectoral and company level also supports this view. In particular, a survey of the financial services and pharmaceutical/chemical industries shows that companies have responded with different product market and innovation strategies in the two countries.

10.3.2 Financial Services

In the post-war period, banking was one of the most profitable sectors in industrialized countries. As a result of the post-1929 worldwide financial crisis regulatory regimes were established to enhance the stability of banking systems. Formal and informal barriers to entry were increased and mechanisms such as maximum interest rates on deposits helped control costs. At the same time, demand for loans for corporations and consumers was high due to rapid economic growth and consumption. The rate of innovation was low, in part because of regulatory opposition to new products. The largest banks focused mainly on 'traditional' commercial banking activities, i.e. taking in deposits from and making loans to corporations and retail customers.[4]

In the past two decades, however, a number of trends have changed the nature of product markets in banking and related financial service areas. First, there has been a strong trend toward deregulation of deposit interest rates and barriers to entry in banking. Second, as economic growth has slowed, demand for bank loans has been reduced and bank competition for loans has increased, thereby driving down the interest rate margin (i.e. profits made on the gap between interest paid on deposits and interest received on loans) and thus the profitability of banks. Third, while traditional banking business (deposit-taking and loan origination) has been stagnating, demand for investment banking and asset management products has increased. This has resulted from the increased pace of corporate restructuring activities (mergers and acquisitions and associated financing packages), the greater sophistication of middle- and upper middle-class households (mutual funds and financial planning), and more demand for hedging against or speculating on greater financial instability (derivatives and swaps). Finally, the development of information technology has simultaneously increased the ability both to customize financial products and to save labor in the provision of simpler services, for example through automated tellers (ATMs), call centers, and paperless processing of transactions.

Large German and British banks have responded to these general developments in very different ways. In the UK, the 'Big Four' banks (Barclays, National Westminster, Midland, and Lloyds) responded to new opportunities in investment banking and asset management very rapidly.[5] All four entered investment banking with 'Big Bang' and have strongly moved into asset management activities.[6]

At the same time, these banks aggressively took advantage of information technology to save labor in more traditional banking areas. In particular during the recession of the early 1990s heavy investments were made in automated tellers and electronic transactions in order to reduce workforce and close down many retail branches.

---

[4] According to a popular anecdote, bank managers during this era could be successful simply by following the '3–6–3 rule'—take in deposits at 3% interest, lend out the money at 6% interest, and be at the golf course by 3 in the afternoon.

[5] Midland has been subsequently acquired by Hong Kong Shanghai Bank (HSBC Holdings), originally a British colonial bank centered in Hong Kong.

[6] As many other banks are entering investment banking and thus competition is increasing, it now appears that some of these banks are already selectively exiting this area. Barclays, for example, has sold much of its capital markets operations.

The 'Big Three' German banks (Deutsche Bank, Dresdner Bank, and Commerzbank) responded to these similar pressures in a very different way than the British banks. First, these banks developed significant international investment banking operations much later.[7] The Deutsche Bank, the largest German bank, relied on the purchase of the British merchant bank Morgan Grenfell in 1989 as its main mechanism for entry. Dresdner Bank, the second largest German bank, also took a similar path six years later by acquiring another British merchant bank, Kleinwort Benson, in 1995. Commerzbank, which to date has not made such an acquisition, is relying on internal growth to build up its (still insignificant) international investment banking activities.

At the same time, the Big Three German banks have been much slower in 'rationalizing' retail banking than their British counterparts. In the late 1970s and 1980s these banks had actually combined investments in information technology with a mass upskilling of the bank workforce (Oberbeck and Baethge 1989). The proportion of bank employees trained through a three-year apprenticeship increased dramatically. Information technology was used to increase the proportion of workforce in customer service occupations (as opposed to 'backroom' functions) and to enable these customer service employees to in principle sell all of the bank's products to a customer ('one-stop-shopping'). While significant investments in ATMs have been made and some division of labor between customized and more routine tasks introduced, the pace of workforce reductions is much more moderate than in the British case.

These differences can be seen in the aggregate data. One widespread measure of profitability, return on equity (RoE), shows that UK banks are about twice as profitable as German banks. UK banks receive only half of their profits from interest income (i.e. traditional deposit-taking and loan-making business) as opposed to two-thirds for German banks.

These different patterns of change can in large part be attributed to the different corporate governance system in Germany. A key characteristic of change at the UK banks is that it has been very much been tied up with one individual, who (if need be) can restructure the company board and implement change despite employee opposition. For example, Martin Taylor, CEO of Barclays, played such a key role.

In Germany in contrast the nature of change has been influenced by all three elements of the corporate governance system, including strategic ownership, corporatist employee representation, and the structure of

---

[7] This late entry took place despite the fact that these banks are 'universal banks' and have thus always been involved in investment banking as well as commercial banking at the domestic level.

management. Despite their poor profit performance, German banks have felt little pressure to improve profitability. Although not as extensive as the Japanese *keiretsu*, the core shareholders of the large German banks include other banks (through cross-shareholdings) as well as the insurance companies such as Allianz.

The strength of employee representation through co-determination has also played an important role. These representatives initially insisted on the 'mass upskilling' strategy for implementing information technology in the late 1970s and early 1980s. In the 1990s they have insisted on slowing the pace of workforce layoffs and branch closings. They have also opposed important management demands for promoting Frankfurt as an international financial market, e.g. in extending working hours or in increasing the amount of incentive pay.

Finally, the post-war internal culture of these banks has been heavily biased toward commercial banking; involvement in corporate lending was seen as the best way to promote one's career within the bank and to increase chances of promotion to the management board. These 'traditionalists' have been able to slow the pace of change despite the full commitment of the management board chairs of Deutsche Bank in the 1990s (Herrhausen, Kopper, Breuer) to a shift to a focus on investment banking.[8]

10.3.3 Chemical/Pharmaceutical Industry

Large companies in the German and UK chemical/pharmaceutical industries generally follow the same national patterns of change as the banking industry. The similarity of these divergent patterns in these two sectors—despite very different technical bases—strengthens the case for the argument that national institutions are the key influence on corporate innovation and product market strategies.

As in the case of the banking industry, pharmaceuticals has undergone great changes in the recent past. Pharmaceuticals originally emerged as a special branch of the chemical industry. With the exception of testing on humans or animals, research was basically done the same way as for chemistry in general—dedicated research laboratories followed their own agenda of 'hit-or-miss' discovery of new compounds. With the growth of extensive healthcare systems (including public financing and widespread access), sales of pharmaceutical products expanded rapidly

---

[8] For example, it was widely reported that the recent resignation of one of the Deutsche Bank's management board members would reduce the opposition to the implementation of the investment bank strategy.

in the post-war period. In part due to the fragmentation of ownership as a result of the world wars, pharmaceutical firms were largely national players focusing on their own national markets. Leading companies were typically highly diversified, with pharmaceuticals just one of a number of divisions such as organic and inorganic chemicals ('diversified chemical conglomerates with a pharmaceutical division').

However, in the past one or two decades, the nature of the chemical/pharmaceutical industry has changed dramatically. First, medications have been discovered for the treatment of most of the 'simpler' medical problems. The shift in focus to solving more complex problems means that the costs of discovery, testing and approval, and marketing of a new drug have increased dramatically. The costs of R&D alone for large companies have increased to well over 10 per cent of sales. The complexity of solutions means that a premium is put on highly specialized expertise. In particular, the field of biotechnology has taken a special role in helping discover new compounds. At the same time, researchers with this specialized expertise need to be carefully coordinated through project teams. In order to limit losses on fruitless research, financial commitments need to be carefully and periodically reviewed in a series of 'go/no-go' decisions on individual products.

At the same time, competitive pressures in standard pharmaceutical products and simpler chemicals have increased. One factor here is the internationalization of product markets. A second is the attempt of national governments to contain the costs of healthcare, e.g. through encouraging the use of 'generic' drugs.

As in the case of the banking industry, British companies in chemicals/pharmaceuticals are characterized by more rapid entry into new growth fields through the radical innovation of new products and more rapid rationalization in the production of simpler products. At ICI, the leading British chemical/pharmaceutical company, the decision was made in the late 1980s to separate chemical and pharmaceutical activities by 'demerger'; pharmaceutical activities were concentrated in a subsidiary which was subsequently listed on the stock exchange and sold off to the public. The resulting company (Zeneca) is the second largest British pharmaceutical company after Glaxo-Wellcome. In the meantime, rationalization activities in ICI (now solely chemicals) have continued rapidly, either through cost-cutting or through the sale of divisions not achieving profit targets.

The pace of change at the largest German chemical/pharmaceutical companies (Hoechst, Bayer, and BASF) has been considerably slower, but the clear tendency is that the importance of pharmaceuticals vis-à-vis chemicals in Germany is decreasing quite substantially. An initial 'exit' mechanism was the tendency of all three companies to relocate their innovative activity in pharmaceuticals to the USA, either through the establishment of new research facilities there or through the acquisition of existing firms (particularly in the biotechnology area).

A second, more recent, 'exit' mechanism is that German companies are simply disappearing from the pharmaceutical industry. The most advanced changes occurred at Hoechst, which in the mid-1990s adopted the goal of becoming a 'pure life sciences' (pharmaceuticals plus agricultural compounds) concern. The pace of disposal of chemical subsidiaries was initially slow, but in 1999 the announcement was made that Hoechst would be merging with the French pharmaceuticals/chemicals company Rhône-Poulenc. Since the new company, Aventis, is headquartered in France, Hoechst as a German pharma company has simply disappeared. Although both Bayer and BASF publicly rejected the strategy of radical company refocus and instead claimed that they would be following a 'balanced' growth strategy in both sectors, in late 2000 BASF made the surprise announcement that it would be selling off all of its pharmaceutical operations to a US company. Bayer is also reportedly coming under pressure from shareholders to increase its focus on core competencies, and the current preference is towards maintaining chemicals activities and selling off pharmaceuticals. If these plans come to fruition, then all three of the major German diversified chemical/pharmaceutical companies will have exited from pharmaceuticals, a more radically innovative activity than chemicals.

Again, differences in corporate governance institutions are crucial for explaining the differences in patterns of change in this sector. ICI, which used to consider itself too large to be taken over, was in fact the object of a hostile takeover bid in the late 1980s. Although unsuccessful, this bid convinced the CEO that shareholder interests (namely higher profitability and share price) had to be taken into account more fully in order to discourage future hostile takeover attempts. He thus set into motion the machinery for formulating and implementing the demerger plan.

In Germany, in contrast, the closed market for corporate control has meant that hostile takeovers have not been a mechanism for encouraging corporate change.[9]

---

[9] The recent takeover bid for the German company Mannesmann by the British telecommunications company Vodaphone/Airtouch has opened a debate on whether German capital markets have fundamentally changed and whether German companies are now exposed to the threat of hostile takeovers. However, it should be noted that (1) the works council at Mannesmann was fully involved in negotiating the merger and effectively

The example of Hoechst is particularly instructive for illustrating the influence of corporate governance institutions. Of the largest German companies, the initial plans for restructuring at Hoechst come closest to the UK model of change. These plans were drawn up largely by Jürgen Dormann, who was appointed speaker of the management board in the early 1990s. These plans initially foresaw the introduction of a radical 'shareholder value' strategy, which would assign the highest priority among corporate goals to increasing share price, and to a concentration on life sciences activities through the rapid sale of chemical divisions. Furthermore, pharmaceutical divisions not achieving minimum profit goals would also be sold off.

These plans, however, were strongly opposed by employee representatives, who feared the mass layoffs associated with such radical restructuring and who organized short mass strikes by employees. These representatives effectively blocked the exit of Hoechst from chemicals and the entry into new pharmaceutical areas by insisting that underperforming subsidiaries be sold off only to 'good' employers willing to take over existing labor agreements and by opposing the introduction of radical performance incentives for researchers. Attempts at Bayer and BASF to restructure their pharmaceuticals operations more along US-style lines—mainly by introducing strong performance incentives for researchers and by weakening the long-standing principle of 'lifetime employment'—also were blocked or watered down by the works councils. The inability to get these changes implemented or the unwillingness to try to push through such changes against opposition contributed to the German companies' decisions to exit from the pharmaceuticals sector.

10.3.4 Summing Up

This section explored the relationship between these institutions and company strategy regarding product markets and innovation. Though dispersed shareholders exercise little direct voice in company decision-making, their interests are largely aligned with top managers in pursuing high-profitability strategies involving certain levels of risk. One of the most common strategies for achieving such high profitability is rapid entry into promising new sectors and radical cost-cutting in or exit from stagnating or declining sectors. The voluntarist labor-relations system

exercised a 'veto right' over the merger if it was not satisfied with the outcome, and (2) Mannesmann was a successful company with a very high share price, not the classic 'underperforming' company with poor management and share price far below the 'breakup' value of the firm.

supports this strategy by allowing companies to rapidly acquire and (through high-performance incentives) reward specialized talent needed for the radical innovation involved in exploiting new fields. At the same time the costs of exit from declining areas are low due to the inability of unions to prevent mass layoffs and rationalization. German shareholders in contrast generally balance share price with other strategic considerations and employee representatives are in a position to block or impose high costs on rationalization measures. Thus German company strategies generally reflect less concern with share price and profitability and a greater concern with goals such as market share in existing markets, technological superiority, and employee security than is the case for British firms. Thus British companies have a comparative advantage in radical innovation in new sectors and price competition in stagnating or declining sectors while German companies have a comparative advantage in so-called medium-tech sectors characterized by incremental innovation and large firm-specific human capital investments.

10.4 Conclusion

This chapter has attempted to demonstrate the utility of applying the varieties of capitalism approach to the study of corporate governance in different countries. First, the chapter described the large differences between two large industrialized countries, the UK and Germany, with regard to the key institutions in corporate governance: equity markets, employee representation, and the organization of management. Two ideal-typical national models of corporate governance were identified, a 'shareholder' model characterized by market regulation of relationships between companies and their constituents, and a 'stakeholder' model characterized by non-market institutions. The British company is dominated by a CEO with strong performance incentives linked to share price, owned by dispersed portfolio shareholders interested mainly in share price and willing to support riskier strategies, and faced with a labor force responding positively to performance incentives and only weakly able to oppose restructuring plans. The German company in contrast is characterized by consensus decision-making among top management, core shareholders for whom share price is only one of a number of goals, and strong employee representatives who can block or moderate the pace of corporate change.

Secondly, an analysis of the political process of change in institutions showed that the UK and Germany do not appear to be converging to a 'one best' model of corporate governance. Rather, the majority of key actors in both systems appear to be cognizant of the comparative advantages of their system and strive to make incremental improvements in existing institutions rather than wholesale change and convergence toward one set of institutions.

Finally, this variation in corporate governance institutions can be linked to differences in corporate strategy and innovation. Aggregate data show that British companies have a greater concern with profitability and dividends than German companies. Furthermore, Germany shows a greater comparative specialization in medium-tech industry versus a greater British specialization in high-tech industries and lower presence in industry in general. Comparative studies of large companies in the financial services and chemical/pharmaceutical industries illustrate the role of corporate governance institutions in influencing these different strategies. The current trend under the pressure of internationalizing capital markets is towards a pattern of greater specialization in national industrial profiles rather than convergence towards a specific pattern.

11

Macro-varieties of Capitalism and Micro-varieties of Strategic Management in European Airlines

Mark Lehrer

The study of macro institutional differences is to date poorly developed in the field of strategic management. It is fair to say that the bulk of strategists, both practitioners and academics, focus more heavily on industry- and firm-level attributes like market share and R&D capabilities than they do on variables like industrial relations and financial systems. Strategy scholars who examine the impact of macro institutional factors (Lenway and Murtha 1994) remain a tiny minority in the field. Strategy scholars have remained generally oblivious even to contributions of comparative institutional analysis that are manifestly germane for core questions of strategic management (Sorge and Streeck 1988; Streeck 1992*b*; Soskice 1994*a*).

The evolution of competition in the European air transport sector bears out the relevance of the varieties of capitalism approach to strategic management. Until the mid-1980s, when the sector was highly regulated and fares fixed, Lufthansa was a clear stand-out (along with Swissair) in an industry environment characterized by *incremental innovation* (mainly in aeronautics engineering). Embedded in its CME environment, Lufthansa prospered in providing the comfort, reliability, and punctuality which formed the basis of competition as long as prices were fixed. After deregulation in western European air transport markets began in the mid-1980s, however, price competition quickly took hold, so that areas like selling systems, distribution channels, and marketing techniques rapidly acquired central strategic importance. In this altered industry context, Lufthansa was unable to adopt *radical innovations* in its commercial systems as easily as competitors like British Airways (Lehrer 1997*b*). This was, as will be fleshed out in some detail, largely due to differences in the institutional environment.

The ascent of British Airways from 'Bloody Awful' to leading European carrier in the 1980s contrasts with the relative decline of Lufthansa in that decade and near bankruptcy after the Gulf War—and also with the sheer economic disaster of Air France, which required a state bail-out of FF 20 billion in 1994 in order to survive (Lehrer 1997*a*). By the mid-1980s British Airways had built up a five- to ten-year lead over its rivals in the areas of information systems, organization structure, hub planning, flight scheduling, and global selling across its network, all amounting to a profound innovation in its commercial practices. LME institutional patterns were crucial enabling conditions for British Airways' management to orchestrate the organizational experiments and firm-internal power shifts needed to undertake radical innovations and break with the conventional industry configuration. By contrast, Germany's CME and France's 'statist' institutional patterns hindered more than they facilitated the adjustment of Lufthansa and Air France to the altered industry environment.

Once the competitive environment again stabilized, to be sure, BA's institutional advantages eroded. By 1997, Lufthansa and Air France reached technological parity with BA in yield management and sales distribution technologies (Lehrer 2000). Thereafter, Lufthansa and Air France not only rapidly equaled, but surpassed the profitability levels of BA, which began to lose much of its previous aura. In other words, BA's comparative institutional advantages were only as long lived as the general turbulence of the civil aviation sector and diminished once the industry reached a new steady state. Still, it will be seen that while Lufthansa and Air France did eventually catch up with BA organizationally and technologically, they did so only after losing inordinate amounts of money.

11.1 Applying the Comparative Institutional Approach to Strategic Management

Before proceeding with the empirical analysis, it is worth contrasting the comparative institutional approach to business strategy with the two dominant paradigms in the strategy field. In both paradigms, the dependent variable is ultimately individual firm performance, but strategists more generally speak of the way firms can obtain a 'competitive advantage.' The dominant strategy paradigm of the late 1970s and early 1980s can be called the 'industry positioning' approach. This approach links firm profitability to industry conditions like intensity of rivalry and product differentiation that shield the firm's economic profits from erosion through competition. This approach was rooted in the study of industrial organization and found its best-known exposition in Porter's

Competitive Strategy (1980), most famous for advising firms to choose decisively between either a low-cost or differentiation posture within their industry and avoid being 'caught in the middle.'

Since the mid-1980s, however, an alternative paradigm has come to the forefront of strategic management, the resource-based view of the firm (Wernerfelt 1984; Rumelt 1987). Whereas the industry positioning view had emphasized oligopolistic *market power* and imperfections in *product* markets, the resource-based view emphasizes *rents* from firm-specific resources and imperfections in *factor* markets as critical determinants of competitive advantage. In this view, sustainable profitability arises from firm-specific ways of doing things that are difficult for competitors to observe and emulate. Proponents of this view attribute competitive advantage to a firm's 'core competences' or 'capabilities' and to the role of complexity and tacit knowledge in camouflaging these capabilities (Reed and DeFillippi 1990; Winter 1995).

Economically speaking, the industry positioning and the resource-based approaches are clear competitors; proponents of these mainstream views argue about whether industry-specific or firm-specific effects are more statistically significant in explaining firm profitability (Porter and McGahan 1997). Yet there is a common denominator to both approaches that helps illuminate the comparative political economy approach to strategic management. This common denominator is the concept of *barriers to imitation* (McGee and Thomas 1986). A firm's competitive advantage is only sustainable to the extent that certain forces prevent the firm's competitors from adopting similar strategies and thereby eroding the basis of the firm's superior performance. In the industry positioning view of strategy, the most familiar barriers to imitation are *entry and mobility barriers* inherent in the structure of the industry (Caves and Porter 1977). In the resource-based view, various *isolating mechanisms* (Rumelt 1987) such as firm-specific skills, patents, or complexity shield the firm's strategic rent-generating resources from easy imitation by other firms.

The concept of barriers to imitation is useful for explaining the distinctiveness of the comparative political economy approach to strategy. Barriers to imitation of institutional advantages (and disadvantages) arise because of the embeddedness of companies within their institutional context. In particular, macro institutional factors constitute barriers to imitation because of the patterned variation they introduce into the constraints and resources affecting the strategic choices made by company management. In the 1980s, for example, macro institutional factors inclined Japanese, German, and other northern European firms

toward differentiation and niche strategies based on incremental innovation and heavy investments in human capital, while Anglo-Saxon labor
institutions seemed more conducive to a low-wage/low-skill equilibrium of low-cost producers (Finegold and Soskice 1988; Lazonick and
O'Sullivan 1996). On the other hand, in contexts where competitive
advantage is driven by radical innovation and first-mover advantages in
the development of rapidly changing technologies, liberal market environments sometimes appear more enabling than coordinated ones
(Lehrer 1997*b*; Casper et al. 1999).

Among other things, differing macro institutional arrangements place
varying costs to *top management* on the pursuit of alternative ways of running the company. In European air transport, as later discussed, cross-
national differences in stakeholder rights and prerogatives were found
to encourage distinctly different *top management styles*, and hence varying
kinds of strategic choices in the airlines studied. As a first step in explaining why comparative institutions matter in this regard, let us consider
the distinction between *formulation* and *implementation* of the firm's business policy. In principle, formulation and implementation of company
strategy are the responsibility of the firm's top management. Yet in practice, top executives can carry out neither formulation nor implementation
merely by issuing edicts. On the formulation side, top executives in firms
of any size at all are beset by substantial *knowledge limitations* concerning
both the firm's internal operations and the external markets in which
the firm must compete; they depend heavily on input provided by other
parties to make informed decisions about issues concerning resource
allocation, technology, approaches to the firm's different geographic
markets, and so forth. Managing knowledge involves multiple 'relational'
challenges. Expressed in economic parlance, the challenge is to overcome
asymmetric information between top management and other parties within
and outside the firm: particularly employees, but also strategic partners,
customers and suppliers, and so forth. On the implementation side,
top executives are beset by substantial *authority limitations*. As Chester
Barnard (1968) noted in a classic management text, regardless of what
company statutes say, top executives are *de facto* not free to impose their
will on subordinates by any means they choose, but can maintain their
own legitimacy and control of the organization only by inducing subordinate parties in the firm to cooperate. Thus, another set of vital relational challenges that top managers face concerns ensuring cooperation
and, in economic terms, *overcoming potential hold-up problems* at lower
levels of the hierarchy and between the firm and outside parties (partners,
suppliers, customers, etc.).

Macrosocial institutions are relevant to the analysis of strategy because of the way they mediate the firm's ability to cope with relational challenges in the formulation and implementation of the firm's business policy. As this volume's editors indicate in their introduction, macro institutional factors have a patterned impact on the mode of coordination between the top management and other key firm stakeholders —employees, providers of finance, partners, customers, suppliers, etc.— and introduce an important level of international variation in the capacity of firms to resolve 'managerial dilemmas' (Miller 1992) such as asymmetric information and hold-up threats. A showcase example of the nexus between a firm's institutional environment and its business policy is undoubtedly 'diversified quality production' (Sorge and Streeck 1988; Streeck 1992b) which emerged as a widely adopted strategy of German firms in coping with the market opportunities and constraints of the 1980s.[1]

In summary, the comparative political economy perspective draws a link between a firm's institutional environment on the one hand and its capacity to develop difficult-to-imitate solutions to intra-organizational relational challenges on the other. This view underlines the *locational institutional resources* that firms can draw upon to mediate relational challenges in the formulation and implementation of strategy. Locational institutional factors have been largely overlooked in the field of strategic management. A 1991 admission by three leading strategy scholars in the *Strategic Management Journal* remains no less true today: 'Today's strategic issues (e.g. the growth of new "network" empires in Europe and Asia, time-based competition) are only dimly perceived by anyone within the academy' (Rumelt et al. 1991: 22). The varieties of capitalism perspective, in contrast, is clearly very much attuned to understanding the new 'network' empires in Europe and Asia, both their strengths and their weaknesses.

11.2 Locational Institutional Resources in Britain, Germany, and France

The setting for the author's comparative study of strategic reorientation at British Airways, Lufthansa, and Air France was provided by regulatory and technological changes in the European civil aviation industry

---

[1] The fact that diversified quality production turned out to be less effective in the face of altered macro-environmental conditions in the 1990s does not detract from the general utility and validity of the underlying theoretical approach.

of the 1980s. Before turning to the particulars of this industry, let us attempt some predictions about how the formulation and implementation of company strategy are likely to proceed in firms in key sectors of the three countries involved (Britain, Germany, and France). These predictions can be based upon the basic institutional frameworks predominant in each of these countries: the LME framework of the UK, the CME framework of Germany, and the 'elite-governed statist' framework of France. By 'key' sectors I mean the publicly traded companies of Britain, the major exporting sectors of Germany, and those large French industrial enterprises governed by France's *grands corps* elite. Institutional patterns exhibited in these sectors have only little in common, in contrast, with entrepreneurial start-ups in the UK, Germany's non-exporting service sector, or France's family-run companies.

Institutions can be expected to influence both strategy formulation (knowledge and information) and strategy implementation (authority) issues.

The effects of institutional frameworks on the formulation of firm strategy. As mentioned earlier, proper strategy formulation involves overcoming the problem of *asymmetric knowledge* between top management and other actors. While the knowledge problem is multifaceted, as a first stab let us consider the distinction between vertical asymmetric knowledge (asymmetries in knowledge between hierarchical levels of the organization) and horizontal asymmetric knowledge (defined here as asymmetries in knowledge between the managers of the firm and managers of other firms).

Arguably, one of the great industrial strengths of Germany's coordinated market economy resides in the way its institutional frameworks help German firms to overcome *both* kinds of information asymmetries. Democratic patterns of industrial relations and firm governance (co-determination) alleviate information asymmetries between management and employees with the firm (vertical dimension), while neo-corporatist patterns of sectoral self-governance foster inter-firm coordination (horizontal dimension) and moderate the impact of information asymmetries between firms in the same industry (Hollingsworth et al. 1994; Soskice 1994*a*).

In contrast, the macro institutional resources for overcoming asymmetric information of firms may be generally more limited in the liberal market economy of Britain and the 'elite-governed statist' economy of France. Enshrined in the UK's more decentralized economic organization is the sacrosanct principle of autonomous decision-making by firms, where neither industry associations nor governments play much of a role in coordinating strategies among firms (Grant 1989). Yet while liberal market institutions thus do little to alleviate *horizontal* information asymmetries *across firms*, they do facilitate *vertical* information flows *within the managerial hierarchy*, albeit not necessarily down to the shop floor. In the liberal market environments of the UK and USA, the combination of deregulated labor and capital markets along with liberal arts and MBA-granting educational institutions creates both a demand for and supply of generalist managers at all levels (Lane 1989). While generalist MBA-type managerial education in the USA and UK has often been criticized as superficial, it arguably fits the type of labor and capital markets that firms in these countries operate in and furnishes firms with a coherent managerial world view to accomplish the needed 'organizational integration' (Lazonick and West 1995; Lam 2000).

The dilemma facing French firms is likely to be just the opposite. In France, the governing *grandes écoles* and *grands corps* elite facilitates the exchange of (horizontal) information between administrative leaders among firms, banks, and government ministries (Thoenig 1987; Ziegler 1997), but the social stratification it entails has been frequently observed to impair the exchange of (vertical) information between the upper and lower levels of the managerial hierarchy. French business leaders thus possess a poor level of knowledge concerning their firm's internal operations (Cohen and Bauer 1980; Bauer and Bertin-Mourot 1995).

The effects of institutional frameworks on the implementation of firm strategy. The main distinction drawn here is between unilateral and consensual implementation patterns. Both the liberal market (British) and elite-governed statist (French) institutional frameworks accord significant unilateral discretion to the top managers of firms to decree what strategy to implement, albeit for different reasons: in Britain's LME because top management acts as an agent of powerful shareholder-owners, and in France because decision-making authority across French society (including firms, banks, and the state) is concentrated in the hands of the selective *grandes écoles* and *grands corps* elite (Cohen and Bauer 1980; Thoenig 1987). In contrast, the CME framework of Germany (and other northern European countries) requires a more consensual approach: once top management has formulated a strategy, the agreement of other stakeholders to implement the strategy has to be negotiated.

Both unilateral and consensual patterns of implementation have advantages. Unilateral authority to decree the implementation of a given strategy has the benefit of speed, which is important in fast-moving markets or in industries where first-mover advantages are substantial. In contrast, consensual patterns of implementation help forestall resistance down the road and facilitate the delegation of decision-making to lower levels, particularly in dealing with unforeseen contingencies (Aoki 1994; Soskice 1994a). In economic terms, unilateral authority to implement strategy is useful for overcoming hold-up problems in the initial phases of implementation, whereas consensual processes are more helpful in overcoming hold-up problems in the later phases of implementation.

Which type of authority pattern is apt to foster superior performance in the implementation of firm strategy will therefore vary according to the technical nature of the production problems that have to be solved. The authority structure of both Anglo-Saxon and French firms is more conducive to the mastery of 'tightly coupled' technologies in which the various components of the production process require centralized control and synchronization. In contrast, the structure of German or Japanese firm governance lends itself to sequential-stage production processes and 'loosely linked' technologies where workers can be granted extensive autonomy (Kitschelt 1991a). Similarly, the authority structure of Anglo-Saxon and French firms is more conducive to radical innovation, while German and Japanese firms clearly excel more in incremental types of innovation (Hollingsworth 1991: 65–73; Kitschelt 1991a; Soskice 1994a).

These stylized facts suggest the patterns of institutional influence on strategy formulation and implementation shown in Table 11.1. These are admittedly coarse generalizations but useful for analyzing the context of European civil aviation in the 1980s. I will essentially argue in the following narrative that industry changes in air transport favored firms operating in the institutional environment of the upper left quadrant. Deregulation in Europe and North America had unleashed a wave of rapid change (hence calling for very rapid adjustments by airlines), while the nature of the requisite changes did not require extensive coordination with other firms nor consultation of the rank and file of the airline (civil aviation is not a shop-floor industry). This configuration of circumstances happened to match the comparative strengths of Britain's LME environment.

In previous eras where commercial and technical efficiency was a function of engineering prowess and efficient operation of the latest generation of aircraft, British institutional patterns were arguably not particularly advantageous for competing in the airline industry. However, market liberalization and technological change in the 1980s created an altered industry environment in which British Airways could build substantial competitive advantage by experimenting in the commercial

TABLE 11.1 Coordination characteristics for comparative institutional advantage

Authority dimension	Knowledge dimension	
	Vertical (hierarchical) knowledge-sharing within managerial hierarchy	Horizontal knowledge-sharing with managers outside the firm
Tightly coupled coordination through high unilateral control by top management	UK	France
Loosely linked coordination through consensus decision-making		Germany

area and by rapidly shifting power from the technical to the commercial side of the airline. This helps explain BA's phenomenal financial performance up until recently (one of the most profitable airlines in the world from the mid-1980s to mid-1990s) and the equally catastrophic performance of Air France. Lufthansa's financial performance fell in the middle, with the airline facing the threat of bankruptcy in 1992, but managing to stage a surprising turnaround thereafter (Lehrer 1997*b*). As argued below, these differences cannot be satisfactorily explained just by differing levels of state ownership.

11.3 The Concrete Setting of European Air Transport

It is at this juncture that we can add flesh to the skeletal outline of how institutional factors influenced strategic competition between British Airways, Air France, and Lufthansa. Beginning in 1987, the European Commission gradually liberalized western Europe's air transport sector, superseding the previously restrictive bilateral agreements on intra-Community routes. Given the three airlines' similarity along many dimensions (turnover, size of domestic market, heritage as national carriers of the largest three EC countries), one would have expected the three carriers to formulate and implement strategy in very similar ways to prepare for the 1 January 1993 target date for full market liberalization on intra-Community flights.[2] In an age of global competition, it is logical to assume that firms in the same industry should converge in their practices.

Yet in many ways the liberalization of scheduled services actually induced the three flag carriers to *enhance* their reliance on their traditional institutional resources and thereby *diverge* in the formulation and implementation of strategy. The British flag carrier relied on management patterns characteristic of liberal market economies (centralized leadership, hire-and-fire and highly autonomous decision-making by top executives), the French carrier on management patterns observed systematically in the firms of France's elite-governed statist economy (a highly top-down management style, with top management summoning the state to limit domestic competition and compel other French airlines to merge with the 'national champion'), and the German carrier on the management patterns we might expect to find in coordinated market economies (consensus-based decision-making favoring incremental rather than radical changes). These patterned differences not only concerned the style of strategy-making, but spilled over into the content of strategy as well: British Airways emphasized commercial innovation, Air France focused on controlling its domestic market, and Lufthansa attempted to institute a high-quality 'made in Germany' strategy in emulation of BMW and Mercedes.

Those not acquainted with decision-making processes in large companies may be surprised that such differences in strategy formulation and implementation should matter in the end. Yet it was clear from this research (over a year of fieldwork, archival research, and more than eighty interviews in the airline sector) that these airlines were anything but simple economic input-output machines consisting of costs, markets, and route structures. Changes in technology and markets in the 1980s shifted the industry's critical parameters of competition from aircraft and flying to areas like information systems, marketing, and pricing. In a deregulated industry environment, an international airline serves tens of thousands of different markets (since every city-pair in its network constitutes a potential separate market) in which competing airlines make thousands of price changes per day on computer reservation systems (CRS). As a former British Airways executive explained: 'When

---

[2] The only exception was cabotage (flights within countries), which was liberalized in April 1997. Considerable barriers to entry continue to exist due to slot saturation at the major European airports.

I prepared the first fare system for British European Airways (BEA), all the fares fit onto one sheet of paper. By the mid 70s there were half a million fares, today there are maybe 100 million fares.'

Given the complexities of the business, no management team could hope to steer the airline directly from the top, but was obliged to coordinate a set of delegated processes within the organization. It was in the vastly different ways the top management of the three airlines coordinated these delegated processes that such notable variation in the strategies, and ultimately in the competitive advantages, of these airlines could be observed to arise. Faced with highly complex, rapidly changing environments, top executives did not have the time, means, nor specialized expertise to micro-manage adjustments in company strategy, but had to manipulate various levers of action available to top management in the hope that a healthy dynamic of organizational change and strategic evolution would emerge.

To take first the issue of *authority*, the macro framework of *industrial relations* and *national company law* had a very substantial impact on the resources and constraints facing top management in the three airlines. Both before and after privatization in 1987, top management at British Airways enjoyed considerable autonomy in decision-making, with neither the state, nor banks, nor employees having much input into decision-making or representation on the top board (aside from a seat reserved for a pilot, who of course did not represent employee interests generally). The chief executive officer (CEO) in particular wielded considerable unilateral authority, as is common in British and American companies. The diametrically opposed situation could be observed at Lufthansa, whose chief executive is not a CEO at all in an Anglo-American sense, but merely the chairman of the executive board (*Vorstand*) which decides by consensus or, if necessary, by majority vote. The unilateral decision-making authority of German top executives in general and of the CEO in particular is further circumscribed by co-determination on the supervisory board (*Aufsichtsrat*), ten of whose twenty members represent employees. Closer to the BA case was the role of the CEO of Air France whose discretion was quite high in some respects — the company's *conseil d'administration*, like most company boards in France (Charkham 1994), exercised little real power.

As far as the *knowledge* resources that top management had access to are concerned, *educational institutions* as well as the nature of *labor markets for managers* appeared to matter. In explaining how knowledge resources varied among the airlines, it is helpful to distinguish between 'specialist' managers—that is, managers who accumulate specialized knowledge in relatively compartmentalized tasks and are not highly mobile between different functional departments within the firm—and more 'generalist' managers whose knowledge is stronger in breadth than in depth and thus enables them to fulfill multiple roles within the company. British Airways featured 'generalist' top and middle managers of the kind pervasive in Britain, the USA, and also Japan, where companies recruit young managers from the universities.[3] Yet not only education, but highly fluid internal and external labor markets made generalist managers a necessity for BA: as managerial mobility and turnover were high, which is characteristic for British managers generally (Nicholson and West 1988), BA depended on managers who could rotate quickly to fill vacated positions in the hierarchy.

The BA managers contrasted with the much less mobile 'specialist' managers of Lufthansa, mirroring the orientation of German managers generally towards technical specialization (Lane 1989). This specialist orientation reinforced Lufthansa's 'BMW strategy' of the 1980s, i.e. targeting an upscale, high-price product niche backed up by operational and engineering excellence. Further reflecting the technical orientation, Lufthansa's prestigious and large maintenance division (*Technik*) supplied a series of influential top managers to the *Vorstand*, including the highly respected Reinhardt Abraham as deputy chairman in the 1980s and the current CEO Jürgen Weber, the *Vorstand* chairman since 1991. Whereas the sales and marketing side of Lufthansa, as discussed below, struggled to field successful leaders in the 1980s and 1990s, the *Technik* division provided a steady stream of orderly internal successions throughout this period.

This generalist/specialist distinction can be applied to Air France in yet a different sense. As previously mentioned, the French administrative elite occupies and rotates across top posts in both the state and industry. In France generally and at Air France in particular, the generalist orientation of France's top managers contrasted with the narrower range of experience of French middle managers excluded from this selective elite. Indeed, the thick glass ceilings placed on middle managers and their concomitant lack of broad experience actually reinforces the demand for *grands corps* generalists at the top (Cohen and Bauer 1980; Thoenig 1987). Sharp social stratification within French company hierarchies produces a characteristically different breed of French generalist top manager from

---

[3] Japanese generalists differ from US and UK generalist managers, however, in that they are likely to spend their entire careers within a single firm, whereas US and UK managers are notable for their inter-firm mobility.

a British top manager. Whereas British top managers tend to be somewhat *inward-looking* and staunchly defensive of their company's autonomy (Grant 1989), the socialization and relational assets of French top managers encourages an often dysfunctionally *outward-looking* mindset, out of touch with the company's internal operations at lower levels and more comfortable approaching company strategy by means of high-level contacts in politics, finance, and the ministries to help limit domestic competition and acquire competitors (Bauer and Bertin-Mourot 1995). This was clearly true of Air France's CEOs from 1983 to 1993, all recruited from the *grands corps* (Lehrer 1997*a*).

All this explains why top managers in the three studied flag carriers coped with industry changes in the 1980s not by adopting convergent practices, but instead by following divergent paths of adaptation reflecting an almost instinctive reliance on the different endowments of institutional resources to be found in their macro environments. British Airways intensified its traits as a 'professionally managed' LME-embedded firm: an already strong CEO became even stronger, while the high mobility and turnover of managers became even higher. Air France intensified rather than moderated its reliance on the top-down style of administration practiced by parachuted members of the *grands corps* elite. Lufthansa tried to enhance its profitability by leveraging, not mitigating the highly technical engineering skills and consensus-based company culture which is common among firms in the CMEs of northern Europe. The hypothesis that follows from this is that firms faced with uncertainty in their industries are apt to try and strengthen themselves by relying on familiar principles of action that match the resources of their macro institutional environment.

At British Airways, CEO Colin Marshall (1983–95) orchestrated an extensive shake-up of the managerial hierarchy that allowed the company to engage in organizational experiments and major intra-firm power shifts. These power shifts enabled BA to break with the operations-driven culture prevalent in the industry and devote strategic resources—most especially young, fresh minds—to commercial innovations in marketing, routing, product design, and use of information technology. Radical changes in organizational structure were announced in 1983 and again in 1986 that promoted promising young managers in their thirties and forties almost overnight to top positions. The organizational 'revolutions' of 1983 and 1986 were announced with little advance warning (1986) or as a complete surprise (1983) after being formulated by a tiny circle of the CEO's closest advisers. The 1983 reorganization resulted in the termination of 161 executives (some 60–70 of the top 100) in a single 24-hour period. This abundant use of hire-and-fire, unthinkable at Air France or Lufthansa, was accomplished while BA was still 100 per cent state-owned (it was privatized in 1987).

BA's heavy reliance on hire-and-fire and rapid promotions proved appropriate in an airline industry environment undergoing extremely rapid change (Lehrer and Darbishire 2000). British Airways was far quicker than either Air France or Lufthansa in handing over control of the airline's technical functions to managers with marketing expertise, although all three airlines were ultimately compelled by their competitive environment to do so. Important power shifts from Operations to Marketing were institutionally facilitated by the exceptional authority vested in the CEO of a British company. After becoming a new locus of power upon Marshall's arrival in 1983, Marketing gained greater control over the commercial and planning functions. In 1986 Marketing gained control over BA's ground services at the London airports. In 1990, Marketing actually took over all of Operations. Another significant institutional pattern revealed by research was BA's use of generalist university-trained managers. Generalists were instrumental in allowing Marketing to take over Operations and proved useful to the company in other ways to coordinate and share information across departmental boundaries. BA was one of the first airlines to offer a 'seamless' service product unifying the look and service provisions across the different departments responsible for the customer's 'experience' (ground service, cabin configuration, meals, etc.).

The management style of Air France was very different. Its CEO Bernard Attali (1988–93) enjoyed significant discretion. Yet this discretion was not exercised in the same way as at BA. Air France's 'generalist' CEO of the post-liberalization years conducted a great deal of decision-making in investment, acquisitions, alliances, and political lobbying by himself. The result was a style of management in which strategic goals were formulated at the top and then issued in top-down fashion to a managerial hierarchy that was quite detached from its leader. This type of approach was observed to retard commercial experimentation and learning. It also meant that Air France's top management devoted far more effort to neutralizing competitive threats from other French carriers in the sector (UTA, Air Inter) than to identifying new commercial opportunities. In neutralizing threats, Attali was definitely effective: the government agreed to block regulatory reforms to the point of forcing the privately owned carrier UTA to sell out to Air France, giving Air France control over virtually the entire French scheduled service sector and a majority stake in Air Inter, the dominant domestic carrier.

Meanwhile, though, in the commercial areas of hub development, revenue management, and selling practices, Air France fell up to ten years behind British Airways. This management style failed to match the requirements of the sector—though it has proven effective in very different industrial settings like nuclear power, telecommunications, and high-speed rail where the requisite knowledge resides in France's engineering *grands corps* (Ziegler 1997).

At Lufthansa, lesser unilateral CEO control hindered the *Vorstand* chairman in the 1980s from fostering a more market-driven orientation which he clearly recognized to be necessary. Consensus decision-making and a specialist orientation in the *Vorstand* made it difficult for Lufthansa's CEO Heinz Ruhnau (1982–91) to match many moves of his counterpart at BA, particularly moves to strengthen and upgrade the commercial side of the airline. Demonstrably, he was deeply concerned about the company's lack of commercial acumen, but it was the engineering and technical side of the airline that held sway within Lufthansa.

Furthermore, locked as it was into costly co-specific human capital investments, Lufthansa's management focused on high value-added segments so as to best leverage its engineering and technical capabilities. This was nothing other than the attempt to apply to civil aviation the 'diversified quality production' successfully employed in other German sectors (Sorge and Streeck 1988; Streeck 1992*b*). In the face of progressive liberalization of the European market from 1987 on, Lufthansa actually *enhanced* the centrality of 'German quality' and 'German productivity' in its strategic thinking. Indeed, it took the parallel with car manufacturers so seriously that it appointed a BMW marketing man to a newly created *Vorstand* position in 'product development and marketing' in May 1989, and after the *Vorstand* director of Sales resigned in early 1990, Lufthansa eyed a top Volkswagen manager as a replacement candidate. However, this strategy, and Lufthansa's focus on classic German strengths, were out of sync with the evolution of airline industry economics (Lehrer 1997*b*). In fact, Lufthansa's 'German quality strategy' reflected a certain void in Lufthansa's commercial strategy and Lufthansa, like Air France, lagged British Airways seriously in a number of commercial systems.

11.4 The Interplay of Comparative Institutional Advantage and Industry Context

The foregoing discussion merely alluded to British Airways' headstarts in commercial innovation and to corresponding lags on the part of Air France and Lufthansa. At this point it is worth providing data about these different rates of innovation. To put the nature of these commercial innovations in perspective, it is helpful to review briefly the industry context of European civil aviation in the 1980s and early 1990s.

Logically, the US experience of airline deregulation ought to have given European carriers a good idea of how to adapt to a less regulated market. Yet the US experience proved not to be so easily transferable. For example, most European carriers expected a shake-out to occur in Europe as it had in the USA and thus they embarked on ambitious expansion plans; yet when an industry crisis came in the wake of the Gulf War, European governments simply bailed out the troubled carriers. Similarly, the hubs-and-spokes strategy of US carriers was difficult to apply: the small number of runways at European airports (only two to three) made it physically impossible to bundle arrivals and departures in the fashion of a US hub airport.

The result was that commercial innovation in the 1980s involved a great deal of uncertainty: the appropriate solutions could not be foreseen or purchased off the shelf. It was very unclear, for example, whether market liberalization required European airlines to further *decentralize* control over their geographic operations (in the interest of giving regional managers more entrepreneurial autonomy to compete on their particular bundles of routes) or whether, on the contrary, they needed to *centralize* control over their geographic operations (in order to optimize planning and selling across the overall route network). In the 1980s and early 1990s, all three airlines experimented (or at times refused to experiment) with a wide variety of organizational structures, from highly decentralized geographical profit centers to highly centralized decision-making units.

As documented in fine detail elsewhere (Lehrer 1997*b*), British Airways essentially won a race of trial-and-error learning in figuring out the optimal structure and strategy for competing in the altered industry environment. This helped to make BA the first of the three airlines to adopt what might be called a 'network-based strategy' as opposed to the former 'route-based strategy' in its operations. The old ('route-based') and new ('network-based') commercial strategies in European civil aviation corresponded only partly to the shift from point-to-point to hub-and-spokes configurations in the USA. While the new commercial strategies adopted by these airlines in the 1980s and 1990s did entail intensifying the strategic centrality of the central airports at London, Paris, and Frankfurt, the challenge was not really one of constructing a hub (as in the USA) but rather of optimizing an already pre-existing hub using high-powered information technology (IT) tools.

TABLE 11.2 Strategy shift in European civil aviation

System affected	Route-based strategy	Network-based strategy
View of market	Separate markets to and from home country	Home-country hub serving global market
Number of markets	100–200	10,000–20,000
Optimization of schedule and prices	On route by route basis	On O&D basis (origin and destination of passengers)
Sales organization	Decentralized	Centralized to optimize network
Scheduling, pricing, selling	Separate, sequential tasks in different departments	Tight integration and control by the Marketing Department

The emergent strategy required extensive experimentation in selling practices and the use of IT to optimize scheduling and pricing so as to squeeze the maximum possible revenue out of precious airport slots and runways. Instead of analyzing just 100 to 200 different markets (corresponding to the number of destinations served from the home country), European airlines were forced to develop the capacity to analyze the revenue implications of serving the 10,000 to 20,000 different city-pairs that could be served by exploiting their main airport as an international hub. With hubbing possibilities limited by runway constraints, IT was crucial for selecting which of these different potential markets it was profitable to serve. The old and new commercial strategies are summarized in Table 11.2.

In retrospect, the network-based strategy may look like an obvious choice, and all three airlines ultimately adopted the network-based strategy—BA proactively, Lufthansa and Air France in imitation of British Airways (with a five- to ten-year lag) and other successful airlines. Yet as earlier indicated, this strategic adjustment was anything but obvious *ex ante*. The bread-and-butter services of European airlines continued to consist of direct connections to and from the home country, so that gaining a consensus on the wisdom of pursuing marginal revenue from transfer traffic was invariably controversial, as interviews at the three airlines revealed. Centralizing the sales force, in particular, ran contrary to the wisdom of developing less bureaucratic structures, which all airlines considered a necessity for competing in a deregulated market. Not technical expertise, but commercial experimentation and innovation

TABLE 11.3 Timing of commercial innovation

Airline	Year in which the need to adopt the new paradigm was clearly recognized	Years of critical organizational reforms for implementation of the new paradigm
British Airways	1984	1983−6
Lufthansa	1992	1992−5
Air France	1994	1994−7

Source: Lehrer (1997*b*).

was what enabled BA to centralize its sales force eight years ahead of Lufthansa and ten years prior to Air France, allowing it to race ahead along the learning curve in running the airline as a network business, as summarized in Table 11.3.

That BA's early adoption of the network-based strategy was a source of true competitive advantage and not merely a reflection of BA-specific circumstances is amply documented by Air France's and Lufthansa's estimate of what tardy adoption of the network-based strategy cost them: about $500 million yearly in forgone revenues (Lehrer 1997*b*). It is therefore a misconception—albeit an extremely common one—to assume that BA's constantly high profitability since 1983 is attributable only to BA's massive headcount reduction in the years 1980–3 or to lower British wage costs. Nor can these revenue-enhancing innovations be attributed only to privatization, for the critical managerial actions and commercial innovations came in the years 1983–6 when BA was still entirely state-owned. Rather, LME institutional features proved particularly advantageous to BA for building its competitive advantage in commercial systems. Indeed, the role of Thatcherism and BA's run-up to privatization in this was to accentuate the traits of 'Anglo-Saxon' capitalism in the way BA was managed.

Why did Lufthansa and Air France fall so far behind British Airways? BA was fortunate that its industry environment happened to favor the institutional framework in which it operated (Lehrer and Darbishire 2000). Not only did commercial innovation matter more than technical excellence (Lufthansa's specialty) and national market share (Air France's specialty), but the nature of commercial innovation in European civil aviation called for a willingness to engage in substantial trial-and-error learning and experimentation. Under these circumstances, where strategy could not follow the simple two stages of formulation followed by implementation, but required an iterative learning process of multiple formulation and implementation attempts, 'Anglo-Saxon' institutional patterns proved advantageous. Anglo-Saxon patterns were ideal for managing a strategy process where neither formulation nor implementation necessarily had to proceed *smoothly*, but where they could proceed *quickly*, so that the requisite feedback on what to do next could be generated.

To see why this is so, we can segment the problem into the knowledge (formulation) and authority (implementation) dimensions discussed earlier. To take first the issue of knowledge, BA's combination of a fluid internal labor market and generalist managers at all levels of management was found to be highly conducive to the exploration of new commercial ideas. A typical qualification for joining the managerial ranks was simply a university degree. An examination of the most important commercial experiments at BA in the 1980s determined that they were generally entrusted to young managers fresh out of the university who were chosen precisely because they had fewer preconceptions of how things should be done; for example, the assignment of exploring the viability of building more systematic hub connections at Heathrow was given to a fresh university graduate who had previously not even heard of the word 'hub' (Lehrer 1997a: 107). While generalist education and high managerial mobility may not necessarily promote knowledge *depth*, they visibly did promote *openness to fresh ideas* as well as the diffusion of ideas across functional boundaries within BA. Discovery of the network-based strategy required neither craft skills, nor specialized engineering knowledge, nor a high-trust system of industrial relations.

In contrast, the managerial hierarchies of Air France and Lufthansa were more compartmentalized, induced to a significant extent by macro institutional patterns: by a tradition of managerial specialists in the case of Lufthansa and by the deep divide between top and middle management in the case of Air France. These traits, it must be underlined, are not fatal in all industry contexts. Technical specialization and an engineering focus are undoubtedly assets in many of Germany's shop-floor industries; even in civil aviation, technical specialization was undoubtedly an asset for Lufthansa's highly reputed maintenance operations (*Technik*) and for maintaining the company's reputation for safety and punctuality. Yet when Lufthansa was faced with the threat of bankruptcy in 1992, top management concluded that the company required a drastic 'mental change' from compartmentalized responsibility to spontaneous informal networking across departmental boundaries (INSEAD 1995).

At Air France, the institutional handicaps were even worse in this respect, clearly inappropriate for orchestrating company-wide learning processes. Though some middle managers at Air France argued for the need to make substantial changes in IT and commercial practices, these ideas received insufficient top management attention for much to happen. The top-down approach exemplified by Air France was predicated on the possession by top management of the knowledge required to formulate the appropriate organizational and strategic adjustments. Post-mortem studies by Air France after paralyzing strikes and the resignation of CEO Bernard Attali in September 1993 showed, however, that management had simply not comprehended its industry environment and the actions required of the company. These studies were written by the head of the pilots' union on the basis of his personal contacts at Lufthansa (Lehrer 1997*b*).

Considering the authority (implementation) dimension, we find another major reason why the context of civil aviation in the 1980s favored BA's Anglo-Saxon type of management patterns. The transition from a route-based to a network-based strategy presupposed a 'tight coupling' of company systems, that is, it involved simultaneous implementation of change across many different departments. Investments in IT, centralization of the sales force, and reworking of the planning procedures were ineffectual when done in isolation and thus required extensive synchronization. It is well established that the substantial authority and decision-making autonomy with which top management is vested in Anglo-Saxon and French business organizations provide a comparative advantage in the development of tightly coupled, 'complex' systems (e.g. aerospace), the very area where German and Japanese business systems, with their more consensus-based patterns of decision-making, are comparatively weak (Kitschelt 1991*a*). In the case of British Airways, the high unilateral discretion of the CEO appeared to be an essential enabling condition in allowing implementation of the network-based strategy by 1986. In that year, based on input from his chief consultant, the CEO of British Airways announced a major organizational reform that in a stroke altered the distribution of power within the company in a radical way and would have been difficult to accomplish by consensus in the absence of crisis.

Table 11.4 summarizes the timing of the three airlines in implementing two crucial organizational changes needed to implement the network-based strategy: first, the creation of a central network department to link together the core 'brain' functions involved in managing the capacity and

TABLE 11.4 Differential rates of commercial innovation

Airline	Creation of a central network department	Centralization of the sales organization
British Airways	1986	1986
Lufthansa	1993	1995
Air France	1995	1997

Source: Lehrer (1997*b*).

setting the ticket prices on the airline's route network; and second, the creation of a centralized sales organization to optimize selling across the network. These organizational changes invariably involved major shake-ups in the managerial hierarchy and shifts of authority that reduced the power of some managers and enhanced the authority of others. Partly as a result of BA's ability to impose major organization-wide changes by simple CEO fiat, British Airways was able to build up a five- to ten-year lead over its rivals in adopting critical technological and organizational innovations. Unilateral CEO control was a major asset in allowing BA to decree orchestrated, synchronized changes across a number of departments in order to implement the network-based strategy rapidly.

This argument helps explain why British Airways was institutionally advantaged and Lufthansa institutionally disadvantaged in the capacity of its leadership to impose the network-based strategy and overcome resistance from individuals and sub-units who had much to lose in the process. But why was the considerable unilateral authority of French CEOs not an asset for Air France? The answer is simply that it probably would have been, but was of little avail because of the lags in organizational learning previously described. Indeed, when Attali was replaced by a new CEO, Christian Blanc, in September 1993, a very major shake-up of the organization *was* quickly announced: a completely new organizational structure accompanied, of course, by replacement of virtually all the top managers. The problem was that Blanc had no time to familiarize himself with the details of the industry and hence announced a massive *decentralization* of the airline as a classic maneuver for uprooting the old, entrenched power structure. Yet just a few weeks later, as the head of the pilots' union began issuing his impressive analysis of changes at British Airways and Lufthansa, top management realized that this was precisely the wrong kind of structure for competing in a network business.

11.5 Some Final Observations: From Initial Differences in Strategy to Sustained Differences in Competitive Advantage

By 1997, Lufthansa and Air France did attain technological parity with British Airways in all the areas described above (Lehrer 2000). By this time, the basic industry tools needed to compete in a deregulated industry environment had diffused among all major European airlines. Thereafter, the strategies and even the profitability of the three airlines quickly converged, with Lufthansa and Air France even surpassing an increasingly troubled British Airways by the end of the 1990s. When the civil aviation sector reverted from a phase characterized by radical innovations back to one of more incremental innovations, BA's institutionally conditioned competitive advantages evidently evaporated.

Nonetheless, one question remains open. Once Lufthansa and Air France fell behind BA, why did it take them so long to catch up? As argued, the poor performance of these airlines (both close to bankruptcy in the early 1990s) was not only due to rigidities in staffing levels deriving from state ownership (99 per cent at Air France, 51 per cent at Lufthansa until 1994), but to a significant extent to lags in commercial innovation. The author's research revealed that Air France and Lufthansa were surprisingly slow to catch on to what British Airways was actually doing. The reasons behind these recognition lags lead to a deeper understanding of why institutional factors may be strategically more important than generally admitted.

In a nutshell, many of British Airways' strategic moves were camouflaged in the complexity of the hidden-from-view management processes underlying them, as were the institutional factors that proved to be such important enabling conditions or constraints on the role and discretion of top management. Recent contributions in strategic management help to place this interesting finding into context. These contributions underline the innovative, 'dynamic' capabilities of firms rather than static one-time advantages (Teece et al. 1997). These capabilities reside in complex 'routines' by which the organization carries out its various tasks; these complex routines are difficult for competing firms to copy because the nature of the knowledge involved is often tacit and embedded in daily practice rather than formally codified (Nelson and Winter 1982; Winter 1995). Competitive advantage achieved through dynamic and innovative capabilities is often sustained by complexity and knowledge limitations that act as obstacles to imitation (Reed and DeFillippi 1990).

Applied to the case of European civil aviation, British Airways, Lufthansa, and Air France can monitor one another's prices, levels of service, and fleets with relative ease. It is more difficult for them, however, to monitor their competitors' complex organizational routines by which prices are decided, service levels upgraded, or the deployment of the fleet negotiated by managers from Marketing and Operations. And it is harder still for these airlines to accurately assess the impact of routines of leadership, power-sharing, and corporate culture which induce revision in how these activities are conducted at lower levels of the company.

To understand the competitive processes observed in European air transport, it is useful to postulate a *hierarchical ordering* of key organizational activities. We can distinguish between higher-order and lower-order dimensions of airline strategy; specific decisions about acquisitions or aircraft orders are clearly lower-level decisions, whereas decisions about whether the airline should be fundamentally run by the Marketing or Operations Department reflect higher-order processes with important consequences for later lower-level decisions. Table 11.5 summarizes the relationship between the hierarchy of organizational activities ('routines')

TABLE 11.5 Hierarchy of organizing activities

	Nature of activities	Examples in civil aviation	Link with top management style	Observability of effects to competitors
Higher-order	Leadership, power relations, corporate culture, etc.	Distribution of power between Operations and Marketing, generalist vs. specialist orientation in management ranks	Direct	Very low
	Decision routines and capabilities	Yield management capabilities, product development skills, fleet planning procedures	Indirect	Low
Lower-order	Outputs of decision routines (discrete decisions)	Prices, service levels, fleet planning procedures	Indirect	High

and their observability to competitors. These routines are hierarchical in the sense that higher-order activities have some direct or indirect effect on lower-level ones, whereas the reverse is far less likely to be the case. This table is *not* meant to suggest that lower-order activities are *exclusively* affected by higher-order ones, only that a significant causal influence in the downward direction is present.

One problem faced by Air France and Lufthansa in competing with British Airways was that they could observe lower-order changes in their competitors' strategies—issues like staffing levels, aircraft orders, and takeovers—much more easily than they could higher-order changes in their competitors' decision routines. For example, the top managers of Air France and Lufthansa were demonstrably obsessed by British Airways' takeover of British Caledonian in 1987, and like most industry observers they saw this as the beginning of a major concentration process in European aviation. Air France and Lufthansa began placing hefty orders for new aircraft, and Air France proceeded to acquire the other major French carriers, UTA and Air Inter, in 1990.

A finding of both theoretical and practical interest is that Air France and Lufthansa were at a competitive disadvantage to the extent their top managers remained fixated on 'lower-level' phenomena as explanations for intra-industry differences in profitability. When Air France's CEO Bernard Attali was asked in late 1992 about the 'miracle' of BA's continued profitability, he replied:

There's no miracle. Certainly, BA has made good progress. First, the concentration of English companies began earlier than in France: BA is the result of two successive mergers. I'll add two reasons that weigh more heavily. The social charges in Great Britain amount to 17% of the wage mass. In France, they are 37%. If we had the British system, the charges of Air France would be lightened by 2 billion francs . . . Second difference: by virtue of the 1977 agreement, called Bermuda 2, BA is protected on the North Atlantic by the limited number of designated American carriers. (Cited in Lehrer 1997*b*)

As discussed earlier, Attali had simply failed to understand the nature of commercial innovations at BA. This quotation sheds light on the reasons for this CEO's lack of industry understanding.

In contrast, when the same question was posed to Jürgen Weber, the CEO of Lufthansa, at roughly the same time, he gave a very different kind of answer, one emphasizing BA's higher-order capabilities, not just the lower-order factors of wage costs and market structure. Asked at a Lufthansa 'town meeting' in Frankfurt, 'What does BA do differently to make profits?' Weber replied that there were three reasons:

1. BA long possesses a sophisticated yield management system with 20 booking classes, giving BA a seat-load factor [i.e. percentage of the plane filled] of 14% higher than Lufthansa.
2. BA's centralized hub structure in London, whereas decentralized services are becoming less profitable.
3. Profitable North Atlantic operations, thanks to the UK–US bilateral, much more favorable than the Germany–US bilateral. (Cited in Lehrer 1997*b*: 122)

As suggested in previous sections, the first two reasons for BA's competitive advantage cited by Weber derived from complex organizational processes and 'higher-order' leadership patterns. By 1992, Lufthansa's management was likewise engaged in changing its higher-order activities, not only upgrading its revenue management, scheduling, and hubbing capabilities, but, significantly, also orchestrating a process of 'mental change' within the company (INSEAD 1995). Lufthansa by 1992 had moved up the 'activity hierarchy' in understanding its loss of competitive advantage and in adapting to the new industry environment, whereas Air France remained fundamentally on the lowest rung of understanding until at least 1994.

In summary, the pace of commercial innovation depended critically on the nature of 'higher-order routines' and higher-order changes occurring within the organization. Institutional factors clearly affected the higher-order routines of leadership and power relations in the airlines studied. British Airways was institutionally doubly protected from imitation and erosion of its competitive advantage by Air France and Lufthansa. First, Anglo-Saxon institutional patterns such as high unilateral CEO control and high mobility of generalist managers were difficult for Air France and Lufthansa to emulate because of their different institutional environments. Second, institutional differences exacerbated cognitive barriers to imitation as well. Environmental complexity and the hierarchical structuring of organizational routines made many strategically significant organizational changes largely unobservable to BA's competitors.

11.6 Conclusion

The airline cases constitute a comparative inquiry into what Gary Miller (1992) in his book *Managerial Dilemmas* calls the 'political economy of hierarchy.' In the language of microeconomics, top managers confront organizational problems of asymmetric information, hold-up, adverse selection, and joint team production (Milgrom and Roberts 1992). As

Miller argues, no designed system of incentives can possibly eliminate all the perverse effects arising from these factors. 'The firm must be regarded as an arena for political leadership, ideology, and goal setting rather than simply for managerial manipulation of economic incentives and formal structure' (1992: 13).

The preceding discussion has alluded to the way macrosocial institutional factors influenced the variation in strategy formulation and implementation among the three airlines, including in these 'soft' areas of executive leadership, beliefs, and goal-setting. Although British Airways, Air France, and Lufthansa were all in the same industry and faced very similar competitive challenges, the top management of these companies, influenced by varying constellations of institutional resources and constraints, developed very different styles in the way they orchestrated organizational processes—with significant consequences for the airlines' ability to compete and innovate.

The foregoing analysis has endeavored to apply the lens of comparative political economy in a novel way. Previously, to the extent this lens has been used to illuminate the inner working of firms, the usual focus has been on bargaining between capital and labor. Whether framed in terms of industrial relations or corporate governance, on the alternatives to mass production or the negotiation over working conditions, the usual center of interest has by and large been the interaction of employers and employees and the shop-floor outcome of that interaction. The preceding analysis of European airlines, in contrast, has looked at an industry environment where knowledge and authority limitations ('asymmetric information' and 'hold-up problems') apply to the managerial hierarchy itself.

European civil aviation presents a case where crucial knowledge is not only distributed across individuals and groups, but is highly emergent in nature and depends critically on the dynamic processes available for *connecting* groups and individuals. Generating strategically important knowledge depends not only on 'cooperation' in the sense of social harmony and trust, but on coordination in the more managerial sense of organizing interactions. Here, too, macro institutions matter: the nature of labor markets, educational systems, and the manner of corporate control (as influenced by the nature of company law and the financial system) all affect the resources available for structuring interactions within the organization.

12

The Legal Framework for Corporate Governance: The Influence of Contract Law on Company Strategies in Germany and the United States

Steven Casper

12.1 Introduction

To date, scholars working within the comparative political economy field have tended to treat the issue of firm strategy and economic performance largely in isolation from any consideration of legal structures. The purpose of this chapter is to show that legal frameworks play a key role in the construction of the political economy and, more specifically, in the determination of corporate strategy.

When political economists refer to the law or the courts, they tend to construe them as institutions whose effects follow from the dictates they issue regarding firm behavior: they are seen as something like 'the long arm of the law.' In fact, however, the way in which legal frameworks condition firm behavior is more complex, and one of the purposes of this chapter is to reveal more precisely the dimensions of their influence. It does so by viewing the courts in the context of coordination problems faced by firms, and more specifically by modeling, in simple game-theoretic terms, the interaction that takes place between courts and firms in the context of the decisions the latter must make about corporate strategy.

Analysts have long recognized that the legal system has a major impact on the type of market and non-market relationships that occur among firms. In Germany, the character of legal regulation is said to facilitate many kinds of non-market coordination, and the legal enforcement of contracts is central even to the market coordination found in liberal market economies. How does the German legal system support non-market

I would like to thank the participants at both Berlin conferences on 'varieties of capitalism,' and especially Peter Hall, David Soskice, and Gunther Teubner, for helpful comments and criticisms on earlier drafts.

coordination? The chapter addresses this issue. In particular, it examines how the institutions of the German system tend to lead firms towards particular kinds of strategies that entail a relatively high level of non-market coordination, while those of the United States tend to reinforce other sets of firm strategies that depend primarily on market forms of coordination.

The second major theme addressed within the chapter is the degree to which institutions in one sphere of the political economy relate to those in other spheres, what this volume terms 'institutional complementarities.' Institutions shaping the form of business coordination in the political economy strongly influence the patterns by which laws may be organized. Again, the analysis points to a more subtle view of the role of law within the political economy. Scholars working in the legal studies field tend to assume that the orientation of the law is relatively autonomous from the activities of societal actors (Ewald 1995). The analysis here suggests that certain legal approaches are feasible only given the existence of complementary forms of economic organization within the political economy.

The effective implementation of certain forms of legal regulation found in Germany is contingent on the choice by firms of strategies that rely on non-market forms of coordination. Thus, while some analysts have argued that Germany's distinctive forms of industrial organization are made possible by 'beneficial constraints' imposed by German laws (Streeck 1997*a*), a more accurate statement is that the relationship between the character of laws and patterns of industry co-ordination within a society is codetermined. While laws strongly shape the strategic decisions of firms, in Germany the decision by firms to engage in non-market forms of coordination is also influenced by the existence of economic institutions that dramatically lower the cost of non-market coordination. As a liberal market economy, the United States lacks similar economic institutions, making non-market forms of coordination costly to firms. If US courts imitated German laws, it is unlikely that firms would abandon market forms of coordination. Instead, such attempts would lead to inefficient laws that would ultimately be abandoned by US courts.

German courts effectively employ regulatory contract law doctrines based on social market economy norms that are routinely dismissed by US legal experts as untenable. How can German courts effectively implement regulatory laws? This is the key question motivating the first parts of the chapter. The answer to this question centers on the strategic capacity of German firms, primarily found within networks of trade associations, to create non-market forms of coordination. In the area of inter-firm relations, non-market forms of coordination consist of sophisticated but standardized contractual structures that facilitate the construction of new forms of industrial organization within the economy. Once firms collectively develop these frameworks, courts in Germany use them to impose strong legal regulation. As the economic institutions facilitating these non-market forms of inter-firm collaboration do not exist in the United States, attempts to impose regulatory contract laws are undermined by information barriers faced by courts. In general, this analysis illustrates that the different legal solutions adopted in the USA and Germany can only be understood through locating legal institutions within the broader political economy.

The second part of the chapter examines how the character of contract law influences firm strategies. Certain forms of regulatory laws preferred by German courts are effective only if German firms create strategies that depend on non-market forms of coordination. This leads to the development of an implicit strategic bargaining game between courts and large firms in Germany. The results of this game lead to the development of institutional frameworks governing inter-firm relations. A detailed micro-analysis of strategic interaction between firms and courts shows directly why institutional structures in Germany typically evolve to support what Streeck (1992*a*) has labeled 'diversified quality production,' a company strategy strongly dependent upon competencies produced through non-market forms of business coordination. Firms in the United States tend to conduce towards company strategies that rely primarily on market forms of coordination and corporate flexibility. These include highly innovative strategies but also opportunistic strategies based on price competition. The chapter concludes through examining the stability of these institutional outcomes, particularly within a heightened debate on industrial competitiveness in Germany.

12.2 Contract Law Regulation in the USA and Germany

The central problems in contract law are those that flow from the high incidence of contractual incompleteness in modern industrial societies. In the context of complex production systems and multiple kinds of firm–supplier relations, unforeseen contingencies are likely to occur. High transaction costs often mean that all contingencies cannot be covered by written contracts (Williamson 1975). The problem of incomplete contracts poses a fundamental challenge to legal systems. How are the courts to cope with the contingencies that arise as a result of incomplete contracting?

In essence, there are two solutions to the problem of incomplete contracting. The first, usually called the 'classical' approach to contract law, attempts to protect each party's freedom to contract (see Macneil 1978). Classical legal doctrine assumes that all market participants are sophisticated agents. The role of courts is to enforce the written contract, even if there appear to be bargaining imbalances between the parties or if contingencies not anticipated in the contract favor one party in ways that were probably not taken into account when the contract was designed. A second, 'regulatory' approach focuses more on the problem of power imbalances within contracts. It attempts to police the distribution of risk within contracts, often in order to implement broad societal norms calling for the fair or just fulfillment of contracts. Courts do this through prohibiting powerful market actors from delegating unspecified risks caused by contractual incompleteness to weaker market players. Following fairness norms, courts implementing the regulatory approach will also attempt to 'repair' contracts that have been disrupted by unforeseen contingencies.

The US contract law philosophy has long been identified with the classical approach, while German contract law is based on a regulatory doctrine. While the basic principles of the US legal system are widely known, the key legal underpinnings of German contract law are rarely discussed outside of technical legal journals. When adjudicating disputes, German courts have long used the norm of 'good faith,' Article 242 of the German Civil Code (BGB), as a primary instrument to adjust contracts (Dawson 1983; Goldberg 1985). However, even more striking is the widespread use by German courts of the Law Regulating Standardized Contracts (known in Germany as the *AGB-Gesetz*). This 1976 law unified a large body of legal precedent applying Ar. 242 BGB to standardized contracts (Martinek 1991). The widespread usage of standardized contracts, combined with the very wide scope the *AGB-Gesetz* gives courts to police contracts, has made the law the center of recent contract law developments in Germany. The *AGB-Gesetz* allows courts to void or adjust any standardized contract in which unspecified risks are delegated to the receiver of the contract (Martinek 1991). The law severely limits the ability of large firms to design contracts granting control rights over incomplete contracting risks to themselves. Furthermore, the *AGB-Gesetz* prohibits the inclusion of clauses in standardized contracts that change the distribution of legal entitlements set out in either the Civil Code (BGB) or Commercial Code (HGB). Particularly in distributing liability for a range of defects between suppliers and final assemblers, this law severely constrains the ability of final assemblers to delegate important liability risks to suppliers.

In order to investigate the relationship between each of these approaches to contract law and the broader organization of the political economy, a good place to start is by asking what prerequisites must be fulfilled before a court will attempt to apply a given law. Courts must apply laws in such a way as to protect judicial process. Protecting process norms is a core preference of all courts, regardless of legal approach. Decisions must be based on a consistent application of laws. Violation of judicial process norms prevents courts from creating a consistent body of precedent. Precedent serves as the 'shadow of the law' (Mnookin and Kornhauser 1979), structuring private dispute resolution among private actors. This is one of the most important functions of private law systems that courts must protect. A court will hesitate in applying any law that necessitates breaking judicial process norms.

Judicial process norms are most likely to be broken in cases where the court does not have the information necessary to apply laws consistently. Courts potentially face the same incomplete information problems as firms. When constructing complex technical arrangements, high transaction costs often force firms to supplement the necessarily incomplete formal contracts with private norms that are developed in the course of the relationship. For example, because companies often work closely together to develop products or maintain quality control systems used for just-in-time delivery, objective evidence assigning liability for damages is often difficult to obtain. Minor problems are easily solved by the parties themselves through invoking private norms, often based on technical rules or indices developed by the parties. However, when major problems occur, such as serial errors during production or defective designs that cause product recalls, private norms between firms may become disputed. At this point, non-contractual norms may become difficult for courts to identify and correctly interpret.

The classical and regulatory approaches to contract law impose substantially different information requirements upon courts. Courts operating under the classical approach are required only to help guarantee that the exchange stipulated in the written contract is fulfilled. As a result, courts rely primarily on the easily obtainable information contained in the written contract. In cases where the written contract does not specifically identify the particular contingency that occurs, US courts will rely on the contract, usually ruling in favor of the firm that appears to have control rights over unforeseen contingencies, no matter how vaguely these rights may be defined (see Schwartz 1992; Macneil 1978). In the preceding example, US courts would ignore disputed private norms. They would instead rely on broad control rights set out in the contract or assign liability on the company that can objectively be shown to be most culpable (such as, for example, the company that conducted product testing or was responsible for quality control).

Courts using the regulatory approach have much higher information requirements than those using the classical approach. They must take into account broader societal norms regarding fair contracting when adjudicating disputes and, moreover, assess information pertaining to the relationship as a whole. This includes the formal contract, but also technical provisions and private norms that may have supplemented the written understanding. Additionally, courts must decide whether power balances exist between the parties and, if so, how they have influenced the distribution of risks across the parties.

While the court system is more centralized in Germany, with most precedent deriving from the High Court (BGH), the organization of judicial processes for private law in Germany is not fundamentally different than in the United States (see Langenfeld 1991). German courts do not have substantially different information-gathering or technical competencies than US courts. How, then, can German courts effectively develop and apply laws with very high information requirements? To understand how this system can persist, we must widen our analysis, examining how legal institutions are embedded within the broader organization of the political economy. In Germany networks of trade associations with the ability to construct standardized industry frameworks act as complements to the legal system, allowing regulatory legal frameworks to be efficiently implemented by courts.

12.3 The Intersection of Law and Comparative Political Economy

An important reason complex contracting structures are difficult for US courts to decipher (why information asymmetries exist) is because the governance structures companies use to manage their relationships vary widely. The institutional structure of the US political economy creates incentives for companies to compete on the basis of creating innovative contractual structures designed to support new forms of industrial organization. The resulting forms of industrial organization used by US companies differ tremendously across the economy. Because differences in contractual structures develop on a case-by-case basis, it is difficult for US courts to gain an understanding of how particular governance structures are typically used to manage various technical contingencies. Such knowledge could inform courts how particular control structures for incomplete contracting actually function. Have bargaining imbalances between the parties influenced how control rights are organized? Are the circumstances causing the dispute common for the form of governance structure used? If so, courts could develop a more subtle understanding of the adequacy of the private rules or technical standards used. Because of the extreme customization of contractual structures in the USA, it is very difficult for courts to develop such knowledge within contract law and most other corporate law domains (product liability is an important exception, see Priest 1985).

The primary reason why German law can adopt a regulatory approach is that most contracts German courts adjudicate are standardized, conforming to a limited set of governance structures with well-known technical and legal properties that courts can understand and thus effectively regulate. Companies have incentives to use a relatively limited number of standardized contractual structures. Doing so simplifies the problem of legal regulation for courts. Complicated inter-firm practices are similar across companies. The use of standardized contracts lowers information costs, allowing courts to more easily understand the consequences of these practices in terms of the distribution of legal and market risks across firms.

While courts and other legal actors play an important role regulating standardized contractual frameworks, large companies dominate the process. Compared to the immense freedom of action companies enjoy in the American legal environment, large German companies exist within a legal straitjacket. Yet, despite this, German companies have a tremendous collective law-making role. They collectively create new contracting structures, then, in a prolonged legal exchange with courts, federal agencies, and sometimes the legislature, see their creations molded into forms that comply with the broader system of legal restraints. These standardized agreements or *industry frameworks* consist of interdependent legal and technical rules that are used to manage complex inter-firm relationships. Industry frameworks differ from private contractual structures only in that they are standardized structures commonly used by firms throughout industry and in that they are also often used as the basis by which courts develop strong legal regulations.

How does the institutional organization of the German political economy facilitate the creation of industry frameworks? Within the strict principles regulating the division of risk between companies, the German

legal system grants German companies a collective law-making capability
within trade associations and other institutions that does not exist in the
United States. This allows German companies to collectively develop and
use industry frameworks regulating important parts of both the legal
and technical division of labor between companies. When disputes over
new industry frameworks reach the legal system, courts investigate the
technical and legal distribution of risks within the new framework and
then apply German legal regulations. If accepted by the broader legal
community (legal scholars and often higher courts through the appeals
process), the resulting precedent is then applied more generally.

Regulatory contract laws in Germany are thus strongly dependent on
the existence of a complementary set of institutions that facilitate the
creation of industry frameworks by large firms. In terms of facilitating
the coordination of non-market forms of business activity, the German
system of business associations can be broken into three distinct areas:

(a) *Capacities of individual social actors*: In Germany social actors such as
unions, employer federations, and, of most concern here, trade associations have competencies in a variety of technical and legal areas that
typically do not exist in the USA. Trade associations in both countries
engage in marketing and some types of research for companies, such as
gathering industry sales data (see Scheiberg and Hollingsworth 1990).
German trade associations possess additional capabilities, such as the
ability to create technical standards, help diffuse new technologies, or in
some cases run common technology projects sponsored by the state (Lütz
1993; Herrigel 1993). In addition, they have strong law-making capabilities, such as the ability to create legal frameworks governing trading
relationships within or across industries and competency in adjudicating
disputes between members. Each of these added competencies requires
expertise about the industry, and thus intricate knowledge about company technologies, organizational structures, and product market strategies. This knowledge only develops through extensive engagement of
trade associations by companies.

In Germany most specialized legal expertise in the area of complex contracting law is concentrated in a small number of trade associations and
a number of very large companies. Lawyers from these companies participate in working groups within trade associations to create new industry frameworks. The technical and legal resources of German trade
associations provide the resources needed to create sophisticated legal
frameworks that large companies often adopt. Trade associations can
develop industry frameworks combining legal and technical rules. The

capacity to provide comprehensive governance structures increases the attractiveness of industry frameworks, particularly to firms without the resources to develop them privately. Furthermore, when firms use industry frameworks, the legal and technical arrangements they adopt become transparent to third-party observers. Through examining the standardized practices generated by industry frameworks, courts can effectively regulate their provisions.

(*b*) *Horizontal coordination*: This refers to the ability of a trade association or other representative body to coordinate its activities with other social actors, and occurs at two levels. First, individual trade associations (or other social actors, such as unions) join a broader group of associations in the same sector of the economy and create a peak association. For example, in Germany individual trade associations in the industrial sector of the economy belong to the BDI (*Bundesverband der deutsche Industrie*). Peak associations have resources allowing individual associations to share information and coordinate their activities. The legal and technical staffs of the BDI often work with individual associations to ensure that their industry frameworks are portable across the industry.

At the second level, various peak associations coordinate their activities. Of particular importance here is the practice of peak associations bargaining with each other to make their individual legal frameworks compatible through using common terms, legal concepts, and rules distributing risks. As a result, modern commercial codes in Germany have an interlocking quality not seen in the United States. The possibility to create interlocking laws is important because it results in yet more standardization of contractual practice, again simplifying the judicial regulation of contracts. Furthermore, interlocking legal frameworks create substantial collective goods for companies and are thus a major reason why large companies participate in projects to create industry frameworks.

(*c*) *Para-public links between industry and the state (vertical coordination)*: While in the USA trade associations or other societal actors routinely lobby legislative and administrative officials over prospective regulation, their status is no different than any other interest group (Schmitter and Streeck 1985). In Germany there exist numerous formal and informal linkages between social actors and the state (Katzenstein 1989). Particularly in labor law, unions and employers' associations are explicitly recognized within law and encouraged to create private agreements, which are then legitimized by the state (Keller 1991). Though the policy process is not so explicit within corporate law areas, it is similar. The primary linkage between trade associations and the state is through the *Bundeskartellamt* (Cartel Office), which has the official task of evaluating and then legalizing industry frameworks to ensure that they do not violate Germany's strict post-war cartel laws. In addition to examining the impact of all industry frameworks on market structure, the Cartel Office also must assure that frameworks are voluntary in nature. In the context of these official inquiries, it employs a much broader informal review. Legal experts at other trade associations, private law firms, and university law departments are asked to scrutinize the broader legal status of the proposed agreement, in particular to see if it would violate the *AGB-Gesetz* and other contract laws.

This review process has two important implications. First, it internalizes contract law considerations that could be brought up in eventual court reviews from an early stage. By creating a strong 'shadow of the law,' the review process ensures that *AGB-Gesetz* and other related regulations on contracts are of primary consideration when constructing industry frameworks. Furthermore, trade associations representing one particular class of companies, such as final assemblers, cannot easily legalize industry frameworks that would violate contract laws and then use the legitimacy of the agreement combined with bargaining power to impose it on companies in another sector. Second, companies using industry frameworks will be highly confident that they are legally permissible. When introducing new technical practices that impinge upon existing legal rules, the risk of using industry frameworks (or private contracts explicitly modeled after them) is less than private arrangements.

By comparison, US institutional environments differ in each of these three respects. Trade associations and other social actors are weak and, particularly in corporate law areas, lack strong law-making capacities. Tremendous legal resources exist in the USA, but these are decentralized throughout the private economy. Except in some legislative lobbying domains, trade associations do not horizontally coordinate their activities. Finally, trade associations, unions, and other collective actors do not have privileged access to the government or legal system. They must engage the political and legal systems through formal channels that any other interest group can use. Overall, trade associations in the United States do not contain the competency or inter-organizational networks needed to create German-style industry frameworks or other forms of non-market business coordination.

To summarize, legal institutions and economic institutions exist in a complementary relationship. Regulatory approaches to contract laws are only viable when economic institutions facilitating non-market forms of business coordination exist. However, it would be mistaken to simply 'read off' the variation in legal outcomes across Germany and the United States from the differences in the institutional capacity for non-market forms of business coordination. It is also necessary to examine the range of circumstances in which it is in the interest of the actors involved to choose strategies that will lead to these outcomes. If German firms did not engage networks of trade associations to create industry frameworks, then German courts could not impose regulatory contract laws. Why do German firms choose corporate strategies that conduce towards the creation of industry frameworks, while firms in the United States do not?

12.4 The Strategic Interaction Between Courts and Large Firms in Germany and the United States

This section develops a micro-level analysis explaining how institutional frameworks governing inter-firm relationships are generated in Germany and the effect these frameworks have on corporate strategy. The argument unfolds through a three-step process. First it examines three generic types of company strategy that firms may select to compete on world markets. Second, using this typology to generate institutional preferences by firms, a simple three-stage bargaining game is developed to examine patterns of strategic interaction between courts and firms. The choices made by courts and firms within this game determine the configuration of institutional frameworks governing inter-firm relations. Finally, having shown that courts and firms are likely to develop dominant strategies within the game, we can examine how the national institutional frameworks that are generated influence corporate strategy in Germany.

12.4.1 Company Strategies

Institutional frameworks influence the governance costs of embarking on particular company strategies (Milgrom and Roberts 1992). The mode of analysis used here assumes that company management, faced with international competition, can survey the spectrum of possible organizational arrangements prevalent within their industry, and attempt to shape a coherent strategy. Institutional frameworks play a strong role through influencing the relative cost of building the organizational competencies needed to pursue each strategy.

To simplify analysis three broad strategies are discussed. Though ideal-typical, they broadly conform to the spectrum of real-world strategies that are conceptualized within the strategic management literature.

1. Innovation. Innovative companies compete by creating new forms of 'best practice' within an industry. Best practice is defined through advances in product technology itself or through advances in the technical organization of the production process. While product advances often result from radical innovation within the company, inter-firm links are increasingly a source of innovation. Within the automobile and most other complex manufacturing industries, the increased technological complexity of different components within the final product has created an incentive for final assemblers to decentralize operations by allowing suppliers to design important subassemblies. In the area of inter-firm relationships, product advances are often achieved through highly collaborative design relationships (see Sabel 1994; Ulrich 1995). Advances in simultaneous engineering, benchmarking, and other collaborative design techniques allow companies to achieve a market advantage through the introduction of products with more sophisticated systems integration than competitors. A parallel strategy is to focus on process enhancements. For example, the introduction of 'just-in-time' delivery systems has allowed innovative companies to radically reduce inventory costs, while allowing consumers more flexibility in customizing product specifications. Heightened quality control risks created by JIT delivery have also created competition across companies to introduce 'quality management systems' with their suppliers. Companies compete on the overall effectiveness and efficiency of quality management regimes. In this case, the innovative strategy is characterized by ongoing quality dialogues designed to continuously reduce quality control costs while reducing defect rates.

2. Price-competition (opportunism). This is a general term for all strategies that create market advantages through the delegation of risks to weaker market participants, whether these are internal employees or, of more relevance here, suppliers. Particularly when there exists a large pool of potential suppliers for each subcontracted component, final assemblers have substantial bargaining advantages over suppliers that may be used to develop opportunistic governance structures. The control rights contained in these structures allow the final assembler to externalize the costs of industrial adjustment to suppliers. Legal clauses do this through delegating to the final assembler unilateral control rights over incomplete contracting contingencies. These typically include rights to change the price of parts or quantity ordered when market conditions change or the delegation of various liability risks to the supplier (see Popp 1993).

Within Germany and other countries with regulatory contract law systems, the introduction of new supplier network concepts often creates an opportunity to redistribute legal and market risks to suppliers under the pretense of innovation. For example, many German companies have created minimal versions of JIT delivery systems in order to reduce inventory costs and improve product variety while simultaneously delegating important legal liability risks to suppliers. German private law obligates final assemblers in most subcontracting relationships to conduct 'entry inspections' of all goods upon delivery. These inspections force final assemblers to assume important legal liability risks. If inspections are not completed and defective goods subsequently damage machine tools, create work delays, or escape unnoticed into final products and eventually harm customers, the final assembler must assume partial liability. German final assemblers have used the introduction of minimal forms of JIT delivery as a mechanism to improve the technical efficiency of their supplier networks, but also transfer these legal liability risks fully to suppliers. They argue that the technical organization of JIT delivery, by definition, precludes the performance of 'entry inspections.' New contracts designed by large auto assemblers replace 'entry inspections' with 'exit inspections' to be performed by suppliers and contain clauses abrogating standard German liability laws in favor of customized clauses transferring legal liability risks normally assumed by final assemblers to suppliers (see Casper 1997: ch. 3).

3. Diversified quality production (DQP). This company strategy augments attempts to combine standardized forms of new industrial practices with non-market goods created collectively by groups of firms (see Streeck 1992*a*). The provision of non-market goods is crucially dependent on the existence of a coordinating capacity among firms. While individual firms can implement the innovative and price competition strategies, DQP strategies require substantial coordination across companies in the sector. Thus, the majority of companies within any sector must choose the strategy if industry frameworks are to be developed.

In the area of inter-firm relations, companies choosing the DQP strategy attempt to create an advantage over international competitors through the use of industry frameworks. Considerable benefits often emerge through the use of industry frameworks. Most importantly, large firms and their suppliers obtain viable governance structures to organize inter-firm relationships at a much lower cost than that of developing them privately. Trade associations use membership fees to create specialized legal and technical competencies, in effect socializing the cost of creating new technical and legal frameworks. Important bargaining cost savings may also emerge. Companies using industry frameworks with their suppliers largely avoid distributional conflict over the distribution of various legal entitlements (Knight 1992; Goldberg 1985). In addition, trade associations often negotiate specialized arrangements with insurance companies. Companies using industry frameworks obtain standardized, and usually much cheaper, insurance premiums than other firms, which must negotiate generally more expensive customized arrangements.

Industry frameworks also create important information externalities for firms. The process of developing industry frameworks, even if many firms do not subsequently adopt them, helps develop and diffuse information about complex interlinkages between contract laws, liability laws, and technical arrangements between companies. Trade associations have the competency to gather expertise needed to propose different models of cooperation and examine the likely effects they will have on different types of companies. Because trade associations have expertise in both technical and legal areas, the often complex interaction between different parts of governance structures can be gauged. This knowledge is costly for companies to develop privately.

To give an illustrative example, firms in the German electronics industry have recently developed an industry framework for JIT delivery (see Casper 1997: ch. 3). The agreement integrates technical provisions over quality control with legal clauses distributing legal liability risks across companies. It necessitates that final assemblers maintain a less stringent form of the 'entry inspections' mandated under German commercial law while also requiring suppliers to introduce a systematic quality management system, certified by accredited auditors on a regular basis, that meets the quality demands created by JIT delivery. On the advice of the industry association, firms usually implement the ISO 9000 quality management system. Though not as efficient as the more customized quality systems introduced by innovative firms, most firms using ISO 9000 can adequately perform as JIT supplier firms. However, because this industry agreement has undergone a thorough judicial review under the Cartel Office and other industry associations, the legal implications of using this agreement are clear. Firms using the agreement preserve normal liability rights that protect suppliers. Once the standardized agreement was created, trade associations became able to

TABLE 12.1 Company strategies and associated supplier network
           practices

Company strategy	Definition	Supplier network practices
Innovation	Create new forms of 'best practice'	Create new governance structure arrangements (usually highly collaborative supplier relationships)
Price competition	Emulate existing forms of best practice but externalize risks/costs to suppliers and workers	Opportunism: distribute market and legal risks to supplier companies
'Diversified quality production'	Emulate existing forms of best practice, but enhance them with non-market goods	Rely on standardized industry frameworks for governance structures

negotiate agreements with the insurance industry to maintain normal, standardized, insurance rates for companies using the industry framework. Table 12.1 summarizes this discussion of company strategies and related supplier network practices.

12.4.2 The Creation of Institutional Frameworks Governing Inter-firm Relationships in Germany

Fig. 12.1 diagrams the strategic interaction between firms and courts that leads to the creation of national institutional frameworks governing the introduction of new forms of inter-firm organization in Germany. This game is played repeatedly over time. A new game begins whenever firms begin developing contractual structures governing major new forms of industrial organization. For example, in empirical research supporting this analysis, I found that the introduction of long-term price clauses within supplier contracts, just-in-time logistical systems, and highly collaborative product development relationships across firms each created episodes of strategic interaction between courts and firms (Casper 1997). In each of these cases, important legal and technical challenges existed for firms and legal actors that warranted the introduction of new institutional frameworks targeted at governing the new form of industrial organization.

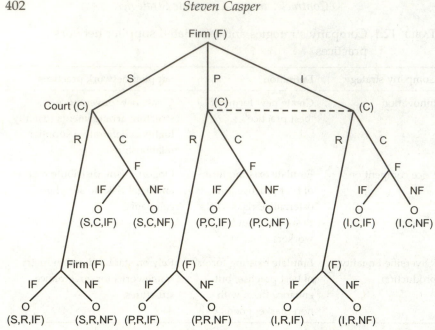

Fig. 12.1 Legal regulation game in Germany

The game has three stages:

1. In the first move, companies choose one of the three company strategies. They may attempt to innovate (I), to compete on the basis of price
by externalizing costs to suppliers whenever possible (P), or chose a DQP
strategy that uses standardized governance structures that are produced
as part of industry frameworks (S).

2. In the second move, courts decide which type of contract law
approach to impose. Courts adopt a legal strategy (R, C), where R
denotes a strategy of regulating the distribution of legal entitlements
within a contract while C refers to the classical approach based on
freedom to contract. When disputed contracts are adjudicated before
courts, I assume that the courts can judge the type of company strategy
chosen only if it is the DQP strategy (S). This follows from the earlier
analysis of information costs faced by courts. Only when firms develop
standardized contractual structures can courts accurately examine the
technical practices and private norms developed between firms, and in
turn situate these practices within the broader context of risk distribution within the relationship. In other cases, the only information courts
have is the written contract, which does not contain sufficient informa-

tion for courts to know which company strategy is being used. Courts cannot differentiate between companies choosing to compete on price (P) or on innovative governance structures (I). The slashed line that connects the P and I choices on Fig. 12.1 illustrates this information set.

3. In the third and final move, companies decide whether or not to create industry frameworks (IF, NF), where IF denotes a strategy of engaging networks of trade associations to create an industry framework and NF refers to a strategy of not creating an industry framework.

Collectively, these decisions determine the institutional framework constellation developed for the new form of inter-firm relations. There are four possible constellations:

C,IF—classical contract law, industry framework
R,IF—regulatory contract law, industry framework
R,NF—regulatory contract law, no industry framework
C,NF—classical contract law, no industry framework

Table 12.2 groups each of the four possible institutional framework possibilities with the associated pattern of business coordination and the efficiency of the resulting laws. The development of market or non-market forms of business coordination follows directly from the decision by firms to develop industry frameworks or not. To describe the effectiveness of laws within each institutional framework possibility, the term 'efficiency' is used. Efficient law-making occurs when courts obtain all information about the relationship that is presupposed within the

TABLE 12.2 Institutional framework possibilities for Germany

Court legal approach	Company framework decision	
	Create industry framework	Do not create industry framework
Regulatory law	— Efficient laws (1) — Non-market forms of industry coordination (R, IF)	— Inefficient laws (2) — Market forms of industry coordination (R,NF)
Classical law	— Efficient laws (3) — Non-market forms of industry coordination (C,IF)	— Efficient laws (4) — Market forms of industry coordination (C,NF)

contract law doctrine that they are enforcing. If courts do not have the information necessary to apply laws consistently, judicial process norms will be broken and inefficient legal outcomes will ensue. Classical contract laws are always efficiently implemented, since there are usually few information requirements besides the written contract. Because the information requirements are higher for the efficient functioning of regulatory laws, courts must rely on the decision of firms to develop industry frameworks. Efficient implementation of regulatory laws ensues only when this condition is met (cell 1).

Institutional Framework Preferences of Firms and Courts

In order to understand the logic of strategic interaction within the game, it is first necessary to examine the preferences that courts and firms have over different institutional framework outcomes. Firm preferences may be derived through considering how each possible framework outcome influences their ability to successfully develop particular company strategies. Judicial preferences may be derived through examining how the different framework constellations influence the ability of courts to efficiently impose different forms of contract law.

Institutional framework preferences of firms

Company preferences are shaped by the competitive strategy selected. The following examines how each possible form of contract law and business coordination influences the ability of firms in each company strategy type to create legal and technical structures to govern inter-firm relationships. Examining these preferences thus allows a direct examination of the influence of particular institutional framework constellations on company strategy. Preferences for contract law and form of business coordination are examined separately, and then combined to create an aggregate preference ordering ranking over each of the four possible national institutional framework possibilities examined in Table 12.2.

1. Innovation. Firms using the innovation strategy have a strong preference for a classical system of contract law $(C > R)$. While innovative companies often employ cooperative supplier relationships and may support the spirit of fair trading laws, they strongly oppose the actual practice by which legal regulation is employed. German courts often impose legal regulation through impinging upon the technical organization of inter-firm relationships. An example discussed earlier is the legal requirement that final assemblers conduct 'entry inspections' of all goods purchased as soon as they are delivered by the supplier to the final assembler. These inspections create technical rigidities firms face when designing innovative versions of just-in-time delivery (see Casper and Hancké 1999). In addition, legal regulation limits the type of legal categories available to firms. By restricting the use of other basic legal categories the complexity of legal regulation is reduced. This impacts the ability of companies to customize incentive structures through creating novel legal forms. The contractual structures created by innovators usually include customized legal clauses needed to create frameworks of incentives that are often necessary to sustain volatile and risky new forms of collaboration. If courts will not recognize the legal categories or underlying division of technical labor between highly innovative large firms and their suppliers, these companies must then opt out of the normal system of legal entitlements and remedies governing inter-firm relationships and create private contracting rules to manage relationships.

Innovators also have little to gain from the development of industry frameworks. The primary goal of industry frameworks is to create tool kits showing other firms how to emulate new forms of industrial organization. Why should an innovative company directly help other firms appropriate its inventions (see Teece 1986)? Innovators thus have a preference for no industry frameworks (NF > IF).

Combining these individual preferences over the form of law and form of industry coordination generates an aggregate preference ordering for innovative firms. Since innovators prefer classical law and do not benefit from industry frameworks, their first preference is for the (C,NF) institutional framework outcome, or cell 4 in Table 12.2. The least desired framework outcome is (R,IF), or cell 1. The second and third preferences could be argued either way, depending on which of the two individual national institutional framework preferences the innovative firm most values. For most innovative firms, the legal preference should outweigh the preference over the form of industry coordination. Innovators are crucially dependent on a classical system of contract law to create customized governance structures. Without a facilitative system of contract law, innovative firms could be forced to depend on private forms of contract and dispute resolution, presumably at great cost to the firm. It then follows that the second preference is (C,IF) or cell 3 and the third preference is (R,NF) or cell 2. The framework preference ordering for innovators is thus: C,NF > C,IF > R,NF > R,IF.

2. Price-competition. For companies concerned with the ability to retain control rights over legal and market risks, the threat of legal regulation is paramount. Regulatory contract laws reduce the flexibility of large firms in distributing legal entitlements with suppliers. While raw bargaining power might allow large companies to include illegal or quasi-legal contract clauses in cases of extreme bargaining asymmetry, most supplier companies will understand their legal rights and can insist on maintaining normal practice. As the goal of legal regulation is primarily to deter firms from adopting opportunistic strategies towards suppliers, price competitors strongly prefer a classical system of contract law (C > R). Companies choosing cost-based product market strategies are usually not innovative in creating their own supplier network structures, and thus could appropriate most of the benefits created by industry structures. Such firms often participate in technical standardization projects and also benefit from the creation of interlocking legal frameworks. Price competitors thus prefer industry frameworks (IF > NF).

It follows that the (C,IF) institutional framework is most preferred. For companies choosing to compete on price, the (C > R) legal preference strongly outweighs the (IF > NF) business coordination preference. The second most favored outcome is thus the (C,NF) institutional framework, which also preserves freedom to delegate contractual control rights. Because the legal preference is valued very highly by price-competitors, the core goal of these firms should be to secure an institutional outcome that includes classical contract laws. If legal regulation is nevertheless imposed, then these firms still prefer legal regulation with industry frameworks (R,IF) over legal regulation without industry frameworks (R,NF). The resulting regulatory framework preference ordering is: C,IF > C,NF > R,IF > R,NF.

3. *Diversified quality production.* Companies using the DQP strategy attempt to fully take advantage of non-market forms of coordination. Their core strategy depends upon the use of standardized contractual structures embedded within industry frameworks to complement generally long-term, cooperative relationships with suppliers. DQP firms thus have a strong preference for industry frameworks (IF > NF). As a result, regulative laws impinge on DQP firms far less than for innovators or price competitors. Nevertheless, DQP firms oppose the imposition of legal clauses defining the distribution of risks across large and small firms by courts. They prefer that firms define risk-sharing parameters privately or through trade association bargaining. DQP firms thus prefer classical contract laws to regulatory laws (C > R).

For DQP firms the benefits gained from industry frameworks strongly outweigh the costs of legal regulation. The most preferred framework outcome is no legal regulation with industry frameworks (C,IF). However, because DQP companies usually have cooperative supplier relationships and use standardized contractual structures, the costs of legal regulation are much smaller than for either innovators or price competitors. As a result, the regulation with industry framework outcome (R,IF) is preferred over the no regulation and no industry framework outcome (C,NF). Regulation with no industry framework (R,NF) is the least favored outcome. Here legal regulation will be both costly and inefficient, creating additional governance costs in addition to the lack of industry framework benefits. The resulting regulatory preference ordering of companies with the DQP company strategy is C,IF > R,IF > C,NF > R,NF.

National institutional framework preferences of courts

An important problem facing courts is that they cannot tailor contract law to suit particular company strategies. For example, courts might prefer to punish price competitors through imposing legal regulation while simultaneously creating classical contract law doctrines for innovative companies. While there might exist public pressure to accommodate both strategies, in practice courts can only adopt one form of contract law to deal with particular contract structures. This follows partly from the high information costs faced by courts in identifying price competitors and innovators, but more fundamentally from the need to create clear bodies of precedent for each area of the law.

In Germany broad social norms underlying the idea of the 'social market economy' have combined with specific 'fair trading' laws such as the *AGB-Gesetz* to provide a clear public mandate for courts to apply regulatory contract laws (R > C). Courts might also have private motives to prefer regulatory contract laws. Legal regulation allows courts to develop an activist legal agenda that increases their power and prestige within society. However, courts must also value the development of efficient legal processes. If courts cannot enforce laws and precedent efficiently, then they have failed in their core function of dispute resolution. Companies would not be able to use the 'shadow of the law' to solve disputes. If the costs of legal inefficiency are high enough, firms might develop alternative dispute resolution procedures. Accordingly, it must be assumed that courts value the efficiency of the law over the ability to implement a particular approach to contract law. It then follows that courts will refuse to develop regulatory laws if they cannot be implemented efficiently. A full preference ordering for courts is thus: efficient regulatory law > classical law > inefficient regulatory laws.

TABLE 12.3 Framework preferences for German courts and large firms

Actor	Framework preferences
Courts	R,IF > C,IF > C,NF > R,NF
Large firms by product market strategy	
DQP	C,IF > R,IF > C,NF > R,NF
Price-based (opportunism)	C,IF > C,NF > R,IF > R,NF
Innovation	C,NF > C,IF > R,NF > R,IF

These legal preferences may be expanded into aggregate institutional framework preferences. Courts can only efficiently implement regulatory laws if companies create industry frameworks. As a result, courts must always prefer that firms create industry frameworks (IF > NF). Combining legal with business coordination preferences, the first framework preference for courts must be (R,IF). Only this framework constellation allows courts to efficiently implement regulatory laws. Of the four possible outcomes, (R,NF) must be the least preferred outcome, since it is only here that inefficient laws are created. This leaves the (C,IF) and (C,NF) outcomes. Courts can always efficiently implement classical contract laws, in which they merely enforce the written rules of contracts. Thus, either the (C,IF) or (C,NF) outcome produces an efficient legal result. As industry frameworks have diffuse public policy benefits (lower transaction costs to industry and small-firm competitiveness), it is plausible to assume that as agents of the state courts prefer (C,IF) over (C,NF), but this is inconsequential to the logic of strategic interaction that occurs. The regulatory preferences of courts are thus: R,IF > C,IF > C,NF > R,NF. Table 12.3 summarizes the framework preferences for German courts and large firms.

Strategic Interaction in Germany

Referring back to Fig. 12.1, we can now examine the strategic interaction between courts and large firms. The game is not solved formally. The goal of the following analysis is to illuminate a strategic dilemma faced by German courts. We will see that courts have the strategic capability to produce their most desired national institutional framework possibility, (R,IF) or cell 1 in Table 12.2. However, to accomplish this goal courts must adopt a strategy of *always* choosing regulatory contract law as the game is repeated over time. This leads to institutional framework outcomes that reward firms that choose DQP strategies while punishing price competitors. However, this court strategy also produces the least favored national institutional framework conditions for innovative companies.

The strategic dilemma facing courts can be illustrated through examining the game by using backward induction. Referring once again to Fig. 12.1, first examine the branch of the decision tree stemming from the decision by a firm to adopt a DQP strategy (choice S). Once this decision has been made, courts and firms both have dominant strategies. DQP firms always prefer to create industry frameworks, regardless of the orientation of contract law. Because this dominant strategy exists, courts can always commit to create regulatory contract law when dealing with known DQP firms. The court will know that DQP companies will always choose to create industry frameworks and that the resulting legal regulation will be efficient. This generates the (R,IF) framework outcome (cell 1 in Table 12.2), producing the second most favored outcome for DQP firms, and the most favored outcome for courts.

The analysis becomes more complicated on the other side of the decision tree, when the court does not know the type of company strategy selected. When a court finds itself within the information set contained in the game, it knows that the firm has not chosen DQP, but does not know if it is a price competitor or an innovator. To examine the possible strategies, we can examine what strategy a court might pursue if it *believes* that the firm is a particular company strategy type.

What should a court do if it believes the company is a price competitor? Because price competitors value the existence of classical contract laws much more than the gains from industry frameworks, they have an incentive to commit to a no framework policy, since they must assume that courts will always regulate any industry frameworks created. Even though legal regulation could then lead to their least preferred outcome (P,R,NF), companies know that this is an inefficient outcome for courts as well. If courts believed this threat, they would be forced to select a classical contract law approach, creating the second most favored outcome for companies (P,C,NF), which must be seen as far superior to any outcome that includes regulatory laws.

Nevertheless, if a court believes that the firm is a price competitor, it might still choose a strategy of legal regulation. From a German public policy perspective, courts have a strong mandate to punish companies adopting the price competition strategy. This might be interpreted to mean that the cost to courts of arriving at the (P,R,NF) outcome is not as high as in the other cases, since inefficient legal decisions in effect add to the 'punishment' imposed upon companies adopting industrial practices defined as socially illegitimate. But besides this point, if courts *always* adopt a policy of legal regulation, companies competing on price must realize that their threat not to create industry frameworks is not credible. Courts know that price competitors prefer the existence of industry frameworks. Faced with legal regulation in any case, companies will then create industry frameworks, since then they receive their third most preferred institutional outcome (R,IF) instead of their least preferred outcome (R,NF). Of course, once firms adopt this strategy, courts achieve their preferred outcome.

Courts face a different problem when they believe the firm has chosen the innovative strategy. Innovators have a strong rationale to always choose market forms of business coordination (NF). Doing so ensures that the least favored R,IF outcome is avoided, and creates a possibility that courts, fearing the creation of inefficient law, will help innovators achieve their most favored outcome through choosing a classical legal approach. Because innovators always prefer institutional frameworks with no industry frameworks, courts cannot cajole innovators to create industry frameworks through repeatedly choosing regulatory contract laws. An additional difference between this and the price-competitor case is that there exists no social legitimacy for a punishment strategy against innovators. So long as courts believe that they are dealing with innovators, they should understand that enabling laws are needed to facilitate the creation of customized contractual structures needed to support new forms of organization, not to opportunistically redistribute risks to weaker suppliers.

Thus, if courts want to create national institutional frameworks hospitable to innovation, they must select a classical approach (C). Given that innovators have a dominant strategy of always choosing NF, there is no possibility for courts to efficiently develop regulatory contract laws. By developing classical contract laws, courts preserve a large role for law in promoting innovation, and avoid the possibility that they will obtain their least preferred R,NF framework outcome. The problem with this approach is that it undermines the 'commit to regulation' strategy that could effectively restrain price competitors. Once a court attempts to reward innovators, price competitors may attempt to signal to the court that they are also innovators. They could do this through consistently choosing the NF strategy as the game is repeated over time.

We can now go back to the beginning of the game, in which the firm must choose a competitive strategy. This decision will be contingent on the firm's calculus of the likelihood that favorable institutional frameworks for the given strategy will develop. The repeated nature of the game can be crucial. If courts have consistently played one strategy over the other, this could strongly influence the firm's company strategy decision.

From the court's perspective, choosing regulatory contract law has the positive effect of raising the cost of opportunism, in effect creating incentives for companies contemplating DQP or price competition to select DQP. However, we know from the partial analysis that this threat is only viable when large firms know that choosing P will *always* lead to a punishment outcome. Because courts cannot distinguish innovators from price competitors, if courts chose to create favorable framework conditions for innovators, they must reward price competitors as well. A court strategy of creating favorable legal conditions for potential innovators through choosing a classical approach all or most of the time would lead some firms that are not innovative, but have a choice between DQP or price-competitive strategies, to choose P. They can do this by choosing P and then NF. The (P,C,NF) outcome is likely to outweigh the (S,R,IF) outcome for many firms. This is particularly true for companies experiencing substantial competition from low-cost foreign producers.

By eliminating the possibility of a strongly preferred outcome within the price competitive strategy option, courts that repeatedly decide to pursue regulatory contract laws give companies an incentive to choose S and create industry frameworks. Doing so creates a pooling equilibrium. Remember that industry frameworks can only be created when there is a consensus among large firms within particular industry associations. For different reasons, both innovators and price competitors are opposed to legal regulation, and thus have an incentive to undermine associational governance projects. Since, for cartel law reasons, the associational governance system is organized on consensus principles, a small coalition of large firms can easily thwart any industry framework project. As long as there is no way for courts to prevent price competitors from attempting to pool with innovators, courts have a strong incentive to develop a signaling strategy of always adopting legal regulation, since this promotes a pooling equilibrium around diversified quality production (S). Because companies choosing S will always generate industry frameworks, only this outcome assures that courts will always be in a position to efficiently regulate contracts—their most desired outcome.

From a public policy perspective, the difficulty with this strategy is that a fixed move by courts towards legal regulation punishes innovation companies as well as companies attempting to compete on the basis of costs. Potential innovators must also cope with legal regulation designed to sway potential price competitors to adopt the DQP strategy. Whenever the R,IF equilibrium prevails, national institutional frameworks become a constraint on innovation. Innovators must circumvent

legal regulation by creating private governance structures to support
new forms of organization. Given this decision calculus, it should not be
surprising if potential innovators also decide to choose the DQP strategy.
This is a core dilemma of legal regulation in Germany—bolstering DQP
types of corporate organization systematically punishes innovation. The
broad public policy problem is that the cost of this strategy—punishing
innovative companies—is borne by the public and not courts.

12.4.3 Contract Law and Corporate Strategy in the United States

Because the institutional infrastructure in the United States lacks
networks of trade associations with strong legal competencies, firms
cannot cheaply collaborate to create industry frameworks. This eliminates DQP as a viable company strategy, since the institutional frameworks needed to support this strategy are unlikely to be created. As
there can only be variance on the form of contract law, the analysis of
strategic interaction between firms and courts is much simpler in the US
case. Dominant strategies exist for both courts and large firms, in effect
eliminating the complex strategic interaction made possible within
Germany's business coordinated political economy.

Institutional Framework Preferences

In the absence of a possibility for firms to collectively create industry
frameworks, there are only two possible institutional framework
outcomes:

C, NF—no legal regulation, no industry frameworks
R, NF—legal regulation, no industry frameworks

Companies: For all firms, the preferred institutional framework outcome
is C,NF > R,NF. The reasoning is identical to that in Germany. Innovators
and price competitors each have a strong preference for classical contract
law.

Courts: The preferences of US courts are similar to those in Germany.
If they could be implemented efficiently, US courts would also favor the
imposition of regulatory contract laws. However, in the United States
decentralized forms of industrial organization and the lack of industry
frameworks create information asymmetries that are difficult for courts
to overcome. US courts have refused to implement regulatory contract
laws in cases in which they lack private information about industrial
practices (Schwartz 1992). The reason again is that these laws would

violate judicial process norms, undermining the consistency of legal reasoning within the precedent system. We may assume that US courts have a preference ordering of NR > R when dealing with innovative companies. When dealing with companies with opportunistic price-based strategies, courts probably would prefer effective regulatory laws. However, since non-market forms of industry coordination are not possible in the United States, this outcome is eliminated. Courts must again prefer NR > R.

Strategic Interaction in the United States

Strategic interaction between courts and large companies is simple, as companies can always credibly commit to their preferred company strategy. Courts might prefer the stricter regulation of contracts. However, they lack the ability to implement regulatory contracting doctrines in all areas where the governance structures used by firms are complex and embedded with information not available to courts. Furthermore, the institutions facilitating the creation of industry frameworks lie outside the legal system and, due to a combination of the United States' historical development and the current strategies of companies, do not exist. Legal actors thus lack the necessary policy instruments to promote their favored strategies. They will choose to maximize efficiency. This can be achieved through developing classical contract laws that promote flexibility by companies and then enforcing the formal rules companies choose to create. The resulting regulatory climate for inter-firm relations fully supports both the innovative and price-based product market strategies.

To summarize, US courts can create a strong role for the legal system in the area of dispute resolution, but cannot mandate how firms distribute contracting risks among themselves. Rather paradoxically, this promotes the creation of a form of industrial dualism in the United States. Institutional frameworks are primarily legal in nature, allowing firms to create customized contractual structures needed to promote highly innovative company strategies, but at the same time also facilitating the development of opportunistic contractual structures demanded by price-competitive strategies.

12.5 Conclusion

This chapter has examined why important differences exist in the configuration of institutional frameworks governing inter-firm relations in

Germany and the United States and explored the effect these frameworks have on company strategies. The governance of today's decentralized economy strongly depends on strategies developed to adjudicate incomplete contracts. The legal system is not an autonomous institution. Rather, the character of laws is strongly determined by the broader configuration of the political economy. An institutional complementarity exists between the legal system and the system of business coordination within the economy. In the United States regulatory contract laws cannot be efficiently implemented because firms privately develop most complex contract structures, which helps create a highly differentiated landscape of industrial organization. Facing high information costs, courts are unable to meet the high information requirements presupposed within regulatory contract law and are forced to apply classical doctrines. National institutional frameworks in the United States subsequently support innovative and price-competitive strategies, but are incapable of promoting the 'DQP' company strategies.

In the United States courts and firms have dominant strategies that depend on no implicit bargaining. Lacking fundamental institutional change, the USA is locked in a very stable regulatory outcome. Most firms in the United States are not interested in copying German-style industrial arrangements. This is because most firms obtain their preferred outcome under the present institutional arrangements: few regulations on their freedom to contract. In terms of the company strategies supported, this freedom is much more than the ability to adopt product market strategies based on delegating risks to weaker partners. The US institutional infrastructure has created incentives for firms to choose fundamentally different strategies than in Germany. US contract law, as one aspect of a broader body of corporate law that is broadly 'enabling' in character (see Easterbrook and Fischel 1991), allows firms to compete over the organization and thus effectiveness of governance structures. Particularly in the 1980s and 1990s, the flexibility that US-based companies have shown in creating highly innovative forms of industrial organization is a key factor allowing many of these companies to dominate a range of high-technology industries characterized by innovative strategies.

Because legal resources are decentralized, it is very hard to imagine the underlying logic of American contract law changing. Legal innovation is driven by thousands of private decisions by companies and courts. Individual companies create new contracting structures which, if successful, other companies might mimic. No collective action is necessary, and innovation usually occurs through competition. Furthermore, once companies embark on the competitive strategies encouraged by these institutional arrangements, they develop private legal competencies and other resources allowing them to compete primarily on the basis of market-based contractual structures. These sunk costs create an additional source of stability. Even if changes to the US institutional infrastructure radically lowered the costs of creating industry frameworks, many large US firms are unlikely to engage these institutions to create industry frameworks. This is because most large firms already have the competencies needed to create and compete on the basis of complex private governance structures. Unless the gains from coordination are high enough to motivate companies to adopt different company strategies and different internal resources to support them, large US firms would be unlikely to develop non-market forms of industry coordination.

Due to differences in historical development, German companies are embedded within complex networks of trade associations that firms may engage to create standardized contractual structures, or industry frameworks. The existence of standardized forms of industrial organization within the economy lowers the information costs faced by courts when imposing regulatory forms of contract law. This institutional complementarity between the legal system and the system of business coordination is crucial to the development of Germany's distinct institutional framework configuration. It creates a capacity for German courts to implement regulatory contract laws that cannot be efficiently implemented in the United States. Analysis of the strategic interaction between courts and firms leads to the conclusion that courts can induce large firms to consistently create industry frameworks through creating laws that favor DQP company strategies while creating hurdles to the successful pursuit of price-competitive and innovative strategies. Because it leads to the investment of substantial collective benefits for firms, German public policy tends to favor DQP firms (see Streeck 1992*a*).

The trajectory of German institutional frameworks is more volatile than that in the United States. While there is at present little evidence that the system is changing, large firms and public actors both have the potential to change the system. The creation of industry frameworks requires collective action by large companies. The probability of strong legal regulation will continue to create incentives for companies to choose DQP strategies, while the system of business coordination allows DQP firms to continue to create important collective benefits that are not available to international competitors. While these factors lend stability to the system, they will also continue to produce institutional frameworks inhospitable to innovators. However, as the bargaining analysis made clear, even 'typical' German DQP companies do not get their preferred outcome: the development of industry frameworks without strong legal regulation. As international competition continues to intensify, firms may feel compelled to develop strategies that are not advantaged by German national institutional frameworks. German companies may increasingly be willing to pay the governance costs of opting out of German institutional frameworks in order to choose innovative or price competition strategies. Even if cooperation is cheap and rewarding, if enough important companies are not interested for other reasons, the German system of non-market-based business coordination could weaken.

Pressures for change could also emerge through public policy. The German public policy debate is increasingly focused on the perceived failure of German firms to compete in a number of high-technology sectors in which continual innovation appears to be paramount (Casper et al. 1999; Casper and Vitols 1997). The analysis here points to the disturbing conclusion that German policy-makers face a difficult dilemma. The disincentives to innovation in Germany arise from the existence of legal regulation and the reliance by firms on standardized industry frameworks. These are the exact framework conditions that advantage the DQP strategy. Thus, to promote widespread innovation within the economy, German public policy would have to encourage courts to pursue classical contract laws. Doing so would encourage potential price competitors and innovators to defect from the creation of industry frameworks, and eventually lead to the creation of market-based institutional frameworks resembling those in the United States. This is a core public policy dilemma in Germany—bolstering DQP types of corporate organization systematically punishes innovation.

13

Legal Irritants: How Unifying Law Ends up in New Divergences

Gunther Teubner

13.1 Legal Transplant: A Misleading Metaphor

Good faith is irritating British law. Recently, the (in)famous European Consumer Protection Directive 1994[1] transplanted the continental principle of *bona fides* directly into the body of British contract law where it has caused a great deal of irritation. A contractual term is unfair if 'contrary to the requirement of good faith, it causes significant imbalances in the parties' rights and obligations arising under the contract, to the detriment of the consumer.' The infecting virus had already earlier found inroads into the common law of contracts, especially in the United States where the Uniform Commercial Code and the Restatement (2d) of Contracts provide for a requirement of good faith in the performance and enforcement of contracts.[2] British courts have energetically rejected this doctrine on several occasions, treating it like a contagious disease of alien origin, as 'inherently repugnant to the adversarial position of the parties' and as 'unworkable in practice.'[3] But they are now at a loss how to deal with the EU Directive. And there is more to come, extending good faith well beyond consumer protection. Article 1.106 of the Principles of European Contract Law states:

(1) In exercising his rights and performing his duties each party must act in accordance with good faith and fair dealing.
(2) The parties may not exclude or limit this duty.

This chapter is an adaptation of an article that appeared in the *Modern Law Review* 61 (1998): 11–32 copyright the Modern Law Review Ltd.
  [1] Regulation 4 of the Unfair Terms in Consumer Contracts, SI 1994 No 3159, implementing the EU Directive on Unfair Terms in Consumer Contracts, Council Directive 93/13/EEC of 5 Apr. 1993 (OJ L95, 21 Apr. 1993: 29).
  [2] Uniform Commercial Code, UCC s. 1-203; Restatement (2d) of Contracts, s. 205.
  [3] *Walford* v. *Miles* [1992] 1 All ER 453, at 460–1.

Finally, in international commercial law, good faith is playing an increasingly important role.[4]

Some academic commentators have expressed deep worries: 'Good faith could well work practical mischief if ruthlessly implanted in our system of law' (Bridge 1984; cf. also Goode 1992). Others have welcomed good faith as a healthy infusion of communitarian values, hoping that it will cure the ills of contractual formalism and interact productively with other substantive elements in British contract law (Brownsword 1994: 197, 1996: 111). The whole debate is shaped by the powerful metaphor of the 'legal transplant.' Will good faith, once transplanted, be rejected by an immune reaction of the *corpus iuris britannicum*? Or will it function as a new organ interacting productively with other elements of the legal organism?

Repulsion or interaction? In my view, this is a false dichotomy because the underlying metaphor of legal transplants, suggestive as it is, is in itself misleading. I think 'legal irritant' expresses things better than 'legal transplant.' To be sure, transplant makes sense in so far as it describes legal import/export in organismic, not in machinistic, terms. Legal institutions cannot be easily moved from one context to another, like the 'transfer' of a part from one machine into another (Kahn-Freund 1978). They need careful implantation and cultivation in the new environment. But 'transplant' creates the wrong impression that after a difficult surgical operation the transferred material will remain identical with itself, playing its old role in the new organism. Accordingly, it comes down to the narrow alternative: repulsion or integration. However, when a foreign rule is imposed on a domestic culture, I submit, something else is happening. It is not transplanted into another organism, rather it works as a fundamental irritation which triggers a whole series of new and unexpected events. It irritates, of course, the minds and emotions of tradition-bound lawyers; but in a deeper sense—and this is the core of my thesis—it irritates law's 'binding arrangements.' It is an outside noise which creates wild perturbations in the interplay of discourses within these arrangements and forces them not only to reconstruct internally their own rules but to reconstruct from scratch the alien element itself. 'Legal irritants' cannot be domesticated, they are not transformed from something alien into something familiar, not adapted to a new cultural context, rather they will unleash an evolutionary dynamics in which the external rule's meaning will be reconstructed and the internal context will undergo fundamental change.

---

[4] On Art. 1.7 UNIDROIT Principles of International Commercial Contracts and Art. 7 (1) CISG, see Farnsworth (1995: 153); Schlechtriem (1997).

Thus, the question is not so much whether British contract doctrine will reject or integrate good faith. Rather, what kind of transformations of meaning will the term undergo, how will its role differ, once it is reconstructed anew under British law? And here is the point where the crucial question of 'production regimes' comes in.[5] In legal contexts, the different impact of various production regimes has rarely been discussed. In this chapter an attempt will be made to enquire into the significance of this concept for the transfer of private law rules from one economic culture to the other. The imperatives of a specific Anglo-American economic culture as against a specific continental one will bring about a fundamental reconstruction of good faith under the new conditions. This is why I think that, in spite of all benign intentions towards an 'Ever Closer Union,' attempts at unifying European contract law will result in new cleavages.

With this argument I take issue with two fundamental assumptions that are popular today in comparative law. One is the 'convergence thesis.'[6] In the current movements toward internationalization, Europeanization, and globalization, industrial nations are supposed to converge toward similar socio-economic structures. Consequently, socio-economic convergence makes uniformization of law as a primary objective appear simultaneously possible and desirable. The other is 'functional equivalence.' While national legal orders are still founded on diverse doctrinal traditions, they face the same structural problems which they have to resolve. Accordingly, they will find different doctrinal solutions as functional equivalents to the same problems which again results in convergence.[7] I question these assumptions because they are not aware of ongoing debates in the social sciences on globalization which make it plausible that the exact opposite of both assumptions is true. From these debates it seems that contemporary trends toward globalization do not necessarily result in a convergence of social orders and in a uniformization of law. Rather, new differences are produced by globalization itself.[8] These trends lead to a double fragmentation of world society into functionally

[5] See Hall and Soskice in the Introduction to this volume.

[6] *Locus classicus* is Kerr et al. (1960): Global cultural convergence is the result of industrialization processes. Its juridical resonances can be heard in Markesinis (1994: 30). He sees a convergence of sources of law, procedures, drafting techniques, and judicial views. Cf. also Helmholz (1990: 1207).

[7] Ancel (1971: 101–3); Zweigert and Kötz (1992: 31 n. 16); Bogdan (1994: 60); Glendon et al. (1994: 12 f.). Critical: Frankenberg (1985: 438); Hill (1989: 106 f.); Ewald (1995*a*: 1986); Legrand (1996: 55).

[8] Huntington (1993: 22) paints a rather dramatic scenario of global cleavages. More realistic appears a simultaneous increase of both convergence and divergence tendencies as a result of globalization: Friedman (1990); Featherstone and Lash (1995); Robertson (1995).

differentiated global sectors and a multiplicity of global cultures. Worse still, they result in a new exclusion of whole segments of the population from the modernizing effects (Luhmann 1994, 1995: 37; Sinha 1995). Accordingly, different sectors of the globalized society do not face the same problems for their laws to deal with, but highly different ones. The result is not more uniform laws but more fragmented laws as a direct consequence of globalizing processes.

While there is evidence of such fragmentation on the level of the global society, it is less apparent on the regional level. In Europe, especially, there is a movement towards unification through law. This appears to lend support to the view that there is increasing convergence and functional equivalence of different national solutions. Of course, differences in fragmentation on the global level and the European level are enormous. Nevertheless, I want to take good faith, an important element of the ongoing harmonization of European contract law, as my test case and put forward the argument that not only globalizing tendencies but also the efforts of Europeanization of national legal orders produce new divergences as their unintended consequences.

13.2 Context versus Autonomy

In stark contrast to mainstream comparative law, some outsiders have recently developed ambitious theoretical perspectives dealing with legal irritants and at the same time irritating the mainstream. I single out three authors: Pierre Legrand, Alan Watson, and William Ewald.

From an anthropologically informed 'culturalist' perspective Pierre Legrand stresses the idiosyncrasies of diverse legal cultures and irritates the European-minded consensus of comparativists with his provocative thesis that 'European legal systems are not converging' (Legrand 1995*a*, 1995*b*: 262, 1997). Of course, he argues, convergences are observable on the level of legal rules and institutions, but the deep structures of law, legal cultures, legal mentalities, legal epistemologies, and the unconscious of law as expressed in legal mythologies remain historically unique and cannot be bridged:

cultures are spiritual creations of their relevant communities, and products of their unique historical experience as distilled and interpreted over centuries by their unique imagination. (Bhikou Parekh, 1994, cited by Legrand 1995*a*: 10)

The crucial question is then how to identify conditions of convergence/divergence. The text identifies major conditions of convergence within the legal system and major conditions of divergence in its binding arrangements with other social systems.

These fundamental differences do not only exist between very distant world cultures, but between the laws of modern industrialized societies as well, and they are particularly strong between the common-law and the civil-law culture. Accordingly, legal transplants are exposed to the insurmountable differences of cultural organisms; they cannot survive, unchanged, the surgical operation:

Rather, the rule, as it finds itself technically integrated into another legal order, is invested with a culture-specific meaning at variance with the earlier one. Accordingly, a crucial element of the ruleness of the rule—its meaning—does not survive the journey from one legal culture to another. (Legrand 1995a: n. 33)

This is an exciting perspective which promises new insights from an adventurous journey through deeper and darker areas of comparative law. It is a contemporary reformulation of Montesquieu's culturalist skepticism against the easy transfer of legal institutions, but with the important modification that the *esprit des lois* is less a reflection of a national culture, but rather, of a specific legal culture. And it radically reconstructs legal transplants anew. This is done not from the author-perspective of the superimposing legal order, but from the viewpoint of the receiving legal culture, which is reading anew, reconstructing, recreating the text of the transplant.[9]

Promising as it is, this approach is however vulnerable to some important objections. How will it avoid the fatal calamities of any approach to *gesellschaftliche Totalität*, to 'totality of society' in which each legal element reflects the whole societal culture and vice versa? How will such an appeal to the totality of cultural meaning, to the ensemble of deep structures of law, and to society's culture *tout court* be translated into detailed analyses of interaction between law and culture? Legrand's still rather modest efforts stand in a somewhat strange contrast to the sweeping claims of his general program.[10] Secondly, how will he account for the manifold successful institutional transfers among western societies that have taken place rapidly and smoothly? And thirdly, does his own transfer into legal discourse of anthropological culturalist knowledge, which presumes that legal phenomena are deeply culturally embedded, take into account the fragmentation, differentiation, separation, closure of discourses that is so typical for the modern and postmodern

---

[9] The inspirational source is of course Stanley Fish and his reader-response theory, see Fish (1989, 1994).

[10] See Legrand (1995a, 1996), for a somewhat 'schematic' attempt at sorting out the differences between the civil law and the common law culture.

experience?[11] Does Legrand adequately reflect the double fragmentation of global society which consists not only in polyculturalism which he speaks about, but also in deep cleavages between discourses which he tends to neglect?[12]

In direct contrast to Legrand, the legal historian Alan Watson has an easy way to deal with these three objections. He provides rich historical evidence showing that transferring legal institutions between societies has been an enormous historical success despite the fact that these societies display a bewildering diversity of socio-economic structures. He explains the success of legal transplants by the highly developed autonomy of the modern legal profession (Watson 1985, 1987, 1993). He confronts functionalist comparativists with the theoretical argument that convergence of socio-economic structures as well as functional equivalence of legal institutions in fact do not matter at all. Neither does—this is his message to the culturalists—the totality of a society's culture.

These claims are based on three main arguments which deserve closer scrutiny. First, Watson asserts, comparative law should no longer simply study foreign laws but study the interrelations between different legal systems (Watson 1993: 1–21). In my view, this argument reflects rightly a major historical shift in the relation between nations and their laws and is apt to reduce inflated culturalist claims. Montesquieu, in his 'esprit des lois,' could still maintain that laws are the expression of the spirit of nations, that they are deeply embedded in and inseparable from their geographical peculiarities, their customs and politics. Therefore the transfer of culturally deeply embedded laws from one nation to the other was a *grand hasard*. Today, due to long-term historical processes of differentiation and globalization, the situation is indeed different. The primary unit is no longer the nation which expresses its unique spirit in a law of its own as a cultural experience which cannot be shared by other nations with different cultural traditions. Rather, national laws—similar to national economies—have become separated from their original comprehensive embeddedness in the culture of a nation. And globalizing processes have created one worldwide network of legal communications which downgrades the laws of the nation-states to mere regional parts

---

[11] Lyotard (1987) speaks of hermetic closure of discourses; Luhmann (1995) sees in the global society a double fragmentation: cultural polycentricity and functional differentiation; Habermas (1996) identifies within the lifeworld a multiplicity of discourses.

[12] Legrand needs to explain why he sees almost insuperable cleavages between different legal cultures while he negates similar cleavages between legal cultures on the one hand, political, economic, academic, aesthetic cultures on the other (Legrand 1995a). Particularly under postmodernist claims which accentuate the fragmentation of diverse discourses (Lyotard), this position is difficult to defend.

of this network which are in close communication with each other.[13] Therefore the transfer of legal institutions is no longer a matter of an interrelation of national societies where the transferred institution carries the whole burden of the original national culture. Rather it is a direct contact between legal orders within one global legal discourse. This explains the frequent and relatively easy transfer of legal institutions from one legal order to the other.

However, at the same time their ties to the 'life of nations' have not vanished. Although having become rather loose they still exist, but in a different form. And it must be said against Watson in his engaged polemics against mirror-theories of law and society that in spite of all differentiation and all autonomy of law we should not lose sight of the cultural ties of the laws and closely observe what happens to them when laws are decoupled from their national roots.

Second, Watson identifies transplants as the main source of legal change (Watson 1993: 95). The legal profession prefers to imitate and take over rules and principles from foreign legal orders rather than reacting directly to external stimuli from society. Watson traces this to the peculiarities of the legal profession who need to argue from precedent and authority. They prefer to derive their solutions from legal traditions and abhor a *creatio ex nihilo*. Again, he has a point here. However, the idiosyncrasies of the profession seem to me a secondary phenomenon. It is the inner logic of the legal discourse itself that builds on normative self-reference and recursivity and thus creates a preference for internal transfer within the global legal system as opposed to the difficult new invention of legal rules out of social issues. But once again, this preference of the legal discourse for its own products should not blind the analysis to the fact that usually in case of transplants the law reacts to external pressures that are then expressed in a recourse to foreign legal rules. And if one wants to understand the dynamics of legal transplants one must analyze those external pressures from culture and society carefully.

Third, Watson generalizes from his historical materials that legal evolution takes place rather insulated from social changes, that it tends to use the technique of 'legal borrowing' and can be explained without reference to social, political, or economic factors (Watson 1981: 38). Again, with the richness of his studies on the history of private law he scores a point against contextualists and culturalists who see law as mirroring

---

[13] For the debate on globalization and law, see Röhl and Magen (1996: 1); Twining (1996: 1); Teubner (1997).

culture and society. And his findings resonate with sociological theories
about cultural evolution which reject a historical trajectory for the whole
of society and identify, instead, separate evolutionary paths for different
sectors of society, among them law. Indeed, legal transplants seem to be
one main source for a specific legal evolution because they create variety
of meaning in law. However, here again, Watson has not finished his
task. In his polemics against contextualism he overgeneralizes and is not
willing to scrutinize more indirect, more subtle ways of law and society
interrelations.[14] He makes only one attempt when he describes the legal
professional elite as the translator of general culture to legal culture. But
here he identifies a surface phenomenon instead of scrutinizing the links
between the deep structure of different discourses (Watson 1985: ch. 5;
Watson 1987: 568 ff.). How will he integrate obvious counterexamples of
politically induced changes of the law, like the political transformation
of American public law in the Revolution, as analyzed by Ewald?[15] He
seems to be obsessed with the somewhat sterile alternative of cultural
dependency versus legal insulation, of social context versus legal
autonomy, an obsession which he shares, of course, with his opponents
(Abel 1982). The whole debate, it seems to me, needs some conceptual
refinement that would allow us to analyze institutional transfer in terms
different from the simple alternative context versus autonomy. Hopefully,
the refinement will not end up in the compromising formula that legal
transfers take place in 'relative autonomy'. . .

13.3 Binding Arrangements in a Fragmented Society

The impasse of context versus autonomy may be overcome by distinguishing two types of institutional transfer which Otto Kahn-Freund
suggested twenty years ago (Kahn-Freund 1978: 298 f.). He proposed to
distinguish between legal institutions that are culturally deeply embedded and others that are effectively insulated from culture and society.
Legal institutions are ordered alongside a spectrum which ranges from
the 'mechanical' where transfer is relatively easy to the 'organic' where
transfer is very difficult, if not outright excluded. At the same time Kahn-
Freund reformulated drastically the meaning of the 'organic,' shifting it
from the traditional comprehensive social embeddedness of law to a new

[14] This argument is made forcefully by Ewald (1994: 1, 1995*b*: 489), in his detailed critique
of Watson's work.

[15] Ewald (1994) uses historical studies of legal changes in the American Revolution which
corroborate roughly Watson's findings in the field of private law but contradict them
directly in the field of public law.

selective connectivity. Legal institutions are no longer totally intertwined in the whole fabric of society and culture; their primary interdependency is concentrated on politics. Thus, institutional transfers of the organic type depend mainly on their interlocking with specific power structures of the societies involved (Kahn-Freund 1978, 303 ff.).

I would like to build on these distinctions—mechanic/organic and comprehensive/selective—modifying them, however, to a certain degree. They provide indeed for the missing link in Watson's account of autonomous transplants and allow for a more sociologically informed formulation of Legrand's culturalism. They attempt to grasp what happened to the social ties of law in the great historical transformation from embeddedness to autonomy—something that I would call law's 'binding arrangements' (for this concept see Teubner 1992: 1443). True, Montesquieu's vision of a total union of law and national culture is no longer adequate for the formalized, technicized, professionalized law of our times which has achieved operational closure in the process of positivization. But, where something is excluded, it often returns through a back door. Law's old connections reappear in new disguises in which they are barely discernible.

I would like to put forward four theses of how the new ties of law look and elaborate on these in the remainder of the chapter:

1. Law's contemporary ties to society are no longer comprehensive, but are highly selective and vary from loose coupling to tight interwovenness.
2. They are no longer connected to the totality of the social, but to diverse fragments of society.
3. Where, formerly, law was tied to society by its identity with it, ties are now established via difference.
4. They no longer evolve in a joint historical development but in the conflictual interrelation of two or more independent evolutionary trajectories.

These four properties of law's binding arrangements share with a culturalist perspective the assumption that law is intricately interwoven with culture, but they differ when it comes to high selectivity of the bonds which excludes any talk about the 'totality of society.' They share with an autonomist perspective the assumption that it is naive to speak of law mirroring society, but they differ in their assessment of legal autonomy. Greater autonomy does not mean greater independence of law, rather a greater degree of interdependence with specific discourses in society.

What do these four properties of the new ties of law and society imply
for the transfer of legal institutions? In particular, how will the transfer
of continental good faith to British law be influenced by these selective
bonds?

13.4 Tight and Loose Coupling

The new ties are highly selective. Since contemporary legal rule production is institutionally separate from cultural norm production, large areas
of law are only in loose, non-systematic contact with social processes. It
is only on the ad hoc basis of legal 'cases' that they are confronted with
social conflicts. They reconstruct them internally as 'cases', deciding
them via the reformulation of preexisting rules. However, as opposed to
these spaces of loose coupling there are areas where legal and social
processes are tightly coupled. Here, legal rules are formulated in ultracyclical processes between law and other social discourses which bind
them closely together while maintaining at the same time their separation and mutual closure.[16]

Various formal organizations and processes of standardization as well
as references of law to social norms work as extra-legal rule-making
machines. They are driven by the inner logic of one specialized social
domain and compete with the legislative machinery and the contracting
mechanism (Teubner 1991: 134 ff.; Sand 1995: 85). This difference between
loose and tight coupling has implications for the institutional transfer
from one legal order to the other. Kahn-Freund's suggestion that institutional transfer may be of a 'mechanic' type or of a more 'organic' type
makes sense in the light of this difference. While in the loosely coupled
areas of law a transfer is comparably easy to accomplish, the resistance
to change is high when law is tightly coupled in binding arrangements
to other social processes.

We should, however, be aware that, even in areas of loose coupling,
where an institutional transfer is easier to accomplish, this is not as
'mechanical' as Kahn-Freund suggested, such as the analogy of changing
a carburetor in an engine. William Ewald in his subtle critique of both
legal contextualism and legal autonomism makes a forceful argument
against a purely mechanic transfer. Even in those situations when the
law is rather 'technical,' insulated from its social context, legal transfer
is not smooth and simple but has to be assimilated to the deep structure
of the new law, to the social world constructions that are unique to the

---

[16] For an analysis of ultracyclical processes in law and society see Teubner (1991).

different legal culture (Ewald 1995*a*: 1943 ff.). Here, in the difference of legal *epistemes*, in the different styles of legal reasoning, modes of interpretation, views of the social world, Legrand's culturalist ideas find their legitimate field of application, particularly under contemporary conditions. After the formal transfer, the rule may look the same but actually it has changed with its assimilation into the new network of legal distinctions. In such situations, the transfer is exposed to the differences of episode linkages that are at the root of different legal world constructions.[17] Legal cultures differ particularly in the way in which they interconnect their episodes of conflict solution. Here, the great historical divide between common-law and civil-law culture still has an important role to play.

Returning to our example, the famous *bona fides* principle is clearly one of the unique expressions of continental legal culture. The specific way in which continental lawyers deal with such a 'general clause' is abstract, open-ended, principle-oriented, but at the same time strongly systematized and dogmatized. This is clearly at odds with the more rule-oriented, technical, concrete, but loosely systematized British style of legal reasoning, especially when it comes to the interpretation of statutes. Does then the inclusion of such a broad principle in a British statute also imply that British lawyers are now supposed to 'concretize' this general clause in the continental way? Will British judges now 'derive' their decisions from this abstract and vague principle moving from the abstract to the concrete via different and carefully distinguished steps of concretization? Will they reconstruct good faith in a series of abstract well-defined doctrinal constructs, translate it into a system of conditional programmes, apply to it the obscurities of teleological reasoning, and indulge in pseudo-historical interpretation of the motives why good faith had been incorporated into the Euro-Directive? From my impressions of British contract law I would guess that good faith will never be 'transplanted' this way. But it will 'irritate' British legal culture considerably. Under the permanent influence of continental noise this culture is undergoing indeed considerable change and is developing a new order of principle-oriented statutory interpretation which is, however, remarkably different from its continental counterpart. New dissonances from harmonization!

Under present conditions it is inconceivable that British good faith will be the same as *Treu und Glauben* German style which has been developed

---

[17] See Teubner (1987, 1989: 727) for the relation of episode linkages to social world constructions of law.

in a rather special historical and cultural constellation. *Treu und Glauben* has been the revolutionizing instrument by which the formalistic civil code of 1900 has been 'materialized' and adapted to the convulsions of Germany's history in the twentieth century.[18] During this time German legal culture developed an intimate 'symbiotic relationship' between the new powers that the national constitution and the Civil Code had given to the judiciary and the old powers invested in the authorities of pandectic legal scholarship (Ewald 1995a: 2087). The result of this unique type of episode linkage was that the highly ambivalent and open-ended good faith principle, which was originally supposed to flexibly counteract on an ad hoc basis the rigidities of formal law, was actually propelled into an incredible degree of conceptual systematization and abstract dogmatization.[19] The law of good faith as it has been developed through extensive case law is divided into three functions: (1) expansion and establishment of contractual duties (*officium iudicis*); (2) limitation of contractual rights (*praeter legem*); (3) transformation of contract (*contra legem*).

The first function, which establishes an expansive doctrine of relational contracting, is divided into a series of doctrinal constructs: secondary duties of performance, duties of information, of protection, of cooperation. The second function deals with the doctrine of individual and institutional abuse of rights: disloyal acquisition of rights, violations of own duties, lack of legitimate interest, proportionality, contradictory behaviour. The third one expands the judicial power to rewrite contracts in the light of supervening events: imbalance of equivalence, frustration of contractual purpose, fundamental social changes (Soergel 1991: § 242, 6, 132 ff.; Staudinger 1995: § 242, 71, 969; Palandt 2001: § 242, 112 ff.). This thorough dogmatic systematization of good faith, a *contradictio in adiectu*, was possible only via a mutual reinforcement of judicial and professorial activism. Bold judicial decisions were sanctified under the condition that they obeyed the rigorous requirements of 'dogmatization' and vice versa. The trend continues; in the most recent round, academics criticize the judge-made law on good faith for its free-style argument, they lament that good faith is still lacking sufficient dogmatization, and push for a closer reintegration into the doctrinal system of German private law.[20]

---

[18] For a brilliant account of the materialization of private law and the role of good faith in this process, see Wieacker (1996: chs. 27–30).

[19] For an English language account of good faith in German Law, see Ebke and Steinhauer (1995); cf. also Schlechtriem (1997: 9 ff.).

[20] See the attempt at a systematic reintegration of good faith into the civil code by J. Schmidt in: Staudinger (1995: §242, 322–1556).

In Britain, it may well be that 'good faith' (together with 'legitimate expectation,' 'proportionality,' and other continental general clauses) will trigger deep, long-term changes from highly formal rule-focused decision-making in contract law toward a more discretionary principle-based judicial reasoning (see Levitsky 1994: 368–78). But it will probably move into a direction quite different from German-style dogmatization. Given the distinctive British mode of episode linkages, good faith will be developed rather in forms of judicial activism similar to those other common-law countries have adopted, combining close fact-oriented case analysis with loosely arranged arguments from broad principles and policies. Lawyers will avoid the recourse to elaborate intermediate structures, dogmatic constructs, juridical theories, and conceptual systematization which is so close to the heart of German law. The predictable result will be a judicial doctrine of good faith that is much more 'situational' in character.[21] 'English courts will inevitably prefer to imply more precise terms governing particular aspects of the business relation.'[22] As opposed to abstract and general 'conditional programmes' and to a series of finely circumscribed doctrinal figures based upon good faith, they will distinguish and elaborate different factual situations of contracting. They will not rely primarily on abstract distinctions developed by legal and economic theory (complete/incomplete, discrete/relational, consumer/commercial), rather begin to typify different 'relationships which are of common occurrence'[23] (landlord and tenant, doctor and patient, carrier and shipper, etc.) and will see the pressures of the factual situations.

On the basis of this type of information English law will develop on an analogical basis new rules coming out of a close analysis of the factual situations involved. And principles will enter the scene which will not be translated into strictly conceptualized and systematized doctrines, but rather appear as loosely organized ad hoc arguments that do not deny their political-ethical origin.

13.5 Tying Law to Social Fragments

Such an exposure to the deep structures of legal culture will take place in any type of institutional transfer, whether they are 'mechanic' or 'organic' in Kahn-Freund's sense, or whether they occur in situations of loose coupling or of tight coupling. Tight coupling will, however, pose

---

[21] For such a situational approach to good faith, see Rakoff (1994: 201 ff.).

[22] Collins (1997: 271).

[23] *Liverpool City Council* v. *Irwin* [1977] AC 239; *Shell UK Ltd.* v. *Lostock Garage Ltd.* [1976] 1 WLR 1187, at 1196 f.

additional difficulties. Transfers will not only be confronted with the idio-syncrasies of the new legal culture, they will have to face resistance which is external to the law. To identify the sources of resistance one must understand that today law meets its society as a fragmented multi-plicity of discourses.

Contemporary legal discourse is no longer an expression of society and culture *tout court*; rather it ties up closely only with some of its areas, only on specific occasions, and only to different fragments of society.[24] Today's society does not present itself to law as the mystical unity of nation, language, culture, and society, as *Volksgeist* in the sense of Savigny and Herder, but rather as a fractured multitude of social systems which allows accordingly only for discrete linkages with these fragments. Kahn-Freund expressed a similar idea, maintaining that among the many social factors Montesquieu had made responsible for the *esprit des lois*, today only certain ones matter. He singled out the political power discourse as law's primary link to society (Kahn-Freund 1978: 303 ff.).

This is an important insight which must however be modified. Kahn-Freund formulated his account in the early 1970s, and the emphasis on the law's political connections reflects the all-important political differ-ences of the Cold War, the ever-present heritage of Europe's political totalitarian regimes, the obsession with political institutions as the almost exclusive expression of society's relevant conflicts, and the high aspir-ations for political planning and steering which were prevalent in those days. From the somewhat sobering perspective of the new century, this seems to overestimate the importance of the political system at the expense of other social systems. These other subsystems have by no means lost their importance through a process of socio-economic conver-gence which would leave us only with differences in institutionalized politics, as Kahn-Freund argued. On the contrary, while political liberal constitutionalism has now become the dominant global norm, differences in respect of other discourses have gained in prominence. This is true especially for the different types of economic regimes under victorious global capitalism.

This has implications for institutional transfer. True, some legal insti-tutions are so closely coupled to the political culture of a society that their transfer to another society would require simultaneous profound changes of its political system if they are supposed to work properly in the new environment. This is the reason why Kahn-Freund was highly critical about the import of collective labor law rules from the United

---

[24] For an elaboration of this point, see Teubner (1992).

States to Britain. He denounced this as a (politically motivated) 'misuse' of comparative law.[25] But there are other legal institutions—especially in private law—whose ties to politics are rather loose while they are at the same time closely intertwined with economic processes. Others are tightly coupled to technology, to health, science, or culture. It is in their close links to different social worlds that we can see why legal institutions resist transfer in various ways. The social discourse to which they are tightly connected will not respond to the signals of legal change. It obeys a different internal logic and responds only to signals of change of a political, economic, technological, or cultural nature. Transfer will be effectively excluded without a simultaneous and complementary change in the other social field.

Good faith is a splendid example of this fundamental transformation from law's comprehensive social embeddedness to a more selective and fractured connectivity. While contract law in general can be adequately described as consisting of 'principles of voluntarism superimposed on underlying social patterns and statuses' (Rakoff 1995: 221), good faith has always been the element in contract law that directly connects with these patterns. But over time this recourse has taken on different forms co-varying with different forms of social organization. Historically, *bona fides* had been contract law's recourse to social morality (Esser 1956: 151–2; Wieacker 1996: ch. 25 III 3). Whenever the application of strict formal contract rules led to morally unacceptable results, *bona fides* was invoked to counteract the formalism of contract law doctrine with a substantive social morality. Contracts were performed in good faith when the participants behaved in accordance with accepted standards of moral behaviour.

Under contemporary conditions of moral pluralization and social fragmentation, good faith cannot play this role any more. There have been attempts to take into account these historical changes and to replace recourse to morality by recourse to the 'purpose' of the legal institutions involved. Contracts are performed in good faith when the participants are responsive to the policy of the rules, the *telos* of their rights, the *idées directrices* of the institutions, the elements of *ordre public*, the values of the political constitution within private arrangements.[26] This new policy-oriented interpretation of good faith which gained high prominence in this century, especially in the debate about institutional *abus des droits*,

---

[25] Kahn-Freund (1978: 316 ff.) it is another question, of course, whether they were ever supposed to work 'properly'.

[26] For a thorough rethinking of German contract law and good faith in such a policy-oriented perspective, see Esser and Schmidt (1991: § 1 II, § 2 II, § 4 IV).

reflected indeed the more selective nature of law's social ties. It concentrated them on the policies of institutionalized politics. But in a sense it privileged the political ties of law, neglecting ties to other discourses.

Formal contractual obligations are not only linked to substantive policy requirements and the *ordre public* of institutionalized politics, they are equally exposed to substantive demands of other social institutions. Markets and organizations, the professions, the health sector, social security, family, culture, religion—they all impose certain requirements on the 'private' contractual relation. Invoking good faith in such situations means making visible how contractual expectations depend upon a variety of non-contractual social expectations, among them (but not exclusively) policy expectations, and their reconstruction within the contract. Unbounded priority of the individual consensus between parties to the contract cannot be insisted upon, whether one is dealing with matters of individual conscience, strict religious prohibitions, political freedoms, regulatory policies, or economic institutions. Good faith complements contractual duties with social expectations stemming from those various fields. Due to its high degree of indeterminacy, the general clause of good faith is particularly suited to link contracts selectively to their unstable social environments with constantly shifting and conflicting requirements.[27]

It is this selective and fractured linkage of good faith to highly diverse social environments that will be responsible for newly emerging cleavages. If, under European law, good faith is transferred from the Continent to British law and if it is supposed to play also in the new context its role of linking contracts to a variety of different discourses, then it is bound to produce results at great variance with continental legal orders. Good faith will reproduce in legal form larger differences of the national cultures involved, and it will do so, paradoxically, because it was meant to make their laws more uniform.

In the considerations to follow we cannot deal with the many links that good faith establishes toward different discourses. We will concentrate on only one of the links good faith is creating, that is the link of contracts to the production regimes in their economic environment. What happens to the institutional transfer of good faith clauses when they are indeed tightly coupled to the production regimes of the countries involved?

---

[27] For a reformulation of good faith in contemporary society, see Teubner (1980: 32–91, 1993: ch. 6 IV, V).

13.6 Divergent Production Regimes

Here we are confronted with results in comparative political economy which undermine the assumptions of mainstream comparative law about 'convergence' and 'functional equivalence' mentioned above (e.g. Porter 1990; Albert 1993; Crouch and Streeck 1995; Soskice 1999). Against all expectations that globalization of the markets and computerization of the economy will lead to a convergence of legal regimes and to a functional equivalence of legal norms in responding to their identical problems, the opposite has turned out to be the case. Against all talk of 'regulatory competition' which is supposed to wipe out institutional differences, legal regimes under advanced capitalism have not converged. Instead, new differences have been created, even under the unifying attempts of the European Common Market. Despite liberalization of the world markets and the legal establishment of the Common Market, the result of the last thirty years is the establishment of more than one form of advanced capitalism. And the differences in production regimes seem to have increased (Soskice 1997*a*). Obviously, production regimes are the place where private law comes into play. The principles of good faith play the role of the major binding arrangement between the rules of private law and economic production regimes.

If we look at the German context, where good faith has been a driving force in contract law, we find that the developments of this legal principle are closely linked to a specific production regime (see Streeck 1995). Here, the judicial requirements of performing a contract in good faith have been deeply influenced by an economic culture which is best described as a coordinated market economy (Soskice 1997: 75). In general, it can be said that this production regime has been facilitated and supported by a system of private law in which the courts used particularly the good faith principle to legally respond to the risks and opportunities which the mixture of autonomy and trust produced in the specific production regime.

More specifically, the following characteristics of the German production regime find their structural correlates in an extensive series of good faith obligations which have been developed by the courts.[28]

1. German corporate governance and corporate finance tend to favor long-term financing of firms. Private law supports this by good faith

---

[28] The text builds especially on Soskice (1997*a*, 1997*b*), and expands his analyses in the direction of private law requirements.

obligations which the participant owners, companies and banks, owe to each other. Under the umbrella of good faith, not only partners of a business association are under a general duty of mutual loyalty; German law acknowledges a far-reaching obligation upon the owners of capital and other constituencies of the firm to further actively the long-term 'company interest' as opposed to their partial self-interest (see Teubner 1994). An extensive system of duties of disclosure and provision of information has been developed in the relation between bank and company.

2. Industrial relations within the firm and in the industry are highly cooperative relations in which labor unions play an important part. As a corollary of employees' high autonomy, the courts have developed extensive good faith duties of loyalty toward the organization which mitigate the risk of moral hazard inherent in their autonomous position. In turn the law gives them a protected status within the firm. There are equally extensive legal duties of responsibility and care of managers toward the employees.[29]

3. Inter-company relations tend to be cooperative networks with relational long-term contracting, horizontally within markets as well as vertically between different suppliers, producers, and distributors. Under the good faith clause, courts have imposed duties of cooperation which are geared toward the common purpose of the contract. In relational contracts they have developed the general duty *ex lege* to renegotiate contractual terms if a new situation arises. And one of the most important judicial innovations has been to reintroduce the old *clausula rebus sic stantibus* which the Civil Code had excluded. Judges take the freedom to rewrite contractual terms in case of supervening events.[30]

4. Business associations and large firms coordinate markets via technical standard-setting, business standard contracting, and dispute resolution. In support of this self-coordination of industries, courts have recognized and reconstructed multilateral firm relations well beyond the wording of bilateral contracts.[31] However, their most important contribution to associational market coordination was to acknowledge standard terms as binding and to regulate them by taking certain interests, particularly that of the consumer, into account.[32]

5. Business associations negotiate technical and business standards with government. Other non-economic interest groups, such as consumer

---

[29] See e.g. Zöllner and Loritz (1998: §§ 12–17).
[30] For an overview, see Schlechtriem (1997: 9 ff.).
[31] For an extensive treatment see Gernhuber (1989).
[32] Ursula Stein in: Soergel (1991), Schuldrecht II, *AGB-Gesetz*, Einl. 3–8.

associations and ecological movements, favour a 'neo-corporatist' culture of mediating economic transactions with their outside world, with political, social, and ecological concerns. The courts can build on such a body of negotiated *ordre public* and reconstruct good faith standards on its basis to counteract excessive economic transactions (see Teubner 1980).

An implantation of this 'living law' into the British soil simply would not find its roots in a corresponding economic culture. How would good faith duties of cooperation, information, renegotiation, contractual adaptation 'fit' into a production regime that is characterized by the traits of a LME?[33] The British economic culture does not appear to be a fertile ground on which continental *bona fides* would blossom. Thus, the 'legal transplant' approach would lead us to expect repulsion, not interaction. The good faith clause will remain an exotic exception in the British landscape. Alternatively, what is the narrative that emerges from the 'legal irritant' metaphor?

13.7 Coevolving Trajectories

Here we have to take a further complication into account: the Janus-like character of law's binding arrangements. Economic 'rules of the game' are not identical with legal rules; economic institutions are different from legal institutions. An economic transaction needs to be distinguished from a legally valid contract, even if they occur at the same instant. The difference in a nutshell is that economic institutions are constraint and incentive structures that influence cost–benefit calculations of economic actors, while legal institutions are ensembles of legally valid rules that structure the resolution of conflicts. While being in a relation of tight structural coupling, economic institutions and legal ones are not only analytically but empirically distinct from each other.[34]

Structural coupling does not create a new identity, rather it binds via a difference—via the difference that distinguishes law from the discourse to which it is bound. Binding arrangements do not create a new unity of law and society, unified socio-legal operations, or common socio-legal structures. While their events happen simultaneously, they remain distinct parts of their specific discourse with a different past and a different future. The only condition for their synchronization is this: they need to be compatible with each other. Binding arrangements are Janus-headed,

---

[33] For the following see particularly Soskice (1991: 45, 1997*a*, 1997*b*).
[34] For details see Teubner (1992).

they have a legal face and a social face. And unfortunately, the two faces of Janus tend to change their minds in different directions.

Now, when in case of a legal transfer the legal side of the relation is changed this compatibility of diverse units can no longer be presupposed; it would have to be recreated in the new context, which is a difficult and time-consuming process. It would involve a double transformation, a change on both sides of the distinction of the transferred institution, not only the recontextualization of its legal side within the new network of legal distinctions but also the recontextualization of its social side in the other discourse. There is no unilateral determination of the direction in which the change of the other side will take place. Their interrelation cannot be described as institutional identity. It is equally wrong to describe it as causal dependency between an independent and a dependent variable, not to speak of a 'last instance' relation between economic base and legal superstructure. Rather, it is a symbolic space of compatibility of different meanings which allows for several possible actualizations.

A binding arrangement, tying law to a social discourse, does not develop in one single historical trajectory but in two separate and qualitatively different evolutionary paths of the two sides which are reconnected via coevolution. Their legal side takes part in the evolutionary logics of law while the social side obeys a different logic of development. Their changes however interact in so far as due to their close structural coupling they permanently perturb each other and provoke change on the other side.

Now it becomes clear why the transferred rule can only serve as an irritation, and never as a transplantation, if a transfer of legal rules is supposed to change a binding arrangement between law and another social discourse. It irritates a coevolutionary process of separate trajectories. On the legal side of the binding institution, the rule will be recontextualized in the new network of legal distinctions and it may still be recognizable as the original legal rule even if its legal interpretation changes. But on the social side, something very different will take place. The legal impulse, if it is recognized at all, will create perturbations in the other social system and will trigger there some changes governed by the internal logics of this world of meaning. It will be reconstructed in the different language of the social system involved, reformulated in its codes and programmes, which leads to a new series of events. This social change in its turn will work back as an irritation to the legal side of the institution thus creating a circular coevolutionary dynamics that comes to a preliminary equilibrium only once both the legal and the social discourse will have evolved relatively stable eigenvalues in their respective sphere. This shows how improbable it is that a legal rule will be successfully transplanted into a binding arrangement of a different legal context. If it is not rejected outright, either it destroys the binding arrangement or it will result in a dynamics of mutual irritations that alter its identity fundamentally.

And good faith? It will not even be an irritant to the British production regime if it presents itself as a bundle of legal duties of mandatory cooperation, German style, imposed on the parties to a contract. The British regime would react with cool indifference. However—and this is my concluding thesis—good faith will become a strong irritation to the market-driven production regime in Britain if the new context transforms good faith from a facilitative rule into a prohibitive rule. Instead of facilitating autonomy, trust, and cooperation, its effect would be to outlaw certain excesses of economic action. Good faith would become a quasi-constitutional constraint on two central elements of the production regime: a constraint on strong hierarchies of private government and a constraint on certain expansionist tendencies of competitive processes.

The continental production regime to which *Treu und Glauben* responded, as we said, was characterized by high autonomy and high trust relations within the market and within the organizations. They carry specific risks and dangers which were mitigated by an elaborate system of legal cooperation duties. The risks and dangers that the British production regime carries are not problems of high autonomy and high trust, but rather the opposite. This production regime is governed by the risks of 'financial Fordism' where low-cost standardized production requires detailed work regulation and frequent personnel change, by the dangers of project organizations that manage complex tasks by a strong managerial prerogative, by the steep hierarchy within economic organization, and asymmetric relations between powerful companies and their dependent satellites (see Soskice 1999). The role of the good faith principle cannot conceivably be to transform these tightly coordinated organizations into cooperative arrangements.[35] Rather, the task for contract law would be to define quasi-constitutional rights and to protect them against encroachments of private government, to set low-discretionary rules that

---

[35] Production regimes are not easy to change by political action. And there is an in-built asymmetry. While it is comparably easy to switch from an association-driven regime to a market-driven regime, just by politically dismantling existing intermediary structures, it is infinitely more difficult, time and energy consuming, to move from market coordination to business coordination by political will. See Soskice (1997a).

draw clearly defined legal limits to quasi-administrative discretion.[36] The good faith principle would have to develop into judicial constraints on arbitrary decisions of private government. As opposed to activating the communitarian traditions of 'duties' of trustful cooperation, the judiciary would have to activate the tradition of constitutional 'rights' which historically have been invoked against governmental authority, and reinforce them in the private law context.

There is a second reinterpretation of good faith which seems equally relevant in the new production regime. It takes into account the fundamental difference between associational coordination and market-driven coordination in standard-setting—in the broad sense of technical, intra-organizational, and contractual standards. While on the Continent the judiciary frequently refers to neo-corporatist processes of standardization where negotiations between associations result in a certain mediation of social and political interests with market results,[37] standard-setting in Britain is basically driven by market processes. Thus, according to its production regime, British law tends to invalidate standard terms when business associations have been involved unilaterally in the uniformization of standard terms in the whole market. In *George Mitchell (Chesterhall) Ltd.* v. *Finney Lock Seeds Ltd.* the court saw it as an invalidating factor that 'a similar limitation of liability was universally embodied in the terms of trade between seedsmen and farmers and had been so for many years.'[38] Under the British production regime, business associations are not supposed to play a decisive role in the formulation of standard contracts. The courts see it as a market failure when business associations produce uniform standard contracts which exclude competition between diverse contractual regimes (Collins 1997: 242). This is in striking contrast to the German situation where business associations play a crucial role in the unilateral standardization of business conditions (Casper 1996). As a consequence, under German good faith rules it does not make a difference whether the standard contracts have been formulated by one enterprise or by business associations for the whole market.[39]

Under the British production regime, it is exceptional for standard terms to be bilaterally negotiated by the relevant interest associations to

---

[36] So-called horizontal effect of constitutional rights. For a sociological discussion, Selznick (1969: ch. 7); for an application of basic rights as legal constraints on private government, Collins (1992). A recent comparative analysis of horizontal effects of fundamental rights is Clapham (1996).

[37] BGHZ 102, 41, 51; Ursula Stein in: Soergel (1991: § 9, 22).

[38] Lord Bridge, [1983] 2 AC 803, [1983] 2 All ER 737 (HL).

[39] Ursula Stein in Soergel (1991: § 1, 11, § 9, 22).

which the courts could then refer as a fair compromise. Standardization is more or less exclusively left to market mechanisms. In such a situation, it would be disastrous if the judiciary understood good faith as an incorporation of spontaneously developed standards into private law. The law would simply sanction the standard-eroding effects of market competition and would effectively rule out non-economic political and cultural aspects of standardization. In such a situation, the role of the judiciary becomes much closer to that of an external political regulatory agency which sets firm boundaries to market dynamics when they work against the fundamental requirements of other social spheres.[40] In conjunction with government, regulatory agencies, and quasi-public organizations, the judiciary of the British production regime needs to set on its own external standards to economic action without having recourse to social norms that have been preformulated in inter-associational negotiations.

Thus, the procedural dimension of good faith is profoundly influenced by the difference of production regimes. If good faith means among other things that one party has to take the other party's legitimate interest into account, and in the case of consumer contracts that standardized contracts must reflect the consumer interest,[41] then the central question is what kind of procedures are effectively working to satisfy this requirement. This is, to be sure, a more demanding procedural requirement of good faith than the usual question of absence of pressure and deception. Under an association-driven production regime the courts have to monitor whether the negotiations between different associations and regulatory agencies fulfill the procedural requirement of an adequate and effective representation of consumer interests in the process of standardization. Their corrective action would primarily consist in changing the rules of the game and redefining the property rights of the collective actors involved. Under a market-driven production regime, the courts will have to take a more active approach in order to make sure that standardized contracts fulfill the procedural requirements of good faith. In the absence of associational negotiations they have to rely on a division of labor with regulatory agencies, particularly the Office of Fair Trading and the Trading Standards Departments of local government authorities.[42] However, as has been well documented, those procedures seem to have 'serious defects' (Beale 1995; Office of Fair Trading 1990). This

---

[40] Brownsword (1997: 271): 'the law of consumer contracts must be seen nowadays as a regulatory regime in its own right.'

[41] Preamble, s. 16 to the Council Directive n. 1 above.

[42] See the annual report, Office of Fair Trading (1996).

implies that for the time being the courts themselves will have to carry the main burden of making sure that the procedural requirements of good faith are satisfied. Instead of monitoring a negotiation process, the courts will have to answer themselves the substantive questions involved and decide about how to account for the legitimate interest of the other party to the contract.

Such an interpretation of good faith which is oriented to the peculiarities, opportunities, risks, and dangers of a specific production regime would indeed result in widely divergent rules in different countries, even in contradictory decisions in apparently equal cases. These cleavages cannot and should not be papered over by the European zeal for harmonization of laws. If there is a role for the European legal authorities to play, it would be to strengthen the capacity for irritation of the good faith clause instead of neutralizing it when they try to enforce its unitarian interpretation.

European efforts at harmonization have not yet seriously taken into account the 'varieties of capitalism', the difference of production regimes. If there is a lesson to learn then it would be a new interpretation of the subsidiarity principle, understood no longer only in terms of political decentralization, rather of respect for the autonomy of social, economic, and cultural sectors, devolution of rule-making powers to social groups, and a reinterpretation of conflict of laws no longer in terms of national laws but of different production regimes.[43]

And maybe the young emerging network of European nations may learn a lesson from the experiences of another slightly older federation of nations, the Commonwealth. Recently the Privy Council allowed for the possibility that a House of Lords decision about the general clause of negligence need not be adopted throughout the Commonwealth if this were not warranted by the 'general pattern of socio-economic behaviour'.[44] This sounds a bit like the diversity of production regimes: A general legal principle allows for a diversity of concrete decisions once it is respecified in different social and economic cultural contexts. This is not a question of Euro-philia or Euro-phobia, rather a question of Euro-paradoxia, the paradox of the *unitas multiplex* which requests the integrating law against all the rhetorics of an 'ever closer union' to pay utmost respect to the autonomy and diversity of European cultures:

Le devoir de répondre à l'appel de la mémoire européenne. . . . dicte de respecter

---

[43] For a new perspective on European integration in terms of pluralization, fragmentation utilizing the idea of network, see Ladeur (1997: 33); Joerges (1996).

[44] *Invercargill City Council* v. *Hamlin* (1994) 3 NZLR 513; (1996) AC 264.

la différence, l'idiome, la minorité, la singularité . . . commande de tolérer tout ce qui ne se place pas sous l'autorité de la raison.[45]

To summarize our more abstract reflections, attempts at institutional transfer seem to produce a double irritation in the new context. They irritate law's binding arrangements to society. Foreign rules are irritants not only in relation to the domestic legal discourse itself but also in relation to the social discourse to which law is, under certain circumstances, closely coupled. As legal irritants, they force the specific *episteme* of domestic law to a reconstruction in the network of its distinctions. As social irritants they provoke the social discourse to which law is closely tied to a reconstruction of its own. Thus, they trigger two different series of events whose interaction leads to an evolutionary dynamics which may find a new equilibrium in the eigenvalues of the discourse involved. The result of such a complex and turbulent process is rarely a convergence of the participating legal orders, rather the creation of new cleavages in the interrelation of operationally closed social discourses.

[45] Derrida (1991). For such a perspective in contract law, see Collins (1995: 353).

14

National Varieties of Standardization

Jay Tate

14.1 Introduction

Industrial revolutions are revolutions in standardization. The industrial revolution of the late eighteenth and early nineteenth centuries depended upon fabrication standards for relatively unitary products such as textiles, pins, and firearms. The revolution of the mid-nineteenth century, driven by scientific advances in chemistry, steam power, and electricity, relied in part upon measurement standards for a broad array of fundamental quantities including time, distance, energy, electrical charge, and atomic weight. A third revolution dating from the beginning of the twentieth century transformed assembly industries by employing compatibility standards for complex devices such as automobiles. The late twentieth century's revolution in information technology and telecommunications spread on the basis of interoperability standards.

Standards provide linchpins for sustainable change. Standards support individual and organizational learning, monitoring, benchmarking, and collaboration. Firms use standards to reduce internal and external transaction costs; to drive down prices from suppliers; to block or circumvent competitors; to lock in quasi-monopoly profits through control of a proprietary standard; to gain greater control over employees, suppliers, and customers; and to set baselines for subsequent rounds of innovation. Economies of scale, scope, speed, and quality are all built on the use of standards.

And yet, standards and even standards institutions are themselves anything but standard. Instead, national arrangements for standardization vary according to historically rooted, and often nationally distinct, institutional trajectories (Zysman 1996*a*). A distinction between liberal market economies (LMEs) and coordinated market economies (CMEs) offers a useful way to compare these national varieties and to analyze their interactions.

National approaches to standards crystallized during the first half of the twentieth century in ways that reflected their respective chronological, legal, and socio-political origins (cf. Verman 1973; Cargill 1989). Timing mattered because although standardization in all countries has always involved a mixture of competitive, cooperative, and coercive elements (Greenstein 1992), the mixture of these elements has varied, both worldwide over time (the relative importance of direct coercion has declined) and within individual countries as they compared themselves to one another. Countries earliest to develop national market standards were most likely to favor liberal approaches based on markets and competition. Follower countries, already possessing a partial roadmap to the future, could develop more cooperative/coordinated approaches. Countries furthest behind were most likely to rely to a larger degree upon direct state coercion (cf. Gerschenkron 1962). Thus, many capitalist countries in Asia have state-run standards-setting institutions while in western Europe only Portugal does so.

However, timing provided at most a set of starting points. Law, itself an early bastion of national standardization, mattered more. Particularly important were the legal approaches to negligence and liability that began to be elaborated as nineteenth-century industries generated unprecedented occasions for previously unheard-of injuries. In Germany, France, Japan, and other countries reliant upon a national code, producer negligence was specified in detailed and a priori regulations that governed not only standard-setting, but also standards-testing and certification.

Within this code-based ('continental') family, at least two types of standardization developed. In Germany and Japan, code-based regulations supported a conservative, fault-based approach to product liability and a producer-oriented tolerance for sectoral (Germany) or intersectoral (Japan) cartels. Firms in those countries enjoyed broad leeway to engage in relatively intensive standards coordination. However, in post-revolutionary France and to a lesser degree in quasi-revolutionary countries influenced by France's Code Napoléon (e.g. Italy and Spain), code-based regulations supported a stricter approach to product liability resembling that in common-law countries, as well as an active ban on many pre-revolutionary ('feudal') types of inter-firm collaboration. Standard-setting in these latter countries was more likely to be mediated through a third party, typically an agent of the state, rather than arranged purely by economic actors themselves, resulting in what might be called a *mediated market economy*.

Common-law traditions in countries such as Britain and the USA did not attempt to specify negligence precisely in advance. Liability remained open ('strict')—it could be found even in the absence of intent or negligence—and shifted according to whatever accumulated case law said it

was. By being less settled, common law encouraged firms to be more creative, but by leaving liability unspecified, it also encouraged them to
avoid any hint of legally actionable collaboration with one another. At
least two types of liberal standardization developed. In Britain, generalized management standards help mitigate the liability risks and related
insurance costs engendered under a common-law system. In the USA,
where federalism has encouraged a highly decentralized, even fragmented, standards system (Krislov 1997), British-style economy-wide
management standards have played less of a role than mergers. US
firms historically avoided inter-firm liability and antitrust prosecution
through acquisitions that brought collaboration in-house. Since US
firms preferred to combine rather than face the legal uncertainties of
collaboration, they favored manufacturers' self-certification over third-
party certification.

Politics mattered in all countries, not only in channeling how a code
or common-law legal tradition could play out, but also in shaping the
character of standardization itself. National approaches to standards
tended to crystallize during whichever period (usually the first third of
the twentieth century) national standards institutions were first created.
In countries where the hegemony of middle-class professions *preceded*
industrialization, the choice was open for essentially pre-industrial free
professions to become the template that later structured engineering and
other technical occupations (Haber 1991), thereby supporting an endur-
ingly liberal approach to standards. Britain, France, and the United States
were such countries, although the liberal settlement was weak in France,
where the Vichy regime's anti-liberal subordination of professionals
had effects that lasted long after 1940–4. By contrast, in countries where
the initial elaboration of national standards institutions took place
under aliberal political regimes, free markets and free professionals were
rejected in favor of a political subordination of markets (cf. Luebbert
1991). Indeed, wherever a legacy of serious challenges to business
hegemony was greater, whether from the right or the left, a more coordinated approach to standards arose and tended to persist. Combined with
a history of reinventing (rather than undermining) guilds, societies such
as Germany and Japan developed a more coordinated approach to standardization based upon continued, and occasionally intensified, subordination of experts within particular organizations. In these countries,
cooperative standardization tended to become the domain of industrial
associations rather than individual-oriented professional societies.

In short, both liberal and coordinated market economies engage in
standardization, but the ease of 'exit,' and the character of 'voice,' and

the basis of 'loyalty' all differ. In a liberal market economy, it is relatively easy to abandon the formal standards-setting process in favor of a proprietary alternative. The most devoted standards participants tend to be motivated by professional and individualistic incentives such as personal reputation, disciplinary networking, and opportunities to monitor employment alternatives (cf. Blau and Scott 1962: 60–3; Wilson 1989: 60). Standards institutions tend to be run like for-profit institutions and are expected to 'compete' for customers. Even when standardization takes place within an industry association and participants are funded by their respective companies, liberal institutional constraints can force participants to behave more like professionals: US Supreme Court decisions, for example, have made it clear that standardization participants within an industry association, under threat of antitrust prosecution, are expected to behave as neutral experts (Curran 1998). State actors with needs unmet by a relatively uncoordinated economy may intervene directly to secure a particular standard, though this in turn tends to weaken efforts at broader coordination. Firms are inclined to view standards, and even standards institutions, less as an opportunity for collaboration and more as an occasion for tactical opportunism. At the low end, opportunistic firms in LME settings use standards simply to increase price competition. At the high end, firms use standards, often in tandem with intellectual property rights, to control radical innovations. At either end, standards in an LME tend to become merely another object of strategic manipulation, whether predatory or innovative.

In a coordinated market economy, by contrast, standardization participants are less directly exposed to markets, less capable of defecting from existing institutional arrangements, more likely to be rooted in particular organizations (cf. Wilson 1989: 58), and more likely to seek anticipatory standardization (or at least pre-competitive efforts to narrow the range of possible standards). Standards institutions themselves are run less like a profit center and more like an underlying part of the economic infrastructure. State actors tend to utilize, reinforce, and extend the existing standards infrastructure. Even nominally professional organizations may be organized, as in Japan, so as to support standardization on an organizational rather than individual or professional basis. Because those working on standards are bound more securely to particular firms, and firms are bound more securely to the national standards system, defections are rarer, and reliance upon market-based *de facto* standardization less common. Long-standing collaborative relationships and encompassing institutions encourage firms in CME settings to treat standards and standards institutions as parametric 'rules of the game,' i.e. as a shared infrastructure for further incremental innovation. By collaborating in the creation of detailed standards that weed out technically inferior outcomes, firms minimize the opportunities for price-based competition and facilitate higher value-added production strategies.

Standards are one of the leading challenges in contemporary capitalism. National differences in standardization have already had profound consequences for firm behavior and performance, and may continue to do so, especially since it appears that *these differences can persist even at a transnational level*. For example, a liberal approach may favor standards arising from a variety of competing sources ('global standards') while a coordinated approach may favor standards that are more formally and centrally coordinated ('international standards'). Moreover, in addition to becoming a central component of firm strategy, national differences in standardization also have important implications for everything from privacy and consumer behavior to patterns of nation-building, international relations, and global social movements. A closer understanding of national approaches to standards can offer many rewards.

14.2 Britain

British firms have supported, and as a result been trapped within, a lowest-common-denominator approach to standardization that has proven relatively incapable of providing the range and quality of product and process standards available to firms in other leading industrial countries. Indeed, rigidities in the British standardization system may have been a proximate cause of Britain's long-standing relative industrial decline.

Such a conclusion is initially surprising. Britain has the oldest, largest, best-funded ($150 million annual budget) national standards organization in the world, the British Standards Institution (BSI). Through at least the 1960s, BSI was widely considered the world's leading standards institution; it was often the model for other countries, not only in Europe but also throughout the Commonwealth. It continues to have the largest number of paying members and what it claims to be the largest library collection of standards in the world. BSI's example informally established principles adopted by many other, especially European, national standards organizations. (1) The peak standards institute is an independent private organization that receives some public financing. (2) The institute is granted an effective monopoly over standards development across a broad swath of economic activity. (3) Participants develop standards within technical committees according to formal procedures that seek to

assure consensus-oriented, voluntary, unpaid participation by all interested parties. (4) Draft standards are publicly disseminated to increase
the probability that all adopted standards are effectively consensus standards. (5) Completed standards are diffused by means of for-profit sales.

Despite superior staff and financial resources, however, the number of
British standards (even including all standards adopted from the
European and international level) is 30 per cent lower than the corresponding figure in France and 40 per cent lower than in Germany. Ties
between industry and BSI have long been relatively weak and subject to
easy 'exit'; indeed, BSI has had relatively little formalized relations of
any kind with the some forty other standards-related organizations in
Britain despite state designation in 1942 as the 'sole organisation' responsible for standards (Hesser and Inklaar 1997: 75).[1]

British firms arrived at this impasse by pursuing liberal market strategies in standardization. British firms were historically lured by the easy
money to be made through their superior connections in the rapidly
developing but less sophisticated markets of the British Empire. The
extreme 'finance- and commerce-driven economy' that Weiss and
Hobson suggest (1995: 235) differentiates Britain from the US version of
liberal capitalism derived in part from the unparalleled market access
Empire and Commonwealth gave British firms in less developed countries. Firms wanted standards that supported exports to less developed
countries. Some of the earliest BSI standards were developed for the
Indian Railways (Woodward 1972: 49), and BSI had begun to establish
standards committees in former Dominions of the Empire (beginning
with South Africa in 1908) a decade before most countries had established even a domestic standards organization.

The imperial approach to standards not only persisted during the shift
to Commonwealth institutions in the 1950s, there was a sharp increase
in state support for BSI outreach abroad. A series of Commonwealth-
level standardization conferences took place in 1946, 1951, 1953 (the year
BSI opened a new 45,000-square-foot facility), 1957, and 1962. These
efforts to maintain imperial-era markets, while popular with many
British firms, did nothing to advance the quality of British standardization relative to that in other advanced industrial countries. Moreover,
even when Britain joined the European Free Trade Association (EFTA) in
1960 and dropped Commonwealth-level standardization in 1962, the turn

---

[1] When BSI's authority *did* expand, as when BSI assumed full responsibility for civil
engineering Codes of Practice on 16 Oct. 1973 (Lukes 1979: 70), it did so not by coordinating industry-level efforts, but by displacing them.

to 'international' standardization at ISO was in fact mostly—especially since British firms often continued to neglect the largest European countries—a reincarnation of the old emphasis on less developed markets; British firms were often merely attempting to increase their presence in newly postcolonial countries that had previously been outside the British sphere of influence. Although the original European Economic Community (EEC) members had established a standards committee in 1957, Britain had no contact with these discussions until 1961, the year that the standards committees of EFTA and the EEC merged. Affiliated with EFTA rather than the EEC, British firms tended to neglect European standardization even after the merger, preferring to concentrate on ISO and IEC standards. BSI became the leading holder of secretariats at ISO and IEC and by the early 1970s was already devoting more effort to 'international' standards than to national or European standards.

As it became clearer that BSI standards and firms were losing ground to major European counterparts, a fundamentally liberal innovation in standardization was gradually crafted. In 1962, the president of the National Council for Quality and Reliability complained that 'although British Standards were respected all over the world, standardization was having less impact on British industry than in many countries' (Woodward 1972: 83). Years of ensuing discussions culminated in a national Quality and Reliability Year in 1966–7, which in turn spurred the Department of Technology and the Confederation of British Industry to create a committee in September 1968 to investigate quality and reliability.

With characteristically liberal flair, the British response—far from devoting greater resources to ordinary product and process standardization—was to create generalized management standards. Not only would management standards support the flexible purchasing strategies of British firms, they might also, however partially, obviate the need for more detailed product and process standards. Thus when the Menforth Committee report, issued in 1970, called for the creation of a 'federal quality organization,' this instead gave rise in 1971 to a Quality Assurance Council *within* BSI as well as the abolition of BSI's product-oriented Certification Mark Committee. Product and process standards were on the way out, management standards were on the way in. By 1974, BSI issued its first quality assurance standard, the first private-sector quality management standard to appear anywhere outside the nuclear power industry (Woodward 1972: 84). Five years later, BSI issued a broader 'quality assurance' standard (BS 5750) that has been BSI's flagship standard—and leading cash cow—ever since.

The 'quality' label has been profoundly misleading. What the British called 'quality' in fact referred only to the *consistency* of overall management operations, procedures such as ensuring that suppliers are clearly advised of purchasing requirements, or that customer orders are examined to confirm that they can in fact be met. In other words, 'quality management' merely aimed to establish a certifiably standard way to manage consistently and reliably; the standard never aimed to assess the quality of products or spur ongoing product and process improvements. British firms embraced these generic management standards because certified reliability would simplify their increasingly far-flung purchasing in open markets. They also liked the fact that the standard could be used defensively, to reduce potential legal and insurance expenses.

Because British firms wished to reduce costs and liability overseas, efforts were made to have British liberalism's innovative approach to standardization adopted by the International Organization for Standardization (ISO). Following almost a decade of British maneuvering, the contents of the British quality management standard (BS 5750) were finally issued, with modifications, as the ISO 9000 series of standards for quality management systems (QMS) in 1987. BSI's long experience with the British version of the standard quickly allowed it to become the world's leading provider of ISO 9000 certification.

The explosion of ISO 9000 certification, in turn, encouraged British firms to back BSI's efforts to develop environmental and other management standards. British firms were supportive, rightly expecting that an environmental management standard would be only incrementally more expensive than the quality management standard while offering even greater opportunities to reduce potential liability. BSI itself, responding to a stagnation in government subsidies during the Thatcher and Major era, was eager to find further opportunities to expand its service and certification business. BSI issued an environmental management standard in 1992 (BS 7750), thereby allowing BSI and British firms to build a five-year record of certification experience before the ISO 14001 environmental management standard finally appeared in 1996 (BS 7750 was promptly withdrawn the following year). The trend continued as BSI's standard for project management (BS 6079), issued in May 1996, provided another generalized management standard linked to BSI certification activities.

BSI increasingly neglected ordinary technical standards in favor of its quasi-proprietary certification business. The shift away from standards work was already evident in the organization's 1986 decision to change its official name from 'British Standards Institution' to 'BSI' (a change analogous to US Steel's decision to call itself 'USX'), and confirmed by a more recent official statement of BSI's mission: 'to maximize global influence in order to increase UK competitive advantage and protect consumer interests, through the full range of quality services' (BSI 1997: p. v). Standards development is not even mentioned in this statement of BSI's mission!

Meanwhile, BSI's certification activities have become a major business, with a vast network of overseas branch offices. In 1991, BSI created 'BSI, Inc.' with headquarters in the USA, to market BSI registration services. By the end of the decade, BSI employed 4,000 people worldwide in 93 countries (800 in the USA), most of whom served BSI's registry business. By 1997, BSI had registered a total of 30,000 organizations to management standards including ISO 9000, QS-9000, ISO 14000, and the Eco-management Audit Scheme. Even BSI's certification for product testing has become subordinated to what amounts to a cult of management systems certification: all of BSI's product certification services, as well as several other more specialized offerings for electronics and software, 'are based on assessments against ISO 9000' (BSI 1996: viii).

Although it nurtures consistency, ISO 9000 certification is expensive and often too general. The cost of initial certification is especially burdensome for small firms, who pay anywhere from a minimum of $10,000 to $40,000; large firms pay hundreds of thousands of dollars. The British government attempted to offset the hardship to smaller firms by offering subsidies toward certification, but maintaining current certification and being recertified to any revised versions of the standards require additional expenditures. BSI's emphasis on ISO 9000 certification also tends to encourage a complacent belief that consistent management and product uniformity is a sufficient proxy for overall quality and innovation. Rather than simply accept the over-generality of the ISO 9000 series, firms in other countries developed more industry-specific implementations for medical devices, automobiles (QS-9000 and TS 16949), aerospace (AS 9000), telecommunications (TL 9000), and eventually for ISO itself (ISO 9000-2000). BSI, as usual, was eager to become the leading registrar for those standards as well.

British firms are relatively free to 'exit' from the BSI framework since 'membership' is primarily an accounting device used to increase BSI's government subsidy, which for decades was pegged to the level of funds raised from membership dues. Indeed, even during the collectivist heyday of nationalized industry from the 1940s to the 1960s, British firms successfully sought a relatively liberal, and ultimately uncoordinated, approach to standardization.[2] Conversely, during the Thatcher–Major era, when BSI quite successfully reinvented itself as a free-market provider of certification services, state intervention continued to play a modest role.[3] The famous quality management standards, for example, were arguably more dependent on the state than on business coordination: quality management had its origins in a military standard,[4] and the costs of certification were partially offset by government subsidies to smaller firms, and the Department of Trade and Industry maintained a steady stream of promotional advertising on behalf of 'quality management' certification into the mid-1990s (Lane 1997: 210, 212).

The apparent contradictions of collectivist liberalism, or liberal collectivism, help explain, or at least restate, the apparent paradox of British standardization—that a large, centralized, professionally staffed, well-funded peak standards organization nonetheless fell so far behind other countries in the development of national product and process standards. British firms responded to weaknesses in national standardization by supporting 'international' standards that favored British access to less developed markets. As other countries advanced in international standards, British firms responded by seeking to shift international standardization away from specific product and process standards toward generic management standards. Operating within a domestic market generally too small to nurture global *de facto* standards, British firms have sought, with some success, to impose liberal features on international standardization.

14.3 Germany

German capitalism has often been regarded as a coordinated, 'social', or 'organized' market economy, but the degree to which this condition stems from the sustained efforts of German industry to retain control over standardization has received little attention. German firms have

[2] Some fifty industries including telecom, petroleum, and automobiles were nationalized after World War II. The big nationalized firms tended to develop their own standards through their respective national boards rather than work through, or support, the BSI framework.

[3] In 1970, fully 40% of the BSI budget of £2.83 million came from the state. By 1992, only 8% of the total budget of £42 million came from state support.

[4] The earliest quality system standard of any sort was a 1963 US Department of Defense standard (MIL-Q-9858), which in turn grew out of military quality improvement programs dating back to World War II. NATO standard AQAP 1-9, issued during 1972 to 1976, was the prototype for the British Defence Standard 05-21 of 1973. Britain's Quality Assurance Council based its quality standard of 1974 (BS 5179 P1-3), on the British military standard of the previous year.

repeatedly supported sustained industry-based standards coordination in order to counter a series of external threats, whether from Wilhelmine bureaucrats, Weimar reformers, Nazis, Allied occupiers, socialists, or EU officials. The repeatedly high degree of environmental uncertainty surrounding standardization in Germany throughout the twentieth century encouraged most firms to relinquish whatever attachment they might otherwise have had to a more liberal approach to standardization.

World War I was arguably the crucial formative experience for German standardization. Production in state factories accounted for 40 per cent of military output at the war's outbreak (Wölker 1992: 53), but efforts to coordinate with private producers were often disastrous, partly because state procurement was fragmented across four different war ministries (Wölker 1992: 47). Communication between firms and the procurement offices was hindered by the absence of standards for paper formats, paper colors, symbols, and conventions for graphic representation (Wölker 1992: 47). Even worse, the lack of standards for items such as ammunition, weapons caliber, firing mechanisms, telephone equipment, and military vehicles chronically complicated the production and distribution of replacement parts throughout the war. Government procurement offices initially had not even known the names of reliable private-sector suppliers and in desperation were forced to ask the Berlin office of the main engineering association (VDI) for a list of suitable firms. VDI, which had itself undertaken some standards work as early as 1860, eventually responded to the plodding and ineffectual incursions of state procurement offices by establishing a private-sector standards committee for machinery in Berlin on 17 May 1917 (Buder 1976: 14), which by 22 December had become a standards committee for all of German industry (Normenausschuß der Deutschen Industrie: NDI) (Hesser and Inklaar 1997: 32). Although too late to salvage the German war effort, the new organization laid the foundation for subsequent industry-based coordination of standards in Germany.

During Weimar, firms supported NDI against the Economics Ministry, which together with a peak association of professional/technical societies established a liberal-statist Reichskuratorium für Wirtschaftlichkeit in Industrie und Handwerk (RKW) in 1921. Firms resisted this state incursion by broadening NDI's work with industry associations into administration, *Handwerk*, and science, in 1926 renaming NDI the German Standards Committee (Deutscher Normenausschuß: DNA). Rising unemployment, especially from 1929, actually helped DNA in this rivalry: rationalization measures promoted by RKW professionals were accused (along with other things liberal) of contributing to rising unemployment and a widening economic crisis, whereas industry's DNA's standards avoided such criticism. Although DNA lost any formal independence under the Nazis, it continued to operate with no major change in personnel until destroyed by Allied bombs (DIN 1992: 111–12).

After the war, German firms sought to defend private-sector coordination against the Occupation by supporting a revived DNA. Almost as soon as the Occupation ended, business turned to fend off Social Democrats, who began agitating for greater government involvement in standardization, especially after their entry into government in the 'Grand Coalition' of 1966–9.[5]

Business again united to defeat such measures with a series of alliances that culminated in a contract (*Vereinbarung*) signed by the Federal Economics Minister and the DIN president on 5 June 1975 that designated DIN (assisted by DKE in electro-technology) as *the* competent national standards body for the Federal Republic of Germany (Reihlen 1977).[6] This was a quintessentially coordinated-market approach to standardization. The word 'Norm' was from this time effectively reserved to documents produced in association with DIN.[7] The federal government, implicitly following a Prussian precedent from 1929, declared its intention to reference DIN standards in legal provisions and to follow DIN standards in its own administration and purchasing (Buder 1976: 5). Even German military standards (*Verteidigungsnormen*) are developed in accordance with DIN procedures and published by Beuth, the DIN communications wing. Business coordination through DIN also gained responsibility for 'the public interest' in safety, health, the environment, consumer protection, and energy (Voelzkow 1996: 245, 247–8, 254). Conversely, DIN standardization would be merely reported to the appropriate ministry; no ministerial supervision or consultation was required (Voelzkow 1996: 96–7).

---

[5] Proposals ranged from modest adjustments—publishing all technical standards in a to-be-added part IV of the federal legal register (*Bundesgesetzblatt*)—to sweeping plans for the creation of new public entities such as 'chambers of technology' (*Technologiekammern*) staffed by legal experts and engineers, or even a 'technical sub-Parliament' (*technisches Unterparlament*) (Voelzkow 1996: 227).

[6] The organization's name was changed from Deutscher Normenausschuß (DNA) to Deutsche Institut für Normung (DIN), thereby gaining an acronym with the same letters as their already well-known Deutsche Industrie Norm (DIN) standards.

[7] A standard not under the DIN purview would thenceforth be known as a technical rule (*technische Regel*), a supplier specification (*Lieferbedingung*), or an administrative guideline (*Richtlinie*).

In short, DIN coordination became authoritative and binding for virtually all government and private-sector standardization. The calls for
enhanced *public* oversight in standardization had been cleverly met with
a public framework that ratified existing *private-sector* coordination of
standardization. Firms, of course, were delighted with this outcome—a
business-led standards organization had gained greater influence, legal
standing, public legitimacy, and funding, all without becoming subject
to any law on the subject (DIN 1995: 59).[8]

The strengthened but still decentralized institutional framework for
standardization, in turn, provided German firms with exceptional
scaffolding for inter-firm alliances during the rest of the 1970s and
throughout the 1980s. DIN standards became part of the curricula at
apprenticeship programs, technical colleges, and universities. National
surveys consistently reported DIN name recognition at incredible levels
of well over 90 per cent. Diversified quality production strategies originally unleashed by more flexible work agreements within large firms
(Streeck 1989) could suddenly use the ready-made standards framework
to include a widening array of suppliers. German mass producers
and customized producers alike suddenly enjoyed an integrated standardization framework for the entire economy that set high-level baselines, whether for mass-market goods or more specialized products. Both
'autarkic' firms and 'decentralized' firms (cf. Herrigel 1996)—often working through quite distinct standards committees—utilize a shared and
increasingly reticulated DIN framework as the basis for increasingly
flexible and innovative joint production arrangements.

The prospect of European integration on statist terms spurred German
business to unite once again in defense of coordinated standardization.
By 1985, German firms had pressed successfully for a 'New Approach'
to European standardization, and by the 1990s, DIN had become the
leading sponsor of standards committees at both the European (CEN/
CENELEC) and international (ISO/IEC) levels.

German unification was perhaps the first major change in the German
business environment that—by suggesting regulatory rollback rather
than incursion—has encouraged defection. Simultaneously, in a small
but growing number of instances during the 1990s, large companies (e.g.
Bosch in the automobile industry) successfully demanded that one or
more DIN standards committees be placed under their direct control in

---

[8] Austria, which *had* created a law regulating standardization (*Normengesetz*) in 1955,
with revisions in 1971, was a common reference point in these discussions. See Reihlen
(1974, 1977).

return for continued funding of standards work. Although direct sponsorship by a single company violates DIN's long-standing rule that the appropriate industry association supervise any standards committee, these new arrangements went unchallenged.

DIN has attempted to adapt to the faster pace of change in information technology by creating a fast track for R&D-based anticipatory standardization (EBN). IT standardization during the 1990s was typically the preserve of two vertically integrated producers, Siemens and IBM, and the EBN track met their needs. Slower-changing R&D-based industries such as micro-technology and nano-technology could also benefit. However, German software houses, including giant SAP, and other firms interested in IT interoperability standards, far from uniting behind a more radical restructuring of the DIN framework, tended to abandon DIN entirely. Intellectual property posed an unresolved problem, e.g. the world-famous MP3 audio file standard developed by a Fraunhofer institute was initially released with no strategy to capitalize on the intellectual property, then later just as clumsily encumbered with claims for patent license fees.

Far from being caught up in such issues, most of German industry continues to rely upon the sturdy but somewhat sluggish DIN framework from 1975, now largely transposed to the European and international level. So far, German firms have not found it necessary to undergo the wrenching changes in standardization that have meanwhile taken place, in different ways, in France, Japan, or the United States.

14.4 France

French firms have been sharply divided over whether to pursue a liberal or a coordinated approach to standardization. The character of this divide has varied, but its persistence has led to a recurrent resort to 'surveillance liberalism' (Burrin 1995)—whether Bonapartist or Gaullist—in which firms accept third-party monitors backed by the state rather than pursue either fully liberal or fully coordinated strategies.

The Revolution divided French business for two centuries in ways that tainted both liberal and coordinated solutions; the code-based legal system often became the default locus of standardization. Excoriated by the Loi Le Chapelier (1791), industry associations faced especially inhospitable conditions: progressive industrial sectors thereafter tended to rely on the liberal atomism of *patron* corporate governance (Jones 1986). Elite professionalism in technical standard-setting was much stronger in France than in Britain (Kindleberger 1976), aided in part by a system of *pantouflage* (mid-career retirements into top private-sector jobs) that 'produced a loyalty which was astonishingly similar to, and perhaps stronger than, loyalty to professions in societies like the United States and Great Britain' (Silberman 1993: 156). However, at non-elite levels of society 'organizational' rather than professional rationality was characteristic (Silberman 1993: 82); inter-firm coordination was more common, but the sectors were more traditional, even backward-looking.

French firms were also divided over which sorts of markets to pursue. Standards for low-end imperial markets mattered more than in Germany but less than in Britain—the French empire was only one-fourth as large as the British—while standards for the sophisticated markets of neighboring Belgium, Germany, and Switzerland played more of a role than was the case in Britain. While Germany moved toward private-sector coordination toward the end of World War I, France moved in the opposite direction, establishing a state standards body (Commission Permanente de Standardisation: CPS) in 1918, whose first standard did not appear until 1920. Support for CPS evaporated by 1924, and in 1926 firms established a private national standards organization (Association Française de Normalisation: AFNOR). By the end of the 1920s, AFNOR had only a single engineer on staff compared to sixteen at its German counterpart (AFNOR 1970; Kuisel 1981: 66, 86, 293).

Eager to preempt more direct intervention during the Nazi occupation, French firms—with mediation from the Vichy state—developed a more coordinated approach to standards. In August 1940, with the northern parts of France under direct occupation, French business organized Paris-based sectoral organization committees (*comités d'organisation*: COs) with public power to impose dues and propose sanctions. A coordinated approach to 'collaboration' even seemed to bring technical gains; by early 1941, routine bilateral conferences to harmonize French and German standards were giving French firms unprecedented glimpses into German technology (Burrin 1995: 234–5).

As the struggle for materials and mere survival in a wartime economy intensified (Vinen 1991: 143–5), the Vichy government intervened, with support from firms such as Peugeot. The standardization decree of 24 May 1941 (confirmed by a 1944 ordinance) interposed Vichy government supervision of standardization against (1) German domination of French firms in the occupied northern zone, and (2) increasing company opportunism throughout France. A standards commissar (*commissaire général à la normalisation*) was created to oversee the liaison between private standardization and the state, and the state supposedly approved the opening or closing of any standardization project, the appointments of all key personnel, and even the scheduling of meetings (Lukes 1979: 310).

Ironically, the Vichy approach to standards lasted *four decades* beyond Liberation. During Vichy, French firms 'had become accustomed to see their affairs administered by competent professionals' at the COs—over half of the CO members seem to have been *polytechniciens* (Jones 1986: 10)—so while industry associations were regarded as Nazi collaborators, 'outside' professionals—often the same people who had staffed the COs during the war—continued to run post-war standardization (Ehrmann 1957: 81).[9] French firms liked technocratic mediation since it gave them explicitly political allies. The coalition behind the alternative French standard for color television standard (SECAM: Sequential Color with Memory) in 1960 is perhaps the best-known example (Crane 1979), but technocratic mediation was very widespread. The famous 'Label Rouge' standards for high-quality agricultural products created in 1960 by the Agriculture Ministry demonstrate mediated standardization in a very different industry.

The arrival of a left-wing government in 1981 presented the first serious challenge to the Vichy settlement. After lurching unsuccessfully in more statist directions, the Socialists turned to cultivating self-development within each technological *filière*; French firms eager to get beyond the increasingly ossified *dirigisme* of the center-right and expand into Europe lent some support. In a retreat by the state so drastic that perhaps only a Socialist government could have carried it out, much of the state's supervision of standardization shifted to AFNOR in 1984. The Vichy-created Commissaire à la Normalisation ceased issuing new 'registered' standards (*normes enregistrées*).[10] Detailed national regulation of standards was replaced by a 'nouvelle approche' that placed more authority with AFNOR; simultaneously, French firms successfully backed a comparable 'New Approach' at the European level (Pelkmans 1987).

The process set in motion under the Socialists continued without them. In 1992, the state standards policy organ (Conseil Supérieur de la Normalisation) was abolished and its functions were transferred to AFNOR. The proportion of AFNOR's standards development devolved to the external *bureaux de normalisation* (BNs) rose from one third in 1980 to one half in the 1990s.

---

[9] The contrast with German industry associations is stark. German associations had been newly reconstituted both during and after the war, had an unusually high degree of legitimacy and influence conferred by the post-war Basic Law, and readily became leading stakeholders in modernization.

[10] By the late 1990s, most existing 'registered' standards had been replaced.

Despite this cascade of devolution, standardization remained subject to mediation by the state: the couple dozen Vichy-era *bureaux de normalisation* (BN) retained their designation as part of the 'service publique,' and state funding continued to flow to AFNOR and the BNs (AFNOR 1970). Direct state support for AFNOR remained almost twice as large as comparable funding in the UK and 50 per cent larger than in Germany. Government officials continued to issue general directives defining public policy on the subject of standards and to attempt to ensure the coherence of the various standards activities (Igalens and Penan 1994: 18 –22). Ministry officials continued to engage in regular reviews to decide, for example, whether the government would overrule a standard established by AFNOR, or even by the EU.

Ultimately, standards mediation became *more* complex. With four levels of 'strategic' personnel—the state, the AFNOR directorate, twenty strategic sectoral committees (COS), and thirty-eight administrative committees—their leading task often became merely interacting with one another. Unlike the several hundred German associations working with the DIN framework, the few dozen BNs in France have never operated according to common organizational principles. Eleven are indirectly supervised by private industrial associations, six are independent professional organizations, and ten are further mediated by state-supported *centres techniques* (CTs) (see Ehrmann 1957: 336–9).

Despite the 'new approach', the vast majority of French firms participating in standardization still regard it as burdensome and a pestering annoyance (Duffaux 1995: 15). Nonetheless, they stay because state incentives keep them there. In 1992, for example, tax write-offs became available for expenses related to participation in AFNOR standardization, with the result that the number of 'participants' in French standardization suddenly rose to German levels.

French firms are embedded in a shifting, heterogeneous environment for standardization where strategic mediation sometimes offers rewards greater than those from mere markets or inter-firm coordination. Thus, French firms are especially prominent in industries where this sort of mediation is most pronounced, e.g. volume production by 'national champions', luxury goods, and 'high infrastructure' sectors, especially transport and communication. World leaders in the smart card industry, for example, Schlumberger and Gemplus, benefited inadvertently from French regulations on ordinary checking accounts and were nourished for many years on infrastructural contracts for public telephone and transportation companies.

Standardization incentives are mixed, often high both for 'participate' *and* for 'defect.' Third-party professionals, both in and out of the state (regional governments add an additional wrinkle), generate exogenous, 'mission-oriented' pressures for standardization, yet the availability of state mediation also attracts firms seeking standards-based trade protection and other tactical advantages. French firms have sometimes successfully used the state to gestate a mediated form of coordination, yet just as often their umbilical cord to the state, attenuated but still uncut, continues to choke off a more fully coordinated approach to standardization.

14.5 Japan

Engrossed during most of their history with the challenges of catch-up industrialization, Japanese firms supported a coordinated approach to standardization that relied less upon liberal professionalism than any other advanced country. Firms favored rapid incremental innovation strategies based on bottom-up coordination. Reflecting these preferences, they developed a layered approach to standards, sometimes in intricate alliance with ministry officials, starting at the shop floor and rising through *keiretsu* groups, industry associations, national standards, and even international standards (JISC 1994). As a result, relatively well-coordinated oligopolistic races to set and use standards have been a central feature of Japanese capitalism.

Japan's 'bottom-up' approach to standards was rooted in the way Meiji Japan's political revolution 'from above' reconfigured the old polycentric *daimyou* political economy. Multiple and newly uprooted centers of political and economic power coalesced during the Meiji period to form competing *zaibatsu* conglomerates in new industries. A national standards office was established in 1921, thereby giving Japanese firms a way to monitor such organizations in other countries, but inter-war *zaibatsu* remained far more focused on standardizing company-level workplace practices (*hyoujun-ka*) rather than on development of a nationally unified set of formal standards (*kikaku-ka*) (cf. Johnson 1982: 27, 31). *Zaibatsu* rivalries—e.g. open sponsorship of different political parties—tended to overshadow efforts at broader coordination.

During two decades of anti-*zaibatsu* radicals, militaristic coercion, and foreign occupation, however, most Japanese firms learned, in alliance with elite bureaucrats, to form strong associations modeled on those in traditional industries. As in Germany, older social relations could be adapted to serve new purposes: guilds in sophisticated traditional industries such as textiles (cf. Rosovsky 1961) were reinvented as industrial associations. During the war, and again following *zaibatsu* dissolution by the post-war Occupation, these associations became the model for industry-wide standards coordination in all industries—albeit often with an exceptional 'maverick' firm willing to bear the high costs of 'exit' from industry association governance (Noble 1998).

Yet the older oligopolistic rivalries also persisted, somewhat rationalized, in the form of vertical and horizontal *keiretsu*. *Keiretsu* alliances, in turn, created competition in which the rapid diffusion and elaboration of standards became central. Shop-floor workers became responsible for iteratively documenting, and incrementally revising, the standards governing their own work (Nakamura 1993). Standards campaigns by the Japan Standards Association (JSA), a public foundation (*zaidan houjin*) with ministerial approval dating from 6 December 1945, targeted progressively smaller firms and attracted widespread interest as large firms sought to rationalize their vertical *keiretsu* supply chains (JSA 1995).

A striking feature of inter-firm coordination in Japan is that the national standards organization and representative to international standards meetings remains a government ministry.[11] Placing ultimate responsibility for standards coordination with the Japan Industrial Standards Committee (JISC), a section within the Ministry of International Trade and Industry (MITI), has had—*in combination with coordination by Japanese business itself*—at least four significant consequences. First, the Japanese form of coordinated market capitalism has relied more heavily on regulations and administrative guidance. Both Germany and Japan were quick to integrate regulatory and voluntary standards, but where they draw the line differed. In Japan, the total number of national voluntary standards has remained relatively small, and the state continues to regulate many areas directly. In Germany, voluntary national standards are far more numerous and have themselves become the technical content referenced in a broader range of regulations.

Second, firms can pursue coordinated standardization in a somewhat more targeted and strategic fashion. As with MITI as a whole (cf. Johnson 1982), JISC is less a regulatory agency than a small 'think tank' (ninety people) to help firms to coordinate long-term standardization. It has issued national five-year standardization plans regularly since 1961; other advanced countries, by contrast, typically have only a two- or

---

[11] For years, the only other OECD (i.e. 'advanced') countries represented at ISO by state officials were Turkey, Portugal, and Finland. However, recent OECD entrants including Mexico, the Czech Republic, Poland, Hungary, and South Korea have all sent representatives from state-run standards organizations to ISO.

three-year planning horizon and make little or no effort to link advanced research with standards development (cf. Bogod 1989: 33). JISC provides overall coordination for work that is typically initiated, undertaken, and supported by firms acting through one of several hundred industry associations. The 'self-regulation' (*jishu kisei*) of Japanese industry associations differs from the 'self-administration' (*Selbstverwaltung*) of German industry associations because in Japan virtually all major industry associations are 'approved' associations (*shadan houjin*) whose top staff are overwhelmingly early retirees from MITI (Tate 1997). Well-institutionalized 'old boy' ties (Schaede 1995) link JISC officials with their 'retired' MITI colleagues at industry associations. These links have enhanced the ability of firms to accelerate inter-firm coordination. Firms also develop a substantial, though nowhere meaningfully totaled, number of special-purpose national standards, with varying degrees of involvement from JISC, in quality control commissions, meetings of company presidents, research consortia (*kenkyuu kumiai*), ad hoc commissions, and foundations (*zaidan houjin*) such as the Japan Information Processing Development Center (est. 1967, 240 staff). Projects that span several sectors (e.g. adoption of ISO 9000 standards as JIS standards) are funneled through the Japan Standards Association (JSA), while those requiring more preliminary research can be hosted at one of the research labs run by MITI's Agency for Industrial Science and Technology (AIST) or a specially designated private or quasi-governmental institute.

Third, Japanese standards, particularly in conjunction with government-sponsored testing and certification, have readily served as trade barriers against imports. During the first five years after the Occupation—a period Johnson (1982) described as MITI's 'golden years'—the number of JIS standards had leapt from 2,509 to 4,561, further increasing to 5,831 standards by 1962 and 6,681 standards by 1967. With increasing trade friction over Japanese standards, however, the production of national-level standards began to stagnate, increasing only 8 per cent between 1975 and 1989 before *declining* absolutely in the 1990s (Fukuhara 1994: 91–101). Japanese firms supported the GATT Standards Code Agreement on Technical Barriers to Trade (TTB) in April 1980, as a way to reduce European technical barriers to trade (Lecraw 1987), but they also hoped to devolve their own potentially controversial standardization activities from the national level—where they were more conspicuously actionable under international agreements—to industry associations.[12] Obstacles to

---

[12] In 1997 the Industrial Standardization Law was amended to eliminate JISC preliminary assessments of draft standards sponsored by industry associations.

foreign participation in JISC declined,[13] but so did the importance of JIS standards.

Fourth, standards have served as a nationalistic 'sword for Japanese exports' (Stern 1997: 83). Coordination has enabled more rapid innovation and massive export drives which together make it possible to dominate an industry, e.g. facsimile machines, computer displays, and data storage technology. In the most successful cases, such as facsimile standardization, Japanese firms coordinated not only in the development of a clear national standard but also on a more flexible strategy for international standardization while firms in other countries rarely developed pronounced national positions at all (Schmidt and Werle 1998: 204). When Japanese standards did not spread beyond Japan, e.g. medical imaging (Yoshikawa 1997) or cellular phones, those tended to be industries where Japanese coordination was confronted by an equally coordinated approach, usually emanating from Europe.[14]

Standards races are an ongoing, but changing, feature of Japanese capitalism. Into the 1980s, firms coordinated on standards within industry associations or research consortia (*kenkyuu kumiai*) — often fertilized with a bit of start-up money from a government ministry — competing with one another based on manufacturing, added features, and marketing. Coordination allowed individual firms to develop *complementary* standards. As interoperability and network effects became more important over the 1980s, however, such coordination became less sustainable, and standards races began to enter the marketplace. Companies increasingly sought the advantages of tacit knowledge and market tipping from having an in-house standard triumph over rival offerings (cf. Callon 1995).

Video presents a good overview of the change. Whereas the Electronics Industries Association of Japan (EIAJ), with urging from MITI and the Ministry of Education, successfully set uniform standards for professional-quality video cassette recorders, by the time of consumer video standardization, even vigorous last-minute intervention from MITI in

---

[13] In 1983, non-Japanese firms were allowed to participate in JIS drafting committees; in 1985, non-Japanese firms were allowed to propose JIS drafts and attend Technical Committees and Division of Council meetings; only in 1987 were non-Japanese firms allowed to participate in Technical Committees as Registered Members.

[14] In medical imaging, Japanese government and industry association coordination behind the Image Save & Carry (IS&C) standard challenged a standard originally developed by professional associations in the USA (ACR/NEMA), but it faltered when the US standard was extensively modified by the European standards organization (CEN), was issued as the Digital Imaging and Communications in Medicine (DICOM) standard in 1994, and went on to become the accepted standard everywhere outside Japan.

1976, though winnowing the four contending standards down to two, was unable to forestall the decade-long market contest between Betamax and VHS (Gabel 1991: esp. 64–5; Noble 1998: 96–100). A delicate balance between coordination and oligopolistic competition was beginning to tip toward greater competition. Across a growing number of Japanese product markets, standards races, while still bounded by coordination, increasingly left competing standards in place for many years, e.g. cellular telephones, compact VCR tapes (Sony vs. Matsushita), or game machines (Nintendo vs. Sega vs. Sony). Coordination is more likely to involve companies pursuing *alternative* standards as part of a larger project; for example, in the Real Internet Consortium's next-generation router project, Hitachi pursues a supercomputer-based approach, while NEC tries parallel processing.

Increasingly networked product markets and the declining value of nationalistic standards—Japanese companies themselves increasingly disagree about the value of maintaining distinct national standards (Stern 1997)—have encouraged Japanese firms to utilize international standards more aggressively. Japanese firms initially criticized ISO 9000 standards as a redundant expense, for example, but by the late 1990s Japanese firms had become the leading holders of ISO certifications worldwide: companies such as NEC and Mitsutoyo had discovered not merely that certification improved market access, especially in Europe, but that by developing their own ISO certification services, they could use those services to create new tie-ins and incentives to increase the market penetration of their core businesses (Stern 1997: 82–3). In short, on top of long-standing company-level, industry association, and national-level standards coordination, Japanese firms have increasingly integrated international standards within their overall coordination strategies. The best firms have made the transition smoothly, but for others the effort to make international standards more central to corporate strategy has merely diminished Japan's utility as a first-stage launching market. The future of Japanese-style coordination will depend, ironically, on firms successfully making that transition.

14.6 United States

US firms have supported an approach to standards that is by far the most institutionally heterogeneous and fragmented of all advanced industrial countries. Whereas firms in other countries have a peak standards organization that supervises the development of a broad majority of national standards, US firms have never united behind more than an accreditor of other standards organizations: the American National Standards Institute. ANSI is forbidden to develop any standards by its charter, the accreditation it offers is merely optional, and it is the only national standards organization in the world that receives no regular and direct governmental support. US government agencies, both at the federal and the state levels, far from making use of private-sector standards, have traditionally exacerbated standards fragmentation by developing their own alternative standards. Only during the 1990s did the US Department of Defense (DoD), which is the single most prolific standards organization in the United States, begin to wean itself from an insistence on special-purpose standards for military applications—e.g. specialized machine-tool standards for the US Air Force (Noble 1984)—that was perhaps the leading cause of standards fragmentation in the USA.[15] (Because military standards in Britain, Germany, Japan, and even France relied heavily upon NATO standards transposed from the US DoD, standardization in those countries was never affected by defense requirements to the same degree.) The top fourteen US standards organizations account for only 85 per cent of all formal standards (Toth 1996: 176).

For decades many of the foremost formal standards organizations in the USA did not bother to affiliate with ANSI. The single largest private-sector standards organization in the USA, the American Society for Testing and Materials (ASTM), withdrew from ANSI for over a decade in protest against ANSI's allegedly lax accreditation procedures, returning only in 1995. Ninety per cent of US standards were not issued as American National Standards that year, 50 per cent of the 400 standards-developing organizations in the USA were not accredited by ANSI, and over a quarter of all standards in the USA were not even issued in accordance with ANSI accreditation.

The liberal, uncoordinated approach to standards in the USA was shaped by antitrust laws (1890) that hindered cooperation within industry associations but encouraged firms to merge, giving rise to a 'managerial' version of liberal capitalism (Lazonick 1991: 31–6) in which inter-firm standards became intra-firm standards. Standards became primarily the responsibility of professional (what Frederick Taylor called 'scientific') managers within multi-divisional corporations, who naturally favored self-certification ('manufacturer's declaration')—a preference they have more recently sought to impose on standards outside the USA

[15] As defense contractors began to develop significant markets outside the defense industry during the mid-1980s, they began to urge the DoD to make greater use of private-sector standards. The Technology Transfer and Advancement Act of 1996 is the most recent effort to align US government standards with private-sector standards.

(National Research Council 1995). Two-thirds of all formal consensus standards produced in the USA come from professional organizations compared to only one third from industry associations.

Two early efforts to achieve broader US standards coordination collapsed in quick succession. Herbert Hoover, both during his long tenure as Secretary of Commerce (1921–8) and later as President, had favored an increased role for the Commerce Department's National Bureau of Standards (NBS). Roosevelt Democrats, whether for partisan reasons or merely under Depression budget pressures, abandoned Hoover's quasi-statist approach in 1933 by defunding most NBS standards efforts. However, Roosevelt's preference for a coordinated-managerial approach, with elements resembling Italian fascism, collapsed just as quickly due to court challenges (Garcia 1992: 533). Courts have remained a major influence on US standardization, not only because of antitrust but also due to rising judicial activism in product liability cases during the 1960s and 1970s.

Complaints about the liberal, uncoordinated approach to US standards continued in later decades (see US Senate 1975: 1; Garcia 1992: 534; OTA 1992), but despite major proposals (e.g. in 1968, 1974, 1980, 1994) to enhance standards coordination, US firms could never agree on a single framework that would accommodate the enormous heterogeneity in US standardization. Indeed, rather than reduce fragmentation, the characteristic American response has been to treat it as a commercial opportunity. A largely US-based service industry, led by Global Engineering Documents/Information Handling Services, has developed that is devoted simply to finding relevant standards for retail customers. ANSI established an electronic National Standards System Network (NSSN) in 1994, but by 1998, the NSSN itself had become another commercial service.

As with the British quality management standard, some of the most outstanding examples of formal standards coordination in the USA were originally government initiatives. Internet standards such as TCP-IP nourished by ARPANET and NSFNET are perhaps the most famous and successful example. Nonetheless, during the 1990s, a striking reversal took place: US firms' liberal approach to standards began to be seen as a strength. Europeans began complaining that the fragmented approach to standards in the USA constituted an unfair *advantage* in trade (Holm 1996; Nicholas 1996) even as US officials began to *praise* the lack of central coordination (e.g. the US Deputy Secretary of Commerce, in Leuteritz et al. 1999: 67).

This reversal followed from a *fivefold* shift in US standardization. First, the character of cutting-edge standards work changed. The government-sponsored[16] Internet Engineering Task Force (IETF) pioneered a new, just-in-time approach to standards that made traditional trade-offs seem obsolete: it was faster yet also more thorough; participants use the Internet itself as an ongoing test bed while requiring demonstration that at least two working implementations of any proposed standard can in fact inter-operate before the standard is accepted (Nielson 1996: 38). IETF standardization was more intensive, since it could take place throughout the year, yet also more inclusive, since it was open to all interested individuals. IETF also inspired the creation of other formal organizations, most notably the World Wide Web Consortium (W3C), a company-membership consortium hosted at MIT[17] that maintained a strong commitment to open, consensus-based standards (e.g. HTML, HTTP, XML) in part because many W3C participants were simultaneously involved in IETF.

Second, decades-long efforts to regulate the monopoly power of AT&T and IBM gradually transferred areas of standardization previously controlled by the 'Ma Blue' duo to a larger range of firms. These include: Microsoft (Plug and Play; Simple Object Access Protocol), Intel (Mobile Data Initiative), Sun (Java), Apple (FireWire), Xerox (Ethernet; XrML), Cisco (Web Content Caching Protocol), Unisys (LZW image compression for GIF files), Adobe (PostScript), Macromedia (Flash), and AOL (Instant Messenger). In addition, as the range of participants expanded, US firms found that the multiplicity of US standards organizations offered numerous opportunities to experiment with formal just-in-time standardization.

Third, a loosening of antitrust regulation, granted most prominently under the 1993 National Cooperative Research and Production Act (NCRPA), made it safer for US firms to abandon formal standards organizations entirely to create a variety of informal standards alliances (known variously as consortia, forums, clubs, coalitions, and ad hoc standards groups), and thereby engage in even more wide-ranging experimentation. At least 150 such standards groups had been formed in the USA by the mid-1990s (Toth 1996: 171). Some consortia differed little from formal organizations, but many deliberately aimed to develop *limited* consensus standards under the control of a few large companies. Intel and Microsoft each sponsored several dozen standards consortia, often called 'initiatives.' Big contributors might receive director seats, special voting privileges, earlier technical access, and greater access to

---

[16] National Science Foundation subsidies to IETF continued until 1995.
[17] W3C later added branches at INRIA (France) and Keio University (Japan).

any resulting licenses; smaller firms might join, if at all, only as observers with highly restricted rights. Consortia can work quickly, but they are also much more expensive than a traditional standards organization (which relies heavily on volunteerism). At many consortia, initial contributions of $25,000 to $50,000 per firm are not uncommon, amounts that are hundreds of times larger than the nominal contributions firms make to formal standards organizations such as ASTM (Cargill 1997a: 145). The Open Software Foundation, an early consortium founded by DEC, IBM, and HP in 1988, had initial funding of $121 million, an amount equivalent to ANSI's entire information technology budget for thirty-five years (Cargill 1997a: 130).

Fourth, aided by a Patent Office and appellate judiciary increasingly and almost uniquely eager to say 'yes', US firms found themselves in a gold rush over intellectual property stakes to the standards they (or their competitors) generated. Control of 'owned but open' standards (Borrus and Zysman 1997) became a central pillar of strategy for many leading US firms (Betancourt and Walsh 1995).

Fifth, leading-edge markets became network markets. *De facto* standard-setting by a single dominant firm had a long and prominent history in many US sectors, but as the number of firms seeking to control standards increased, several types of complex standards wars broke out. These sometimes took the form of 'battle-of-the-sexes' competitions in which the two sides were reluctant to cooperate simply because they preferred different standards, e.g. the cellular telephone competition between Qualcomm's CDMA versus AT&T's TDMA. Other times, the rivals also differed over what role *any* standard would play in their overall business strategy, as when a dominant firm seeking to exploit a proprietary standard was challenged by one or more lesser firms favoring more 'open' standards.

US companies have developed a vast armamentarium of ways to favor 'open' standards while retaining some sort of proprietary advantage (cf. Cargill 1997a). Sun Microsystems, for example, sought to have its tightly controlled, in-house development of Java software formally recognized as an international standard, first by ISO, then by ECMA. For Sun, 'openness' consisted in gaining the imprimatur of a formal organization for standards that Sun would continue to develop internally. Netscape went further, establishing a consortium (Mozilla.org) in 1998 that gives outsiders access to pieces of proprietary source code in products such as the company's Communicator browser in the hopes that including people outside the company will help develop a better product and stronger brand than could Netscape alone.

Microsoft's dominance in proprietary operating system standards has placed it on the conspicuously proprietary side in a number of prominent contests: its NT operating system versus Sun's UNIX-based operating system, its integrated browser versus Netscape's open-code Mozilla project; its Media Player Active Streaming Format streaming media standard versus RealNetworks Real Time Streaming Protocol. However, where firms standardize depends on how they are situated. Microsoft itself has sought help from the IETF when promoting a more 'open' standard against AOL's proprietary control of the two leading instant messaging standards (IM and ICQ). Autodesk's proprietary standard for computer-aided design (DWG) was challenged by an OpenDWG Alliance led by Visio, a firm that was shortly thereafter acquired by Microsoft. AOL reversed its long-standing advocacy of 'open access' to cable after merging with cable leader TimeWarner.

For US firms, standards are less the solution to a collective action problem than a new and sometimes decisive competition over the sources of proprietary advantage (Shapiro and Varian 1999). Formal standards organizations matter less than informal standards consortia—whether closed or relatively open—and standardization centers less around what standard is chosen than around who controls the standard. US firms have pioneered a competitive rather than coordinated approach to standards that responds well to increasingly global markets, the importance of rapid innovation, and the increasingly enormous costs of solo product development. However, the sustainability of US-style standardization is challenged by the more coordinated approaches favored in much of the rest of the world.

14.7 One World? Liberal or Coordinated?

The world shows no sign of developing a single approach to standardization, so it is useful to disentangle the several lines of division more explicitly. Within Europe, the principal contrast is between the liberalism of British firms, the coordination of German firms, and the reliance on state and professional mediation by French firms. British firms, favoring price competition and open markets, support the use of generalized management standards in place of specific product and process standards. European unification has helped British firms 'export' their generalized management standards to the continent while they remain free to ignore the more specialized and detailed Continental standards, whether because the imported standards are voluntary, are neutralized by mutual recognition agreements, or involve industries where Britain has no domestic firms. German firms, conversely, while digesting the British management standards, have steadily transplanted much of their coordinated approach across the full range of detailed product and process standards to the European and international levels: German firms host more technical committees, both within CEN/CENELEC and within ISO/IEC, than do firms from any other country. French firms, eager to expand their inter-firm networks to the European level, support EU directives, mandates, and other forms of standards mediation analogous to those within France. European standardization represents an amalgam of disparate national approaches, whose signal achievement has been to *combine* these alternatives rather than abolish them.

From a broader view, however, European standardization is itself a distinct form of coordination. To understand how this was possible, it is useful to recall that British firms, though clearly in a liberal market economy, are also embedded in a residually collectivist (both conservative and socialist) institutional heritage—for example, a single, relatively authoritative national standards institution. This context made it easier for Europe *to assimilate Britain's liberal approach as another strand within Europe's coordinated standardization*. British firms themselves sought this outcome.

In the larger world, Europe's multi-coordinated approach to standardization confronts a congeries of nationally coordinated market economies in Asia, led by Japan and China, as well as a hyper-liberal approach to standardization rooted in the USA. Do these varieties converge simply because firms from all of these countries participate in a trio of Geneva-based international organizations—the International Organization for Standardization (ISO), the International Electrotechnical Committee (IEC), and the International Telecommunications Union (ITU-T)? Not really.[18] Membership in these organizations is for countries (rather than firms or individuals), which limits the influence of firms from large countries such as Japan and the USA. As NIST director Raymond Kammer said in 1998: 'ISO and IEC standards tend to be responsive to European needs and only sometimes responsive to US industrial needs' (ASTM 1998: 16). The same could be said *a fortiori* about Japanese needs, despite the fact that Japanese firms have been avid participants, often sending delegations far larger (at far greater cost) than any other country. Moreover, since 1991, the formal international standards system has increasingly become an outpost of the European

---

[18] After all, the Soviet Union was a permanent and leading member of all ISO and IEC supervisory bodies for decades without ever becoming *any* variety of capitalism.

standards system.[19] Europe's national (BSI, DIN, AFNOR, etc.), regional (CEN, CENELEC), and international (ISO, IEC) standards are now closely coordinated with one another to a degree that is not remotely approximated by other parts of the world.

Naturally, firms can experiment with standards strategies that diverge from their home base—perhaps at their peril. US firms trying coordinated strategies have suffered some spectacular failures. During the 1980s, several East Coast firms committed to Europe (e.g. IBM, DEC) invested enormous resources in the Corporation for Open Systems (COS), a group supporting Open Systems Interconnect (OSI), an ISO-IEC seven-layer communications schema of formal standards that aimed, but failed, to allow computer operating systems to communicate with one another. The spectacular failure of the effort by 1990, whose costs totaled an estimated $500 million, convinced many US information technology firms that formal standardization itself had become a very dead end. The US backlash against formal standards thereafter led to radically liberal approaches to standardization—proprietary consortia that were sometimes actively hostile toward formal standards development (Cargill 1994: 6). Even cheap and innocuous standards projects, such as the 1995 creation of an ISO system to categorize standards, have failed to draw any US participation whatsoever.

The most promising way to integrate liberal and coordinated approaches seems to involve a whole-cloth incorporation of a liberal strand within a coordinated framework. The US-based Unicode consortium quickly developed a 16-bit character set standard, for example, that was ultimately incorporated as the first section of a more formal and comprehensive 32-bit ISO standard (Hayes 1992). Similarly, and more directly, Sun Microsystems almost succeeded in getting its JavaSoft corporate unit designated an official ISO standards committee, all without releasing proprietary claims to its Java software (Cargill 1997b; Lemley and McGowan 1998). In general, US firms prefer to leave *all* standards routes open: they want increased access to international standardization for their many standards organizations, consortia, and in-house projects, yet they also want to retain the option of offering 'global' standards directly.

Firms in coordinated markets, conversely, can offer 'global' standards without relying on strictly international organizations (OTA 1992). The

---

[19] In 1991, following two years of less formal collaboration, both the 'Vienna Agreement' between CEN and ISO and the 'Lugano Agreement' between CENELEC and IEC were signed; the latter was revised via a 'Dresden Agreement' in 1996.

development of Japanese production networks electronics in Asia (e.g. in electronics) as well as the establishment of the European Telecommunications Standards Institute (ETSI), whose work on GSM standards put European cellular telephony ahead, both suggest that coordinated approaches to 'global' standards are possible. Japanese firms maintained coordination by establishing remarkably 'closed' cross-border production networks (Borrus 1997). To take a more promising example, ETSI, whose members are firms rather than countries, has taken aggressive stands (some of which it has been forced to retract, e.g. against Motorola) to weaken US intellectual property protections on behalf of coordination desired by European firms. What these two brief examples suggest is that coordinated approaches to 'global' standards are no less likely than liberal approaches to 'international' standardization.

14.8 Conclusion: When Norms Collide

National varieties of standardization, faced with shrinking opportunities for autonomy, are increasingly in collision. The European varieties of standardization, whether alone or in combination at the European level, have never converged with Japan's more 'bottom-up' approach to inter-firm coordination nor with the extreme liberalism of the US approach. National varieties of standardization (continue to) vary for at least three reasons.

1. Perhaps surprisingly, national *standards themselves* continue to differ. Although European firms made heroic efforts to harmonize formal national standards during the 1990s—indeed, firms in some smaller European countries relinquished national standards almost entirely—in larger countries, standards remain different. National standards bodies reported that an average of 57 per cent of their standards are *not* identical to, technically equivalent to, or even based on international standards (Toth 1996: 176). Japan (despite making substantial efforts to harmonize JIS with international standards during the 1990s) and the United States (which made relatively little effort to change domestic standards) are even less reliant on international standards. Moreover, China and other rapidly developing countries in Asia have sought, within whatever bounds are set by the WTO, IMF, and other international organizations, to imitate Japan's aggressive use of national standards.

2. National *standards institutions* continue to differ, remaining at least as diverse as the governments under which they operate. 'Peak' standards institutions can be liberal, whether marketing organizations (Britain's

BSI) or accrediting bodies that certify competing standards organizations (the American National Standards Institute); they can serve as the primary focus of national coordination, whether as an autonomous coordinator of industry associations (Germany's DIN) or a government think tank (Japan's JIS); or they can be professional societies that mediate between firms (France's AFNOR). Liberal standards institutions rely primarily on relatively autonomous professionals, coordinated standards institutions rely primarily on organizational representatives from industry associations, and mediated standards institutions rely primarily on neutral third parties to reconcile inter-firm differences. Even when firms in some smaller European countries (most notably the Netherlands) decided to abandon national standards work in favor of work on European standards, they did not close their national standards organization or abandon efforts to impose national preferences.

3. Most important, national approaches to *the purpose of standards* are increasingly in collision. Corporate strategies in liberal market economies treat standards as a proprietary good or service to be traded like any other. In Britain, the most important standards are a commercial service for reducing insurance and liability costs. In the USA, precisely because of its more fragmented, open, proprietary, and 'professional' institutional landscape, standards have become pieces of intellectual property, alternately guarded and contested. Corporate strategies in coordinated market economies, by contrast, treat standards as an infrastructure for deeper cooperation. In Germany, firms have been world leaders at creating a transnational infrastructure for standards, transferring their routine national standards work to the European and international levels which in turn remain closely integrated with more specialized national standards capable of supporting diversified quality strategies. In Japan, where firms pursue flexible mass production, standards coordination is distinctive for the degree to which national and industry association standards are integrated with incremental innovation on the individual shop floor, in a way that facilitates oligopolistic competition. Firms in mediated market economies such as France appear liberal when standards mediation is statist, coordinated when mediation is not statist, but somewhere in between when both aspects are kept in mind.

Harmonization at the European level is resulting in a compression, but not elimination, of national varieties within Europe. British firms' emphasis upon standards as a commercial service continues to vie with the efforts of French firms to utilize standards as a form of strategic mediation and the needs of German firms for a comprehensive standards infrastructure capable of supporting high-level product engineering.

Although European harmonization might also be seen as creating a hybrid European variety, Mendelian metaphors risk obscuring the ongoing clash of national varieties sequestered in the hundreds of CEN and ISO technical committees where national representatives actually confront one another.

Standards are an increasingly crucial component of economic competition in many industries. One consequence is that the national rules and institutions through which standards are created are themselves increasingly becoming objects of strategic activity. Seen from a broader perspective, coordinated market advances such as European harmonization or Japan's 'bottom-up' integration of shop-floor workers, and liberal market advances based on proprietary standards, can together be regarded as simply the first steps in an ongoing rivalry that seems very far from over. Nationally rooted collisions of divergent approaches to standardization may be with us for quite some time to come.

BIBLIOGRAPHY

ABEL, RICHARD. 1982. 'Law as a Lag: Inertia as a Social Theory of Law.' *Michigan Law Review* 80: 785–809.

ABRAMSON, N., J. ENCARNACAO, P. REID, and U. SCHMOCH, eds. 1997. *Technology Transfer Systems in the United States and Germany*. Washington: National Academy Press.

ACEMOGLU, D., and J. PISCHKE. 1998. 'Why do Firms Train? Theory and Evidence.' *Quarterly Journal of Economics* 108: 983–1014. [113 (Feb.): 79–119.]

AFNOR (Association Française de Normalisation). 1970. *Cinquante Ans de normes françaises 1920–1970*. Paris: AFNOR, Tour Europe, 92-Courbevoie.

AGELL, JONAS, and BENGT-CHRISTER YSANDER. 1993. 'Should Governments Learn to Live with Inflation? Comment.' *American Economic Review* 83 (1): 305–11.

AGHION, PHILIPPE, and PETER HOWITT. 1998. *Endogenous Growth Theory*. Cambridge, Mass.: MIT Press.

ALBERT, MICHEL. 1991. *Capitalisme contre capitalisme*. Paris: Le Seuil.

—— 1993. *Capitalism against Capitalism*. London: Whurr.

ALESINA, ALBERTO, and DANI RODRIK. 1994. 'Distributive Politics and Economic Growth.' *Quarterly Journal of Economics* 109 (May): 465–90.

—— and LAWRENCE H. SUMMERS. 1993. 'Central Bank Independence and Macroeconomic Performance.' *Journal of Money, Credit, and Banking* 25 (2): 151–63.

ALLMENDINGER, JUTTA. 1989. 'Educational Systems and Labor Market Outcomes.' *European Sociological Review* 5 (3): 231–50.

ALT, JAMES E., JEFFRY FRIEDEN, MICHAEL GILLIGAN, DANI RODRIK, and RONALD ROGOWSKI. 1996. 'The Political Economy of International Trade: Enduring Puzzles and an Agenda for Inquiry.' *Comparative Political Studies* 29 (6): 689–717.

—— FREDRIK CARLSEN, PER HEUM, and KÅRE JOHANSEN. 1999. 'Asset Specificity and the Political Behavior of Firms: Lobbying for Subsidies in Norway.' *International Organization* 53 (1): 99–116.

ALVAREZ, R. MICHAEL, GEOFFREY GARRETT, and PETER LANGE. 1991. 'Government Partisanship, Labor Organization, and Macroeconomic Performance.' *American Political Science Review* 85 (June): 539–56.

AMAR, MICHEL, and BRUNO CRÉPON. 1990. 'Les Deux Visages de la concentration industrielle: efficacité et rente de situation.' *Économie & statistique* 229: 5–20.

ANCEL, MARC. 1971. *Utilité et méthodes du droit comparé*. Neuchâtel: Ides et Calendes.

ANDERSEN, SVEIN S., and KJELL A. ELIASSEN, eds. 1993. *Making Policy in Europe: The Europeification of National Policy-Making*. London: Sage.

ANDERSON, JEFFREY J. 1997. 'Hard Interests, Soft Power, and Germany's Changing

Role in Europe.' In *Tamed Power: Germany in Europe*, ed. Peter J. Katzenstein. Ithaca, NY: Cornell University Press: 80–107.

AOKI, MASAHIKO. 1988. *Information, Incentives and Bargaining in the Japanese Economy*. Cambridge: Cambridge University Press.

—— 1990. 'Toward an Economic Model of the Japanese Firm.' *Journal of Economic Literature* 28 (March): 1–27.

—— 1994. 'The Japanese Firm as a System of Attributes: A Survey and Research Agenda.' In *The Japanese Firm: Sources of Competitive Strength*, ed. Masahiko Aoki and Ronald Dore. Oxford: Clarendon Press: 11–40.

Arbeitsausschuß 'Mitbestimmung und Tarifwesen.' 1997. '2. Bericht für die Mitbestimmungskommission.' Paper presented at the 15 October meeting of the Mitbestimmungskommission, Gütersloh.

ASTM (American Society for Testing and Materials). 1998. *Standardization News* 26 (June).

AUERBACH, SIMON. 1990. *Legislating for Conflict*. Oxford: Clarendon Press.

AYRES, I., and J. BRAITHWAITE. 1992. *Responsive Regulation: Transcending the Deregulation Debate*. New York: Oxford University Press.

BABSON, STEVE, ed. 1995. *Lean Work: Empowerment and Exploitation in the Global Auto Industry*. Detroit: Wayne State University Press.

BADE, ROBIN, and MICHAEL PARKIN. 1982. 'Central Bank Laws and Monetary Policy.' Department of Economics, University of Western Ontario. Typescript.

BADIE, BETRAND, and PIERRE BIRNBAUM. 1979. *La Sociologie de l'État*. Paris: Grasset.

BALDWIN, DAVID A., ed. 1993. *Neorealism and Neoliberalism: The Contemporary Debate*. New York: Columbia University Press.

BALDWIN, PETER. 1990. *The Politics of Social Solidarity: Class Bases of the European Welfare State 1875–1975*. New York: Cambridge University Press.

BARNARD, CHESTER. 1968. *The Functions of the Executive*. Cambridge, Mass.: Harvard University Press.

BARRO, ROBERT J., and DAVID B. GORDON. 1983*a*. 'Rules, Discretion, and Reputation in a Model of Monetary Policy.' *Journal of Monetary Economics* 12 (1): 101–21.

—— —— 1983*b*. 'A Positive Theory of Monetary Policy in a Natural Rate Model.' *Journal of Political Economy* 91 (4): 589–610.

—— and XAVIER SALA-I-MARTIN. 1995. *Economic Growth*. New York: McGraw-Hill.

BATES, ROBERT. 1997. *Open-Economy Politics: The Political Economy of the World Coffee Trade*. Princeton: Princeton University Press.

—— P. BROCK, and J. TIEFENTHALER. 1991. 'Risk and Trade Regimes: Another Exploration.' *International Organization* 45 (1): 1–18.

BAUER, MICHEL. 1988. 'The Politics of State-Directed Privatization: The Case of France. 1986–88.' *West European Politics* 11 (4): 49–60.

—— and BÉNÉDICTINE BERTIN-MOUROT. 1995. *L'Accès au sommet des grandes entreprises françaises 1985–1994*. Paris: Seuil.

BEALE, HUGH. 1995. 'Legislative Control of Fairness: The Directive on Unfair

Terms in Consumer Contracts.' In *Good Faith and Fault in Contract Law,* ed. Jack Beatson and Daniel Friedmann. Oxford: Clarendon: 231–88.

BECKER, GARY. 1964. *Human Capital: A Theoretical and Empirical Analysis, with Special Reference to Education.* New York: Columbia University Press.

BEESON, MARK. 1999. *Competing Capitalisms: Australia, Japan and Economic Competition in the Asia Pacific.* London: Macmillan.

BÉNABOU, ROLAND. 1996. 'Inequality and Growth.' In *National Bureau of Economic Research Macro Annual,* ed. Ben S. Bernanke and Julio J. Rotemberg. 11: 11–74.

BENDERS, JOS, FRED HUIJGEN, ULRICH PEKRUHL, and KEVIN P. O'KELLY. 1999. *Useful but Unused—Group Work in Europe: Findings from the EPOC Survey.* Dublin: European Foundation for the Improvement of Living and Working Conditions.

BÉRET, PIERRE. 1992. 'Salaires et marchés internes: quelques évolutions récentes en France.' *Économie Áppliquée* 45 (2): 5–22.

BERGER, SUZANNE. 1972. *Peasants against Politics.* Cambridge: Cambridge University Press.

—— ed. 1981. *Organizing Interests in Western Europe: Pluralism, Corporatism, and the Transformation of Politics.* Cambridge: Cambridge University Press.

—— 1995. 'Trade and Identity: The Coming Protectionism?' In *Remaking the Hexagon: The New France in the New Europe,* ed. Gregory Flyn. Boulder, Colo.: Westview Press: 195–210.

—— and RONALD DORE, eds. 1996. *National Diversity and Global Capitalism.* Ithaca, NY: Cornell University Press.

—— and MICHAEL J. PIORE. 1980. *Dualism and Discontinuity in Industrial Societies.* Cambridge, Mass.: Cambridge University Press.

BERLE, ADOLPH A., and G. C. MEANS. 1932. *The Modern Corporation and Private Property.* New York: Macmillan.

BETANCOURT, DIEGO, and ROBERT WALSH. 1995. 'The Evolution of Strategic Standardization Management.' *StandardView* 3 (September): 117–26.

BEUTER, RITA. 1994. 'Germany and the Ratification of the Maastricht Treaty.' In *The Ratification of the Maastricht Treaty: Issues, Debates and Future Implications,* ed. Finn Laursen and Sophie Vanhoonacker. Dordrecht: Martinus Nijhoff Publishers: 87–112.

BIRNBAUM, PIERRE. 1994. *Les Sommets de l'état: essai sur l'élite du pouvoir en France.* Paris: Le Seuil.

BLAU, PETER M., and W. RICHARD SCOTT. 1962. *Formal Organizations: A Comparative Approach.* San Francisco: Chandler Publishing Company.

BLEANEY, MICHAEL. 1996. 'Central Bank Independence, Wage-Bargaining Structure, and Macroeconomic Performance in OECD Countries.' *Oxford Economic Papers* 48 (1): 20–38.

BLOSSFELD, HANS-PETER, and KARL ULRICH MAYER. 1988. 'Labor Market Segmentation in the Federal Republic of Germany: An Empirical Study of Segmentation Theories from a Life Course Perspective.' *European Sociological Review* 4 (2): 123–40.

BMBW (Bundesministerium für Bildung, Wissenschaft, Forschung und Technologie), ed. 2000. *Berufsbildungsbericht.* Bonn: BMBF.

BOGDAN, MICHAEL. 1994. *Comparative Law*. Deventer: Kluwer.

BOGOD, JULIAN. 1989. *Information Technology Standardization: A Report to BSI and DTI*. London: Department of Trade and Industry Information Technology Division, 9 February.

BOIX, CARLES. 1998. *Political Parties, Growth and Equality: Conservative and Social Democratic Strategies in the World Economy*. New York: Cambridge University Press.

BOLTHO, ANDREA. 1996. 'Has France Converged on Germany?' In *National Diversity and Global Capitalism*, ed. Suzanne Berger and Ronald Dore. Ithaca, NY: Cornell University Press: 89–104.

BONOLI, GIULIANO. 1999. 'State Structures and the Process of Welfare State Adaptation.' Department of Social and Policy Sciences, University of Bath. Mimeograph.

BORRUS, MICHAEL. 1997. 'Left for Dead: Asian Production Networks and the Revival of US Electronics.' BRIE Working Paper 100 (April). Berkeley, Calif.: BRIE.

—— and JOHN ZYSMAN. 1997. 'Wintelism and the Changing Terms of Global Competition: Prototype of the Future?' BRIE Working Paper 96B (February). Berkeley, Calif.: BRIE.

BOURDIEU, PIERRE. 1989. *La Noblesse d'état: Grandes écoles et esprit de corps*. Paris: Éditions de Minuit.

BOYER, ROBERT. 1988. *The Search for Labour Market Flexibility*. Oxford: Clarendon Press.

—— 1990. *The Regulation School: A Critical Introduction*. New York: Columbia University Press.

—— 1995. 'Wage Austerity and/or an Education Push: The French Dilemma.' *Labour* (Special Issue): 19–66.

—— 1996. 'The Convergence Hypothesis Revisited: Globalization but Still the Century of Nations?' In *National Diversity and Global Capitalism*, ed. Suzanne Berger and Ronald Dore. Ithaca, NY: Cornell University Press: 29–59.

—— 1997. 'French Statism at the Crossroads.' In *Political Economy of Modern Capitalism: Mapping Convergence and Diversity*, ed. Colin Crouch and Wolfgang Streeck. London: Sage: 71–101.

—— and DANIEL DRACHE, eds. 1996. *States against Markets*. New York: Routledge.

—— and JEAN-PIERRE DURAND. 1993. *L'Après-fordisme*. Paris: Syros.

BRAUNTHAL, GERARD. 1996. *Parties and Politics in Modern Germany*. Boulder, Colo.: Westview Press.

BREGER, MONIKA. 1982. *Die Haltung der Industriellen Unternehmer zur staatlichen Sozialpolitik in den Jahren 1878–1891*. Frankfurt: Haag & Herchen.

—— 1994. 'Der Anteil der deutschen Großindustriellen an der Konzeptualisierung der Bismarckschen Sozialgesetzgebung.' In *Bismarcks Sozialstaat: Beiträge zur Geschichte der Sozialpolitik und zur sozialpolitischen Geschichtsschreibung*, ed. Lothar Machtan. Frankfurt: Campus: 25–60.

BRIDGE, MICHAEL G. 1984. 'Does Anglo-Canadian Contract Law Need a Doctrine of Good Faith?' *Canadian Business Law Journal* 9: 385–426.

BROWN, WILLIAM, PAUL MARGINSON, and JANET WALSH. 1995. 'Management: Pay Determination and Collective Bargaining.' In *Industrial Relations: Theory and Practice in Britain*, ed. Paul Edwards. Oxford: Blackwell: 123–50.

BROWNSWORD, ROGER. 1994. 'Two Concepts of Good Faith.' *Journal of Contract Law* 7: 197–206.

—— 1996. 'Good Faith.' *Current Legal Problems* 49 (2): 111–34.

—— 1997. 'Contract Law, Cooperation and Good Faith.' In *Contracts, Co-operation and Competition*, ed. Simon Deakin and Jonathan Mitchie. Oxford: Oxford University Press: 255–84.

BRUNO, MICHAEL, and JEFFREY SACHS. 1987. *The Economics of Worldwide Stagflation*. Cambridge, Mass.: Harvard University Press.

BSI. 1996. *Annual Report*. London.

—— 1997. *BSI Standards Catalogue 1997–1998*. London.

BUCKLEY, PETER, and JONATHAN MICHIE, eds. 1996. *Firms, Organization and Contracts: A Reader in Industrial Organization*. Oxford: Oxford University Press.

BUDER, MARIANNE. 1976. *Das Verhältnis von Dokumentation und Normung von 1927 bis 1945 in nationaler und internationaler Hinsicht*. DIN Normungskunde 7. Berlin: Beuth.

BUECK, HENRY AXEL. 1901. *Der Centralverband Deutscher Industrieller 1876–1905*. Berlin: Deutscher Verlag.

BULMER, SIMON, and WILLIAM PATTERSON. 1987. *The Federal Republic of Germany and the European Community*. Boston: Allen & Unwin.

Bundesarbeitgeberverband Chemie. 1997. 'Die Zukunft der Alterssicherung in Deutschland.' Unpublished manuscript. BDA Archiv, Cologne.

Bundessozialgericht, ed. 1970. *Entscheidungen des Bundessocialgerichtes*, 30. Cologne: Carl Heymans: 167–209.

Bundesvereinigung der Deutschen Arbeitgeberverbände. 1997. 'Grundsatzpositionen der Bundesvereinigung der Deutschen Arbeitgeberverbände zur Rentenreform.' Unpublished manuscript. BDA Archiv, Cologne.

—— 1998. 'Sozialpolitik für mehr Wettberwerbsfähigkeit und Beschäftigung. Ordnungspolitische Grundsätze der BDA.' Cologne: BDA.

BUNEL, J. 1995. *La Transformation de la représentation patronale en France: CNPF et CGPME*. Paris: Commissariat Général du Plan.

BURRIN, PHILIPPE. 1995. *France under the Germans: Collaboration and Compromise*. New York: New Press.

BUSCH, MARC. 1999. *Trade Warriors*. New York: Cambridge University Press.

BUXTON, TONY, PAUL CHAPMAN, and PAUL TEMPLE. 1994. 'Overview: The Foundations of Competitiveness.' In *Britain's Economic Performance*, ed. Tony Buxton, Paul Chapman, and Paul Temple. London: Routledge: 101–27.

CABALLERO, R., and M. HAMOUR. 1998. 'The Macroeconomics of Specificity.' *Journal of Political Economy* 106 (August): 724–67.

CALLON, SCOTT. 1995. *Divided Sun: MITI and the Breakdown of Japanese High-Tech Industrial Policy, 1975–1993*. Stanford, Calif.: Stanford University Press.

CALMFORS, LARS. 1993. *Centralization of Wage Bargaining and Macroeconomic*

Performance: A Survey. Seminar Paper No. 536. Stockholm: Institute for International Economic Studies.

—— 1998. 'Macroeconomic Policy, Wage Setting, and Employment: What Difference Does the EMU Make?' *Oxford Review of Economic Policy* 14 (3): 125–51.

—— and JOHN DRIFFILL. 1988. 'Centralisation of Wage Bargaining and Macroeconomic Performance.' *Economic Policy* 6 (April): 13–61.

CALVERT, R. 1995. 'The Rational Choice Theory of Social Institutions: Cooperation, Coordination, and Communication.' In *Modern Political Economy*, ed. J. Banks and E. Hanushek. New York: Cambridge University Press: 216–67.

CAMERON, DAVID R. 1984. 'Social Democracy, Corporatism, Labor Quiescence, and the Representation of Economic Interest in Advanced Capitalist Society.' In *Order and Conflict in Contemporary Capitalism: Studies in the Political Economy of Western European Nations*, ed. John H. Goldthorpe. New York: Oxford University Press: 143–78.

—— 1996. 'Exchange Rate Politics in France, 1981–1983: The Regime-Defining Choices of the Mitterrand Presidency.' In *The Mitterrand Era: Policy Alternatives and Political Mobilization in France*, ed. Anthony Daley. London: Macmillan: 56–82.

CAMPBELL, JOHN L., ROGERS HOLLINGSWORTH, and LEON LINDBERG. 1991. *Governance of the American Economy.* New York: Cambridge University Press.

CARGILL, CARL F. 1989. *Information Technology Standardization: Theory, Process and Organizations.* Bedford, Mass.: Digital Equipment Corporation.

—— 1994. 'Evolution and Revolution in Open Systems.' *StandardView* 2 (March): 3–13.

—— 1997a. *Open Systems Standardization: A Business Approach.* Upper Saddle River, NJ: Prentice Hall PTR.

—— 1997b. 'Standardizing Java.' *StandardView* 5 (4) (December): 127–200.

CARLIN, WENDY, and DAVID SOSKICE. 1990. *Macroeconomics and the Wage Bargain: A Modern Approach to Employment, Inflation and the Exchange Rate.* Oxford: Oxford University Press.

—— —— 1997. 'Shocks to the System: The German Political Economy Under Stress.' *National Institute Economic Review* 159 (January): 57–76.

CARO, PHILIPPE. 1993. 'Les Usines Citroën de Rennes: origines, implantation et évolutions (1951 à 1974).' Ph.D. thesis, EHESS, Paris.

CASPER, STEVEN. 1996. *German Industrial Associations and the Diffusion of Innovative Economic Organisation.* Berlin: Wissenschaftszentrum Berlin.

—— 1997. 'Reconfiguring Institutions: The Political Economy of Legal Development in Germany and the United States.' Ph.D. dissertation, Cornell University, Ithaca, NY.

—— 1999. 'High Technology Governance and Institutional Adpativeness.' Discussion Paper 99-307. Wissenschaftszentrum, Berlin.

—— and BOB HANCKÉ. 1999. 'Global Quality Norms within National Production Regimes: ISO 9000 Standards in the French and German Car Industries.' *Organizational Studies* 20 (6): 961–86.

CASPER, STEVEN and SIGURT VITOLS. 1997. 'The German Model in the 1990s: Problems and Prospects.' *Industry and Innovation* 4: 1–14.

—— MARK LEHRER, and DAVID SOSKICE. 1999. 'Can High-Technology Industries Prosper in Germany? Institutional Frameworks and the Evolution of the German Software and Biotechnology Industries.' *Industry and Innovation* 6 (1): 5 –24.

CAUCHON, CHRISTOPHE. 1997. 'La Hiérarchie face aux réformes de la grande entreprise de service public en réseau et de son marché interne de travail: les cadres de la SNCF.' Ph.D. thesis, University of Aix-Marseille.

CAVES, RICHARD E., and MICHAEL E. PORTER. 1977. 'From Entry Barriers to Mobility Barriers: Conjectural Decisions and Contrived Deterrence to New Competition.' *Quarterly Journal of Economics* 91 (2): 241–61.

CBI (Confederation of British Industry). 1981. *Green Paper on Democracy in Trade Unions: Response from Confederation of British Industry*. June. London: CBI Social Affairs Directorate.

Centralverband Deutscher Industrieller 1881. *Verhandlungen, Mitteilungen und Berichte des Centralverbandes Deutscher Industrieller*. Berlin: CDI.

CHANDLER, ALFRED. 1974. *The Visible Hand*. Cambridge, Mass.: Harvard University Press.

—— and HAROLD DAEMS, eds. 1980. *Managerial Hierarchies: Comparative Perspectives on the Rise of the Modern Corporation*. Cambridge, Mass.: Harvard University Press.

CHANG, CHUN, and YIJIAN WANG. 1995. 'A Framework for Understanding Differences in Labor Turnover and Human Capital Investment.' *Journal of Economic Behavior and Organization* 28 (1): 91–105.

CHARKHAM, JONATHAN. 1994. *Keeping Good Company: A Study of Corporate Governance in Five Countries*. Oxford: Oxford University Press.

CHARPAIL, C., and S. ZILBERMAN. 1998. 'Diplôme et insertion professionnelle après un contrat de qualification.' In *Bilan de la politique de l'emploi 1997*. Paris: DARES: 187–93.

CHURCH, CLIVE H., and DAVID PHINNEMORE. 1994. *European Union and European Community: A Handbook and Commentary on the 1992 Maastricht Treaties*. London: Prentice Hall and Harvester Wheatsheaf.

CLAPHAM, ANDREW. 1996. *Human Rights in the Private Sphere*. Oxford: Oxford University Press.

CLARK, WILLIAM ROBERTS, USHA NAIR REICHERT, SANDRA LYNN LOMAS, and KEVIN L. PARKER. 1998. 'International and Domestic Constraints on Political Business Cycles in OECD Economies.' *International Organization* 52 (1): 87–120.

COHEN, ELIE. 1989. *L'État Brancardier*. Paris: Calmann-Levy.

—— 1996. *La Tentation hexagonale*. Paris: Fayard.

—— and MICHEL BAUER. 1980. *Qui gouverne les grands groupes industriels français?* Paris: Seuil.

COHEN, J., and J. ROGERS. 1992. 'Secondary Associations and Democratic Governance.' *Politics and Society* 20 (4): 393–472.

COHEN, STEPHEN. 1977. *Modern Capitalist Planning*. Berkeley and Los Angeles: University of California Press.

—— JAMES GALBRAITH, and JOHN ZYSMAN. 1985. 'The Control of Financial Policy in France.' In *The State in Capitalist Europe*, ed. Steven Bornstein, David Held, and Joel Krieger. London: Allen & Unwin: 21–53.

COLLINS, HUGH. 1992. *Justice in Dismissal: The Law of Termination of Employment*. Oxford: Oxford University Press.

—— 1995. 'European Private Law and the Cultural Identities of States.' *European Review of Private Law* 3 (2): 353–65.

—— 1997. *The Law of Contract*. 3rd edn. London: Butterworths.

Comité de Coordination. 1996. *Évaluation des politiques régionales de formation professionnelle*. Paris: Government Report.

Commissariat Général du Plan. 1996. *Globalisation, mondialisation, concurrence: la planification française a-t-elle encore un avenir?* Paris: Commissariat Général du Plan.

COURTOIS, GÉRARD. 1995. 'Éducation et formation: grandes tendances.' In *L'État de la France 95–96*. Paris: La Découverte: 85–90.

COWHEY, PETER F. 1993. 'Domestic Institutions and the Credibility of International Commitments: Japan and the United States.' *International Organization* 47 (2): 299–326.

COX, ANDREW. 1986. *The State, Finance and Industry*. Brighton: Wheatsheaf.

CRANE, RHONDA. 1979. *The Politics of International Standard Setting: France and the Color TV War*. Norwood, NJ: Ablex.

CROUCH, COLIN, and WOLFGANG STREECK. 1997a. 'Introduction: The Future of Capitalist Diversity.' In *Political Economy of Modern Capitalism: Mapping Convergence and Diversity*, ed. Colin Crouch and Wolfgang Streeck. London: Sage: 1–18.

—— —— eds. 1997b. *Political Economy of Modern Capitalism: Mapping Convergence and Diversity*. London: Sage.

CROZIER, MICHEL. 1964. *Le Phénomène bureaucratique*. Paris: Le Seuil.

—— 1970. *La Société bloquée*. Paris: Le Seuil.

CUBITT, ROBIN P. 1989. 'Precommitment and the Macroeconomic Policy Game.' D.Phil. thesis, Oxford University.

—— 1992. 'Monetary Policy Games and Private Sector Precommitment.' *Oxford Economic Papers* 44 (3): 513–30.

—— 1995. 'Corporatism, Monetary Policy and Macroeconomic Performance: A Simple Game Theoretic Analysis.' *Scandinavian Journal of Economics* 97 (2): 245–59.

CUKIERMAN, ALEX. 1992. *Central Bank Strategy, Credibility, and Independence: Theory and Evidence*. Cambridge, Mass.: MIT Press.

—— 1996. 'The Economics of Central Banking.' Working Paper No. 36-96, Tel Aviv: Stackler Institute for Economic Studies, Tel Aviv University.

—— and FRANCESCO LIPPI. 1999. 'Central Bank Independence, Centralization of Wage Bargaining, Inflation and Unemployment: Theory and Evidence.' *European Economic Review* 43 (7): 1395–434.

CUKIERMAN, ALEX, BILIN NEYAPTI, and STEVEN B. WEBB. 1992. 'Measuring the Independence of Central Banks and its Effect on Policy Outcomes.' *World Bank Economic Review* 6 (3): 353–98.

CULLY, MARK, STEPHEN WOODLAND, ANDREW O'REILLY, and GILL DIX. 1999. *Britain at Work: As Depicted by the 1998 Employee Relations Survey.* London: Routledge.

CULPEPPER, PEPPER D. 1998. 'Rethinking Reform: The Politics of Decentralized Cooperation in France and Germany.' Ph.D. dissertation, Harvard University.

—— 1999. 'Individual Choice, Collective Action, and the Problem of Training Reform.' In *The German Skills Machine,* ed. Pepper D. Culpepper and David Finegold. Oxford: Berghahn: 269–325.

—— 2000. 'Can the State Create Cooperation? Problems of Reforming the Labor Supply in France.' *Journal of Public Policy* 20 (3): 223–45.

—— Forthcoming. *Rethinking Reform: The Politics of Decentralized Cooperation in the Advanced Industrial Countries.*

—— and DAVID FINEGOLD, eds. 1999. *The German Skills Machine.* Oxford: Berghahn.

CURRAN, WILLIAM J., III. 1998. 'Mystery or Magic? The Intriguing Interface of Antitrust Law and Today's Information Technologies.' *Antitrust Bulletin* (Fall/Winter): 775–99.

CUSACK, THOMAS R., and ALEXANDRA FROSCH. 2000. 'Sample-Based Weightings of Scientific Linkage Scores for US Patent Data: A Comparison with Grupp *et al.*'s Assessments Based on Data from the European Patent Office.' Berlin: Wissenschaftszentrum. Working Paper.

CUTCHER-GERSHENFELD, JOEL, DONALD POWER, and MAUREEN MCCABE-POWER. 1996. 'Global Implications of Recent Innovations in U.S. Collective Bargaining.' *Industrial Relations (Canadian)* 51 (2): 281–302.

DALEY, ANTHONY. 1996. *Steel, State, and Labor: Mobilization and Adjustment in France.* Pittsburgh: University of Pittsburgh Press.

—— 1999. 'The Hollowing out of French Unions.' In *The Brave New World of European Labor: European Trade Unions at the Millennium,* ed. Andrew Martin and George Ross. New York: Berghahn: 167–216.

DALY, MARY. 1994. 'A Matter of Dependency? The Gender Dimension of British Income-Maintenance Provision.' *Sociology* 28 (3): 779–97.

DAVIES, PAUL, and MARK FREEDLAND. 1993. *Labour Legislation and Public Policy: A Contemporary History.* Oxford: Clarendon Press.

DAWSON, JOHN. 1983. 'Judicial Revision of Frustrated Contracts: Germany.' *Boston University Law Review* 63 (5): 1039–98.

DEEG, RICHARD, and SUSANNE LUTZ. 1998. 'Internationalization and Financial Federalism: The United States and Germany at the Crossroads?' Discussion Paper, Max Planck Institut für Gesellshaftsforschung, Cologne.

DEININGER, KLAUS, and LYN SQUIRE. 1996. 'Measuring Income Inequality: A New Data-Base.' Development Discussion Paper No. 537, Harvard Institute for International Development.

Deregulierungskommission. 1991. *Marktöffnung und Wettbewerb.* Stuttgart: C. E. Poeschel Verlag.

DERRIDA, JACQUES. 1991. *L'Autre Cap.* Paris: Minuit.

Deutsche Bundesbank. 1997. 'Die Aktie als Finanzierungs- und Anlageinstrument.' *Monatsbericht* 49 (January): 23–47.

DICKENS, LINDA, and MARK HALL. 1995. 'The State: Labour Law and Industrial Relations.' In *Industrial Relations: Theory and Practice in Britain*, ed. Paul Edwards. Oxford: Blackwell: 255–303.

DIMAGGIO, PAUL, and WALTER POWELL. 1991. 'Introduction.' In *The New Institutionalism in Organizational Analysis*. Chicago: University of Chicago Press: 1–40.

DIN. 1992. *75 Jahre DIN 1917 bis 1992: ein Haus mit Geschichte und Zukunft*. Berlin: Beuth Verlag.

—— 1995. *Grundlagen der Normungsarbeit des DIN*. DIN Normenheft 10. Berlin: Beuth.

D'IRIBARNE, ALAIN. 1989. *La Compétitivité: défi social, enjeu éducatif*. Paris: Presses du CNRS.

DOERINGER, PETER B., and MICHAEL J. PIORE. 1971. *Internal Labor Markets and Manpower Analysis*. Lexington, Mass.: Heath.

DORE, RONALD. 1986. *Flexible Rigidities*. Stanford, Calif.: Stanford University Press.

—— and MARI SAKO. 1989. *How the Japanese Learn to Work*. London: Routledge.

DOSI, GIOVANNI, C. FREEMAN, R. NELSON, G. SILVERBERG, and L. SOETE. 1988. *Technical Change and Economic Theory*. London: Pinter.

—— DAVID TEECE, and JOSEF CHYTRY, eds. 1998. *Technology, Organization and Competitiveness*. Oxford: Oxford University Press.

DRIVER, STEPHEN, and LUKE MARTELL. 1998. *New Labour: Politics after Thatcherism*. Malden: Polity Press.

DUCHÉNEAUT, BERTRAND. 1995. *Enquête sur les PME françaises: identités, contextes, chiffres*. Paris: Maxima.

DUCLOS, LAURENT, and NELLY MAUCHAMP. 1994. *Bilan-perspectives des relations sociales et professionnelles à EDF-GDF*. Paris: GIP-Mutations Industrielles.

DUFFAUX, KARINE. 1995. 'La Démarche productique: une approche en terme d'héritage, la perspective allemagne.' Unpublished paper.

DU TERTRE, CHRISTIAN. 1989. *Technologie, flexibilité, emploi: une approche sectorielle du post-taylorisme*. Paris: L'Harmattan.

DUVAL, GUILLAUME. 1996. 'Les Habits neufs du taylorisme.' *Alternatives Économiques*, 137: 30–9.

—— 1998. *L'Entreprise efficace à l'heure de Swatch et McDonalds: la seconde vie du taylorisme*. Paris: Syros.

EASTERBROOK, FRANK, and DANIEL FISCHEL. 1991. *The Economic Structure of Corporate Law*. Cambridge, Mass.: Harvard University Press.

EBBINGHAUS, BERNHARD, and JELLE VISSER. 2000. *Trade Unions in Western Europe since 1945*. London: Macmillan.

EBKE, WERNER F., and BETTINA M. STEINHAUER. 1995. 'The Doctrine of Good Faith in German Contract Law.' In *Good Faith and Fault in Contract Law*, ed. Jack Beatson and Daniel Friedmann. Oxford: Clarendon: 171–90.

EDQUIST, CHARLES. 1997. *Systems of Innovation*. London: Pinter.

EDWARDS, PAUL. 1995. 'Strikes and Industrial Conflict.' In *Industrial Relations: Theory and Practice in Britain*, ed. Paul Edwards. Oxford: Blackwell: 434–60.

—— MARK HALL, RICHARD HYMAN, PAUL MARGINSON, KEITH SISSON, JEREMY

WADDINGTON, and DAVID WINCHESTER. 1992. 'Great Britain: Still Muddling Through.' In *Industrial Relations in the New Europe*, ed. Anthony Ferner and Richard Hyman. Oxford: Blackwell: 1–68.

EDWARDS, RICHARD C., MICHAEL REICH, and DAVID M. GORDON. 1975. *Labor Market Segmentation*. Lexington, Mass.: Heath.

EHRMANN, HENRY WALLACE. 1957. *Organized Business in France*. Princeton: Princeton University Press.

EICHENGREEN, BARRY. 1997. 'Institutions and Economic Growth after World War II.' In *Economic Growth in Europe since 1945*, ed. Nicholas Crafts and Gianni Toniolo. Cambridge: Cambridge University Press: 38–72.

EIJFFINGER, SYLVESTER C. W., and JAKOB DE HAAN. 1996. *The Political Economy of Central Bank Independence*. Princeton: Special Papers in International Economics 19 (May). Princeton University, Department of Economics, International Finance Section.

ELLIS, JAMES W. 1998. 'Voting for Markets or Marketing for Votes: The Politics of Neo-Liberal Economic Reform'. Ph.D. Dissertation, Department of Government, Harvard University.

ELSTER, JON, ed. 1998. *Deliberative Democracy*. New York: Cambridge University Press.

ELVANDER, NILS. 1997. 'The Swedish Bargaining System in the Melting Pot.' In *The Swedish Bargaining System in the Melting Pot: Institutions, Norms and Outcomes in the 1990s*, ed. Nils Elvander and Bertil Holmlund. Solna: Arbetslivsinstitutet: 11–89.

ERGAS, HENRI. 1987. 'Does Technology Policy Matter?' In *Technology and Global Industry*, ed. Bruce R. Guile and Harvey Brooks. Washington: National Academy Press: 191–245.

ESPING-ANDERSEN, GØSTA. 1985. *Politics against Markets*. Princeton: Princeton University Press.

—— 1990. *Three Worlds of Welfare Capitalism*. Princeton: Princeton University Press.

—— 1999. *Social Foundations of Postindustrial Economies*. Oxford: Oxford University Press.

ESSER, JOSEF. 1956. *Grundsatz und Norm in der richterlichen Fortbildung des Privatrechts: Rechtsvergleichende Beiträge zur Rechtsquellen- und Interpretationslehre*. Tübingen: Mohr & Siebeck.

—— and EIKE SCHMIDT. 1991. *Schuldrecht: Allgemeiner Teil*. 8th edn. Heidelberg: C. F. Müller.

ESTEVEZ-ABE, MARGARITA. 1999a. 'Welfare and Capitalism in Contemporary Japan.' Ph.D. dissertation, Department of Government, Harvard University.

—— 1999b. 'Comparative Political Economy of Female Labor Force Participation.' Paper presented at the meeting of the American Political Science Association, Atlanta, 2–5 September.

ESTRIN, SAUL, and PETER HOLMES. 1983. *French Planning in Theory and Practice*. London: Allen & Unwin.

ETTL, W., and A. HEIKENROTH. 1995. 'Strukturwandel, Verbandsabstinenz, Tarifflucht: zur Lage ostdeutscher Unternehmen und Arbeitgeberverbände.'

Working Paper 95/3, Max Planck Gesellschaft, Arbeitsgruppe Transformations-prozesse in den neuen Bundesländern.

European Commission. *Unemployment in Europe* (various years).

EVANS, PETER, DIETRICH RUESCHEMEYER, and THEDA SKOCPOL, eds. 1985. *Bringing the State Back in*. New York: Cambridge University Press.

EWALD, FRANÇOIS. 1986. *L'État providence*. Paris: Grasset.

—— 1991. 'Insurance and Risk.' In *The Foucault Effect: Studies in Governmentality*, ed. Graham Burchell, Colin Gordon, and Peter Miller. London: Harvester: 197-211.

—— 1996. *Histoire de l'État providence: les origines de la solidarité*. Paris: Grasset.

EWALD, WILLIAM. 1994. 'The American Revolution and the Evolution of Law.' *American Journal of Comparative Law* 42 (1): 1–14.

—— 1995a. 'Comparative Jurisprudence I: What Was It Like to Try a Rat.' *University of Pennsylvania Law Review* 143 (June): 1889–2149.

—— 1995b. 'Comparative Jurisprudence II: The Logic of Legal Transplants.' *American Journal of Comparative Law* 43 (Fall): 489–510.

EYRAUD, FRANÇOIS, and ROBERT TCHOBANIAN. 1985. 'The Auroux Reforms and Company Level Industrial Relations in France.' *British Journal of Industrial Relations* 23: 241–59.

FARNSWORTH, ALLAN E. 1995. 'Good Faith in Contract Performance.' In *Good Faith and Fault in Contract Law*, ed. Jack Beatson and Daniel Friedmann. Oxford: Clarendon: 153–70.

FEATHERSTONE, MIKE, and SCOTT LASH. 1995. 'Globalization, Modernity and the Spatialization of Social Theory.' In *Global Modernities*, ed. Mike Featherstone, Scott Lash, and Roland Robertson. London: Sage: 1–24.

FEHN, RAINER. 1998. 'Capital Market Imperfections, Greater Volatilities and Rising Unemployment: Does Venture Capital Help?' Working Paper, Bayerische Julius-Maximillians-Universität Würtzburg.

FERNER, ANTHONY, and RICHARD HYMAN, eds. 1992a. *Industrial Relations in the New Europe*. Oxford: Blackwell.

———— 1992b. 'Italy: Between Political Exchange and Micro-corporatism.' In *Industrial Relations in the New Europe*, ed. Anthony Ferner and Richard Hyman. Oxford: Blackwell: 524–600.

FICHTER, M. 1997. 'Unions in the New Länder: Evidence for the Urgency of Reform.' In *Negotiating the New Germany*, ed. L. Turner. Ithaca, NY: Cornell University Press: 87–112.

FINEGOLD, DAVID, and DAVID SOSKICE. 1988. 'The Failure of Training in Britain: Analysis and Prescription.' *Oxford Review of Economic Policy* 4 (3): 21–53.

FIORETOS, KARL ORFEO. 1998. 'Anchoring Adjustment: Globalization, Varieties of Capitalism, and the Domestic Sources of Multilateralism'. Ph.D. Dissertation, Columbia University.

—— 2000. 'Creative Reconstruction: National Capitalisms and European Integration, 1957–99.' University of Wisconsin-Madison. Typescript.

FISH, STANLEY. 1989. *Doing What Comes Naturally: Change, Rhetoric, and the Practice of Theory in Literary and Legal Studies*. Oxford: Oxford University Press.

FISH, STANLEY. 1994. *There's No Such Thing as Free Speech.* Oxford: Oxford University Press.

FORTEZA, ALVARO. 1998. 'The Wage Bargaining Structure and the Inflationary Bias.' *Journal of Macroeconomics* 20 (3): 599–614.

FRANCKE, L. 1881. 'Die Stimmen der deutschen Handels- und Gewerbekammern über das Haftpflichtgesetz vom 7. Juni 1871 und den Reichs-Unfallsversicherungs-Gesetzentwurf vom 8. 03. 1881.' *Zeitschrift des Königlich-Preussischen Statistischen Büros* 21: 39–416.

FRANKENBERG, GÜNTER. 1985. 'Critical Comparisons: Re-thinking Comparative Law.' *Harvard International Law Journal* 26 (2): 411–55.

Frankfurter Allgemeine. 1985. 'Auch Arbeitgeber gegen Bonner Pläne für ein neues Betriebsverfassungsrecht.' 2 February.

FRANZESE, ROBERT J., Jr. 1994. 'Central Bank Independence, Sectoral Interest, and the Wage Bargain.' Working Paper 56, Harvard Center for European Studies.

—— 1996. 'The Political Economy of Over-commitment: A Comparative Study of Democratic Management of the Keynesian Welfare State.' Ph.D. dissertation, Harvard University.

—— 1999a. 'Exchange-Rate Regimes and Inflation in the Open and Institutionalized Economy.' Paper presented at the annual meeting of the American Political Science Association.

—— 1999b. 'Partially Independent Central Banks, Politically Responsive Governments, and Inflation.' *American Journal of Political Science* 43 (3): 681–706.

—— 2000. 'Credibly Conservative Monetary Policy and Labor–Goods Market Organization: A Review with Implications for ECB-Led Monetary Policy in Europe.' In *Fifty Years of the Bundesbank: Lessons for the European Central Bank,* ed. Jakob de Haan. London: Routledge: 97–124.

—— Forthcoming. *Explaining Macroeconomic Policies: Institutional Interactions in the Evolving Political Economies of Developed Democracies.* New York: Cambridge University Press.

—— and PETER A. HALL. 2000. 'The Institutional Interaction of Wage-Bargaining and Monetary Policy.' In *Unions, Employers and Central Banks: Macroeconomic Coordination and Institutional Change in Social Market Economies,* ed. Torben Iversen, Jonas Pontusson, and David Soskice. Cambridge: Cambridge University Press: 173–204.

—— CINDY D. KAM, and AMANEY A. JAMAL. 1999. 'Modeling and Interpreting Interactive Hypotheses in Regression Analysis.' Paper presented at the annual meeting of the American Political Science Association.

FREEMAN, RICHARD B., and EDWARD P. LAZEAR. 1995. 'An Economic Analysis of Works Councils.' In *Works Councils: Consultation, Representation, and Cooperation in Industrial Relations,* ed. Joel Rogers and Wolfgang Streeck. Chicago: University of Chicago Press: 27–52.

FREYSSENET, MICHEL. 1998. 'Renault: From Diversified Mass Production to Innovative Flexible Production.' In *One Best Way? Trajectories and Industrial Models of the World's Automobile Producers,* ed. Michel Freyssenet, Andrew Mair, Koichi Shimizu, and Giuseppe Volpato. Oxford: Oxford University Press: 365–94.

FRIEDEN, JEFFRY. 1991. 'Invested Interests: The Politics of National Income Policies in a World of Global Finance.' *International Organization* 45 (4) (Autumn): 425–51.

—— 1999. 'Actors and Preferences in International Relations.' In *Strategic Choice and International Relations*, ed. David A. Lake and Robert Powell. Princeton: Princeton University Press: 39–76.

—— and RONALD ROGOWSKI. 1996. 'The Impact of the International Economy on National Policies: An Analytical Overview.' In *Internationalization and Domestic Politics*, ed. Robert Keohane and Helen Milner. New York: Cambridge University Press: 25–47.

FRIEDMAN, JONATHAN. 1990. 'Being in the World: Globalization and Localization.' In *Global Culture: Nationalism, Globalisation and Modernity*, ed. Mike Featherstone. London: Sage: 311–28.

FRIEDMAN, THOMAS. 1999. *The Lexus and the Olive Tree*. New York: Farrar, Strauss & Giroux.

FUDENBERG, DREW, and ERIC MASKIN. 1986. 'The Folk Theorem in Repeated Games with Discounting and Incomplete Information.' *Econometrica* 54 (May): 533–54.

FÜHRER, CARL. 1990. *Arbeitslosigkeit und die Enstehung der Arbeitslosenversicherung in Deutschland 1902–1927*. Berlin: Colloquium.

FUKUHARA, KENICHI. 1994. 'Das System der industriellen Standardisierung in Japan und die Rolle der Japanese Standards Association (Japanischer Normenausschuß–JSA).' In *Bedeutung der Normung und Zertifizierung in Bezug auf den Europäischen Binnenmarkt und Japan*, trans. Bernd Rießland. Normungskunde Band 32. Berlin: Beuth Verlag: 91–101.

GABEL, H. LANDIS. 1987. *Product Standardization and Competitive Strategy*. Amsterdam: Elsevier Science Publishers.

—— 1991. *Competitive Strategies for Product Standards: The Strategic Use of Compatibility Standards for Competitive Advantage*. London: McGraw-Hill.

GAMBLE, ANDREW, and STUART WALKLAND. 1984. *Britain's Party System and Economic Policy 1945–1983*. Oxford: Clarendon.

GANNE, BERNARD. 1992. 'Place et évolution des systèmes industriels locaux en France: Économie politique d'une transformation.' In *Les Régions qui gagnent: districts et réseaux: les nouveaux paradigmes de la géographie économique*, ed. Georges Benko and Alain Lipietz. Paris: Presses Universitaires de France: 315–45.

GARCIA, D. LINDA. 1992. 'Standard Setting in the United States: Public and Private Sector Roles.' *Journal of the American Society for Information Science* 43 (8): 531–7.

GARRETT, GEOFFREY. 1998. *Partisan Politics in the Global Economy*. Cambridge: Cambridge University Press.

—— and P. LANGE. 1991. 'Political Responses to Interdependence: What's Left for the Left?' *International Organization* 45 (4): 539–64.

—— —— 1996. 'Internationalization, Institutions, and Political Change.' In *Internationalization and Domestic Politics*, ed. Robert O. Keohane and Helen V. Milner. New York: Cambridge University Press: 48–75.

—— and CHRISTOPHER WAY. 1995a. 'Labor Market Institutions and the Economic

Consequences of Central Bank Independence.' Paper presented at the annual meeting of the American Political Science Association.

GARRETT, GEOFFREY and CHRISTOPHER WAY. 'The Sectoral Composition of Trade Unions, Corporatism and Economic Performance.' In *Monetary and Fiscal Policy in an Integrated Europe*, ed. Barry Eichengreen, Jeffry Frieden, and Jürgen von Hagen. New York: Springer-Verlag: 38–61.

—— —— 1999. 'The Rise of Public Sector Unions, Corporatism, and Macroeconomic Performance.' *Comparative Political Studies* 32 (4): 411–34.

—— —— 2000. 'Public Sector Unions, Corporatism, and Wage Determination.' In *Unions, Employers and Central Banks: Macroeconomic Coordination and Institutional Change in Social Market Economies*, ed. Torben Iversen, Jonas Pontusson, and David Soskice. Cambridge: Cambridge University Press: 267–91.

GEARY, JOHN F. 1995. 'Work Practices: The Structure of Work.' In *Industrial Relations: Theory and Practice in Britain*, ed. Paul Edwards. Oxford: Blackwell: 368–96.

GÉHIN, J.-P., and P. MÉHAUT. 1993. *Apprentissage ou formation continue? Stratégies éducatives des entreprises en Allemagne et en France*. Paris: Éditions l'Harmattan.

GEORGE, STEPHEN. 1990. *An Awkward Partner: Britain in the European Community*. New York: Oxford University Press.

GERNHUBER, JOACHIM. 1989. *Das Schuldverhältnis: Begründung und Änderung, Pflichten und Strukturen, Drittwirkungen*. Tübingen: Mohr & Siebeck.

GERSCHENKRON, ALEXANDER. 1962. *Economic Backwardness in Historical Perspective*. Cambridge, Mass.: Harvard University Press.

GERSTENBERGER, WOLFGANG. 1992. 'Zur Wettbewerbsposition der deutschen Industrie im High-Tech-Bereich.' *ifo Schnelldienst* 45 (13): 14–23.

Gesamtmetall. 1999. *Geschäftsbericht 1997–1999*. Cologne: Gesamtmetall.

GLENDON, ANN, MICHAEL W. GORDON, and CHRISTOPHER OSAKWE. 1994. *Comparative Legal Traditions*. St Paul, Minn.: West.

Global Economic Forum. 2000. *World Competitiveness Report*. New York: Oxford University Press.

GLYN, ANDREW. 1997. 'Does Aggregate Profitability *Really* Matter?' *Cambridge Journal of Economics* 219 (September): 593–616.

GOLDBERG, VICTOR. 1985. 'Price Adjustments in Long-Term Contracts.' *Wisconsin Law Review* 54 (3): 527–43.

GOLDEN, MIRIAM. 1993. 'The Dynamics of Trade Unionism and National Economic Performance.' *American Political Science Review* 87 (June): 439–54.

—— and MICHAEL WALLERSTEIN. 1995. 'Trade Union Organization and Industrial Relations in the Post-war Era in 16 Nations.' Paper presented at the annual meeting of the Midwest Political Science Association.

—— LANGE, PETER, and WALLERSTEIN, MICHAEL. 1997. 'Union Centralization among Advanced Industrial Societies: An Empirical Study.' Dataset available at http://www.shelley.sscnet.ucla.edu/data.

GOLDSTEIN, ANDREA. 1996. 'Privatizations and Corporate Governance in France.' *Banca Nazionale del Lavoro Quarterly Review* 44: 455–88.

GOLDTHORPE, JOHN H., ed. 1984. *Order and Conflict in Contemporary Capitalism*. New York: Oxford University Press.

GOODE, ROY. 1992. *The Concept of 'Good Faith' in English Law*. Rome: Centro di Studi e Ricerche di Diritto Comparato e Straniero.

GORDON, COLIN. 1991. 'New Deal, Old Deck: Business and the Origins of Social Security 1920–1935.' *Politics and Society* 19 (June): 165–207.

—— 1994. *New Deals: Business, Labor and Politics in America 1920–1935*. New York: Cambridge University Press.

GORGEU, ARMELLE, and RENÉ MATHIEU. 1993. 'Dix Ans de relations de sous-traitance dans l'industrie française.' *Travail* 28: 23–44.

—— —— 1995. 'Stratégies d'approvisionnement des grandes firmes et livraisons juste à temps: quel impact spatial?' *L'Espace géographique* 24 (3): 245–59.

—— —— 1996. 'Les Ambiguités de la proximité: les nouveaux établissements d'équipement automobile.' *Actes de la recherche en sciences sociales* 114: 44–53.

GOTTSCHALK, PETER, and T. M. SMEEDING. 2000. 'Empirical Evidence on Income Inequality in Industrialized Countries.' In *The Handbook of Income Distribution*, ed. A. B. Atkinson and F. Bourgignon. London: North Holland Press.

GOUREVITCH, PETER ALEXIS. 1996. 'Squaring the Circle: The Domestic Sources of International Cooperation.' *International Organization* 50 (2): 349–73.

GOYER, MICHEL. 1998. 'Governments, Markets, and Growth Revisited: Corporate Governance in France and Japan, 1965–98.' Paper presented at the annual meeting of the American Political Science Association, Boston.

—— 2001. 'Corporate Governance under Stress: France and Germany in Comparative Perspective.' Ph.D. dissertation, Department of Political Science, Massachusetts Institute of Technology.

—— Forthcoming. 'Corporate Governance and the Innovation System in France: The Development of Firms' Capabilities and Strategies, 1985–2000.' *Industry and Innovation*.

GRANOVETTER, MARK. 1985. 'Economic Action and Social Structures: The Problem of Embeddedness.' *American Journal of Sociology* 91 (3): 481–510.

GRANT, WYN. 1989. *Government and Industry: A Comparative Analysis of the US, Canada, and the UK*. Aldershot: Edward Elgar.

GRAUBARD, STEPHEN, 1964. *A New Europe?* Boston: Beacon Press.

GREENSTEIN, SHANE M. 1992. 'Invisible Hands and Visible Advisors: An Economic Interpretation of Standardization.' *Journal of the American Society for Information Science* 43 (8): 538–49.

GREWLICH, KLAUS W. 1984. 'EG-Forschung- und Technologiepolitik.' In *EG-Mitgliedschaft: Ein vitales Interesse der Bundesrepublik Deutschland*, ed. Rudolf Hrbek and Wolfgang Wessels. Bonn: European Union Verlag: 221–68.

GRIECO, JOSEPH M. 1995. 'The Maastricht Treaty, European Economic and Monetary Union and the Neo-realist Research Programme.' *Review of International Studies* 21 (January): 21–40.

GRIFFIN, JOHN. 1997. 'National Capitalisms? Toward a Comparison of Tenuous States from a Modern Perspective of Ownership Politics.' Paper presented at the meeting of the American Political Science Association, Washington.

—— 2000. 'Making Money Talk: A New Bank–Firm Relationship in German Banking?' Paper presented to the Annual Conference of the Society for the Advancement of Socio-economics, London, July.

GRILLI, VITTORI, DONATO MASCIANDARO, and GUIDO TABELLINI. 1991. 'Political and Monetary Institutions and Public Financial Policies in the Industrial Countries.' *Economic Policy* 13: 341–92.

GROSSMAN, GENE, and ELHANAN HELPMANN. 1992. *Innovation and Growth in the Global Economy*. Cambridge, Mass.: MIT Press.

GRÜNER, HANS-PETER, and CARSTEN HEFEKER. 1999. 'How Will EMU Affect Inflation and Unemployment in Europe?' *Scandinavian Journal of Economics* 101 (1): 33–47.

GRUNFELD, CYRIL, and LIONEL BLOCH. 1986. *Law Reform and the Mining Dispute 1984–5*. London: Institute of Directors.

GRUPP, HARIOLF, GUNNAR MÜNT, and ULRICH SCHMOCH. 1995. *Wissenintensive Wirtschaft und Resourcenschonende Technik*. Parts D and E. Report to the BMBF. Karlsruhe: FhG-ISI.

GUILLEMARD, ANNE-MARIE. 1991. 'France: Massive Exit through Unemployment Compensation.' in *Time for Retirement: Comparative Studies of Early Exit from the Labor Force*, ed. Martin Kohli, Martin Rein, Anne-Marie Guillemard, and Herman van Gunsteren. Cambridge: Cambridge University Press: 127–80.

—— 1997. 'Sorties précoces d'activité.' Projet 249: 15–30.

GYLFASON, THORVALDUR, and ASSAR LINDBECK. 1994. 'The Interaction of Monetary Policy and Wages.' *Public Choice* 79 (1–2): 33–46.

HABER, SAMUEL. 1991. *The Quest for Authority and Honor in the American Professions, 1750–1900*. Chicago: University of Chicago Press.

HABERMAS, JÜRGEN. 1996. *Between Facts and Norms: Contributions to a Discourse Theory of Law and Democracy*. Cambridge, Mass.: MIT.

HACKER, JACOB, and PAUL PIERSON. 2000. 'Business Power and Social Policy: Employers and the Formation of the American Welfare State.' Paper presented at the annual meeting of the American Political Science Association, Wardman Park.

HALIMI, SERGE. 1992. *Sisyphe est fatigué: les échecs de la gauche au pouvoir*. Paris: Robert Laffont.

HALL, PETER A. 1986. *Governing the Economy: The Politics of State Intervention in Britain and France*. New York: Oxford University Press.

—— 1990. 'The State and the Market.' In *Developments in French Politics*, ed. Peter A. Hall, Jack Hayward, and Howard Machin. London: Macmillan: 171–87.

—— 1994. 'Central Bank Independence and Coordinated Wage Bargaining: Their Interaction in Germany and Europe.' *German Politics and Society* (Winter): 1–23.

—— 1997. 'The Political Economy of Adjustment in Germany.' In *Ökonomische Leitstungsfahigkeit und institutionelle Innovation*, ed. Frieder Naschold, David Soskice, Bob Hancké, and Ulrich Jurgens. Berlin: Sigma: 293–317.

—— 1999. 'The Political Economy of Europe in an Era of Interdependence.' In *Continuity and Change in Contemporary Capitalism*, ed. Herbert Kitschelt et al. Cambridge: Cambridge University Press: 135–63.

—— 2000. 'Organized Market Economies and Unemployment in Europe: Is It Finally Time to Accept Liberal Orthodoxy.' In *Context and Consequence: The Effects of Unemployment in the New Europe*, ed. Nancy Bermeo. New York: Cambridge University Press: 52–86.

—— 2001. 'The Evolution of Economic Policy in the European Union.' In *From Nation-State to European Union,* ed. Anand Menon and Vincent Wright. Oxford: Oxford University Press: 214–45.

—— and ROBERT FRANZESE, Jr. 1998. 'Mixed Signals: Central Bank Independence, Coordinated Wage Bargaining, and European Monetary Union.' *International Organisation* 52 (Summer): 502–36.

HANCKÉ, BOB. 1998. 'Trust or Hierarchy? Changing Relationships between Large and Small Firms in France.' *Small Business Economics* 11 (3): 237–52.

—— Forthcoming. 'Many Roads to Flexibility. How Large Firms Built Flexible Regional Production Systems in France.'

—— and SYLVIE CIEPLY. 1996. 'Bridging the Finance Gap for Small Firms.' Discussion Paper 96-311, Wissenschaftszentrum, Berlin.

—— and DAVID SOSKICE. 1996. 'Coordination and Restructuring in Large French Firms: The Evolution of French Industry in the 1980s.' Discussion Paper 96-303, Wissenschaftszentrum, Berlin.

Handelskammer Bremen. 1920. 'Bericht der Handelskammer Bremen.' Zentrales Staatsarchiv Potsdam. Reichswirtschaftsministerium 2078.

Handelskammer Hannover. 1922. 'Entschliessung zum Referentenentwurf uber eine vorlaufige Arbeitslosenversicherung.' Zentrales Staatsarchiv Potsdam. Reichswirtschaftsrat 664.

Handelskammer Leipzig. 1920. 'Denkschrift an das Arbeitsministerium Dresden.' Zentrales Staatsarchiv Potsdam. Reichsarbeitsamt 4310.

Handelskammer Lübeck. 1920. 'Denkschrift über die Arbeitslosenversicherung.' Zentrales Staatsarchiv Potsdam. Reichsarbeitsamt 4311.

Handwerkskammer Kassel. 1921. 'Bericht über die Vollversammlung der Handwerkskammer Kassel.' Zentrales Staatsarchiv Potsdam. Reichswirtschaftsministerium 2071.

—— 1925. *Bericht über die Vollversammlung der Handwerkskammer Kassel.* Zentrales Staatsarchiv Potsdam. Reichswirtschaftsministerium 2073.

HARHOFF, D., and T. KANE. 1997. 'Is the German Apprenticeship System a Panacea for the US Labor Market?' *Journal of Population Economics* 10 (May): 171–96.

HART, JEFFREY A. 1992. *Rival Capitalists: International Competitiveness in the United States, Japan, and Western Europe.* Ithaca, NY: Cornell University Press.

HAYES, FRANK. 1992. 'Superalphabet Compromise is Best of Two Worlds.' *UnixWorld* (January): 99–100.

HEADEY, BRUCE. 1970. 'Trade Unions and National Wage Policies.' *Journal of Politics* 32 (2): 407–39.

HEFERMEHL, WOLFGANG, ed. 1991. *Aktiengesetz und GmbH-Gesetz.* Munich: Deutscher Taschenverlag.

HELMHOLZ, RICHARD. 1990. 'Continental Law and Common Law: Historical Strangers or Companions.' *Duke Law Journal* 39 (December): 1207–68.

HELPMANN, ELHANAN. 1984. 'Increasing Returns, Imperfect Markets, and Trade Theory.' In *Handbook of International Economics,* ed. R. W. Jones and P. B. Kenen. Amsterdam: North Holland: 325–66.

HENNESSY, PETER. 1994. *The Hidden Wiring: Unearthing the British Constitution.* London: Indigo.

HERRIGEL, GARY. 1993. 'Large Firms, Small Firms, and the Governance of Flexible Specialization: The Case of Baden Württenberg and Socialized Risk.' In *Country Competitiveness,* ed. Bruce Kogut. New York: Oxford University Press: 15–35.

—— 1996. *Industrial Constructions: The Sources of German Industrial Power.* Cambridge: Cambridge University Press.

HESSER, WILFRIED, and ALEX INKLAAR. 1997. *An Introduction to Standards and Standardization.* DIN Normungskunde 36. Berlin: Beuth.

HEYLEN, FREDDY, and ANDRÉ VAN POECK. 1995. 'National Labour Market Institutions and the European Economic and Monetary Integration Process.' *Journal of Common Market Studies* 33 (4): 573–95.

HILDEBRANDT, SWEN. 1996. 'Berufsausbildung in Frankreich zwischen Staat, Region und Unternehmen: Neuere Entwicklungen in der Region Provence-Alpes-Côte d'Azur.' Discussion Paper 96-101, Wissenschaftszentrum, Berlin.

HILL, JONATHAN. 1989. 'Comparative Law, Law Reform and Legal Theory.' *Oxford Journal of Legal Studies* 9: 101–15.

HMSO. 1994. *Competitiveness: Helping Business to Win.* London: HMSO.

—— 1996a. *Competitiveness: Creating the Enterprise Centre of Europe.* London: HMSO.

—— 1996b. *A Partnership of Nations: The British Approach to the European Union Intergovernmental Conference 1996.* Cm. 3181 (March). London.

HOANG-NGOC, LIÊM. 1998. *La Facture sociale: sommes-nous condamnés au libéralisme?* Paris: Arléa.

HOFSTEDE, G. 1980. *Culture's Consequences.* London: Sage.

HOLLINGSWORTH, J. ROGERS. 1991. 'The Logic of Coordinating American Manufacturing Sectors.' In *Governance of the American Economy,* ed. John L. Campbell, J. Rogers Hollingsworth, and Leon N. Lindberg. New York: Cambridge University Press: 35–73.

—— PHILIPPE C. SCHMITTER, and WOLFGANG STREECK, eds. 1994. *Governing Capitalist Economies.* New York: Oxford University Press.

—— 1997. 'Continuities and Changes in Social Systems of Production: The Cases of Germany, Japan, and the United States.' In *Contemporary Capitalism,* ed. Rogers Hollingsworth and Robert Boyer. Cambridge: Cambridge University Press: 265–310.

—— and ROBERT BOYER, eds. 1997. *Contemporary Capitalism: The Embeddedness of Institutions.* Cambridge: Cambridge University Press.

HOLM, NIELS W. 1996. 'Standardization towards the Year 2000: A CEN Perspective.' *Normung in Europa und das DIN: Ziele für Jahr 2005.* Bericht über die ausserordentliche Sitzung des DIN-Presidium am 23. April 1996 in Berlin. DIN-Manuskriptdruck 13689. Berlin: Beuth: 51–6.

HOLMES, MARTIN. 1991. 'Mrs Thatcher, Labour and the EEC.' *The Bruges Group Occasional Papers* (12).

HOMBACH, BODO. 2000. *The Politics of the New Centre.* Cambridge: Polity Press.

HOWELL, CHRIS. 1992. *Regulating Labour: The State and Industrial Relations in France.* Princeton: Princeton University Press.

—— 1995. 'Trade Unions and the State: A Critique of British Industrial Relations.' *Politics and Society* 23 (June): 149–83.

—— 1996. 'Women as the Paradigmatic Trade Unionists? New Work, New Workers, and New Trade Union Strategies in Conservative Britain.' *Economic and Industrial Democracy* 17 (November): 511–43.

—— 1999. 'Unforgiven: British Trade Unionism in Crisis.' In *The Brave New World of European Labor: European Trade Unions at the Millennium*, ed. Andrew Martin and George Ross. New York: Berghahn: 26–74.

—— 2000. 'Is There a Third Way for the Party–Union Relationship? The Industrial Relations Project of New Labour.' Paper presented at the annual conference of the Political Studies Association, London.

HUBER, EVELYNE, and JOHN D. STEPHENS. 1999. 'Welfare States and Production Regimes in the Era of Retrenchment.' Occasional Papers, Institute for Advanced Study, Princeton.

—— —— 2001. *Development and Crisis of the Welfare State: Parties and Policies in Global Markets*. Chicago: University of Chicago Press.

—— CHARLES RAGIN, and JOHN STEPHENS. 1993. 'Social Democracy, Christian Democracy, Constitutional Structure and the Welfare State.' *American Journal of Sociology* 99 (3): 711–49.

—— —— —— 1997. *Comparative Welfare States Data Set*. Evanston, Ill.: Northwestern University and University of North Carolina.

HUNTINGTON, SAMUEL P. 1993. 'The Clash of Civilizations.' *Foreign Affairs* 72 (Summer): 22–49.

HUTTON, WILL. 1995. *The State We're in*. London: Vintage.

HYMAN, RICHARD. 1994. 'Industrial Relations in Western Europe: An Era of Ambiguity?' *Industrial Relations* 33 (January): 1–24.

IAB Kurzbericht. 1988*a*. 'Aktualisierte Befunde zur Vorruhestandsregelung: Globale und wirtschaftszweigspezifische Ergebnisse'. Nuremberg: Institut für Arbeitsmarkt- und Berufsforschung.

—— 1988*b*. 'Zur Konkurrenz zwischen Vorruhestand und "59-er Regelung".' Nuremberg: Institut für Arbeitsmarkt- und Berufsforschung.

IGALENS, JACQUES, and HERVÉ PENAN. 1994. *La Normalisation*. Paris: Que sais-je?

IIDA, K. 1993. 'Analytic Uncertainty and International Cooperation: Theory and Application to International Economic Policy Coordination.' *International Studies Quarterly* 37 (December): 431–57.

ILO. 1989–90. *Yearbook of Labour Statistics*. Geneva: ILO.

Income Data Services. 1996. *Industrial Relations and Collective Bargaining*. London: Institute of Personnel and Development.

INSEAD. 1995. *Lufthansa: The Turnaround*. Case Study. INSEAD.

INSEE. 1993. *Tableaux de l'économie française 1993–1994*. Paris: INSEE.

—— 1996. *Tableaux de l'économie française 1996–1997*. Paris: INSEE.

IoD (Institute of Directors). 1985. *Settling Disputes Peacefully II: Procedure Agreements*. London: Institute of Directors.

ITAMI, HIROYUKI. 1999. 'Concept of the Firm and Corporate Governance in Japan.' Paper presented at the First Humboldt Forum on Economics and Management on Corporate Governance, Berlin, 4–5 June.

IVERSEN, TORBEN. 1996. 'Power, Flexibility, and the Breakdown of Centralized Wage Bargaining: Denmark and Sweden in Comparative Perspective.' *Comparative Politics* 28 (July): 399–436.

—— 1998*a*. 'Wage Bargaining, Central Bank Independence and the Real Effects of Money.' *International Organization* 52 (3): 469–504.

—— 1998*b*. 'Hard Choices for Scandinavian Social Democracy in Comparative Perspective.' *Oxford Review of Economic Policy* 14 (2): 59–75.

—— 1998*c*. 'Wage Bargaining, Hard Money and Economic Performance: Theory and Evidence for Organized Market Economies.' *British Journal of Political Science* 28 (January): 31–61.

—— 1999*a*. *Contested Economic Institutions: The Politics of Macroeconomics and Wage Bargaining in Advanced Democracies*. New York: Cambridge University Press.

—— 1999*b*. 'The Political Economy of Inflation: Bargaining Structure or Central Bank Independence?' *Public Choice* 99 (2): 237–58.

—— 2000. 'Decentralization, Monetarism, and the Social-Democratic Welfare State in the 1980s and 90s.' In *Unions, Employers and Central Banks: Macroeconomic Coordination and Institutional Change in Social Market Economies*, ed. Torben Iversen, Jonas Pontusson, and David Soskice. Cambridge: Cambridge University Press: 205–31.

—— and JONAS PONTUSSON. 2000. 'Comparative Political Economy: A Northern European Perspective.' In *Unions, Employers and Central Banks*, ed. Torben Iversen, Jonas Pontusson, and David Soskice. Cambridge: Cambridge University Press: 1–37.

—— and DAVID SOSKICE. 2000. 'An Asset Theory of Social Policy Preferences.' Paper presented at the annual meeting of the American Political Science Association, Wardman Park.

—— JONAS PONTUSSON, and DAVID SOSKICE, eds. 2000. *Unions, Employers and Central Banks: Macroeconomic Coordination and Institutional Change in Social Market Economies*. Cambridge: Cambridge University Press.

—— and ANNE WREN. 1998. 'Equality, Employment, and Budgetary Restraint: The Trilemma of the Service Economy.' *World Politics* 50 (July): 507–46.

JACOBS, KLAUS, and WINFRIED SCHMÄHL. 1988. 'Der Übergang in den Ruhestand: Entwicklung, öffentliche Diskussion und Möglichkeiten seiner Umgestaltung.' *Mitteilungen aus dem Arbeitsmarkt und Berufsforschung*. 2 (April): 196–205.

—— et al. 1991. 'Germany: The Diversity of Pathways.' In *Time for Retirement: Comparative Studies of Early Exit from the Labor Force*, ed. Martin Kohli et al. Cambridge: Cambridge University Press: 181–221.

JACOBY, SANFORD. 1997. *Modern Manors*. Princeton: Princeton University Press.

JAIKUMAR, R. 1986. 'Postindustrial Manufacturing.' *Harvard Business Review* (November–December): 69–76.

JEFFERS, E., and D. PLIHON 2000. 'Les Fonds d'investissement étrangers, fers de lance du pouvoir de la finance.' University of Paris-Nord. Manuscript.

JEFFERY, CHARLIE. 1996. 'The Territorial Dimension.' In *Developments in German Politics 2*, ed. Gordon Smith, William E. Paterson, and Stephen Padgett. London: Macmillan: 76–95.

JENKINS, PETER. 1991. 'Major Coup on Road to a Flexible and Pragmatic Union.' *Independent* (11 December).

JENSEN, HENRIK. 1997. 'Monetary Policy Coordination May Not Be Counter-productive.' *Scandinavian Journal of Economics* 99 (1): 73–80.

JERVIS, ROBERT. 1988. 'Realism, Game Theory, and Cooperation.' *World Politics* 40 (3): 317–49.

JISC. 1994. *JIS Yearbook*. Tokyo: Japan Industrial Standards Committee.

JOERGES, CHRISTIAN. 1996. 'Taking the Law Seriously: On Political Science and the Role of Law in the Process of European Integration.' *European Law Journal* 2 (2): 105–35.

JOHNSON, CHALMERS. 1982. *MITI and the Japanese Miracle: The Growth of Industrial Policy 1925–1975*. Stanford, Calif.: Stanford University Press.

—— 1995. 'Die Rolle intermediärer Organisationen beim Wandel des Berufs-bildungssystems.' In *Einheit als Interessenpolitik*, ed. H. Wiesenthal. Frankfurt: Campus: 126–59.

JONES, ADRIAN. 1986. 'Illusions of Sovereignty: Business and Organization of Committees of Vichy France.' *Social History* 11 (1) (January): 1–31.

JONSSON, GUNNAR. 1995. 'Institutions and Macroeconomic Outcomes: The Empirical Evidence.' *Swedish Economic Policy Review* 2 (1): 181–212.

JSA (Japan Standards Association—Nihon Kikaku Kyoukai). 1995. *Nihon Kikaku Kyoukai 50-nen no ayumi* [a 50-year history of JSA]. Tokyo: Nihon Kikaku Kyoukai.

JÜRGENS, ULRICH, KATRIN NAUMANN, and JOACHIM RUPP. 2000. 'Shareholder Value in an Adverse Environment: The German Case.' *Economy and Society* 29 (1): 54–59.

KADUSHIN, CHARLES. 1995. 'Friendship among the French Financial Elite.' *American Sociological Review* 60 (April): 202–21.

KAHLER, MILES. 1995. *International Institutions and the Political Economy of Integration*. Washington: Brookings Institution.

KAHN-FREUND, OTTO. 1978. 'On Uses and Misuses of Comparative Law.' In *Selected Writings*, ed. Otto Kahn-Freund. London: Stevens: 294–319.

KATZ, HARRY, and OWEN DARBISHIRE. 1999. *Converging Divergences: Worldwide Changes in Employment Systems*. Ithaca, NY: Cornell University Press.

KATZENSTEIN, PETER J., ed. 1978a. *Between Power and Plenty*. Madison: University of Wisconsin Press

—— 1978b. 'Conclusion: Domestic Sources and Strategies of Foreign Economic Policy.' In *Between Power and Plenty: Foreign Economic Policies of Advanced Industrial States*, ed. Peter J. Katzenstein. Madison: University of Wisconsin Press: 295–336.

—— 1985a. *Corporatism and Change*. Ithaca, NY: Cornell University Press.

—— 1985b. *Small States in World Markets*. Ithaca, NY: Cornell University Press.

—— 1987. *Policy and Politics in West Germany: The Growth of a Semi-Sovereign State*. Philadelphia: Temple University Press.

—— 1989. 'Stability and Change in the Emerging Third Republic.' In *Industry and Politics in West Germany*, ed. Peter Katzenstein. Ithaca, NY: Cornell University Press: 307–53.

KAVANAGH, DENIS. 1998. 'Power in the Parties: R.T. McKenzie and After.' *West European Politics* 21 (1): 55–78.

KEASY, KEVIN, and MIKE WRIGHT, eds. 1997. *Corporate Governance: Responsibilities, Risks and Remuneration*. Chichester: John Wiley & Sons.

KEELER, JOHN T. S. 1987. *The Politics of Neocorporatism in France: Farmers, the State, and Agricultural Policy-Making in the Fifth Republic.* New York: Oxford University Press.

KELLER, BERND. 1991. *Einführung in die Arbeitspolitik*. Munich: Oldenbourg.

KELLY, GAVIN, DOMINIC KELLY, and ANDREW GAMBLE, eds. 1997. *Stakeholder Capitalism*. London: Macmillan Press.

KENNEDY, ELLEN. 1991. *The Bundesbank: Germany's Central Bank in the International Monetary System*. London: Pinter.

KEOHANE, ROBERT. 1984. *After Hegemony*. Princeton: Princeton University Press.

—— and STANLEY HOFFMANN. 1991. 'Institutional Change in Europe in the 1980s.' In *The New European Community: Decisionmaking and Institutional Change*, ed. Robert O. Keohane and Stanley Hoffmann. Boulder, Colo.: Westview Press: 1–40.

—— and HELEN V. MILNER, eds. 1996. *Internationalization and Domestic Politics*. New York: Cambridge University Press.

KERR, CLARK, JOHN DUNLOP, FREDERICK HARBISON, and CHARLES MYERS. 1960. *Industrialism and Industrial Man*. Cambridge, Mass.: Harvard University Press.

KINDLEBERGER, CHARLES P. 1976. 'Technical Education and the French Entrepreneur.' In *Enterprise and Entrepreneurs in Nineteenth- and Twentieth-Century France*, ed. Robert Foster and James Moody. Baltimore: Johns Hopkins University Press: 3–40.

KING, DESMOND. 1993. 'The Conservatives and Training Policy: From a Tripartite to a Neoliberal Regime.' *Political Studies* 41: 214–35.

—— 1995. *Actively Seeking Work? The Politics of Unemployment and Welfare Policy in the United States and Great Britain*. Chicago: University of Chicago Press.

—— and STEWART WOOD. 1999. 'The Political Economy of Neoliberalism: Britain and the United States in the 1980s.' In *Continuity and Change in Contemporary Capitalism*, ed. Herbert Kitschelt, Peter Lange, Gary Marks, and John D. Stephens. Cambridge: Cambridge University Press: 371–97.

KITSCHELT, HERBERT. 1991a. 'Industrial Governance, Innovation Strategies, and the Case of Japan: Sectoral or Cross-national Analysis?' *International Organization* 45 (4): 453–93.

—— 1991b. *The Transformation of Social Democracy*. Cambridge: Cambridge University Press.

—— 1994. 'Austrian and Swedish Social Democrats in Crisis: Party Strategy and Organization in Corporatist Regimes.' *Comparative Political Studies* 27 (1): 3–39.

—— PETER LANGE, GARY MARKS, and JOHN D. STEPHENS. 1999a. 'Convergence and Divergence in Advanced Capitalist Democracies.' In *Continuity and Change in Contemporary Capitalism*, ed. Herbert Kitschelt, Peter Lange, Gary Marks, and John D. Stephens. Cambridge: Cambridge University Press: 427–60.

—— —— —— —— 1999b. *Continuity and Change in Contemporary Capitalism*. Cambridge: Cambridge University Press.

KJELLBERG, ANDERS. 1998. 'Sweden: Restoring the Model?' In *Changing Industrial Relations in Europe*, ed. Anthony Ferner and Richard Hyman. 2nd edn. Oxford: Blackwell: 57–117.

KNETTER, M. 1989. 'Price Discrimination by US and German Exporters.' *American Economic Review* 79 (1): 198–210.

KNIGHT, JACK. 1992. *Institutions and Social Conflict*. New York: Cambridge University Press.

KOCHAN, THOMAS, HARRY KATZ, and ROBERT MCKERSIE. 1986. *The Transformation of U.S. Industrial Relations*. New York: Basic Books.

KOHLI, MARTIN, MARTIN REIN, ANNE-MARIE GUILLEMARD, and HERMAN VAN GUNSTEREN, eds. 1991. *Time for Retirement: Comparative Studies of Early Exit from the Labor Force*. Cambridge: Cambridge University Press.

KOIKE, KAZUO. 1981. *Nihon no Jukuren: Sugureta Jinzai Keisei Shisutemu* [Skills in Japan: An Effective Human Capital Formation System]. Tokyo: Yuhikaku.

—— 1994. 'Learning and Incentive Systems in Japanese Industry.' In *The Japanese Firm*, ed. Masahiko Aoki and Ronald Dore. Oxford: Clarendon Press: 41–65.

KORPI, WALTER. 1989. 'Power, Politics, and State Autonomy in the Development of Social Citizenship: Social Rights during Sickness in 18 OECD Countries since 1930.' *American Sociological Review* 54 (3): 309–28.

KRASNER, STEPHEN D. 1983*a*. 'Structural Causes and Regimes Consequences: Regimes as Intervening Variables.' In *International Regimes*, ed. Stephen D. Krasner. Ithaca, NY: Cornell University Press: 1–22.

—— ed. 1983*b*. *International Regimes*. Ithaca, NY: Cornell University Press.

—— 1991. 'Global Communication and National Power: Life on the Pareto Frontier.' *World Politics* 43: 336–66.

KREPS, DAVID. 1990. 'Corporate Culture and Economic Theory.' In *Perspectives on Positive Political Economy*, ed. James E. Alt and Kenneth A. Shepsle. New York: Cambridge University Press: 90–143.

KRISLOV, SAMUEL. 1997. *How Nations Choose Product Standards and Standards Change Nations*. Pittsburgh: University of Pittsburgh Press.

KRUGMAN, PAUL, ed. 1986. *Strategic Trade Policy and the New International Economics*. Cambridge, Mass.: MIT Press.

—— 1991. *Geography and Trade*. Cambridge, Mass.: MIT Press.

KÜHLEWIND, GERHARD. 1986. 'Beschäftigung und Ausgliederung älterer Arbeitsnehmer.' *Mitteilungen aus der Arbeitsmarkt- und Berufsforschung* 2 (April): 209–32.

KUISEL, RICHARD F. 1981. *Capitalism and the State in Modern France: Renovation and Economic Management in the Twentieth Century*. Cambridge: Cambridge University Press.

KUME, IKUO. 1998. *Disparaged Success: Labor Politics in Postwar Japan*. Ithaca, NY: Cornell University Press.

LABBÉ, DANIEL. 1992. 'Renault: les trois âges de la négociation.' *Travail* 26: 73–95.

LADEUR, KARL-HEINZ. 1997. 'Towards a Legal Theory of Supranationality: The Viability of the Network Concept.' *European Law Journal* 3 (1): 33–54.

LAM, ALICE. 2000. 'Tacit Knowledge, Organizational Learning and Societal Institutions: An Integrated Framework.' *Organization Studies* 21 (3): 487–513.

LANE, CHRISTEL. 1989. *Management and Labor in Europe: The Industrial Enterprise in Germany, Britain and France.* Aldershot: Edward Elgar.

—— 1997. 'The Social Regulation of Inter-firm Relations in Britain and Germany: Market Rules, Legal Norms and Technical Standards.' *Cambridge Journal of Economics* 21 (March): 197–215.

LANGE, PETER. 1984. 'Unions, Workers, and Wage Regulation: The Rational Bases of Consent.' In *Order and Conflict in Contemporary Capitalism: Studies in the Political Economy of Western European Nations,* ed. John H. Goldthorpe. New York: Oxford University Press: 98–123.

—— and GEOFFREY GARRETT. 1985. 'The Politics of Growth: Strategic Interaction and Economic Performance in Advanced Industrial Democracies, 1974–80.' *Journal of Politics* 47 (3): 792–827.

—— MICHAEL WALLERSTEIN, and MIRIAM GOLDEN. 1995. 'The End of Corporatism? Wage Setting in the Nordic and Germanic Countries.' In *Workers of Nations: Industrial Relations in a Global Economy,* ed. Sanford M. Jacoby. Oxford: Oxford University Press: 101–26.

LANGENFELD, GERIT. 1991. *Vertragsgestaltung: Methode, Verfahren, Vertragstypen.* Munich: C. H. Beck.

LAYARD, RICHARD, STEPHEN NICKELL, and RICHARD JACKMAN. 1991. *Unemployment: Macroeconomic Performance and the Labour Market.* New York: Oxford University Press.

—— K. MAYHEW, and G. OWEN, eds. 1994. *Britain's Training Deficit.* Aldershot: Ashgate Publishing Limited.

LAZEAR, EDWARD, and RICHARD FREEMAN. 1996. 'Relational Investing: The Workers' Perspective.' NBER Working Paper 5346.

LAZONICK, WILLIAM. 1991. *Business Organization and the Myth of the Market Economy.* Cambridge: Cambridge University Press.

—— and MARY O'SULLIVAN. 1996. 'Organization, Finance, and International Competition.' *Industrial and Corporate Change* 5 (1): 1–49.

—— —— 2000. 'Maximizing Shareholder Value: A New Ideology for Corporate Governance.' *Economy and Society* 29 (February): 13–35.

—— and JONATHAN WEST. 1995. 'Organizational Integration and Competitive Advantage: Explaining Strategy and Performance in American Industry.' *Industrial and Corporate Change* 4 (2): 229–70.

LECRAW, DONALD J. 1987. 'Japanese Standards: A Barrier to Trade.' In *Product Standardization and Competitive Strategy,* ed. H. Landis Gabel. Amsterdam: Elsevier Science Publishers: 29–46.

LEGRAND, PIERRE. 1995a. 'Comparatists-at-Law and the Contrarian Challenge.' Working Paper, Tilburg University.

—— 1995b. 'Comparative Legal Studies and Commitment to Theory.' *Modern Law Review* 58: 262–73.

—— 1996. 'European Legal Systems Are Not Converging.' *International and Comparative Law Quarterly* 45 (1): 52–81.

—— 1997. 'Against a European Civil Code.' *Modern Law Review* 60 (1): 44–63.

LEHMBRUCH, GERHARD, and PHILIPPE SCHMITTER, eds. 1982. *Patterns of Corporatist Policy-Making.* Beverly Hills, Calif.: Sage.

LEHRER, MARK. 1997*a*. 'Comparative Institutional Advantage in Corporate Governance and Managerial Hierarchies: The Case of European Airlines.' Unpublished doctoral dissertation, INSEAD.

—— 1997*b*. 'German Industrial Strategy in Turbulence: Corporate Governance and Managerial Hierarchies in Lufthansa.' *Industry and Innovation* 4 (1): 115–40.

—— 2000. 'The Organizational Choice between Evolutionary and Revolutionary Capability Regimes: Theory and Evidence from European Air Transport.' *Industrial and Corporate Change* 9 (3): 489–520.

—— and OWEN DARBISHIRE. 2000. 'Comparative Managerial Learning in Germany and Britain: Techno-organizational Innovation in Network Industries.' In *National Capitalisms, Global Competition and Economic Performance*, ed. Sigrid Quack, Glenn Morgan, and Richard Whitley. Amsterdam: John Benjamins: 79–104.

LEIBFRIED, STEPHAN, and PAUL PIERSON. 1995. 'Semisovereign Welfare States: Social Policy in a Multitiered Europe.' In *European Social Policy: Between Fragmentation and Integration*, ed. Stephan Leibfried and Paul Pierson. Washington: Brookings Institution: 43–77.

LEMLEY, MARK A., and DAVID McGOWAN. 1998. 'Could Java Change Everything? The Competitive Propriety of a Proprietary Standard.' *Antitrust Bulletin* (Fall/Winter): 715–73.

LENWAY, STEFANIE ANN, and THOMAS P. MURTHA. 1994. 'The State as Strategist in International Business Research.' *Journal of International Business Studies* 25 (3): 513–35.

LERUEZ, JACQUES. 1975. *Economic Planning and Politics in Britain*. London: Martin Robertson.

LEUTERITZ, KRISTA, J. JOHNSEN, and WALTER G. LEIGHT. 1999. *Toward a National Standards Strategy*. Conference Report. NISTIR 6290. Gaithersburg, Md.: NIST (National Institute of Standards and Technology), February.

LEVITSKY, JONATHAN. 1994. 'The Europeanization of the British Legal Style.' *American Journal of Comparative Law* 42: 347–80.

LEVY, JONAH. 1999*a*. *Tocqueville's Revenge: Dilemmas of Institutional Reform in Post-dirigiste France*. Cambridge, Mass.: Harvard University Press.

—— 1999*b*. 'Vice into Virtue? Progressive Politics and Welfare Reform in Continental Europe.' *Politics and Society* 27 (2): 239–74.

LEWEK, PETER. 1992. *Arbeitslosigkeit und Arbeitslosenversicherung in der Weimarer Republik 1918–1927*. Stuttgart: Franz Steiner.

LINDBLOM, CHARLES. 1977. *Politics and Markets: The World's Political-Economic Systems*. New York: Basic Books.

LINHART, DANIÈLE. 1991. *Le Torticolis de l'autruche: l'éternelle modernisation des entreprises françaises*. Paris: Le Seuil.

LIPIETZ, ALAIN. 1998. *La Société en sablier*. Paris: La Découverte.

LOCKE, RICHARD. 1995. *Remaking the Italian Economy*. Ithaca, NY: Cornell University Press.

—— and LUCIO BACCARO. 1999. 'The Resurgence of Italian Unions?' In *The Brave New World of European Labor*, ed. Andrew Martin and George Ross. New York: Berghahn: 217–68.

LOHMANN, SUSANNE. 1992. 'Optimal Commitment in Monetary Policy: Credibility Versus Flexibility.' *American Economic Review* 82 (1): 273–86.

LOUBET, JEAN-LOUIS. 1995. *Citroën, Peugeot, Renault et les autres: soixante ans de stratégies*. Paris: Le Monde-Édition.

—— 1998. 'Peugeot meets Ford, Sloan, and Toyota.' In *One Best Way? Trajectories and Industrial Models of the World's Automobile Producers*, ed. Michel Freyssenet, Andrew Mair, Koichi Shimizu, and Giuseppe Volpato. Oxford: Oxford University Press: 339–64.

LUEBBERT, GREGORY M. 1991. *Liberalism, Fascism, or Social Democracy: Social Classes and the Political Origins of Regimes in Interwar Europe*. New York: Oxford University Press.

LUHMANN, NIKLAS. 1994. 'Inklusion und Exklusion.' In *Nationales Bewußtsein und kollektive Identität*, ed. Helmut Berding. Frankfurt: Suhrkamp: 15–45.

—— 1995. 'The Paradoxy of Observing Systems.' *Cultural Critique* 31: 37–55.

LUKES, RUDOLF. 1979. *Überbetriebliche technische Normung in den Rechtsordungen ausgewählter EWG- und EFTA-Staaten; Frankreich, Großbritannien, Italien, Oesterreich, Schweden; Organisation der Normung; Einfluß des Staates; Beziehungen zum Verbraucherschutz*. Cologne: Carl Heymanns Verlag.

LUTZ, B., and H. GRÜNERT. 1999. 'Evaluierung der Vorhaben der beruflichen Erstausbildung.' *Forschungsbeiträge zum Arbeitsmarkt in Sachsen-Anhalt* 14 (October): 1–128.

LÜTZ, SUSANNE. 1993. *Die Steuerung industrieller Forschungskooperation*. Frankfurt am Main: Campus.

—— 1996. 'The Revival of the Nation-State? Stock Exchange Regulation in an Era of Internationalized Financial Markets.' MPIFG Discussion Paper 96/9. Cologne.

LYOTARD, JEAN-FRANÇOIS. 1987. *The Differend: Phrases in Dispute*. Manchester: Manchester University Press.

MCARTHUR, JOHN, and BRUCE SCOTT. 1969. *Industrial Planning in France*. Boston: Harvard Business School.

MCGEE, JOHN, and HOWARD THOMAS. 1986. 'Strategic Groups: Theory, Research and Taxonomy.' *Strategic Management Journal* 7: 141–60.

MACLEAN, MAIRI. 1995. 'Privatization in France 1993–94: New Departures or a Case of Plus ça change?' *West European Politics* 18 (2): 273–90.

MACNEIL, IAN. 1978. 'Contracts: Adjustment of Long-Term Economic Relations under Classical, Neoclassical, and Relational Contract Law.' *Northwestern University Law Review* 72: 854–905.

MAGEE, STEPHEN P., WILLIAM A. BROCK, and LESLIE YOUNG. 1989. *Black Hole Tariffs and Endogenous Policy Theory: Political Economy in General Equilibrium*. Cambridge: Cambridge University Press.

MANOW, PHILIP. 1997. *Social Insurance and the German Political Economy*. Discussion Paper, Max Planck Institute for the Study of Societies. Cologne.

—— 2000. 'Social Protection, Capitalist Production.' Manuscript. Cologne: Max Planck Institute for the Study of Societies.

—— and BERNHARD EBBINGHAUS, eds. Forthcoming. *The Varieties of Welfare*

Capitalism: Social Policy and Political Economy in Europe, Japan and the USA. London: Routledge.

MANOW, PHILIP., and ERIC SEILS. 1999. *Adjusting Badly: The German Welfare State, Structural Change and an Open Economy.* Max-Planck Institute for the Study of Societies, Cologne. Manuscript.

—— —— 2000. 'Adjusting Badly: The German Welfare State, Structural Change and the Open Economy.' In *Welfare and Work in the Open Economy: Diverse Responses to Common Challenges,* ed. Fritz Scharpf and Vivien Schmidt. Oxford: Oxford University Press: 264–307.

MARCH, JAMES G., and JOHAN P. OLSEN. 1989. *Rediscovering Institutions: The Organizational Basis of Politics.* New York: Free Press.

MARES, ISABELA. 1996. 'Firms and the Welfare State: The Emergence of New Forms of Unemployment.' Discussion Paper 96-308, Wissenschaftszentrum, Berlin.

—— 1997*a*. 'Business (Non)Coordination and Social Policy Development: The Case of Early Retirement.' Paper presented at the 'Varieties of Capitalism' conference, Wissenschaftszentrum, Berlin.

—— 1997*b*. 'Is Unemployment Insurable? Employers and the Introduction of Unemployment Insurance.' *Journal of Public Policy* 17 (December): 299–327.

—— 1998. 'Negotiated Risks: Employers' Role in Social Policy Development.' Ph.D. dissertation, Department of Government, Harvard University.

—— 2000. 'Strategic Alliances and Social Policy Reform: Unemployment Insurance in Comparative Perspective.' *Politics and Society* 28 (June): 223–44.

—— Forthcoming. 'Interwar Responses to the Problem of Unemployment: A Game-Theoretic Analysis.' In *The Varieties of Welfare Capitalism: Social Policy and Political Economy in Europe, Japan and the USA,* ed. Philip Manow and Bernhard Ebbinghaus. London: Routledge.

MARKESINIS, BASIL S. 1994. 'Learning from Europe and Learning in Europe'. In *The Gradual Convergence: Foreign Ideas, Foreign Influences, and English Law on the Eve of the 21st Century,* ed. Basil S. Markesinis. Oxford: Oxford University Press: 1–32.

MARTIN, CATHIE JO. 1995. 'Nature or Nurture? Sources of Firm Preferences for National Health Reform.' *American Political Science Review* 89 (December): 898–913.

—— 1999. *Stuck in Neutral: Business and the Politics of Human Capital Investment Policy.* Princeton: Princeton University Press.

MARTINEK, MARTIN. 1991. *Zulieferverträge und Qualitätssicherung.* Cologne: Verlag Kommunikationsforum.

MATRAVES, CATHERINE. 1997. 'German Industrial Structure in Comparative Perspective.' *Industry and Innovation* 4 (1): 37–51.

MAURICE, M., F. SELLIER, and J.-J. SILVESTRE. 1986. *The Social Foundations of Industrial Power.* Trans. A. Goldhammer. Cambridge, Mass.: Cambridge University Press.

—— et al. 1988. 'The Search for a Societal Effect in the Production of Company Hierarchy: A Comparison of France and Germany.' In *Internal Labour Markets,* ed. Paul Osterman. Cambridge, Mass.: MIT Press: 231–70.

MÉHAUT, PHILIPPE. 1986. 'Production et gestion des formations post-initiales: règles, instances, nouvelles implications du système productif.' In *Le Travail: marchés, règles, conventions*, ed. Robert Salais and Laurent Thévenot. Paris: Economica: 161–77.

MELTZER, ALLAN H., and SCOTT F. RICHARDS. 1981. 'A Rational Theory of the Size of Government.' *Journal of Political Economy* 89 (5): 914–27.

MIDDLEMAS, KEITH. 1991. *Power, Competition and the State*, iii: *The End of the Post-war Era*. London: Macmillan.

MIDLER, CHRISTOPHER, and FLORENCE CHARUE. 1993. 'A French-Style Sociotechnical Learning Process: The Robotization of Automobile Body Shops.' In *Country Competitiveness: Technology and the Organizing of Work*, ed. Bruce Kogut. Oxford: Oxford University Press: 156–75.

MILGROM, PAUL, and JOHN ROBERTS. 1990. 'The Economics of Modern Manufacturing: Technology, Strategy and Organization.' *American Economic Review* 80: 511–28.

—— —— 1992. *Economics, Organization and Management*. Englewood Cliffs, NJ: Prentice Hall.

—— —— 1995. 'Complementarities, Industrial Strategy, Structure and Change in Manufacturing.' *Journal of Accounting and Economics* 19: 179–208.

MILLER, GARY J. 1992. *Managerial Dilemmas: The Political Economy of Hierarchy*. Cambridge: Cambridge University Press.

MILLWARD, NEIL, MARK STEVENS, DAVID SMART, and W. R. HAWES. 1992. *Workplace Industrial Relations in Transition*. Aldershot: Dartmouth Publishing Company.

MILNER, HELEN V. 1988. *Resisting Protectionism: Global Industries and the Politics of International Trade*. Princeton: Princeton University Press.

—— 1992. 'International Theories of Cooperation among Nations.' *World Politics* 44 (April): 466–96.

—— 1997. *Interests, Institutions, and Information: Domestic Politics and International Relations*. Princeton: Princeton University Press.

MNOOKIN, R., and L. KORNHAUSER. 1979. 'Bargaining in the Shadow of the Law: The Case of Divorce.' *Yale Law Journal* 88: 950–97.

MÖBUS, MARTINE, and ERIC VERDIER. 1997. *Les Diplômes professionnels en Allemagne et en France: conception et jeux d'acteurs*. Paris: Harmattan.

MOENE, KARL OVE, and MICHAEL WALLERSTEIN. 1999. 'Inequality, Social Insurance and Redistribution.' Paper presented at the European Political Economy Workshop, Center for European Studies, Harvard University.

MORAVCSIK, ANDREW. 1991. 'Negotiating the Single European Act: National Interests and Conventional Statecraft in the European Community.' *International Organization* 45 (1): 19–56.

—— 1997. 'Taking Preferences Seriously: A Liberal Theory of International Politics.' *International Organization* 51 (4): 513–53.

—— 1998. *The Choice for Europe: Social Purpose and State Power from Messina to Maastricht*. Ithaca, NY: Cornell University Press.

MORIN, FRANÇOIS. 1989. 'Le Nouveau Pouvoir financier en France ou "l'autogestion" du capital.' *Revue d'économie industrielle* 41 (1): 44–51.

MORIN, FRANÇOIS. 1995. 'Les Mutations au cœur financier et son rôle dans les privatizations.' In *L'État de la France 1995–96*. Paris: La Découverte: 427–30.

—— 2000. 'A transformation in the French Model of Shareholding and Management.' *Economy and Society* 1 (29): 36–53.

MORIN, MARIE-LAURE. 1994. 'Sous-traitance et relations salariales: aspects de droit du travail.' *Travail et emploi* 60: 23–431.

MORVILLE, PIERRE. 1985. *Les Nouvelles Politiques sociales du patronat*. Paris: La Découverte.

MOSELY, HUGH, and THOMAS KRUPPE. 1992. 'Employment Protection and Labor Force Adjustment. A Comparative Evaluation.' Discussion Paper 92-9, Wissenschaftszentrum, Berlin.

MULLER, MICHAEL. 1997. 'Institutional Resilience in a Changing World Economy? The Case of the German Banking and Chemical Industries.' *British Journal of Industrial Relations* 35 (4): 609–26.

MYLES, JOHN, and JILL QUADAGNO, eds. 1991. *States, Labor Markets and the Future of Old-Age Policy*. Philadelphia: Temple University Press.

NAKAMURA, SHIGEHIRO. 1993. *The New Standardization: Keystone of Continuous Improvement in Manufacturing*. Portland, Ore.: Productivity Press.

NASCHOLD, FRIEDER, and BERT DE VROOM, eds. 1994. *Regulating Employment and Welfare: Company and National Policies of Labor Force Participation at the End of Worklife in Industrial Countries*. Berlin: Walter de Gruyter.

National Research Council. 1995. *Standards, Conformity Assessment, and Trade: Into the Twenty-First Century*. Washington: National Conformity Press.

NELSON, RICHARD R. 1991. 'Why Do Firms Differ, and How Does It Matter?' *Strategic Management Journal* 12: 61–91.

—— ed. 1993. *National Innovation Systems*. New York: Oxford University Press.

—— and SIDNEY WINTER. 1982. *An Evolutionary Theory of Economic Change*. Cambridge: Belknap Press.

NI CHEALLAIGH, MARTINA. 1995. *Apprenticeship in the EU Member States: A Comparison*. Berlin: European Center for the Development of Vocational Training.

NICHOLAS, FLORENCE. 1996. 'The United States: A Standardized Vision of International Relations.' *StandardView* 4 (December): 179–82.

NICHOLSON, NIGEL, and MICHAEL A. WEST. 1988. *Managerial Job Change: Men and Women in Transition*. Cambridge: Cambridge University Press.

NICOLAIDES, KALYPSO. 1993. 'Mutual Recognition among Nations.' Ph.D. dissertation, Harvard University.

NICOLAIDES, PHEDON, ed. 1993. *Industrial Policy in the European Community: A Necessary Response to Economic Integration?* Maastricht: European Institute of Public Administration.

NIELSON, FRANN. 1996. 'Human Behavior: Another Dimension of Standards Setting.' *StandardView* 4 (March): 36–41.

NOBLE, DAVID F. 1984. *Forces of Production: A Social History of Industrial Automation*. New York: Knopf.

NOBLE, GREGORY W. 1998. *Collective Action in East Asia: How Ruling Parties Shape*

Industrial Policy. Ithaca, NY: Cornell University Press.

NORDLINGER, ERIC. 1981. *On the Autonomy of the Democratic State.* Cambridge, Mass.: Harvard University Press.

NORTH, DOUGLASS C. 1990. *Institutions, Institutional Change and Economic Performance.* New York: Cambridge University Press.

—— 1993. 'Institutions and Credible Commitments.' *Journal of Institutional and Theoretical Economics* 149: 11–23.

NORTON, PHILIP, ed. 1996. *The Conservative Party.* London: Prentice-Hall.

OBERBECK, H., and M. BAETHGE. 1989. 'Computer and Pinstripes: Financial Institutions.' In *Industry and Politics in West Germany*, ed. P. Katzenstein. Ithaca, NY: Cornell University Press: 275–303.

OECD. 1991. 'Unemployment Benefit Rules and Labour Market Policy.' *OECD Employment Outlook.* Paris: OECD: 199–236.

—— 1992. *Industrial Policy in OECD Countries: Annual Review 1994.* Paris: OECD.

—— 1994*a*. *Apprenticeship: Which Way Forward?* Paris: OECD.

—— 1994*b*. *The OECD Jobs Study: Evidence and Explanations.* Paris: OECD.

—— 1996*a*. *OECD Economies at a Glance: Structural Indicators.* Paris: OECD.

—— 1996*b*. *OECD International Sectoral Data Base.* Paris: OECD.

—— 1997*a*. *Statistical Compendium.* Paris: OECD.

—— 1997*b*. *The OECD STAN Database for Industrial Analysis, 1976–1995.* Paris: OECD.

—— 1997*c*. 'Economic Performance and the Structure of Collective Bargaining.' *OECD Employment Outlook.* Paris: OECD: 63–92.

—— 1999. *OECD Education Database.* Paris: OECD.

—— 2000. *Literacy in the Information Age.* Paris: OECD and Statistics Canada.

—— *OECD Employment Outlook.* Paris: OECD (various years).

—— *Labour Force Statistics.* Paris: OECD (various years).

—— *National Accounts, Part II: Detailed Tables.* Paris: OECD (various years).

OFFE, CLAUS. 1981. 'The Attribution of Public Status to Interest Groups: Observations on the West German Case.' In *Organizing Interests in Western Europe*, ed. Suzanne Berger. Cambridge: Cambridge University Press: 123–58.

Office of Fair Trading. 1990. *Trading Malpractices.* London: Office of Fair Trading.

—— 1996. *Unfair Contract Terms, Bulletin Issue No. 1.* London: Office of Fair Trading.

OHASHI, ISAO, and TOSHIAKI TACHIBANAKI, eds. 1998. *Internal Labor Markets, Incentives and Employment.* New York: St Martin's Press.

OHMAE, KENICHI. 1991. *The Borderless World.* New York: Harper.

OLSON, MANCUR. 1965. *The Logic of Collective Action: Public Goods and the Theory of Groups.* Cambridge, Mass.: Harvard University Press.

OSTERMAN, PAUL, THOMAS KOCHAN, RICHARD LOCKE, and MICHAEL PIORE. Forthcoming. *Working in America.* Cambridge, Mass.: MIT Press.

OSTERMAN, PETER. 1987. 'Choice of Employment Systems in Internal Labour Markets.' *Industrial Relations* 26 (1): 46–67.

OSTROM, ELINOR. 1990. *Governing the Commons: The Evolution of Institutions for Collective Action.* New York: Cambridge University Press.

—— 1998. 'A Behavioral Approach to the Rational Choice Theory of Collective Action.' *American Political Science Review* 92 (1): 1–22.

OTA (Office of Technology Assessment), US Congress. 1992. *Global Standards: Building Blocks for the Future*. TCT-512. Washington: US Government Printing Office, March.

OZKAN, F. GULCIN, ANNE C. SIBERT, and ALAN SUTHERLAND. 1997. 'Monetary Union, Entry Conditions, and Economic Reform.' Discussion Paper, Centre for Economic Policy Research.

PALANDT, OTTO. 2001. *Bürgerliches Gesetzbuch*. Munich: Beck.

PATERSON, WILLIAM E., and DAVID SOUTHERN. 1994. *Governing Germany*. Oxford: Blackwell.

PELKMANS, JACQUES. 1987. 'The New Approach to Technical Harmonization and Standardization.' *Journal of Common Market Studies* 25 (March): 249–69.

PÉREZ, SOFIA A. 1999. 'The Resurgence of National Social Bargaining in Europe: Explaining the Italian and Spanish Experiences.' Working Paper of the Instituto Juan March, Madrid.

—— 2000. 'From Decentralization to Reorganization: Explaining the Return to National Bargaining in Italy and Spain.' *Comparative Politics* 32 (July): 437–58.

PEROTTI, ROBERTO. 1996. 'Growth, Income Distribution and Democracy: What the Data Say.' *Journal of Economic Growth* 1 (2): 149–87.

PESTOFF, VICTOR A. 1991. 'The Demise of the Swedish Model and the Resurgence of Organized Business as a Major Political Actor'. Working Paper PP1991: 2, Stockholm University, Department of Business Administration.

PIERSON, PAUL. 1995a. 'The Scope and Nature of Business Power: Employers and the American Welfare State 1900–1935.' Paper presented at the annual Conference of the American Political Science Association, Chicago.

—— 1995b. 'Fragmented Welfare States: Federal Institutions and the Development of Social Policy.' *Governance* 8 (4): 449–78.

—— 1996a. 'The New Politics of the Welfare State.' *World Politics* 48 (2): 143–79.

—— 1996b. 'The Path to European Integration: A Historical Institutionalist Approach.' *Comparative Political Studies* 29 (April): 123–63.

—— 2000. 'Increasing Returns, Path Dependence, and the Study of Politics.' *American Political Science Review* 94 (June): 251–67.

PIORE, MICHAEL, and CHARLES SABEL. 1984. *The Second Industrial Divide*. New York: Basic.

PIRKER, THEO. 1979. *Die blinde Macht: die Gewerkschaftsbewegung in der Bundesrepublik*. Vols. i and ii. Berlin: Verlag Olle & Wolter.

PIZZORNO, ALESSANDRO. 1978. 'Political Exchange and Collective Identity in Industrial Conflict.' In *The Resurgence of Class Conflict in Western Europe*, vol. i, ed. Colin Crouch and Alessandro Pizzorno. London: Macmillan: 277–98.

POLANYI, KARL. 1944. *The Great Transformation*. New York: Rinehart & Co.

POLEYN, J. 1996. 'L'Industrie du décolletage: au fil de l'Arve.' *Le 4 Pages des statistiques industrielles* 57 (January): 1–4.

POLLACK, MARK A. 1996. 'The New Institutionalism and EC Governance: The Promise and Limits of Institutional Analysis.' *Governance* 9 (4): 429–58.

POLLACK, MARK A. 1997. 'Delegation, Agency and Agenda-Setting in the European Community.' *International Organization* 51: 99–134.

PONTUSSON, JONAS. 1997. 'Between Neo-liberalism and the German Model: Swedish Capitalism in Transition.' In *Political Economy of Modern Capitalism*, ed. Colin Crouch and Wolfgang Streeck. Thousand Oaks, Calif.: Sage: 55–70.

—— and PETER SWENSON. 1996. 'Labor Markets, Production Strategies, and Wage Bargaining Institutions: The Swedish Employer Offensive in Comparative Perspective.' *Comparative Political Studies* 29 (April): 223–50.

POPP, KARL. 1993. *Die Qualitätssicherungsvereinbarung*. Munich: Carl Hanser Verlag.

PORTER, MICHAEL E. 1980. *Competitive Strategy: Techniques for Analyzing Industries and Competitors*. New York: Free Press.

—— 1990. *The Competitive Advantage of Nations*. New York: Free Press.

—— and ANITA MCGAHAN. 1997. 'How Much Does Industry Matter, Really?' *Strategic Management Journal* 18 (Special Summer Issue): 15–30.

PRIEST, GEORGE. 1985. 'The Invention of Enterprise Liability: A Critical History of the Intellectual Foundations of Modern Tort Law.' *Journal of Legal Studies* 14: 461–527.

Protocol of conference of German employers of Bochum. 1880. 'Protokoll der Konferenz zur endgültigen Beratung des von einer engeren Komission vorbereiteten Gesetzentwurfes, betreffend der Einrichtung einer Arbeiter-Unfall-Versicherungskasse, Bochum, 2. November 1880', reprinted *Bismarcks Sozialstaat: Beiträge zur Geschichte der Sozialpolitik und zur sozialpolitischen Geschichtsschreibung* (1994), ed. Lothar Machtan. Frankfurt: Campus: 48–66.

PROWSE, STEPHEN. 1994. *Corporate Governance in an International Perspective: A Survey of Corporate Control Mechanisms among Large Firms in the US, the UK, Japan and Germany*. Basle: Bank for International Settlements.

PRZEWORSKI, ADAM, and MICHAEL WALLERSTEIN. 1982. 'The Structure of Class Conflict in Democratic Capitalist Societies.' *American Political Science Review* 76 (2): 215–38.

PUTNAM, ROBERT. 1988. 'Diplomacy and Domestic Politics.' *International Organization* 42 (3): 427–60.

—— 1993. *Making Democracy Work*. Princeton: Princeton University Press.

QUADAGNO, JILL S. 1984. 'Welfare Capitalism and the Social Security Act of 1935.' *American Sociological Review* 49 (5): 632–47.

QUÉLENNEC, MICHEL. 1997. *L'Industrie en France*. Paris: Nathan.

RABINBACH, ANSELM. 1996. 'Social Knowledge, Social Risk and the Politics of Industrial Accidents in Germany and France.' In *States, Social Knowledge and the Origin of Modern Social Policies*, ed. Dietrich Rueschemeyer and Theda Skocpol. Princeton: Princeton University Press: 48–89.

RAKOFF, TODD. 1995. 'The Implied Terms of Contracts: Of "Default Rules" and "Situation Sense".' In *Good Faith and Fault in Contract Law*, ed. Jack Beatson and Daniel Friedmann. Oxford: Clarendon: 191–228.

RAMA, MARTIN. 1994. 'Bargaining Structure and Economic Performance in the Open Economy.' *European Economic Review* 38 (2): 403–15.

RAMIREZ-RANGEL, HIRAM. 2000. 'Microconstitutionalism: The Politics of Co-operation among Spanish Small Firms.' Ph.D. dissertation, Department of Government, Harvard University.

REED, RICHARD, and ROBERT J. DEFILLIPPI. 1990. 'Causal Ambiguity, Barriers to Imitation, and Sustainable Competitive Advantage.' *Academy of Management Review* 15 (1): 88–102.

REGALIA, IDA. 1995. 'Italy: The Costs and Benefits of Informality.' In *Works Councils: Consultation, Representation, and Cooperation in Industrial Relations*, ed. Joel Rogers and Wolfgang Streeck. Chicago: University of Chicago Press: 217–42.

—— and MARINO REGINI. 1995. 'Between Voluntarism and Industrialization: Industrial Relations and Human Resource Practices in Italy.' In *Employment Relations in a Changing World Economy*, ed. Richard Locke, Thomas Kochan, and Michael Piore. Cambridge, Mass.: MIT Press: 131–64.

REGINI, MARINO. 1984. 'The Conditions for Political Exchange: How Concertation Emerged and Collapsed in Britain and Italy.' In *Order and Conflict in Contemporary Capitalism: Studies in the Political Economy of Western European Nations*, ed. J. H. Goldthorpe. New York: Oxford University Press: 124–42.

—— 1997a. 'Different Responses to Common Demands: Firms, Institutions, and Training in Europe.' *European Sociological Review* 13 (3): 267–82.

—— 1997b. 'Still Engaging in Corporatism? Recent Italian Experience in Comparative Perspective.' *European Journal of Industrial Relations* 3 (November): 259–78.

—— 2000. 'Between Deregulation and Social Pacts: The Responses of European Economies to Globalization.' *Politics & Society* 28 (March): 5–33.

—— and IDA REGALIA. 1997. 'Employers, Unions, and the State: The Resurgence of Concertation in Italy?' *West European Politics* 20 (October): 210–30.

REICH, R. 1991. *The Work of Nations: Preparing Ourselves for 21st-Century Capitalism*. New York: A. A. Knopf.

Reichsverband der Deutschen Industrie. 1920. 'Denkschrift betreffend der Arbeitslosenversicherung'. Zentrales Staatsarchiv Potsdam, Reichsarbeitsministerium 4311.

Reichsverband des Deutschen Handwerks. 1923. 'Denkschrift des Reichsverbandes des Deutschen Handwerks an das Reichsarbeitsministerium'. Zentrales Staatsarchiv Potsdam, Reichsarbeitsministerium 1017.

—— 1925. 'Tätigkeitsbericht des Reichsverbandes des Deutschen Handwerks'. Zentrales Staatsarchiv Potsdam, Reichswirtschaftsministerium 2073.

—— 1926. 'Tätigkeitsbericht des Reichsverbandes des Deutschen Handwerks 1926'. Zentrales Staatsarchiv Potsdam, Reichswirtschaftsministerium 2073.

—— 1927. 'Tätigkeitsbericht des Reichsverbands des Deutschen Handwerks 1927'. Zentrales Staatsarchiv Potsdam, Reichswirtschaftsministerium 2074.

REIHLEN, HELMUT. 1974. *Struktur und Arbeitsweise der Normenorganisationen westeuropaeischer Nachbarstaaten*. DIN Normenheft 2. Berlin: Beuth.

—— 1977. 'Die Auswirkungen des Normenvertrages zwischen der Bundesrepublik Deutschland und dem DIN auf das DIN.' *DIN-Mitteilungen* 56: 339.

RHODES, MARTIN. 1997. 'Globalisation, Labour Markets and Welfare States: A Future of "Competitive Corporatism"?' In *The Future of European Welfare*, ed. Martin Rhodes and Yves Meny. London: Macmillan.

RICHARDSON, G. B. 1990. *Information and Investment: A Study in the Working of the Competitive Economy*. New York: Clarendon.

RICHTER, ANSGAR. 1997. *Restructuring or Restrukturierung: Corporate Change in the UK and Germany*. London: Centre for Economic Performance.

ROBERTSON, ROLAND. 1995. 'Globalization: Time-Space and Homogeneity-Heterogeneity'. In *Global Modernities*, ed. Mike Featherstone, Scott Lash, and Roland Robertson. London: Sage: 15–30.

ROCHARD, M. B. 1987. *La Sous-traitance: entreprises et emplois: le secteur de l'électronique professionelle*. Paris: CEE-CEREQ-SESSI.

RODRIK, DANI. 1997. *Has Globalization Gone Too Far?* Washington: Institute for International Economics.

—— 1998. 'Why Do More Open Economies Have Larger Governments?' *Journal of Political Economy* 106 (October): 997–1032.

ROGOFF, KENNETH. 1985. 'The Optimal Degree of Commitment to an Intermediate Monetary Target.' *Quarterly Journal of Economics* 100 (4): 1169–90.

ROGOWSKI, RONALD. 1987. 'Political Cleavages and Changing Exposure to Trade.' *American Political Science Review* 81 (December): 1121–37.

—— 1989. *Commerce and Coalitions: How Trade Affects Domestic Political Alignments*. Princeton: Princeton University Press.

RÖHL, KLAUS F., and STEFAN MAGEN. 1996. 'Die Rolle des Rechts im Prozeß der Globalisierung.' *Zeitschrift für Rechtssoziologie* 17 (1): 1–57.

ROMER, PAUL. 1986. 'Increasing Returns and Long-Run Growth.' *Journal of Political Economy* 94 (5): 1002–37.

—— 1994. 'The Origins of Endogenous Growth.' *Journal of Economic Perspectives* 8 (1): 3–22.

ROSEN, RÜDIGER VON. 1997. *Chancengemeinschaft: Deutschland braucht die Aktie*. Munich: Wirtschaftsverlag Langen Müller/Herbig.

ROSOVSKY, HENRY. 1961. *Capital Formation in Japan*. Glencoe, Ill.: Free Press.

ROWTHORN, ROBERT. 1992. 'Corporatism and Labour Market Performance.' In *Social Corporatism: A Superior Economic System?*, ed. Jukka Pekkarinen, Matti Pohjola, and Bob Rowthorn. Oxford: Clarendon Press: 44–81.

RUBERY, JILL. 1994. 'The British Production Regime: A Societal-Specific System?' *Economy and Society* 23 (August): 335–54.

—— COLETTE FAGAN, and FRIEDERIKE MAIER. 1996. 'Occupational Segregation, Discrimination and Equal Opportunity.' In *International Handbook of Labour Market Policy and Evaluation*, ed. Gunther Schmid, Jacqueline O'Reilly, and Klaus Schomann. Cheltenham: Edward Elgar: 431–61.

RUBINSTEIN, ARIEL. 1982. 'Perfect Equilibrium in a Bargaining Model.' *Econometrica* 50 (1): 97–109.

RUEDA, DAVID, and JONAS PONTUSSON. 2000. 'Wage Inequality and Varieties of Capitalism.' *World Politics* 52 (April): 350–83.

RUGGIE, JOHN GERARD. 1993. 'Multilateralism: The Anatomy of an Institution.' In

Multilateralism Matters: The Theory and Praxis of an Institutional Form, ed. John Gerard Ruggie. New York: Columbia University Press: 3–48.

RUMELT, RICHARD. 1987. 'Theory, Strategy and Entrepreneurship.' In *The Competitive Challenge: Strategies for Industrial Innovation and Renewal*, ed. David J. Teece. New York: Harper & Row: 137–58.

—— DAN SCHENDEL, and DAVID J. TEECE. 1991. 'Strategic Management and Economics.' *Strategic Management Journal* 12: 5–29.

SABEL, CHARLES F. 1992. 'Studied Trust: Building New Forms of Cooperation in a Volatile Economy.' In *Industrial Districts and Local Economic Reorganization*, ed. Frank Pyke and Werner Sengenberger. Geneva: International Institute for Labor Studies: 215–50.

—— 1994. 'Learning by Monitoring: The Institutions of Economic Development.' In *The Handbook of Economic Sociology*, ed. Neil Smelser and Richard Swedberg. Princeton: Princeton University Press: 137–65.

SACKS, PAUL M. 1980. 'State Structure and the Asymmetrical Society.' *Comparative Politics* (April): 349–76.

SADOWSKI, DIETER, USCHI BACKES-GELLNER, and BERNARD FRICK. 1995. 'Works Councils: Barriers or Boosts for the Competitiveness of German Firms?' *British Journal of Industrial Relations* 33 (September): 493–513.

SALAIS, ROBERT. 1988. 'Les Stratégies de modernisation de 1983 à 1986.' *Économie et statistique* 213: 51–74.

—— 1992. 'Modernisation des entreprises et Fonds National de l'Emploi: une analyse en terme de mondes de production.' *Travail et emploi* 51: 49–69.

—— and MICHAEL STORPER. 1993. *Les Mondes de production: enquête sur l'identité économique de la France*. Paris: Éditions de l'École des Hautes Études en Science Sociales.

SAND, INGER-JOHANNE. 1995. 'From the Distinction between Public Law and Private Law to Legal Categories of Social and Institutional Differentiation in a Pluralistic Legal Context.' In *Legal Polycentricity: Consequences of Pluralism in Law*, ed. Hanne Petersen and Henrik Zahle. Aldershot: Dartmouth: 85–101.

SANDHOLTZ, WAYNE, and JOHN ZYSMAN. 1989. '1992: Recasting the European Bargain.' *World Politics* 42 (1): 95–128.

SCHAEDE, ULRIKE. 1995. 'The "Old Boy" Network and Government–Business Relationships in Japan.' *Journal of Japanese Studies* 21 (Summer): 293–317.

SCHARPF, FRITZ W. 1984. 'Economic and Institutional Constraints of Full-Employment Strategies: Sweden, Austria, and West Germany, 1973–82.' In *Order and Conflict in Contemporary Capitalism: Studies in the Political Economy of Western European Nations*, ed. John H. Goldthorpe. New York: Oxford University Press: 257–90.

—— 1987. 'Game-Theoretical Interpretations of Inflation and Unemployment in Western Europe.' *Journal of Public Policy* 7 (3): 227–57.

—— 1991. *Crisis and Choice in European Social Democracy*. Ithaca, NY: Cornell University Press.

—— 1995. *Governing in Europe*. Oxford: Oxford University Press.

—— 1997a. *Games Real Actors Play: Actor-Centered Institutionalism in Policy Research*. Boulder, Colo.: Westview Press.

SCHARPF, FRITZ W. 1997*b*. 'Introduction: The Problem-Solving Capacity of Multi-level Governance.' *Journal of European Public Policy* 4 (4): 520–38.

—— and VIVIEN A. SCHMIDT, eds. 2000. *Welfare and Work in the Open Economy: Diverse Response to Common Challenges*. Vol ii. Oxford: Oxford University Press.

SCHEIBERG, MARC, and ROGERS HOLLINGSWORTH. 1990. 'Can Transaction Cost Economics Explain Trade Associations?' In *The Firm as a Nexus of Treaties*, ed. Masahiko Aoki, Bo Gustafsson, and Oliver E. Williamson. London: Sage Publications: 320–46.

SCHETTKAT, RONALD. 1993. 'Compensating Differentials? Wage Differentials and Employment Stability in the US and German Economies.' *Journal of Economic Issues* 27 (1): 153–70.

SCHEVE, KENNETH F., and MATTHEW J. SLAUGHTER. 1999. 'What Determines Individual Trade-Policy Preferences?' Paper presented at the 1998 annual meeting of the Midwest Political Science Association.

SCHLECHTRIEM, PETER. 1997. *Good Faith in German Law and in International Uniform Laws*. Rome: Centro di Studi e Ricerche di Diritto Comparato e Straniero.

SCHMÄHL, WINFRIED. 1993. 'The 1992 Reform of Public Pensions in Germany: Main Elements and Some Effects.' *Journal of European Social Policy* 3 (January): 39 –51.

SCHMIDT, SUSANNE K., and RAYMOND WERLE. 1998. *Coordinating Technology: Studies in the International Standardization of Telecommunications*. Cambridge, Mass.: MIT Press.

SCHMIDT, VIVIEN A. 1996. *From State to Market? The Transformation of Business in France*. Cambridge: Cambridge University Press.

—— 1997. 'Discourses and (Dis)Integration in Europe: The Cases of France, Great Britain and Germany.' *Daedalus* (Summer): 167–97.

SCHMITTER, PHILIPPE. 1974. 'Still the Century of Corporatism.' *Review of Politics* 36: 85–131.

—— and GERHARD LEHMBRUCH, eds. 1979. *Trends toward Corporatist Intermedia-tion*. Beverly Hills, Calif.: Sage.

—— and WOLFGANG STREECK. 1985. *Private Interest Government*. London: Sage.

SCHRAMEDEI, H. 1995. 'Ungünstige politische Rahmenbedingungen für die Wirtschaftsentwicklung in Sachsen-Anhalt.' *VME Sachsen-Anhalt* 5 (8): 1–2.

SCHROEDER, WOLFGANG, and BURKARD RUPPERT. 1996. *Austritte aus Arbeitge-berverbände: Eine Gefahr für das deutsche Modell?* Marburg: Schüren.

SCHUMPETER, JOSEPH. 1950. *Capitalism, Socialism and Democracy*. 3rd edn. New York: Harper.

SCHWARTZ, ALAN. 1992. 'Relational Contracts and the Courts.' *Journal of Legal Studies* 21 (2): 271–318.

SCOTT, JAMES C. 1998. *Seeing like a State: How Certain Schemes to Improve the Human Condition have Failed*. New Haven: Yale University Press.

SEIBERT, ULRICH. 1997. 'Kontrolle und Transparenz im Unternehmensbereich (KonTraG). Der Referenten-Entwurf zur Aktienrechtsnovelle.' *Zeitschrift für Wirtschafts- und Bankrecht* 51 (January): 1–48.

SELZNICK, PHILIP. 1969. *Law, Society and Industrial Justice*. New York: Russell Sage.

SENGENBERGER, WERNER. 1984. 'West German Employment Policy: Restoring Worker Competition.' *Industrial Relations* 23 (3): 323–43.

SESSI. 1997. *L'Industrie française*. Paris: Ministère de l'Économie, des Finances et de l'Industrie, Service des Statistiques Industrielles.

SHAFER, D. MICHAEL. 1994. *Winners and Losers: How Sectors Shape the Developmental Prospects of States*. Ithaca, NY: Cornell University Press.

SHALEV, MICHAEL. 1983. 'The Social Democratic Model and Beyond: Two Generations of Comparative Research on the Welfare State.' *Comparative Social Research* 6: 315–51.

SHAPIRO, CARL, and JOSEPH E. STIGLITZ. 1984. 'Equilibrium Unemployment as a Worker Discipline Device.' *American Economic Review* 74 (June): 433–44.

—— and HAL R. VARIAN. 1999. *Information Rules: A Strategic Guide to the Network Economy*. Cambridge, Mass.: Harvard Business School Press.

SHIBATA, HIROMICHI. 1999. 'Comparison of American and Japanese Work Practices: Skill Formation, Communications and Conflict Resolution.' *Industrial Relations* 38 (2): 192–214.

SHONFIELD, ANDREW. 1965. *Modern Capitalism*. New York: Oxford University Press.

SIBERT, ANNE C. 1999. 'Monetary Integration and Economic Reform.' *Economic Journal* 109 (452): 78–92.

—— and ALAN SUTHERLAND. 2000. 'Monetary Union and Labor Market Reform.' *Journal of International Economics* 51 (2): 421–35.

SIEBERT, HORST. 1997. 'Labor Market Rigidities: At the Root of Unemployment in Europe.' *Journal of Economic Perspectives* 11 (3): 37–54.

SILBERMAN, BERNARD. 1993. *Cages of Reason*. Chicago: University of Chicago Press.

SILVIA, STEPHEN J. 1988. 'The West German Labor Law Controversy: A Struggle for the Factory of the Future.' *Comparative Politics* 20 (January): 155–73.

—— 1997. 'German Unification and Emerging Divisions within German Employers' Associations.' *Comparative Politics* 29 (January): 187–208.

SIMMONS, BETH A. 1996. 'Rulers of the Game: Central Bank Independence during the Interwar Years.' *International Organization* 50 (3): 407–43.

—— 1999. 'The Internationalization of Capital.' In *Continuity and Change in Contemporary Capitalism*, ed. Herbert Kitschelt et al. Cambridge: Cambridge University Press: 39–69.

SINHA, SURYA P. 1995. 'Legal Polycentricity.' In *Legal Polycentricity: Consequences of Pluralism in Law*, ed. Hanne Petersen and Henrik Zahle. Aldershot: Dartmouth: 31–69.

SINN, HANS-WERNER. 1995. 'A Theory of the Welfare State.' *Scandinavian Journal of Economics* 97 (4): 495–526.

SISSON, KEITH, and PAUL MARGINSON. 1995. 'Management: Systems, Structures and Strategy.' In *Industrial Relations: Theory and Practice in Britain*, ed. Paul Edwards. Oxford: Blackwell: 89–122.

SKOCPOL, THEDA, and EDWIN AMENTA. 1985. 'Did Capitalists Shape Social Security?' *American Sociological Review* 50 (4): 572–5.

—— and JOHN IKENBERRY. 1983. 'The Political Formation of the American Welfare

State in Historical and Comparative Perspective.' *Comparative Social Research* 6: 87–148.

SKOTT, PETER. 1997. 'Stagflationary Consequences of Prudent Monetary Policy in a Unionized Economy.' *Oxford Economic Papers* 49 (4): 609–22.

SMITH, W. RAND. 1998. *The Left's Dirty Job: The Politics of Industrial Restructuring in France and Spain*. Pittsburgh: University of Pittsburgh Press.

SOERGEL, HANS T. 1991. *Bürgerliches Gesetzbuch mit Einführungsgesetzen und Nebengesetzen: Kohlhammer-Kommentar*. Stuttgart: Kohlhammer.

SOLTWEDEL, RÜDIGER. 1989. 'Supply-Side Policies since 1982? The Lessons are Still to be Learned.' In *A Supply-Side Agenda for Germany*, ed. Gerhard Fels and George M. Furstenberg. Berlin: Springer Verlag: 73–100.

SORGE, ARNDT, and WOLFGANG STREECK. 1988. 'Industrial Relations and Technical Change: The Case for an Extended Perspective.' In *New Technology and Industrial Relations*, ed. Richard Hyman and Wolfgang Streeck. Oxford: Basil Blackwell: 19–47.

—— and MICHAEL WARNER. 1986. *Comparative Factory Organization*. Aldershot: Gower.

SOSKICE, DAVID. 1990a. 'Wage Determination: The Changing Role of Institutions in Advanced Industrialized Countries.' *Oxford Review of Economic Policy* 6 (4): 36–61.

—— 1990b. 'Reinterpreting Corporatism and Explaining Unemployment: Coordinated and Non-coordinated Market Economies.' In *Labour Relations and Economic Performance*, ed. Renato Brunetta and Carlo Dell'Aringa. Proceedings of a conference held by the International Economics Association in Venice, Italy. Vol. 95. London: Macmillan: 170–214.

—— 1991. 'The Institutional Infrastructure for International Competitiveness: A Comparative Analysis of the UK and Germany.' In *Economics for the New Europe*, ed. Anthony B. Atkinson and Renato Brunetta. London: Macmillan: 45–66.

—— 1994a. 'Innovation Strategies of Companies: A Comparative Institutional Approach of Some Cross-country Differences.' In *Institutionenvergleich und Institutionendynamik: WZB Jahrbuch 1994*, ed. Wolfgang Zapf and Meinholf Dierkes. Berlin: Sigma: 271–89.

—— 1994b. 'Reconciling Markets and Institutions: The German Apprenticeship System.' In *Training and the Private Sector: International Comparisons*, ed. Lisa M. Lynch. Chicago: Chicago University Press: 25–60.

—— 1996a. 'German Technology Policy, Innovation, and National Institutional Frameworks.' Discussion Paper 96-319, Wissenschaftszentrum, Berlin.

—— 1996b. 'National Patterns in Company Innovation Strategies: A Comparative Institutional Approach'. Wissenschaftszentrum, Berlin. Typescript.

—— 1996c. 'The Stake We're in.' *Prospect* (April): 39–42.

—— 1997. 'German Technology Policy, Innovation, and National Institutional Frameworks.' *Industry and Innovation* 4 (1): 75–96.

—— 1999. 'Divergent Production Regimes: Coordinated and Uncoordinated Market Economies in the 1980s and 1990s.' In *Continuity and Change in Contemporary Capitalism*, ed. Herbert Kitschelt et al. Cambridge: Cambridge University Press: 101–34.

—— and TORBEN IVERSEN. 1998. 'Multiple Wage-Bargaining Systems in the Single European Currency Area.' *Oxford Review of Economic Policy* 14 (3): 110–24.

—— —— 2000. 'The Non-neutrality of Monetary Policy with Large Price or Wage Setters.' *Quarterly Journal of Economics* 115 (1): 265–84.

SPD. 1998. *SPD-Programm für die Bundestagswahl 1998*. Bonn.

SPENCE, MICHAEL. 1973. 'Job Market Signaling.' *Quarterly Journal of Economics* 87 (3): 355–74.

STAUDINGER, JULIUS V. 1995. *Kommentar zum Bürgerlichen Gesetzbuch: mit Einführungsgesetz und Nebengesetzen*. Berlin: Sellier de Gruyter.

STEINMO, SVEN, KATHLEEN THELEN, and FRANK LONGSTRETH, eds. 1992. *Structuring Politics: Historical Institutionalism in Comparative Analysis*. New York: Cambridge University Press.

STEPHENS, JOHN D. 1979. *The Transition from Capitalism to Socialism*. London: Macmillan Press Ltd.

—— EVELYNE HUBER, and LEONARD RAY. 1999. 'The Welfare State in Hard Times.' In *Continuity and Change in Contemporary Capitalism*, ed. Herbert Kitschelt, Peter Lange, Gary Marks, and John Stephens. Cambridge: Cambridge University Press: 164–93.

STERN, JOHN P. 1997. 'The Japanese Technology Infrastructure: Issues and Opportunities.' *Japan's Technical Standards: Implications for Global Trade and Competitiveness*, ed. John R. McIntyre. Westport, Conn.: Quorum: 75–86.

STOLPER, WOLFGANG FRIEDRICH, and PAUL SAMUELSON. 1941. 'Protection and Real Wages.' *Review of Economic Studies* 9: 58–73.

STONE, ALEC. 1994. 'Judging Socialist Reform: The Politics of Coordinate Construction in France and Germany.' *Comparative Political Studies* 26 (January): 443–69.

STORY, JONATHAN, and INGO WALTER. 1997. *Political Economy of Financial Integration in Europe*. Manchester: Manchester University Press.

STREECK, WOLFGANG. 1981. *Gewerkschaftliche Organisationsprobleme in der sozialistischen Demokratie*. Königstein/Ts: Athenäum.

—— 1983. 'Between Pluralism and Corporatism: German Business Associations and the State.' *Journal of Public Policy* 3 (3): 265–84.

—— 1987. 'The Uncertainties of Management in the Management of Uncertainty: Employers, Labor Relations and Industrial Adjustment in the 1980s.' *Work, Employment and Society* 1 (September): 281–308.

—— 1989. 'Successful Adjustment to Turbulent Markets: The Automobile Industry.' In *Industry and Politics in West Germany: Toward the Third Republic*, ed. Peter J. Katzenstein. Ithaca, NY: Cornell University Press: 113–56.

—— 1991. 'On the Institutional Conditions of Diversified Quality Production.' In *Beyond Keynesianism: The Socio-economics of Production and Full Employment*, ed. Egon Matzner and Wolfgang Streeck. Aldershot: Elgar: 21–61.

—— 1992a. 'Productive Constraints: On the Institutional Preconditions of Diversified Quality Production.' In *Social Institutions and Economic Performance*, ed. W. Streeck. London: Sage: 1–40.

STREECK, WOLFGANG. 1992*b*. *Social Institutions and Economic Performance: Studies on Industrial Relations in Advanced European Capitalist Countries*. London: Sage.

—— 1994. 'Pay Restraint without Incomes Policy: Institutionalized Monetarism and Industrial Unionism in Germany?' In *The Return of Incomes Policy*, ed. Ronald Dore, Robert Boyer, and Zoë Mars. London: Pinter: 118–40.

—— 1995. 'From Market-Making to State-Building: Reflections on the Political Economy of European Social Policy.' In *European Social Policy*, ed. Stephan Leibfried and Paul Pierson. Washington: Brookings Institution: 359–431.

—— 1996*a*. *Mitbestimmung: Offene Fragen*. Gütersloh: Verlag Bertelsmann.

—— 1996*b*. 'Public Power beyond the Nation-State: The Case of the European Community.' In *States against Markets*, ed. Robert Boyer and Daniel Drache. New York: Routledge: 299–316.

—— 1997*a*. 'Beneficial Constraints: On the Economic Limits of Rational Voluntarism.' In *Contemporary Capitalism: The Embeddedness of Institutions*, ed. Rogers Hollingsworth and Robert Boyer. Cambridge: Cambridge University Press: 197–219.

—— 1997*b*. 'The German Economic Model: Does it Exist? Can it Survive?' In *Political Economy of Modern Capitalism: Mapping Convergence and Diversity*, ed. Colin Crouch and Wolfgang Streeck. London: Sage: 33–54.

—— and PHILIP SCHMITTER, eds. 1986. *Private Interest Government: Beyond Market and State*. Beverly Hills, Calif.: Sage.

—— J. HILBERT, K.-H. VAN KEVALAER, F. MAIER, and H. WEBER. 1987. *The Role of the Social Partners in Vocational Training and Further Training in the Federal Republic of Germany*. Berlin: CEDEFOP.

SULEIMAN, EZRA. 1979. *Les Élites en France*. Paris: Le Seuil.

—— 1995. *Les Ressorts cachés de la réussite française*. Paris: Le Seuil.

SWEDBERG, RICHARD. 1994. 'Markets as Societies.' In *The Handbook of Economic Sociology*, ed. Neil J. Smelser and Richard Swedberg. Princeton: Princeton University Press: 255–82.

SWENSON, PETER. 1989. *Fair Shares: Unions, Pay, and Politics in Sweden and West Germany*. Ithaca, NY: Cornell University Press.

—— 1991. 'Bringing Capital Back in, or Social Democracy Reconsidered: Employer Power, Cross-class Alliances and Centralization of Industrial Relations in Denmark and Sweden.' *World Politics* 43 (July): 513–44.

—— 1997. 'Arranged Alliance: Business Interests in the New Deal.' *Politics and Society* 25 (March): 66–116.

—— 2001. *Capitalists against Markets: The Making of Labor Markets and Welfare States in the United States and Sweden*. New York: Oxford University Press.

SWIDLER, ANN. 1986. 'Culture in Action: Symbols and Strategies.' *American Sociological Review* 51 (2): 273–86.

TADDÉI, DOMINIQUE, and BENJAMIN CORIAT. 1993. *Made in France: l'industrie française dans la compétition mondiale*. Paris: Librairie Générale Française.

TATE, JOHN JAY. 1997. 'Who Governs Whom? Business Associations and the State in Germany and Japan.' Paper presented at the annual meeting of the American Political Science Association, Washington.

TAYLOR, ROBERT. 1993. *The Trade Union Question in British Politics: Government and Unions since 1945*. Oxford: Blackwell.

TEECE, DAVID. 1986. 'Profiting from Technological Innovation: Implications for Integration, Collaboration, Licensing, and Public Policy.' *Research Policy* 15: 285–305.

—— and GARY PISANO. 1998. 'The Dynamic Capabilities of Firms.' In *Technology, Organization and Competiveness*, ed. Giovanni Dosi, David J. Teece, and Josef Chytry. Oxford: Oxford University Press: 193–212.

—— —— and AMY SHUEN. 1997. 'Dynamic Capabilities and Strategic Management.' *Strategic Management Journal* 18: 509–34.

TENNSTEDT, FLORIAN, and HEIDI WINTER. 1993. *Quellensammlung zur Geschichte der deutschen Sozialpolitik 1867 bis 1914*. Vol. ii. Stuttgart: Gustav Fischer.

TERRY, MICHAEL. 1995. 'Trade Unions: Shop Stewards and the Workplace.' In *Industrial Relations: Theory and Practice in Britain*, ed. Paul Edwards. Oxford: Blackwell: 203–28.

TEUBNER, GUNTHER. 1980. 'Die Generalklausel von "Treu und Glauben".' In *Alternativkommentar zum Bürgerlichen Gesetzbuch*, vol. ii: *Allgemeines Schuldrecht*, ed. Rudolf Wassermann. Neuwied: Luchterhand: 32–91.

—— 1987. 'Episodenverknüpfung: Zur Steigerung von Selbstreferenz im Recht.' In *Theorie als Passion*, ed. Dirk Baecker, Jürgen Markowitz, Rudolf Stichweh, Hartmann Tyrell, and Helmut Willke. Frankfurt: Suhrkamp: 423–46.

—— 1989. 'How the Law Thinks: Towards a Constructivist Epistemology of Law.' *Law and Society Review* 23 (December): 727–57.

—— 1991. 'Autopoiesis and Steering: How Politics Profits from the Normative Surplus of Capital.' In *Autopoiesis and Configuration Theory: New Approaches to Societal Steering*, ed. Roeland J. in't Veld, Linze Schaapp, Catrien Termeer, and Mark van Twist. Dordrecht: Kluwer: 127–41.

—— 1992. 'The Two Faces of Janus: Rethinking Legal Pluralism.' *Cardozo Law Review* 13 (March): 1443–62.

—— 1993. *Law as an Autopoietic System*. London: Blackwell.

—— 1994. 'Company Interest: The Public Interest of the Enterprise "in Itself".' In *Reflexive Labour Law*, ed. Ralf Rogowski and Tomas Wilthagen. Deventer: Kluwer: 21–52.

—— ed. 1997. *Global Law without a State*. Aldershot: Dartmouth Gower.

THELEN, KATHLEEN. 1991. *Union of Parts: Labor Politics in Postwar Germany*. Ithaca, NY: Cornell University Press.

—— 1993. 'West European Labor in Transition: Sweden and Germany Compared.' *World Politics* 46 (October): 23–49.

—— 1994. 'Beyond Corporatism: Toward a New Framework for the Study of Labor in Advanced Capitalism.' *Comparative Politics* 27 (October): 107–24.

—— 1996. 'The Changing Character of Industrial Relations in Contemporary Europe.' Paper presented at the 2nd workshop on 'The New Europe: Rethinking the Collective Response to Change,' Harvard University.

—— 2000. 'Why German Employers Cannot Bring Themselves to Abandon the German Model.' In *Unions, Employers and Central Banks*, ed. Torben Iversen,

Jonas Pontusson, and David Soskice. New York: Cambridge University Press: 138–69.

THELEN, KATHLEEN., and IKUO KUME. 1999a. 'The Effects of Globalization on Labor Revisited: Lessons from Germany and Japan.' *Politics and Society* 27 (December): 477–505.

—— —— 1999b. 'The Rise of Non-market Training Regimes: Germany and Japan Compared.' *Journal of Japanese Studies* 25 (Winter): 33–64.

—— and LOWELL TURNER. 1997. *German Codetermination in Comparative Perspective*. Gütersloh: Verlag Bertelsmann.

—— and CHRISTA VAN WIJNBERGEN. 2000. 'The Paradox of Globalization: Turning the Tables on Labor and Capital in German Industrial Relations.' Evanston, Ill.: Northwestern University. Typescript.

THOENIG, JEAN-CLAUDE. 1987. *L'Ère des technocrates*. Paris: L'Harmattan.

TODD, EMMANUEL. 1998. *L'Illusion économique*. Paris: Gallimard.

TOTH, BOB. 1996. 'Putting the U.S. Standardization System into Perspective: New Insights.' *StandardView* 4 (December): 169–78.

TROY, LEO. 1999. *Beyond Unions and Collective Bargaining*. Armonk, NY: M. E. Sharpe.

TRUMBULL, GUNNAR. 2001. 'France's 35 Hour Work Week: Flexibility through Regulation.' Brookings Institution Center on the United States and France. http://www.brook.edu/fp/cusf/analysis/workweek.htm

TSEBELIS, GEORGE. 1990. *Nested Games: Rational Choice in Comparative Perspective*. Berkeley and Los Angeles: University of California Press.

TURNER, LOWELL. 1991. *Democracy at Work: Changing World Markets and the Future of Labor Unions*. Ithaca, NY: Cornell University Press.

TWINING, WILLIAM. 1996. 'Globalization and Legal Theory: Some Local Implications.' *Current Legal Problems* 49 (1): 1–42.

ULLMANN, HANS-PETER. 1979. 'Industrielle Interessen und die Entstehung der deutschen Sozialversicherung 1880–1889.' *Historische Zeitschrift* 229 (3): 574–610.

ULRICH, KARL. 1995. 'The Role of Product Architecture in the Manufacturing Firm.' *Research Policy* 24 (3): 419–40.

UNDY, ROGER, PATRICIA FOSH, HUW MORRIS, PAUL SMITH, and RODERICK MARTIN. 1996. *Managing the Unions: The Impact of Legislation on Trade Unions' Behaviour*. Oxford: Clarendon Press.

UNESCO. 1999. *UNESCO Statistical Yearbook*. New York: UNESCO.

UNGERER, HORST. 1997. *A Concise History of European Monetary Integration: From EPU to EMU*. Westport, Conn.: Quorum Books.

US Senate. 1975. *Voluntary Industrial Standards: Hearings before the Subcommittee on Antitrust and Monopoly of the Committee on the Judiciary United States Senate*.

VELASCO, ANDRÉS, and VINCENZO GUZZO. 1999. 'The Case for a Populist Central Banker.' *European Economic Review* 43 (7): 1317–44.

VELTZ, PIERRE. 1996. *Mondialisation, villes et territoires: l'économie d'archipel*. Paris: Presses Universitaires de France.

Verband Mitteldeutscher Industriellen. 1920. 'Erklärung betreffend des Gesetzentwurfes der Arbeitslosenversicherung.' Zentrales Staatsarchiv Potsdam, Reichsarbeitsministerium 4311.

VERDIER, ERIC. 1997. 'L'Action publique en matière de formation professionnelle et les grandes entreprises: entre normes et décentralisation.' Paper presented at the workshop on 'Mutations industrielles et dynamiques territoriales.' Nantes, 28–9 March.

Verein Deutscher Eisen- und Stahlindustrieller. 1884*a*. 'Vorstandssitzung des Vereins Deutscher Eisen- und Stahlindustrieller, Berlin, 10. February 1884.' *Stahl und Eisen* 11: 177–9.

—— 1884*b*. 'Die Grundzüge für den Entwurf eines Gesetzes über die Unfallversicherung der Arbeiter.' *Stahl und Eisen* 11: 103–7.

Vereinigung der Deutschen Arbeitgeberverbände. 1920. 'Denkschrift der Vereinigung der Deutschen Arbeitgeberverbände.' Zentrales Staatsarchiv Potsdam, Reichsarbeitsamt 4310.

—— 1925. 'Stellungnahme zu den Grundfragen der Arbeitslosenversicherung.' Zentrales Staatsarchiv Potsdam, Deutsches Arbeitswissenschaftliches Institut 2575.

—— 1927. 'Geschäftsbericht der Vereinigung der Deutschen Arbeitgeberverbände 1925–1926.' Berlin.

VERMAN, LAL C. 1973. *Standardization: A New Discipline*. Hamden, Conn.: Archon Books.

VINEN, RICHARD. 1991. *Politics of French Business, 1936–1945*. New York: Cambridge University Press.

VISSER, JELLE. 1996. 'Unionization Trends Revisited.' Unpublished paper, University of Amsterdam.

—— and ANTON HEMERIJCK. 1997. *A Dutch Miracle?* Amsterdam: University of Amsterdam Press.

VITOLS, SIGURT. 1997. 'The German Industrial Strategy: An Overview.' *Industry and Innovation* 4 (1): 15–36.

—— 2000. 'Germany's Neuer Markt: Radical Transformation or Incremental Change in a National Innovation System?' Paper presented to the Annual Conference of the Society for the Advancement of Socio-economics, London, July.

—— STEVEN CASPER, DAVID SOSKICE, and STEPHEN WOOLCOCK. 1997. *Corporate Governance in Large British and German Companies: Comparative Institutional Advantage or Competing for Best Practice*. London: Anglo German Foundation.

VOELZKOW, HELMUT. 1996. *Private Regierungen in der Techniksteuerung: eine sozialwissenschaftliche Analyze der technischen Normung*. Cologne: Max-Planck Institut für Gesellschaftliche Forschung.

VOGEL, DAVID. 1995. *Trading up: Consumer and Environmental Regulation in a Global Economy*. Cambridge, Mass.: Harvard University Press.

VOGEL, STEVEN. 1996. *Freer Markets, More Rules*. Ithaca, NY: Cornell University Press.

VON ALEMANN, ULRICH. 1989. *Organisierte Interessen in der Bundesrepublik*. Opladen: Leske & Budrich.

WADE, ROBERT. 1996. 'Globalization and its Limits: Reports of the Death of the National Economy are Greatly Exaggerated.' In *National Diversity and Global*

Capitalism, ed. Suzanne Berger and Ronald Dore. Ithaca, NY: Cornell University Press: 60–88.

WAGNER, K. 1999. 'The German Apprenticeship System under Strain.' In *The German Skills Machine*, ed. Pepper Culpepper and David Finegold. Oxford: Berghahn: 37–76.

WAIGEL, THEO. 1993. 'Engere Zusammenarbeit in Währungsfragen.' *Arbeitgeber* 25 (45): 854–5.

WALLACE, HELEN. 1996. 'The Institutions of the EU: Experience and Experiments.' In *Policy-Making in the European Union*, ed. Helen Wallace and William Wallace. Oxford: Oxford University Press: 37–70.

WALLERSTEIN, MICHAEL. 1999. 'Wage-Setting Institutions and Pay Inequality in Advanced Industrial Societies.' *American Journal of Political Science* 43 (3): 649–80.

—— and MIRIAM GOLDEN. 1997. 'The Fragmentation of the Bargaining Society: Wage-Setting in the Nordic Countries, 1950–1992.' *Comparative Political Studies* 30 (December): 699–732.

—— —— 2000. 'Postwar Wage Setting in the Nordic Countries'. In *Unions, Employers, and Central Banks*, ed. Torben Iversen, Jonas Pontusson, and David Soskice. New York: Cambridge University Press: 107–37.

—— —— and PETER LANGE. 1997. 'Unions, Employers' Associations, and Wage-Setting Institutions in Northern and Central Europe, 1950–1992.' *Industrial and Labor Relations Review* 50 (April): 379–401.

WATSON, ALAN. 1981. *The Making of the Civil Law.* Cambridge, Mass.: Harvard University Press.

—— 1985. *The Evolution of Law.* Baltimore: Johns Hopkins University Press.

—— 1987. 'Evolution of Law: Continued.' *Law and History Review* 5: 537–70.

—— 1993. *Legal Transplants.* 2nd edn. Atlanta: University of Georgia Press.

WEBER, HENRI. 1990. *Le Parti des patrons.* Paris: Le Seuil.

WEINSTEIN, MARC, and THOMAS KOCHAN. 1995. 'The Limits of Diffusion: Some Recent Developments in Industrial Relations and Human Resource Practices.' In *Employment Relations in a Changing World Economy*, ed. Richard Locke, Thomas Kochan, and Michael Piore. Cambridge, Mass.: MIT Press: 1–32.

WEISS, LINDA, and JOHN M. HOBSON. 1995. *States and Economic Development: A Comparative Historical Analysis.* Cambridge: Polity Press.

WERNERFELT, BIRGIT. 1984. 'A Resource-Based View of the Firm.' *Strategic Management Journal* 5 (2): 171–80.

WEVER, KIRSTEN. 1995. *Negotiating Competitiveness: Employment Relations and Organizational Innovation in Germany and the United States.* Boston: Harvard Business School Press.

WHITLEY, RICHARD. 1999. *Divergent Capitalisms: The Social Structuring and Change of Business Systems.* Oxford: Oxford University Press.

WIEACKER, FRANZ. 1967. *Privatrechtsgeschichte der Neuzeit unter besonderer Berücksichtigung der deutschen Entwicklung.* 2nd edn. Göttingen: Vandenhoeck & Ruprecht.

—— 1996. *A History of Private Law in Europe: With Particular Reference to Germany.* Oxford: Clarendon Press.

WIESENTHAL, H., ed. 1995. *Einheit als Interessenpolitik*. Frankfurt: Campus.

WIEVIORKA, MICHEL, et al. 1989. *Le Modèle EDF: essai de sociologie des organisations*. Paris: La Découverte.

WILENSKY, HAROLD. 1975. *The Welfare State and Equality: Structural and Ideological Roots of Public Expenditures*. Berkeley and Los Angeles: University of California Press.

WILLIAMS, KAREL, COLIN HASLAM, SUKHDEV JOHAL, and JOHN WILLIAMS. 1994. *Cars: Analysis, History, Cases*. Providence, RI: Berghahn Books.

WILLIAMSON, OLIVER. 1975. *Markets and Hierarchies*. New York: Free Press.

—— 1985. *The Economic Institutions of Capitalism: Firms, Markets, Relational Contracting*. New York: Free Press.

—— 1988. 'Corporate Finance and Corporate Governance.' *Journal of Finance* 43 (May): 567–91.

WILSON, JAMES Q. 1989. *Bureaucracy: What Government Agencies Do and Why They Do It*. New York: Basic Books.

WINTER, SYDNEY G. 1995. 'Four Rs of Profitability: Rents, Resources, Routines, and Replication.' In *Resource-Based and Evolutionary Theories of the Firm: Towards a Synthesis*, ed. Cynthia A. Montgomery. Boston: Kluwer: 147–78.

WÖLKER, THOMAS. 1992. *Entstehung und Entwicklung des Deutschen Normenaus-schusses 1917 bis 1925*. Berlin: Beuth.

WOOD, STEWART. 1997. 'Capitalist Constitutions: Supply-Side Reforms in Britain and West-Germany 1960–1990.' Ph.D. dissertation, Department of Government, Harvard University.

—— 1999. 'Building a Governance Structure for Training? Employers, Government and the TEC Experiment in Great Britain.' In *The German Skills Machine: Sustaining Comparative Advantage in a Global Economy*, ed. Pepper D. Culpepper and David Finegold. New York: Berghahn Books: 363–402.

—— 2000. 'Why Indicative Planning Failed: British Industry and the Formation of the National Economic Development Council (1961–65).' *Twentieth Century British History* 11 (4): 431–59.

—— 2001. 'Labour Market Regimes under Threat? Sources of Continuity in Germany, Britain and Sweden.' In *The New Politics of the Welfare State*, ed. Paul Pierson. Oxford: Oxford University Press: 368–409.

WOODWARD, C. DOUGLAS. 1972. *BSI: The Story of Standards*. London: British Standards Institution.

YASHIV, ERAN. 1989. 'Inflation and the Role of Money under Discretion and Rules: A New Interpretation.' Working Paper No. 8-89, PSIE, MIT, November.

YOSHIKAWA, AKI. 1997. 'Introducing a Standard for Digitalized Medical Images in Japan.' In *Japan's Technical Standards: Implications for Global Trade and Competitiveness*, ed. John R. McIntyre. Westport, Conn.: Quorum: 93–106.

Zeit, Die. 1984. 'Ende des Tauwetters.' *Die Zeit* 23 November.

Zeitschrift für Handel und Gewerbe. 1888. 'Mangel des Unfallversicherungsgesetzes.' *Zeitschrift für Handel und Gewerbe* 32: 373–4.

—— 1890. 'Das Inkrafttreten des Invaliditäts- und Altersversicherungsgesetzes.' *Zeitschrift für Handel und Gewerbe* 34: 319–21.

Zentralverband des Deutschen Handwerks. 1982. 'Verkürzung der Lebens-arbeitszeit—kein Beitrag zur Bekämpfung der Arbeitslosigkeit.' In *Argumente zur Handwerkspolitik*, ed. Zentralverbands des Deutschen Handwerks, Bonn: Bundesvereinigung der Fachverbände des Deutschen Handwerks.

—— 1983a. 'Kürzere Arbeitszeit: alle Gründe und Überlegungen sprechen dage-gen.' *Deutsches Handwerksblatt* 12: 416–20.

—— 1983b. 'Das ZDH nimmt zu den Beschäftigungspolitischen Leitlinien und anderen Anträgen Stellung.' *Deutsches Handwerksblatt* 18: 591–3.

—— 1983. 'Handwerk bekräftigt sein Nein zu Arbeitszeitverkürzungen.' *Deutsches Handwerksblatt* 23–4: 754.

—— 1984. 'Vorruhestandsregelung: Handwerk warnt!' *Deutsches Handwerksblatt*: 2–13.

ZERVOYIANNI, ATHINA. 1997. 'Monetary Policy Games and Coalitions in a Two-Country Model with Unionised Wage-Setting.' *Oxford Economic Papers* 49 (1): 57–76.

ZEVIN, ROBERT. 1992. 'Are World Financial Markets More Open? If So, Why and With What Effects?' In *Financial Openness and National Autonomy*, ed. Tariq Banuri and Juliet Schor. Oxford: Oxford University Press: 43–84.

ZIEGLER, J. NICHOLAS. 1997. *Governing Ideas: Strategies for Innovation in France and Germany*. Ithaca, NY: Cornell University Press.

—— 2000. 'Corporate Governance and the Politics of Property Rights in Germany.' *Politics and Society* 28: 195–221.

ZÖLLNER, WOLFGANG, and KARL-GEORG LORITZ. 1998. *Arbeitsrecht: ein Studien-buch*. Munich: Beck.

ZUMPE, LOTTE. 1961. 'Zur Geschichte der Unfallverhältnisse in der deutschen Industrie.' Ph.D. dissertation, Humboldt University, Berlin.

ZWEIGERT, KONRAD, and HEIN KÖTZ. 1992. *An Introduction to Comparative Law*. Oxford: Oxford University Press.

ZYSMAN, JOHN. 1977. *Political Strategies for Industrial Order. State, Market and Industry in France*. Berkeley and Los Angeles: University of California Press.

—— 1983. *Governments, Markets, and Growth: Financial Systems and the Politics of Industrial Change*. Ithaca, NY: Cornell University Press.

—— 1994. 'How Institutions Create Historically Rooted Trajectories of Growth.' *Industrial and Corporate Change* 3 (1): 243–83.

—— 1996a. 'Nations, Institutions, and Technological Development.' *International Journal of Technology Management* 12 (5–6): 651–78.

—— 1996b. 'The Myth of a "Global" Economy: Enduring National Foundations and Emerging Regional Realities.' *New Political Economy* 1 (2): 157–84.

INDEX

Note: **bold** page numbers indicate chapters.